Rick S

EASY ACCESS EUROPE

D0126785

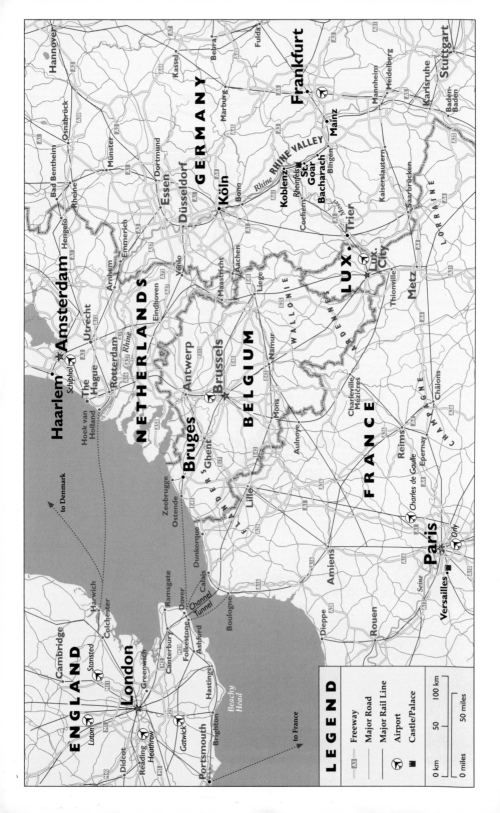

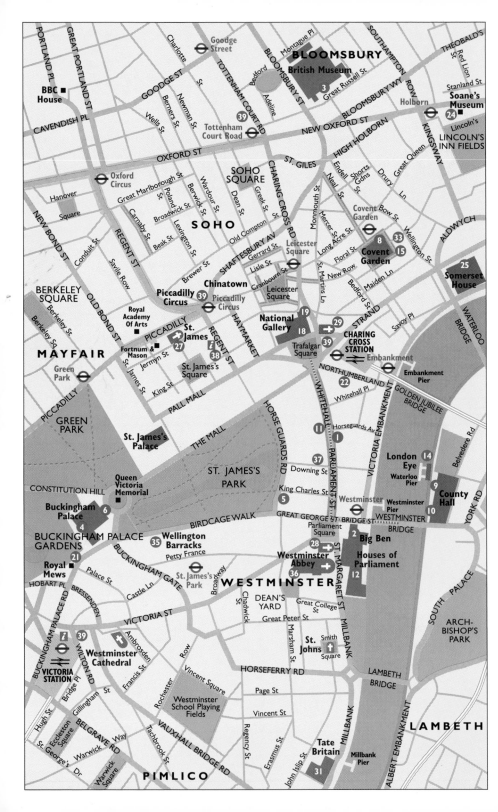

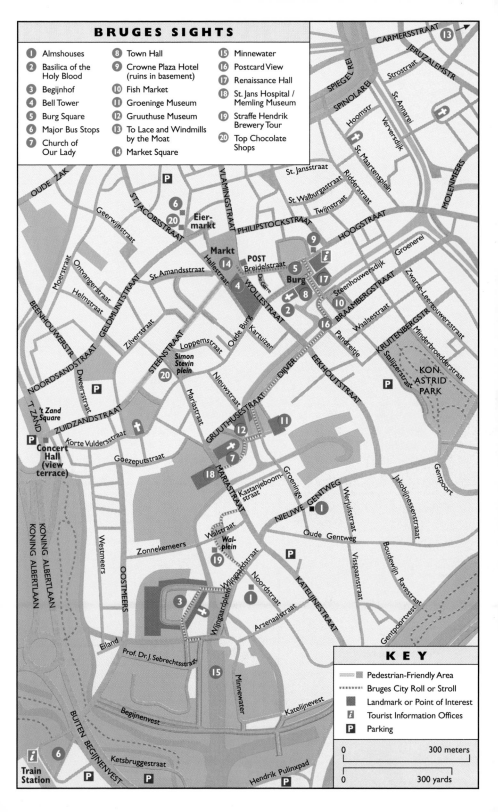

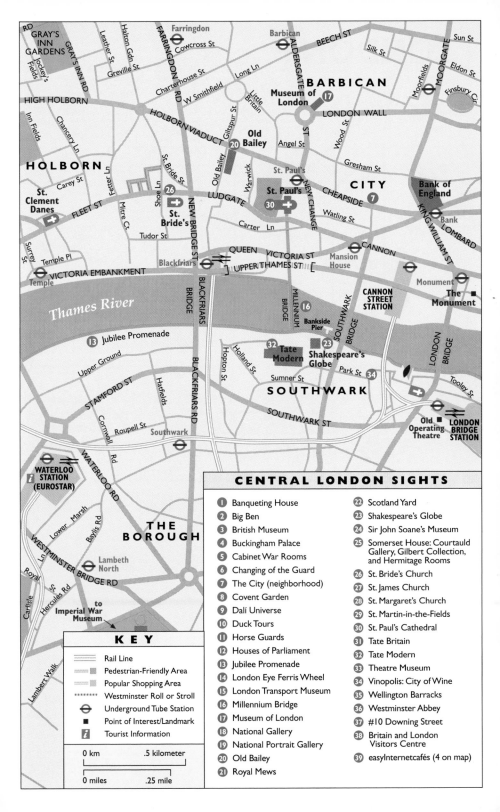

CENTRAL LONDON SIGHTS

1. Banqueting House
2. Big Ben
3. British Museum
4. Buckingham Palace
5. Cabinet War Rooms
6. Changing of the Guard
7. The City (neighborhood)
8. Covent Garden
9. Dalí Universe
10. Duck Tours
11. Horse Guards
12. Houses of Parliament
13. Jubilee Promenade
14. London Eye Ferris Wheel
15. London Transport Museum
16. Millennium Bridge
17. Museum of London
18. National Gallery
19. National Portrait Gallery
20. Old Bailey
21. Royal Mews
22. Scotland Yard
23. Shakespeare's Globe
24. Sir John Soane's Museum
25. Somerset House: Courtauld Gallery, Gilbert Collection, and Hermitage Rooms
26. St. Bride's Church
27. St. James Church
28. St. Margaret's Church
29. St. Martin-in-the-Fields
30. St. Paul's Cathedral
31. Tate Britain
32. Tate Modern
33. Theatre Museum
34. Vinopolis: City of Wine
35. Wellington Barracks
36. Westminster Abbey
37. #10 Downing Street
38. Britain and London Visitors Centre
39. easyInternetcafés (4 on map)

KEY

Rail Line
Pedestrian-Friendly Area
Popular Shopping Area
Westminster Roll or Stroll
Underground Tube Station
Point of Interest/Landmark
Tourist Information

0 km   .5 kilometer

0 miles   .25 mile

LONDON

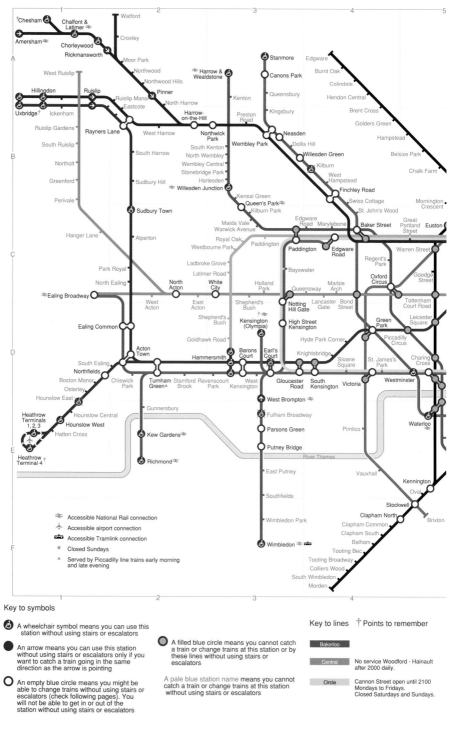

Accessible National Rail connection
Accessible airport connection
Accessible Tramlink connection
★ Closed Sundays
▲ Served by Piccadilly line trains early morning
  and late evening

Key to symbols

A wheelchair symbol means you can use this station without using stairs or escalators

An arrow means you can use this station without using stairs or escalators only if you want to catch a train going in the same direction as the arrow is pointing

An empty blue circle means you might be able to catch trains without using stairs or escalators (check following pages.) You will not be able to get in or out of the station without using stairs or escalators

A filled blue circle means you cannot catch a train or change trains at this station or by these lines without using stairs or escalators

A pale blue station name means you cannot catch a train or change trains at this station without using stairs or escalators

Key to lines   † Points to remember

Bakerloo

Central — No service Woodford - Hainault after 2000 daily.

Circle — Cannon Street open until 2100 Mondays to Fridays. Closed Saturdays and Sundays.

Tube access guide
How to plan a Tube journey avoiding stairs and escalators

November 2002

D2 ○ **Acton Town** ⒸⒶ
Connection only: District line eastbound and Piccadilly line eastbound. District line westbound and Piccadilly line westbound

D6 ○ **Aldgate** ⒷⒷ
Connection only: Circle line and terminating Metropolitan line

C7 ○ **Aldgate East** ⒶⒶ
Connection only: District line eastbound and Hammersmith & City line eastbound. District line westbound and Hammersmith & City line westbound

D7 ♿ **All Saints** Ⓐ ⬆

A1 ➡ **Amersham** Ⓑ ⇌ Ⓟ
Metropolitan line and National Rail southbound only

B5 ○ **Archway** ⒷNB
Connection only between terminating and continuing northbound trains

C4 ○ **Baker Street** ⒷⒷ
Connection only: Bakerloo line northbound and Jubilee line northbound. Bakerloo line southbound and Jubilee line southbound

D6 ♿ **Bank** Ⓐ ⬆
Docklands Light Railway only, lift located in King William Street

C9 ♿ **Barking** ⒸEB ⒷWB Ⓒ ⬆ ⇌ 🔄

B9 ⬆ **Barkingside** Ⓐ Ⓟ
Eastbound Central line only

D3 ○ **Barons Court** ⒸⒷ
Connection only: District line eastbound and Piccadilly line eastbound. District line westbound and Piccadilly line westbound

D9 ♿ **Beckton** Ⓐ

D9 ♿ **Beckton Park** Ⓐ ⬆

D6 ♿ **Bermondsey** Ⓐ ⬆

C7 ○ **Bethnal Green** Ⓑ
Connection only for reverse direction travel to Mile End for eastbound Central, District and Hammersmith & City lines

D5 ○ **Blackfriars** ⒷⒷ
Connection only: District line eastbound and Circle line eastbound. District line westbound and Circle line westbound

D8 ♿ **Blackwall** Ⓐ ⬆

E5 ➡ **Borough** ⒷNB ⬆
Northern line northbound only

C8 ♿ **Bow Church** Ⓐ ⬆small

B6 ♿ **Caledonian Road** Ⓑ ⬆

B5 ♿ **Camden Town** ⒷNB
Connection only: Northern line northbound (Barnet/Mill Hill East services) and Northern line northbound (Edgware branch service)

D7 ♿ **Canada Water** ⒶⒶ ⬆ 🔄

D8 ♿ **Canary Wharf** ⒶⒶ ⬆ WC (ticket hall)
200 metres between Jubilee line and DLR

D8 ♿ **Canning Town** ⒶⒶ ⬆ 🔄 ✈ (via bus)

A3 ○ **Canons Park** ⒷNB
Connection only between terminating and continuing northbound trains

A1 ♿ **Chalfont & Latimer** Ⓒ ⇌ Ⓟ

A1 ♿ **Chesham** ⒷNB Ⓟ

A1 ♿ **Chorleywood** ⒷSB ⒸNB Ⓟ

F5 ○ **Clapham North** ⒷNB
Connection only for reverse direction Northern line travel to Borough from London Bridge

E8 ♿ **Crossharbour & London Arena** Ⓐ ⬆ small

D8 ♿ **Custom House** Ⓐ ⬆

E8 ♿ **Cutty Sark** Ⓐ ⬆

D9 ♿ **Cyprus** Ⓐ ⬆

B9 ○ **Dagenham East** Ⓑ
Connection only between terminating and continuing eastbound trains

B9 ♿ **Dagenham Heathway** Ⓒ

A8 ➡ **Debden** Ⓐ Ⓟ
Central line eastbound only, connection between terminating and continuing eastbound trains

E8 ♿ **Deptford Bridge** Ⓐ ⬆

D8 ♿ **Devons Road** Ⓐ ⬆small

C1 ○ **Ealing Broadway**
Ⓒ Platform 9 Ⓑ Platforms 7&8 ⇌
Connection only between Central and District lines and National Rail eastbound (for Paddington)

D2 ○ **Ealing Common** ⒶⒸ
Connection only: District line eastbound and Piccadilly line eastbound. District line westbound and Piccadilly line westbound

D3 ✖ **Earl's Court** ⒷⒷ ⬆
Access facilities under construction.
○ Connection only: District line (for High St Kensington/Edgware Rd) and District line (for Victoria/Barking/ Upminster), and District line from Olympia. District line (for Richmond/Ealing Broadway) and District line (for Putney Bridge/ Wimbledon), and District line for Olympia

D8 ♿ **East India** Ⓐ ⬆

C4 ○ **Edgware Road** ⒷⒷ
Connection only: Circle line eastbound and Hammersmith & City line eastbound. Circle line westbound and Hammersmith & City line westbound

B9 ♿ **Elm Park** Ⓒ

E8 ♿ **Elverson Road** Ⓐ

D5 ○ **Embankment** Ⓑ Ⓑ
Connection only: Circle line eastbound
and District line eastbound. Circle line westbound
and District line westbound

A8 🚇 **Epping** Ⓐ

C5 ○ **Euston** Ⓑ Ⓑ
Connection only: Victoria line northbound and
Northern line (Bank Branch) northbound. Victoria
line southbound and Northern line (Bank Branch)
southbound

A5 ○ **Finchley Central** ⊖Ⓑ Ⓟ
Connection only between Northern line (Barnet
service) northbound and Northern line (Mill Hill
East service) northbound

B4 ○ **Finchley Road** Ⓑ EB Ⓐ WB Ⓒ
Connection only: Metropolitan line northbound
and Jubilee line northbound. Metropolitan line
southbound and Jubilee line southbound

B6 ○ **Finsbury Park** Ⓑ Ⓑ
Connection only: Victoria line northbound and
Piccadilly line northbound. Victoria line south-
bound and Piccadilly line southbound

E3 🚇 Fulham Broadway Ⓒ EB Ⓐ WB ⬆
Access facilities under construction

D9 🚇 **Gallions Reach** Ⓐ ⬆

D3 🚇 **Gloucester Road** Ⓑ Ⓑ
Connection only between District line eastbound
and Circle line

E8 🚇 **Greenwich** Ⓐ ⇌ ⬆

D4 ○ **Green Park** Ⓑ Ⓑ ⬆
Connection only between Piccadilly and Jubilee
lines. Long walkway between lifts

A9 ○ **Hainault** ⊖Ⓒ Ⓟ
Connection only between terminating eastbound
or starting westbound (certain trains only)

D3 🚇 **Hammersmith** Ⓑ EB Ⓒ WB Ⓐ Ⓒ ⬆ ⓘ ⊝
WC (shopping mall)
Long distance between District and Piccadilly lines
and Hammersmith & City line via street

A3 🚇 **Harrow & Wealdstone** Ⓒ ⇌ ⬆

B2 ○ **Harrow-on-the-Hill** Ⓑ Ⓟ
Connection only between fast, semi-fast and 'all
stations' Metropolitan line services

E1 🚇 **Heathrow Terminals 1, 2, 3** Ⓑ ⬆ ✈ ⓘ ⊝
WC (airport)
Lift on request. Long subway or travalator between
terminals and booking hall

E1 🚇 **Heathrow Terminal 4** Ⓑ ⬆ ✈ ⓘ
WC (airport)
Closed after 2345 Mondays to Saturdays and 2315
Sundays

D8 🚇 **Heron Quays** Ⓐ ⬆
Closed until winter 2002

B6 ○ **Highbury & Islington** Ⓑ ⇌
Connection only: Victoria line northbound and
National Rail (WAGN) northbound. Victoria line
southbound and National Rail southbound

A1 🚇 **Hillingdon** Ⓒ Ⓐ ⬆ Ⓟ

D1 🚇 Hounslow East Ⓐ
Access facilities under construction

E1 🚇 **Hounslow West** Ⓑ ⬆ Ⓟ
Long walkway between booking hall and stairlift

E8 🚇 **Island Gardens** Ⓐ ⬆

E5 ○ **Kennington** ⊖Ⓑ
Connection only between terminating and
continuing southbound trains

D3 🚇 **Kensington (Olympia)** Ⓑ ⇌
Open 0700 to 2345 Mondays to Saturdays and
0800 to 2345 Sundays

E2 🚇 **Kew Gardens** Ⓒ EB Ⓑ WB ⇌

B4 🚇 Kilburn Ⓐ NB Ⓑ SB
Access facilities under construction

C5 ○ **King's Cross St. Pancras** Ⓑ Ⓑ Ⓑ
Connection only between Hammersmith & City,
Circle and Metropolitan lines

E8 🚇 **Lewisham** Ⓐ ⬆ ⇌ ⊝

B8 ○ **Leytonstone** Ⓐ
Connection only from Central line eastbound
Epping branch to trains via Hainault (for
Barkingside)

D7 🚇 **Limehouse** Ⓐ ⬆ small

C6 ➡ **Liverpool Street** Ⓑ Ⓑ Ⓑ ⇌ ⬆ ⓘ
WC (National Rail concourse)
Accessible Circle, Metropolitan and Hammersmith
& City lines eastbound only. Long distance to
National Rail via lift. Connection only between
westbound Circle, Metropolitan and Hammersmith
& City lines

D6 🚇 **London Bridge** Ⓐ ⊖Ⓑ ⇌ ⬆ ⊝
WC (National Rail concourse)
Long distances between Northern line, Jubilee line
and National Rail via street

A8 ○ **Loughton** ⊖Ⓑ
Connection only between terminating and
continuing eastbound trains

D5 ○ **Mansion House** Ⓑ Ⓑ
Connection only: Circle line
eastbound and District line eastbound
(non-terminating). Circle line westbound and
District line westbound

C7 ○ **Mile End** Ⓑ Ⓑ Ⓑ
Connection only: District line, Hammersmith &
City line and Central line eastbound. District
line, Hammersmith & City line and Central line
westbound

D6 ○ **Monument** Ⓑ Ⓑ
Connection only: Circle line eastbound
and District line eastbound. Circle line westbound
and District line westbound

C6 ○ **Moorgate** Ⓑ Ⓑ Ⓑ
Connection only: Hammersmith & City line eastbound, Circle line eastbound and Metropolitan
line eastbound. Hammersmith & City line westbound, Circle line westbound and Metropolitan
line westbound

E8 🚇 **Mudchute** Ⓐ

B3 ○ Neasden ⚫C

Connection only for reverse direction travel to Wembley Park from Stanmore for northbound Metropolitan line. Also connection between terminating and continuing northbound trains

E7 ♿ New Cross ⚫C ≋

East London line and southbound National Rail only

C2 ○ North Acton ⚫C

Connection only between terminating and continuing westbound trains

D1 ○ Northfields ⚫B

Connection only between terminating and continuing westbound trains

D8 ♿ North Greenwich ⚫A ♿ ⊖ WC (ticket hall)

B3 ○ Northwick Park ⚫B

Connection only for reverse direction travel between Amersham, Chesham and Uxbridge

C3 ○ Notting Hill Gate ⚫B ⚫B

Connection only: Circle line northbound and District line northbound. Circle line southbound and District line southbound

C4 ○ Oxford Circus ⚫B ⚫B

Connection only: Victoria line northbound and Bakerloo line northbound. Victoria line southbound and Bakerloo line southbound

C3 ○ Paddington ⚫C ⚫C

Connection only: Circle line eastbound and District line eastbound. Circle line westbound and District line westbound

E3 ○ Parsons Green ⚫B

Connection only between terminating and continuing westbound trains

A2 ⬇ Pinner ⚫B 🅿

Metropolitan line southbound only

C8 ○ Plaistow ⚫C ⚫C

Connection only: District line eastbound, Hammersmith & City line eastbound and between terminating and continuing eastbound trains. District line westbound and Hammersmith & City line westbound

D8 ♿ Poplar ⚫A ♿ small

D9 ♿ Prince Regent ⚫A ♿

C8 ♿ Pudding Mill Lane ⚫A ♿

E3 ○ Putney Bridge ⚫B

Connection only between terminating and continuing westbound District line trains

B3 ○ Queen's Park ⚫A ≋

Connection only: Bakerloo line northbound and National Rail northbound (for Watford Junction) and between terminating and continuing northbound Bakerloo line trains. Bakerloo line southbound and National Rail southbound (for Euston)

B2 ○ Rayners Lane ⚫C ⚫B 🅿

Connection only: Metropolitan line eastbound and Piccadilly line eastbound. Metropolitan line westbound and Piccadilly line westbound

E2 ♿ Richmond ⚫B ≋ ⊖ 🅿 ℹ ♿

A1 ⬇ Rickmansworth ⚫C 🅿

Metropolitan line and National Rail southbound only

A8 ➡ Roding Valley ⚫B

Central line eastbound only. No service after 2000 daily

D9 ♿ Royal Albert ⚫A ♿

D8 ♿ Royal Victoria ⚫A ♿

A1 ➡ Ruislip ⚫C ⚫A 🅿

Metropolitan line eastbound and Piccadilly line eastbound only

B7 ○ Seven Sisters ⚫B

Connection only between terminating and continuing northbound trains

D7 ♿ Shadwell ⚫A ♿ small

Docklands Light Railway only

D4 ○ South Kensington ⚫B ⚫B

Connection only: District line eastbound and Circle line eastbound. District line westbound and Circle line westbound

D8 ♿ South Quay ⚫A ♿ small

E5 ♿ Southwark ⚫A ≋ ♿

Connection via street to National Rail

B8 ⬆ South Woodford ⚫A

Central line eastbound only via George Lane (West) entrance, (closed on Sundays)

A3 ♿ Stanmore ⚫A 🅿 WC (platform)

Long walkway from car park to platforms

F5 ○ Stockwell ⚫B ⚫B

Connection only: Victoria line northbound and Northern line northbound. Victoria line southbound and Northern line southbound

C8 ♿ Stratford ⚫B ⚫A ⚫A ≋ ♿ ⊖ WC (ticket hall)

Long ramp down and subway from entrance and Jubilee line to Central line, DLR and National Rail

C2 ○ Sudbury Town ⚫B EB ⚫A WB 🅿

A8 ➡ Theydon Bois ⚫A EB 🅿

Central line eastbound only

B7 ♿ Tottenham Hale ⚫B ♿ 🅿

D7 ♿ Tower Gateway ⚫A ♿ small

D6 ○ Tower Hill ⚫A ⚫A

Connection only: District line eastbound (non-terminating) and Circle line eastbound. District line westbound and Circle line westbound

D2 ○ Turnham Green ⚫B EB ⚫C WB ⚫B

Connection only: District line eastbound and Piccadilly line eastbound. District line westbound and Piccadilly line westbound. Piccadilly line trains only before 0645 and after 2230 Monday to Saturday and before 0745 and after 2230 Sundays

B9 ♿ Upminster ⚫C ≋ ♿ 🅿

C9 ♿ Upney ⚫C

A1 ♿ Uxbridge ⚫C ⚫B

E5 ♿ Waterloo ⚫A ≋ ♿ ⊖ 🅿

WC (National Rail concourse)

Accessible Jubilee line. Long distance to Eurostar and National Rail via lifts and street

B3 ○ Wembley Park ⒸⒷ℗ WC (platform)

Connection only: Metropolitan line northbound and Jubilee line northbound. Metropolitan line southbound and Jubilee line southbound. Also connection between terminating and continuing northbound trains

D3 ⬆ West Brompton Ⓑ ⇌

District line northbound only. Cross-platform connection to National Rail southbound. Connection to National Rail northbound via lift

D7 ♿ Westferry Ⓐ ⬆ small

A5 ♿ West Finchley Ⓑ

Northbound at all times, southbound Monday to Fridays 7.30am to 9.30am only

C8 ♿ West Ham ⒷⒷⒶ ⇌ ⬆

Access facilities under construction to District and Hammersmith & City line platforms.
Silverlink not accessible

D8 ♿ West India Quay Ⓐ ⬆ small

D5 ♿ Westminster ⒷⒷⒶ ⬆

C7 ○ Whitechapel ⒷⒷ

Connection only: District line eastbound and Hammersmith & City line eastbound and between terminating and continuing eastbound trains. District line westbound and Hammersmith & City line westbound

C3 ○ White City Ⓑ

Connection only between terminating and continuing westbound trains

B3 ○ Willesden Green Ⓑ

Connection only between terminating and continuing northbound trains

B3 ♿ Willesden Junction Ⓒ ⇌ ⬆

F3 ♿ Wimbledon Ⓑ ⇌ ⬆ 🚋 Ⓒ ℗

A8 ♿ Woodford Ⓐ ℗

A5 ♿ Woodside Park Ⓑ SB Ⓐ NB ℗

Key to index

Platform to train step

Colour of circle indicates line

Ⓐ Level to 100mm (4 inches)

Ⓑ 100 to 200mm (4 to 8 inches)

Ⓒ 200 to 300mm (8 to 12 inches)

Ⓐ Minus figures indicate a step down into the train

NB Platform to train measurements indicate the step height only. There may also be a significant gap. See 'Access to the Underground' for more detail

Abbreviations

EB	Eastbound	WB	Westbound
NB	Northbound	SB	Southbound

Explanation of symbols

♿ Step-free access to platforms

➡ Step-free access to platforms in one direction only

○ Some step-free access between connections. Entry and exit not accessible. Always check the index for details

⬆ Access via lift(s). Limited capacity (8 to 12 persons) indicated by 'small'

⇌ Accessible National Rail connections

Ⓒ Accessible station with major bus connections

🚋 Accessible connection to Tramlink

✈ Accessible airport connection

℗ Accessible station with car park

WC Accessible station with toilet on site or nearby (you must have a valid ticket to use toilets in a Compulsory Ticket Area)

🛈 Accessible station with Transport for London Travel Information Centre

Your feedback

This guide has been produced in consultation with disability groups and developed through partnership between TfL, LUL and Scope with the best information available at the time of publication (November 2002). We are keen to hear your comments or suggestions for future updates. Please contact Access & Mobility on **020 7941 4600**

If you have any general comments about your tube journey please contact London Underground Customer Services on **0845 330 9880** or textphone **020 7918 3500** or write to: **LU Customer Services, 55 Broadway, London SW1H 0BD.** If you are not satisfied with their response and wish to take the matter further, contact the London Transport Users Committee on **020 7505 9000**

Scope is a national disability organisation whose focus is people with cerebral palsy. Scope's aim is that disabled people achieve equality. **www.scope.org.uk**

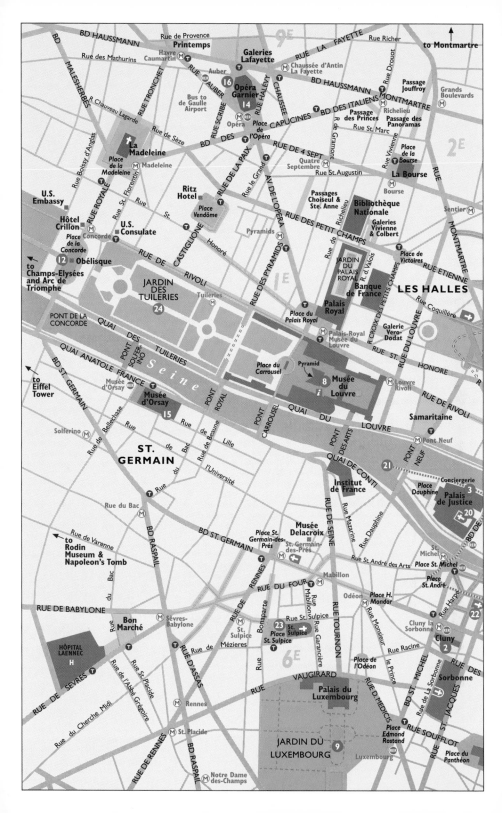

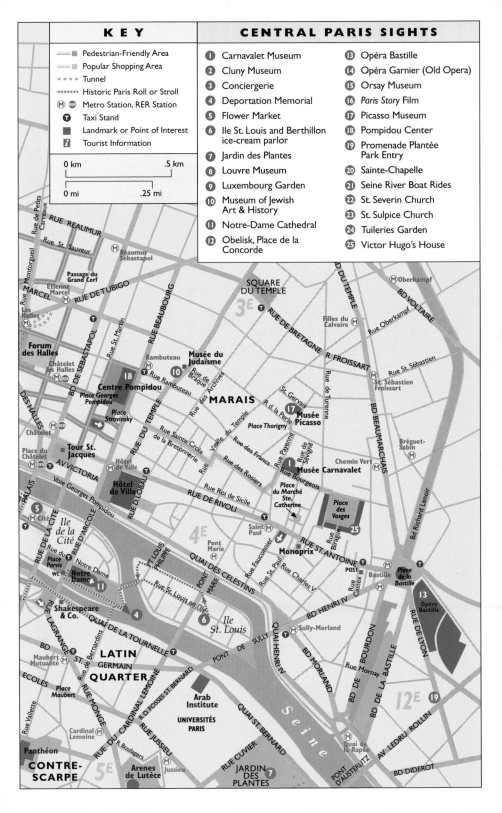

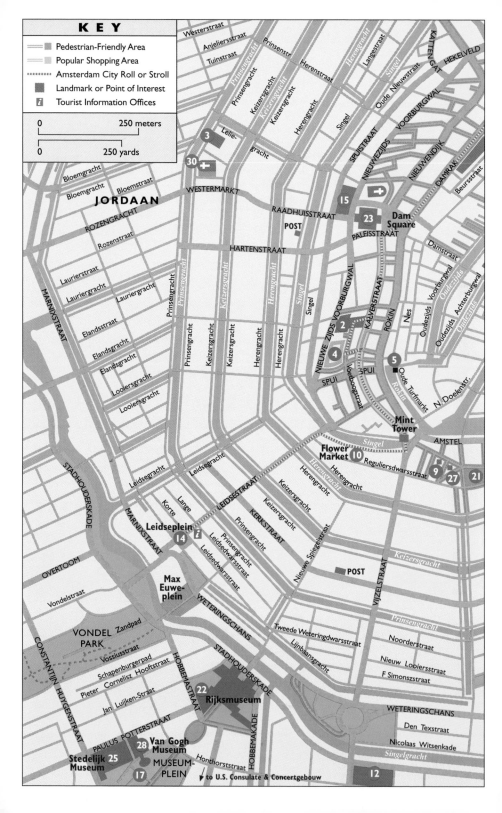

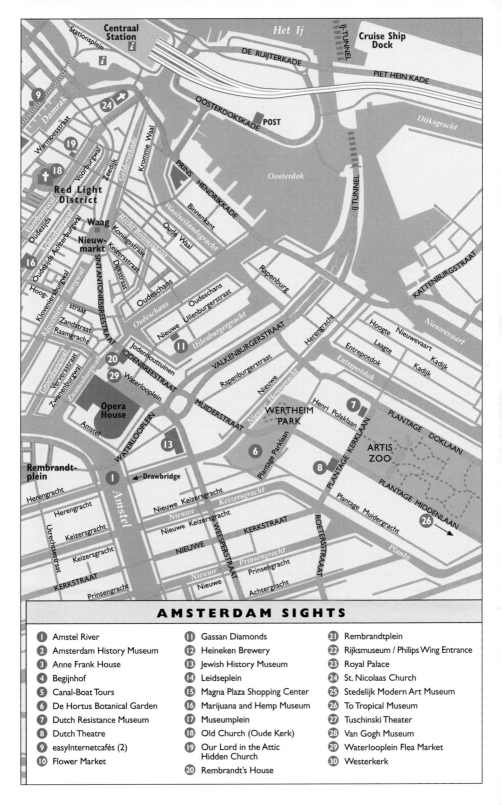

AMSTERDAM SIGHTS

1. Amstel River
2. Amsterdam History Museum
3. Anne Frank House
4. Begijnhof
5. Canal-Boat Tours
6. De Hortus Botanical Garden
7. Dutch Resistance Museum
8. Dutch Theatre
9. easyInternetcafés (2)
10. Flower Market
11. Gassan Diamonds
12. Heineken Brewery
13. Jewish History Museum
14. Leidseplein
15. Magna Plaza Shopping Center
16. Marijuana and Hemp Museum
17. Museumplein
18. Old Church (Oude Kerk)
19. Our Lord in the Attic Hidden Church
20. Rembrandt's House
21. Rembrandtplein
22. Rijksmuseum / Philips Wing Entrance
23. Royal Palace
24. St. Nicolaas Church
25. Stedelijk Modern Art Museum
26. To Tropical Museum
27. Tuschinski Theater
28. Van Gogh Museum
29. Waterlooplein Flea Market
30. Westerkerk

Rick Steves'
EASY
ACCESS
EUROPE

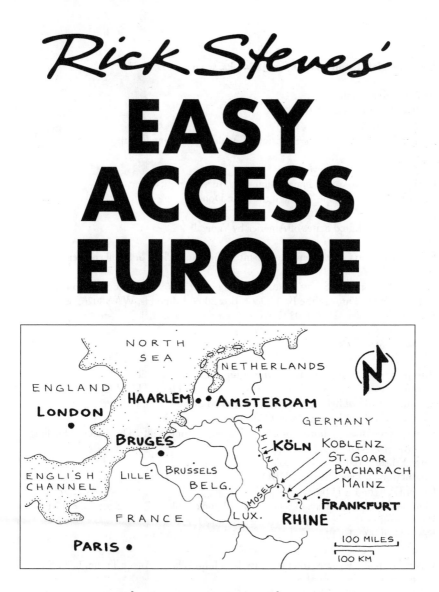

NORTH SEA

NETHERLANDS

ENGLAND

LONDON

HAARLEM • AMSTERDAM

GERMANY

BRUGES

RHINE

KÖLN

KOBLENZ
ST. GOAR
BACHARACH
MAINZ

ENGLISH
CHANNEL

LILLE

BRUSSELS

BELG.

MOSEL

FRANKFURT

FRANCE

LUX.

RHINE

PARIS •

100 MILES

100 KM

Rick Steves & Ken Plattner

AVALON
TRAVEL

For a complete listing of Rick Steves' books, see page 15.

Avalon Travel Publishing
1400 65th Street, Suite 250
Emeryville, CA 94608
Avalon Travel Publishing is a division of Avalon Publishing Group.

Printed in the United States of America by Worzalla

Special thanks to Gene Openshaw for his writing in the Roll or Stroll chapters.

For the latest on Rick Steves' lectures, guidebooks, tours, and public television series, contact Europe Through the Back Door, Box 2009, Edmonds, WA 98020, tel. 425/771-8303, fax 425/771-0833, www.ricksteves.com, or rick@ricksteves.com.

ISBN: 1-56691-668-2 • ISSN: 1549-1811

Europe Through the Back Door Managing Editor: Risa Laib
Europe Through the Back Door Editors: Cameron Hewitt, Jill Hodges
Avalon Travel Publishing Editor and Series Manager: Laura Mazer
Avalon Travel Publishing Project Editor: Patrick Collins
Research Assistance: Jim White, Carol Fisher, Sandra White, Dr. Clarence Snelling, Dr. Shirley Heckman
Copy Editor: Matthew Reed Baker
Production & Typesetting: PDBD
Cover Design: Kari Gim
Maps and Graphics: David C. Hoerlein, Rhonda Pelikan, Zoey Platt, Lauren Mills
Photography: Rick Steves, Cameron Hewitt, Ken Plattner
Front Matter Color Photos: p. i, Bruges Square © Rick Steves; p. xvi, Eiffel Tower © Dominic Bonuccelli
Cover Photos: Flower Market in Brussels © John Elk III; Arc de Triumphe © Steve Allen/Royalty Free/Getty Images
Avalon Travel Publishing Graphics Coordinator: Susan Snyder

Distributed to the book trade by Publishers Group West, Berkeley, California

CONTENTS

Top Easy Access Destinations in Europe

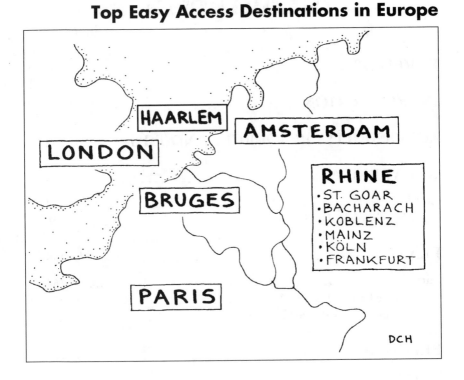

FOREWORD

By Susan Sygall, Executive Director of Mobility International USA

In my 30 years of international travel, I have found there are few things in life as exhilarating as visiting and exploring another culture. I've been traveling the Rick Steves way since 1973, and being a wheelchair rider has not held me back one bit. I was thrilled to be asked to write this foreword, since my most enriching experiences abroad have often been off the beaten path. As a person with a disability, one thing you are almost guaranteed: You will never have an ordinary day.

I cherish my memories of traveling through Europe. I spent a month traveling with no plans or reservations throughout Italy, hopping on different trains, and staying in both accessible and inaccessible hotels. I spoke to strangers in my makeshift Italian and flew down a hill in my wheelchair in Tuscany—to the surprise of whizzing cars—while inhaling the fragrant smells of the vineyards and cows. I was welcomed and befriended by strangers. I was also thrown out of restaurants and left in the rain with flat tires in the middle of a big city. I volunteered in a community-service project with 15 other folks from throughout Europe, sleeping on the floor in a sleeping bag and cooking our dinner of simple boiled potatoes while discussing international politics. I skied using adaptive equipment with other disabled people, and I bicycled and camped for several weeks in Holland and Germany using an adapted bicycle—with my wheelchair (and camping gear) in tow.

Europe is an enchanting place to visit. Where else can you be surrounded by some of the world's most spectacular art and architecture? Where better to dine on fabulous food and experience a slower pace, where sitting for hours at an outdoor café with a cappuccino and rich chocolate dessert is a way of life? I love the excitement of large cities, where you can see an original painting by van Gogh or Chagall. But I'm often drawn to the smaller villages and towns, where pungent cheese and fresh bread from the local bakery, or a picnic lunch surrounded by farmland and snowcapped mountains, makes memories that continue to refresh and renew me long after I have returned home to my busy life.

This book gives you the detailed information to make those life-changing experiences possible, and perhaps a bit easier.

As more people with disabilities enjoy the *real* Europe, they'll also be drawn to other non-traditional travel. Mobility International USA (www.miusa.org) and our National Clearinghouse on Disability and Exchange (NCDE) promote international exchange opportunities for people with disabilities, including study, volunteer, teaching, and internships abroad. An opportunity to live and learn alongside European people may significantly increase the value of your trip, and may also make it more affordable. (For more information, see page 32.)

As more civil rights legislation emerges in Europe and throughout the world, people with disabilities can look forward to a future of greater accessibility wherever we travel. We will undoubtedly be frustrated at times by the lack of access, but it is important that we do not internalize those feelings. Our frustration should be placed on the fact that people with disabilities have not yet achieved our human right to full access. Your travel experiences can become a positive force for changing the world, for fellow travelers as well as for the people with disabilities who live in the countries that you explore—who also want access to hotels, restaurants, historical landmarks, theaters, and campgrounds.

I know that you will enjoy this rich, well-researched book, which offers a rare combination of detailed information on accessibility with true local flavor. In the future, when all guidebooks include accessibility information as a standard feature, *Easy Access Europe* will be a welcome supplement.

Whether you travel alone, in a group of friends or family, or with a personal assistant, this book will assist you in exploring your European dreams. It is up to you to choose your own travel style, how much accessibility you require, and the type of experience you want to have. Use this book as a guide, but don't limit yourself from pursuing whatever wild idea you have. Be safe, be smart, have fun—and through your travels, make this world a better place for all people.

INTRODUCTION

Until now, wheelchair users and slow walkers have not had a resource—designed just for them—to guide them through Europe's highlights. The creaky, cobblestoned Old World has long had a reputation for poor accessibility. But in recent years, Europe has been making impressive strides towards opening its doors to everybody—including travelers with limited mobility. Maybe you're a wheelchair user with an adventurous spirit. Or perhaps you're traveling with a loved one who has limited mobility. Or you simply don't get around as well as you used to, but your sense of wanderlust refuses that rocking chair. This book is written for you.

Easy Access Europe

Since my first guidebook in 1980, my mission has been to make Europe accessible. Until now my books have focused on *economic* accessibility—travel needn't be a rich person's hobby. With this book, I broaden that passion to include *physical* accessibility.

I've teamed up with a committed band of researchers—led by Ken Plattner—who care about those who face extra physical challenges. Together we've written this book to help guide slow walkers and wheelchair users through Europe.

I picked a handful of Europe's best and most accessible destinations: London, Paris, Bruges, Amsterdam, and Germany's Rhine River Valley. Using core material from my existing guidebooks (the most carefully updated books available), Ken and his helpers researched everything a second time for accessibility.

Like an additional fermentation turns a good wine into fine champagne, this second research trip was designed to bring our Easy Access travelers a smooth and bubbly experience.

ACCESSIBILITY IN EUROPE

Compared to the U.S., Europe is not very accessible. It's the very charm of Europe—old, well-preserved, diverse, and very different from home—that often adds to the barriers. Many merchants, museum curators, hoteliers, and restaurateurs don't care about accessibility. Our challenge has been to find and describe the places that are welcoming and properly equipped.

We know levels of personal mobility vary tremendously from person to person. You need to consider your own situation very thoughtfully in choosing which attractions to see, places to stay, and things to avoid. We're not here to tell you what you can and can't do. Instead, we've attempted to give you the lay of the land to help you make informed decisions for yourself.

We've come up with various ways of letting you know what accessibility features you can expect at each building. Most important are Accessibility Levels and Accessibility Codes.

Accessibility Levels

In this book, we rate buildings (sights, hotels, restaurants, facilities, and other venues) using four categories, each one representing a different level of accessibility. Determine which of these levels matches your own level of personal mobility, and use the levels as a shortcut for deciding which buildings are accessible to you.

Level 1—Fully Accessible: A Level 1 building is completely barrier-free, flat, and specifically adapted for wheelchair users. This includes wide doors and elevators that are adapted to accommodate a person using a wheelchair. If the building has a bathroom, it must be adapted for use by a wheelchair rider: an adapted toilet and sink, grab bars, wide doors, and, if applicable, roll-in (no rim) showers. By definition, Level 1 properties are rare in Europe.

Level 2—Moderately Accessible: A Level 2 building is suitable for, but not specifically adapted to accommodate, a person using a wheelchair. This level will work for a wheelchair user who can make transfers and take a few steps. A person who is permanently in a wheelchair may require some assistance here (either from a companion or from staff).

Level 3—Minimally Accessible: A Level 3 building is satisfactory for people who have minimal mobility difficulties (that is, people who usually do not use a wheelchair, but take more time to do things than a non-disabled person). This building may have some steps—but not too many—and has limited barriers to mobility. Level 3 buildings are best suited to slow walkers; wheelchair users will require substantial assistance here. Most of the buildings in this book fall into this category.

Level 4—Not Accessible: There are buildings in these destinations that are simply not accessible to people with limited mobility (for example, a church tower that is reachable only by climbing several flights of steep stairs, or a museum interior that has many levels with lots of steps and no elevator). These buildings—which are, thankfully, quite rare in this book—are categorized as Level 4. We include them because they are important to know about, and because the information might be useful to a non-disabled companion, or to readers with limited mobility but an adventurous spirit (such as slow walkers who can climb several flights of stairs, if given enough time, to reach a worthwhile sight).

Adapted vs. Suitable

Throughout this book, we use two very different terms to describe buildings and facilities that can be used by wheelchair riders: *adapted* and *suitable*.

An **adapted** building has been designed or retrofitted specifically for independent wheelchair users. For example, an adapted bathroom has wide doors, a roll-in shower, a specially adapted sink that can easily be accessed by a wheelchair user, and grab bars to facilitate toilet transfers.

A **suitable** building has not been specifically designed for wheelchair users, but it can still be used by people with limited mobility—that is, wheelchair users who have a greater degree of mobility (can make transfers or walk a few steps without assistance), or wheelchair users with a lesser degree of mobility who have assistance. For example, a suitable bathroom has wide enough doors for a person in a wheelchair to enter, and enough space inside to negotiate the wheelchair—but it does *not* have specially adapted toilets, sinks, or showers (for instance, no grab bars to help with transfers). In Europe, most buildings are suitable rather than adapted.

ACCESSIBILITY CODES

For more specific information on exactly what accessibility features each building has, we use a series of easy-to-understand symbols. These accessibility codes are intended to give you a quick overview of what to expect. If applicable, more specific details about the facility (e.g., exact number and height of steps, special instructions for gaining entry) are explained at the end of the listing.

CODE	MEANING	EXPLANATION
AE	Accessible Entryway	A level entryway with no steps or barriers and a door wide enough for an independent wheelchair user.
AE+A	Accessible Entry with Assistance	An entryway with one or two small steps and a door wide enough for a wheelchair user.
AI	Accessible Interior	A flat, spacious, barrier-free interior with enough room to comfortably negotiate a wheelchair.
AI+A	Accessible Interior with Assistance	An interior that has enough room to negotiate a wheelchair, but is not barrier-free (e.g., a few steps, narrow doors, tight aisles, and so on).
AT	Accessible Toilet	The toilet is at an appropriate height and has grab bars to allow the wheelchair user to transfer without assistance.
AT+A	Accessible Toilet with Assistance	A toilet that is suitable for a wheelchair user, but is not specifically adapted. Wheelchair users will likely need assistance.
AL	Accessible Lift (elevator)	An elevator big enough to be used by an independent wheelchair user.

AL+A	Accessible Lift with Assistance	An elevator that is small or presents other barriers to the wheelchair user, requiring assistance.
AR	Accessible Room	A hotel room big enough for a wheelchair to move around freely. There are no barriers to impede independent wheelchair users.
AR+A	Accessible Room with Assistance	A hotel room that is cramped and not barrier-free, but suitable for a wheelchair user who has assistance.
AB	Accessible Bathroom	A hotel bathroom specially adapted for wheelchair users, with grab bars throughout, wide entry doors, a bathtub or roll-in shower, raised toilet, and adapted sink.
AB+A	Accessible Bathroom with Assistance	The door is wide enough for wheelchair entry, but the wheelchair user will require some assistance to transfer to the tub or toilet (no grab bars).
❤	Heart	An establishment that has a positive, helpful attitude towards travelers with limited mobility.

So, for example, imagine a restaurant with one 8" entry step, a fully accessible interior, toilets that are down a narrow winding stairway of ten 6" steps, and a staff that is warm and welcoming. This place would be coded as: **AE+A, AI, ❤**.

Now imagine a hotel that is fully accessible, with no barriers at the entry or inside; a wheelchair-accessible elevator; a specially adapted room and bathroom designed for wheelchair users; and a friendly staff that welcomes travelers with limited mobility. That hotel would be coded as: **AE, AI, AL, AR, AB, ❤**. There are not a lot of these fully accessible places around, but we were able to sprinkle the book with a few great options found in our explorations.

USING THIS BOOK

The **Accessibility Resources and Tips** chapter includes an array of disability organizations, books, and other resources to help you plan a smooth trip, and contains tips from experienced travelers with limited mobility.

The **Country Introductions** give you a snapshot of each country's culture and include country-specific resources for accessible travel.

Each destination in this book is covered as a mini-vacation on its own, filled with exciting sights and homey, accessible, and affordable places to stay. Using the levels and codes described on previous pages, we provide detailed information on accessibility for sights, restaurants, hotels, tourist offices, and so on. For each destination, you'll find the following:

Accessibility gives you an overview of what kind of access concerns you can expect.

Orientation includes tourist information, city transportation, and an easy-to-read map designed to make the text clear and your arrival smooth.

Sights are rated: ▲▲▲—Don't miss; ▲▲—Try hard to see; ▲—Worthwhile if you can make it; no rating—Worth knowing about.

Sleeping and **Eating** include addresses and phone numbers of our favorite budget and splurge hotels and restaurants.

Transportation Connections covers how to reach nearby destinations by train, bus, or taxi. We've focused our listings on only the most accessible options.

The **Appendix** has a list of national tourist offices and U.S. embassies, telephone tips, and a climate chart.

With the help of this book, you'll travel like a temporary local, getting the most out of every mile, minute, and dollar. You won't waste time on mediocre sights because this guidebook, unlike others, covers only the best. We've worked hard to assemble good-value, fully accessible accommodations and eateries for each stop. And as you travel the route we know and love, we're happy you'll be meeting our favorite Europeans.

Trip Costs

Five components make up your trip cost: airfare, surface transportation, room and board, sightseeing/entertainment, and shopping/miscellany.

Airfare: Don't try to sort through the mess yourself. Get and use a good travel agent. A basic round-trip U.S.A.-to-Europe flight should cost $500 to $1,000 (even cheaper in winter), depending on where you fly from and when. Always consider saving time and money in Europe by flying "open-jaw" (flying into one city and out of another, such as flying into London and out of Frankfurt).

Surface Transportation: Your best mode depends upon accessibility concerns, the time you have, and the scope of your trip.

Trains are often—but not always—moderately accessible or better, and conveniently connect the big cities in this book (especially London and Paris, just 2.5 hrs by Eurostar train). If you go by train, consider a Eurail Selectpass (see page 18). Train passes are normally available only outside of Europe. You may save money by simply buying tickets as you go.

Renting a **car** has its advantages. Most major car-rental agencies have specially adapted vehicles. Though struggling with traffic and parking can be stressful—especially in the big cities covered in this book—having your own adapted rental car means that you don't have to rely on public transportation. Drivers can figure $250 per person per week (based on 2 people splitting the cost of the car, tolls, gas, and insurance). Car rental is cheapest to arrange from the United States. Leasing, for trips over three weeks, is even cheaper.

When it comes to mobility, **taxis** are the great equalizer. Budget a little extra to get around in cities by taxi.

Room and Board: You can thrive in Europe in 2004 on an overall average of $100 a day per person for room and board (more for cities, less for towns). A $100 a day budget allows $10 apiece for lunch, $10 for snacks, $15 for dinner, and $65 for lodging (based on 2 people splitting the cost of a $130 double room that includes breakfast).

Sightseeing and Entertainment: In big cities, figure $5 to $10 per major sight, $2 for minor ones, and $25 for splurge experiences (e.g., bus tours, concerts, and plays). An overall average of $15 a day works for most. Don't skimp here. After all, this category directly powers most of the experiences all the other expenses are designed to make possible.

Shopping and Miscellany: Figure $1 per postcard and $2 per coffee, beer, and ice-cream cone. Shopping can vary in cost from nearly nothing to a small fortune. Good budget travelers find that this category has little to do with assembling a trip full of lifelong and wonderful memories.

Exchange Rates

We list prices in the local currency throughout this book. Of the destinations covered, you'll use pounds sterling in Britain and euros everywhere else.

1 British pound sterling (£) = about $1.70

The British pound, also called a "quid," is broken into 100 pence (p). Pence means "cents." You'll find coins ranging from 1p to £2 and bills from £5 to £50. To very roughly convert pounds to dollars, add 50 percent to British prices: £6 is about $9 (actually $10.20), £3 is about $4.50, and 80p is about $1.20.

1 euro (€) = about $1.15

One euro is broken down into 100 cents. You'll find coins ranging from one cent to two euros, and bills from five euros to 500 euros. To convert prices in euros to dollars, add 15 percent: €20 = about $23, €45 = about $52.

Prices, Times, and Discounts

The accessibility information in this book, as well as the prices, hours, and telephone numbers, are accurate as of mid-2003. Europe is always changing, and I know you'll understand that this, like any other guidebook, starts to yellow even before it's printed. For the latest, see www.ricksteves.com/update. At the Web site, check the Graffiti Wall (select "Rick Steves' Guidebooks," then "Easy Access Europe") for a valuable list of reports and experiences—good and bad—from fellow travelers.

In Europe—and in this book—you'll be using the 24-hour clock. After 12:00 noon, keep going—13:00, 14:00, and so on. For anything over 12, subtract 12 and add p.m. (14:00 is 2 p.m.).

While discounts for sights and transportation are not listed in this book, seniors (60 and over), students (with International Student Identity Cards), and youths (under 18) may snare discounts—but only by asking. Some discounts (particularly for sights) are granted only to European residents.

SIGHTSEEING PRIORITIES

This book covers northern Europe's top destinations, which could be lined up for a quick one-week getaway or a full-blown three-week vacation. Combining London and Paris with the speedy Eurostar train offers perhaps the most exciting 10 days of big-city thrills Europe has to offer.

Of course, you should arrange your itinerary according to your own level of mobility—building in as much rest as you need. But for a relatively fast-paced tour of the destinations in this book, consider this plan:

Day	Plan	Sleep in
1	Arrive in London	London
2	London	London
3	London	London
4	London	London
5	Eurostar to Paris	Paris
6	Paris	Paris
7	Paris	Paris
8	Paris	Paris
9	To Bruges	Bruges
10	Bruges	Bruges
11	Bruges	Bruges
12	To Amsterdam	Amsterdam
13	Amsterdam	Amsterdam
14	Amsterdam	Amsterdam
15	To Köln, then Rhine	Rhine
16	Rhine	Rhine
17	To Frankfurt	Frankfurt
18	Fly home	

Most attractions and events have special discounts for wheelchair users (many are free to you as well as your companion). A traveler with limited mobility generally may go to the head of the line for attractions and events. Don't be shy. Europe may not have as many ramps and elevators as the United States, but it's socially aware.

When to Go

May, June, September, and October are the best travel months. Peak season (July and August) offers the sunniest weather and the most exciting slate of activities, but the worst crowds. Because it's also the most physically grueling time to travel, many travelers with limited mobility prefer to visit outside of summer.

Off-season, October through April, expect generally shorter hours at attractions, more lunchtime breaks, fewer activities, and fewer guided tours in English. If you're traveling off-season, be careful to confirm opening times. In winter, I like to set up a full week in a big city (like Paris or London) to take advantage of fewer crowds and a cultural calendar in full swing.

As a general rule of thumb any time of year, the climate north of the Alps is mild (like Seattle), and south of the Alps it's like Arizona. For specifics, check the climate chart in the appendix.

Red Tape, News, and Electricity

Red Tape: Americans need a passport but no visa and no shots to travel throughout Europe. Crossing borders is easy. Sometimes you won't even realize it's happened. When you do change countries, however, you change phone cards, postage stamps, gas prices, ways to flush a toilet, words for "hello," figurehead monarchs, and breakfast breads. Plan ahead for these changes: Brush up on the new language, and use up stamps, phone cards, and—when you're going between Britain and the continent—any spare coins (spend them on candy, souvenirs, gas, or a telephone call home).

News: Americans keep in touch with the *International Herald Tribune* (published almost daily via satellite throughout Europe). Every Tuesday, the European editions of *Time* and *Newsweek* hit the stands with articles of particular interest to European travelers. Sports addicts can get their fix from *USA Today*. News in English will only be sold where there's enough demand: in big cities and tourist centers. Good Web sites include www.europeantimes.com and http://news.bbc.co.uk. If you're concerned about how some event might affect your safety as an American traveling abroad, call the U.S. consulate or embassy in the nearest big city for advice (see appendix for list).

Watt's up? If you're bringing electrical gear, you'll need an adapter plug (two round prongs for the continent, three flat ones for Britain; sold cheap at travel stores like Rick's at www.ricksteves.com). Travel appliances often have convenient, built-in converters; look for a voltage switch marked 120V (U.S.) and 240V (Europe). If yours doesn't have a built-in converter, you'll have to buy an external one.

Banking

Bring plastic (ATM, credit, or debit cards) along with a couple hundred dollars as a backup. Traveler's checks are a waste of time and money.

To withdraw cash from a bank machine, you'll need a PIN code (numbers only, no letters) and your bankcard. Before you go, verify with your bank that your card will work and alert them that you'll be making withdrawals in Europe; otherwise, the bank may not approve transactions if it perceives unusual spending patterns. Bring two cards in case one gets demagnetized or eaten by a machine. If you plan on getting cash advances with your regular credit card, be sure to ask the card company about fees before you leave.

Visa and MasterCard are more commonly accepted than American Express. Just like at home, credit or debit cards work easily at larger hotels, restaurants, and shops, but smaller businesses prefer payment in local currency.

Regular banks have the best rates for changing money and traveler's checks. For a large exchange, it pays to compare rates and fees. Post offices and train stations usually change money if you can't get to a bank.

You should use a money belt or neck pouch (available at www.ricksteves .com). Thieves target tourists. A money belt provides peace of mind. You can carry lots of cash safely in a money belt.

Don't be petty about changing money. You don't need to waste time every few days returning to a bank or tracking down a cash machine. Change a week's worth of money, get big bills, stuff them in your money belt, and travel!

If Your Credit Cards are Lost or Stolen: If you lose your credit, debit, or ATM card, you can stop people from using your card by reporting the loss immediately to the respective global customer-assistance centers. Call these 24-hour U.S. numbers collect: Visa (410/581-9994), MasterCard (636/722-7111), and American Express (336/393-1111).

Providing the following information will help expedite the process: the name of the financial institution that issued you the card; full card number; the cardholder's name as printed on the card; billing address; home phone number; circumstances of the loss or theft; and identification verification, such as a Social Security number or birth date and your mother's maiden name. (Packing along a photocopy of the front and back of your cards helps you answer the harder questions.) You can generally receive a temporary card within two business days in Europe.

If you promptly report your card lost or stolen, you typically won't be responsible for any unauthorized transactions on your account, although many banks charge a liability fee of about $50.

As you can see...it's smart to wear a money belt. Keep your cards safe inside, not in a wallet or day bag.

VAT Refunds and Customs Regulations

VAT Refunds for Shoppers: Wrapped into the purchase price of your souvenirs is a Value-Added Tax (VAT), ranging from 7 to 22 percent throughout Europe. If you make a purchase that meets your host country's minimum purchase requirement (see sidebar below) at a store that participates in the VAT refund scheme, you're entitled to get most of the tax back. Personally, we've never felt that VAT refunds are worth the hassle, but if you do, here's the scoop.

VAT RATES
AND MINIMUM PURCHASES REQUIRED
TO QUALIFY FOR REFUNDS

Country of Purchase	VAT rate*	Minimum in Local Currency	Minimum in U.S. dollars**
Belgium	17%	€125	$155
France	16.4%	€175	$220
Germany	13.8%	€25	$30
Great Britain	15%	£30	$55
Netherlands	15.9%	€137	$170

*VAT Rate indicates the percentage of the total purchase price that is VAT.
**Exchange rate as of 3/1/04
Source: Global Refund
Please note: Figures are subject to change. For more information, visit www.traveltax.msu.edu or www.globalrefund.com.

If you're lucky, the merchant will subtract the tax when you make your purchase (this is more likely if the store ships the goods to your home). Otherwise, you'll need to:

Get the paperwork. Have the merchant completely fill out the necessary refund document, typically called a "cheque." You'll have to present your passport at the store.

Have your cheque(s) stamped at the border by the customs agent who deals with VAT refunds. If you're in a European Union country, then you get the stamp at your last stop in the European Union. Otherwise, get your cheque stamped when you leave the country.

It's best to keep your purchases in your carry-on for viewing, but if they're too large or considered too dangerous (such as knives) to carry on, then track down the proper customs agent to inspect them before you check your bag. You're not supposed to use your purchased goods before you leave. If you show up at customs wearing your new sweater, officials might look the other way—or deny you a refund.

To collect your refund, you'll need to return your stamped documents to the retailer or its representative. Many merchants work with a service that has offices at major airports, ports, and border crossings, such as Easy Tax Free (www.easytaxfree.com), Global Refund (www.globalrefund .com) or Premier Tax Free (www.premiertaxfree.com). These services, which extract a 4 percent fee, usually can refund your money immediately in your currency of choice or credit your card (within two billing cycles). If you have to deal directly with the retailer, mail the store your stamped documents and then wait. It could take months.

Customs Regulations: You can take home $800 in souvenirs per person duty-free. The next $1,000 is taxed at a flat 3 percent. After that, you pay the individual item's duty rate. You can also bring in duty-free a liter of alcohol (slightly more than a standard-sized bottle of wine), a carton of cigarettes, and up to 100 cigars. To check customs rules and duty rates, visit www.customs.gov.

Travel Smart

Your trip to Europe is like a complex play—easier to follow and really appreciate on a second viewing. While no one does the same trip twice to gain that advantage, reading this book before your trip accomplishes much the same thing.

Reread this book as you travel and visit local tourist information offices. Upon arrival in a new town, lay the groundwork for a smooth departure. Buy a phone card and use it for reservations, reconfirmations, and double-checking hours. Enjoy the friendliness of the local people. Slow down and ask questions. Most locals are eager to point you in their idea of the right direction. Wear your money belt, learn the local currency, and develop a simple formula to quickly estimate rough prices in dollars. Keep a notepad in your pocket for organizing your thoughts. Those who expect to travel smart, do.

As you read this book, note the days of markets and festivals and when sights are closed. Anticipate problem days: Mondays are bad in Bruges, Tuesdays are bad in Paris. Museums and sights, especially large ones, usually stop admitting people 30 to 60 minutes before closing time.

Sundays have the same pros and cons as they do for travelers in the United States. Sightseeing attractions are generally open, shops and banks are closed, and city traffic is light. Rowdy evenings are rare on Sundays. Saturdays in Europe are virtually weekdays with earlier closing hours. Hotels in tourist areas are most crowded on Fridays and Saturdays.

Plan ahead for banking, laundry, post office chores, and picnics. Mix intense and relaxed periods. Every trip (and every traveler) needs at least a few slack days. Pace yourself. Assume you will return.

Tourist Information

The tourist information office is your best first stop in any new city. Try to arrive, or at least telephone, before it closes. In this book, we'll refer to a tourist information office as a TI. Throughout Europe, you'll find TIs are usually well-organized and English-speaking.

As national budgets tighten, many TIs have been privatized. This means they become sales agents for big tours and hotels, and their "information" becomes unavoidably colored. While the TI has listings of all the rooms and is eager to book you one, use their room-finding service only as a last resort. Across Europe, room-finding services are charging commissions from hotels, taking fees from travelers, blacklisting establishments that buck their materialistic rules, and refusing to give hard opinions on the relative value of one place over another. The accommodations stakes are too high to go potluck through the TI. By using the listings in this book, you can avoid that kind of "help."

Tourist Offices, U.S. Addresses: Each country has a national tourist office in the U.S. (see the appendix for addresses). Before your trip, you can ask for the free general-information packet and for specific information, such as city maps and schedules of upcoming festivals.

Rick Steves' Books, Videos, and DVDs

While Rick's other guidebooks are written for a general audience—and are not mobility-specific—they may be helpful in your travels.

Rick Steves' Europe Through the Back Door gives you budget-travel skills, such as minimizing jet lag, packing light, planning your itinerary, traveling by car or train, finding rooms, changing money, avoiding rip-offs, using

---

RICK STEVES' GUIDEBOOKS

Country Guides
Rick Steves' Best of Europe
Rick Steves' Best of Eastern Europe
Rick Steves' France
Rick Steves' Germany, Austria & Switzerland
Rick Steves' Great Britain
Rick Steves' Ireland
Rick Steves' Italy
Rick Steves' Scandinavia
Rick Steves' Spain & Portugal

City and Regional Guides
Rick Steves' Amsterdam, Bruges & Brussels
Rick Steves' Florence & Tuscany
Rick Steves' London
Rick Steves' Paris
Rick Steves' Provence & the French Riviera
Rick Steves' Rome
Rick Steves' Venice
Rick Steves' Easy Access Europe

(Avalon Travel Publishing)

mobile phones, hurdling the language barrier, staying healthy, taking great photographs, using a bidet, and much more. The book also includes chapters on 38 of Rick's favorite "Back Doors."

Rick Steves' Country Guides, an annually updated series that covers Europe, offer you the latest on the top sights and destinations, with tips on how to make your trip efficient and fun. You'll learn the best places to stay, eat, enjoy, and explore.

Rick's **City and Regional Guides,** freshly updated every year, focus on Europe's most compelling destinations. Along with specifics on sights, restaurants, hotels, and nightlife, you'll get self-guided, illustrated tours of the outstanding museums and most characteristic neighborhoods.

Rick's *London, Paris,* and *Amsterdam, Bruges & Brussels* city guidebooks are beefy yet pocketsize editions covering these destinations with more depth than this *Easy Access* book does. The main difference is that the individual city guides have many more museum tours and self-guided walks.

Rick Steves' Europe 101: History and Art for the Traveler (with Gene Openshaw, 2000) gives you the story of Europe's people, history, and art. Written for smart people who were sleeping in their history and art classes before they knew they were going to Europe, *101* helps Europe's sights come alive.

Rick Steves' Mona Winks (with Gene Openshaw, 2001) gives you fun, easy-to-follow self-guided tours of the major museums in London, Paris, Amsterdam, Venice, Florence, Rome, and Madrid. When you're touring museums, *Mona* becomes a valued friend.

After more than 25 years as an English-only traveler struggling with other phrase books, Rick designed a series of practical, fun, and budget-oriented phrase books to help you ask the gelato man for a free little taste and the hotel receptionist for a room with no street noise. If you want to chat with your cabbie and make hotel reservations over the phone, the pocket-sized **Rick Steves' Phrase Books** (French, German, Italian, Portuguese, Spanish, and French/Italian/German) will come in handy.

Rick's new public television series, *Rick Steves' Europe,* keeps churning out shows. Many of the 82 episodes (from the new series and from *Travels in Europe with Rick Steves*) explore the destinations featured in this book. These air nationally on public television and are also available in information-packed home videos and seven- or eight-episode DVDs (available online at www.ricksteves.com).

Rick Steves' Postcards from Europe (1999), Rick's autobiographical book, packs 25 years of travel anecdotes and insights into the ultimate 2,000-mile European adventure. Through Rick's guidebooks, he shares his favorite European discoveries with you. *Postcards* introduces you to Rick's favorite European friends.

All Rick Steves books are published by Avalon Travel Publishing (www.travelmatters.com).

Other Guidebooks

You may want some supplemental information, especially if you'll be traveling beyond our recommended destinations. When you consider the improvements they'll make in your $3,000 vacation, $25 or $35 for extra maps and books is money well spent. Especially for several people traveling by car, the weight and expense are negligible.

There are a handful of good books written for travelers with limited mobility. We enjoy Candy Harrington's *Barrier-Free Travel: A Nuts and Bolts Guide for Wheelers and Slow Walkers*. For travel in London and Paris, we also highly recommend *Access in London* and *Access in Paris* (by Gordon Couch; Access Project, 39 Bradley Gardens, West Ealing, London W13 8HE, www.accessproject-phsp.org, gordon.couch@virgin.net).

Patrick Simpson's *Wheelchair Around the World* includes an extensive bibliography with resources to help people with disabilities plan their trip ($29.70 postpaid, Pentland Press, 5122 Bur Oak Circle, Raleigh, NC 27612, tel. 919/782-0281). The *Around the World Resource Guide,* published by Access for Disabled Americans, is an easy-to-use bibliography of services and resources (both print and Internet) for disabled people.

For specifics, Fodor's Gold Guides always have a section on travel for people with disabilities.

Maps

The black-and-white maps in this book, drawn by Dave Hoerlein, are concise and simple. Dave, who is well-traveled in Europe, has designed the maps to help you locate recommended places and get to the tourist information offices, where you can pick up a more in-depth map (usually free) of the city or region.

For maps of Europe and individual European countries, consider the Rick Steves' Planning Map series—geared to travelers' needs—with sightseeing destinations listed prominently (visit www.ricksteves.com).

European bookstores, especially in tourist areas, have good selections of maps. For drivers, we'd recommend a 1:200,000- or 1:300,000-scale map for each country. Train travelers can usually manage fine with the freebies they get with their train pass and at local tourist offices.

Transportation in Europe
By Car or Train?
Each has pros and cons. Cars are an expensive headache in big cities but are fully accessible. Groups of three or more go cheaper by car. If you're packing heavy, go by car. Trains are best for city-to-city travel and give you the convenience of doing long stretches overnight. By train, we arrive relaxed and well-rested—not so by car. Note that most larger European train stations are fully accessible, but many others are not.

If visiting only the destinations covered in this book, you're probably best off simply buying train tickets. A car is worthless in the cities, where taxis and public transit make more sense. Connecting London and Paris is clearly easiest by Eurostar train. And train connections for Bruges, Amsterdam, and the Rhine are convenient with good access.

Traveling by Train
A major mistake Americans make in Europe is relating public transportation in Europe to the pathetic public transportation they're used to at home. By rail you'll have Europe by the tail. To study train schedules in advance on the Web, look up http://bahn.hafas.de/english.html.

While you can buy tickets as you go ("point to point"), you can save money by getting a railpass if you plan to travel beyond the destinations in this book.

If you want to travel first-class between the destinations in this book, a Eurail Selectpass for five or six days of travel in France, Benelux, and Germany is convenient and worthwhile (starts at $304 per person for 2 or more traveling together, 5 days within a 2-month travel period). If you plan to travel beyond these destinations, the pass can actually save you money, particularly for long rides in Germany or France. However, if you're happy in second class, or if you can take advantage of discounts for wheelchair users, then point-to-point tickets are cheaper for this route. Note that a Eurostar ticket from London to the continent is not covered by any railpass, but railpass holders and wheelchair users get discounts.

For a summary of railpass deals and point-to-point ticket options (available in the U.S. and in Europe), check our free Railpass Guide at www.ricksteves.com.

Car Rental

It's cheaper to arrange European car rentals in the United States, so check rates with your travel agent or directly with the companies. Most car-rental agencies offer cars that are adapted for drivers with disabilities. Rent by the week with unlimited mileage. If you'll be renting for three weeks or more, ask your agent about leasing, which is a scheme to save on insurance and taxes. I normally rent the smallest, least expensive model. Explore your drop-off options (and costs).

Driving: Distance and Time

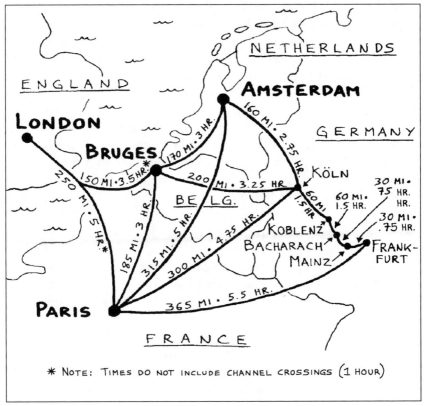

For peace of mind, I spring for the Collision Damage Waiver insurance (CDW, about $15 per day), which has a zero- or low-deductible rather than the standard value-of-the-car "deductible." Ask your travel agent about money-saving alternatives to CDW. A few gold credit cards cover CDW insurance; quiz your credit-card company on the worst-case scenario. Or consider Travel Guard, which offers CDW insurance for $7 a day (U.S. tel. 800/826-1300, www.travelguard.com); it'll cover you throughout most of Europe, but is not honored in Scotland, Ireland, and Italy.

Driving

For much of Europe, all you need is your valid U.S. driver's license and a car. Confirm with your rental company if an international driver's license is required in the countries you plan to visit. You probably won't need it for the destinations in this book other than Germany. If you're traveling further, you'd also need it for Austria, Italy, Portugal, Spain, and Eastern Europe (at your local AAA office—$10 plus the cost of two passport-type photos).

While gas is expensive, if you keep an eye on the big picture, paying $4 per gallon is more a psychological trauma than a financial one. Use the freeways whenever possible. They are free in the Netherlands and Germany. The French autoroutes are punctuated by tollbooths (charging about $1 for every 10 minutes). The alternative to these superfreeways often is being marooned in rural traffic. The autostrada/autoroute usually saves enough time, gas, and nausea to justify its expense. Mix scenic country-road rambling with high-speed autobahning, but don't forget that in Europe, the shortest distance between two points is the autobahn.

Metric: Outside of Britain, get used to metric. A liter is about a quart, four to a gallon. A kilometer is six-tenths of a mile. I figure kilometers to miles by cutting them in half and adding back 10 percent of the original (120 km: 60 + 12 = 72 miles; 300 km: 150 + 30 = 180 miles).

Parking: Parking is a costly headache in big cities. You'll pay about $20 a day to park safely. Ask at your hotel for advice. Keep a pile of coins in your ashtray for parking meters, public phones, launderettes, and wishing wells.

Transportation at Your Destination

The most accessible way to get around town is usually by taxi (though often you'll have to transfer into the car and have the driver fold your

wheelchair to put it in the trunk). Some cities have some fully accessible buses and subway routes. Other cities' transportation systems—like Paris' Métro—have very poor accessibility. We've explained your options for each destination, and recommended what works best.

Telephones, Mail, and E-mail

Smart travelers learn the phone system and use it daily to reserve or reconfirm rooms, find tourist information, or phone home. Many European phone booths take insertable phone cards rather than coins.

Phone Cards: There are two kinds of phone cards: official phone cards that you insert into the phone (which can only be used in phone booths), and scratch-off PIN cards that can be used from virtually any phone, even your hotel room (you dial a toll-free number and enter your PIN code). Both kinds of cards work only in the country where you bought them (for example, a Dutch phone card works when you're making calls in the Netherlands, but is worthless in France).

You can buy **insertable phone cards** from post offices, newsstands, or tobacco shops. Insert the card into the phone and make your call; the value is deducted from your card. These are a good deal for calling within Europe, but it's cheaper to make international calls with a PIN card.

PIN cards, which have a scratch-off Personal Identification Number, allow you to call home at the rate of about a dime a minute. To use a PIN card, dial the toll-free access number listed on the card; then, at the prompt, enter your Personal Identification Number (also listed on card) and dial the number you want to call. These are sold at newsstands, exchange bureaus, souvenir shops, and mini-marts. There are many different brands. Ask for a "cheap international calling card." Make sure you get a card that allows you to make international calls (some types permit only local calls). Buy a lower denomination in case the card is a dud. Note that in Germany, due to a crackdown by the phone company, these cheap cards are no longer a good deal if used from payphones; use them instead for calling from hotel-room phones.

If you use **coins** to make your calls, have a bunch handy. Avoid using hotel-room phones for anything other than local calls and PIN card calls.

Making Calls within a European Country: You'll save money by dialing direct. You just need to learn to break the codes. About half of all European countries use area codes; the other half use a direct-dial system without area codes.

In countries that use area codes (such as Austria, Britain, Germany, Ireland, and the Netherlands), you dial the local number when calling within a city, and you add the area code if calling long-distance within the country. For example, Amsterdam's area code is 020, and the number of one of our recommended Amsterdam hotels is 622-6352. To call it from Rotterdam, dial 020/622-6352.

To make calls within a country that uses a direct-dial system (Belgium, the Czech Republic, Denmark, France, Italy, Spain, and Switzerland), you dial the same number whether you're calling across the country or across the street.

Making International Calls: You always start with the international access code (011 if you're calling from America or Canada, or 00 from Europe), then dial the country code of the country you're calling (see chart in appendix).

What you dial next depends on the phone system of the country you're calling. If the country uses area codes, drop the initial zero of the area code, then dial the rest of the number. To call the Amsterdam hotel from Paris, dial 00, 31 (the Netherlands' country code), 20/622-6352 (omitting the initial zero in the area code).

Countries that use direct-dial systems (no area codes) vary in how they're accessed internationally by phone. For instance, if you're making an international call to Denmark, Italy, Spain, or the Czech Republic, simply dial the international access code, country code, and phone number. But if you're calling Belgium, France, or Switzerland, drop the initial zero of the phone number. Example: To call a Paris hotel (tel. 01 47 05 49 15) from London, dial 00, 33 (France's country code), then 1 47 05 49 15 (the phone number without the initial zero).

To call Rick's office from Europe, we dial 00 (Europe's international access code), 1 (U.S.'s country code), 425 (Edmonds, WA's area code), and 771-8303.

European time is six/nine hours ahead of the east/west coast of the U.S.

U.S. Calling Cards: Calling home from Europe is easy but expensive with AT&T, MCI, or Sprint calling cards. Since direct-dial rates have dropped, U.S. calling cards are no longer a good value. It's also outrageously expensive to use your calling card to make calls between European countries. It's much cheaper to make your calls using a phone card or PIN card purchased in Europe.

Mobile Phones: Many travelers now buy cheap mobile phones in Europe to make both local and international calls. (Typical American mobile phones don't work in Europe, and those that work have horrendous per-minute costs.) For about $75, you can get a phone with $20 worth of calls that will work in the country where you purchased it. (You can buy more time at newsstands or mobile-phone shops.) For about $100, you can get a phone that will work in most countries once you pick up the necessary chip per country (about $20). If you're interested, stop by any European shop that sells mobile phones (you'll see prominent store-window displays). Depending on your trip and budget, ask for a phone that works only in that country or one that can be used throughout Europe. If you're on a budget, skip mobile phones and use PIN cards instead.

Mail: To arrange for mail delivery, reserve a few hotels along your route in advance and give their addresses to friends or use the American Express Company's mail services (free for AmEx cardholders and available at a minimal fee for others). Allow 10 days for a letter to arrive. Federal Express makes two-day deliveries—for a price. Phoning and e-mailing are both so easy that I've dispensed with mail stops altogether.

E-mail: More and more hotels have e-mail addresses and Web sites (included in this book). We've listed some Internet cafés, but your hotelier or TI can steer you to the nearest Internet access point.

Sleeping

In the interest of smart use of your time, we favor hotels and restaurants handy to your sightseeing activities. Rather than list hotels scattered throughout a city, we describe one or two favorite neighborhoods and recommend the best accommodations values in each.

This book lists accommodations of various accessibility levels. We've listed several cheaper, small-hotel options. But because truly accessible rooms are at a premium in some destinations, we've also listed some expensive—but plush and fully adapted—splurges.

Rooms with private bathrooms are often bigger, more recently renovated, and more likely to be accessible, while the cheaper rooms without bathrooms often will be on the top floor or not yet refurbished—and usually not accessible. Any room without a bathroom has access to a bathroom in the corridor (free, unless otherwise noted). Rooms with tubs often cost more than rooms with showers. All rooms have a sink.

Before accepting a room, confirm your understanding of the complete price. The only tip our recommended hotels would like is a friendly, easygoing guest. We appreciate feedback on your hotel experiences.

Hotels

While most hotels listed in this book cluster around $70 to $100 per double, they can be as much as $200-plus (maximum plumbing and more)

SLEEP CODE

To give maximum information in a minimum of space, we use this code to describe accommodations listed in this book. Prices listed are per room, not per person. When there is a range of prices in one category, the price will fluctuate with the season, size of room, or length of stay.

S = Single room (or price for one person in a double).

D = Double or twin. Double beds are usually big enough for non-romantic couples.

T = Triple (often a double bed with a single bed moved in).

Q = Quad (an extra child's bed is usually less).

b = Private bathroom with toilet and shower or tub.

s = Private shower or tub only (the toilet is down the hall).

no CC = Does not accept credit cards; you'll need to pay with the local currency.

SE = Speaks English. This code is used only when it seems predictable that you'll encounter English-speaking staff.

NSE = Does not speak English. Used only when it's unlikely you'll encounter English-speaking staff.

According to this code, a couple staying at a "Db-€90, SE" hotel in Bruges would pay a total of 90 euros (about $105) for a double room with a private bathroom. The staff speaks English. The hotel accepts credit cards or cash in payment; you can assume a hotel takes credit cards unless you see "no CC" in the listing.

per double. The cost is higher in big cities and heavily touristed cities and lower off the beaten track. Three or four people can save money by requesting one big room. Traveling alone can get expensive: A single room is often only 20 percent cheaper than a double. If you'll accept a room with twin beds and you ask for a double, you may be turned away. Ask for "a room for two people" if you'll take a twin or a double.

Rooms are generally safe, but don't leave valuables lying around. More (or different) pillows and blankets are usually in the closet or available on request. Remember, in Europe, towels and linen aren't always replaced every day. Drip-dry and conserve.

A very simple continental breakfast is almost always included. If you like juice and protein for breakfast, supply it yourself. Buy a box of juice for your hotel room and supplement the skimpy breakfast with a piece of fruit and cheese.

Pay your bill the evening before you leave to avoid the time-wasting crowd at the reception desk in the morning.

Making Reservations

It's possible to travel at any time of year without reservations (especially if you arrive early in the day), but given the high stakes, relatively few accessible options, erratic accommodations values, and the quality of the gems we've found for this book, we'd highly recommend calling for rooms at least a day or two in advance as you travel (your fluent receptionist will likely help you call your next hotel if you pay for the call). Even if a hotel clerk says the hotel is fully booked, you can try calling between 9:00 and 10:00 on the day you plan to arrive. That's when the hotel clerk knows who'll be checking out and just which rooms will be available. We've taken great pains to list telephone numbers with long-distance instructions (see "Telephones," page 22, and in the appendix). Use the telephone and the convenient phone cards. Most hotels listed are accustomed to English-only speakers. A hotel receptionist will trust you and hold a room until 16:00 (4:00 p.m.) without a deposit, though some will ask for a credit-card number. Honor (or cancel by phone) your reservations. Long distance is cheap and easy from public phone booths. Don't let these people down—we promised you'd call and cancel if for some reason you won't show up. Don't needlessly confirm rooms through the tourist office; they'll take a commission.

If you know exactly which dates you need and really want a particular place, reserve a room well in advance before you leave home. To reserve from home, e-mail, call, or fax the hotel. Phone and fax costs are reasonable, e-mail is a steal, and simple English is usually fine. To fax, use the form in the appendix (or find it online at www.ricksteves .com/reservation). A two-night stay in August would be "2 nights, 16/8/04 to 18/8/04" (Europeans write the date in this order—day/month/year—and hotel jargon counts your stay from your day of arrival through your day of departure).

If you e-mail or fax a reservation request and receive a response with rates stating that rooms are available, this is not a confirmation. You must confirm that the rates are fine and that indeed you want the room. You'll often receive a response requesting one night's deposit. A credit card number and expiration date will usually suffice. If you use your credit card for the deposit, you can pay with your card or cash when you arrive; if you don't show up, you'll be billed for one night. Ask about the cancellation policy when you reserve; sometimes you may have to cancel as much as two weeks ahead to avoid paying a penalty. Reconfirm your reservations several days in advance for safety.

Hostels

For $10 to $20 a night, you can stay at one of Europe's 2,000 youth hostels. Of course, these vary widely in accessibility—but many are more modern and likely to have at least moderately accessible facilities. While most hostels admit nonmembers for an extra fee, it's best to join the club and buy a youth-hostel card before you go (call Hostelling International at 202/783-6161 or order online at www.hiayh.org). Except in Bavaria (where you must be under 27 to stay in a hostel), travelers of any age are welcome as long as they don't mind dorm-style accommodations and making lots of traveling friends. Cheap meals are sometimes available, and kitchen facilities are usually provided for do-it-yourselfers. Expect crowds in the summer, snoring, and lots of youth groups giggling and making rude noises while you try to sleep. Family rooms and doubles are often available on request, but it's basically boys' dorms and girls' dorms. Many hostels are locked up from about 10:00 until 17:00, and a 23:00 curfew is often enforced. Hostelling is ideal for those traveling single: Prices are per bed, not per room, and you'll have an instant circle of friends. More and more hostels are getting their business acts together, taking credit-card reservations over the phone and leaving sign-in forms on the door for each available room. If you're serious about traveling cheaply, get a hostel card.

Eating European

Europeans are masters at the art of fine living. That means eating long and eating well. Two-hour lunches, three-hour dinners, and endless hours sitting in outdoor cafés are the norm. Americans eat on their way to an evening event and complain if the check is slow in coming. For Europeans, the meal is an end in itself, and only rude waiters rush you.

Even those of us who liked dorm food will find that the local cafés, cuisine, and wines become a highlight of our European adventure. This is sightseeing for your palate, and even if the rest of you is sleeping in cheap hotels, your taste buds will want an occasional first-class splurge. You can eat well without going broke. But be careful: You're just as likely to blow a small fortune on a mediocre meal as you are to dine wonderfully for $15.

Restaurants

To conserve your time and energy, we've focused on restaurants that are in the neighborhood close to your hotel or handy to your sightseeing. For each one, we've indicated the specific accessibility features you can expect to find.

If restaurant hunting on your own, choose a place filled with locals, not the place with the big neon signs boasting "We Speak English and Accept Credit Cards." Look for menus posted outside; if you don't see one, move along.

When you're in the mood for something halfway between a restaurant and a picnic meal, look for take-out food stands, bakeries (with sandwiches and small pizzas to go), delis, a department-store cafeteria, or simple little eateries for fast and easy restaurant food.

Picnics

So that we can afford the occasional splurge in a nice restaurant, we like to picnic. In addition to the savings, picnicking is a great way to sample local specialties. And, in the process of assembling your meal, you get to plunge into local markets like a European.

Gather supplies early. Many shops close for a lunch break. While it's fun to visit the small specialty shops, a *supermarché* gives you more efficiency with less color for less cost.

When driving, we organize a backseat pantry in a cardboard box: plastic cups, paper towels, a water bottle (the standard disposable European half-liter plastic mineral water bottle works fine), a damp cloth

TIPS ON TIPPING

Tipping in Europe isn't as automatic and generous as it is in the U.S., but for special service, tips are appreciated, if not expected. As in the U.S., the proper amount depends on your resources, tipping philosophy, and the circumstances, but some general guidelines apply.

Restaurants: In general, if service is not included, tip up to 10 percent (15 percent for France). We've included tipping guidelines at the beginning of the restaurant listings for each destination.

Taxis: To tip the cabbie, round up. For a typical ride, round up to the next euro on the fare (to pay a €13 fare, give €14); for a long ride, to the nearest 10 (for a €75 fare, give €80). If the cabbie hauls your bags and zips you to the airport to help you catch your flight, you might want to toss in a little more. But if you feel like you're being driven in circles or otherwise ripped off, skip the tip.

Special services: Tour guides at public sites often hold out their hands for tips after they give their spiel; if we've already paid for the tour, we don't tip extra, though some tourists do give a euro or two, particularly for a job well done. We don't tip at hotels, but if you do, give the porter a euro for carrying bags and leave a couple of euros in your room at the end of your stay for the maid if the room was kept clean. In general, if someone in the service industry does a super job for you, a tip of a couple of euros is appropriate...but not required.

When in doubt, ask. If you're not sure whether (or how much) to tip for a service, ask your hotelier or the TI; they'll fill you in on how it's done on their turf.

in a Ziploc baggie, a Swiss Army knife, and a petite tablecloth. To take care of juice once and for all, stow a rack of liter boxes of orange juice in the trunk. (Look for "100%" on the label or you'll get a sickly sweet orange drink.)

Picnics (especially French ones) can be an adventure in high cuisine. Be daring: Try the smelly cheeses, midget pickles, ugly pâtés, and minuscule yogurts. Local shopkeepers sell small quantities of produce and even slice and stuff a sandwich for you.

A typical picnic for two might be fresh bread (half loaves on request), two tomatoes, three carrots, 100 grams of cheese (about a quarter-pound), 100 grams of meat, two apples, a liter box of orange juice, and yogurt. Total cost for two: about $10.

Stranger in a Strange Land

We travel all the way to Europe to enjoy differences—to become temporary locals. You'll experience frustrations. Certain truths that we find "God-given" or "self-evident," like cold beer, ice in drinks, bottomless cups of coffee, hot showers, and bigger being better, are suddenly not so true. One of the benefits of travel is the eye-opening realization that there are logical, civil, and even better alternatives. A willingness to go local ensures that you'll enjoy a full dose of local hospitality.

If there is a negative aspect to the European image of Americans, we can appear loud, aggressive, impolite, rich, and a bit naive. While Europeans look bemusedly at some of our Yankee excesses—and worriedly at others—they nearly always afford us individual travelers all the warmth we deserve.

Send Us a Postcard, Drop Us a Line

If you enjoy a successful trip with the help of this book and would like to share your discoveries, please fill out the survey at the end of this book (or find it online at www.ricksteves.com/feedback) and send it to Europe Through the Back Door, Box 2009, Edmonds, WA 98020. We personally read and value all feedback.

For our latest travel information, tap into our Web site: www.ricksteves .com. To check on updates for this book, visit www.ricksteves.com/update. Rick's e-mail address is rick@ricksteves.com. Anyone is welcome to request a free issue of our *Back Door* newsletter.

Judging from all the positive feedback we receive from travelers who have used Rick's books, it's safe to assume you'll enjoy a great, affordable, and accessible vacation—with the finesse of an experienced, independent traveler. Thanks, and happy travels!

BACK DOOR TRAVEL PHILOSOPHY

From *Rick Steves' Europe Through the Back Door*

Travel is intensified living—maximum thrills per minute and one of the last great sources of legal adventure. Travel is freedom. It's recess, and we need it.

Experiencing the real Europe requires catching it by surprise, going casual..."Through the Back Door."

Affording travel is a matter of priorities. (Make do with the old car.) You can travel—simply, safely, and comfortably—anywhere in Europe for $100 a day plus transportation costs. In many ways, spending more money only builds a thicker wall between you and what you came to see. Europe is a cultural carnival and, time after time, you'll find that its best acts are free and the best seats are the cheap ones.

A tight budget forces you to travel close to the ground, meeting and communicating with the people, not relying on service with a purchased smile. Never sacrifice sleep, nutrition, safety, or cleanliness in the name of budget. Simply enjoy the local-style alternatives to expensive hotels and restaurants.

Extroverts have more fun. If your trip is low on magic moments, make things happen. If you don't enjoy a place, maybe you don't know enough about it. Seek the truth. Recognize tourist traps. Give a culture the benefit of your open mind. See things as different but not better or worse. Any culture has much to share.

Of course, travel, like the world, is a series of hills and valleys. Be fanatically positive and militantly optimistic. If something's not to your liking, change your liking. Travel is addicting. It can make you a happier American as well as a citizen of the world. Our Earth is home to six billion equally important people. It's humbling to travel and find that people don't envy Americans. They like us, but with all due respect, they wouldn't trade passports.

Globetrotting destroys ethnocentricity. It helps you understand and appreciate different cultures. Travel changes people. It broadens perspectives and teaches new ways to measure quality of life. Many travelers toss aside their hometown blinders. Their prized souvenirs are the strands of different cultures they decide to knit into their own character. The world is a cultural yarn shop. And Back Door travelers are weaving the ultimate tapestry. Come on, join in!

ACCESSIBILITY RESOURCES AND TIPS

European countries, at various speeds, are doing what they can to open their doors and make their cobbled streets negotiable for more visitors. It's smart to do some advance groundwork. We've listed useful resources to help you plan ahead. The tips come from a variety of sources, including Susan Sygall, the Executive Director of Mobility International USA (MIUSA) and writer of this book's Foreword; the National Clearinghouse on Disabilities and Exchange (run by MIUSA); and Rick's readers.

For more advice on the ups and downs of Europe via walker or wheelchair, visit the Graffiti Wall at www.ricksteves.com.

PLANNING YOUR TRIP

Organizations

These organizations can help you plan an accessible, enjoyable journey.

Mobility International USA runs the National Clearinghouse on Disabilities and Exchange (NCDE), a free service for individuals with disabilities (thanks to funding by the Bureau of Education and Cultural Affairs of the U.S. State Department). If you're interested in participating in international programs, they'll help you find the right one. NCDE also offers disability-related contacts worldwide. Consider getting their Global Impact newsletter, *A World Awaits You* journal, or their useful books, such as *A World of Options: A Guide to International Educational Exchange, Community Service, and Travel for Persons with Disabilities.* Another is *Survival Strategies for Going Abroad: A Guide for People with Disabilities* (P.O. Box 10767, Eugene, OR 97440, tel. 541/343-1284 voice and TTY, www.miusa.org, info@miusa.org).

Access-Able Travel Source sponsors a useful Web site with access information and resources for travelers with disabilities, as well as a free e-mail newsletter. They have information about guidebooks, accessible transportation, wheelchair travel, scooter rental, disabled-travel forums, accessible transportation, and more (tel. 303/232-2979, www.access-able .com, carol@access-able.com, Bill and Carol Randall).

The **Society for Accessible Travel & Hospitality** (SATH), a non-profit membership organization, publishes a travel magazine *(Open World)* and offers travel advice ($45 membership, $30 for students and seniors, includes magazine; $13 for magazine subscription only; tel. 212/447-SATH, fax 212/725-8253, www.sath.org, info@sath.org).

The **European Commission** has produced a series of travel guides for tourists with disabilities, including information about accessibility, facilities, tour operators, travel agents, and more. The countries covered include Belgium, Britain, France, and the Netherlands (http://europa .eu.int/comm/enterprise/services/tourism/policy-areas/guides.htm).

Several organizations specialize in **health** issues: The **International Association for Medical Assistance to Travelers (IAMAT)** provides a directory of English-speaking doctors in 500 cities in 120 countries who charge affordable, standardized fees for medical visits (membership free but donation requested, 417 Center Street, Lewiston, NY 14092, tel. 716/754-4883, www.iamat.org, info@iamat.org). The **Centers for Disease Control and Prevention (CDC)** maintain health-related information online, including travel preparation and health information for travel worldwide (www.cdc.gov/travel). **PersonalMD.com** provides information on a wide variety of health topics. The main feature is the PersonalMD Emergency Card, a free service that allows users to enter their medical information into a secure database that can be accessed anywhere in the world via the Internet, in case of an emergency. **Shoreland's Travel Health Online** offers health tips, a planning guide, and country information (www.tripprep.com).

Susan Sygall, the Executive Director of Mobility International USA, suggests the following: "I always get information about disability groups where I am going. They have the best access information, and many times they will become your new traveling partners and friends. Remember that you are part of a global family of disabled people. It can also be helpful to contact tourism offices and local transit providers before you travel. Some even include information about accessibility for people with disabilities on their Web sites." (See the appendix for a list of tourist information offices and their Web sites.)

Web Sites

In addition to the organizations listed above, you can find helpful resources and links pages on the Web sites for **Emerging Horizons** (www.emerginghorizons.com), **Half the Planet** (www.halftheplanet .org), **Gimp on the Go** (www.gimponthego.com), **Disabled Peoples' International** (www.dpi.org), and **MossRehab ResourceNet** (www .mossresourcenet.org/travel.htm). **AARP**'s Web site features articles written for seniors and slow walkers (www.aarp.org/destinations). **Access Abroad** is a good resource for students with disabilities planning to study abroad (www.umabroad.umn.edu/access).

GETTING THERE

Here are some resources and tips for getting to Europe, whether on your own or with a tour.

Air Travel

The **U.S. Department of Transportation**'s "New Horizons" guide provides information for air travelers with disabilities, including navigating security, getting on and off aircraft, and handling seating assignments (available online at http://airconsumer.ost.dot.gov/publications/horizons.htm).

Thanks to the National Clearinghouse on Disabilities and Exchange, run by Mobility International USA (www.miusa.org), for this helpful information:

Though many transatlantic air carriers try to accommodate disabled travelers, airline policies are inconsistent. They change often and can vary from company to company and terminal to terminal.

Regardless of the inconsistencies, be aware that the Air Carrier Access Act of 1986 prohibits airlines from discriminating on the basis of disability (see www.faa.gov/acr/dat.htm). Airlines can no longer require that passengers with disabilities travel with attendants, carry medical certificates, or agree to assume liability for the damage of mobility equipment.

Be Assertive: If you have a disability, traveling by plane can be an exercise in relinquishing control. You temporarily surrender autonomy in exchange for necessary assistance and compliance with policies. Be flexible and ready to deal with frustrating situations.

It is important to know the policies of an airline before arriving at the airport. Unfortunately, it is not uncommon for a passenger with a disability to be assured over the phone that his or her needs can be accommodated, only to find that employees at the gate have a different understanding of policies and procedures. Be assertive about your needs and insist upon the services necessary to complete a flight.

If you feel you've been discriminated against because of your disability, document your experience. Complaints should first go to an airline's complaint resolution officer on site. Later, try the airline's community-relations department. If these approaches are not successful, file a complaint with the U.S. Department of Transportation's Aviation Consumer Protection Division (tel. 202/366-2220, http://airconsumer.ost.dot.gov, airconsumer@ost.dot.gov) or the Disability Rights Education and Defense Fund (voice telephone & TTY: 800/466-4232, www.dredf.org).

You can also call a toll-free hotline at 800/778-4838 or TTY 800/455-9880, seven days a week (answered 7:00–23:00 EST), run by the U.S. Department of Transportation. They can provide immediate and pre-travel assistance in resolving disability-related air-travel problems by suggesting and facilitating alternative solutions for you and the airline.

Choosing an Airline: Organizations that advocate for disabled air travelers are reluctant to recommend a specific air company, because even the "good" ones are inconsistent. Having a positive air-travel experience depends to a great extent on the needs of the individual, the departure and destination cities, and the particular staff on duty.

Air carriers abroad have significantly different policies regarding people with disabilities than U.S. air carriers. Some European airlines have excellent reputations for being very helpful to customers with disabilities. Other companies may have virtually no experience with disabled passengers.

Some foreign airlines may require a doctor's certificate for all independent air travel. Other foreign airlines may require that a person with a disability travel with a personal assistant. Advance research and comparison-shopping are crucial to having a successful trip.

Fortunately, the European Commission recently drafted legislation—that will go into effect in 2006—to force airlines to meet the needs of people with disabilities.

Planning Ahead: Whenever possible, plan and book flights well in advance. It is important to inform the travel agent and airline representative of the following information:

- Your type of disability and equipment aids used for locomotion, such as a cane, crutches, manual wheelchair, or electric wheelchair.
- Your special dietary requirements or need for assistance at meals (airline personnel are not required to help with eating, but should assist with preparing to eat).
- Whether another person will accompany you.

It is essential to call the airline directly to make sure all disability-related needs will be met. Always ask for the name and position of each airline employee and record this information with the time, day, and content of the call. It can be helpful to work with an airline special-services representative who can assist with facilitating arrangements.

Think carefully about flight length. You may find long flights uncomfortable if you can't use cramped airline toilets. Shorter connecting flights can be a good alternative. It's a good idea to schedule at least two hours between flights in case of delays or boarding and de-boarding problems—especially if you want your wheelchair, scooter, or other mobility equipment delivered to the gate at each stop (see below). Be sure your wheelchair is marked with your name and contact information, including those parts that can become separated.

Most airplanes lack accessible bathrooms. Either work out alternative systems for dealing with this issue (such as limiting fluids immediately before a flight) or book flights on planes with accessible bathrooms.

At the Airport: On the day of departure, consider arriving at least an hour earlier than the normal flight check-in time.

You'll probably need local accessible transportation for going to or from airports. Many major transportation companies, like airport shuttles, offer accessible vans with advance reservations.

If you don't own a wheelchair, but need to use one at the airport, request a wheelchair and assistance from the airline. On the plane, canes or crutches can be kept under the seat, provided that the equipment does not block the aisles.

If you can't walk onto the plane, you'll be transported to your seat on an aisle chair (a narrow chair on wheels) by airline personnel. Be prepared to instruct the staff on the best transfer method and to assist with the boarding process.

If you have your own manual wheelchair, you'll generally be allowed to use it until you reach the door of the airplane. Your wheelchair will then be stowed with luggage in the baggage compartment or placed in an onboard storage space. Insist that your wheelchair be brought to the *gate* upon landing, rather than to the baggage-claim area. Request this arrangement between flights and at the final destination.

More Air Travel Tips

Rick's readers offer these suggestions for people with limited mobility traveling by air:

"If possible, speak to the ramp/baggage personnel who will be loading your chair (especially important for power chairs). Let them know how to take it out of gear, how to push it, and anything else of importance. Be sure you know what kind of battery you have. If your battery is a sealed, gel-cell type, it will have to be disconnected from your chair and boxed up—and you generally won't get help at the other end to put it back together. If your chair has removable leg rests, armrests, and the like, bring a separate bag to hold them. Ask the baggage handlers about the size of the opening to the baggage compartment and make any adjustments necessary to your chair yourself, such as reclining a high backrest."

"Power chairs and scooters can easily be damaged on airplanes. Having damage-proof packaging for your scooter or wheelchair can provide big relief."

"When making ticket reservations, request a bulkhead aisle seat, and take a plane that is nonstop."

"If you wear a catheter leg bag onto a plane, make sure it is connected tight and TAPED. Otherwise you will have a big wet mess (I learned this one from experience)."

"Know your rights. Demand (politely at first) your rights. Know that every U.S.-based airline is obligated to follow the laws as set forth in the ACAA (Air Carrier Access Act). If you run into a problem, ask immediately for the Complaints Resolution Officer. Every U.S.-based airline is required to have a CRO on duty, and they have the authority to make sure your rights are respected."

"A word of caution about European 'no-frills' airlines: While mainstream airlines employ their own customer-service assistants to help wheelchair passengers from check-in to boarding, no-frills airlines use a pool of people employed by the airport for a variety of duties. If you're flying a no-frills airline and you have asked for wheelchair assistance, you are not by any means guaranteed to receive that service. As a wheelchair passenger flying no-frills, it's a good idea to check in as early as possible, since smaller airports (the kind cheap airlines fly out of) often use old mobile steps to board the aircraft or require passengers to take a bus to the aircraft. Both methods obviously have implications for wheelchair passengers, who may need to be carried."

Tours

If you'd rather not go it alone, you'll find a selection of groups that run accessible tours to Europe, including **Accessible Journeys** (wheelchair trips to Britain, France, and Holland, 35 West Sellers Avenue, Ridley Park, PA 19078, tel. 800/846-4537, www.disabilitytravel.com, sales @disabilitytravel.com), **Flying Wheels Travel** (escorted tours to Great Britain and France, plus custom itineraries, P.O. Box 382, Owatonna, MN 55060, tel. 507/451-5005, www.flyingwheelstravel.com, thq@ll.net), and **Nautilus Tours and Cruises** (tours to France, Belgium, and the Netherlands, plus cruises to other destinations, 22567 Ventura Boulevard, Woodland Hills, CA 91364, tel. outside California 800/797-6004, in California 818/591-3159, www.nautilustours.com).

Access/Abilities offers information and custom searches on accessible-travel opportunities (tel. 415/388-3250). **Accessible Europe** is a collection of European travel agents and tour operators who specialize in disabled travel (www.accessibleurope.com). **Accessible City Breaks,** based in Britain, runs trips to all the cities covered in this book and has a Web site with travel tips and some destination information (www .accessiblecitybreaks.co.uk).

In Case of Discrimination: Under the Americans with Disabilities Act, if you feel you have been discriminated against (such as not being allowed on a U.S. tour company's tour of Europe), contact the U.S. Department of Justice ADA Information Line at 800/514-0301 or the Disability Rights Education and Defense Fund at voice telephone & TTY: 800/466-4232 (www.dredf.org).

ON THE ROAD

These resources and tips will help keep your on-the-road experiences smooth and fun.

Accommodations

A growing number of hotels have elevators and rooms with accessible bathrooms. But hotels aren't your only option.

Hostelling International provides a guide to hostels around the world that indicates which hostels are accessible (tel. 202/783-6161, www.hiayh.org).

The Sweden-based **Independent Living** Institute's Accessible Vacation Home Exchange Web site can put you in touch with disabled Europeans looking to swap homes or help you find an assistant overseas (www.independentliving.org).

Here are some more **tips** about accommodations from Rick's readers:

"I strongly suggest that you confirm all 'accessible' rooms by phone prior to booking. It is worth it to do this and make absolutely sure that there are no unhappy surprises when you show up!"

"Do your research. The Internet is a wonderful resource, but be sure you talk to people on the phone or by e-mail to ask specific questions, especially about accommodations. Get dimensions of doorways and elevators especially. Elevators in Europe tend to be quite small, which can really be a problem if you are in a power chair. Ask, ask, ask."

Parking

Parking spaces reserved for people with disabilities are commonly available throughout Europe. If you have a permit to use these spaces in the U.S., it is also valid in Europe. For more information on parking in Europe, see www.oecd.org/cem/topics/handicaps/parking.htm.

Wheelchairs

Some museums (listed in this book) offer free loaner wheelchairs for mobility-impaired vistors. Be prepared to leave a photo ID as a deposit.

Here are some tips for Europe-bound wheelchair users:

"Electric wheelchairs must be recharged every one to two days depending on use. Compare the voltage requirements (120V in the United States and 220V in Europe) and be sure you have the proper voltage transformer and type of adapter plug: three flat prongs for Britain, two round prongs for the Continent." (From NCDE)

"Repairs for electric or 'power' wheelchairs are more expensive than for manual wheelchairs. Electric-wheelchair parts may be difficult to find when traveling abroad. Assembling an emergency kit of basic tools and frequently-broken, hard-to-get parts for power-wheelchair users is a smart idea." (From NCDE)

"I use a lightweight manual wheelchair with pop-off tires. I take a backpack that fits on the back of my chair and store my daypack underneath my chair in a net bag. Since I usually travel alone, if I can't carry it myself, I don't take it. I keep a bungee cord with me for the times I can't get my chair into a car and need to strap it in the trunk or when I need to secure it on a train." (From Susan Sygall)

"If the weather turns poor and you're traveling with a power chair or scooter, get a poncho that covers the occupant and the batteries to stay dry." (From a reader)

"Bring information about your wheelchair equipment and repair shop with you. Find out if the manufacturers sell equipment in Europe and get their contact information." (From a reader)

"Low-slung backs are great when the wheelchair users push on their own. In cases where they may need assistance, it would be great to be able to attach some higher handles for assistants to use as pushing and leverage points." (From NCDE)

"We often discovered that doorways into restaurants or funiculars were too narrow, but, upon looking again, we found that there were second narrow doors next to the main door that can open up if unlocked, therefore creating a wider entrance." (From NCDE)

Restrooms

"Bathrooms are often a hassle so I have learned to use creative ways to transfer into narrow spaces. To be blatantly honest, when there are no accessible bathrooms in sight I have found ways to pee discreetly just about anywhere (outside the Eiffel Tower or on a glacier in a national park). Bring along an extra pair of pants and a great sense of humor." (From Susan Sygall)

"There are plenty of accessible restrooms in Paris and London. The restrooms are usually locked with entrance limited to people who really need them. At the Eiffel Tower, there is an elevator to the restroom, which is below ground. You must ask the matron who will then 'beam you down.' WCs in Europe tend to be smaller than those in the United States (probably because we tend to have more girth in general), so if you use a chair larger than 29 inches total width, you may want to bring a smaller one for your trip. Cambered wheels usually make the difference." (From a reader)

Overcoming Challenges

For anyone, challenges are a part of travel. Here are some pointers on traveling well.

"If a museum lacks elevators for visitors, be sure to ask about freight elevators. Almost all have them somewhere, and that can be your ticket to seeing a world-class treasure." (From Susan Sygall)

"Bring non-disabled friends. Having more helping hands with you if you need a quick lift up a curb, or if you have trouble handling your luggage, is always good. Also, when things go wrong, having a support group cuts down on panic and increases the number of ideas for solving problems." (From a reader)

"Consider making your first trip to a country where you know someone. Visiting friends is great, and having a local to check things out for you before you come is very helpful. They also know you and know the local sources of help if you get in trouble." (From a reader)

"Don't confuse being flexible and having a positive attitude with settling for less than your rights. I expect equal access and constantly let people know about the possibility of providing access through ramps or other modifications. When I believe my rights have been violated, I do whatever is necessary to remedy the situation so the next traveler, or disabled people in that country, won't have the same frustrations." (From Susan Sygall)

"If you get in trouble or need supplies, ask for help. Being shy is a real liability in traveling to a foreign place. Most people are very friendly and helpful. If someone isn't, shrug it off and keep asking. In many cases, you will not need to ask—people will jump to your aid." (From a reader)

"Keep in mind that accessibility can mean different things in different countries. In some countries people rely more on human-support systems than on physical or technological solutions. People may tell you their building is accessible because they're willing to lift you and your wheelchair over the steps at the entryway. Be open to trying new ways of doing things, but also ask questions to make sure you are comfortable with the access provided." (From Susan Sygall)

"I always try to learn some of the language of the country I'm in, because it cuts through the barriers when people stare at you (and they will) and also comes in handy when you need assistance in going up a curb or a flight of steps. Don't accept other people's notions of what is possible—I have climbed Masada in Israel and made it to the top of the Acropolis in Greece." (From Susan Sygall)

GREAT BRITAIN

- Great Britain is 88,000 square miles (a little bigger than Idaho)
- Population is 58 million (about 660 per square mile)
- One British pound sterling (£1) = about $1.70

Regardless of the revolution we had 200 years ago, many American travelers feel that they "go home" to Britain. This most popular tourist destination has a strange influence and power over us.

Geographically, the isle of Britain is small—600 miles long and 300 miles at its widest point. Its highest mountain is 4,400 feet, a foothill by our standards. The population is a fifth that of the United States. At its peak in the mid-1800s, Britain owned one-fifth of the world and accounted for more than half of the planet's industrial output. Today, the empire has been reduced to the isle of Britain itself, a troubled province in Northern Ireland, and small, distant outposts like Gibraltar and the Falklands.

Economically, Great Britain's industrial production is about 5 percent of the world's total. For the first time in history, Ireland has a higher per-capita income than Britain. Still, the economy is healthy, and inflation, unemployment, and interest rates are all low.

Culturally, Britain is still a world leader. Her heritage, her culture, and her people cannot be measured in traditional units of power. London is a major exporter of actors, movies, and theater, of rock and classical music, and of writers, painters, and sculptors.

British television is so good—and so British—that it deserves a mention as a sightseeing treat. After a hard day of sightseeing, watch the telly over tea in the living room of your B&B. England has five channels. BBC-1 and BBC-2 are government regulated, commercial free, and traditionally highbrow. Channels 3, 4, and 5 are private, are a little more Yankee, and have commercials—but those commercials are clever and sophisticated and provide a fun look at England. Broadcasting is funded by a £100-per-year-per-household tax. Hmmm, 40 cents per day to escape commercials and public-television pledge drives.

Great Britain

Oscar Wilde said, "The English have everything in common with the Americans—except, of course, language." Traveling through England is an adventure in accents and idioms. Every day you'll see babies in prams, sucking dummies as mothers change wet nappies. Soon the kids can trade in their nappies for smalls and spend a penny on their own. "Spend a penny" is British for a visit to the loo (bathroom). In England, chips are fries, and crisps are potato chips. A hamburger is a bomb on a toasted bap. One of the beauties of touring the British Isles is the illusion of hearing a foreign language and actually understanding it—most of the time.

People of leisure punctuate their afternoon with a "cream tea" at a tearoom. You'll get a pot of tea, small finger foods (like cucumber sandwiches), homemade scones, jam, and thick clotted cream. For maximum pinkie-waving taste per calorie, slice your scone thin like a miniature loaf of bread. Tearooms, which often serve appealing light meals, are usually open for lunch and close around 17:00, just before dinner.

Our chocoholic readers are enthusiastic about English chocolates. Their favorites include Cadbury Wispa Gold bars (filled with liquid caramel), Cadbury Crunchie bars, Nestle's Lion bars, Cadbury's Boost bars (a shortcake biscuit with caramel in milk chocolate), and Galaxy chocolate bars (especially the ones with hazelnuts). Thornton shops (in larger train stations) sell a box of sweets called the Continental Assortment, which comes with a tasting guide. The highlight is the mocha white-chocolate truffle. British M&Ms (Smarties) are better than American ones. For a few extra pence, adorn your ice cream cone with a "flake"—a chocolate bar stuck right into the middle.

ACCESSIBILITY IN GREAT BRITAIN

Great Britain is one of the world's more accessible countries in terms of attractions, accommodations, and transportation. London, easily the best destination for a first-time visitor, is the epicenter of all things British—one of Europe's most accessible and most enjoyable cities.

The **British Tourist Authority** can provide information to help people with disabilities plan a visit to the United Kingdom (551 Fifth Avenue, Suite 701, New York, NY 10176, U.S. tel. 800/462-2748, U.S. fax 212/986-1188, www.visitbritain.com, travelinfo@visitbritain.org). For help on disabled travel, see the special section of their Web site at www.travelbritain.org/NewHome/Mature/tcdisabl.htm). For an over-view of the UK's DDA/Special Educational Needs and Disability Act of 2001, see www.strath.ac.uk/Departments/specneeds/quiz/DDA.htm (full text at www.hmso.gov.uk/acts/acts2001/20010010.htm).

Transportation

Great Britain provides some helpful resources for people with disabilities: For example, London Taxi International's "black cabs" are wheelchair-accessible. Eurostar, which runs the "Chunnel" train to Paris or Brussels, offers special fares of $54 apiece for wheelchair users and their compan-ions (see www.ricksteves.com/eurostar). If traveling by rail within Britain, wheelchair users and one companion can automatically receive a 34 per-cent discount on point-to-point tickets or 50 percent off same-day round-trips.

Transport for London Access & Mobility provides maps, station guides, and information on access to the London Underground, buses, and river services for people with disabilities. Recent improvements include better wheelchair accessibility and the introduction of audio and visual cues to announce stops on the Tube. This organization will help keep you up-to-date on all the changes (42/50 Victoria Street, London SW1H OTL, tel. 020/7941-4600, fax 020/7941-4605, www.tfl.gov.uk, access&mobility @tfl.gov.uk). For more details on available resources, see page 61.

Wheelchair Travel rents adapted, lift-equipped vans (with or without driver) that can accommodate up to three wheelchairs. They also rent cars with hand controls and "Chairman" cars (1 Johnston Green, Guildford, Surrey, GU2 6XS, near London, tel. 01483/233-640, fax 01483/237-772, www.wheelchairtravel.co.uk, info@wheelchairtravel.co.uk).

Guidebooks and Publications

This guidebook should fulfill your needs for a visit to London. But here are a few to consider, especially if you're lingering in London or venturing further into the British Isles.

Access in London, written by Gordon Couch, William Forrester, and David McGaughey, and published by Pauline Hephaistos Survey Projects, provides detailed information on London accessibility for people with disabilities (Access Project, 39 Bradley Gardens, West Ealing, London W13 8HE, www.accessproject-phsp.org, gordon.couch @virgin.net). The same team also produces the book *Access in Paris.*

Smooth Ride Guides: UK is a guidebook on accessibility in the United Kingdom (England, Scotland, Wales, and Northern Ireland), covering accommodations, tourist attractions, wheelchair-equipment rental and repair, and more (Duck Street Barns, Furneux Pelham, Hertfordshire SG9 0LA, tel. 01279/777-966, fax 01279/777-995, www.smoothride guides.com, info@smoothrideguides.com).

Holidays in Britain and Ireland: A Guide for Disabled People, which features more than 1,400 places to stay in the U.K. and Ireland, is published by the Royal Association for Disability and Rehabilitation (see below for more on RADAR; book costs £15, tel. 020/7250-322, fax 020/7250-0212, TTY 020/7250-4119, www.radar.org.uk, radar@radar .org.uk). You can also search RADAR's Web site for accessible accommodations (www.radarsearch.org).

The National Trust Disability Office annually publishes the booklet *Information for Visitors with Disabilities,* which contains useful information on the accessibility of National Trust properties (get it free online at www.nationaltrust.org.uk/main/placestovisit/disability.pdf, also available in standard or large print and on audiocassette; National Trust Disability Office, 36 Queen Anne's Gate, London SW1H 9AS, tel. 020/7447-6742, accessforall@ntrust.org.uk).

Organizations

Great Britain has numerous organizations designed to support the needs of disabled travelers.

General

British Council of Organizations of Disabled People (BCODP) provides information to those with disabilities (Litchurch Plaza, Litchurch Lane, Derby DE24 8AA, tel. 01332/295-551, TTY 01332/295-581, www.bcodp.org.uk, general@bcodp.org.uk). Also consider the **Disability Rights Commission** (www.drc-gb.org).

DIAL (National Association of Disablement Information and Advice Lines) can direct you to local groups in the United Kingdom that offer free information and advice on all aspects of disability (www.dialuk .org.uk).

GLAD (Greater London Action on Disability) is a voluntary organization that provides valuable information for disabled visitors and residents. It publishes the biweekly *Disability Update* (relevant excerpts from national newspapers), the monthly *London Disability News,* and the bimonthly *Boadicea* for disabled women (www.glad.org.uk).

RADAR (Royal Association for Disability and Rehabilitation) provides information and referral to resources for people with disabilities in the United Kingdom. They operate a National Key Scheme (NKS), allowing people with disabilities to get a map and key for 5,000 accessible toilets throughout the U.K. (£8, tel. 020/7250-3222, fax 020/7250-0212, TTY 020/7250-4119, www.radar.org.uk, radar@radar .org.uk). RADAR also offers a search engine for finding accessible accommodations (www.radarsearch.org).

You're Able offers disability-related information, news, chat rooms, and other resources (www.youreable.com).

Holiday Care Service is an advisory service specializing in disabled holiday accommodation, offering phone support and a handy series of information sheets (www.holidaycare.org.uk).

Travel

Can Be Done arranges tours in London that are tailored to the needs of disabled people (www.canbedone.co.uk).

Undiscovered Britain is a travel agent with an emphasis on accessible travel (www.undiscoveredbritain.com/access).

Arts

Artsline has information on disabled access to arts and entertainment events in London and on adapted facilities in cinemas, art galleries, and theatres (www.artsline.org.uk).

London Disability Arts Forum (LDAF) produces a 32-page monthly magazine—*Disability Arts in London,* or *DAIL*—with listings, reviews, and articles on disabled artists (£10/yr, or £30/yr for overseas subscribers, www.ldaf.net).

Comments from Readers

These thoughts on traveling in Britain were submitted by Rick's readers, mostly through his Graffiti Wall Web site (www.ricksteves.com).

"At the Tower of London, we were approached by a Beefeater guard who took us on a private tour and assisted by pushing the chair over the rough terrain. Every place we visited in London was terrific with the assistance and the accessibility. The Londoners came to us everywhere we went; we never needed to ask for help. America could learn some lessons!"

"The Museum of London has free electric carts for visitors. You have to use the freight elevator because the passenger elevator is too small, but the staff was really great."

"Figuring out the city buses in London was agonizing until we had the bright idea to just call up the phone number in the brochure we picked up (tel. 020/7941-4600). I spoke to a very helpful person who mapped our routes out for us, checked on the accessibility of the lines we needed to use, and gave us good general info on using the buses."

"The Tube was a good option, and we used the Westminster, South Kensington, and Olympia routes at least three times to get around the city. (Lifts always were in good working order when we were there.) But had I not had an able-bodied companion to jump the 'gap,' I don't think I would have used it. My wheelie skills are not that good!"

"A word about London's Tube stations: The Westminster stop has elevator access from every level to the street, but you have to find someone to operate the elevator most of the time. Covent Garden has a staircase. Both Hammersmith Tube stations have good access, and Liverpool Street eastbound isn't bad (about three steps up, then turnstiles, then an elevator to the main station and to the street). Canary Wharf and the other new stations on the Jubilee Line are very good. East Croydon has ramps up and down and a cool trolley service right by the front door."

"My companion and I used London city buses, the Tube, the railway, black cabs, and a Thames riverboat, as well as renting a car and driving in and around Somerset and Yorkshire. A few standout memories include the 45 minutes it took for the National Express coach driver (and several other coach staff) to figure out how to operate the beautiful brand-new wheelchair lift on the coach from

Heathrow to Bath—with teamwork, it finally got figured out and the commuters on the coach were quite understanding about the delay...and we got to Bath!"

"London's Gatwick Airport was a nightmare. Make sure you are dropped off at the wheelchair-carriage terminal entrance. This is the only location to find porters (skycaps). The porter was not allowed to go through security, unlike in the U.S. and Mexico, so I had to push my husband for about 20 minutes to the boarding gate. I would pay more to avoid Gatwick."

LONDON

London is more than 600 square miles of urban jungle. With 9 million people—many of whom don't speak English—it's a world in itself and a barrage on all the senses. London is much more than its museums and famous landmarks. It's a living, breathing, thriving organism.

Culturally, London has changed dramatically in recent years, and many visitors are surprised to find how "un-English" it is. Whites are now a minority in major parts of the city that once symbolized white imperialism. Arabs have nearly bought out the area north of Hyde Park. Chinese take-outs outnumber fish-and-chips shops. Many hotels are run by people with foreign accents (who hire English chambermaids), while outlying suburbs are home to huge communities of Indians and Pakistanis. London is learning—sometimes fitfully—to live as a microcosm of its formerly vast empire. Many see the English Channel Tunnel as another foreign threat to the Britishness of Britain.

With just a few days here, you'll get no more than a quick splash in this teeming human tidal pool. But, with a quick orientation, you'll get a good look at its top sights, history, and cultural entertainment, as well as its ever-changing human face.

Have fun in London. Blow through the city on the open deck of a double-decker orientation tour bus, cruise down the Thames River, or tour the town by taxi. Take a pinch-me-I'm-in-Britain roll or stroll through downtown. Ogle the crown jewels at the Tower of London, hear the chimes of Big Ben, and see the Houses of Parliament in action. Hobnob with the tombstones in Westminster Abbey, duck WWII bombs in Churchill's underground Cabinet War Rooms, and brave the earthshaking Imperial War Museum. Visit with Leonardo da Vinci, Botticelli, and

Rembrandt in the National Gallery. Whisper across the dome of St. Paul's Cathedral and rummage through our civilization's attic at the British Museum. Cruise down the Thames River. You'll enjoy some of Europe's best people-watching at Covent Garden and snap to at Buckingham Palace's Changing of the Guard. Just sit in Victoria Station, at a major Tube station, at Piccadilly Circus, or in Trafalgar Square, and observe. Spend one evening at a theater and the others catching your breath.

ACCESSIBILITY IN LONDON

A staggering 20 million people visit London every year, and many of them have disabilities. With recent improvements and a barrier-free mentality, the city makes a great first stop for your trip. Mention accessibility, and hoteliers, restaurateurs, and civil servants snap to attention. Many services and venues are geared to wheelchair users. The city tours help you taste the fabled history of this diverse and multicultural city. The central restaurants, pubs, and hotels put you in the midst of London's sights and attractions. Taxis are convenient, inexpensive, and fully accessible, as are many Tube stations. The airports are accessible, from customs to baggage claim to queuing for a taxi.

Most of London's big sights are fully accessible (Level 1): Cabinet War Rooms, National Gallery, National Portrait Gallery, Somerset House, London Transport Museum, Theatre Museum, British Museum, British Library, Madame Tussaud's waxworks, Buckingham Palace, Royal Mews, Victoria and Albert Museum, Natural History Museum, St. Paul's Cathedral (main floor only), Tower of London, London Eye Ferris Wheel, Imperial War Museum, Tate Britain, Tate Modern, Shakespeare's Globe, and Vinopolis City of Wine.

A few London sights will work for wheelchair users who have some assistance (Level 2): Westminster Abbey, Houses of Parliament, St. Martin-in-the-Fields Church, Museum of London, and Dalí Universe. Travelers with limited mobility will only have to skip a few minor attractions (Level 3 or 4): Banqueting House, Sir John Soane's Museum, Old Bailey, and the top of St. Paul's dome.

To help you prioritize and plan your time, note the ranking that accompanies each sight listing (ranging from ▲▲▲—a can't-miss sight—to zero, for a sight that is easily skippable).

ACCESSIBILITY CODES

These codes offer a quick overview of what to expect. If applicable, more specific details about the facility (e.g., exact number and height of steps, special instructions for gaining entry) are explained in each listing.

CODE	MEANING
AE	Accessible Entryway
AE+A	Accessible Entry with Assistance
AI	Accessible Interior
AI+A	Accessible Interior with Assistance
AT	Accessible Toilet
AT+A	Accessible Toilet with Assistance
AL	Accessible Lift (elevator)
AL+A	Accessible Lift with Assistance
AR	Accessible Hotel Room
AR+A	Accessible Hotel Room with Assistance
AB	Accessible Hotel Bathroom
AB+A	Accessible Hotel Bathroom with Assistance
♥	Caring, welcoming attitude regarding accessibility

For more detailed information, please refer to the full Accessibility Codes chart on page 4 of the Introduction. For more information on Accessibility Levels, see page 2.

ORIENTATION

(area code: 020)

To grasp London comfortably, see it as the old town in the city center without the modern, congested sprawl. The River Thames runs roughly west to east through the city, with most of the visitor's sights on the north bank. Mentally, maybe even physically, trim down your map to include only the area between the Tower of London (to the east), Hyde Park (west), Regent's Park (north), and the Thames (south). (This is roughly the area bordered by the Tube's Circle Line.) This three-mile stretch

London Overview

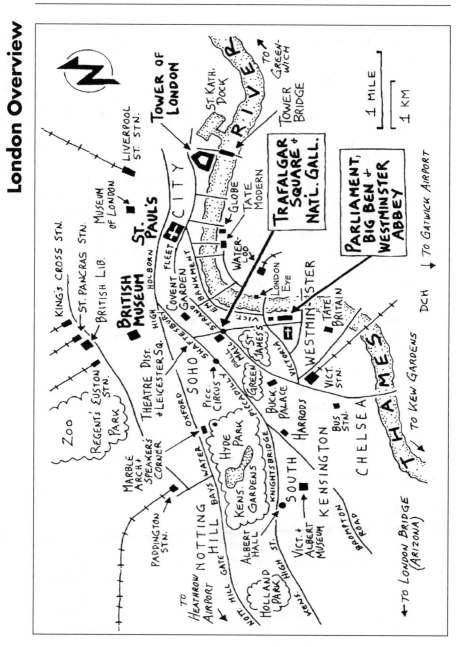

between the Tower and Hyde Park holds 80 percent of the sights mentioned in this chapter.

London is a collection of neighborhoods:

Westminster: This neighborhood includes Big Ben, Parliament, Westminster Abbey, and Buckingham Palace, the grand government buildings from which Britain is ruled.

The City: Shakespeare's London was a walled town clustered around St. Paul's Cathedral. Today, it's the modern financial district.

The West End: Lying between Westminster and the City (that is, at the "west end" of the original walled town), this is the center of London cultural life. Trafalgar Square has major museums. Piccadilly Circus and Leicester Square host tourist traps, cinemas, and nighttime glitz. Soho and Covent Garden are thriving people-zones housing theaters, restaurants, pubs, and boutiques.

The South Bank: Until recently, the entire south bank of the Thames River was a run-down, generally ignored area, but now it's the hottest real estate in town, with upscale restaurants, major new sightseeing attractions, and pedestrian bridges allowing easy access from the rest of London.

Residential neighborhoods to the west: Though they lack major tourist sights, South Kensington, Notting Hill, Chelsea, and Belgravia are home to London's wealthy and trendy, as well as many shopping streets and enticing restaurants.

With this focus and a good orientation, you'll find London manageable and even fun. You'll get a sampling of the city's top sights, history, and cultural entertainment, and a good look at its ever-changing human face.

Tourist Information

The **Britain and London Visitors Centre** is the best tourist information service in town (**AE, AI, AL+A, AT+A,** Level 2—Moderately accessible, no adapted toilet, but small lift leads to suitable upper-level toilet; Mon–Fri 9:00–18:30, Sat–Sun 10:00–16:00, phone not answered after 17:00 Mon–Fri or at all Sat–Sun, booking service, just off Piccadilly Circus at 1 Lower Regent Street, tel. 020/8846-9000, www.visitbritain. com, www.visitlondon.com). If you're traveling beyond London, take advantage of the Centre's well-equipped England desk. Bring your itinerary and a checklist of questions. Pick up these publications: *London Planner* (a great free monthly that lists all the sights, events, and hours),

IF YOU NEED MEDICAL HELP

Your first point of contact is your hotel. They are accustomed to dealing with medical emergencies. Here are some other resources:

Local hospitals have 24-hour-a-day emergency care centers where any tourist who needs help can drop in and, after a wait, be seen by a doctor. The quality is good and the price is right (free). Your hotel has details. St. Thomas' Hospital, immediately across the river from Big Ben, has a fine reputation (Lambeth Palace Road, tel. 020/7928-9292).

Pharma-Center is on call 24 hours a day (no appointment necessary, toll-free tel. 0808-108-5720). You can have a medical consultation at your hotel or visit a clinic (travel vaccinations, health screening, and same-day blood-test results).

For dental emergencies, consider the 24-Hour Accident and Acute Dental Emergency Service (75 Gloucester Road, opposite Gloucester Road Tube station, tel. 020/7373-3744 or 020/7373-6708).

guided-tour schedule fliers, a theater guide, "Central London Bus Guide," and the Thames River Services brochure. If you'll be taking the Tube, pick up a free copy of the Accessible Tube Map.

The Britain and London Visitors Centre sells long-distance bus tickets and passes, train tickets (convenient for reservations), British Heritage Passes, and tickets to plays (20 percent booking fee). They also sell **Fast Track tickets** to some of London's attractions (at no extra cost), allowing you to skip the queue at the sights. These can be worthwhile for places that sometimes have long ticket lines, such as the Tower of London, London Eye Ferris Wheel, and Madame Tussaud's wax museum. These advance tickets usually aren't necessary for wheelchair users, who often skip to the head of the line at such attractions anyway. While the Visitors Centre books rooms, you can avoid their £5 booking fee by calling hotels direct.

The **London Pass** provides free entrance to most of the city's sights, but since many museums are free, it's hard to justify the purchase. Still, fervent sightseers can check the list of covered sights and do the arithmetic (£27/1 day, £42/2 days, £52/3 days, £72/6 days, includes 128-page guidebook, tel. 0870-242-9988 for purchase instructions, www. londonpass.com).

Nearby you'll find the **Scottish Tourist Centre** (**AE, AI,** Level 2— Moderately accessible; May–Sept Mon–Fri 9:30–18:30, Sat 10:00–17:00, off-season Mon–Fri 10:00–18:00, Sat 12:00–17:00, 19 Cockspur Street, tel. 0845-225-5121, www.visitscotland.com) and the slick **French National Tourist Office** (**AE, AI,** Level 2—Moderately accessible; Mon–Fri 10:00–18:00, Sat until 17:00, closed Sun, 178 Piccadilly, tel. 0906-824-4123).

Unfortunately, **London's Tourist Information Centres** (which present themselves as TIs at major train and bus stations and airports) are now simply businesses selling advertising space to companies with fliers to distribute.

Local bookstores sell London guides and maps; **Bensons Mapguide** is the best (£2.25, also sold at newsstands).

Helpful Hints

Accessibility Resources: Call the Accessibility Officer of London if you need help with any accessibility issue (tel. 020/7332-1995 or tel. 020/7332-1933). The extremely helpful *Access in London* guidebook is a deal for £10 at Waterstone's and other good London bookstores (see "Travel Bookstores," below; see also www.accessproject-phsp.org).

U.S. Embassy: The embassy is fully accessible (**AE, AI, AL, AT,** Level 1; open Mon–Fri 8:30–11:00 plus Mon and Fri 14:00–16:00, 24 Grosvenor Square, Tube: Bond Street, tel. 020/7499-9000).

Theft Alert: The Artful Dodger is alive and well in London. Be on guard, particularly on public transportation and in places crowded with tourists. Tourists, considered naive and rich, are targeted. More than 7,500 handbags are stolen annually at Covent Garden alone.

Changing Money: ATMs are the way to go. For changing traveler's checks, standard transaction fees at banks are £2 to £4. The always-accessible Marks & Spencer department stores give good rates with no fees.

What's Up: For the best list of what's happening and a look at the trendy London scene, pick up a current copy of *Time Out* (£2.20, www .timeout.com) or *What's On* at any newsstand. The TI's free, monthly *London Planner* covers sights, events, and plays at least as well. For plays, also visit www.officiallondontheatre.co.uk. For a chatty, *People*

Magazine-type Web site on London's entertainment, look up www.thisislondon.com.

Sights: Free museums include the British Museum, British Library, National Gallery, National Portrait Gallery, Tate Britain (British art), Tate Modern (modern art), Imperial War Museum, Natural History Museum, Science Museum, Victoria and Albert Museum, and the Royal Air Force Museum Hendon. Special exhibitions cost extra. Telephoning first to check hours and confirm plans, especially off-season, when hours can shrink, is always smart.

Internet Access: The astonishing easyInternetcafé offers up to 500 computers per store and is open long hours daily (**AE**, Level 2—Moderately accessible). Depending on the time of day, a £2 ticket buys anywhere from 80 minutes to six hours of computer time. The ticket is valid for four weeks and multiple visits at any of their five branches: Victoria Station (across from front of station, near taxis and buses, long lines), Trafalgar Square (456 Strand), Tottenham Court Road (#9-16), Oxford Street (#358, opposite Bond Street Tube station), and Kensington High Street (#160-166). They also sell 24-hour, seven-day, and 30-day passes (www.easyinternetcafe.com). All of the stores have accessible entries, but the interiors are compact and crowded enough that it can be hard to get around; none has an accessible toilet. Disabled travelers often find that smaller Internet outlets offer more attentive service than these large, jam-packed places.

Travel Bookstores: Stanfords Travel Bookstore (**AE, AI,** Level 2—Moderately accessible) is good and stocks current editions of Rick Steves' books at Covent Garden (Mon–Fri 9:00–19:30, Sat 10:00–19:00, Sun 12:00–18:00, 12 Long Acre, tel. 020/7836-1321). There are two impressive Waterstone's bookstores (**AE, AI,** Level 2—Moderately accessible): the biggest in Europe on Piccadilly (Mon–Sat 10:00–22:00, Sun 12:00–18:00, 203 Piccadilly, tel. 020/7 851-2400) and one on the corner of Trafalgar Square (Mon–Sat 9:30–21:00, Sun 12:00–18:00, next to Costa Café, tel. 020/7839-4411). Other, smaller locations include a branch inside Harrods.

Left Luggage: As security concerns heighten, train stations have replaced their lockers with left-luggage counters. Each bag must go through a scanner (just like at the airport), so lines can be long. Expect a wait to pick up your bags, too (each item-£5/24 hrs, daily 7:00–24:00). You can also check bags at the airports (£4/day). If leaving

London and returning later, you may be able to leave a box or bag at your hotel for free—assuming you'll be staying there again.

Arrival in London

By Train: London has eight train stations, all connected by the Tube (subway) and all with exchange offices and luggage storage (see above). From any station, ride the taxi or Tube to your hotel.

By Bus: The bus station is one block southwest of Victoria Station, which has a TI, taxi stand, and Tube entrance.

By Plane: For detailed information on getting from London's airports to downtown London, see "Transportation Connections" at the end of this chapter.

Getting around London

To travel smart in a city this size, you must get comfortable with public transportation. London's excellent taxis, buses, and subway system make a private car unnecessary. In fact, the new "congestion charge" of £5 levied on any private car entering the city center has been effective in cutting down traffic jam delays and bolstering London's public transit. The revenue raised subsidizes the buses, which are now cheaper, more frequent, and even more user-friendly than before. Today the vast majority of vehicles in the city center are buses, taxis, and service trucks. (Drivers, for all the details on the congestion charge, see www.cclondon.com.)

By Taxi

London is the easiest taxi town in Europe, with big, black, carefully regulated cabs everywhere. Best of all, every taxi in London is required to be wheelchair-accessible.

We've never met a crabby cabbie in London. They love to talk, and they know every nook and cranny in town. We like to ride in one each day just to get our London questions answered.

Access: AE, Level 1—Fully accessible. All "Black Cabs" have ramps that pull down on the side of the car so you can wheel right in. The older cabs carry a ramp in the trunk, which they will get out when needed. Cab drivers have sometimes been known to switch off their light when they see a wheelchair user on the road, but this is unusual. If a taxi driver is reported to be discourteous to a wheelchair user (or anyone else, for that matter), he can lose his license. You can call for a taxi (tell them if

ACCESSIBILITY ON LONDON'S PUBLIC TRANSPORTATION

London has one of the world's best public transportation networks—and making all of the trains, buses, and boats fully accessible to all visitors is a priority. There are gaps in the network, but they are quickly being filled. New Tube stations and buses are fully adapted, and old ones are continually being retrofitted to meet accessibility standards.

If you have specific questions about accessibility on London's public transportation, call **Transport for London** at 020/7222-1234. There is also accessibility information on their Web site: www.tfl.gov.uk (click on "Passenger Help," then "Access and Mobility").

Transport for London offers several free resources for travelers with limited mobility, including a Tube map listing all accessible stations (see the color Tube map at the front of this book), and a list of accessible buses. You can call Transport for London to request any of these materials (from the U.S., dial 011-44-20-7222-1234). Once in London, you can get the latest Accessible Tube Map at any Tube station. For the other materials, or for questions, visit a Travel Information Center (at various Tube stations around London, including Victoria Station, Victoria Coach Station, both Tube stations at Heathrow Airport, Piccadilly Circus, Liverpool Street, Euston, West Croydon, Bromley, and Camden Town Hall).

For a specific trip within London, Transport for London's online **Journey Planner** will figure out if you can get to your destination without encountering barriers (http://journeyplanner.tfl.gov.uk; click on "Journey Planner," then on "More Options" to specify your mobility level).

you are using a wheelchair; Radio Taxi, tel. 020/7272-0272; or Dial-a-Cab, tel. 020/7253-5000).

Cost and Procedure: Rides start at £2 and cost about £1.50 per Tube stop. Connecting downtown sights is quick and easy and will cost you about £4 (e.g., St. Paul's to the Tower of London). For a short ride, three people in a cab travel at Tube prices. If a cab's top light is on, just wave it down. (Drivers flash lights when they see you.) They have a tiny turning radius, so you can wave at cabs going in either direction. If waving doesn't work, ask someone where you can find a taxi stand. While telephoning a cab gets one in minutes, it's generally not necessary and adds to the cost. London is such a great wave-'em-down taxi town that most cabs don't even have a radio phone.

Don't worry about meter cheating. British cab meters come with a sealed computer chip and clock that ensures you'll get the regular tariff #1 most of the time, tariff #2 during "unsociable hours" (18:00–6:00 and Sat–Sun), and tariff #3 only on holidays. All extra charges are explained in writing on the cab wall. The only way a cabbie can cheat you is to take a needlessly long route. There are alternative cab companies driving normal-looking, non-metered cars that charge fixed rates based on the postal codes of your start and end points. These are generally honest and can actually be cheaper when snarled traffic drives up the cost of a metered cab. Tip a cabbie by rounding up (maximum 10 percent).

By Bus

London's extensive bus system is easy to follow. Just pick up a free "Central London Bus Guide" map from a TI or Tube station. Signs at stops list routes clearly. On most buses (marked on sign), you'll pay at a machine at the bus stop (exact change only), then show your ticket as you board. On other buses, you can pay the conductor (take a seat, and he'll come and collect £1). Any ride in downtown London costs £1. If you have a Travel Card (see below), get in the habit of using buses for even little straight shots. But during bump-and-grind rush hours (8:00–10:00 and 16:00–19:00), you'll go faster by Tube. Consider two special bus deals: all day for £2 and a ticket six-pack for £4 (also see "London Tube and Bus Passes," below).

Access: Range from Level 3—Minimally accessible to Level 1—Fully accessible. Most London buses are already fully accessible, and they plan to reach 100 percent accessibility by 2005. The few older buses have only stairs, but the newer low-floor buses have a ramp. You can get a free timetable of accessible bus routes through Transport for London (see sidebar, previous page).

HANDY BUSES

Since the institution of London's "congestion charge" for cars, the bus system is faster, easier, and cheaper than ever. Tube-oriented travelers need to make a point to get over their tunnel vision, learn the bus system, and get around fast and easy.

Here are some of the most useful routes:

Route #9: Harrods to Hyde Park Corner to Piccadilly Circus to Trafalgar Square.

Routes #11 and #24: Victoria Station to Westminster Abbey to Trafalgar Square (#11 continues to St. Paul's).

Route #RV1: Tower of London to Tower Bridge to Tate Modern/Shakespeare's Globe to London Eye/Waterloo Station/County Hall Travel Inn to Trafalgar Square to Covent Garden (a scenic joyride).

Route #15: Paddington Station to Oxford Circus to Regent Street/TI to Piccadilly Circus to Trafalgar Square to Fleet Street to St. Paul's to Tower of London.

Route #188: Waterloo Station/London Eye to Trafalgar Square to Covent Garden to British Museum.

In addition, several buses (including #6, #12, #13, #15, #23, #139, and #159) make the corridor run from Trafalgar, Piccadilly Circus, and Oxford Circus to Marble Arch.

By Tube

London's subway system (called the Tube or Underground, but never "subway") is one of this planet's great people-movers and the fastest—and cheapest—long-distance transport in town (runs Mon–Sat about 5:00–24:00, Sun about 7:00–23:00).

Access: Ranges from Level 4—Not accessible to Level 1—Fully accessible. The Accessible Tube Map (see the color Tube map at the front of this book) shows which Tube stops are accessible. It can be hit-or-miss downtown. The handy Jubilee line has accessible stations at several important downtown stops, including Westminster, Waterloo, Southwark, and London Bridge; several other outlying stops on other lines are also accessible (including both Heathrow Airport stops on the

Piccadilly Line). Even at "accessible" stations, you will have to conquer the famous "gap" between the platform and the train, which can be as big as 12 inches.

Using the Tube: Looking at a Tube map, you'll see that each line has a name (such as Jubilee, Circle, Northern, or Bakerloo) and two directions (indicated by the end-of-the-line stop). Find the line that will take you to your destination, and figure out roughly what direction (north, south, east, west) you'll need to go to get there.

In the Tube station, feed your ticket into the turnstile, reclaim it, and hang onto the ticket—you'll need it to get through the turnstile at the end of your journey. Find your train by following signs to your line and the (general) direction it's headed (e.g., Central Line: East).

Since some tracks are shared by several lines, you'll need to double-check before boarding a train: First, make sure your destination is one of the stops listed on the sign at the platform. Also, check the electronic signboards that announce which train is next, and make sure the destination (the end-of-the-line stop) is the one you want. Each train has its final destination above its windshield. When in doubt, ask a local or a blue-vested staff person for help.

Trains run roughly every three to 10 minutes. If one train is absolutely packed and you notice another to the same destination is coming in three minutes, you can wait to avoid the sardine experience. The system can be fraught with construction delays and breakdowns, so pay attention to signs and announcements explaining necessary detours, etc. The Circle Line is notorious for problems. Bring something to do to make your waiting time productive.

You can't leave the system without feeding your ticket to the turnstile. (The turnstile will either eat your now-expired single-trip ticket, or spit your still-valid pass back out.) Save time by choosing the best accessible street exit—check the maps on the walls or ask any station personnel. "Subway" means "pedestrian underpass" in "English." For Tube and bus information 24 hours a day, call 020/7222-1234 (www.transportfor london.gov.uk). And always...mind the gap.

Cost: Any ride in Zone 1 (on or within the Circle Line, including virtually all of our recommended sights and hotels) costs £1.60. Tube tickets are also valid on city buses.

You can avoid ticket-window lines in Tube stations by buying tickets from coin-operated machines; practice on the punchboard to see how the system works (hit *Adult Single* and your destination). Note that tickets bought from a machine are valid only on the day of purchase.

Again, nearly every ride will be £1.60. Beware: Overshooting your zone nets you a £10 fine.

Carnet of 10 tickets: If you want to travel a little each day or if you're part of a group, an £11.50 carnet (CAR-net) is a great deal: You get 10 separate tickets for Tube travel in Zone 1, paying £1.15 per ride rather than £1.60. Wait for the machine to lay all 10 tickets.

London Tube and Bus Passes: Consider using the following passes, valid on both the Tube and buses (all passes are available for more zones, can be purchased as easily as a normal ticket at any station, and can get you a 33 percent discount on most Thames cruises):

One-Day pass: If you figure you'll take three rides in a day, a day pass is a good deal. The One-Day Travel Card, covering Zones 1 and 2, gives you unlimited "off-peak" travel for a day, starting after 9:30 on weekdays and anytime on weekends (£4.10). The all-zone version of this card costs £5.10 (and includes Heathrow Airport). The unrestricted version, covering six zones (including Heathrow) at all times, costs £10.70. Families save with the One-Day Family Travel Card (price varies depending on number in family). For details, including a handy journey planner, see www.thetube.com.

Weekend pass: The Weekend Travel Card, covering Saturday, Sunday, and Zones 1 and 2 for £6.10, costs 25 percent less than two one-day cards.

Seven-Day pass: The 7-Day Travel Card costs £19.60 and covers Zones 1 and 2.

Group deals: Groups of 10 or more can travel all day on the Tube for £3.10 each (but not on buses).

TOURS

▲▲▲**Hop-on, Hop-off Double-Decker Bus Tours**—Two competitive companies (Original and Big Bus) offer essentially the same tours with buses that have either live (English-only) guides or a tape-recorded, dial-a-language narration. The "Original" company is the better choice for wheelchair users (see below). This light, once-over bus tour drives by all the famous sights, providing a stress-free way to get your bearings and at least see the biggies. You can relax and enjoy the entire two-hour orientation tour (a good idea if you like the guide and the weather), or get on or off at any of the nearly 30 stops and catch a later bus. Buses run about every 10-15 minutes in summer, every 20 minutes in winter. It's an inexpensive form of transport as well as an informative tour. Buses operate daily (from about 9:00 until early evening in summer, until late afternoon in winter) and stop at Victoria Street (1 block north of Victoria Station), Marble Arch, Piccadilly Circus, Trafalgar Square, and elsewhere.

Each company offers a core two-hour overview tour, two other routes, and a narrated Thames boat tour covered by the same ticket (buy ticket from driver, credit cards accepted at major stops such as Victoria Station, ticket good for 24 hrs, bring a sweater and extra film). Pick up a map from any flier rack or from one of the countless salespeople and study the complex system. Note: If you start at Victoria Station at 9:00, you'll finish near Buckingham Palace in time to see the Changing of the Guard (at 11:30); ask your driver for the best place to get off. Sunday morning—when the traffic is light and many museums are closed—is a fine time for a tour. The last full loop leaves Victoria at 17:00. Both companies have entertaining as well as boring guides. The narration is important. If you don't like your guide, get off and find another. If you like your guide, settle in for the entire loop.

The **Original London Sightseeing Bus Tour** is the more accessible option. Live guided buses have a Union Jack flag and a yellow triangle on the front of the bus. If the front has many flags or a green or red triangle, it's a tape-recorded multilingual tour—avoid it, unless you have kids who'd enjoy the entertaining recorded kids' tour (£15, £2.50 discount with this book, limit 2 discounts per book, they'll rip off the corner of this page—raise bloody hell if they don't honor this discount, ticket good for 24 hours, tel. 020/8877-1722, www.theoriginaltour.com). Your ticket includes a 50-minute-long round-trip boat tour from Westminster Pier or Waterloo Pier (departs hourly, tape-recorded narration).

Access: AE+A, Level 2—Moderately accessible. The driver will assist the wheelchair user on to the bus. They have one space available per bus for a wheelchair.

Big Bus Hop-on, Hop-off London Tours are also good, but are less accessible to wheelchair users. For £17, you get the same basic tour plus coupons for three different one-hour London "walks" and the scenic and usually amusingly guided Thames boat ride (normally £5) between

Westminster Pier and the Tower of London. The pass and extras are valid for 24 hours. Buses with live guides are marked in front with a picture of an orange bus; buses with tape-recorded spiels display a picture of a blue bus and headphones. While the price is steeper, Big Bus guides seem more dynamic than the Original guides (daily 8:30–18:00, July-Aug until 18:00, winter until 16:30, from Victoria Station, tel. 020/7233-9533, www.bigbus.co.uk).

Access: Level 3—Minimally accessible. There are no wheelchair-accessible buses, so the wheelchair user must be able to climb on the bus.

At Night: The London by Night Sightseeing Tour runs basically the same circuit as the other companies, but after hours and with poor accessibility. The narration is lame (the driver does little more than call out the names of famous places as you roll by), but the views at twilight are grand (£9.50, pay driver or buy tickets at Victoria Station or Paddington Station TI, April–Oct only, 2-hr tour with live guide, departs at 19:30, and 21:30 from Victoria Station, Taxi Road, at front of station near end of Wilton Road, tel. 020/8646-1747, www.london-by-night.net).

Access: Level 3—Minimally accessible. There are no wheelchair-accessible buses; you'll need to be able to climb on the bus.

▲▲**Walking Tours**—Several times a day, top-notch local guides lead (often big) groups through specific slices of London's past. Wheelchair users are welcome to roll along on these walks. Check with the individual companies to be sure that their tours are appropriate for your mobility level. Schedule fliers litter the desks of TIs, hotels, and pubs. *Time Out* lists many, but not all, scheduled tours. You don't need to register; simply show up at the announced location, pay £5, and enjoy two chatty hours of Dickens, the Plague, Shakespeare, Legal London, the Beatles, Jack the Ripper, or whatever is on the agenda. Original London Walks, the dominant company, lists its extensive daily schedule in a beefy, plain, black-and-white *The Original London Walks* brochure—which you'll see at the TI and on racks in every hotel (tours offered year-round—even Christmas, private tours for £90, tel. 020/7624-3978, for a recorded listing of today's tours call 020/7624-9255, www.walks.com). They also run moderately accessible **Explorer day trips** (AE, Level 2), a good option for those with limited time and transportation (different trip daily: Stonehenge/Salisbury, Oxford/Cotswolds, York, Bath, and so on).

The Beatles: Fans of the still-Fab Four can take one of the Beatles tours (5/week, offered by Original London Walks, above). While these

LONDON AT A GLANCE

▲▲▲**British Museum** The world's greatest collection of artifacts from Western Civilization, including the Rosetta Stone and the Parthenon's Elgin Marbles. **Hours:** Daily 10:00–17:30, Thu–Fri until 20:30, but only a few galleries open after 17:30. **Access:** Level 1—Fully accessible.

▲▲▲**National Gallery** Remarkable collection of European paintings (1250-1900), including Leonardo da Vinci, Sandro Botticelli, Diego Velázquez, Rembrandt, J.M.W. Turner, Vincent van Gogh, and the Impressionists. **Hours:** Daily 10:00–18:00, Wed until 21:00. **Access:** Level 1—Fully accessible.

▲▲▲**British Library** Impressive collection of the most important literary treasures of the Western world, from the Magna Carta to Handel's *Messiah*. **Hours:** Mon–Fri 9:30–18:00, Tue until 20:00, Sat 9:30-17:00, Sun 11:00-17:00. **Access:** Level 1—Fully accessible.

▲▲▲**Westminster Abbey** Britain's finest church, and the site of royal coronations and burials since 1066. **Hours:** Mon–Fri 9:00–16:45, Wed also 18:00–19:45, Sat 9:30–14:45, closed Sun to sightseers but open for services. **Access:** Level 2—Moderately accessible.

▲▲▲**St. Paul's Cathedral** The main cathedral of the Anglican Church, designed by Christopher Wren, with a grand dome and daily evensong services. **Hours:** Mon–Sat 8:30–16:30, closed Sun except for worship. **Access:** Main Floor is Level 1—Fully accessible; dome is Level 4—Not accessible.

▲▲▲**Tower of London** Historic castle, palace, and prison, today housing the crown jewels and a witty band of Beefeaters. **Hours:** March–Oct Mon–Sat 9:00–18:00, Sun 10:00–18:00; Nov–Feb Tue–Sat 9:00–17:00, Sun–Mon 10:00–17:00. **Access:** Level 1—Fully accessible.

▲▲▲**London Eye Ferris Wheel** Enormous observation wheel, dominating—and offering commanding views over—London's skyline. **Hours:** April–mid-Sept daily 9:30–22:00, mid-Sept-March 9:30-20:00, closed Jan. **Access:** Level 1—Fully accessible.

▲▲▲**Tate Modern** Works by Claude Monet, Henri Matisse, Salvador Dalí, Pablo Picasso, and Andy Warhol, displayed in a converted power house. **Hours:** Daily 10:00–18:00, Fri–Sat until 22:00. **Access:** Level 1—Fully accessible.

▲▲**Tate Britain** Collection of British painting from the 16th century through modern times, including works by William Blake, the Pre-Raphaelites, and J.M.W. Turner. **Hours:** Daily 10:00–17:50. **Access:** Level 1—Fully accessible.

▲▲**Houses of Parliament** London's famous neo-Gothic landmark, topped by Big Ben and occupied by the Houses of Lords and Commons. **Hours:** House of Commons—Mon 14:30–22:30, Tue–Thu 11:30–19:30, Fri 9:30–15:00; House of Lords—Mon–Wed 14:30–22:30 or until they finish, Thu from 12:00 on, sometimes Fri from 10:00. **Access:** Level 2—Moderately accessible.

▲▲**Imperial War Museum** Examines the military history of the bloody 20th century. **Hours:** Daily 10:00–18:00. **Access:** Level 1—Fully accessible.

▲▲**Cabinet War Rooms** Underground WWII headquarters of Churchill's war effort. **Hours:** Daily April–Sept 9:30–18:00, Oct–March 10:00–18:00. **Access:** Level 1—Fully accessible.

▲▲**National Portrait Gallery** *Who's Who* of British history, featuring portraits of this nation's most important historical figures. **Hours:** Daily 10:00–18:00, Thu–Fri until 21:00. **Access:** Level 1—Fully accessible.

▲▲**Buckingham Palace** Britain's royal residence with the famous Changing of the Guard. **Hours:** Palace—Aug–Sept only, daily 9:30–17:00; Guard—Almost daily in summer at 11:30, every other day all year long. **Access:** Level 1—Fully accessible.

▲▲**Shakespeare's Globe** Timbered, thatched-roofed reconstruction of the Bard's original wooden "O." **Hours:** Actor-led tours mid-May–Sept Mon–Sat 9:30–12:00, Sun 9:30–11:30; virtual tours daily 12:30–16:00; actor tours Oct–mid-May daily 10:30–17:00; also regular performances (see "Entertainment and Theater," page 108). **Access:** Level 1—Fully accessible.

▲▲**Victoria and Albert Museum** The best collection of decorative arts anywhere. **Hours:** Daily 10:00–17:45, Wed until 21:30. **Access:** Level 1—Fully accessible.

continued on next page

continued from previous page

▲▲**Somerset House** Grand 18th-century civic palace housing three fine art museums: Courtauld Gallery (decent painting collection), Hermitage Rooms (rotating exhibits from the famous St. Petersburg museum), and the Gilbert Collection (decorative arts). **Hours:** Daily 10:00–18:00. **Access:** Level 1—Fully accessible.

▲▲**Vinopolis: City of Wine** Offers a breezy history of wine with plenty of tasting opportunities. **Hours:** Daily 11:00–18:00, Sat and Mon until 21:00. **Access:** Level 1—Fully accessible.

"walks" include wheelchair-using participants (Level 2—Moderately accessible), the route ends with an inaccessible Tube ride to Abbey Road (skip this ending, or take a taxi to meet the group at your own expense).

Private Guides: Standard rates for London's registered guides are £97 for four hours, £146 for eight hours (tel. 020/7403-2962, wheelchair users can call tel. 020/7495-5504 to request a guide that suits your needs; www.touristguides.org.uk). William Forrester, one of the authors of *Access in London* and a wheelchair user himself, is a London Registered Guide. He offers tailor-made day tours as well as group tours (early booking necessary, mobile 0148-357-5401). Robina Brown leads tours with small groups in her Toyota Previa. She has led tours for deaf, blind, and other travelers with disabilities, and wheelchair users are welcome—though they must be able to climb into her car (£200/3 hrs, £300–450/day, tel. 020/7228-2238, www.driverguidetours.com, robina@driverguidetours.com).

▲▲**Cruises**—Boat tours with entertaining commentaries sail regularly from many points along the Thames.

Access: All passenger boats on the Thames (including all listed below, except on Regent's Canal) are legally required to be wheelchair-accessible (Level 1). Boats are accessed via ramps (no steps or other barriers), but the steepness of the ramp depends on the level of the water. At the lowest tide, the ramp is much steeper than at high tide—so some wheelchair users might require assistance. While some boats have accessible toilets, not all do. If finding a boat with an adapted toilet is important to you, or if you want to check on when the ramp will be the least

London Center

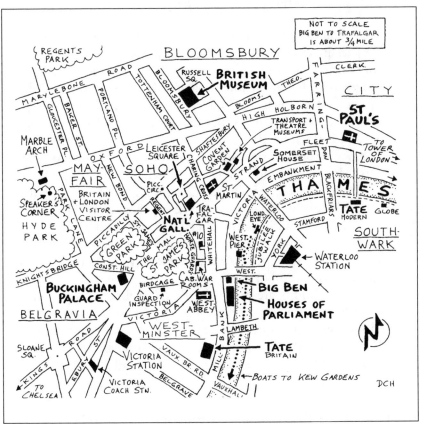

steep, call the individual companies (listed below). For general questions, contact London River Services at 020/7941-2400.

Options: It's confusing, since there are several companies offering essentially the same thing. Your basic options are downstream (to the Tower and Greenwich), upstream (to Kew Gardens and Hampton Court), and round-trip scenic tour cruises. Most people depart from the Westminster Pier (**AE, AI, AT,** dock area and boat ramp are Level 1—Fully accessible; at the base of Westminster Bridge under Big Ben). You can catch most of the same boats—with less waiting—from Waterloo Pier at the London Eye Ferris Wheel across the river (Level 1—Fully accessible dock area and boat ramp). For pleasure and efficiency, consider combining a one-way cruise (to Kew, Greenwich, or wherever) with a Tube

DAILY REMINDER

Sunday: Some sights don't open until noon. The Tower of London is especially crowded today. Hyde Park Speakers' Corner rants from early afternoon until early evening. These are closed: Banqueting House, Sir John Soane's Museum, and legal sights (Houses of Parliament, Old Bailey, the City is dead). Evensong is at 15:00 at Westminster Abbey (plus organ recital at 17:45 for a fee) and 15:15 at St. Paul's (plus free organ recital at 17:00); both churches are open during the day for worship but closed to sight-seers. Many stores and theaters are closed. Street markets flourish: Camden Lock, Spitalfields, Greenwich, and Petticoat Lane.

Monday: Virtually all sights are open except for Apsley House, the Theatre Museum, Sir John Soane's Museum, and a few others. The St. Martin-in-the-Fields church offers a free 13:05 concert. At Somerset House, the Courtauld Gallery is free until 14:00. Vinopolis is open until 21:00.

Tuesday: All sights are open; the British Library is open until 20:00. St. Martin-in-the-Fields has a free 13:05 concert.

Wednesday: All sights are open, plus evening hours at Westminster Abbey (until 19:45), the National Gallery (until 21:00), and Victoria and Albert Museum (until 22:00).

ride back. While Tube and bus tickets don't work on the boats, a Travel Card can snare you a 33 percent discount on most cruises. Buy boat tickets at the small ticket offices on the docks. Children and seniors get discounts. You can buy drinks and scant, pricey snacks on board. Clever budget travelers pack along a small picnic and munch while they cruise.

Here are some of the most popular cruise options.

To Tower of London: **City Cruises** boats sail 30 minutes to the Tower from Westminster Pier (£5.20 one-way, £6.30 round-trip, one-way included with Big Bus London tour; covered by £8.50 "River Red Rover" ticket that includes Greenwich—see next paragraph; 3/hr during June–Aug daily 10:00–20:40, 2/hr and shorter hours rest of year, tel. 020/7740-0400, www.citycruises.com).

To Greenwich: Two companies head to Greenwich from Westminster Pier. Choose between City Cruises (£6.50 one-way, £8 round-

Thursday: All sights are open, British Museum until 20:30 (selected galleries), National Portrait Gallery until 21:00. St. Martin-in-the-Fields hosts a 19:30 evening concert (for a fee).

Friday: All sights are open, British Museum until 20:30 (selected galleries only), National Portrait Gallery until 21:00, Tate Modern until 22:00. Best street market: Spitalfields. St. Martin-in-the-Fields offers two concerts (13:05-free, 19:30-fee).

Saturday: Most sights are open except legal ones (Old Bailey; Houses of Parliament—open summer Sat for tours only; skip the City). Vinopolis is open until 21:00, Tate Modern until 22:00. Best street markets: Portobello, Camden Lock, Greenwich. Evensong is at 15:00 at Westminster Abbey, 17:00 at St. Paul's. St. Martin-in-the-Fields hosts a concert at 19:30 (fee).

Notes: Evensong occurs daily at St. Paul's (Mon–Sat at 17:00 and Sun at 15:15) and daily except Wednesday at Westminster Abbey (Mon–Tue and Thu–Fri at 17:00, Sat–Sun at 15:00). London by Night Sightseeing Tour buses leave from Victoria Station every evening at 20:00, 21:00, and 22:00. The London Eye Ferris Wheel spins nightly until 22:00 in summer, until 20:00 in winter (closed Jan).

trip; or get their £8.50 all-day, hop-on, hop-off "River Red Rover" ticket to have option of getting off at London Eye and Tower of London; June–Aug daily 10:00–17:00, less off-season, every 40 min, 70 min to Greenwich, usually narrated only downstream—to Greenwich, tel. 020/7740-0400) and **Thames River Services** (£6.50 one-way, £8 round-trip, April–Oct daily 10:00–16:00, July–Aug until 17:00, 2/hr, 50 min, has shorter hours and runs every 40 min rest of year, usually narrated only to Greenwich, tel. 020/7930-4097).

To Kew Gardens: Westminster Passenger Services Association leaves for Kew Gardens from Westminster Pier (£9 one-way, £15 round-trip, 4/day, generally departing 10:30–14:00, 90 min, narrated for 30 min, tel. 020/7930-2062, www.wpsa.co.uk). Some boats continue on to **Hampton Court Palace** for an additional £3 (and 90 min). Because of the river current, you'll save 30 minutes cruising from Hampton Court back into town.

Round-Trip Cruises: Fifty-minute round-trip cruises of the Thames leave hourly from Westminster and Embankment Piers (£7.50, included with Original London Bus tour—listed above, tape-recorded narration, Catamaran Circular Cruises, tel. 020/7987-1185). The London Eye Ferris Wheel operates its own "River Cruise Experience," offering a similar 45-minute circular tour from Waterloo Pier (must be done in combination with Ferris Wheel, £20 includes both, reservations recommended and cost 50p, tel. 0870-443-9185, www.ba-londoneye.com).

From Tate to Tate: This new boat service for art-lovers connects the Tate Modern and Tate British galleries in 18 scenic minutes (departing every 40 min from 10:00–17:00, also stops at London Eye Ferris Wheel, £4.50, £10 per family, buy ticket at gallery desk or on board, tel. 020/7887-8008).

On Regent's Canal: Consider exploring London's canals by taking a cruise on historic Regent's Canal in north London. The good ship *Jenny Wren* (**AE+A,** Level 2—Moderately accessible) offers 90-minute guided canal boat cruises from Walker's Quay in Camden Town to Little Venice (3 steps to board boat; £6.50, March–Oct daily 12:30, 14:30, Sat–Sun also 10:30, 16:30, Walker's Quay, 250 Camden High Street, Tube: Camden Town, tel. 020/7485-4433 or 020/7485-6210, www.walkers quay.com). While in Camden Town, have a look at the popular Camden Lock Market, selling trendy arts and crafts (daily 10:00–18:00, busiest on weekends, a block from Walker's Quay).

London Duck Tours—A bright-yellow amphibious vehicle takes a gang of 30 tourists past some famous sights on land (Big Ben, Buckingham Palace, Piccadilly Circus), then splashes into the Thames for a 30-minute cruise (Level 3—Minimally accessible, 5 steps to enter; £17, 2/hr, daily 10:00–18:00, 75 min, live commentary, these book up in advance, departs from Chicheley Street behind County Hall near London Eye Ferris Wheel, Tube: Waterloo or Westminster, tel. 020/7928-3132, www .londonducktours.com).

SIGHTS

From Westminster Abbey to Trafalgar Square

These sights are linked by the Westminster Roll or Stroll chapter on page 146.

▲▲▲**Westminster Abbey**—As the greatest church in the English-speaking world, Westminster Abbey has been the place where England's kings and queens have been crowned and buried since 1066. A thousand years of English history—3,000 tombs, the remains of 29 kings and queens, and hundreds of memorials—lie within its walls and under its stone slabs. Like a stony refugee camp huddled outside St. Peter's gates, this place has a story to tell and the best way to enjoy it is with a **tour** (audioguide-£2, live-£3; many prefer the audioguide because it's self-paced, both tours include entry to cloister museums). Experience an **evensong** service—awesome in a nearly empty church (weekdays except Wed at 17:00, Sat–Sun at 15:00). The **organ recital** on Sunday at 17:45 is another highlight (fee, 40 min). Organ concerts here are great and inexpensive; look for signs with schedule details (or visit www.westminster-abbey.org).

Access: AE, AI, Level 2—Moderately accessible. Most of the museum is wheelchair-accessible. There are loaner wheelchairs, but no accessible toilets. Wheelchair riders use the main entrance on the north (Big Ben) side of the museum.

Cost, Hours, and Location: Abbey entry free for wheelchair user and companion, otherwise £6, Mon–Fri 9:00–16:45, Wed also 18:00-19:45, Sat 9:30–14:45, last admission 60 min before closing, closed Sun to sightseers but open for services and organ recital (photography prohibited, coffee available in cloister, Tube: Westminster or St. James's Park, call for tour schedule, tel. 020/7222-7110). Since the church is often closed to the public for special services, it's wise to call first.

Three tiny **museums** ring the cloister (all **AE, AI, AT,** Level 1—Fully accessible; £1 covers all, on top of your abbey ticket; or free with either the audioguide or live tour): The **Chapter House,** where the monks held their daily meetings, is notable for its fine architecture and well-described but faded medieval art. The **Pyx Chamber** contains an exhibit on the king's treasury. The **Abbey Museum** tells of the abbey's history, royal coronations, and burials; look into the impressively realistic eyes of Henry VII's funeral effigy, one of a fascinating series of wax-and-wood statues that, for three centuries, graced royal coffins during funeral processions.

Enter the abbey on the Big Ben side (often with a sizable line, visit early to avoid crowds) and then follow a one-way route through this English hall of fame around the church and cloisters (with the 3 small museums), back through the nave, and out (see map on page 148).

▲▲Houses of Parliament (Palace of Westminster)—This neo-Gothic icon of London, the royal residence from 1042 to 1547, is now the meeting place of the legislative branch of government. Tourists are welcome to view debates in either the bickering House of Commons or the genteel House of Lords (when in session—indicated by a flag flying atop the Victoria Tower). While the actual debates are generally extremely dull, it is a thrill to be inside and see the British government inaction. The House of Lords has more pageantry, shorter lines, and less interesting debates.

Just past security to the left, study the big dark **Westminster Hall,** which survived the 1834 fire. The hall was built in the 11th century, and its famous self-supporting hammer-beam roof was added in 1397. The Houses of Parliament are located in what was once the Palace of Westminster, long the palace of England's medieval kings, until it was largely destroyed by fire in 1834. The palace was rebuilt in Victorian Gothic style (a move away from neo-classicism back to England's Christian and medieval heritage, true to the Romantic Age). It was completed in 1860.

Big Ben, the clock tower (315 feet high), is named for its 13-ton bell, Ben. The light above the clock is lit when the House of Commons is sitting. The face of the clock is huge—you can actually see the minute hand moving. For a better view of it, go halfway over Westminster Bridge (also the beginning of the Westminster Roll or Stroll, page 146).

Access: AE+A, AI, AT, AL+A, Level 2—Moderately accessible. To enter either House of Parliament, you need to alert the main entrance guards to your presence. You will be escorted to a separate entry and guided to your choice of House. Security is very tight and body searches should be expected, especially if the House of Commons is in session.

Cost, Hours, and Location: Free. Hours of House of Commons— Mon 14:30–22:30; Tue, Wed, Thu 11:30–19:30; Fri 9:30–15:00 (generally less action and no lines after 18:00, use St. Stephen's entrance, tel. 020/7219-4272 for schedule). Hours of House of Lords—Mon–Wed 14:30–22:30 or until they finish, Thu from 12:00 on, sometimes Fri from 10:00 on (tel. 020/7219-3107 for schedule). Tube: Westminster, www .parliament.uk.

If there's only one line outside, it's for the House of Commons. Wheelchair users can go to the head of the line (see above). Slow walkers and non-disabled travelers can go to the gate and tell the guard you want the Lords (that's the second "line" with no people in it). You may pop right in—that is, after you've cleared the security gauntlet. Once you've seen the Lords (hide your HOL flier), you can often slip directly over to the House of Commons and join the gang waiting in the lobby. Inside the lobby, you'll find an announcement board with the day's line-up for both houses.

▲▲**Cabinet War Rooms**—This is a fascinating look at the underground headquarters of the British government's fight against the Nazis in the darkest days of the Battle for Britain. The 27-room nerve center of the British war effort was used from 1939 to 1945. Churchill's room, the map room, and other rooms are just as they were in 1945. For all the details of blood, sweat, toil, and tears, pick up an audioguide at the entry and follow the included and excellent 60-minute tour. Be patient—it's worth it.

Access: AE, AI, AT, AL, ♥ Level 1—Fully accessible. Loaner wheelchairs are available. The lift will get you to the underground headquarters.

Cost, Hours, and Location: £7, half-price for wheelchair user and companion, daily April–Sept 9:30–18:00, Oct–March 10:00–18:00, last entry 45 min before closing, on King Charles Street 200 yards off Whitehall, follow the signs, Tube: Westminster, tel. 020/7930-6961, www.iwm.org.uk.

Horse Guards—The Horse Guards change daily at 11:00 (10:00 on Sun), and there's a colorful dismounting ceremony daily at 16:00 (you view it from the sidewalk). The rest of the day, they just stand there—terrible for camcorders (on Whitehall, between Trafalgar Square and #10 Downing Street, Tube: Westminster). While Buckingham Palace pageantry is canceled when it rains, the horse guards change regardless of the weather.

▲**Banqueting House**—England's first Renaissance building was designed by Inigo Jones around 1620. It's one of the few London landmarks spared by the 1666 fire and the only surviving part of the original Palace of Whitehall. Don't miss its Rubens ceiling, which, at Charles I's request, drove home the doctrine of the legitimacy of the divine right of kings. In 1649—divine right ignored—Charles I was beheaded on the balcony of this building by a Cromwellian Parliament. Admission includes a restful 20-minute audiovisual history, which shows the place in banqueting action; a 30-minute audio tour (interesting only to history buffs); and a look at the exquisite banqueting hall.

Access: AE+A, Level 4—Not accessible. There is one 4" step to enter the lobby. From then on, the building is divided into upper and lower levels with no lifts or ramps.

Cost, Hours, and Location: £4, Mon–Sat 10:00–17:00, closed Sun, last entry at 16:30, subject to closure for government functions, aristocratic toilet, immediately across Whitehall from the Horse Guards, Tube: Westminster, tel. 020/7930-4179.

Trafalgar Square

▲▲**Trafalgar Square**—London's central square, the climax of most marches and demonstrations, is a thrilling place to simply hang out. Lord Nelson stands atop his 185-foot-tall fluted granite column, gazing out to Trafalgar, where he lost his life but defeated the French fleet. Part of this 1842 memorial is made from his victims' melted-down cannons. He's surrounded by giant lions, hordes of people, and—until recently—even more pigeons. London's Mayor Livingstone, nicknamed "Red Ken" for his passion for an activist government, decided that London's "flying rats" were a public nuisance and evicted the venerable seed salesmen (Tube: Charing Cross).

▲▲▲**National Gallery**—Displaying Britain's top collection of European paintings from 1250 to 1900 (works by Leonardo, Sandro Botticelli, Diego Velázquez, Rembrandt, J. M. W. Turner, Vincent van Gogh, and the Impressionists), this is one of Europe's great galleries. While the collection is huge, following the route suggested on the map on page 80 will give you the best quick visit. The audioguide tours are the finest I've used in Europe (suggested £4 donation). Don't miss the Micro Gallery, a computer room even your dad could have fun in (closes 30 min earlier than museum); you can study any artist, style, or topic in the museum

and even print out a tailor-made tour map.

Access: AE, AI, AL, AT, Level 1—Fully accessible. Loaner wheelchairs are available.

Cost, Hours, and Location: Free, daily 10:00–18:00, Wed until 21:00, free one-hour overview tours daily at 11:30 and 14:30 plus Wed at 18:30, photography prohibited, on Trafalgar Square, Tube: Charing Cross or Leicester Square, tel. 020/7747-2885, www.nationalgallery.org.

▲▲**National Portrait Gallery**—Put off by halls of 19th-century characters who meant nothing to me, I used to call this "as interesting as someone else's yearbook." But a selective visit to this 500-year-long *Who's Who* of British history is quick and free and puts faces on the story of England. A bonus is the chance to admire some great art by painters such as Hans Holbein, Anthony Van Dyck, William Hogarth, Joshua Reynolds, and Thomas Gainsborough. The collection is well-described, not huge, and in historical sequence, from the 16th century on the second floor to today's royal family on the ground floor.

Some highlights: Henry VIII and wives; several fascinating portraits of the "Virgin Queen" Elizabeth I, Sir Francis Drake, and Sir Walter Raleigh; the only real-life portrait of William Shakespeare; Oliver Cromwell and Charles I with his head on; self-portraits and other portraits by Gainsborough and Reynolds; the Romantics (William Blake, Lord Byron, William Wordsworth, and company); Queen Victoria and her era; and the present royal family, including the late Princess Diana.

The excellent audioguide tours (£3 donation requested) describe each room (or era in British history) and more than 300 paintings. You'll learn more about British history than art and actually hear interviews with 20th-century subjects as you stare at their faces. The elegant Portrait Restaurant on the top floor comes with views and high prices (cheaper Portrait Café in basement).

Access: AE, AI, AL, AT, Level 1—Fully accessible. Loaner wheelchairs are available.

National Gallery

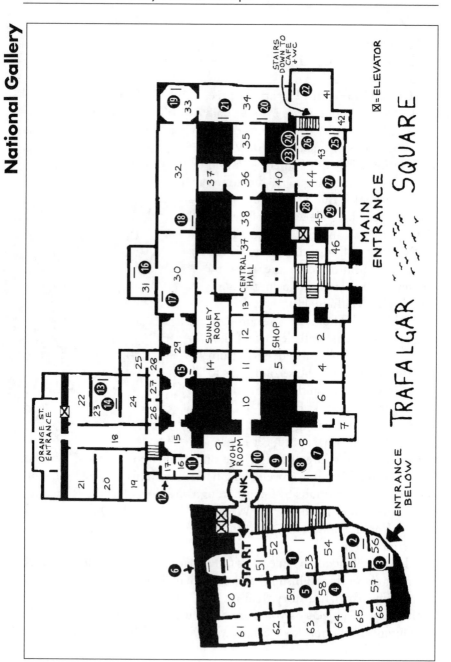

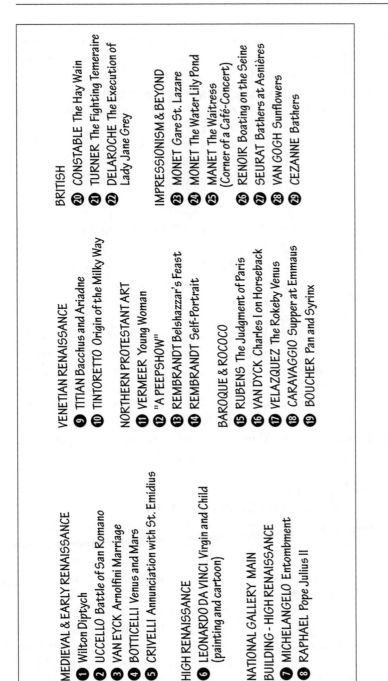

MEDIEVAL & EARLY RENAISSANCE
1. Wilton Diptych
2. UCCELLO Battle of San Romano
3. VAN EYCK Arnolfini Marriage
4. BOTTICELLI Venus and Mars
5. CRIVELLI Annunciation with St. Emidius

HIGH RENAISSANCE
6. LEONARDO DA VINCI Virgin and Child (painting and cartoon)

NATIONAL GALLERY MAIN BUILDING - HIGH RENAISSANCE
7. MICHELANGELO Entombment
8. RAPHAEL Pope Julius II

VENETIAN RENAISSANCE
9. TITIAN Bacchus and Ariadne
10. TINTORETTO Origin of the Milky Way

NORTHERN PROTESTANT ART
11. VERMEER Young Woman
12. "A PEEPSHOW"
13. REMBRANDT Belshazzar's Feast
14. REMBRANDT Self-Portrait

BAROQUE & ROCOCO
15. RUBENS The Judgment of Paris
16. VAN DYCK Charles I on Horseback
17. VELAZQUEZ The Rokeby Venus
18. CARAVAGGIO Supper at Emmaus
19. BOUCHER Pan and Syrinx

BRITISH
20. CONSTABLE The Hay Wain
21. TURNER The Fighting Temeraire
22. DELAROCHE The Execution of Lady Jane Grey

IMPRESSIONISM & BEYOND
23. MONET Gare St. Lazare
24. MONET The Water Lily Pond
25. MANET The Waitress (Corner of a Café-Concert)
26. RENOIR Boating on the Seine
27. SEURAT Bathers at Asnières
28. VAN GOGH Sunflowers
29. CEZANNE Bathers

Cost, Hours, and Location: Free, daily 10:00–18:00, Thu–Fri until 21:00, entry 100 yards off Trafalgar Square, around corner from National Gallery, opposite Church of St. Martin-in-the-Fields, tel. 020/7306-0055, recorded info tel. 020/7312-2463, www.npg.org.uk.

▲**St. Martin-in-the-Fields**—This church, built in the 1720s with a Gothic spire atop a Greek-type temple, is an oasis of peace on the wild and noisy Trafalgar Square. St. Martin cared for the poor. "In the fields" was where the first church stood on this spot (in the 13th century), between Westminster and the City. As you enter, you still feel a compassion for the needs of the people in this community. A free flier provides a brief yet worthwhile self-guided tour. The church is famous for its concerts. Consider a free lunchtime concert (Mon, Tue, and Fri at 13:05) or an evening concert (£6–18, Thu–Sat at 19:30, box office tel. 020/7839-8362). Downstairs (and not accessible for wheelchair users) is a ticket office for concerts (wheelchair users call tel. 020/7839-8362 for tickets), a gift shop, a brass-rubbing center, and a fine support-the-church cafeteria (see "Eating," page 127).

Access: AE+A, AI+A, AL+A, ♥ Level 2—Moderately accessible. There is a rather steep ramp on the north side of the building for wheelchair users that takes you directly into the sanctuary/concert hall. There are plans for full accessibility by 2005. Fourteen steps lead downstairs (Level 4—Not accessible) to the café, bookstore, exhibit hall, and brass-rubbing center. The toilets are clean and free, but not accessible.

Cost, Hours, and Location: Free, donations welcome, open daily, tel. 020/7766-1100, www.stmartin-in-the-fields.org.

More Top Squares:
Piccadilly, Soho, and Covent Garden

▲▲**Piccadilly Circus**—London's most touristy square got its name from the fancy ruffled shirts—*picadils*—made in the neighborhood long ago. Today the square is surrounded by fascinating streets swimming with youth on the rampage. For overstimulation, drop by the extremely trashy **Pepsi Trocadero Center's** (AE, AI+A, AL, Level 2—Moderately accessible) "theme park of the future" for its Segaworld virtual-reality games, nine-screen cinema, and thundering IMAX theater (admission to Trocadero is free; individual attractions cost £2–8; before paying full price for IMAX, look for a discount ticket at brochure racks at the TI or hotels; located between Coventry Street and Shaftesbury Avenue, just

Top London Squares

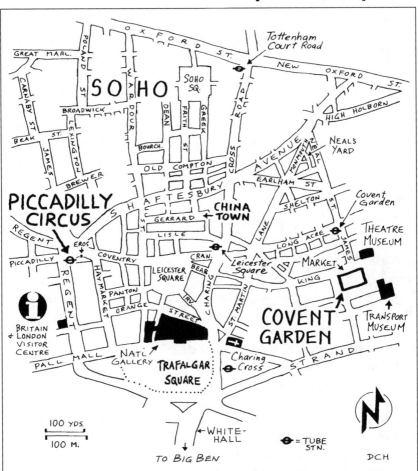

off Piccadilly). Chinatown, to the east, has swollen since Hong Kong lost its independence. Nearby Shaftesbury Avenue and Leicester Square teem with fun-seekers, theaters, Chinese restaurants, and street singers. **Soho**—North of Piccadilly, motley Soho is becoming trendy and is well worth a gawk. Most sidewalk corners have curb cuts, and the sidewalks are very negotiable. Some of the streets have been made into pedestrian malls, so the sidewalk and the road are all on one level. Soho is London's red light district, where voluptuous con artists sell strip shows. Anyone who goes into any one of the shows will be ripped off. Every time. Even a £5 show in a "licensed bar" comes with a £100 cover or minimum (as it's printed on the drink menu) and a "security man." You may accidentally buy a £200 bottle of bubbly. And suddenly, the door has no handle.

Telephone sex is hard to avoid these days in London. Phone booths are littered with racy fliers of busty ladies "new in town." Some travelers gather six or eight phone booths' worth of fliers and take them home for kinky wallpaper.

▲▲**Covent Garden**—This boutique-ish shopping district is a people-watcher's delight, with cigarette eaters, Punch-and-Judy acts, food that's

good for you (but not your wallet), trendy crafts, sweet whiffs of marijuana, two-tone hair (neither color natural), and faces that could set off a metal detector (Tube: Covent Garden). For better Covent Garden lunch deals, get a block or two away from the eye of this touristy hurricane (check out the places north of the Tube station along Endell and Neal Streets).

Museums near Covent Garden

▲▲**Somerset House**—This grand 18th-century, fully accessible civic palace offers a marvelous public space, three fine art collections, and a riverside terrace. The palace once housed the national registry that records Britain's births, marriages, and deaths ("where they hatched 'em, latched 'em, and dispatched 'em"). Enter the courtyard to enjoy the fountain. The 55 jets get playful twice an hour.

Surrounding you are three small and sumptuous sights: the Courtauld Gallery (paintings), the Gilbert Collection (fine arts), and the Hermitage Rooms (the finest art of czarist Russia).

The **Courtauld Gallery** is less impressive than the National Gallery, but its wonderful collection of paintings is still a joy. The gallery is part of the Courtauld Institute of Art, and the thoughtful description of each piece of art reminds visitors that the gallery is still used for teaching. You'll see medieval European paintings and works by Rubens, the Impressionists (Manet, Monet, Degas, Seurat), Post-Impressionists (such as Cézanne), and more.

The **Hermitage Rooms** offer a taste of Romanov imperial splendor. As Russia struggles and tourists are staying away, someone had the bright idea of sending the best of its art to London to raise some hard cash. These five rooms host a different collection every six months, with a standard intro to the czar's winter palace in St. Petersburg.

The **Gilbert Collection** displays 800 pieces of the finest in European decorative arts, from diamond-studded gold snuffboxes to intricate Italian mosaics. Maybe you've seen Raphael paintings and Botticelli frescoes...but this lush collection is refreshingly different.

Access: AE, AI, AL, AT, Level 1: All of the Somerset House galleries are fully accessible. The west door provides accessible entry to the complex, and you can take the lift to the accessible toilet in the basement. Accessible parking and loaner wheelchairs are also available.

Cost, Hours, and Location: Courtauld Gallery—£5, free Mon until 14:00 (downstairs cafeteria, cloakroom, lockers, and toilet). Hermitage Rooms—£6 (tel. 020/7420-9410, www.hermitagerooms.org.uk). Gilbert Collection—£5, free after 16:30 (includes free audioguide with a highlights tour and a helpful loaner magnifying glass). If you buy a ticket at one gallery, you get a £1 discount off admission to either or both of the other two on the same day. All galleries are open daily 10:00–18:00 (last admission 17:15). Tel. 020/7848-2526 or 020/7845-4600. The Web site (www.somerset-house.org.uk) lists a busy schedule of tours, kids' events, and concerts. The riverside terrace is picnic-friendly (deli inside lobby). Somerset House is located between the Strand and the Thames, off Waterloo Bridge. Coming from Trafalgar Square, catch bus #6, #9, #11, #13, #15, or #23. Tube: Temple (closer) or Covent Garden.

▲**London Transport Museum**—This wonderful museum is a delight for kids. Whether you're cursing or marveling at the buses and the Tube, the growth of Europe's biggest city has been made possible by its public transit system. Watch the growth of the Tube, then sit in the simulator to "drive" a train.

Access: AE, AI, AL, AT, Level 1—Fully accessible. Loaner wheelchairs are available.

Cost, Hours, and Location: £6, kids under 16 free, Sat–Thu 10:00–18:00, Fri 11:00–18:00, 30 yards southeast of Covent Garden's marketplace, tel. 020/7565-7299.

Theatre Museum—This earnest museum, worthwhile for theater buffs, traces the development of British theater from Shakespeare to today.

Access: AE, AI, AL, AT, ♥ Level 1—Fully accessible. Loaner wheelchairs are available.

Cost, Hours, Location: Free, Tue–Sun 10:00–18:00, closed Mon, free guided tours at 11:00, 12:00, and 16:00, a block east of Covent Garden's marketplace down Russell Street, tel. 020/7943-4700, www.theatremuseum.org.

North London

▲▲▲**British Museum, Great Court, and Reading Room**—Simply put, this is the greatest chronicle of civilization...anywhere. A visit here is

like a long roll or stroll through Encyclopedia Britannica National Park. Entering on Great Russell Street, you'll come into the Great Court, the glass-domed hub of a two-acre cultural complex, containing restaurants, shops, and lecture halls plus the Round Reading Room.

Access: AE, AI, AT, AL, Level 1: The museum and the Great Court are both fully accessible. The main entry on Great Russell Street and the entry on Montague Place are both fully accessible.

Cost, Hours, and Location: The British Museum is free (£2 donation requested, daily 10:00–17:30, Thu–Fri until 20:30—but only a few galleries open after 17:30, least crowded weekday late afternoons, Great Russell Street, Tube: Tottenham Court Road, tel. 020/7323-8000 or recorded information 020/7388-2227, www.thebritishmuseum.ac.uk). The Reading Room is free and open daily 10:00–17:30 (Thu until 20:30). Computer terminals within the Reading Room offer COMPASS, a database of information about selected museum items. The Great Court has longer opening hours than the museum (daily 9:00–18:00, Thu–Sat until 23:00).

Tours: Guided **eyeOpener tours** (free, nearly hrly, 50 min) are each different, focusing on one particular subject within the museum. These leave throughout the day and can make the visit much more meaningful. There are also three types of **audioguide tours:** Top 50 highlights (90 min, pick up at Great Court information desks), the Parthenon Sculptures (60 min, get at desk outside Parthenon Galleries), and the family tour, with themes such as "bodies, boardgames, and beasts" (length

British Museum

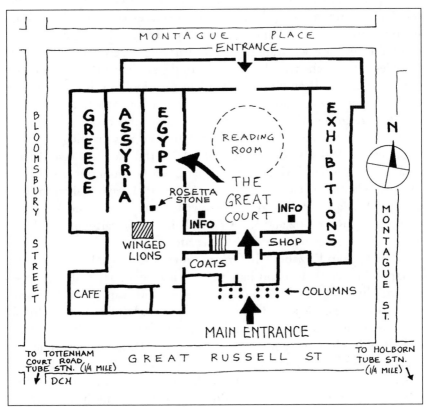

varies, pick up at Great Court information desks). To rent an audioguide (£3.50), you'll need to leave a photo ID and £10 for a deposit.

Self-Guided Tour: The most popular sections of the museum fill the ground floor: Egyptian, Mesopotamian, and ancient Greek—with the famous Elgin Marbles from the Athenian Parthenon. Huge winged lions (which guarded Assyrian palaces 800 years before Christ) guard these great ancient galleries. For a brief tour, connect these ancient dots:

Start with the **Egyptian** (Room 4). Wander from the Rosetta Stone past the many statues. If you visit the upper level later (see below), be sure to take a roll or stroll through mummy land (Rooms 62 and 63).

Make your way to room 7 (back at the winged lions) and wander through the dark, violent, and mysterious **Assyrian** rooms. The Nimrud Gallery is lined with royal propaganda reliefs and wounded lions.

The most modern of the ancient art fills the **Greek** section. Find room 11 behind the winged lions and start your exploration of Greek art history with the simple and primitive Cycladic fertility figures. Later, painted vases show a culture really into partying. The finale is the Elgin Marbles. The much-wrangled-over bits of the Athenian Parthenon (from 450 B.C.) are even more impressive than they look. To best appreciate these ancient carvings, take the audioguide tour (available in this gallery).

Be sure to venture to the upper level (accessible by elevator) to see artifacts from **Roman Britain** (Room 50) that surpass anything you'll see at Hadrian's Wall or elsewhere in Britain. Nearby, the Dark Age Britain exhibits offer a worthwhile peek at that bleak era; look for the Sutton Hoo Ship Burial artifacts from a seventh-century royal burial on the east coast of England (Room 41). If you want more Egypt, check out the mummies in Rooms 62 and 63. A rare Michelangelo cartoon is in Room 90 (one more level up, accessible by elevator).

The **Queen Elizabeth II Great Court** is Europe's largest covered square—bigger than a football field. This people-friendly court—delightfully out of the London rain—was for 150 years one of London's great lost spaces...closed off and gathering dust. While the vast British Museum wraps around the court, its centerpiece is the stately and accessible **Reading Room,** famous as the place Karl Marx hung out while formulating his ideas on communism and writing *Das Kapital.* The Reading Room—one of the fine cast-iron buildings of the 19th century—is free to explore, but there's little to see that you can't see from the doorway.

▲▲▲**British Library**—The British Empire built its greatest monuments out of paper. And it's in literature that England made her lasting contribution to civilization and the arts. Britain's national archives has more than 12 million books, 180 miles of shelving, and the deepest basement in London. But everything that matters for your visit is in one delightful room labeled "The Treasures." This room is filled with literary and historical documents that changed the course of history. You'll trace the evolution of European maps over 800 years.
Follow the course of the Bible—from the earliest known gospels (written on scraps of papyrus) to the first complete Bible to the original King James Version and the Gutenberg Bible. You'll see Leonardo da Vinci's doodles, the Magna Carta, Shakespeare's First Folio, the original *Alice*

British Library

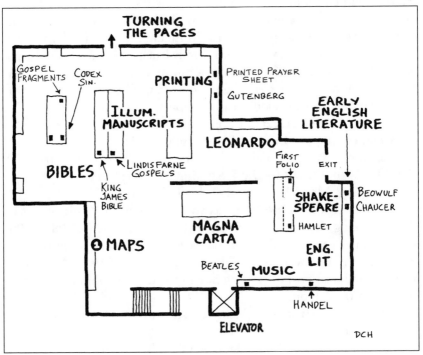

in Wonderland in Lewis Carroll's handwriting, and manuscripts by Beethoven, Mozart, Lennon, and McCartney. Finish in the fascinating "Turning the Pages" exhibit, which lets you actually browse through virtual manuscripts of a few of these treasures on a computer. The ground-floor café is next to a vast and fun pull-out stamp collection, and the upper-level cafeteria serves good hot meals.

Access: AE, AI, AT, AL, ♥ Level 1—Fully accessible.

Cost, Hours, and Location: Free, Mon–Fri 9:30–18:00, Tue until 20:00, Sat 9:30–17:00, Sun 11:00–17:00; 60-min tours for £5 usually Mon, Wed, and Fri–Sun at 15:00, also Tue 18:30, Sat 10:30, and Sun 11:30; call 020/7412-7332 to confirm schedule and reserve; £3.50 audioguide, £1 lockers, Tube: King's Cross, turn right out of station and continue a block to 96 Euston Road, library tel. 020/7412-7000, www.bl.uk.

▲**Madame Tussaud's Waxworks**—This is expensive but dang good. The original Madame Tussaud did wax casts of heads lopped off during the French Revolution (such as Marie Antoinette's). She took her show on the road and ended up in London. And now it's much easier to be featured. The gallery is one big *Who's Who* photo-op—a huge hit with the kind of travelers who skip the British Museum. Don't miss the gallery of has-been heads that no longer merit a body (such as Sammy Davis Jr. and Nikita Khrushchev). After looking a hundred famous people in their glassy eyes and surviving a silly hall of horror, you'll board a Disney-type ride and cruise through a kid-pleasing "Spirit of London" time trip.

Access: AE, AI, AT, AL, Level 1—Fully accessible.

Cost, Hours, and Location: £20, children-£15, under 5 free, tickets include entrance to the London Planetarium, Jan-Sept daily 9:00–17:30, Oct–Dec Mon–Fri 10:00–17:30, Sat–Sun 9:30–17:30, last entry 30 min before closing, Marylebone Road, Tube: Baker Street.

Crowd-Beating Tips: The waxworks are popular. Avoid a wait by either booking ahead to get a ticket with an entry time (tel. 0870-400-3000, online at www.madame-tussauds.com for a £2 fee, or at no extra cost at the Britain and London Visitors Centre or the TIs at Waterloo or Victoria train stations) or arriving late in the day—90 minutes is plenty of time for the exhibit.

Sir John Soane's Museum—Architects and fans of eclectic knickknacks love this quirky place.

Access: Level 3—Minimally accessible. The entrance has eight steps up, and the ground floor is 80 percent on one level. The other two levels require a trip up or down narrow flights of stairs, and the doors are narrow. Once inside, loaner wheelchairs are available.

Cost, Hours, and Location: Free, Tue–Sat 10:00–17:00, first Tue of the month also 18:00–21:00, closed Sun–Mon, £3 guided tours Sat at 14:30, 5 blocks east of British Museum, Tube: Holborn, 13 Lincoln's Inn Fields, tel. 020/7405-2107.

Buckingham Palace

▲**Buckingham Palace**—This lavish home has been Britain's royal residence since 1837. When the queen's at home, the royal standard flies; otherwise the Union Jack flaps in the wind.

Access: AE, AI, AL, AT, Level 1—Fully accessible.

Cost, Hours, and Location: £12 for state apartments and throne room, open Aug–Sept only, daily 9:30–17:00, only 8,000 visitors a day— to get an entry time, come early or for £1 extra book ahead by phone or online, Tube: Victoria, tel. 020/7321-2233, www.the-royal-collection

Buckingham Palace

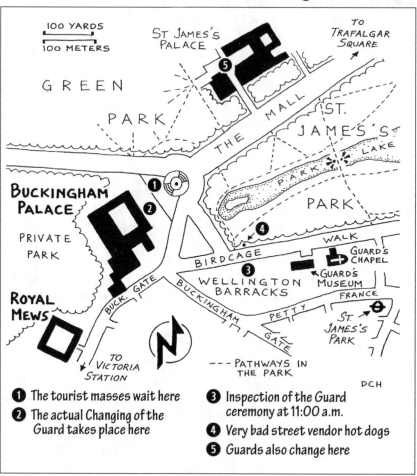

100 YARDS
100 METERS

ST JAMES'S PALACE

TO TRAFALGAR SQUARE

GREEN PARK

THE MALL

ST. JAMES'S

LAKE

PARK

BUCKINGHAM PALACE

PRIVATE PARK

BIRDCAGE WALK

GUARD'S CHAPEL

GUARD'S MUSEUM

WELLINGTON BARRACKS

FRANCE

ROYAL MEWS

BUCK. GATE

BUCKINGHAM GATE

PETTY

ST. JAMES'S PARK

TO VICTORIA STATION

--- PATHWAYS IN THE PARK

DCH

❶ The tourist masses wait here

❷ The actual Changing of the Guard takes place here

❸ Inspection of the Guard ceremony at 11:00 a.m.

❹ Very bad street vendor hot dogs

❺ Guards also change here

.com/royaltickets, buckinghampalace@royalcollection.org.uk.

Royal Mews—Actually the queen's working stables, the "mews" are open to visitors to wander, talk to the horse-keeper, and see the well-groomed horses. Marvel at the gilded coaches paraded during royal festivals, see fancy horse gear—all well-described—and learn how skeptical the attendants were when the royals first parked a car in the stables.

Access: AE, AI, Level 1—Fully accessible.

Cost, Hours, and Location: £5, April–Oct 11:00–16:00, closed Nov–March, Buckingham Palace Road, tel. 020/7321-2233.

▲▲**Changing of the Guard at Buckingham Palace**—The guards change with much fanfare at 11:30 almost daily in the summer and at a minimum, every other day all year long (no band when wet). Each month it's either daily or on odd or even days. Call 020/7321-2233 for the day's plan. Join the mob behind the palace (the front faces a huge and extremely private park). You'll need to be early or tall to see much of the actual Changing of the Guard, but for the pageantry in the street you can pop by at 11:30. The marching troops and bands are colorful and even stirring, but the actual Changing of the Guard is a nonevent. It is interesting, however, to see nearly every tourist in London gathered in one place at the same time. Wave down a big black taxi and say, "Buck House, please." The show lasts about 30 minutes: Three troops parade by, the guard changes with much shouting, the band plays a happy little concert, and then they march out. On a balmy day, it's a fun happening.

For all the pomp with none of the crowds, see the colorful **Inspection of the Guard** ceremony at 11:00 in front of the **Wellington Barracks,** 500 yards east of the palace on Birdcage Walk. Afterward, roll or stroll through nearby St. James' Park (Tube: Victoria, St. James' Park, or Green Park).

West London
▲**Hyde Park and Speakers' Corner**—London's "Central Park," originally Henry VIII's hunting grounds, has more than 600 acres of lush greenery, a huge man-made lake, the royal Kensington Palace (not worth touring), and the ornate neo-Gothic Albert Memorial across from the Royal Albert Hall. Early afternoons on Sunday (until early evening), Speakers' Corner offers soapbox oratory at its best (Tube: Marble Arch). "The grass roots of democracy" is actually a holdover from when the gallows stood here, and the criminal was allowed to say just about anything he wanted to before he swung. We dare you to raise your voice and gather a crowd—it's easy to do.

Access: Level 1—Fully accessible.
▲▲**Victoria and Albert Museum**—The world's top collection of decorative arts (vases, stained glass, fine furniture, clothing, jewelry, carpets, and more) is a surprisingly interesting assortment of crafts from the West as well as Asian and Islamic cultures.

The V&A, which grew out of the Great Exhibition of 1851—that ultimate festival celebrating the Industrial Revolution and the greatness

West London

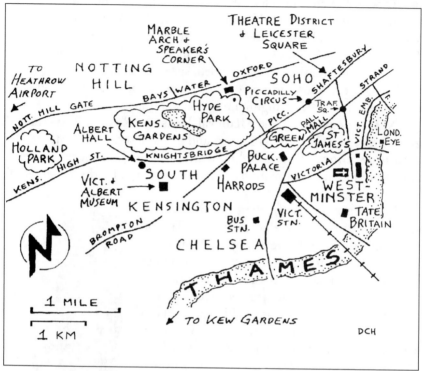

of Britain—was originally for manufactured art, but fine-art sculptures (and copies) were soon added. After much support from Queen Victoria and Prince Albert, it was renamed after the royal couple, and its present building was opened in 1909. The idealistic Victorian notion that anyone can be continually improved by education and example remains the driving force behind this museum.

Access: AE, AI, AT, AL, Level 1—Fully accessible. There are two accessible entrances to the museum. An accessibility information sheet and loaner wheelchairs are available.

Cost, Hours, and Location: Free, possible fee for special exhibits (reduced for wheelchair users), daily 10:00–17:45, Wed until 21:30 (Tube: South Kensington, a long tunnel leads directly from the Tube station to the museum, tel. 020/7942-2000, www.vam.ac.uk).

Museum Overview and Tours: The museum is large and gangly, with 150 rooms and more than 12 miles of corridors. While just exploring works well here, consider catching one of the free 60-minute orientation tours (daily, on the half hour from 10:30–15:30, also daily at 13:00, Wed at 16:30, and a half-hour version at 19:30) or buying the fine £5 *Hundred Highlights* guidebook, or the handy £1 "What to See at the V&A" brochure (outlines 5 self-guided, speedy tours).

To tour this museum on your own, grab a museum map and start with these ground-floor highlights:

Near the entrance: The **Medieval Treasury** (Room 43) has stained glass, bishops' robes, old columns, and good descriptions. Statues by **Antonio Canova** (Room 50A)—white, polished, and pretty Greek graces, minotaurs, and nymphs—are rare originals by the neoclassical master.

Southeast corner (to the right of entrance, at the end of the hall): Plaster casts of **Trajan's Column** (Room 46A) are a copy of Rome's 140-foot spiral relief telling the story of the conquest of Romania. (The V&A's casts are copies made for the benefit of 19th-century art students who couldn't afford a railpass.) Plaster casts of **Renaissance sculptures** (Room 46B) let you compare Michelangelo's monumental *David* with Donatello's girlish *David;* see also Lorenzo Ghiberti's bronze Baptistery doors that inspired the Florentine Renaissance. The hall of **Great Fakes and Forgeries** (Room 46) chronicles concocted art and historical objects passed off as originals.

Southwest corner (left of entrance, end of hall): **Raphael's "cartoons"** (Room 48A) are seven huge watercolor designs by the Renaissance master for tapestries meant for the Sistine Chapel. The cartoons were sent to Brussels, cut into strips (see the lines), and placed on the looms. Notice that the scenes, the Acts of Peter and Paul, are the reverse of the final product (lots of left-handed saints). The **Dress Gallery** (in Room 40) has 400 years of English fashion corseted into 40 display cases.

The rest of the ground floor: Room 41 has the finest collection of Indian decorative art outside India. There's medieval **stained glass** in room 28 (and much more upstairs, accessible via elevator).

Upstairs you can visit the **British Galleries** for centuries of British furniture, clothing, glass, jewelry, and sculpture. The **Musical Instruments** section displays lutes, harpsichords, early flutes, big violins, and strange, curly horns—some recognizable, some obsolete (Room 40A).

▲**Natural History Museum**—Across the street from the Victoria and Albert, this mammoth museum is housed in a giant and wonderful Victorian, neo-Romanesque building. Built in the 1870s specifically to house the huge collection (50 million specimens), it has two halves: the Life Galleries (creepy-crawlies, human biology, the origin of species, "our place in evolution," and awesome dinosaurs) and the Earth Galleries (meteors, volcanoes, earthquakes, and so on). Exhibits are wonderfully explained, with lots of creative interactive displays. Pop in, if only for the wild collection of dinosaurs and the roaring *Tyrannosaurus rex*. Free 45-minute highlights tours occur daily about every hour from 11:00 to 16:00.

Access: AE, AI, AT, AL, Level 1—Fully accessible. There are multiple entrances to the museum, and all are accessible. Loaner wheelchairs and brochures about museum access are available.

Cost, Hours, and Location: Free, possible fee for special exhibits (reduced for wheelchair user and companion), Mon–Sat 10:00–18:00, Sun 11:00–18:00, last entrance 17:30, a long tunnel leads directly from South Kensington Tube station to museum, tel. 020/7942-5000, exhibit info and reservations tel. 020/7942-5011, www.nhm.ac.uk.

East London: "The City"

▲▲**The City of London**—When Londoners say "The City," they mean the one-square-mile business, banking, and journalism center that 2,000 years ago was Roman Londinium. The outline of the Roman city walls can still be seen in the arc of roads from Blackfriars Bridge to Tower Bridge. Within the City are 24 churches designed by Christopher Wren, mostly just ornamentation around St. Paul's Cathedral. Today, while home to only 5,000 residents, the City thrives with more than 500,000 office workers coming and going daily. It's a fascinating district to wander on weekdays, but since almost nobody actually lives there, it's dull in the evenings and on Saturday and Sunday.

▲**Old Bailey**—To view the British legal system in action—lawyers in little blond wigs speaking legalese with a British accent—spend a few minutes in the visitors' gallery at the Old Bailey.

East London

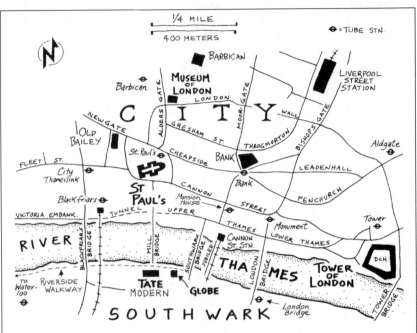

Access: Level 4—Not accessible. With lots of winding stairs and many levels, Old Bailey will challenge any traveler with limited mobility.

Cost, Hours, and Location: Free, no kids under 14, Mon–Fri 10:30–13:00 & 14:00–16:30 most weeks, closed Sat–Sun, reduced hours in Aug; no bags, mobile phones, or cameras, but small purses OK; you can check your bag at the bagel shop next door—or any other entrepreneurial place nearby—for £1; Tube: St. Paul's, 2 blocks northwest of St. Paul's on Old Bailey street, follow signs to public entrance, tel. 020/7248-3277.

▲▲▲**St. Paul's Cathedral**—Wren's most famous church is the great St. Paul's, its elaborate interior capped by a 365-foot dome. The crypt (included with admission) is a world of historic bones and memorials, including Admiral Nelson's tomb and interesting cathedral models. The great West Door is opened only for great occasions, such as the wedding of Prince Charles and the late Princess Diana in 1981. Go to the back of the church, look up the nave, and imagine how Diana felt before making the trip to the altar with the world watching. Relax under the second-

St. Paul's Cathedral

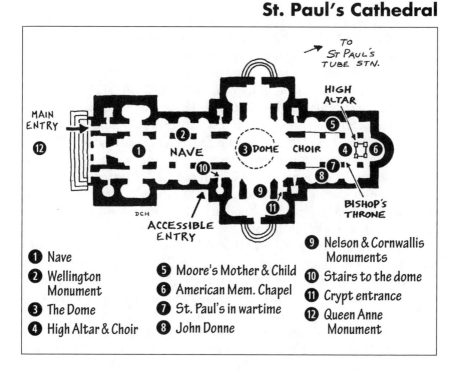

TO
ST PAUL'S
TUBE STN.

HIGH
ALTAR

MAIN
ENTRY

⑫

① NAVE

②

③ DOME   CHOIR   ④ ⑥

⑤

⑩

⑦

⑧

⑨

⑪

BISHOP'S
THRONE

DCH

ACCESSIBLE
ENTRY

❶ Nave
❷ Wellington
   Monument
❸ The Dome
❹ High Altar & Choir

❺ Moore's Mother & Child
❻ American Mem. Chapel
❼ St. Paul's in wartime
❽ John Donne

❾ Nelson & Cornwallis
   Monuments
❿ Stairs to the dome
⓫ Crypt entrance
⓬ Queen Anne
   Monument

largest dome in the world and eavesdrop on guided tours.

Since World War II, St. Paul's has been Britain's symbol of resistance. Despite 57 nights of bombing, the Nazis failed to destroy the cathedral, thanks to the St. Paul's volunteer fire watch, who stayed on the dome.

Non-disabled travelers can climb the dome for a great city view and some fun in the Whispering Gallery—where the precisely designed barrel of the dome lets sweet nothings circle audibly around to the opposite side.

Access: AE, AI, AL, AT, The accessible entrance is to the right of the main entrance (it's locked, but a bell by the door will bring assistance). The main floor (Level 1—Fully accessible) can be reached by lift. Follow signs to the accessible toilet. The dome and Whispering Gallery (Level 4—Not accessible) can be reached only by climbing many flights of stairs.

Cost, Hours, and Location: £6, includes church entry and dome climb, Mon–Sat 8:30–16:30, last entry 16:00, closed Sun except for worship and organ recital, no photography allowed, £2.50 for guided 90-min "super tours" of cathedral and crypt Mon–Sat at 11:00, 11:30, 13:30, and 14:00, confirm schedule at church or call 020/7236-4128; £3.50 for audioguide tour available Mon–Sat 8:45–15:00; Tube: St. Paul's.

Services: Sunday services are at 8:00, 10:15, 11:30 (sung Eucharist), 15:15 (evensong), and 18:00, with a free organ recital at 17:00. The **evensong** services are free, but nonpaying visitors are not allowed to linger afterward (Mon–Sat at 17:00, Sun at 15:15, 40 min).

▲**Museum of London**—London, a 2,000-year-old city, is so littered with Roman ruins that when a London builder finds Roman antiquities, he doesn't stop work. He simply documents the finds, moves the artifacts to a museum, and builds on. If you're asking, "Why did the Romans build their cities underground?" a trip to the creative and entertaining London Museum is a must. You'll time-travel through London history from pre-Roman times through the 1920s. This regular stop for the local school kids gives the best overview of London history in town.

Access: AE+A, AI, AT, AL, Level 2—Moderately accessible.

Cost, Hours, and Location: Free, Mon–Sat 10:00–18:00, Sun 12:00–18:00, Tube: Barbican or St. Paul's, tel. 020/7600-3699.

▲▲▲**Tower of London**—The tower has served as a castle in wartime, a king's residence in peace, and, most notoriously, as the prison and execution site of rebels. This historic fortress is host to more than three million visitors a year. Enjoy the free and entertaining 50-minute Beefeater tour (leaves regularly from inside the gate, first one usually at 9:30, last one usually at 15:30, 14:30 off-season). The crown jewels, dating from the Restoration, are the best on Earth—and come with hour-long lines for most of the day.

Access: AE, AI, AT, AL, Level 1—Fully accessible.

Cost, Hours, and Location: £13.50 (1-day combo-ticket with Hampton Court Palace-£18), March–Oct Mon–Sat 9:00–18:00, Sun 10:00–18:00; Nov–Feb Tue–Sat 9:00–17:00, Sun–Mon 10:00–17:00; last entry 60 min before closing. The long but fast-moving ticket line is

worst on Sunday. No photography is allowed of jewels or in chapels. Skip the £3 audioguide. Tube: Tower Hill, tel. 0870-751-5177, recorded info: 020/7680-9004, booking: 020/7488-5681.

Crowd-Beating Tips: To avoid the crowds, arrive when the Tower opens and go straight for the jewels, doing the Beefeater tour and White Tower later—or do the jewels after 16:30. The long but fast-moving ticket line is worst on Sunday. You can avoid lines by picking up your ticket at any London TI or the Tower Hill Tube station ticket office.

Ceremony of the Keys: Every night at precisely 21:30, with pageantry-filled ceremony, the Tower of London is locked up, as it has been for the last 700 years. To attend this free 30-minute event (which some find dull and others thrilling), you need to request an invitation at least two months before your visit. Write to Ceremony of the Keys, H.M. Tower of London, London EC3N 4AB. Include your name; the addresses, names, and ages of all people attending (up to 6 people, non-transferable, no kids under 8 allowed); requested date; alternative dates; and two international reply coupons (buy at U.S. post office—if your post office doesn't have the $1.75 coupons in stock, they can order them; the turnaround time is a few days).

South London, on the South Bank

The South Bank is a thriving arts and cultural center tied together by a riverside path. This popular, accessible, pub-happy route—called the Jubilee Promenade—stretches from the Tower Bridge past Westminster Bridge, where it offers grand views of the Houses of Parliament. (The promenade hugs the river except just east of London Bridge, where it cuts inland for a couple of blocks.)

▲▲▲**London Eye Ferris Wheel**—Built by British Airways, the wheel towers above London opposite Big Ben. This is the world's highest observational wheel, giving you a chance to fly British Airways without

leaving London. Designed like a giant bicycle wheel, it's a pan-European undertaking: British steel and Dutch engineering, with Czech, German, French, and Italian mechanical parts. It's also very "green," running extremely efficiently and virtually silently. Twenty-five people ride in each of its 32 air-condi-

London's South Bank

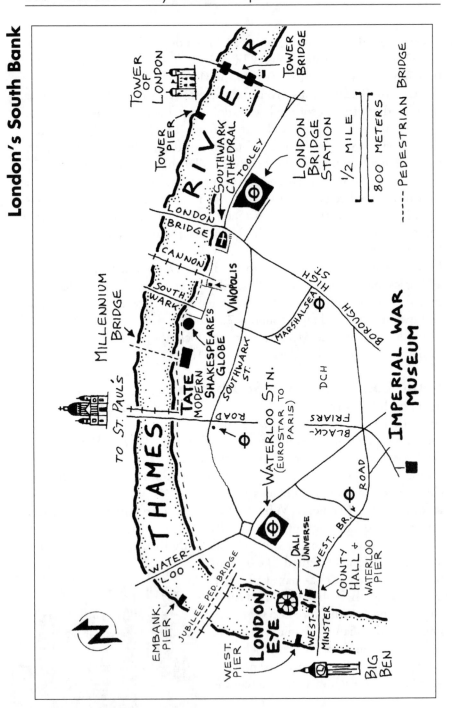

tioned capsules for the 30-minute rotation (each capsule has a bench, but most people stand). From the top of this 450-foot-high wheel—the highest public viewpoint in the city—Big Ben looks small. You only go around once; save a shot on top for the glass capsule next to yours. Its original five-year lease has been extended to 25 years and it looks like this will become a permanent fixture on the London skyline. Thames boats come and go from here using the Waterloo Pier (fully accessible dock area and ramp) at the foot of the Wheel.

Access: AE, AI, AT, AL, Level 1—Fully accessible. People with limited mobility can reserve a free "fast track" service to allow them to skip the line by calling 0870-990-8885.

Cost, Hours, and Location: £11, £2 discount for wheelchair user and free ticket for companion if you book in advance by calling 0870-990-8885. April–mid-Sept daily 9:30–22:00, mid-Sept–March 9:30–20:00, closed Jan for maintenance. Tube: Waterloo or Westminster, www.ba-londoneye.com.

Crowd-Beating Tips: While huge lines made advance booking smart in past years, today you can generally just buy your ticket and get right on (never more than a 30-min wait, worst on weekends and school holidays). To book a ticket (with an assigned time) in advance, buy one at a London TI, call, or go online (50p charge, automated booking tel. 0870-500-0600 or www.ba-londoneye.com). Upon arrival, you either pick up your pre-booked ticket (if you've reserved ahead) or wait in the line inside to buy tickets. Then you join the ticket-holders' line at the wheel (starting 10 min before your assigned half-hour time slot).

Dalí Universe—Cleverly located next to the hugely popular London Eye Ferris Wheel, this exhibit features 500 works of mind-bending art by Salvador Dalí. While pricey, it's entertaining if you like Surrealism and want to learn about Dalí.

Access: AE, AI, AL, AT, Level 2—Moderately accessible. Wheelchair users should call ahead to let them know you are coming. When you arrive, go to the box office, where you will be assisted.

Cost, Hours, and Location: £8.50, daily 10:00–18:30, generally summer eves until 20:00, last entry 1 hr before closing, tel. 020/7620-2720.

▲▲**Imperial War Museum**—This impressive museum covers the wars of the last century, from heavy weaponry to love notes and Vargas Girls, from Monty's Africa campaign tank to Schwartzkopf's Desert Storm uniform. You can trace the development of the machine gun, watch footage of the first tank battles, see one of more than a thousand V2 rockets Hitler rained on Britain in 1944 (each with more than a ton of explosives), hold your breath through the gruesome WWI trench experience, and buy WWII-era toys in the fun museum shop. The "Secret War" section gives a fascinating peek into the intrigues of espionage in World Wars I and II. The section on the Holocaust is one of the best on the subject anywhere. Rather than glorify war, the museum does its best to shine a light on the powerful human side of one of mankind's most persistent traits.

The museum is housed in what was the Royal Bethlam Hospital. Also known as "the Bedlam asylum," the place was so wild it gave the world a new word for chaos: "bedlam." Back in Victorian times, locals— without trash-talk shows and cable TV—came here for their entertainment. The asylum was actually open to the paying public on weekends.

Access: AE, AI, AT, Level 1—Fully accessible.

Cost, Hours, and Location: Free, daily 10:00–18:00, 90 min is enough time for most visitors, Tube: Lambeth North or bus #12 from Westminster, tel. 020/7416-5000.

▲▲▲**Tate Modern**—Dedicated in the spring of 2000, this striking museum across the river from St. Paul's opened the new century with art from the old one. Its powerhouse collection of Claude Monet, Henri Matisse, Dalí, Pablo Picasso, Andy Warhol, and much more is displayed in a converted power house.

Access: AE, AI, AL, AT, Level 1—Fully accessible.

Cost, Hours, and Location: Free, fee for special exhibitions, daily 10:00–18:00, Fri–Sat until 22:00—a good time to visit, audioguide-£1, free 1-hr guided tours at 11:00 and 14:00, call to confirm schedule, view café on top floor. Cross the Millennium Bridge from St. Paul's; or take the Tube to Southwark, plus a half-mile roll or stroll; or take the fully accessible Tate-to-Tate ferry from Tate Britain for £4.50. Tel. 020/7887-8008, www.tate.org.uk.

▲**Millennium Bridge**—The pedestrian bridge links St. Paul's Cathedral and the Tate Modern across the Thames. This is London's first new bridge in a century. When it first opened, the $25 million bridge wiggled when people walked on it, so it promptly closed for a $7 million stabilization; now it's stable and back open (free). Nicknamed "a blade of light" for its sleek minimalist design—370 yards long, four yards wide, stainless steel with teak planks—it includes clever aerodynamic handrails to deflect wind over the heads of pedestrians.

Access: AE, AI, Level 1—Fully accessible.

▲▲**Shakespeare's Globe**—The original Globe Theater has been rebuilt—half-timbered and thatched—as it was in Shakespeare's time. (This is the first thatched roof in London since they were outlawed after the great fire of 1666.) The Globe originally accommodated 2,000 seated and another 1,000 standing. (Today, leaving space for reasonable aisles, the theater holds 900 seated and  600 groundlings.) Its promoters brag that the theater melds "the three A's"—actors, audience, and architecture—with each contributing to the play. Open as a museum and a working theater, it hosts authentic old-time performances of Shakespeare's plays. The theater can be toured when there are no plays. The Globe's exhibition on Shakespeare is the world's largest, with interactive displays and film presentations, a sound lab, a script factory, and costumes. For details on seeing a play here, see "Entertainment and Theater," page 108. The Globe Café is open daily (10:00–18:00, tel. 020/7902-1433).

Access: AE, AI, AT, AL, ♥, Level 1—Fully accessible. You can download an "Access Guide" from the Globe's Web site (www.shakespeares -globe.org). For specific accessibility questions, call the Access Information Line at 020/7902-1409.

Cost, Hours, and Location: £8; mid-May–Sept Mon–Sat 9:30–12:00, Sun 9:30–11:30, free 30-min actor-led tour offered on the half hour; also open daily 12:30–16:00 but only for disappointing virtual tours; Oct–mid-May daily 10:30–17:00, free 30-min tour offered on the half hour; on the South Bank directly across Thames over Southwark Bridge from St. Paul's; Tube: London Bridge plus a half-mile roll or stroll; tel. 020/7902-1500; www.shakespeares-globe.org.

▲▲**Vinopolis: City of Wine**—While it seems illogical to have a huge wine museum in London, Vinopolis makes a good case. Built over a Roman wine store and filling the massive vaults of an old wine warehouse, the museum offers an excellent audioguide with a light yet earnest history of wine. Sipping various reds and whites, ports, and champagnes—

immersed in your headset as you explore—you learn about the libation from its Georgian origins to Chile, including a Vespa ride through Chianti country in Tuscany. Allow some time, as the audioguide takes 90 minutes—and the sipping can slow things down wonderfully.

Access: AE, AI, AT, ♥, Level 1—Fully accessible. This place is wheelchair-friendly, all on one level, fun, and hospitable.

Cost, Hours, and Location: £11.50 with 5 tastes, £14 with 10, don't worry...for £2.50 you can buy 5 more tastes inside, daily 11:00–18:00, Sat and Mon until 21:00, last entry 2 hrs before closing, Tube: London Bridge, between the Globe and Southwark Cathedral at 1 Bank End, tel. 0870-241-4040 or 020/7940-8301, www.vinopolis.co.uk.

South London, on the North Bank

▲▲**Tate Britain**—One of Europe's great art houses, Tate Britain specializes in British painting from the 16th century through modern times. The museum has a good representation of William Blake's religious sketches, the Pre-Raphaelites' realistic art, and J.M.W. Turner's swirling works.

Access: AE, AI, AL, AT, Level 1— Fully accessible, but there is a limit of six wheelchairs at a time.

Cost, Hours, and Location: Free, daily 10:00–17:50, last admission 17:00, fine £3 audioguide, free tours normally Mon–Fri at 11:00—16th, 17th, and 18th centuries; at noon—19th century; at 14:00—Turner; at 15:00—20th century; Sat–Sun at noon and 15:00—highlights; call to confirm schedule; no photography allowed, Tube: Pimlico, then a quarter-mile roll or stroll; or arrive directly at museum by taking bus #88 from Oxford Circus or #77A from National Gallery; or catch the fully accessible Tate-to-Tate ferry from Tate Modern for £4.50, tel. 020/7887-8000, recorded info tel. 020/7887-8008, www.tate.org.uk.

Greater London

▲**Kew Gardens**—For a visit to a fine riverside park and a palatial greenhouse jungle, take the Tube or the boat to every botanist's favorite escape, Kew Gardens. While to most visitors the Royal Botanic Gardens of Kew are simply a delightful opportunity to wander among 33,000 different types of plants, to the hardworking organization that runs the gardens, it's a way to promote understanding and preservation of the botanical diversity of our planet. The Kew Gardens Tube station drops you in an herbal little business community a two-block roll or stroll from Victoria Gate (the main garden entrance). Pick up a map brochure and check at the gate for a monthly listing of the best blooms.

Garden-lovers could spend days exploring Kew's 300 acres. For a quick visit, spend a fragrant hour wandering through three buildings: the Palm House, a humid Victorian world of iron, glass, and tropical plants, built in 1844; a Waterlily House that would impress Monet; and the Princess of Wales Conservatory, a modern greenhouse with many different climate zones growing countless cacti, bug-munching carnivorous plants, and more.

Access: AE, AI, AT, Level 1—Fully accessible. Imagine peaceful, flat, gorgeous, and green (with only occasional areas of inaccessibility). For the most part, you can roll wherever you please—and there are accessible toilets, too. Loaner wheelchairs are available.

Cost, Hours, and Location: £7.50, £5.50 at 16:45 or later, Mon–Fri 9:30–18:30, Sat–Sun 9:30–19:30, until 16:30 or sunset off-season, galleries and conservatories close at 17:30, consider £3 narrated floral 35-minute joyride on little train departing on the hour until 16:00 from Victoria Gate, Tube: Kew Gardens, tel. 020/8332-5000). For a sun-dappled lunch, roll or stroll a half-mile from the Palm House to the Orangery (£6 hot meals, daily 10:00–17:30).

Disappointments of London

The venerable BBC broadcasts from the Broadcasting House. Of all its productions, the "BBC Experience" tour for visitors is among the worst. On the South Bank, the London Dungeon, a much-visited but amateurish attraction, is just a highly advertised, overpriced haunted house—certainly not worth the £12 admission, much less your valuable London time. It comes with long and rude lines. Wait for Halloween and see one in your hometown to support a better cause. "Winston Churchill's

Britain at War Experience" (next to the London Dungeon) wastes your time. The Kensington Palace State Apartments are lifeless and not worth a visit.

SHOPPING

Marks & Spencer—No one in London is doing a better job with confronting accessibility issues than Marks & Spencer department stores, even sponsoring an annual contest where major hotels compete for accessible designs. Their stores are sprinkled throughout London, and each one has an accessible food-and-wine section for gathering your picnic goodies (main store in South Kensington, store finder at www2.marksand spencer.com/stores).
　　Access: AE, AI, AL, AT, ♥, Level 1—Fully accessible.
Harrods—Harrods is London's most famous and touristy department store. With a million square feet of retail space on seven floors, it's a place where some shoppers could spend all day. Big yet classy, Harrods has everything from elephants to toothbrushes.
　　Sightseers should pick up the free Store Guide at any info post. Here's what we enjoyed: On the Ground and Lower Ground Floors, find the Food Halls, with their Edwardian tiled walls, creative and exuberant displays, and staff in period costumes—not quite like your local supermarket back home.
　　Descend to the Lower Ground Floor and follow signs to the Egyptian Escalator—lined with pharaoh-headed sconces, papyrus-plant lamps, and hieroglyphic balconies (Harrods'

owner, Mohamed Al Fayed, is from Egypt). There you'll find a memorial to Dodi Al Fayed and Princess Diana. Photos and flowers honor the late Princess and her fiancé (the son of Harrods' owner), who both died in a car crash in Paris in 1997. See the wine glass from their last dinner and the engagement ring that Dodi purchased the day before they died.
　　Ascend to the 4th Floor. Go to the toys section to find child-size luxury cars that actually work. A Junior Jaguar or Mercedes will set you

back about $13,000. The child's Hummer is big and expensive ($30,000).

Also on the 4th Floor is The Georgian Restaurant. Enjoy a fancy tea under a skylight as a pianist tickles the keys of a Bösendorfer, the world's most expensive piano (tea-£19, includes finger sandwiches and pastries, served after 15:45).

Harrods is overpriced (its accessible £1 toilets are the most expensive in Europe), snooty, and teeming with American and Japanese tourists. Still, it's the palace of department stores. The nearby Beauchamp Place is lined with classy and fascinating shops.

Access: AE, AI, AT, AL, ♥, Level 1—Fully accessible. All floors are accessible by elevator, and the toilets are easily accessible.

Hours and Location: Mon–Sat 10:00–19:00, closed Sun, mandatory storage for big backpacks-£2.50, on Brompton Road, Tube: Knightsbridge, tel. 020/7730-1234.

Harvey Nichols—Once Princess Diana's favorite, "Harvey Nick's" remains the department store *du jour*. Want to pick up a little £20 scarf for the wife? You won't do it here, where they're more like £200. The store's fifth floor is a veritable food fest, with a gourmet grocery store, a fancy (smoky) restaurant, a Yo! Sushi bar, and a lively café. Consider a take-away tray of sushi to eat on a bench in the Hyde Park rose garden two blocks away.

Access: AE, AI, AT+A, AL, Level 1—Fully accessible.

Hours and Location: Mon, Tue, Sat 10:00–19:00, Wed–Fri until 20:00, Sun 12:00–18:00, near Harrods, Tube: Knightsbridge, 109 Knightsbridge, www.harveynichols.com).

Toys—The biggest toy store in Britain is Hamleys, with seven floors buzzing with 28,000 toys managed by a staff of 200. At the "Bear Factory," kids can get a made-to-order teddy bear by picking out a "bear skin" and watch while it's stuffed and sewn.

Access: AE, AI, AL, AT, Level 1—Fully accessible. The accessible toilet is on the fourth floor.

Hours and Location: Mon–Fri 10:00–20:00, Sat 9:30–20:00, Sun 12:00–18:00, 188 Regent, tel. 0870-333-2455, www.hamleys.com.

Carnaby Street—This pedestrian mall has big, flat cobblestones and no break between sidewalk and street area. Most stores have a flat entry (or one step of less than 6"), and all corners have curb cuts. It's a short distance from here to Regent Street, where the sidewalks are wide and interesting shops abound.

Street Markets—Antique buffs, people-watchers, and folks who brake for garage sales love to haggle at London's street markets. While some nooks and crannies may be difficult for wheelchair users to reach, the markets generally have decent accessibility. There's good early-morning market activity somewhere any day of the week. The best are **Portobello Road** (roughly Mon–Sat 10:00–17:00, closed Sun, go on Sat for antiques—plus the regular junk, clothes, and produce; Tube: Notting Hill Gate, tel. 020/7229-8354) and **Camden Lock Market** (daily 10:00–18:00, arts and crafts, Tube: Camden Town, tel. 020/7284-2084, www.camdenlock.net). The TI has a complete, up-to-date list. Warning: Markets attract two kinds of people—tourists and pickpockets.

ENTERTAINMENT AND THEATER

London bubbles with top-notch entertainment seven days a week. Everything's listed in the weekly entertainment magazines (e.g., *Time Out)*, available at newsstands. Choose from classical, jazz, rock, and far-out music, Gilbert and Sullivan, dance, comedy, Baha'i meetings, poetry readings, spectator sports, film, and theater. In Leicester Square, you'll find movies that have yet to be released in the States; if Hugh Grant is attending an opening-night premiere in London, it will likely be at one of the big movie houses here.

London's theater scene rivals Broadway's in quality and beats it in price. Choose from the Royal Shakespeare Company, top musicals, comedy, thrillers, sex farces, and more. We prefer big, glitzy—even bombastic—musicals over serious chamber dramas, simply because London can deliver the lights, sound, dancers, and multimedia spectacle we rarely get back home. Performances are nightly except Sunday, usually with one matinee a week. Matinees, usually held on Wednesday, Thursday, or Saturday, are cheaper and rarely sell out. Tickets range from about £8-40.

Most theaters, marked on tourist maps, are in the Piccadilly/ Trafalgar area. The majority of big venues are accessible and wheelchair-friendly (we've listed pertinent information for the most popular venues in this book); you can also find accessibility information for specific theaters online at www.officiallondontheatre.co.uk or www.theatremonkey.com.

Box offices, hotels, and TIs offer a handy *Theatre Guide*. To book a seat, simply call the theater box office directly, ask about seats and available dates, and for a £2 fee, buy a ticket with your credit card. (To avoid the fee, buy the ticket in person at the box office.) You can make calls from the United States as easily as from England. We listed phone numbers for some box offices; for others, check www.officiallondon theatre.co.uk, the American magazine *Variety*, or photocopy your hometown library's London newspaper theater section. Pick up your ticket 15 minutes before the show.

For a booking fee, you can reserve online (www.ticketmaster.co.uk or www.firstcalltickets.com) or call Global Tickets (U.S. tel. 800/223-6108). While booking through an agency is quick and easy, prices are inflated by a standard 25 percent fee. Ticket agencies (whether in the U.S., at London's TIs, or scattered throughout the city) are scalpers with an address. If you're buying from an agency, look at the ticket carefully (your price should be no more than 30 percent over the printed face value; the 15 percent VAT is already included in the face value) and understand where you're sitting according to the floor plan (if your view is restricted, it will state this on the ticket; for floor plans, see www .theatremonkey.com). Agencies are worthwhile only if a show you've just got to see is sold out at the box office. They scarf up hot tickets, planning to make a killing after the show is sold out. U.S. booking agencies get their tickets from another agency, adding even more to your expense by involving yet another middleman. Many tickets sold on the street are forgeries. Although some theatres have booking agencies handle their advance sales, you'll stand a good chance of saving money and avoiding the middleman by simply calling the box office directly to book your tickets (international phone calls are cheap and credit cards make booking a snap).

Theater Lingo: stalls (ground floor), dress circle (first balcony), upper circle (second balcony), balcony (sky-high third balcony), slips (cheap seats on the fringes). Many cheap seats have a restricted view (behind a pillar).

Cheap Theater Tricks: Some theaters offer discounts for disabled theatergoers—be sure to ask when you're booking your ticket. Most theaters also offer cheap returned tickets, matinee, and senior or student stand-by deals (available to disabled or non-disabled travelers). These "concessions" are indicated with a *conc* or *s* in the listings. Picking up a late return can get you a great seat at a cheap-seat price. If a show is "sold out," there's usually a way to get a seat. Call the theater box office and ask how.

Half-Price "tkts" Booth at Leicester Square: This famous ticket booth at Leicester Square (LESS-ter) sells discounted tickets for top-price seats to shows on the push list the day of the show only (£2.50 service charge per ticket, Mon–Sat 10:00–19:00, Sun 12:00–15:30, matinee tickets from noon, lines often form early, list of shows available online at www.tkts.co.uk).

Here are sample prices: A top-notch seat to the long-running *Les Misérables* (which rarely sells out) costs £40 bought directly from the theater, but only £22.50 from tkts. The cheapest balcony seat (bought from the theater) is £15.

Half-price tickets can be a good deal, unless you want the cheapest seats or the hottest shows. But check the board; occasionally they sell cheap tickets to good shows. Note that the real half-price booth (labeled *tkts*) is a freestanding kiosk at the edge of the garden in Leicester Square. Several dishonest, copy-cat outfits nearby advertise "official half-price tickets." Avoid these.

West End Theaters—The commercial (non-subsidized) theaters cluster around Soho (especially along Shaftesbury Avenue) and Covent Garden. With a centuries-old tradition of pleasing the masses, these present London theater at its glitziest. See the "What's On in the West End" sidebar.

Royal Shakespeare Company—If you'll ever enjoy Shakespeare, it'll be in Britain. The RSC performs at various theaters around London and in Stratford year-round. To get a schedule and accessibility information for each venue, contact the RSC (Royal Shakespeare Theatre, Stratford-upon-Avon, tel. 01789/403-403, ticket hotline tel. 0870-609-1110, www.rsc.org.uk).

Shakespeare's Globe—To see Shakespeare in a replica of the theater for which he wrote his plays, attend a play at the Globe. This thatch-roofed, open-air round theater does the plays much as Shakespeare intended (with no amplification). The play's the thing from mid-May through September (usually Tue–Sat 14:00 and 19:30, Sun at either 13:00 and 18:30 or 16:00 only, no plays on Mon, tickets can be sold out months in advance). A seat will cost you £13–29 (usually on a backless

London Theaters

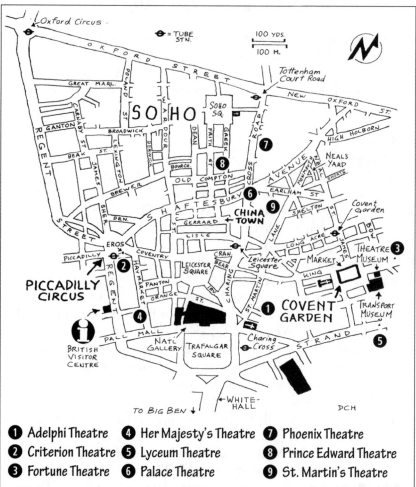

1 Adelphi Theatre **4** Her Majesty's Theatre **7** Phoenix Theatre
2 Criterion Theatre **5** Lyceum Theatre **8** Prince Edward Theatre
3 Fortune Theatre **6** Palace Theatre **9** St. Martin's Theatre

bench; only a few rows and the pricier Gentlemen's Rooms have seats with backs). You can pay £5 to stand (or sit in your wheelchair) in the "groundling" pit; these tickets—while the only ones open to rain—are most fun. We've never enjoyed Shakespeare as much as here, performed as it was meant to be in the "wooden O." Plays can be long. Many groundlings leave before the end. If you like, hang out an hour before the finish and beg or buy a ticket from someone leaving early (groundlings are allowed to come and go).

WHAT'S ON IN THE WEST END

Here are some of the perennial favorites that you're likely to find among the West End's evening offerings. Generally you can book tickets for free at the box office or for a £2 fee by telephone or online. Wheelchair users and their companions are often eligible for discounts; ask when you buy your ticket.

Musicals

Chicago—A chorus-girl-gone-bad forms a nightclub act with another murderess to bring in the bucks (**AE, AI, AT,** Level 1—Fully accessible; £15–40, Mon–Thu and Sat 20:00, Fri 20:30, matinees Fri 17:00 and Sat 15:00, Adelphi Theatre, Strand, Tube: Covent Garden or Charing Cross, booking tel. 020/7344-0055, www.chicagothemusical.com).

Mamma Mia—This high-energy spandex-and-platform-boots musical weaves together 20 or 30 ABBA hits to tell the story of a bride in search of her real dad as her promiscuous mom plans her Greek Isle wedding. The production has the audience dancing by its happy ending (**AE, AI, AT,** Level 1—Fully accessible; £19–40, Mon–Thu and Sat 19:30, Fri 20:30, matinees Fri 17:00 and Sat 15:00, Prince Edward Theatre, Old Compton Street, Tube: Leicester Square, booking tel. 020/7447-5400).

Les Misérables—Claude-Michel Schönberg's musical adaptation of Victor Hugo's epic follows the life of Jean Valjean as he struggles with the social and political realities of 19th-century France. This inspiring mega-hit takes you back to the days of France's struggle for a just and modern society (**AE, AI, AT,** Level 1—Fully accessible; £9–40, Mon–Sat 19:30, matinees Thu and Sat 14:30, Palace

Access: AE, AI, AT, AL, ❤, Level 1—Fully accessible. Wheelchair users have two options: fancy "Gentlemen's Rooms" seating for a discounted £20 (same discount for companion, book in advance), or down in special elevated groundling-pit spaces (though the view of the stage may still be partially obstructed). The staff will gladly assist if necessary.

Theatre, Cambridge Circus, Tube: Leicester Square, box office tel. 0870-160-2878, www.lesmis.com).

The Phantom of the Opera—A mysterious masked man falls in love with a singer in this haunting Andrew Lloyd Webber musical about life beneath the stage of the Paris Opera (**AE, AI,** Level 2—Moderately accessible; £10–40, Mon–Sat 19:30, matinees Wed and Sat 15:00, Her Majesty's Theatre, Haymarket, Tube: Piccadilly Circus, booking tel. 0870-160-2878, www.thephantomofthe opera.com).

The Lion King—In this Disney extravaganza featuring music by Elton John, Simba the lion learns about the delicately balanced circle of life on the savanna (**AE, AI, AT,** Level 1—Fully accessible; £18–43, Mon–Sat 19:30, matinees Wed and Sat 14:00 and Sun 15:00, Lyceum Theatre, Wellington Street, Tube: Charing Cross or Covent Garden, booking tel. 0870-243-9000 or 0161/228-1953, theater info tel. 020/7420-8112, www.thelionking.co.uk).

Thrillers

The Mousetrap—Agatha Christie's whodunit about a murder in a country house continues to stump audiences after 50 years (**AE, AI+A, AT,** Level 2—Moderately accessible; £11.50–30, Mon–Sat 20:00, matinees Tue 14:45 and Sat 17:00, St. Martin's Theatre, West Street, Tube: Leicester Square, box office tel. 0870-162-2878).

The Woman in Black—The chilling tale of a solicitor who is haunted by what he learns when he closes a reclusive woman's affairs (Level 3—Minimally accessible; £10–30, Mon–Sat 20:00, matinees Tue 15:00 and Sat 16:00, Fortune Theatre, Russell Street, Tube: Covent Garden, box office tel. 020/7369-1737, www .thewomaninblack.com).

The theater runs a Disabled Access Information line (tel. 020/7902-1409), and you can download an "Access Guide" from their Web site (www.shakespeares-globe.org).

Location: The theater is on the South Bank directly across the Thames over the Millennium Bridge from St. Paul's Cathedral (Tube:

Mansion House or London Bridge, tel. 020/7902-1500, box office tel. 020/7401-9919, www.shakespeares-globe.org). The Globe is inconvenient for public transport, but the courtesy phone in the lobby gets a minicab in minutes. (These have set fees—e.g., £8 to South Kensington—but generally cost less than a metered cab and provide fine and honest service.)

Fringe Theatre—London's rougher evening-entertainment scene is thriving, filling pages in *Time Out*. Choose from a wide range of fringe theater and comedy acts (generally £5).

Music—For easy, cheap, or free concerts in historic churches, check the TIs' listings for **lunch concerts,** especially St. James at Piccadilly (**AE, AI+A, AT+A,** Level 2—Moderately accessible; free lunch concerts on Mon, Wed, and Fri at 13:10, info tel. 020/7381-0441; two ramps lead from Piccadilly to the church, a few steps inside) and St. Martin-in-the-Fields (**AE, AI+A, AL+A, ♥,** Level 2—Moderately accessible; free lunch concerts on Mon, Tue, and Fri at 13:05, church tel. 020/7766-1100; concerts are accessible but box office is not, so call ahead for tickets, box office tel. 020/7839-8362).

St. Martin-in-the-Fields also hosts fine **evening concerts by candlelight** (£6–18, Thu–Sat at 19:30, box office tel. 020/7839-8362).

At St. Paul's Cathedral (**AE, AI, AL, AT,** Level 1—Fully accessible, except for dome), **evensong** is held Monday through Saturday at 17:00 and on Sunday at 15:15. At Westminster Abbey (**AE, AI,** Level 2—Moderately accessible, loaner wheelchairs), it's sung weekdays at 17:00 (but not on Wed) and Saturday and Sunday at 15:00. **Organ recitals** are held on Sunday at Westminster Abbey (17:45, 40 min, small fee, tel. 020/7798-9055) and at St. Paul's (17:00, 30 min, free, tel. 020/7236-4128).

For a fun classical event (mid-July–early Sept), attend a **"Prom Concert"** during the annual festival at the Royal Albert Hall (**AE, AI, AL, AT,** Level 1—Fully accessible, loaner wheelchairs). Nightly concerts are offered at give-a-peasant-some-culture prices (£4 standing-room spots sold at the door, £7 restricted-view seats, most £22, depending on performance, Tube: South Kensington, tel. 020/7589-8212, www.royalalberthall.com).

Some of the world's best **opera** is belted out at the prestigious Royal Opera House (**AE, AI, AT, AL,** Level 1—Fully accessible), near Covent Garden (box office tel. 020/7304-4000, www.royalopera.org; call ahead to reserve wheelchair space, use accessible Bow Street entrance) and at the less-formal Sadler's Wells Theatre (**AE, AI, AT, AL,** Level 1—Fully accessible; Rosebery Avenue, Islington, Tube: Angel, box office tel. 020/7863-8000, www.sadlers-wells.com; call ahead to reserve wheelchair space).

SLEEPING

London is expensive. For £70 ($110), you'll get a double with breakfast in a safe, cramped, and dreary place with minimal service and difficult accessibility. For £90 ($145), you'll get a basic, clean, reasonably cheery double in a usually cramped, cracked-plaster building with a private bath, or a soulless but comfortable room without breakfast in a huge, mostly accessible Motel 6-type place. Our London splurges, at £100–150 ($160–240), are spacious, thoughtfully appointed, fully accessible places. Hearty English or generous buffet breakfasts are included unless otherwise noted, and TVs are standard in rooms.

Reserve your London room with a phone call or e-mail as soon as you can commit to a date. To call a London hotel from the United States or Canada, dial 011-44-20 (London's area code without the initial zero), then the local eight-digit number. Some hotels will hold a room until 16:00 without a deposit, although most places will ask you for a credit-card number. The pricier ones have expensive cancellation policies (such as no refund if you cancel with less than 2 weeks' notice). Some fancy £120 rooms rent for a third off if you arrive late on a slow day and ask for a deal.

For more options, check out *Access in London*, with information on accessible accommodations, pubs, and toilets in London (£10, by Gordon Couch, William Forrester, and David McGaughey; Access Project, 39 Bradley Gardens, West Ealing, London W13 8HE, www.accessproject-phsp.org, gordon.couch@virgin.net).

Big, Cheap, Modern Hotels
The following hotels—popular with budget tour groups—are well-run and offer elevators and all the modern comforts in a no-frills, practical

SLEEP CODE

(£1 = about $1.70, country code: 44, area code: 020)
Sleep Code: **S** = Single, **D** = Double/Twin, **T** = Triple, **Q** = Quad, **b** = bathroom, **s** = shower only, **no CC** = Credit Cards not accepted. Unless otherwise noted, credit cards are accepted, and prices include a generous breakfast and all taxes.

Please see "Accessibility Codes" sidebar on page 54 of this chapter for a quick guide to codes. For a more detailed explanation of Accessibility Levels and Codes, please see page 2 of the Introduction.

package. Though not quaint, these places offer the best (and cheapest) accessibility in London. Some of the more forward-thinking hotel chains (such as **Ibis, Travel Inn,** and **Forte Travelodge**) have made it corporate policy to provide adapted facilities for persons with limited mobility. Midweek prices are generally higher than weekend rates.

Level 1—Fully Accessible
London County Hall Travel Inn (AE, AI, AL, AR, AB), literally down the hall from a $400-a-night Marriott Hotel, fills one end of London's massive former County Hall building. This place is wonderfully located near the base of the London Eye Ferris Wheel and across the Thames from Big Ben. Its 300 slick, no-frills rooms come with all the necessary comforts (Db-£82 for 2 adults and up to 2 kids under age 15, couples can request a bigger family room—same price, breakfast extra, book in advance, no-show rooms are released at 16:00, elevator, non-smoking rooms, 500 yards from Westminster Tube stop and Waterloo Station, Belvedere Road, you can call central reservations at 0870-242-8000 or 0870-238-3300, you can fax 020/7902-1619 but you might not get a response, it's easiest to book online at www.travelinn.co.uk). There is a special accessible entrance and lift at the rear of the hotel, and there are 16 specially adapted rooms for wheelchair users. Other **Travel Inns** in London are less central, but have at least one room per hotel that is fully adapted (**AE, AI, AL, AR, AB;** figure £70–80 per room). Call ahead at each place to get details and reserve: **London Euston** (a big, blue Lego-

type building on a handy but noisy street packed with Benny Hill families on vacation, 141 Euston Road, Tube: Euston, tel. 0870-238-3301), **Tower Bridge** (Tower Bridge Road, Tube: London Bridge, tel. 0870-238-3303), and **London Putney Bridge** (farther out, 3 Putney Bridge Approach, Tube: Putney Bridge, tel. 0870-238-3302).

Jurys Inn (AE, AI, AL, AR, AB) rents 200 mod, compact, and comfy rooms near King's Cross station (Db/Tb-£104, 2 adults and 2 kids—under age 12—can share 1 room, breakfast extra, non-smoking floors, 60 Pentonville Road, Tube: Angel, tel. 020/7282-5500, fax 020/7282-5511, www.jurysdoyle.com). Built only five years ago, this hotel has 20 fully adapted rooms. The main entrance is also fully accessible.

Hotel Ibis London Euston (AE, AI, AL, AR, AB), which feels classier than a Travel Inn, is located on a quiet street a block behind Euston Station (380 rooms, Db-£80, breakfast-£5, no family rooms, non-smoking floor, 3 Cardington Street, tel. 020/7388-7777, fax 020/7388-0001, www.ibishotel.com, h0921@accor-hotels.com). The hotel has eight accessible rooms (4 twins and 4 doubles). The main entrance on Cardington Street is fully accessible.

Level 2—Moderately Accessible
Premier Lodge (AE, AI, AL, AR, AB+A, ♥) is near Shakespeare's Globe on the South Bank (55 rooms, Db for up to 2 adults and 2 kids-£70, Bankside, 34 Park Street, tel. 0870-700-1456, www.premier-lodge.co.uk). This surprising little gem offers good accessibility, except for the bathrooms, which are suitable, but not adapted.

Victoria Station Neighborhood, Belgravia
The streets behind Victoria Station teem with budget B&Bs. It's a safe, surprisingly tidy, and decent area without a hint of the trashy, touristy glitz of the streets in front of the station. Here in Belgravia, your neighbors include Andrew Lloyd Webber and Margaret Thatcher (her policeman stands outside 73 Chester Square). Decent eateries abound (see "Eating," page 127). Cheaper rooms are relatively dumpy. Don't expect £90 cheeriness in a £60 room. Off-season, it's possible to save money by arriving late without a reservation and looking around. Competition softens prices, especially for multinight stays. On hot summer nights, request a quiet back room. All are within a few blocks of the Victoria Tube, bus, and train stations. There's a £15-per-day (with a hotel voucher) garage

Victoria Station Neighborhood

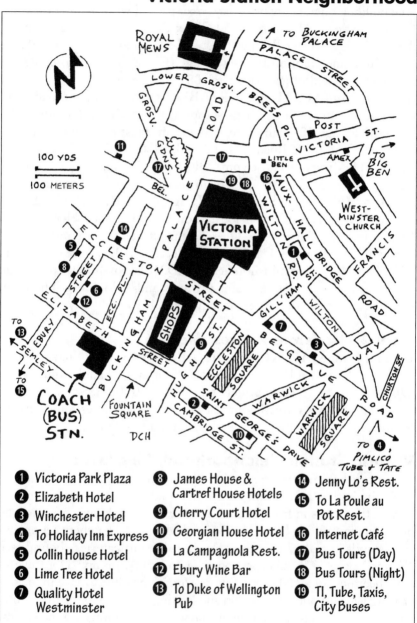

❶ Victoria Park Plaza
❷ Elizabeth Hotel
❸ Winchester Hotel
❹ To Holiday Inn Express
❺ Collin House Hotel
❻ Lime Tree Hotel
❼ Quality Hotel Westminster
❽ James House & Cartref House Hotels
❾ Cherry Court Hotel
❿ Georgian House Hotel
⓫ La Campagnola Rest.
⓬ Ebury Wine Bar
⓭ To Duke of Wellington Pub
⓮ Jenny Lo's Rest.
⓯ To La Poule au Pot Rest.
⓰ Internet Café
⓱ Bus Tours (Day)
⓲ Bus Tours (Night)
⓳ TI, Tube, Taxis, City Buses

and a nearby **launderette** (daily 8:00–20:30, self-service or full service, past Warwick Square at 3 Westmoreland Terrace, tel. 020/7821-8692).

Level 1—Fully Accessible
Victoria Park Plaza (AE, AI, AL, AR, AB) is ideally situated 50 yards from Victoria Station. While on the higher side for room expense (call and check for "bargain rates"), the hotel is excellent for wheelchair users who need fully-adapted rooms (Sb-£119, Db-£200, apartments available, elevator, 239 Vauxhall Bridge Road, tel. 020/7769-9999, fax 020/7769-9820, www.victoriaparkplaza.com, vppres@parkplazahotels.co.uk).

Level 2—Moderately Accessible
Elizabeth Hotel (AE+A, AI, AR, AB+A) is a stately old place overlooking Eccleston Square, with fine public spaces and 38 spacious and decent rooms that could use a minor facelift (D-£72, small Db-£88, big Db-£99, Tb-£110, Qb-£120, Quint/b-£125, 37 Eccleston Square, tel. 020/7828-6812, fax 020/7828-6814, www.elizabethhotel.com, info @elizabethhotel.com). There are four 6" entry steps. Two suitable Level 2 rooms on the ground floor have been used by wheelchair users in the past. Be careful not to confuse this hotel with the nearby Elizabeth House. This one is big and comfy, the other small and dumpy.

    Winchester Hotel (AE+A, AI, AR, AB+A, ♥) is family-run and a good value, with 18 fine rooms, no claustrophobia, and a wise and caring management (Db-£85, Tb-£110, Qb-£140, no CC, no groups, no infants, 17 Belgrave Road, tel. 020/7828-2972, fax 020/7828-5191, www.winchester-hotel.net, enquiry@winchester-hotel.net, commanded by Jimmy with his able first mates: Juanita, Ian, and Paul). While there are no specially adapted rooms, there is a suitable ground-floor room, and the staff is welcoming to wheelchair users.

    Holiday Inn Express (AE+A, AI, AB, AR) fills an old building with 52 fresh, modern, and efficient rooms (Db-£105, Tb-£120, family rooms, up to 2 kids free, some discounts on Web site, non-smoking floor, elevator, Tube: Pimlico, 106 Belgrave Road, tel. 020/7630-8888 or 0800-897-121, fax 020/7828-0441, www.hiexpressvictoria.co.uk, info@hiexpress victoria.co.uk). Aside from steps at the entry, this is a fully accessible hotel (but has only one adapted room—call ahead to reserve it). The wheelchair entry is to the right side of the main door, and the staff will assist in your arrival. For those who enjoy and trust the Holiday Inn

Express chain, note that all of the Express hotels have at least one wheel-chair-accessible room (in London, call 0800-434-040 for reservations).

Level 3—Minimally Accessible

Collin House Hotel (AE+A, AI, AR+A, AB+A), clean, simple and efficiently-run, offers 12 basic rooms with woody, modern furnishings (Sb-£55, D-£68, Db-£82, T-£95, non-smoking rooms, 104 Ebury St, tel.& fax 020/7730-8031, www.collinhouse.co.uk, booking@collinhouse.co.uk). There are two rooms on the ground floor that are suitably accessible, but not adapted. There are two 8" steps at the entrance. They have not had wheelchair users in the past, but they are ready to welcome guests that have limited mobility.

Lime Tree Hotel (AE+A, AI+A), enthusiastically run by David and Marilyn Davies and their daughter Charlotte, comes with spacious and thoughtfully decorated rooms and a fun-loving breakfast room. While priced a bit steep, the place has character and is a good value (30 rooms, Sb-£80, Db-£110–120, Tb-£150, family room-£160, possible discount with cash, all rooms non-smoking, quiet garden, David deals in slow times and is creative at helping travelers in a bind, 135 Ebury Street, tel. 020/7730-8191, fax 020/7730-7865, www.limetreehotel.co.uk, info@limetreehotel.co.uk). There are five 6" entry steps, no interior lifts, and no accessible rooms.

Quality Hotel Westminster (AE+A, AI+A) is big, modern (but with tired carpets), well-located, and a fine value for no-nonsense comfort (Db-£130, on slow days drop-ins can ask for "saver prices," if booking in advance check various specials on the Web, breakfast extra or bargained in, non-smoking floor, elevator, 82 Eccleston Square, tel. 020/7834-8042, fax 020/7630-8942, www.hotels-westminster.com, enquiries@hotels-westminster.com). There are nine 6" entry steps and no accessible rooms.

James House (AE+A, ♥; two 8" entry steps, non-accessible rooms upstairs and breakfast room downstairs) and **Cartref House (AE+A, ♥;** five 6" entry steps, two non-adapted rooms on the ground floor with the breakfast room downstairs) are two nearly identical, well-run, smoke-free, 10-room places on either side of Ebury Street (S-£55, Sb-£65, D-£74, Db-£90, T-£100, Tb-£120, family bunk-bed Qb-£140, 5 percent discount with cash, all rooms with fans, no smoking, James House at 108 Ebury Street, tel. 020/7730-7338; Cartref House at 129 Ebury Street, tel. 020/

7730-6176, fax for both: 020/7730-7338, www.jamesandcartref.co.uk, jandchouse@aol.com, run by Derek and Sharon). While neither house is specifically adapted for accessibility, the management is friendly and inviting.

Cherry Court Hotel (AE+A, AI+A), run by the friendly and industrious Patel family, offers tight, basic rooms for good value in a central location (Sb-£42, Db-£48, Tb-£70, Qb-£85, Quint/b-£100, paying with credit card costs 5 percent extra, fruit-basket breakfast in room, non-smoking, free Internet access, peaceful garden patio, 23 Hugh Street, tel. 020/7828-2840, fax 020/7828-0393, www.cherrycourthotel.co.uk, bookings@cherrycourthotel.co.uk). Five 6" steps greet you at the entry, and there are no specially adapted rooms. But the staff is kind and has hosted persons with varying degrees of disability in the past.

Georgian House Hotel (AE+A, AI+A) has 50 once-grand, now basic rooms; skip the cheaper fourth floor, up lots of stairs (S-£29, Db-£69, Tb-£86, Qb-£94, Internet access, 35 St. George's Drive, tel. 020/7834-1438, fax 020/7976-6085, www.georgianhousehotel.co.uk, reception@georgianhousehotel.co.uk). The hotel has exterior and interior stairs that slow walkers could negotiate.

"South Kensington," She Said, Loosening His Cummerbund.

To live on a quiet street so classy it doesn't allow hotel signs, surrounded by trendy shops and colorful restaurants, call "South Ken" your London home. Shoppers like being close to Harrods and the designer shops of King's Road and Chelsea. When we splurge, we splurge here. Sumner Place is just off Old Brompton Road, 200 yards from the handy South Kensington Tube station (on Circle Line, 2 stops from Victoria Station, direct Heathrow connection). There's a taxi rank in the median strip at the end of Harrington Road. The handy Wash & Dry **launderette** is on the corner of Queensberry Place and Harrington Road (daily 8:00–21:00, bring 20p and £1 coins).

Level 1—Fully Accessible

Jurys Kensington Hotel (AE, AI, AL, AR, AB, ♥) is big, stately, and impersonal, with a greedy pricing scheme—but it's also fully wheelchair-accessible (Sb/Db/Tb-£100–220 depending on "availability," ask for a deal, breakfast extra, piano lounge, non-smoking floor, elevator, Queen's

South Kensington Neighborhood

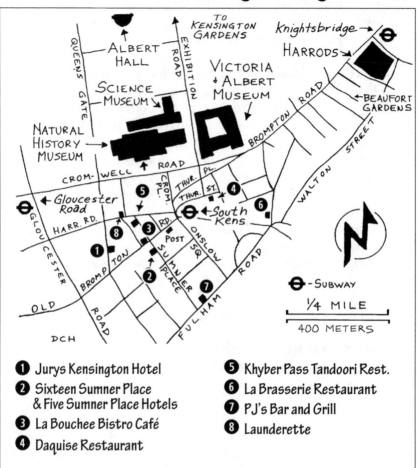

1 Jurys Kensington Hotel
2 Sixteen Sumner Place
   & Five Sumner Place Hotels
3 La Bouchee Bistro Café
4 Daquise Restaurant

5 Khyber Pass Tandoori Rest.
6 La Brasserie Restaurant
7 PJ's Bar and Grill
8 Launderette

Gate, tel. 020/7589-6300, fax 020/7581-1492, www.jurysdoyle.com, kensington@jurysdoyle.com). Though expensive, this place is a worthwhile splurge from an accessibility standpoint—fully adapted from entryway to bathrooms, including a wheelchair-accessible restaurant.

Level 2—Moderately Accessible

Number Sixteen (AE+A, AI, AL, AR, AB+A), for well-heeled travelers, has over-the-top formality and class packed into its 40 rooms, plush lounges, and quiet garden. It's in a labyrinthine building, with modern

Italian decor throughout (Db-£165–200—but squishy, breakfast in your room, elevator, 16 Sumner Place, tel. 020/7589-5232, fax 020/7584-8615, U.S. tel. 800/553-6674, www.firmdale.com/index.html, sixteen @firmdale.com). There is no entry ramp, but if you can negotiate the five 6" entry steps, the rest of the hotel is suitable (though not specially adapted). There are rooms on the ground floor, and an accessible lift to the other floors. Breakfast can be delivered to your room.

Level 3—Minimally Accessible

Five Sumner Place Hotel (AE+A, AI+A, AL+A, AR+A) has received several "best small hotel in London" awards. The rooms in this 150-year-old building are tastefully decorated, and the breakfast room is a conservatory/greenhouse (13 rooms, Sb-£100, Db-£153, third bed-£22, ask for Rick Steves discount; TV, phones, and fridge in rooms by request; non-smoking rooms, elevator, 5 Sumner Place, tel. 020/7584-7586, fax 020/7823-9962, www.sumnerplace.com, reservations@sumnerplace.com, run by John and Barbara Palgan). There are five 8" entry steps and two ground-floor rooms that are suitable (but not specially adapted). The breakfast room is downstairs and not wheelchair-accessible.

Notting Hill Neighborhood

Residential Notting Hill has quick bus and Tube access to downtown, is on the A2 Airbus line from Heathrow, and, for London, is very "homely." It has a self-serve launderette on Moscow Road, an artsy theater, a late-hours supermarket, and lots of fun budget eateries (see "Eating," page 127).

Level 2—Moderately Accessible

Westland Hotel (AE+A, AI, AL, AR, AB+A) is comfortable, convenient, and hotelesque, with a fine lounge and spacious rooms. Cheaper rooms are old and simple; others are quite plush (Sb-£80–90, Db-£95–105, cavernous deluxe Db-£110–125, sprawling Tb-£120–140, gargantuan Qb-£135–160, Quint/b-£150–170, elevator, free garage with 6 spaces, between Notting Hill Gate and Queensway Tube stations, 154 Bayswater Road, tel. 020/7229-9191, fax 020/7727-1054, www.westland hotel.co.uk, reservations@westlandhotel.co.uk). There are plans to replace the current entryway (three 6" steps) with a wheelchair-accessible ramp. Until that time, the staff will assist your entrance. Past wheelchair

Notting Hill Neighborhood

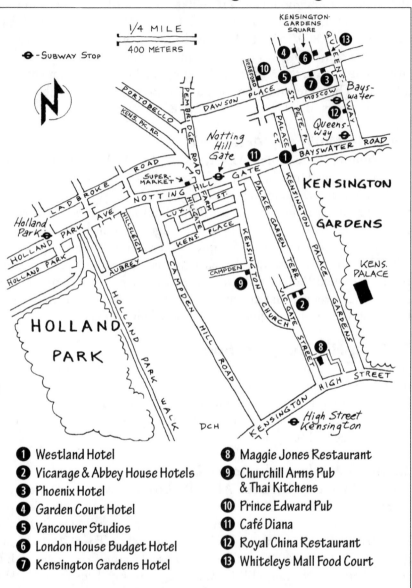

1. Westland Hotel
2. Vicarage & Abbey House Hotels
3. Phoenix Hotel
4. Garden Court Hotel
5. Vancouver Studios
6. London House Budget Hotel
7. Kensington Gardens Hotel
8. Maggie Jones Restaurant
9. Churchill Arms Pub & Thai Kitchens
10. Prince Edward Pub
11. Café Diana
12. Royal China Restaurant
13. Whiteleys Mall Food Court

users have stayed on the ground floor or used the wheelchair-accessible lift. Call ahead to alert the staff of your needs.

Level 3—Minimally Accessible

Vicarage Private Hotel (AE+A, AI, AR, AB+A), understandably popular, is family-run and elegantly British in a quiet, classy neighborhood. It has 17 rooms furnished with taste and quality, a TV lounge, and facilities on each floor. Mandy, Richard, and Krassi maintain a homey and caring atmosphere (S-£46, Sb-£75, D-£78, Db-£102, T-£95, Tb-£130, Q-£102, Qb-£140, no CC, ⅓-mile roll or stroll from the Notting Hill Gate and High Street Kensington Tube stations, near Kensington Palace at 10 Vicarage Gate, tel. 020/7229-4030, fax 020/7792-5989, www.londonvicaragehotel.com, reception@londonvicaragehotel.com). Call ahead to reserve one of the two large ground-floor rooms. Although the staff welcomes wheelchair users, you'll have to negotiate six 6" entry steps.

Abbey House Hotel (AE+A, AI, AR, AB+A), next door, is basic but sleepable (16 rooms, S-£45, D-£74, T-£90, Q-£100, Quint-£110, no CC, 11 Vicarage Gate, tel. 020/7727-2594, fax 020/7727-1873, www.abbeyhousekensington.com, abbeyhousedesk@btconnect.com, Rodrigo). The entry is not wheelchair-accessible (six 6" steps). Call ahead to reserve one of the two large ground-floor rooms. They have hosted wheelchair users in the past, and the staff is willing to assist.

Kensington Gardens

Several big old hotels line the quiet Kensington Gardens, a block off the bustling Queensway shopping street near the Bayswater Tube station. Popular with young international travelers, Queensway is a multicultural festival of commerce and eateries (such as Whiteleys Mall Food Court—see "Eating," page 127). These hotels are very quiet for central London. One of several **launderettes** in the neighborhood is Brookford Wash & Dry, at Queensway and Bishop's Bridge Road (daily 7:00-19:30, service from 9:00-17:30, computerized pay point takes all coins).

Level 3—Minimally Accessible

Phoenix Hotel (AE+A, AI, AL, AR+A, AB+A), a Best Western modernization of a 125-room hotel, offers American business-class comforts; spacious, plush public spaces; and big, fresh, modern-feeling rooms (Sb-

£99, Db-£130, Tb-£165, Qb-£185, flaky "negotiable" pricing list, elevator, 1-8 Kensington Gardens Square, tel. 020/7229-2494, fax 020/7727-1419, U.S. tel. 800/528-1234, www.phoenixhotel.co.uk, info@phoenixhotel.co.uk). There are five 6" entry steps. Call ahead to reserve a suitable ground-floor room. There is an adapted lift to get to the other floors and to the restaurant. Wheelchair users with assistance or a high degree of mobility have stayed here in the past.

Garden Court (AE+A, AI+A, AR+A) rents 34 comfortable, smoke-free rooms and is a fine value. It's friendly and has a garden (S-£39, Sb-£58, D-£58, Db-£88, T-£72, Tb-£99, Q-£82, Qb-£120, 5 percent discount with this book, elevator, 30 Kensington Gardens Square, tel. 020/7229-2553, fax 020/7727-2749, www.gardencourthotel.co.uk, info @gardencourthotel.co.uk). There are four 7" entry steps and two suitable ground-floor rooms. They have not had wheelchair users in the past, and your companion would be expected to assist your entry.

Vancouver Studios (AE+A, AI+A, AR+A, ♥) offers 45 modern rooms with all the amenities, and gives you a fully-equipped kitchenette (utensils, stove, microwave, and fridge) rather than breakfast (small Sb-£57, big Sb-£77, small Db-£97, big Db-£112, Tb-£132, extra bed-£10, 10 percent discount with week-long stay or more, welcoming staff, homey lounge and private garden, 30 Prince's Square, tel. 020/7243-1270, fax 020/7221-8678, www.vancouverstudios.co.uk, info@vancouverstudios .co.uk). There are five 7" entry steps and several ground-floor rooms. They have not had wheelchair users in the past, but the staff is welcoming and willing to assist. A wheelchair user with a high degree of mobility or with a companion would probably be fine here.

London House Budget Hotel (AE+A, AI+A, AR+A) is a threadbare, nose-ringed slumber mill renting 240 beds in 93 stark rooms (S-£40, Sb-£45, twin-£54, Db-£68, dorm bed-£15, prices flex downward with demand, includes continental breakfast, lots of school groups, 81 Kensington Gardens Square, tel. 020/7243-1810, fax 020/7243-1723, londonhousehotel@yahoo.co.uk). There are five 7" entryway steps with rooms on the ground floor. In the past, wheelchair users have been welcomed here. This hotel might work for a wheelchair user with a high degree of mobility or with a companion.

Kensington Gardens Hotel (AE+A, AR+A) laces 16 decent rooms together in a tall, skinny place with lots of stairs and no lift (Ss-£45–50, Sb-£50–55, Db-£75, Tb-£95, 9 Kensington Gardens Square, tel.

020/7221-7790, fax 020/7792-8612, www.kensingtongardenshotel.co.uk, ignore inflated prices on the Web site—the above rates will be honored, info@kensingtongardenshotel.co.uk, charming Rowshanak). There are three 5" entry steps and one ground-floor room (down more steps). They have not had wheelchair users in the past, and your companion would be expected to assist your entry.

EATING

If you want to dine (as opposed to eat), check out the extensive listings in the weekly entertainment guides sold at London newsstands (or catch a train for Paris). The thought of a £30 meal in Britain generally ruins our appetite, so our London dining is limited mostly to easygoing, fun, but inexpensive alternatives. We've listed places by neighborhood—handy to your sightseeing or hotel—and provided accessibility information for each place. Unless otherwise noted (by **AT** or **AT+A**), these restaurants do *not* have accessible toilets.

Pub grub is the most atmospheric budget option. Many of London's 7,000 pubs serve fresh, tasty buffets under ancient timbers, with hearty lunches and dinners for £6–8. For details, see "Pub Pointers," next page. (While pubs are going strong, the new phenomenon is coffee shops: Starbucks and its competitors have sprouted up all over town, providing cushy and social watering holes with comfy chairs, easy toilets, £2 lattes, and a nice break between sights.)

Ethnic restaurants—especially Indian and Chinese—are popular, plentiful, and cheap. Most large museums (and many churches) have inexpensive, cheery cafeterias. Of course, picnicking is the fastest and cheapest way to go. Good grocery stores and sandwich shops, fine park benches, and polite pigeons abound in Britain's most expensive city.

Tipping
Tipping is an issue only at restaurants and fancy pubs that have waiters and waitresses. If you order your food at a counter, don't tip.

If the menu states that service is included, there's no need to tip beyond that. If service isn't included, tip about 10 percent by rounding up. Leave the tip on the table, or hand it to your server with your payment for the meal and say, "Keep the rest, please."

Pub Pointers

Pubs are a basic part of the British social scene, and, whether you're a teetotaler or a beer guzzler, they should be a part of your travel here. "Pub" is short for "public house." It's an extended living room where, if you don't mind the stickiness, you can feel the pulse of London. Smart travelers use the pubs to eat, drink, get out of the rain, watch the latest sporting event, and make new friends.

A cup of darts is free for the asking. People go to a "public house" to be social. They want to talk. Get vocal with a local. This is easiest at the bar, where people assume you're in the mood to talk (rather than at a table, where you're allowed a bit of privacy). The pub is the next best thing to having relatives in town. Cheers!

Pub Grub

Pub grub gets better each year. It's London's best eating value. For £6–8, you'll get a basic, budget hot lunch or dinner in friendly surroundings.

Pubs generally serve traditional dishes, like fish and chips, vegetables, "bangers and mash" (sausages and mashed potatoes), roast beef with Yorkshire pudding (batter-baked in the oven), and assorted meat pies, such as steak-and-kidney pie or shepherd's pie (stewed lamb topped with mashed potatoes). Side dishes include salads (sometimes even a nice self-serve salad bar), vegetables, and—invariably—"chips" (French fries). "Crisps" are potato chips. A "jacket potato" (baked potato stuffed with fillings of your choice) can almost be a meal in itself. A "ploughman's lunch" is a modern "traditional English meal" of bread, cheese, and sweet pickles that nearly every tourist tries...once. These days, you'll likely find more Italian pasta, curried dishes, and quiche on the menu than "traditional" fare.

Meals are usually served from 12:00 to 14:00 and from 18:00 to 20:00, not throughout the day. There's usually no table service. Order at the bar, then go to a table and they'll bring the food when it's ready (or sometimes you pick it up at the bar). Pay at the bar (sometimes when you order, sometimes after you eat). Don't tip unless it's a place with full table service. Servings are hearty, service is quick, and you'll rarely spend more than £8. Your beer or cider adds another couple of pounds. (Free tap water is always available.) Pubs that advertise their food and are crowded with locals are less likely to be the kinds that serve only lousy microwaved snacks. Because they make more money selling drinks, many stop cooking fairly early.

Beer

The British take great pride in their beer. Many Brits think that drinking beer cold and carbonated, as Americans do, ruins the taste. Most pubs will have **lagers** (cold, refreshing, American-style beer), **ales** (amber-colored, room-temperature beer), **bitters** (hop-flavored ale, perhaps the most typical British beer), and **stouts** (dark and somewhat bitter, like Guinness). At pubs, long hand pulls are used to pull the traditional, rich-flavored "real ales" up from the cellar. These are the connoisseur's favorites: fermented naturally, varying from sweet to bitter, often with a hoppy or nutty flavor. Notice the fun names. Short hand pulls at the bar mean colder, fizzier, mass-produced, and less interesting keg beers. Mild beers are sweeter, with a creamy malt flavoring. Irish cream ale is a smooth, sweet experience. Try the draft cider (sweet or dry)...carefully.

Order your beer at the bar and pay as you go, with no need to tip. An average beer costs £2.50. Part of the experience is standing before a line of "hand pulls," or taps, and wondering which beer to choose.

Drinks are served by the pint (20-ounce imperial size) or the half-pint. (It's considered almost feminine for a man to order just a half.) Proper English ladies like a half-beer and half-lemonade **shandy.**

Pubs serve beer daily 11:00–23:00 (Sun 12:00–22:30). As it nears 23:00, you'll hear shouts of "Last orders." Then comes the 10-minute warning bell. Finally, they'll call "Time!" to pick up your glass, finished or not, sometime before 23:25, when the pub closes.

Besides beer, many pubs actually have a good selection of wines by the glass, a fully stocked bar for the gentleman's "G and T" (gin and tonic), and the increasingly popular bottles of alcohol-plus-sugar (such as Bacardi Breezers) for the younger, working-class set. Teetotalers and kids can order from a wide variety of soft drinks. Children are served food and soft drinks in pubs, but you must be 18 to order a beer.

Near Trafalgar Square

The **Clarence Pub,** down Whitehall, a block south of Trafalgar Square toward Big Ben, is touristy but atmospheric with decent grub (**AE+A, AI,** Level 2—Moderately accessible; indoor/outdoor seating, £8 meals, daily 11:00–22:00). Nearby are several cheaper cafeterias and pizza joints.

Crivelli's Garden Restaurant, serving a classy, fully accessible lunch in the National Gallery, is a good place to treat your palate to pricey, light Mediterranean cuisine (**AE, AI, AT, AL,** Level 1—Fully accessible; £15 lunches, daily 10:00–17:00, first floor of Sainsbury Wing).

St. Martin-in-the-Fields Café in the Crypt is just right for a tasty meal on a monk's budget, sitting on somebody's tomb in an ancient crypt (currently Level 4—Not accessible, must climb down 14 steps—but there are plans for full accessibility by 2005; £6–7 cafeteria plates, cheaper sandwich bar, Mon–Wed 10:00–20:00, Thu–Sat 10:00–23:00, Sun 12:00–20:00, profits go to the church, no CC, underneath St. Martin-in-the-Fields church on Trafalgar Square, tel. 020/7839-4342).

Near Piccadilly

Hungry and broke in the theater district? Head for Panton Street (off Haymarket, 2 blocks southeast of Piccadilly Circus) for cheap Thai, Chinese, and two famous London eateries.

Stockpot (**AE+A, AI, ♥,** Level 2—Moderately accessible) is a mushy-peas kind of place, famous and rightly popular for its edible, cheap meals (daily 7:00–22:00, 38 Panton Street). Wheelchair users are frequent patrons here, in spite of the two entry steps and the narrow door. Travelers with any disability can expect a warm welcome.

The **West End Kitchen** (**AE+A, AI,** Level 2—Moderately accessible; across the street at #5, same hours and menu) is a direct competitor that's just as good.

Vegetarians prefer the **Woodland South Indian Vegetarian Restaurant** (**AE+A,** Level 2—Moderately accessible; 1 entry step to a table that is always reserved for anyone with limited mobility), across from the West End Kitchen.

The palatial **Criterion Brasserie** (**AE, AI, AT,** Level 1—Fully accessible) serves a special £15 two-course "Anglo-French" *menu* (or £18 for 3 courses) under gilded tiles and chandeliers in a dreamy Byzantine church setting from 1880. It's right on Piccadilly Circus but a world away from the punk junk. The house wine is great and so is the food (specials available

Mon–Sat 12:00–14:30 & 17:30–19:00, closed Sun lunch, reservations requested, tel. 020/7930-0488). After 19:00, the menu becomes really expensive. Anyone can drop in for coffee or a drink.

The "Food Is Fun" Dinner Tour: From Covent Garden to Soho

London has a trendy, Generation X scene that most Beefeater-seekers miss entirely. For a multicultural, movable feast, consider exploring these. Start around 18:00 to avoid lines, get in on early specials, and find waiters willing to let you split a meal. Prices, while reasonable by London standards, add up. Servings are large enough to share. All are open nightly.

Suggested nibbler's dinner roll or stroll for two: Arrive before 18:00 at **Belgo Centraal** and split the early-bird dinner special: a kilo of mussels, fries, and dark Belgian beer. At **Yo! Sushi,** have beer or sake and a few dishes. Slurp your last course at **Wagamama Noodle Bar.** Then, for dessert, people-watch at Leicester Square.

Belgo Centraal (AE, AI, AL, AT, ♥, Level 1—Fully accessible, people with limited mobility given priority seating and service) dishes hearty Belgian specialties. It's a seafood, chips, and beer emporium dressed up as a mod monastic refectory—with waiters dressed as Trappist monks and noisy acoustics. The classy restaurant section requires reservations, but just grabbing a bench in the boisterous beer hall (no reservations possible) is more fun. The same menu and specials work on both sides. Belgians claim they eat as well as the French and as heartily as the Germans. Specialties include mussels, great fries, and a stunning array of dark, blond, and fruity Belgian beers. Belgo actually makes Belgian things trendy—a formidable feat (£10–14 meals; open daily until 23:00; Mon–Fri 17:30–19:00 "beat the clock" meal specials for £5.30–7.00, and you get mussels, fries, and beer; no meal-splitting after 18:30, and you must buy food with beer; daily £6 lunch special 12:00–17:30; 1 block north of Covent Garden Tube station at intersection of Neal and Shelton Streets, 50 Earlham Street, tel. 020/7813-2233).

Yo! Sushi (AE, AI, AL, Level 2—Moderately accessible) is a futuristic Japanese food-extravaganza experience. With thumping rock, Japanese cable TV, a 195-foot-long conveyor belt, the world's longest sushi bar, a robotic drink trolley, and automated sushi machines, just sipping a sake on a bar stool here is a trip. For £1 each you get unlimited tea,

From Covent Garden to Soho: Food is Fun

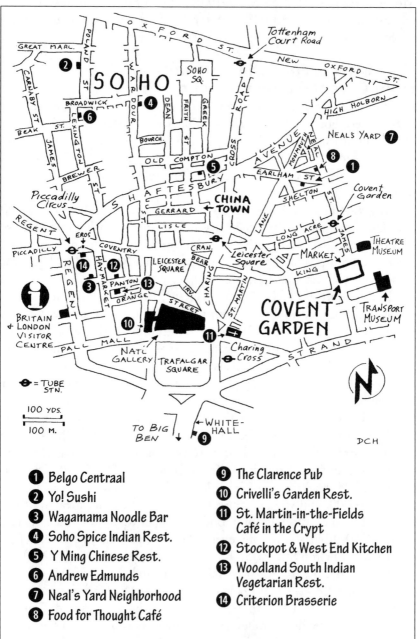

1. Belgo Centraal
2. Yo! Sushi
3. Wagamama Noodle Bar
4. Soho Spice Indian Rest.
5. Y Ming Chinese Rest.
6. Andrew Edmunds
7. Neal's Yard Neighborhood
8. Food for Thought Café
9. The Clarence Pub
10. Crivelli's Garden Rest.
11. St. Martin-in-the-Fields Café in the Crypt
12. Stockpot & West End Kitchen
13. Woodland South Indian Vegetarian Rest.
14. Criterion Brasserie

water (from spigot at bar, with or without gas), or miso soup. Grab dishes as they rattle by (priced by color of dish; check the chart: £1.50–3.50 per dish; daily 12:00–24:00, 2 blocks south of Oxford Street, where Lexington Street becomes Poland Street, 52 Poland Street, tel. 020/7287-0443).

Wagamama Noodle Bar (ranges from Level 1—Fully accessible to Level 4—Not accessible; see below) is a noisy, pan-Asian, organic slurpathon. As you enter, check out the kitchen and listen to the roar of the crowds. Benches rock with happy eaters, and everybody sucks. Feel the energy of all this "positive eating" (£10 meals, daily 12:00–24:00, crowded after 20:00, non-smoking). Wagamama has branches all over town, but not all are accessible. The two most convenient fully accessible branches (**AE, AI, AT,** Level 1) are near Piccadilly Circus at 8 Norris Street (handiest for this "Dinner Tour") and on Wigmore Street (#101-A, Tube: Bond Street). Other central branches are located in basements with no elevator (and therefore Level 4—Not accessible), including 10-A Lexington Street in Soho and 4-A Streatham Street near the British Museum.

Soho Spice Indian (**AE, AI, AT, ♥,** Level 1—Fully accessible, only 1 wheelchair allowed at a time for safety reasons) is where modern Britain meets Indian tradition—fine cuisine in a trendy, jewel-tone ambience. Unlike many Indian restaurants, when you order an entrée here (£10–15), it comes with side dishes (nan, dal, rice, vegetables). The £15 "tandoori selections" meal is the best "variety" dish and big enough for two (Mon–Sat 11:30–24:00, Sun 12:30–22:30, non-smoking section, 5 blocks north of Piccadilly Circus at 124 Wardour Street, tel. 020/7434-0808).

Y Ming Chinese Restaurant (**AE+A, AI,** Level 2—Moderately accessible) has clean European decor, serious but helpful service, and authentic Northern Chinese cooking. It's across Shaftesbury Avenue from the ornate gates, clatter, and dim sum of Chinatown (good £10 meal deal offered 12:00–18:00—last order at 18:00, Mon–Sat 12:00–23:30, closed Sun, 35 Greek Street, tel. 020/7734-2721, www.yming.com).

Andrew Edmunds Restaurant (**AE, AI, ♥** Level 2—Moderately accessible, ask for accessible upstairs table) is a tiny, candlelit place where you'll want to hide your camera and guidebook and act as local as possible. This great little place—with a jealous and loyal clientele—is the closest we found to Parisian quality in a cozy restaurant in London. The modern European cooking with a creative seasonal menu is worth the splurge (3 courses for £25, daily 12:30–15:00 & 18:00–22:45, reservations suggested, 46 Lexington Street in Soho, tel. 020/7437-5708).

Neal's Yard is *the* place for cheap, hip, and healthy eateries on a charming pedestrian mall near Covent Garden, where accessible shops abound. The neighborhood is a tabbouleh of fun, hippie-type cafés. One of the best is **Food for Thought** (**AI,** Level 3—Minimally accessible, narrow door and flight of narrow and steep steps), packed with local health nuts (good £5 vegetarian meals, Mon–Sat 12:00–20:30, Sun 12:00–17:00, non-smoking, 2 blocks north of Covent Garden Tube station, 31 Neal Street, tel. 020/7836-0239).

Eating near Recommended Victoria Station Accommodations

Here are places a couple of blocks southwest of Victoria Station where we've enjoyed eating (see map on page 118).

La Campagnola (**AE+A, AI,** Level 2—Moderately accessible, staff willing to assist with 5" entry step) is small, seriously Italian, and Belgravia's favorite budget Italian restaurant (£8–16, Mon–Sat 12:00–15:00 & 18:00–23:30, closed Sun, 10 Lower Belgrave Street, tel. 020/7730-2057). Local wheelchair users regularly eat here.

Ebury Wine Bar (**AE+A, AI,** Level 2—Moderately accessible), full of young professionals, provides a classy atmosphere, delicious meals, and a £13 two-course special from 18:00–19:30 (£15–18, Mon–Fri 11:00–23:00, Sat 12:00–23:00, Sun 18:00–23:00, 139 Ebury Street, at intersection with Elizabeth Street, near bus station, tel. 020/7730-5447).

Duke of Wellington pub (**AE, AI, AT+A,** Level 2—Moderately accessible) is good, if somewhat smoky, and dominated by local drinkers. It's the neighborhood place for dinner (£6 meals, daily 11:00–15:00 & 18:00–21:00, 63 Eaton Terrace, at intersection with Chester Row, tel. 020/7730-1782). The staff is welcoming and regularly serves local wheelchair users.

Jenny Lo's Tea House (**AE+A, AI, AT,** Level 2—Moderately accessible, one 3" entry step, large entry door) is a simple, budget place serving up reliably tasty £5–8 eclectic Chinese-style meals to locals in the know (Mon–Fri 11:30–15:00 & 18:00–22:00, Sat 12:00–15:00 & 18:00–22:00, closed Sun, no CC, 14 Eccleston Street, tel. 020/7259-0399).

La Poule au Pot (**AE+A, AI,** Level 2—Moderately accessible, friendly staff will assist with the 8" entry step) is ideal for a romantic splurge, offering a classy, candlelit ambience with well-dressed patrons and expensive but fine country-style French cuisine (£15 lunch, £25 dinners, daily 12:30–14:30 & 18:45–23:00, Sun until 22:00, leafy patio dining, reservations smart, end of Ebury at intersection with Pimlico, 231 Ebury Street, tel. 020/7730-7763).

For a quick bite at Victoria Station, try the sandwich vendors on the main floor, easily accessible by wheelchair.

Near Recommended Notting Hill Hotels

Queensway is lined with lively and inexpensive eateries. See map on page 124.

Maggie Jones (AE+A, AI, AT+A, Level 2—Moderately accessible, staff will assist your entry up one 6" step; suitable toilet up 3 small steps) is exuberantly rustic and very English, serving our favorite £20 London dinner. You'll get fun-loving if brash service, solid English cuisine, including huge plates of crunchy vegetables—by candlelight. If you eat well once in London, eat here (daily 12:30–14:30 & 18:30–23:00, less-expensive lunch menu, reservations recommended, friendly staff, 6 Old Court Place, just east of Kensington Church Street, near High Street Kensington Tube stop, tel. 020/7937-6462).

Churchill Arms pub and **Thai Kitchens** is a local hangout (both AE, AI, Level 2—Moderately accessible, enter on Compden Street rather than at corner), with good beer and old-English ambience in front and hearty £6 Thai plates in an enclosed patio in the back. You can eat the Thai food in this tropical hideaway or in the smoky but wonderfully atmospheric pub section. Arrive by 18:00 to avoid a line (Mon–Sat 12:00–21:30, Sun 12:00–16:00, 119 Kensington Church Street, tel. 020/7792-1246). Local wheelchair users like this welcoming place.

Prince Edward Pub (AE, AI, Level 2—Moderately accessible) serves good pub grub in a quintessential pub setting (£8 meals, Mon–Sat 12:00–14:30 & 18:00–21:00, Sun 12:00–18:00, indoor/outdoor seating, 2 blocks north of Bayswater Road at corner of Dawson Place and Hereford Road, 73 Prince's Square, tel. 020/7727-2221).

Café Diana (AE+A, AI, Level 2—Moderately accessible, staff will assist with one 8" entry step) is a healthy little eatery serving sandwiches and Middle Eastern food. It's decorated with photos of Princess Diana, who used to drop by for pita sandwiches (daily 8:00–22:30, 5 Wellington

Terrace, on Bayswater Road, opposite Kensington Palace Garden Gates—where Di once lived, tel. 020/7792-9606).

Royal China Restaurant (**AE+A, AI+A, AT+A,** Level 2—Moderately accessible, staff will assist with one 7" entry step and four 5" steps into the dining area) is filled with London's Chinese, who consider this one of the city's best eateries. It's dressy in black, white, and chrome, with candles, brisk waiters, and fine food (£7–9 dishes, dim sum until 17:00, Mon–Thu 12:00–23:00, Fri–Sat 12:00–23:30, Sun 11:00–22:00, 13 Queensway, tel. 020/7221-2535).

Whiteleys Mall Food Court (**AE, AI, AT, AL,** Level 1—Fully accessible) offers a fun selection of ethnic and fast-food eateries in a fully accessible mall that will remind you of the United States (corner of Porchester Gardens and Queensway).

Near Recommended Accommodations in South Kensington

Popular eateries line Old Brompton Road and Thurloe Street (Tube: South Kensington). See map on page 122.

La Bouchee Bistro Café (**AE+A, AI, ♥,** Level 2—Moderately accessible, staff will assist with one-step entry) is a classy, hole-in-the-wall touch of France serving early-bird, three-course £12 meals before 19:00 and *plats du jour* for £8 all *jour* (daily 12:00–23:00, Sun until 22:00, 56 Old Brompton Road, tel. 020/7589-1929).

Daquise (**AE+A, AI,** Level 2—Moderately accessible, staff will assist with one 4" entry step), a 1930s Polish time-warp, is ideal if you're in the mood for kielbasa and kraut. It's likeably dreary—fast, cheap, family-run, and a part of the neighborhood (£10 meals, daily 11:00–23:00, non-smoking, 20 Thurloe Street, tel. 020/7589-6117). This place entertains a steady flow of regulars who use wheelchairs.

The **Khyber Pass Tandoori Restaurant** (**♥,** Level 3—Minimally accessible) is a nondescript but handy place serving great Indian cuisine. Locals in the know travel to eat here (£10 dinners, daily 12:00–14:30 & 18:00–23:30, 21 Bute Street, tel. 020/7589-7311). The narrow entryway is currently not accessible for wheelchair users, but there is a plan underway to make the place bigger and fully accessible. The staff is attentive and warm.

La Brasserie (**AE, AI,** Level 2—Moderately accessible, one 2" entry step) fills a big, plain room painted "nicotine yellow," with ceiling fans, a

Parisian ambience, and good, traditional French cooking at reasonable prices (salads and veggie plates for £10, 2-course menus for £15 and £18, nightly until 23:00, 272 Brompton Road, tel. 020/7581-3089). Wheelchair users have been welcome here for years.

PJ's Bar and Grill (AE+A, AI, Level 2—Moderately accessible, staff will assist with one 6" entry step) is lively with the yuppie Chelsea crowd for a good reason. Traditional "New York Brasserie"-style, yet trendy, it has dressy tables surrounding a centerpiece bar. It serves pricey, cosmopolitan cuisine from a menu that changes with the seasons (£20 meals, nightly until 24:00, 52 Fulham Road, at intersection with Sydney Street, tel. 020/7581-0025). They have traditionally entertained patients from a nearby hospital who use wheelchairs.

Between St. Paul's and the Tower of London
The **Counting House (AE, AI, AL, AT, ♥,** Level 1—Fully accessible), formerly an elegant old bank, offers great £7 meals, nice homemade meat pies, fish, and fresh vegetables (Mon–Fri 12:00–20:00, closed Sat–Sun, gets really busy with the buttoned-down 9-to-5 crowd after 12:15, near Mansion House in the City, 50 Cornhill, tel. 020/7283-7123).

TRANSPORTATION CONNECTIONS

Heathrow Airport
This airport is the world's fourth busiest. Think about it: 60 million passengers a year on 425,000 flights from 200 destinations riding 90 airlines...some kind of global maypole dance. While many complain about Heathrow, we think it's a great airport. It's user-friendly. Read signs, ask questions. For Heathrow's airport, flight, and transfers information, call the switchboard at 0870-000-0123 (www.baa.co.uk). It has four terminals: T-1 (mostly domestic flights, with some European), T-2 (mainly European flights), T-3 (mostly flights from the United States), and T-4 (British Airways transatlantic flights and BA flights to Paris, Amsterdam, and Athens). Taxis know which terminal you'll need.

Each terminal has an airport information desk, car-rental agencies, exchange bureaus, ATMs, a pharmacy, a **VAT refund desk** (T-4 VAT info tel. 020/8910-3682; you must present the VAT claim form from the retailer here to get your 15 percent tax rebate on items purchased in

Britain, see page 12 for details), and a £4/day **baggage-check desk** (T-1 and T-2 desks open daily 6:00–23:00; T-3 desk opens at 5:15 and T-4 at 5:30). Heathrow's **Internet Exchange** provides access 24 hours a day (T-3). There are **post offices** in T-2 and T-4. Each terminal has cheap **eateries** (such as the cheery Food Village self-service cafeteria in T-3). The **American Express** desk, in the Tube station at Terminal 4 (daily 7:00–19:00), has rates similar to the exchange bureaus upstairs, but doesn't charge a commission (typically 1.5 percent) for cashing any type of traveler's check.

Though Heathrow also has a TI, it's not worth the long trek—make a beeline for downtown London and instead visit the Britain and London Visitors Centre at 1 Lower Regent Street (airport TI open daily 8:30–18:00, a quarter-mile from Terminal 3 in the Tube station, follow signs to *Underground;* bypass the queue for transit info to reach the window for London questions).

If you're taking the Tube into London, buy a one-day Travel Card pass to cover the ride (see below).

Transportation to London from Heathrow Airport

By Taxi: This is the simplest door-to-door option for wheelchair users and other travelers with limited mobility (see "Getting around London," page 60). Taxis from the airport cost about £45. For four people traveling together, this can be a deal. Hotels can often line up a cab back to the airport for about £30. For the cheapest taxi to the airport, don't order one from your hotel. Simply flag down a few and ask them for their best "off-meter" rate. Another good option is **Hotelink,** a door-to-door airport shuttle (**AE, AI,** Level 1—Fully accessible; Heathrow-£15 per person, Gatwick-£22 per person, book the day before departure, buy online and save £1-2, tel. 01293/532-244, www.hotelink.co.uk, reservations@hotelink.co.uk).

By Heathrow Express Train: This slick train service (**AE, AI, AT,** Level 1—Fully accessible) zips you between Heathrow Airport and London's Paddington Station. These trains are wheelchair-accessible and equipped with adapted toilets. You will arrive at Paddington Station on tracks 6-8 (accessible toilet near track 1), and the Express Service Agents are available to assist you. At Paddington, you're close to the city center (handy for an accessible taxi ride) and in the thick of the Tube system (though unfortunately, Paddington's Tube station is not accessible). It's only 15 minutes to downtown from Terminals 1, 2, and 3 and 20 minutes from Terminal 4 (at the airport, you can use the Express as a free transfer between terminals). Buy your ticket to London before you board or pay a £2 surcharge to buy it on the train (£13, but ask about discount promos at Heathrow ticket desk, kids under 16 ride half-price, under 5 ride free, covered by Britrail pass, 4/hr, daily 5:10–23:30, tel. 0845-600-1515, www.heathrowexpress.co.uk). A "Go Further" ticket (£14.60) includes one Tube ride from Paddington to get you to your hotel (valid only on same day and in Zone 1, saves time, but remember that Paddington Tube station is not accessible). For one person on a budget, combining the Heathrow Express with a taxi ride (between your hotel and Paddington) is nearly as fast and half the cost of taking a cab directly to (or from) the airport. The queue for taxis at Paddington Station is located through the *Way Out* exit near track 1.

By Tube (Subway): For £3.70, the Tube takes you the 14 miles to downtown London in 50 minutes (6/hr; depending on your destination, may require a change). Even better, buy a £5 one-day Travel Card that covers your trip into London and all your Tube travel for the day (starting at 9:30). Buy it at the ticket window at the Tube. The Tube stops at all terminals. For information on the Tube, see "Getting around London," page 60. While the Tube stations at the airport are fully accessible, most other stations on that line (Piccadilly) are not (though you can transfer to the accessible Jubilee line at the Green Park stop). You'll find the Accessible Tube Map, showing which stops are accessible, at the front of this book.

By Airport Bus: The Airbus, running between the airport and London's King's Cross station, serves the Notting Hill and Bayswater neighborhoods (manual wheelchairs only: **AI, AE,** Level 1—Fully accessible; £10 one-way, £15 round-trip, 2/hr, 60 min, runs 5:00–21:15, departs from each terminal, buy ticket from driver, tel. 08705-757-747). Buses are equipped with a lift, but only for manual wheelchairs—motorized chairs are too heavy. If you're hauling baggage and choosing between the Tube and Airbus, the Airbus is better (assuming it serves your hotel neighborhood) because there are no connections underground. Ask the driver to remind you when to get off. For people heading to the airport, exact pickup times are clearly posted at each bus stop.

Flying into London's Gatwick Airport

More and more flights, especially charters, land at the fully accessible Gatwick Airport, halfway between London and the southern coast (recorded airport info tel. 0870-000-2468). Wheelchair users go to the head of the line at customs. Express trains—clearly the best and most accessible way into London from here—shuttle conveniently between Gatwick and London's Victoria Station (see below for accessibility information on Victoria Station; £11 one-way, £21.50 round-trip, children under 5 free, 4/hr during day, 1-2/hr at night, 30 min, runs 24 hrs daily, can purchase tickets on train at no extra charge, tel. 0845-850-1530, www.gatwickexpress.co.uk). You can save a few pounds by taking South Central rail line's slower and less-frequent shuttle between Victoria Station and Gatwick (Level 3—Minimally accessible—not good for wheelchair users, but slow walkers can use the South Central in a pinch; £8.20, 3/hr, 1/hr 0:00–04:00, 45 min, tel. 08457-484-950, www.southcentraltrains.co.uk).

Victoria Station (**AE, AI, AL, AT,** Level 2—Moderately accessible) has an accessible lift, accessible snack shops, accessible toilet and showers, and a drop-in Medi Centre doctor's office. At the station, follow signs to the taxi queue and catch a taxi to your hotel. Victoria Station's Tube station is mostly suitable for wheelchair users, but not fully adapted.

London's Other Airports

Both of London's other two major airports are fully accessible: **Stansted** (tel. 0870-0000-303, www.baa.co.uk/main/airports/stansted) and **Luton** (tel. 01582/405-100, www.london-luton.com). Taking a taxi is the easiest way to get into the city from either airport.

Discounted Flights from London

Although bmi has been around the longest, the others generally offer cheaper flights.

With **bmi (British Midland Airways),** you can fly inexpensively to destinations in the U.K. and beyond (fares start around £30 one-way to Edinburgh, Paris, Brussels, or Amsterdam; or around £50 one-way to Dublin; prices can be higher, but there can also be much cheaper Internet specials—check online). For the latest, call British tel. 0870-607-0555 or U.S. tel. 800/788-0555 (check www.flybmi.com and their subsidiary, bmi baby, at www.bmibaby.com). Book in advance. Although you can book right up until the flight departs, the cheap seats will have sold out long before, leaving the most expensive seats for latecomers.

With no frills and cheap fares, **easyJet** flies mostly from Luton and Gatwick. Prices are based on demand, so the least popular routes make for the cheapest fares, especially if you book early (tel. 0870-600-0000, www.easyjet.com).

Ryanair is a creative Irish airline that prides itself on offering the lowest fares. It flies from London (mostly Stansted airport) to often obscure airports in Dublin, Glasgow, Frankfurt, Stockholm, Oslo, Venice, Turin, and many others. Sample fares: London–Dublin—£78 round-trip (sometimes as low as £25), London–Frankfurt—£67 round-trip (Irish tel. 01/609-7881, British tel. 0871-246-0000, www.ryanair .com). Because they offer promotional deals any time of year, it's not essential that you book long in advance to get the best deals.

Virgin Express is a British-owned company with good rates (book by phone and pick up ticket at airport an hour before your flight, tel. 020/7744-0004, www.virgin-express.com). Virgin Express flies from London Heathrow and Brussels. From its hub in Brussels, you can connect cheaply to Barcelona, Madrid, Nice, Málaga, Copenhagen, Rome, or Milan (round-trip from Brussels to Rome for as little as £105). Their prices stay the same whether or not you book in advance.

Crossing the Channel by Eurostar Train

The fastest, most convenient, and most accessible way to get from Big Ben to the Eiffel Tower is by rail. In London, advertisements claim "more businessmen travel from London to Paris on the Eurostar than on all airlines combined."

Eurostar is the speedy passenger train that zips you (and up to 800 others in 18 sleek cars) from downtown London to downtown Paris (12–15/day, last departure 19:23, 2.5 hrs) or Brussels (8/day, 2.5 hrs) faster and easier than flying. The train goes 80 mph in England and

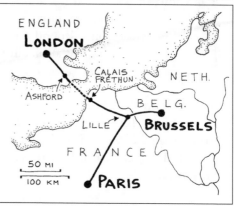

Eurostar Train

STANDARD EUROSTAR FARES

I've listed only standard (second-class) prices between London and Paris or Brussels. Standard class is comfortable, making first class an unnecessary luxury. Compare one-way fares with cheap round-trip fares (especially the Leisure RT Same Day; you can forget to return).

Wheelchair users and their companions ride in accessible first class for reasonable fares ($54 apiece for wheelchair user and companion); unused tickets are 100 percent refundable or exchangeable up to 60 days after the departure date.

Standard Class	Major Restrictions	One-Way	Round-Trip
Full Fare	None (fully refundable even after departure date).	$223	$446
Leisure Flexi	One exchange in Europe before departure; 25 percent refund up to three days before departure. Round-trip discount based on seat availability.	$195	$210/ $300/ $390
Leisure	No refund or exchange.	$90	$180
Leisure RT	No refund or exchange. Round-trip travel and minimum one-night stay required.	N/A	$150
Leisure RT Midweek	No refund or exchange. Round-trip travel and minimum one-night stay required. Travel Mon–Thu only. Round-trip discount based on seat availability.	N/A	$90/ $120

190 mph on the continent. The actual tunnel crossing is a 20-minute, black, silent, 100-mile-per-hour non-event. Your ears won't even pop. You can go direct to Disneyland Paris (1/day, more frequent with transfer at Lille) or change at Lille to catch a TGV to Paris' Charles de Gaulle Airport.

The following fares are accurate as of early 2004 and subject to change. Note that the ticket names, restrictions, and prices listed here are for tickets purchased in the U.S. If you buy your ticket in Europe, your options are similar, though rarely identical. Sometimes it's a better deal to buy your ticket in Britain instead of the United States—or vice-versa. Compare. For European fares, go to www.eurostar.com and input your travel date and time to see the available rates and restrictions. For U.S. fares (including first-class prices), visit www.ricksteves.com/eurostar. A Premier Train Fee of $7 per order applies.

Standard Class	Major Restrictions	One-Way	Round-Trip
Leisure RT Same Day	No refund or exchange. Travel round-trip within one day (ideal for Paris day trip from London).	N/A	$94
Passholder	No refund. One exchange in Europe before departure. Trip must occur during the validity period of a railpass including Britain, France, or Belgium.	$75	$150
Senior	Age 60-plus. No refund. One exchange in Europe before departure.	$90	$180
Youth Peak	Age under 26. No refund, one exchange.	$75	$150
Youth Off-Peak	Age under 26. No refund, one exchange.	$45	$90
Child	Age 4–11. No refund, one exchange.	$38	$76

Access

All Eurostar terminals (**AE, AI, AL, AT,** Level 1—Fully accessible) feature elevators with controls at wheelchair height, ramps with handrails and landings, ramps and wheelchairs for boarding and disembarking (upon request), accessible toilets, and wheelchair-accessible check-in booths.

Eurostar trains themselves are also fully accessible to wheelchair users (**AE, AI, AT,** Level 1). The wheelchair user and a companion pay a set fare of $54 each (one-way), and ride in the accessible first-class cabin (cars 9 and 10 have spaces reserved for wheelchair users and their companions, and there is an adapted toilet between these two cars). To take seats in second class, you must be able to walk a minimum of 200 meters. Wheelchair users should arrive 45 minutes before departure so that the staff can assist with ramps and alert appropriate personnel. Eurostar provides a free assistance service for wheelchair users (arrange when you book ticket, must book at least 48 hrs in advance: call French tel. 08 92 35 35 39, British toll-free tel. 0870-518-6186, or British tel. 1233/617-575).

Fares

Channel fares (essentially the same to Paris or Brussels) are reasonable but complicated. Prices vary depending on when you travel; whether you can live with restrictions; and whether you're eligible for any discounts (youth, seniors, and railpass holders all qualify). Rates are lower for round-trip and off-peak (midday, midweek, low-season, and low-interest) travel.

Note that **wheelchair users** and their companions pay the discounted fare of $54, and ride in accessible first class (see "Access," above).

As with airfares, the most expensive and flexible option is a **full-fare ticket** with no restrictions on refunds (even refundable after the departure date; $223 one-way in second class, $312 in first). A first-class ticket comes with a meal (a dinner departure nets you more grub than breakfast)—but it's not worth the extra expense.

Also like the airlines, **cheaper tickets** come with more restrictions—and are limited in number (so they sell out more quickly). Non-full-fare tickets have severe restrictions on refunds (best-case scenario: you'll get 25 percent back, but with many you'll get nothing). But several do allow you to change the specifics of your trip once before departure. For details, see "Standard Eurostar Fares," page 142.

Those traveling with a railpass for Britain, France, or Belgium should look first at the **passholder fare,** an especially good value for one-way Eurostar trips. In Britain, passholder tickets can be issued only at the Eurostar office in Waterloo Station or the American Express office in Victoria Station—not at any other stations. You can also order them by phone, then pick them up at Waterloo Station.

Refund and exchange restrictions are serious, so don't reserve until you're sure of your plans. If you are confident of the time and date of your crossing, order ahead from the U.S. Only the most expensive ticket (full fare) is fully refundable, so if you want to have more flexibility, hold off—keeping in mind that the longer you wait, the more likely the cheapest tickets will be sold out.

You can check and book fares by phone or online in the United States (order online at www.ricksteves.com/eurostar; order by phone at U.S. tel. 800/EUROSTAR) or in Britain (British tel. 08705-186-186, www.eurostar.com). These are different companies, often with slightly different prices and discount deals on similar tickets (see above)—if you order from the United States, check out both. (If you buy from a U.S. company, you'll pay for ticket delivery in the United States; if you book with the British company, you'll pick up your ticket at Waterloo Station.) In Europe, you can get your Eurostar ticket at any major train station in any country or at any travel agency that handles train tickets (expect a booking fee).

Note that Britain's time zone is one hour earlier than the Continent's. Times listed on tickets are local times.

WESTMINSTER ROLL OR STROLL

From Big Ben to Trafalgar Square

London is the L.A., D.C., and N.Y. of Britain. This tour starts with London's "star" attraction (Big Ben), continues to its "Capitol," passes its "White House," and ends at its "Times Square"—Trafalgar Square. Most of it follows the historic Whitehall boulevard.

Under London's modern traffic and big-city bustle lie 2,000 fascinating years of history. This eight-stop tour gives you a good overview as well as a practical orientation to the city. For information on the sights listed in this tour, see "Sights—From Westminster Abbey to Trafalgar Square," on page 74 of the London chapter.

Start halfway across Westminster Bridge (Tube: Westminster; take the Westminster Pier exit). The bridge itself is wheelchair-accessible, and all of the sidewalks for the remainder of the walk have curb cutouts.

1. On Westminster Bridge

Views of Big Ben and the Parliament

• *First look south (upstream), toward the Parliament.*

Ding dong ding dong. Dong ding ding dong. Yes, indeed, you are in London. **Big Ben** is actually "not the clock, not the tower, but the bell that tolls the hour." However, since the 13-ton bell is not visible,

ACCESSIBILITY CODE CHART

CODE	MEANING
AE	Accessible Entryway
AE+A	Accessible Entry with Assistance
AI	Accessible Interior
AI+A	Accessible Interior with Assistance
AT	Accessible Toilet
AT+A	Accessible Toilet with Assistance
AL	Accessible Lift (elevator)
AL+A	Accessible Lift with Assistance

For the full chart and a more detailed explanation of codes, please see page 2 of the Introduction.

everyone just calls the whole works Big Ben. Ben (named for a fat bureaucrat) is scarcely older than my great-grandmother, but it has quickly become the city's symbol. The tower is 320 feet high, and the clock faces are 23 feet across. The 13-foot-long minute hand sweeps the length of your body every five minutes.

Big Ben is the north tower of a long building, the **Houses of Parliament (AE+A , AI, AT, AL+A,** Level 2—Moderately accessible, see page 76), stretching along the Thames. Britain is ruled from this building, which for five centuries was the home of kings and queens. Then, as democracy was foisted on tyrants, a parliament of nobles was allowed to meet in some of the rooms. Soon, commoners were elected to office, the neighborhood was shot, and the royalty moved to Buckingham Palace. The current building, though it looks medieval with its prickly Flamboyant spires, was built in the 1800s after a fire gutted old Westminster Palace. Its horizontal symmetry is an impressive complement to Big Ben's vertical.

Today, the **House of Commons,** which is more powerful than the queen and prime minister combined, meets in the north half of the building. The rubber-stamp **House of Lords** grumbles and snoozes in the south end of this 1,000-room complex and provides a tempering

Westminster Roll or Stroll

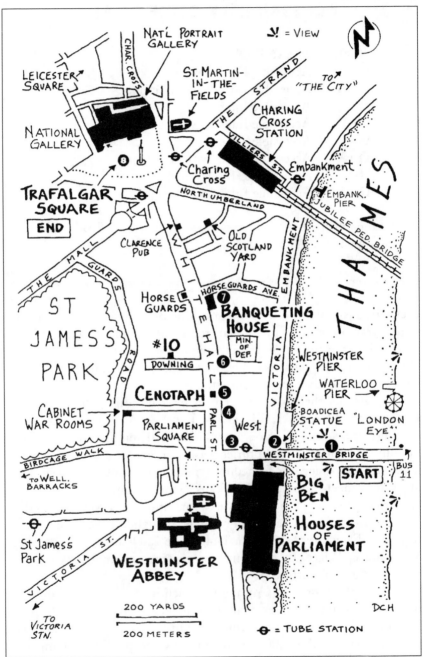

= VIEW

NAT'L PORTRAIT GALLERY

LEICESTER SQUARE

CHAR. CROSS

ST. MARTIN-IN-THE-FIELDS

THE STRAND

TO "THE CITY"

CHARING CROSS STATION

NATIONAL GALLERY

VILLIERS ST.

Embankment

Charing Cross

EMBANK. PIER

TRAFALGAR SQUARE

NORTHUMBERLAND

EMBANKMENT

JUBILEE PED. BRIDGE

END

CLARENCE PUB

OLD SCOTLAND YARD

THAMES

THE MALL

GUARDS

ST JAMES'S PARK

HORSE GUARDS

HORSE GUARDS AVE.

BANQUETING HOUSE

MIN. OF DEF.

WESTMINSTER PIER

WATERLOO PIER

#10 DOWNING

CENOTAPH

CABINET WAR ROOMS

PARLIAMENT SQUARE

West.

BOADICEA STATUE

"LONDON EYE"

BIRDCAGE WALK

VICTORIA

THE MALL ROAD

PARL. ST.

WESTMINSTER BRIDGE

START

BUS 11

TO WELL. BARRACKS

BIG BEN

St James's Park

VICTORIA ST.

HOUSES OF PARLIAMENT

WESTMINSTER ABBEY

TO VICTORIA STN.

200 YARDS

200 METERS

= TUBE STATION

DCH

effect on extreme governmental changes. The two houses are very much separate: Notice the riverside tea terraces with the color-coded awnings—royal red for lords, common green for commoners. If a flag is flying from the Victoria Tower, at the far south end of the building, Parliament is in session.

Views of the London Eye Ferris Wheel, The City, and the Thames
• *Now look north (downstream).*

Built in 2000 to celebrate the millennium, the London Eye—known to some as "the London Eyesore"—stands 443 feet tall and slowly spins 32 capsules, each filled with 25 visitors, up to London's best viewpoint (up to 25 miles on a rare clear day; for more on the London Eye, see page 99). Aside from Big Ben, Parliament, St. Paul's Cathedral, and the wheel itself, London's skyline is not overwhelming; it's a city that wows from within.

Next to the wheel sprawls the huge former **County Hall building,** now a hotel and tourist complex. Shut down a decade ago, this bastion of London liberals still seems to snarl across the river at the home of the national government.

The London Eye marks the start of the accessible **Jubilee Promenade,** a pleasant half-mile riverside path along the South Bank of the Thames, through London's vibrant, gentrified arts and cultural zone. Along the way, you have views across the river of St. Paul's stately dome and the City.

London's history is tied to the **Thames,** the 210-mile river highway linking the interior of England with the North Sea. The city got its start in Roman times as a trade center along this watery highway. As recently as a century ago, large ships made their way upstream to the city center to unload. Today, the major port is 25 miles downstream.

Look for the piers on the Thames. A 50-minute round-trip **cruise** (**AE, AI,** Level 1—Fully accessible, see page 70) geared for tourists departs from the pier near the base of the Ferris wheel. On the other side of the river, at **Westminster Pier,** boats leave for the Tower of London, Greenwich, and Kew Gardens (see page 73).

Lining the river, beneath the lamp posts, are little green copper **lions' heads** with rings for tying up boats. Before the construction of the Thames Barrier in 1982 (the world's largest movable flood barrier, downstream near Greenwich), high tides from the nearby North Sea made floods a recurring London problem. The police kept an eye on these lions: "When the lions drink, the city's at risk."

Until 1750, only London Bridge crossed the Thames. Then a bridge was built here. Early in the morning of September 3, 1803, William Wordsworth stood where you are and described what he saw:

> *This city now doth like a garment wear*
> *The beauty of the morning; silent, bare,*
> *Ships, towers, domes, theaters, and temples lie*
> *Open unto the fields, and to the sky;*
> *All bright and glittering in the smokeless air.*

• *Go to Big Ben's side of the river. Near Westminster Pier is a big statue of a lady on a chariot (nicknamed "the first woman driver"...no reins).*

2. Boadicea, Queen of the Iceni

Riding in her two-horse chariot, daughters by her side, this Celtic Xena leads her people against Roman invaders. Julius Caesar had been the first Roman to cross the Channel, but even he was weirded out by the island's strange inhabitants, who worshiped trees, sacrificed virgins, and went to war painted blue. Later, Romans subdued and civilized them, building roads and making this spot on the Thames—"Londinium"—into a major urban center.

But Boadicea refused to be Romanized. In A.D. 60, after Roman soldiers raped her daughters, she rallied her people and "liberated" London, massacring its 70,000 Romanized citizens. However, the brief revolt was snuffed out, and she and her family took poison rather than surrender.

• *Continue past Big Ben, one block inland to the busy intersection of Parliament Square.*

3. Parliament Square

To your left is the orange-hued **Parliament (AE+A, AI, AT, AL+A,** Level 2— Moderately accessible, see page 76). If Parliament is in session, the entrance is lined with tourists and staked out by camera crews interviewing Members of Parliament (M.P.s). Kittycorner across the Square, the two white towers of **Westminster Abbey (AE, AI,** Level 2— Moderately accessible, loaner wheelchairs, see page 75) rise above the trees. And broad Whitehall (here called Parliament Street) stretches to your right up to Trafalgar Square.

This is the heart of what was once a suburb of London—the medieval City of Westminster. Like Buda and Pest, London is two cities that grew into one. The City of London, centered near St. Paul's Cathedral and the Tower of London, was the place to live. But King Edward the Confessor decided to build a church (minster) and monastery (abbey) here, west of the city walls—hence Westminster. And to oversee its construction, he moved his court here and built a palace. The palace gradually evolved into a meeting place for debating public policy, which is why to this day the Houses of Parliament are known to the Brits as the "Palace of Westminster."

Across from Parliament, the cute little church with the blue sundials, snuggling under the Abbey "like a baby lamb under a ewe," is **St. Margaret's Church.** Since 1480, this has been *the* place for politicians' weddings—such as Churchill's.

Parliament Square, the small park between Westminster Abbey and Big Ben, is filled with statues of famous Brits. The statue of **Winston Churchill,** the man who saved Britain from Hitler, shows him in the military overcoat he wore as he limped victoriously onto the beaches of Normandy after D-Day. According to tour guides, the statue has a current of electricity running through it to honor Churchill's wish that if a statue were made of him, his head shouldn't be soiled by pigeons.

In 1868, the world's first traffic light was installed on the corner here where Whitehall now spills

double-decker buses into the square. And speaking of lights, the little yellow lantern atop the concrete post on the street corner closest to Parliament says *Taxi*. When an M.P. needs a taxi, this blinks to hail one.

• *Consider touring Westminster Abbey. Otherwise, turn right (north), go away from the Houses of Parliament and the abbey, and continue up Parliament Street, which becomes Whitehall.*

4. Whitehall

Today, Whitehall is choked with traffic, but imagine the effect this broad street must have had on out-of-towners a century ago. In your horse-drawn carriage, you'd clop along a tree-lined boulevard past well-dressed lords and ladies, dodging street urchins. Gazing left, then right, you'd try to take it all in, your eyes dazzled by the bone-white walls of this man-made marble canyon.

Whitehall is now the most important street in Britain, lined with the ministries of finance, treasury, and so on. You may see limos and camera crews as an important dignitary enters or exits. Notice the security measures. Iron grates seal off the concrete ditches between the buildings and sidewalks for protection against explosives. London was terrorist-conscious long before September 2001. As the N.Y., L.A., and D.C. of Britain, London is also seen as the "Babylon" of a colonial empire whose former colonies sometimes resent its lingering control.

The black, ornamental arrowheads topping the iron fences were once colorfully painted. In 1861, Queen Victoria ordered them all painted black when her beloved Prince Albert ("the only one who called her Vickie") died. Possibly the world's most determined mourner, Victoria wore black for the standard two years of mourning—and tacked on 38 more.

• *Continue toward the tall, square, concrete monument in the middle of the road. On your right is a colorful pub, the Red Lion. Across the street, a 700-foot detour down King Charles Street leads to the* **Cabinet War Rooms,** *the underground bunker of 21 rooms that was the nerve center of Britain's campaign against Hitler (AE, AI, AT, AL, ♥, Level 1—Fully accessible, loaner wheelchairs, see page 77).*

5. Cenotaph

This big white stone monument (in the middle of the boulevard) honors those who died in the two events that most shaped modern Britain—World Wars I and II. The monumental devastation of these wars helped turn a colonial superpower into a cultural colony of an American superpower.

The actual cenotaph is the slab that sits atop the pillar—a tomb. You'll notice no religious symbols on this memorial. The dead honored here came from many creeds and all corners of Britain's empire. It looks lost in noisy traffic, but on each Remembrance Sunday (closest to November 11), Whitehall is closed off to traffic, the royal family fills the balcony overhead in the foreign ministry, and a memorial service is held around the cenotaph.

It's hard for an American to understand the impact of the Great War (WWI) on Europe. It's said that if all the WWI dead from the British Empire were to march four abreast past the cenotaph, the sad parade would last for seven days.

Eternally pondering the cenotaph is an equestrian statue up the street. Earl Haig, commander-in-chief of the British Army from 1916 to 1918, was responsible for ordering so many brave and not-so-brave British boys out of the trenches and onto the killing fields of World War I.

• *Just past the cenotaph, on the other (west) side of Whitehall, is an iron security gate guarding the entrance to Downing Street.*

6. #10 Downing Street and the Ministry of Defense

Britain's version of the White House is where the current prime minister—Tony Blair—and his family live, at #10 (in black-brick building 300 feet down blocked-off street, on the right). It looks modest, but the entryway does open up into fairly impressive digs. Blair is a young, Clinton-esque politician who prefers persuasive charm to rigid dogma, though he didn't quite charm the public into accepting his participation in America's controversial war on Iraq. There's not much to see here unless a VIP happens to drive up. Then the bobbies (police officers) snap to and check credentials, the gates open, the traffic barrier midway down the street drops into its bat cave, the car drives in, and...the bobbies go back to mugging for the tourists.

The huge building across Whitehall from Downing Street is the

Ministry of Defense (MOD). This bleak place looks like a Ministry of Defense should. In front are statues of illustrious defenders of Britain. "Monty" is **Field Marshal Bernard Montgomery** of WWII. Monty beat the Nazis in North Africa (defeating "the Desert Fox," Erwin Rommel, at El Alamein) and gave the Allies a jumping-off point to retake Europe. Along with Churchill, Monty breathed confidence back into a demoralized British Army, persuading them they could ultimately beat Hitler.

Nearby, the statue of **Walter Raleigh** marks the spot where he was presented in glory to Queen Elizabeth after returning from America. Nothing marks the spot—a few hundred yards back toward Big Ben—where he was beheaded for plotting against James I, her successor, a few years later.

You may be enjoying the shade of London's **plane trees.** They do well in polluted London, thanks to roots that work well in clay, waxy leaves that self-clean in the rain, and bark that sheds and regenerates so pollution doesn't get into their vascular systems.

• *At the equestrian statue, you'll be flanked by the Welsh and Scottish government offices. At the corner (same side as the MOD), you'll find the Banqueting House.*

7. Banqueting House

The Banqueting House (**AE+A,** Level 4—Not accessible, see page 77) is just about all that remains of what was once the biggest palace in Europe—Whitehall Palace, stretching from Trafalgar Square to Big Ben. Henry VIII started it when he moved out of the Palace of Westminster (now the Parliament) and into the residence of the archbishop of York. Queen Elizabeth I and other monarchs added on as England's worldwide prestige grew. Finally, in 1698, a roaring fire destroyed everything at Whitehall except the name and the Banqueting House.

The kings held their parties and feasts in the Banqueting House's grand ballroom on the first floor. At 112 feet wide by 56 feet tall and 56 feet deep, the Banqueting House is a perfect double cube. Today, the exterior of Greek-style columns and pediments looks rather ho-hum,

much like every other white, marble, neoclassical building in London. But in 1620, it was the first, a highly influential building by architect Inigo Jones that sparked London's distinct neoclassical look.

On January 27, 1649, a man dressed in black appeared at one of the Banqueting House's first-floor windows and looked out at a huge crowd that surrounded the building. He stepped out the window and onto a wooden platform. It was King Charles I. He gave a short speech to the crowd, framed by the magnificent backdrop of the Banqueting House. His final word was "Remember." Then he knelt and laid his neck on a block as another man in black approached. It was the executioner—who cut off the King's head.

Plop—the concept of divine monarchy in Britain was decapitated. But there would still be kings after Cromwell. In fact, the royalty was soon restored, and Charles' son, Charles II, got his revenge here in the Banqueting Hall...by living well. His elaborate parties under the chandeliers of the Banqueting House celebrated the Restoration of the monarchy. But from then on, every king knew that he ruled by the grace of Parliament.

Charles I is remembered today with a statue at one end of Whitehall (in Trafalgar Square at the base of the tall column), while his killer, Oliver Cromwell, is given equal time with a statue at the other end (at the Houses of Parliament).

• *Cross the street for a close look at the* **Horse Guards,** *dressed in Charge-of-the-Light-Brigade cavalry uniforms and swords. Until the Ministry of Defense was created, the Horse Guards was the headquarters of the British Army. It's still the home of the queen's private guard. (Changing of the Guard Mon–Sat 11:00, 10:00 on Sun, dismounting ceremony daily at 16:00.)*

Continue up Whitehall, dipping into the guarded entry court of the next big building (probably covered with scaffolding) that has the too-long Ionic columns. This holds the offices of the **Old Admiralty,** *headquarters of the British Navy. Ponder*

Trafalgar Square

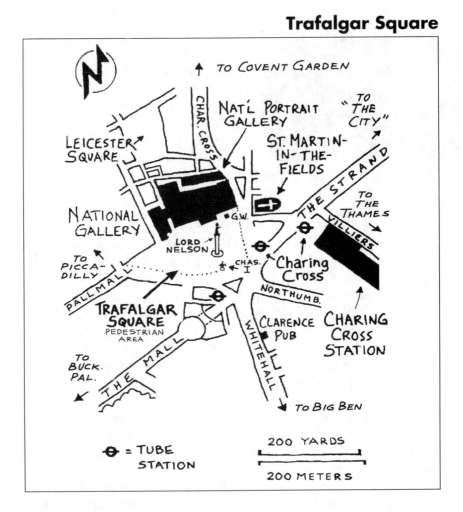

the scheming that must have gone on behind these walls as the British Navy built the greatest empire the world has ever seen. Across the street, behind the old Clarence Pub (**AE+A, AI,** Level 2— Moderately accessible, no accessible toilet; serves lunch only, no dinner), stood the original **Scotland Yard,** headquarters of London's crack police force in the days of Sherlock Holmes. Finally, Whitehall opens up into the grand, noisy, traffic-filled...

8. Trafalgar Square

London's answer to Times Square bustles around the monumental column where Admiral Horatio Nelson stands 170 feet tall in the crow's nest. Nelson saved England at a time as dark as World War II. In 1805, Napoleon (the Mussolini of his day) was poised on the other side of the Channel, threatening to invade England. Meanwhile, more than 900 miles away, the one-armed, one-eyed, and one-minded Lord Nelson attacked the French fleet off the coast of Spain at Trafalgar. The French were routed, Britannia ruled the waves, and the once-invincible French army was slowly worn down, then defeated at Waterloo. Nelson, while victorious, was shot by a sniper in the battle. He died, gasping, "Thank God, I have done my duty."

At the top of Trafalgar Square sits the domed National Gallery (**AE, AI, AL, AT,** Level 1—Fully accessible, loaner wheelchairs, see page 78), and to the right, the steeple of St. Martin-in-the-Fields, built in 1722, inspiring the style of many town churches in New England (**AE+A, AI+A, AL+A, ♥,** Level 2—Moderately accessible; for concert information, see page 82). In between is a small statue of America's George Washington, looking veddy much the English gentleman that he was.

Surrounding Nelson's column are bronze reliefs cast from melted-

down enemy cannons, and four huggable lions, dying to have their photo taken with you. The artist had never seen a lion in person, so he used his dog as a model, giving them doggie paws. In front of the column, Charles I sits on horseback (the oldest such statue in town). Directly behind Charles is a pavement stone marking the center of London.

Trafalgar Square is indeed the center of modern London, connecting Westminster, The City, and the West End. Spin clockwise 360 degrees and survey the city:

To the south (down Whitehall) is the center of government, Westminster. Looking southwest, down the broad boulevard called The Mall, you see Buckingham Palace in the distance. (Down Pall Mall is St. James' Palace, where Prince Charles lives when in London.) A few blocks northwest of Trafalgar Square is Piccadilly Circus. Directly north (2 blocks behind the National Gallery) sits Leicester Square, the jumping-off point for Soho, Covent Garden, and the West End theater district.

The boulevard called the Strand takes you past Charing Cross Station, then eastward to the City, the original walled town of London and today's financial center. In medieval times, when people from the City met with the Westminster government, it was here. And finally, Northumberland Avenue leads southeast to the Golden Jubilee pedestrian bridge (fully accessible) over the Thames.

Soak it in. You're smack-dab in the center of London, a thriving city atop thousands of years of history.

FRANCE

- France is 210,000 square miles (like Texas)
- Population is 60 million (about 276 per square mile)
- 1 euro (€) = about $1.15

France is Europe's most diverse, tasty, and, in many ways, exciting country to explore. It's a multifaceted cultural fondue.

France is nearly as big as Texas, with 60 million people and more than 500 different cheeses. *Diversité* is a French forte. From its Swiss-like Alps to its *molto Italiano* Riviera, and from the Spanish Pyrenees to *das* German Alsace, you can stay in France, feel like you've sampled much of Europe, and never be more than a quiche's throw from a good *vin rouge*.

The key political issues in France today are high unemployment (about 9 percent), a steadily increasing percentage of ethnic minorities, and the need to compete in a global marketplace. The challenge is to address these issues while maintaining the generous social benefits the French expect from their government. As a result, national policies seem to conflict with each other. For example, France supports the lean economic policies of the European Union, but recently reduced the French workweek to 35 hours—in pursuit of good living.

Imitate the French. Try to buy at least one of your picnics at a colorful open-air market street, like the rue Cler in Paris. Relax at a park while children sail toy boats in a pond. Enjoy the subtle pleasure of people-watching from a sun-dappled café. If you prefer to travel at a slower pace, you'll fit in fine in France. With five weeks' paid time off, the French can't comprehend why anyone would rush through a vacation.

Make an effort to understand French culture and you're more likely to have a richer experience. You've no doubt heard that the French are "mean and cold and refuse to speak English." This out-of-date preconception is left over from the de Gaulle days. The French are as sincere as any other people. Polite and formal, the French respect the fine points of culture and tradition. Recognize sincerity and look for kindness. Give them the benefit of the doubt. Parisians are no more disagreeable than

France

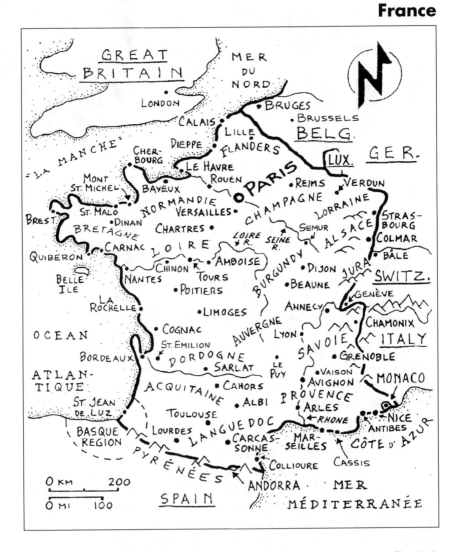

New Yorkers. And, without any doubt, the French speak more English than Americans speak French. Be reasonable in your expectations: Waiters are paid to be efficient, not chatty. And Parisian postal clerks are every bit as speedy, cheery, and multilingual as ours are back home.

Communication difficulties are exaggerated. To hurdle the language barrier, bring a phrase book (look for Rick's) and a good supply of patience. If you learn only five phrases, choose these: *bonjour* (good day), *pardon* (pardon me), *s'il vous plaît* (please), *merci* (thank you), and *au revoir* (good-bye). For more phrases, see the "French Survival Phrases" near the end of this book.

The French are language perfectionists—they take their language (and other languages) seriously. They often speak more English than they let on. This isn't a tourist-baiting tactic, but timidity on their part to speak another language less than fluently. Start any conversation with *"Bonjour, madame/monsieur. Parlez-vous anglais?"* and hope they speak more English than you speak French.

Diners around the world recognize French food as a work of art. The cuisine is sightseeing for your tastebuds. Styles of cooking include *haute cuisine* (classic, elaborately prepared multi-course meals); *cuisine bourgeoise* (the finest-quality home-cooking); *cuisine des provinces* (traditional dishes of specific regions, using the best ingredients); and *nouvelle cuisine* (the pricey "new style" from the 1970s, which breaks from tradition with a focus on small portions and close attention to the texture and color of the ingredients). Each region has its own specialties, and all of the influences come together in Paris.

If you make only one stop in France, make it Paris—the *pièce de résistance*. Paris is quintessential France, deservedly one of the world's most-visited cities.

ACCESSIBILITY IN FRANCE

In France, special consideration is given to travelers with limited mobility. This thoughtfulness is obvious in public spaces and in such adaptations as special-access ramps, lifts, toilets, parking spaces, and telephone booths. However, some tourist attractions are not wheelchair-accessible and some city streets do not feature sufficient curb cuts.

The **French Government Tourist Office** can help you plan your visit (444 Madison Avenue, 16th Floor, New York, NY 10022, tel. 410/286-8310, www.franceguide.com, info@franceguide.com).

You can also check with the **Paris Convention and Visitors Bureau** for advice (127 avenue des Champs-Elysées, 75008 Paris, toll tel. 08 92 68 31 12—€0.33/min, fax 01 49 52 53 00, www.paris-touristoffice.com, info@paris-touristoffice.com).

Transportation

Rail is the most convenient form of travel for disabled travelers in France. Wheelchair compartments are available on all TGV services. Ask for the *Guide du voyageur à mobilité réduite* at train stations. SNCF, France's rail company, runs an accessibility hotline (French only, tel. 08 00 15 47 53). Taxis are obliged to take wheelchair-bound passengers and to help you in and out of their vehicle.

The **Groupement pour l'Insertion des Handicapés Physiques** (**GIHP,** Group for the Inclusion of the Physically Handicapped) runs an accessible transport service in Paris; you'll need to book trips in advance (10 rue Georges de Porto-Riche, tel. 01 43 95 66 36, fax 01 45 40 40 26, gihp.nat@wanadoo.fr). Regional offshoots of this organization also provide transportation services elsewhere in France.

Guidebooks

Pick up a copy of *Paris-Ile-de-France for Everyone,* available at most TIs. It lists accessible sights, hotels, and restaurants in the City of Light.

Before you go: An excellent resource is the guidebook *Access in Paris,* which has detailed information on accessible sights, hotels, and restaurants. The same team wrote *Access in London.* The book can be hard to find in Paris, so get it before you go (Access Project, 39 Bradley Gardens, West Ealing, London W13 8HE, www.accessproject-phsp.org, gordon.couch@virgin.net).

Organizations

The **Association des Paralysés de France** (APF, French Association for the Paralyzed) is an organization of and for people with mobility disabilities. With delegations across France, APF may be able to help find a personal attendant or other resources. Their Web site lists a number of links to other types of disability organizations (17 boulevard Auguste Blanqui, Paris, tel. 01 40 78 69 00, fax 01 45 89 40 57, www.apf.asso.fr, info@apf.asso.fr).

Handitel is also a fine resource for accessibility information (www.socialnet.lu/handitel/).

Comments from Readers

These thoughts on traveling in Paris were submitted by Rick's readers, mainly from his Graffiti Wall Web site (www.ricksteves.com).

"I was very impressed in Paris that every street corner we crossed was wheelchair-accessible. We encountered no unexpected steps and were pleasantly surprised."

"Admission to the Louvre for wheelchair users is free, but its working elevators are few. When we were there, it was possible to see the *Winged Victory* and the *Mona Lisa* (with a lot of pushing), but the elevator didn't go to the *Venus de Milo*. The Louvre is worth visiting, but call first to see if all (or even most) of the elevators are running."

"My 73-year-old mother can not get around well, so I took advantage of the free wheelchairs available at the Louvre and Musée d'Orsay in Paris. All I had to do was leave my passport at the counter—it was returned when I brought the wheelchair back."

PARIS

Paris offers sweeping boulevards, sleepy parks, world-class art galleries, chatty crêpe stands, Napoleon's body, sleek shopping malls, and people-watching from outdoor cafés. Enjoy the Eiffel Tower, cruise the Seine and the avenue des Champs-Elysées, and master the Louvre and Orsay museums. Save some after-dark energy for one of the world's most romantic cities. Many people fall in love with Paris. Some see the essentials and flee, overwhelmed by the huge city. With the proper approach and a good orientation, you'll fall head over heels for Europe's capital city.

ACCESSIBILITY IN PARIS

Paris is more challenging than Belgium or London for people with disabilities. But if you can make a little extra effort and have a healthy sense of humor, you'll find the City of Light is worth it.

Public transportation in Paris can be difficult for wheelchair users. For example, you may need to wait a few extra minutes until a newer, accessible bus comes by. (Consider taking a taxi instead.) Paris' Métro is not accessible, but some RER (suburban subway) lines are. If traveling long distances by rail, you may want to book the Thalys train (first class is wheelchair-accessible).

For hotel and restaurant recommendations, we focus on our two favorite neighborhoods: the rue Cler area (in southwest Paris near the Eiffel Tower) and the Marais area (in northeast Paris near place de la Bastille). In either neighborhood, you'll find a concentration of accessible

ACCESSIBILITY CODES

These codes offer a quick overview of what to expect. If applicable, more specific details about the facility (e.g., exact number and height of steps, special instructions for gaining entry) are explained in each listing.

CODE	MEANING
AE	Accessible Entryway
AE+A	Accessible Entry with Assistance
AI	Accessible Interior
AI+A	Accessible Interior with Assistance
AT	Accessible Toilet
AT+A	Accessible Toilet with Assistance
AL	Accessible Lift (elevator)
AL+A	Accessible Lift with Assistance
AR	Accessible Hotel Room
AR+A	Accessible Hotel Room with Assistance
AB	Accessible Hotel Bathroom
AB+A	Accessible Hotel Bathroom with Assistance
♥	Caring, welcoming attitude regarding accessibility

For more detailed information, please refer to the full Accessibility Codes chart on page 4 of the Introduction. For more information on Accessibility Levels, see page 2.

hotels and restaurants, and some of the best Parisian attractions.

Many of Paris' top sights are fully accessible to wheelchair users (Level 1): the Louvre, the Orsay, Eiffel Tower (up to the second level), Les Invalides (except crypt), Rodin Museum (ground floor only) and garden, Luxembourg Gardens, Montparnasse Tower, Opéra Garnier (entry, but not tours), Grande Arche de La Défense, Victor Hugo House, Pompidou Center, Jewish Art and History Museum, Picasso Museum, and the Palace of Versailles.

Other sights will work for wheelchair users with some assistance (Level 2): Notre-Dame Cathedral interior (not the tower), the lower level of Sainte-Chapelle, Arc de Triomphe (museum level only), and the peaceful park, place des Vosges.

Unfortunately, Paris also has a few sights that are best left to the non-disabled (or the more adventurous slow walkers): Notre-Dame's tower, Paris Archaeological Crypt, Deportation Memorial, Sainte-Chapelle upstairs chapel, Conciergerie, Cluny Musuem, the top level of the Eiffel Tower, the upper level of the Rodin Museum, the top level of the Arc de Triomphe, the *Paris Story* film, Sacré-Cœur, Carnavalet Museum, and Promenade Plantée Park.

ORIENTATION

Paris is split in half by the Seine River, divided into 20 *arrondissements* (proud and independent governmental jurisdictions), and circled by a ring-road freeway (the *périphérique*). You'll find Paris easier to navigate if you know which side of the river you're on, which *arrondissement* you're in, and which subway (Métro) stop you're closest to. If you're north of the river (the top half of any city map), you're on the Right Bank *(rive droite)*. If you're south of it, you're on the Left Bank *(rive gauche)*. Most of your sightseeing will take place within five blocks of the river.

Arrondissements are numbered, starting at Notre-Dame (ground zero) and moving in a clockwise spiral out to the ring road. The last two digits in a Parisian zip code are the *arrondissement* number. The notation for the Métro stop is "Mo." In Parisian jargon, Napoleon's tomb is on *la rive gauche* (the Left Bank) in the *7ème* (7th *arrondissement*), zip code 75007, Mo: Invalides. Paris Métro stops are used as a standard aid in giving directions, even for those not using the Métro. As you're tracking down addresses, these definitions will help: *place* (square), *rue* (road), and *pont* (bridge).

Paris *Arrondissements*

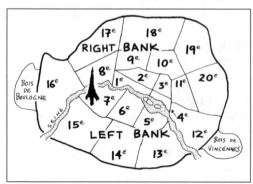

Paris Overview

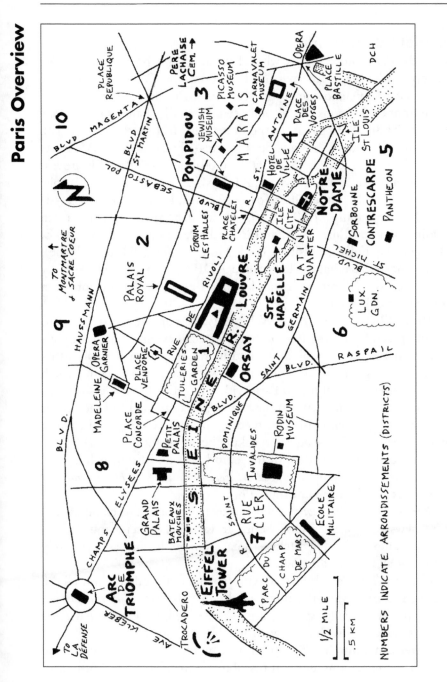

NUMBERS INDICATE ARRONDISSEMENTS (DISTRICTS)

Tourist Information

Avoid the Paris tourist offices, which have long lines, provide short information, and charge for maps. This book, the *Pariscope* magazine (described below), and one of the freebie maps available at any hotel (or in the front of this book) are all you need. Paris TIs share a single phone number: 08 36 68 31 12 (from the States, dial 011 33 8 36 68 31 12). The main TI is at 127 avenue des Champs-Elysées (**AE+A, AI,** Level 2—Moderately accessible; daily 9:00–20:00), but the other TIs are less crowded: at Gare de Lyon (**AE+A, AI,** Level 2—Moderately accessible; daily 8:00–20:00), at the Eiffel Tower (**AE, AI,** Level 1—Fully accessible; May–Sept daily 11:00–18:40, closed Oct–April, in little brown building between Pilier Nord and Pilier Est), and at the Louvre (**AE, AI,** Level 1—Fully accessible; Wed–Mon 10:00–19:00, closed Tue). Both airports have handy TIs, called ADP (**AE, AI,** Level 1—Fully accessible) with long hours and short lines (see "Transportation Connections," below).

Paris' TIs have an official Web site (www.paris-touristoffice.com) offering practical information on hotels, special events, museums, children's activities, fashion, nightlife, and more. Two other Web sites that are entertaining and at times useful are www.bonjourparis.com (which claims to offer a virtual trip to Paris with interactive French lessons, tips on wine and food, and news on the latest Parisian trends) and the similar www.paris-anglo.com (with informative stories on visiting Paris, plus a directory of over 2,500 English-speaking businesses).

For a complete schedule of museum hours and English-language museum tours, pick up the free *Musées, Monuments Historiques, et Expositions* booklet from any museum.

Pariscope: The *Pariscope* weekly magazine (or one of its clones, €0.50 at any newsstand) lists museum hours, art exhibits, concerts, music festivals, plays, movies, and nightclubs. Smart tour guides and sightseers rely on this for all the latest listings.

Maps: While Paris is littered with free maps, they don't show all the streets. You may want the huge Michelin #10 map of Paris. For an extended stay, consider getting the pocket-sized, street-indexed *Paris Pratique* (about €6) with an easy-to-use Métro map.

American Church: The American Church is a nerve center for the American émigré community. It distributes a free, handy, and insightful

IF YOU NEED MEDICAL HELP

First, contact your hotelier, who is accustomed to dealing with emergencies. Here are other resources:

For the American Hospital, call 01 46 41 25 25 (63 boulevard Victor Hugo, 92202 Neuilly-sur-Seine, Mo: Porte Maillot, then bus #82). A handy English-speaking pharmacy, Pharmacie les Champs, is open 24/7 (tel. 01 45 62 02 41, 84 avenue des Champs-Elysées, Mo: George V). To get emergency medical help anywhere in France, dial 15. To summon an ambulance in Paris, call 01 45 67 50 50. To reach an English-language SOS Help crisis line in Paris, call 01 47 23 80 80 (daily 15:00–23:00). For SOS doctors, who charge affordable rates and will even come to your hotel, dial 01 47 07 77 77 or 01 48 28 40 04. To reach the police, call 17.

monthly English-language newspaper called the *Paris Voice* (with useful reviews of concerts, plays, and current events; available at about 200 locations in Paris, www.parisvoice.com) and an advertisement paper called *France—U.S.A. Contacts* (full of useful information for those seeking work or long-term housing). The church faces the river between the Eiffel Tower and Orsay Museum (Level 3—Minimally accessible, fifteen 6" steps to enter; reception open Mon–Sat 9:30–22:30, Sun 9:00–19:30, 65 quai d'Orsay, Mo: Invalides, tel. 01 40 62 05 00, www.acparis.org).

Arrival in Paris

By Train: Paris has six train stations, all connected by taxi (most accessible option), bus (sometimes accessible), and Métro (generally poor access). All stations have ATMs, banks or change offices, information desks, telephones, cafés, lockers *(consigne automatique)*, newsstands, and clever pickpockets. For details about each station, see "Transportation Connections" on page 244.

By Plane: For information on getting from Paris' airports to downtown Paris (and vice versa), see "Transportation Connections" on page 244.

THE PARIS MUSEUM PASS

In Paris, there are two classes of sightseers—those with a Paris museum pass and those who wait in line. Serious sightseers save time and money by getting this pass.

For slow walkers unable to stand for long periods of time, the biggest advantage of the museum pass is avoiding lines. If you use a wheelchair, the reasons to buy a museum pass are less convincing: Wheelchair users—even without the pass—are often allowed to enter museums free and can sometimes (but not always) bypass the line.

Most of the sights listed in this chapter are covered by the Paris museum pass, except for the Eiffel Tower, Montparnasse Tower, Opéra Garnier, Notre-Dame treasury, Jewish Art and History Museum, Grande Arche de La Défense, *Paris Story* film, and the ladies of Pigalle. Outside Paris, the pass covers the château of Versailles.

The pass pays for itself in two admissions (1 day-€18, 3 consecutive days-€36, 5 consecutive days-€54, no youth or senior discount). It's sold at museums, TIs (even at the airports), and major Métro stations (including Ecole Militaire and Bastille stations). Try to avoid buying the pass at a major museum (such as the Louvre), where supply can be spotty and lines long.

The pass isn't activated until the first time you use it (you enter the date on the pass). Think and read ahead to make the most of your pass, since some museums are free (e.g., Carnavalet and Victor Hugo's house), many sights are discounted on Sundays, and your pass must be used on consecutive days.

The pass isn't worth buying for children, as most museums are free for those under 18. Note that kids can skip the lines with their passholder parents.

The free museum and monuments directory that comes with

your pass lists the latest hours, phone numbers, and specifics on what kids pay. The cutoff age for free entry varies from 5 to 18. Most major art museums let young people under 18 in for free, but anyone over age 5 has to pay to tour the sewers—go figure.

Included sights you're likely to visit (and admission prices without the pass): Louvre (€8.50), Orsay Museum (€7), Sainte-Chapelle (€5.50), Arc de Triomphe (€7), Les Invalides/Napoleon's Tomb (€6), Conciergerie (€5.50), Cluny Museum (€7), Pompidou Center (€5.50), Notre-Dame towers (€5.50) and crypt (€3.50), Picasso Museum (€5.50), and the Rodin Museum (€5). Outside Paris, the pass covers the Palace of Versailles (€7.50) and its Trianon châteaux (€5).

Tally up what you want to see—and remember, an advantage of the pass is that you skip to the front of some lines, saving hours of waiting, especially in summer (though everyone must pass through the slow-moving metal-detector lines at some sights, and a few places, such as Notre-Dame's tower, can't accommodate a bypass lane). With the pass, you'll pop freely into sights that you're passing by (even for a few minutes) that otherwise might not be worth the expense (e.g., Notre-Dame crypt, Conciergerie, and the Panthéon).

Museum Tips: The Louvre and many other museums are closed on Tuesday. The Orsay, Rodin, and Carnavalet museums and Versailles are closed Monday. Most museums offer reduced prices on Sunday. Most sights stop admitting people 30–60 minutes before they close, and many begin closing rooms 45 minutes before the actual closing time.

For the fewest crowds, visit very early, at lunch, or very late. Most museums have slightly shorter hours October through March. French holidays can really mess up your sightseeing plans on Jan 1, May 1, July 14, Nov 1, Nov 11, and Dec 25.

Helpful Hints

Paris Museum Pass: This worthwhile pass, covering most sights in Paris, is available at museums, TIs, and major Métro stations. For information, see previous page.

U.S. Embassy: Call 01 43 12 22 22. It's at 2 avenue Gabriel (to the left as you face Hôtel Crillon, Mo: Concorde).

Theft Alert: Pickpockets seem more numerous and determined than ever. Métro and RER lines that serve popular sights are infested with thieves. If you're walking, wear a money belt and put your wallet in your front pocket. Everyone should keep a close eye on their belongings—loop your day bag over your shoulders (consider wearing it in front) and keep a tight grip on a purse or shopping bag. Muggings are rare, but do occur. If you're out late, avoid the dark riverfront quays and anywhere the lighting is dim and pedestrian activity minimal.

Street Safety: Be careful! Parisian drivers are notorious for ignoring pedestrians. Look both ways, as many streets are one-way, and be careful of seemingly quiet bus/taxi lanes. Don't assume you have the right of way, even in a crosswalk. When crossing a street, keep your pace constant and don't stop suddenly. By law, drivers must miss pedestrians by three feet (5 feet in the countryside). Drivers carefully calculate your speed and won't hit you, provided you don't alter your route or pace.

Watch out for a lesser hazard: *merde*. Parisian dogs decorate the city's sidewalks with 16 tons of droppings a day. People get injured by slipping in it.

Toilets: Carry small change for pay toilets, or roll or stroll into any sidewalk café like you own the place and find the toilet in the back. Restaurants with accessible toilets are noted under "Eating," page 231; you may want to seek out American chain restaurants, like McDonald's—more likely than the small, traditional places to have accessible toilets. Museum toilets are free and generally the best you'll find—and are often fully adapted. If you have a museum pass, you can drop into almost any museum just for the toilets. Keep some toilet paper or tissues with you as some toilets are poorly supplied.

Getting around Paris

For wheelchair users, taxis are the best option; if you prefer public transit, opt for the buses and skip the Métro. To save money on a trip to Versailles, it's worth considering the RER, though again, a taxi is easier.

By Taxi

Parisian taxis are reasonable—especially for couples and families. The meters are tamper-proof. Fares and supplements (described in English on the back windows) are straightforward. There's a €5 minimum. A 10-minute ride costs about €8 (versus €1 to get anywhere in town using a *carnet* ticket on the Métro). You can try waving down a taxi, but it's easier to ask for the nearest taxi stand (*Où est une station de taxi?*; oo ay oon stah-see-ohn duh taxi). Taxi stands are indicated by a circled T on many city maps, including Michelin's #10 Paris. A typical taxi takes three people (maybe 4 if you're polite and pay €2.50 extra); groups of up to five can use a *grand taxi,* which must be booked in advance—ask your hotel to call. If a taxi is summoned by phone, the meter starts as soon as the call is received, adding €3–4 to the bill. Higher rates are charged at night from 19:00 to 7:00, all day Sunday, and to either airport. There's a €1 charge for each piece of baggage and for train station pick-ups. To tip, round up to the next euro (minimum €0.50). Taxis are tough to find on Friday and Saturday nights, especially after the Métro closes (around 00:30). If you need to catch a train or flight early in the morning, book a taxi the day before.

Access: Range from Level 2—Moderately accessible to Level 1—Fully accessible. For wheelchair users, taxis **(AE+A)** and minibuses **(AE+A)** are the way to go. Some minibuses **(AE)** even have ramps *(le gambade)*—call ahead to request one (tel. 06 07 49 58 92 or tel. 06 07 22 41 61; best to call up to 4 weeks in advance, but may be possible on short notice; figure €40–55 for a trip across central Paris). Most drivers are happy to assist persons using wheelchairs. Once you're in the taxi, the driver will fold up your wheelchair and place it in the trunk.

By City Bus

The tricky bus system is worth figuring out. Métro tickets are good on both bus and Métro, though you can't use the same ticket to transfer between the two systems. One ticket gets you anywhere in central Paris, but if you leave the city center (shown as zone 1 on the diagram on board the bus), you must validate a second ticket. While the Métro shuts down about 00:30, some buses continue much later.

Schedules are posted at bus stops. Handy bus system maps *(plan des autobus)* are available in any Métro station and are provided in your *Paris Pratique* map book if you invest €6. Big system maps, posted at each bus and Métro stop, display the routes. Individual route diagrams show the exact routes of the lines serving that stop. Major stops are displayed on the side of each bus.

Access: All newer buses are wheelchair-accessible (**AE, AI,** Level 1—Fully accessible, with low floors and hydraulic ramp, identified by the standard wheelchair symbol), but it's difficult to predict exactly when and where the newer buses operate. Generally your odds are best for lines #20 (which runs in the Marais neighborhood), scenic #24, #30, #88, #91, #92, #139, #170, #217, #302, #304, #360, and #393. Older buses (**AE+A,** Level 2—Moderately accessible) have one 8" step to negotiate and an entry pole between the doors, making it a narrow opening, though wheelchair users have been able to board these buses with assistance.

Tickets and Passes: You can buy single tickets from the driver for €1.40. You'll save 40 percent by buying a *carnet* (car-nay) of 10 tickets for €10 (kids 4–10 pay €5), sold at any Métro station by ticket-sellers and machines (some machines also accept credit cards).

If you're staying in Paris for a week or more, consider the **Carte Orange** (kart oh-rahnzh) for about €15, which gives you free run of the bus and Métro system for one week, starting Monday and ending Sunday; ask for the Carte Orange *coupon vert* and supply a passport-size photo. The month-long version costs about €50; request a Carte Orange *coupon orange* (good from the first day of the month to the last). These passes cover only central Paris; you can pay more for passes covering regional destinations (like Versailles). All passes can be purchased at any Métro station, most of which have photo booths where you can get the photo required for the pass. While some Métro agents may hesitate to sell you Carte Orange passes because you're not a resident, Carte Orange passes are definitely not limited to residents; if you're refused, simply go to another station to buy your pass.

The overpriced **Paris Visite** passes were designed for tourists and offer minor reductions at minor sights (1 day-€9, 2 days-€14, 3 days-€19, 5 days-€28), but you'll get a better value with a cheaper *carnet* of 10 tickets or a Carte Orange.

By Métro

The subway is divided into two systems—the Métro (for puddle-jumping everywhere in Paris) and the RER (which connects suburban destinations with a few stops in central Paris). The system operates daily from 5:30 until 00:30.

Access: Level 3—Minimally accessible. Slow walkers will find the Métro challenging, but not impossible. For wheelchair users, the Métro is packed with barriers and very difficult to use, even with the help of a companion. Even though some of the newer trains are designed for accessible boarding, you'll have to negotiate lots of stairs and escalators (often broken)—usually without elevators—at most stations. As an alternative, wheelchair users who can make transfers and climb a few steps could find the RER useful for some trips (see "By RER," next page).

Theft and Panhandler Alert: Thieves spend their days in the Métro. Be on guard. For example, if your pocket is picked as you pass through a turnstile, you end up stuck on the wrong side while the thief strolls away. Any jostle or commotion (especially when boarding or leaving trains) is likely the sign of a thief or team of thieves in action.

Paris has a huge homeless population and higher than 11 percent unemployment; expect a warm Métro welcome by panhandlers, musicians, and those selling magazines produced by the homeless community.

Tickets and Passes: In Paris, you're never more than a few blocks from a Métro station. One ticket (€1.40) takes you anywhere in the system with unlimited transfers. Tickets are also good on the RER suburban trains (see below) and on city buses, although one ticket cannot be used as a transfer between subway and bus. To save money, buy a 10-pack *carnet* or a week-long Carte Orange pass (see "By City Bus—Tickets and Passes," previous page).

Using the Métro: Remember, the Métro does work for slow walkers, but not for wheelchair users. To get to your destination, determine the closest "Mo" stop and which line or lines will get you there. The lines have numbers, but they're best known by their direction or end-of-the-line stop. (For example, the La Défense/Château de Vincennes line runs between La Défense in the west and Vincennes in the east.) Once in the Métro station, you'll see blue-and-white signs directing you to the train going in your direction (e.g., *direction:* La Défense"). Insert your ticket in the automatic turnstile (brown stripe down), pass through, and reclaim and keep your ticket until you exit the system. Fare inspectors regularly check for cheaters and accept absolutely no excuses from anyone. We repeat, keep that ticket until you leave the Métro system.

Transfers are free and can be made wherever lines cross. When you transfer, look for the orange *correspondance* (connections) signs when you exit your first train, then follow the proper direction sign.

While the Métro whisks you quickly from one point to another, be prepared to walk significant distances within stations to reach your platform (most noticeable when you transfer). Escalators are usually available for vertical movement, but they're not always in working order. Elevators are rare. It is very unusual that you will not have to climb at least a few steps in a Métro station or while making a transfer. To limit excessive transfer distances, avoid transferring at these sprawling stations: Montparnasse-Bienvenüe, Chatelet-Les Halles, Charles de Gaulle-Etoile, Gare du Nord, and Bastille.

Before taking the *sortie* (exit) to leave the Métro, check the helpful *plan du quartier* (map of the neighborhood) to get your bearings, locate your destination, and decide which *sortie* you want. At stops with several *sorties,* you can save lots of time and effort by choosing the best exit.

After you exit the system, toss or tear your used ticket so you don't confuse it with your unused ticket—they look virtually identical.

By RER

The RER (Réseau Express Régionale; air-euh-air) is the suburban train system serving destinations such as Versailles and the airports. These routes are indicated by thick lines on your subway map and identified by letters A, B, C, and so on.

Within the city center, the RER works like the Métro but can be speedier (if it serves your destination directly) because it makes only a few stops within the city. It also offers the disabled traveler more accessible stations than the Métro.

Access: Range from Level 3—Minimally accessible to Level 2—Moderately accessible. The RER is not recommended for wheelchair users as a primary means of getting around Paris. Most stations on lines A and B are generally wheelchair-accessible, though they have few stops in the city center. Other lines have a few stops that are wheelchair-accessible. While the RER is cost-effective, it uses up a lot of time and energy. For maximum accessibility, we recommend using taxis—but for the slow walker or adventurous wheelchair user, getting around via the RER is a possibility.

Using the RER: Métro tickets are good on the RER when traveling in the city center. (You can transfer between the Métro and RER systems with the same ticket.) But to travel outside the city (to Versailles

KEY WORDS FOR THE MÉTRO AND RER

- *direction* (dee-rek-see-ohn): direction
- *ligne* (leen-yuh): line
- *correspondance* (kor-res-pohn-dahns): transfer
- *sortie* (sor-tee): exit
- *carnet* (car-nay): cheap set of 10 tickets
- *Pardon, madame/monsieur* (par-dohn, mah-dahm/mes-yur): Excuse me, lady/bud.
- *Je descend* (juh day-sahn): I'm getting off.
- *Donnez-moi mon porte-feuille!* (dohn-nay-mwuh mohn port-foo-ay): Give me back my wallet!

or the airport, for example), you'll need to buy a separate, more expensive ticket at the station window before boarding. Unlike in the Métro, you need to insert your ticket in a turnstile to exit the RER system. Also unlike the Métro, not every train stops at every station along the way; check the sign over the platform to see if your destination is listed as a stop (*toutes les gares* means it makes all stops along the way) or confirm with a local before you board.

TOURS

Bus Tours—Paris Vision (AE+A, Level 2—Moderately accessible) offers handy bus tours of Paris, day and night (advertised in hotel lobbies); their "Paris Illumination" tour is much more interesting (see "Nightlife," page 218). Far better daytime bus tours are the hop-on, hop-off double-decker bus services connecting Paris' main sights while providing running commentary (ideal in good weather if you can climb up to the top deck).

These two companies provide hop-on, hop-off bus service: **Les Cars Rouges** and **L'Open Tours** (pick up their brochures showing routes and stops from any TI or on their buses). Two or three buses depart hourly from about 10:00 to 18:00; expect to wait 10–20 minutes at each stop (they can be tricky to find). You can get off at any stop, then catch a later bus. You'll see these topless double-decker buses all over town; pick one up at the first important sight you visit, or start your tour at the Eiffel Tower stop (on avenue Joseph Bouvard).

Les Cars Rouges' (**AE+A,** Level 2—Moderately accessible) bright red buses are the slightly more accessible option. You'll have to make it up one step into the bus (wide entry). Attendants can help lift the wheelchair onto the bus, but then you'll transfer to a seat and the driver will place your folded wheelchair under the bus (makes fewer stops and costs less than L'Open, 2-day tickets, €22-adult, €11-kids 4–12, tel. 01 53 95 39 53).

L'Open Tours (**AE+A,** Level 2—Moderately accessible), which is a bit less accessible and uses bright yellow buses, provides more extensive coverage and offers three different routes, rolling by most of the important sights in Paris. Their Paris Grand Tour offers the best introduction. You'll have to ascend three steps to get on the bus (attendants will assist and wheelchair must fold to go under bus). Tickets are good for any route. Buy your tickets from the driver (€25/1-day ticket, €27/2-day ticket, kids 4–11 pay €12.50 for 1 or 2 days, 20 percent less if you have a *Carte Orange* Métro pass, allow 2 hours per tour, tel. 01 42 66 56 56).

Boat Tours—Several companies offer one-hour boat cruises on the Seine (by far best at night).

The huge, mass-production **Bateaux-Mouches** boats (**AE, AI, ♥,** Level 1—All boats and docks are fully accessible), which depart every 20–30 minutes from the pont de l'Alma's right bank and also from right in front of the Eiffel Tower, are convenient to rue Cler hotels (€7.50, €4.50 for ages 4–12, daily 10:00–22:30, useless taped explanations in 6 languages and tour groups by the dozens, tel. 01 40 76 99 99).

The smaller and more intimate **Vedettes du Pont-Neuf** (**AE, AI,** Level 1—Fully accessible) depart only once an hour from the center of pont Neuf (twice an hour after dark), but they come with a live guide giving explanations in French and English and are convenient to Marais hotels (€9.50, €5 for ages 4–12, tel. 01 46 33 98 38). To get to the river level, the wheelchair user goes one block upriver on the south side of the island to the ramp. This area has large, rough cobblestones to negotiate.

Walking Tours—The company **Paris Walking Tours** offers a variety of excellent two-hour walks, led by British or American guides, nearly daily for €10 (range from Level 4—Not accessible to Level 1—Fully accessible; tel. 01 48 09 21 40 for recorded schedule in English, fax 01 42 43 75 51, www.paris-walks.com shows schedule). Tours focus on the Marais,

DAILY REMINDER

Monday: These sights are closed today—Orsay, Rodin, Montmartre, Carnavalet, and Versailles; the Louvre is more crowded because of this, but the Denon wing (with *Mona Lisa, Venus de Milo,* and more highlights) stays open until 21:45. Napoleon's Tomb is closed the first Monday of the month. Some small stores don't open until 14:00. Street markets such as rue Cler and rue Mouffetard are dead today. Some banks are closed. It's discount night at most cinemas.

Tuesday: Many museums are closed today, including the Louvre, Picasso, Cluny, and Pompidou Center. The Eiffel Tower, Orsay, and Versailles are particularly busy today.

Wednesday: All sights are open (Louvre until 21:45). The weekly *Pariscope* magazine comes out today. Most schools are closed, so many kids' sights are busy. Some cinemas offer discounts.

Thursday: All sights are open, the Orsay until 21:45. Department stores are open late.

Friday: All sights are open. Afternoon trains and roads leaving Paris are crowded; TGV reservation fees are higher.

Saturday: All sights are open (except the Jewish Art and History Museum). The fountains run at Versailles (July–Sept). Department stores are busy. The Jewish Quarter is quiet.

Sunday: Some museums are two-thirds price all day and/or free the first Sunday of the month, thus more crowded (e.g., Louvre, Orsay, Rodin, Cluny, Pompidou, and Picasso). The fountains run at Versailles (early April–early Oct). Most of Paris' stores are closed on Sunday, but shoppers will find relief in the Marais neighborhood's lively Jewish Quarter and in Bercy Village, where many stores are open. Look for organ concerts at St. Sulpice and possibly other churches. The American Church hosts a free evening concert at 17:00 (Jan–June and Sept–Nov only). Most recommended restaurants in the rue Cler neighborhood are closed for dinner.

Montmartre, Ile de la Cité and Ile St. Louis, and Hemingway's Paris. Call a day or two ahead to learn their schedule and the starting point, and to find out which tour best fits your mobility level. These receptive, warm folks have welcomed wheelchair users on their tours in the past. No reservations are required. The walks are thoughtfully prepared, relaxing, and humorous. Don't hesitate to get close to the guide to hear.

Private Guide Service—For many, Paris merits hiring a Parisian as your personal guide. Two excellent licensed local guides who freelance for individuals and families are Arnaud Servignat, who runs Global Travel Partners (€215/4 hrs, €335/day, also does car tours of countryside around Paris, tel. 06 72 77 94 50, fax 01 42 57 00 38, arnaud.servignat@noos.fr), and Marianne Siegler (€150/4 hrs, €250/day, reserve in advance if possible, tel. 01 42 52 32 51). These guides will take wheelchair users as long as they can transfer into a car or van.

Excursion Tours—Many companies offer minivan and big bus tours to regional sights (most are Level 3—Minimally accessible, best for slow walkers). **Paris Walking Tours** (mentioned on page 178) offer informative though infrequent excursions to the Impressionist artist retreats of Giverny and Auvers-sur-Oise (€47–56, includes admissions, tel. 01 48 09 21 40 for recording in English, www.paris-walks.com).

Paris Vision offers mass-produced, full-size bus and minivan tours to several popular regional destinations, including the Loire Valley, Champagne region, D-Day beaches, and Mont St. Michel. Their minivan tours are more expensive but more personal than their big-bus version; given in English; and offer pick-up at your hotel (€130–200/person). Their full-size bus tours are multilingual and cost about half the price of a minivan tour—worth it for some simply for the ease of transportation to the sights (full-size buses depart from 214 rue de Rivoli, Mo: Tuileries, tel. 01 42 60 30 01, fax 01 42 86 95 36, www.parisvision.com).

SIGHTS

Museums near the Tuileries Garden

The newly renovated Tuileries Garden was once the private property of kings and queens. Paris' grandest public park links these museums.

▲▲▲**Louvre**—This is Europe's oldest, biggest, greatest, and maybe most crowded museum. There is no grander entry than through the

pyramid, but metal detectors create a long line at times. Don't try to cover the entire museum. Pick up the free "Louvre Handbook" in English at the information desk under the pyramid as you enter. Consider taking a tour (see Tours, page 185), or, better yet, follow our suggested Self-Guided Tour (also page 185).

Access: AE, AI, AL, AT, Level 1—Fully accessible. Loaner wheelchairs are available. The museum is fully accessible by elevator, including stores and restaurants on the lower level—though there are few elevators, and readers report that they are sometimes out of order. There are accessible

Museums near the Tuileries Garden

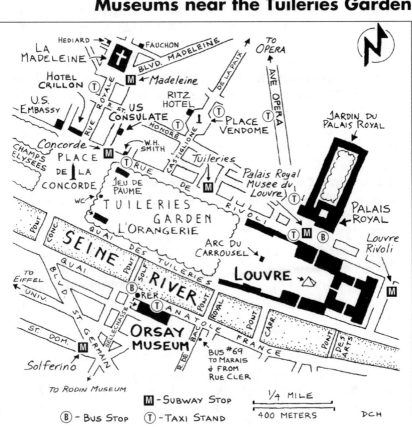

PARIS AT A GLANCE

▲▲▲**Louvre** Europe's oldest and greatest museum, starring *Mona Lisa* and *Venus de Milo*. **Hours:** Wed–Mon 9:00–18:00, closed Tue. Denon wing open Mon until 21:45; all wings open Wed until 21:45. **Access:** Level 1—Fully accessible.

▲▲▲**Orsay Museum** Nineteenth-century art, including Europe's greatest Impressionist collection. **Hours:** June 20–Sept 20 Tue–Sun 9:00–18:00; Sept 21–June 19 Tue–Sat 10:00–18:00, Sun 9:00–18:00; Thu until 21:45 year-round, closed Mon. **Access:** Level 1—Fully accessible.

▲▲▲**Eiffel Tower** Paris' soaring exclamation point. **Hours:** March–Sept daily 9:00–24:00, Oct–Feb 9:30–23:00. **Access:** Up to second level—Fully accessible; top level—Not accessible.

▲▲▲**Arc de Triomphe** Triumphal arch with viewpoint, marking start of Champs-Elysées. **Hours:** Outside always open; inside April–Sept daily 10:00–23:00, Oct–March daily 10:00–22:30. **Access:** Museum only is Level 2—Moderately accessible; viewpoint is Level 4—Not accessible.

▲▲▲**Sainte-Chapelle** Gothic cathedral with peerless stained glass. **Hours:** Daily 9:30–18:00. **Access:** Ground floor only is Level 2—Moderately accessible; upstairs chapel is Level 4—Not accessible.

▲▲▲**Versailles** The ultimate royal palace, with Hall of Mirrors, vast gardens, a grand canal, and smaller palaces. **Hours:** May–Sept Tue–Sun 9:00–18:30, Oct–April Tue–Sun 9:00–17:30, closed Mon. Gardens open early (7:00) and smaller palaces open late (12:00). **Access:** Level 1—Fully accessible.

▲▲**Notre-Dame Cathedral** Paris' most beloved church, with towers and gargoyles. **Hours:** Church daily 8:00–18:45; tower April–Sept daily 9:30–19:30, Oct–March daily 10:00–17:30. **Access:** Level 2—Moderately accessible.

▲▲**Sacré-Cœur** White basilica atop Montmartre with spectacular views. **Hours:** Daily until 23:00. **Access:** Level 4—Not accessible.

▲▲**Napoleon's Tomb** The emperor's imposing tomb, flanked by army museums. **Hours:** April–Sept daily 10:00–18:00, Oct–March daily 10:00–17:00, closed first Mon of month. **Access:** Level 1—Fully accessible (except for crypt).

▲▲**Rodin Museum** Works by the greatest sculptor since Michelangelo. **Hours:** April–Sept Tue–Sun 9:30–17:45; Oct–March Tue–Sun 9:30–17:00, closed Mon. **Access:** Main floor and gardens are Level 1—Fully accessible. Upper floor is Level 3—Minimally accessible.

▲▲**Pompidou Center** Modern art in colorful building with city views. **Hours:** Wed–Mon 11:00–21:00, closed Tue. **Access:** Level 1—Fully accessible.

▲▲**Cluny Museum** Medieval art with unicorn tapestries. **Hours:** Wed–Mon 9:15–17:45, closed Tue. **Access:** Level 3—Minimally accessible.

▲▲**Carnavalet Museum** Paris' history wrapped up in a 16th-century mansion. **Hours:** Tue–Sun 10:00–18:00, closed Mon. **Access:** Level 4—Not accessible.

▲▲**Jewish Art and History Museum** Displays history of Judaism in Europe. **Hours:** Mon–Fri 11:00–18:00, Sun 10:00–18:00, closed Sat. **Access:** Level 1—Fully accessible.

▲▲**Deportation Memorial** Memorial to Holocaust victims, near Notre-Dame. **Hours:** April–Sept daily 10:00–12:00 & 14:00–19:00; Oct–March daily 10:00–12:00 & 14:00–17:00. **Access:** Level 4—Not accessible.

continued on next page

continued from previous page

▲▲Champs-Elysées Paris' grand boulevard. **Hours:** Always open. **Access:** Mostly Level 1: Fully accessible.

▲Old Opera (Opéra Garnier) 19th-century opera house open for tours. **Hours:** Daily 10:00–17:00 except during performances. **Access:** Level 1—Fully accessible.

▲La Défense and La Grande Arche Paris' modern arch on outskirts of city. **Hours:** Elevator daily 10:00–19:00. **Access:** Level 1—Fully accessible.

▲Picasso Museum World's largest collection of Picasso's works. **Hours:** April–Sept Wed–Mon 9:30–18:00; Oct–March 9:30–17:30, closed Tue. **Access:** Level 1—Fully accessible.

toilets throughout the building. Like most of Europe's great museums, the Louvre is a modernized facility designed with the wheelchair user in mind. Still, the museum can be quite crowded, and there are sporadic obstacles that can make it difficult to maneuver a wheelchair.

Cost: Free for wheelchair user and companion, otherwise €8.50, €6 after 18:00 on Mon and Wed, free on first Sunday of month and for those under 18, covered by museum pass. Tickets good all day. Reentry allowed. Tel. 01 40 20 51 51, recorded info tel. 01 40 20 53 17 (www.louvre.fr).

Hours: Wed–Mon 9:00–18:00, closed Tue. All wings open Wed until 21:45. On Mon, only the Denon wing is open until 21:45, but it contains the biggies: *Mona Lisa, Venus de Milo,* and more. Galleries start closing 30 minutes early. Closed Jan 1, Easter, May 1, Nov 1, and Dec 25. Crowds are worst on Sun, Mon, Wed, and mornings. Save money by visiting after 15:00.

Line-beating Tips: Wheelchair users can skip to the front of the line; enter through the pyramid (elevator to the left on entry). If you're a slow walker, you have several options for avoiding the line. Museum passholders can use the group entrance (which has an escalator) at the pedestrian passageway between the pyramid and rue de Rivoli (facing the pyramid with your back to the Tuileries Garden, go to your left, which is north; under the arches, you'll find the entrance and escalator down). Otherwise, you can enter the Louvre underground directly from the Métro stop Palais Royal-Musée du Louvre (exit following signs to *Musée du Louvre*) or from the Carrousel shopping mall, which is connected to the museum. Enter the mall at 99 rue de Rivoli (the door with the red awning, daily 8:30–23:00). The taxi stand is across rue de Rivoli next to the Métro station.

Tours: The 90-minute English-language tours, which leave six times daily except Tuesday (when the museum is closed) and Sunday, boil this overwhelming museum down to size (wheelchair users and slow walkers welcome; normally at 11:00, 14:00, and 15:45, €3 plus your entry ticket, tour tel. 01 40 20 52 63). Clever €5 digital audioguides (after ticket booths) give you a receiver and a directory of about 130 masterpieces, allowing you to dial a (rather dull) commentary on included works as you come upon them.

Self-Guided Tour: Start in the Denon wing and visit the highlights, in the following order.

Wander through the **ancient Greek and Roman works** to see the Parthenon frieze, Pompeii mosaics, Etruscan sarcophagi, and Roman portrait busts. You can't miss lovely *Venus de Milo (Aphrodite)*. This goddess of love (c. 100 B.C., from the Greek island of Melos) created a sensation when she was discovered in 1820. Most "Greek" statues are actually later Roman copies, but *Venus* is a rare Greek original. She, like Golden Age Greeks, epitomizes stability, beauty, and balance. Later Greek art was Hellenistic, adding motion and drama. For a good example, see the exciting *Winged Victory of Samothrace (Victoire de Samothrace,* on the landing). This statue of a woman with wings, poised on the prow of a ship, once stood on a hilltop to commemorate a great naval victory. This is the *Venus de Milo* gone Hellenistic.

The **Italian collection** is on the other side of the *Winged Victory.* The key to Renaissance painting was realism, and for the Italians "realism" was spelled "3-D." Painters were inspired by the realism and balanced beauty of Greek sculpture. Painting a 3-D world on a 2-D surface is tough, and after a millennium of Dark Ages, artists were rusty. Living in a religious age, they painted mostly altarpieces full of saints, angels, Madonnas-and-bambinos, and crucifixes floating in an ethereal gold-leaf heaven. Gradually, though, they brought these otherworldly scenes down

The Louvre

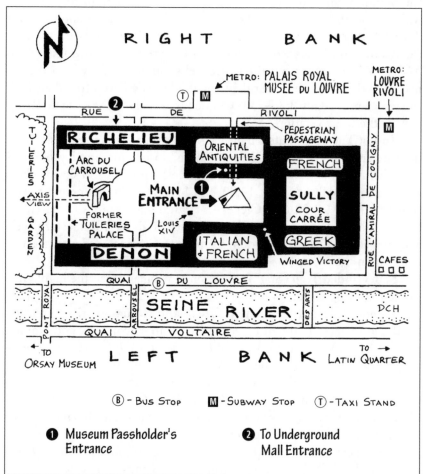

to earth. The Italian collection—including *Mona Lisa*—is scattered throughout rooms *(salles)* 3 and 4, in the long Grand Gallery, and in adjoining rooms.

Two masters of the Italian High Renaissance (1500–1600) were Raphael (see his *La Belle Jardinière,* showing the Madonna, Child, and John the Baptist) and Leonardo da Vinci. The Louvre has the greatest collection of Leonardos in the world—five of them, including the exquisite *Virgin, Child, and St. Anne,* the neighboring *Madonna of the Rocks,* and the androgynous *John the Baptist.* His most famous, of course, is the *Mona Lisa.*

Leonardo was already an old man when François I invited him to France. Determined to pack light, he took only a few paintings. One was a portrait of a Lisa del Giocondo, the wife of a wealthy Florentine merchant. When Leonardo arrived, François immediately fell in love with the painting, making it the centerpiece of the small collection of Italian masterpieces that would, in three centuries, become the Louvre museum. He called it *La Gioconda*. We know it as a contraction of the Italian for "my lady Lisa"—*Mona Lisa*. Warning: François was impressed, but *Mona* may disappoint you. She's smaller and darker than you'd expect, engulfed in a huge room, and hidden behind a glaring pane of glass.

Mona's overall mood is one of balance and serenity, but there's also an element of mystery. Her smile and long-distance beauty are subtle and elusive, tempting but always just out of reach, like strands of a street singer's melody drifting through the Métro tunnel. *Mona* doesn't knock your socks off, but she winks at the patient viewer.

Now for something **neoclassical.** Notice the fine work, such as *The Coronation of Napoleon* by Jacques-Louis David, near *Mona* in the Salle Daru. Neoclassicism, once the rage in France (1780–1850), usually features Greek subjects, patriotic sentiment, and a clean, simple style. After Napoleon quickly conquered most of Europe, he insisted on being made emperor (not merely king) of this "New Rome." He staged an elaborate coronation ceremony in Paris, and rather than let the pope crown him, he crowned himself. The setting is the Notre-Dame cathedral, with Greek columns and Roman arches thrown in for effect. Napoleon's mom was also added, since she couldn't make it to the ceremony. A key on the frame describes who's who in the picture.

The **Romantic** collection, in an adjacent room (Salle Mollien), has works by Théodore Géricault *(The Raft of the Medusa)* and Eugène Delacroix *(Liberty Leading the People)*. Romanticism, with an emphasis on motion and emotion, is the complete flip side of neoclassicism, though they both flourished in the early 1800s. Delacroix's *Liberty,* commemorating the stirrings of democracy in France, is also a fitting tribute to the Louvre, the first museum opened to the common rabble of humanity. The good things in life don't belong only to a small wealthy part of society, but to all. The motto of France is *"Liberté, Egalité, Fraternité"*—liberty, equality, and brotherhood.

Exit the room at the far end (past the café) and take the elevator down to find the large, twisting male nude who looks like he's just waking up after a thousand-year nap. The two *Slaves* (1513–15) by Michelangelo are a fitting end to this museum—works that bridge the ancient and modern worlds. Michelangelo, like his fellow Renaissance artists, learned from the Greeks. The perfect anatomy, twisting poses, and idealized faces look like they could have been done 2,000 years earlier. Michelangelo said that his purpose was to carve away the marble to reveal the figures God put inside. The *Rebellious Slave*, fighting against his bondage, shows the agony of that process and the ecstasy of the result.

Underground Louvre: To explore the accessible subterranean shopping mall, enter through the pyramid, go toward the inverted pyramid, and uncover a post office, a handy TI and SNCF (train tickets) office, glittering boutiques and a dizzying assortment of good-value eateries (one level up by escalator or elevator), and the Palais Royal-Musée du Louvre Métro entrance. An elevator will take you to the Tuileries Garden, a perfect antidote to the stuffy, crowded rooms of the Louvre.

▲▲▲**Orsay Museum**—The Musée d'Orsay (mew-zay dor-say) houses French art of the 1800s (specifically, art from 1848 to 1914),

picking up where the Louvre leaves off. For us, that means Impressionism. The Orsay houses the best general collection anywhere of Manet, Monet, Renoir, Degas, van Gogh, Cézanne, and Gauguin.

The museum shows art that is also both old and new, conservative and revolutionary. You'll start on the ground floor with the Conservatives and the early rebels who paved the way for the Impressionists, then head to the upper level (accessible by elevator) to see how a few visionary young artists bucked the system and revolutionized the art world, paving the way for the 20th century.

For most visitors, the most important part of the museum is the upper-level Impressionist collection. Here, you can study many pictures you've probably seen in books, such as Manet's *Luncheon on the Grass*, Renoir's *Dance at the Moulin de la Galette*, Monet's *Gare St. Lazare*, Whistler's *Mother*, van Gogh's *The Church at Auvers-sur-Oise*, and Cézanne's *The Card Players*. As you approach these beautiful, easy-to-enjoy paintings, remember that there is more to this art than meets the eye. For help appreciating this art, see "Impressionism 101," below.

Access: AE, AI, AL, AT, Level 1—Fully accessible. The modernized Orsay building is designed to accommodate the wheelchair user. The "Museum Guide" has an overlay (available at information counter) that indicates accessible toilets, ramps, and elevators. Loaner wheelchairs are available.

Cost: Free to wheelchair user and companion; otherwise €7; €5 after 16:15, on Sun, and for ages 18 to 25; free for youth under 18 and for anyone first Sun of month; covered by museum pass. Tickets are good all day. Museum passholders can enter to the left of the main entrance.

Hours: June 20–Sept 20 Tue–Sun 9:00–18:00; Sept 21–June 19 Tue–Sat 10:00–18:00, Sun 9:00–18:00; Thu until 21:45 all year, always closed Mon. Last entrance is 45 minutes before closing. The Impressionist Galleries start closing at 17:15, frustrating many unwary visitors. Note that the Orsay is crowded on Tue, when the Louvre is closed.

Location: Bus #69 from the Marais and rue Cler neighborhoods stops at the Orsay on the river side (quai Anatole France). The museum sits above the RER-C stop called Musée d'Orsay. The nearest Métro stop is Solférino, three blocks south of the Orsay. Tel. 01 40 49 48 14, www.musee-orsay.fr.

Tours: Live English-language tours of the Orsay usually run daily (except Sun) at 11:30. Wheelchair users and slow walkers are welcome. The 90-minute tours cost €6 and are also available on audioguide (€5). Tours in English focusing on the Impressionists are offered Tuesdays at 14:30 and Thursdays at 18:30 (sometimes also on other days, €6).

Cafés: The museum has a cheap café on the fourth floor, and the elegant Salon de Thé du Musée is on the second floor (good salad bar; both restaurants **AE, AI, AT,** Level 1—Fully accessible).

Impressionism 101: The camera threatened to make artists obsolete. A painter's original function was to record reality faithfully, like a journalist. Now a machine could capture a better likeness faster than you could say Etch-A-Sketch.

But true art is more than just painted reality. It gives us reality from the artist's point of view, putting a personal stamp on the work. It records not only a scene—a camera can do that—but the artist's impressions of that scene. Impressions are often fleeting, so the artist has to work quickly.

The Impressionist painters rejected camera-like detail for a quick style more suited to capturing the passing moment. Feeling stifled by the rigid rules and stuffy atmosphere of the Academy, the Impressionists took as their motto, "out of the studio, into the open air." They grabbed their berets and scarves and took excursions to the country, where they set up their easels on riverbanks and hillsides, or they sketched in cafés and dance halls. Gods, goddesses, nymphs, and fantasy scenes were out; common people and rural landscapes were in.

The quick style and simple subjects were ridiculed and called childish by the "experts." Rejected by the Salon, the Impressionists staged their own exhibition in 1874. They brashly took their name from an insult thrown at them by a critic, who laughed at one of Monet's impressions of a sunrise. During the next decade, they exhibited their own work independently. The public, opposed at first, was slowly drawn in by the simplicity, color, and vibrancy of Impressionist art.

Historic Core of Paris: Notre-Dame, Sainte-Chapelle, and More

All of these sights are covered in detail in the Historic Paris Roll or Stroll (plus map) on page 255. Only the essentials are listed here.

▲▲Notre-Dame Cathedral—This 700-year-old cathedral is packed with history and tourists. Study its sculpture and windows, take in a Mass, eavesdrop on guides, and walk around the back for a look at the graceful flying buttresses. The church has a treasury inside, a tower climb with an outside entrance (stairs only, no elevator), and a crypt across the square (Mo: Cité, Hôtel de Ville, or St. Michel).

Cathedral Access: AE, AI+A, Level 2—Moderately accessible. The entryway and three-fourths of the main floor are wheelchair-accessible. There are three 6" steps to enter the area of the Mass and the treasury.

Cathedral Cost and Hours: Free, daily 8:00–18:45; treasury-€2.50, not covered by museum pass, daily 9:30–17:30; ask about free English tours, normally Wed and Thu at 12:00 and Sat at 14:30.

Tower Access: Level 4—Not accessible (400 steps). Hardy slow walkers can climb to the top of the facade between the towers and then to the top of the south tower.

Tower Cost and Hours: €5.50, daily April–Sept 9:30–19:30, Oct–March 10:00–18:00, last entry 45 min before closing, covered by museum pass, arrive early to avoid long lines.

Paris Archaeological Crypt: For slow walkers, the crypt (entrance 100 yards in front of the cathedral) is a short, worthwhile stop with your museum pass. You'll visit Roman ruins, trace the street plan of the medieval village, and see diagrams of how early Paris grew and grew, all thoughtfully explained in English.

Crypt Access: Level 4—Not accessible. There are fourteen 6" steps down to the entryway, but the inside is mostly level.

Crypt Cost and Hours: €3.50, Tue–Sun 10:00–18:00, closed Mon.

▲▲**Deportation Memorial (Mémorial de la Déportation)**—This memorial to the 200,000 French victims of the Nazi concentration camps draws you into their experience. See description on page 260.

Access: Level 4—Not accessible. The memorial can be reached only by going down twenty-six 7" stairs.

Cost, Hours, and Location: Free, April–Sept daily 10:00–12:00 & 14:00–19:00, Oct–March daily 10:00–12:00 & 14:00–17:00, east tip of the island Ile de la Cité, behind Notre-Dame and near Ile St. Louis, Mo: Cité.

Ile St. Louis—This residential island behind Notre-Dame is known for its restaurants (see "Eating," page 231), great Berthillon ice cream shop (**AE+A, AI+A,** Level 2—Moderately accessible, one 4" entry doorstep and one interior 4" step; 31 rue St. Louis-en-l'Ile), and fun window-shopping (along rue St. Louis-en-l'Ile). For more information, see page 261.

Cité "Métropolitain" Stop and Flower Market—On place Louis Lépine, between Notre-Dame and Sainte-Chapelle, you'll find an early-19th-century subway entrance and a flower market (that chirps with a bird market on Sun).

▲▲▲**Sainte-Chapelle**—This triumph of Gothic church architecture is a cathedral of glass like no other. For a description, see page 264.

Access: Ground floor only—**AE, AI, AT+A,** Level 2—Moderately accessible. Unfortunately, the upstairs chapel can be reached only by climbing a narrow spiral staircase (Level 4—Not accessible, though slow walkers will find it's worth the climb). Wheelchair-accessible toilets are near the Palace of Justice entrance, with one 4" curb to negotiate and a long ramp with no railing.

Cost and Hours: Free for wheelchair users, otherwise €5.50, €8 combo-ticket covers inaccessible Conciergerie, both covered by museum pass, daily 9:30–18:00, Mo: Cité, tel. 01 44 07 12 38 for concert information.

▲**Conciergerie**—Marie-Antoinette was imprisoned here, as were 2,780 others on the way to the guillotine.

Access: Level 4—Not accessible. Visitors must negotiate a flight of stairs to get into the accessible courtyard and lobby of the Conciergerie.

Cost and Hours: Courtyard and lobby—Free. Interior—€5.50, €8 combo-ticket covers Sainte-Chapelle, both covered by museum pass, daily April–Sept 9:30–18:30, Oct–March 10:00–17:00, good English descriptions.

Southwest Paris: The Eiffel Tower Neighborhood

▲▲▲**Eiffel Tower (La Tour Eiffel)**—It's crowded and expensive, but worth the trouble. The tower is a 1,000-foot-tall ornament. In hot weather, it's six inches taller. It covers 2.5 acres and requires 50 tons of paint. Its 7,000 tons of metal are spread out so well at the base that it's no heavier per square inch than a linebacker on tiptoes. Visitors to Paris may find *Mona Lisa* to be less than expected, but the Eiffel Tower rarely disappoints, even in an era of skyscrapers.

Built a hundred years after the French Revolution (and in the midst of an Industrial one), the tower served no function but to impress. Bridge-builder Gustave Eiffel won the contest for the 1889 Centennial World's Fair by beating out such rival proposals as a giant guillotine. To a generation hooked on technology, the tower was the marvel of the age, a symbol of progress and of man's ingenuity. To others it was a cloned-sheep monstrosity. The writer Guy de Maupassant routinely ate lunch in the tower just so he wouldn't have to look at it.

Delicate and graceful when seen from afar, it's massive—even a bit scary—from close up. You don't appreciate the size until you move toward it; like a mountain, it seems so close but takes forever to reach. There are three observation platforms, at 200, 400, and 900 feet; the higher you go, the more you pay. The top level is not wheelchair-accessible (see "Access," page 194), but for anyone, the view from the 400-foot-high second level is plenty good. Each level requires a separate elevator (and line). As you ascend through the metal beams, imagine being a worker, perched high above nothing, riveting this giant erector

Southwest Paris

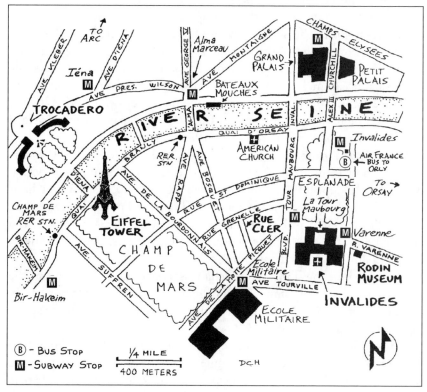

set together. On top, all of Paris lies before you, with a panorama guide. On a good day, you can see for 40 miles.

The **first level** has exhibits, a post office (daily 10:00–19:00, cancellation stamp will read Eiffel Tower), a snack bar, and souvenirs. Read the informative signs (in English) describing the major monuments, see the entertaining free movie on the history of the tower, and don't miss a century of fireworks—including the entire millennium blast—on video. Then consider a drink or a sandwich as you overlook all of Paris at the snack café (outdoor tables in summer) or at the city's best view bar/restaurant, **Altitude 95 (AE, AI, AL, AT,** Level 1—Fully accessible; €21–31 lunches, €55 dinners, dinner seatings at 19:00 and 21:00, reserve well ahead for a view table; before you ascend to dine, drop by the booth between the north/*nord* and east/*est* pillars to buy your Eiffel Tower ticket and pick up a pass that enables you to skip the line; tel. 01 45 55 20 04, fax 01 47 05 94 40).

The **second level** has the best views (non-disabled travelers can walk up the stairway to get above the netting), and a small cafeteria.

Access: Up to the second level—**AE, AI, AL, AT,** Level 1—Fully accessible, including accessible toilets on both levels, restaurants, and shops. The top level is Level 4—Not accessible to wheelchairs, but some slow walkers can make it up the narrow, steep steps from the elevator to the observation deck. If you have your heart set on a high-altitude panorama of Paris, ascend the accessible Montparnasse Tower instead (see "Sights—Southeast Paris," page 198).

Cost and Hours: It costs €4 to go to the first level, €7.50 to the second, and €11 to go all the way (not covered by museum pass). Open daily March–Sept 9:00–24:00, Oct–Feb 9:30–23:00, last entry 1 hour before closing, shorter lines at night. A TI/ticket booth is between the Pilier Nord (north pillar) and Pilier Est (east pillar). A sign in the jammed elevator tells you to beware of pickpockets. Mo: Trocadéro, RER: Champ de Mars-Tour Eiffel, tel. 01 44 11 23 23.

Crowd-Beating Tips: Wheelchair users can go to the head of the line. To avoid crowds, slow walkers should go early (by 8:45) or late in the day (after 18:00, after 20:00 in summer, last entry 1 hour before closing); weekends are worst.

Best View: The best place to view the tower is from **Trocadéro Square** to the north (about a half-mile across the river, and a happening scene at night). Another great viewpoint is the long, grassy field, le parc du Champ de Mars, to the south (after about 20:00, the *gendarmes* look the other way as Parisians stretch out or picnic on the grass). However impressive it may be by day, the tower is an awesome thing to see at twilight, when it becomes engorged with light and virile Paris lies back and lets night be on top.

▲▲**Napoleon's Tomb and Army Museum (Les Invalides)**—The emperor lies majestically dead inside several coffins under a grand dome—a goose-bumping pilgrimage for historians. Napoleon is surrounded by the tombs of other French war heroes and a fine military museum in Hôtel des Invalides. Check out the interesting World War II wing. Non-disabled travelers can follow signs to the "crypt" to find Roman Empire-style reliefs listing the accomplishments of

Napoleon's administration. The restored dome glitters with 26 pounds of gold.

Access: AE, AI, AT, Level 1—Fully accessible (except for crypt). Loaner wheelchairs are available. Most of the museum is accessible for people using wheelchairs. The crypt itself, however, has an entryway of fifteen 4" steps and a 36"-high solid railing around the tomb. Be aware of large areas of rough cobblestone.

Cost, Hours, and Location: Free for wheelchair user and companion, otherwise €6, students-€5, under 18 free, covered by museum pass, daily April–Sept 9:00–18:00, Oct–March 10:00–17:00; closed first Mon of month. Mo: La Tour Maubourg, Varenne or Invalides, tel. 01 44 42 37 72.

▲▲**Rodin Museum (Musée Rodin)**—This user-friendly museum is filled with passionate works by the greatest sculptor since Michelangelo. See *The Kiss, The Thinker, The Gates of Hell,* and many more. Don't miss

Rodin Museum and Gardens

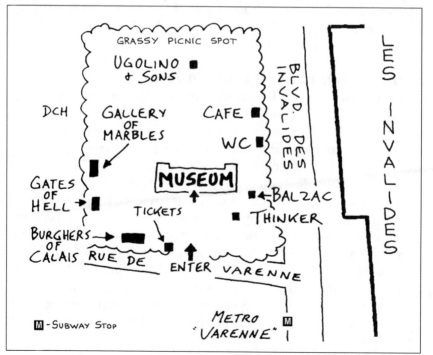

the room full of work by Rodin's student and mistress, Camille Claudel. There's a good self-serve cafeteria as well as idyllic picnic spots in the family-friendly back garden.

Access: Main floor only—**AE, AI, AT,** Level 1—Fully accessible. Only the main floor of the museum is wheelchair-accessible (via an entry ramp); to get to the upper level, you'll have to be able to climb a flight of stairs. The courtyard is made of rough cobblestone. The best part of the museum—the beautiful, sculpture-packed gardens—is fully accessible. Loaner wheelchairs are available.

Cost, Hours, and Location: Free for wheelchair user and companion, otherwise €5, €3 on Sun and for students, free for youth under 18, free for anyone on first Sun of month; covered by museum pass; €1 for gardens only, which may be Paris' best deal as many works are well displayed in the beautiful gardens; April–Sept Tue–Sun 9:30–17:45, closed Mon, gardens close 18:45, Oct–March Tue–Sun 9:30–17:00, closed Mon, gardens close 16:45; near Napoleon's Tomb, 77 rue de Varenne, Mo: Varenne, tel. 01 44 18 61 10.

Southeast Paris: The Latin Quarter

▲**Latin Quarter**—This Left Bank neighborhood just opposite Notre-Dame is the Latin Quarter. (For more information and a guided tour, see Historic Paris Roll or Stroll chapter.) This was a center of Roman Paris. But its touristic fame relates to the Latin Quarter's intriguing, artsy, bohemian character. This was perhaps Europe's leading university district in the Middle Ages—home, since the 13th century, to the prestigious Sorbonne University. Back then, Latin was the language of higher education. And, since students here came from all over Europe, Latin served as their linguistic common denominator. Locals referred to the quarter by its language: Latin. In modern times this was the center of Paris' café culture. The neighborhood's main boulevards (St. Michel and St. Germain) are lined with cafés—once the haunts of great poets and philosophers but now the hangout of tired tourists. While still youthful and artsy, the area has become a tourist ghetto filled with cheap North African eateries.

Southeast Paris

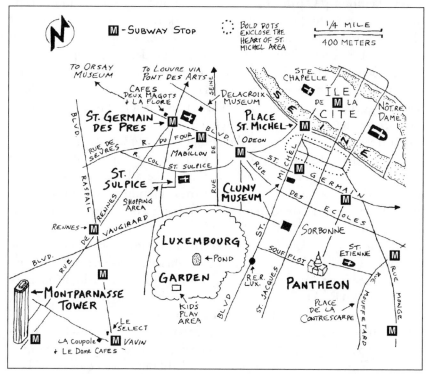

▲▲**Cluny Museum (Musée National du Moyen Age)**—This treasure trove of medieval art fills the old Roman baths, offering close-up looks at stained glass, Notre-Dame carvings, fine goldsmithing and jewelry, and rooms of tapestries—the best of which is the exquisite *Lady with the Unicorn*. In five panels, a delicate-as-medieval-can-be noble lady introduces a delighted unicorn to the senses of taste, hearing, sight, smell, and touch.

Access: Level 3—Minimally accessible. Large, rough cobblestones lead to the entrance, and the interior is even worse—multiple levels and lots of stairs without any elevators. The museum is not accessible for wheelchair users, but works for energetic, art-loving slow walkers.

Cost, Hours, and Location: €7, €5.50 on Sun, free first Sun of month, covered by museum pass, Wed–Mon 9:15–17:45, closed Tue, near corner of boulevards St. Michel and St. Germain, Mo: Cluny-La Sorbonne, St. Michel, or Odéon, tel. 01 53 73 78 00.

▲▲Luxembourg Garden (Jardin du Luxembourg)—Paris' most beautiful, interesting, and enjoyable garden/park/recreational area is a great place to watch Parisians at rest and play (open daily until dusk, Mo: Odéon, RER: Luxembourg). These private gardens are property of the French Senate (housed in the château) and have special rules governing their use (e.g., where cards can be played, where dogs can be walked, where joggers can run, when and where music can be played). The brilliant flower beds are completely changed three times a year, and the boxed trees are brought out of the orangery in May. Challenge the card and chess players to a game (near the tennis courts), rent a toy sailboat, or find a free chair near the main pond and take a breather. Notice any pigeons? The story goes that a poor Ernest Hemingway used to hand-hunt (read: strangle) them here. Paris Walking Tours offers a good tour of the park (see "Tours," page 177).

If you enjoy the Luxembourg Garden and want to see more, visit the nearby, colorful Jardin des Plantes (Mo: Jussieu or Gare d'Austerlitz, RER: Luxembourg) and the more elegant Parc Monceau (Mo: Monceau).

Access: AE, AI, Level 1—Fully accessible. The park has specific, gated entrances that lead to paved or dirt paths.

Montparnasse Tower (La Tour Montparnasse)—This wheelchair-accessible 59-story superscraper is cheaper and easier to get to the top of than the Eiffel Tower, and it has the added bonus of one of Paris' best views—since the Eiffel Tower is in sight, and the Montparnasse Tower isn't. If you couldn't go to the top of the Eiffel Tower to get your panoramic bearings, you can do it here instead with easy access. Buy the photo guide to the city, then go to the rooftop and orient yourself.

Access: AE, AI, AL, AT, Level 1—Fully accessible. Wheelchair users can easily ascend to the top of the tower. You'll also find an accessible toilet in the shopping center below the tower.

Cost, Hours, and Location: €8.20, not covered by museum pass, daily in summer 9:30–23:30, off-season 10:00–22:00, disappointing after dark, entrance on rue de l'Arrivée, Mo: Montparnasse-Bienvenüe.

Northwest Paris

▲▲**Place de la Concorde and the Champs-Elysées**—This famous boulevard is Paris' backbone, and has the greatest concentration of traffic. All of France seems to converge on the place de la Concorde, the city's largest square. It was here that the guillotine took the lives of thousands—

Northwest Paris

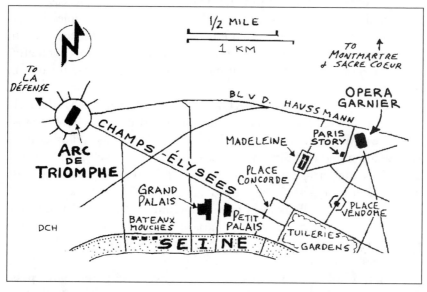

including King Louis XVI and Marie-Antoinette. Back then it was called the place de la Revolution.

Catherine de Médicis wanted a place to drive her carriage, so she started draining the swamp that would become the avenue des Champs-Elysées. Napoleon put on the final touches, and it's been the place to be seen ever since. The Tour de France bicycle race ends here, as do all parades (French or foe) of any significance. While the boulevard has become a bit hamburgerized, a roll or stroll here is great fun. Still, this can be a challenging area for wheelchair users and slow walkers—with lots of traffic (Parisian drivers get the right-of-way) and stairs. For a guided, accessible roll or stroll from the top to the bottom of the Champs-Elysées, see page 268.

▲▲▲**Arc de Triomphe**—Napoleon had the magnificent Arc de Triomphe commissioned to commemorate his victory at the battle of Austerlitz. There's no triumphal arch bigger (164 feet high, 130 feet wide). And, with 12 converging boulevards, there's no traffic circle more thrilling

to experience—either behind the wheel, or on foot (inaccessible by wheelchair). From the base of the arch, a wheelchair-accessible elevator or a spiral staircase leads to a cute museum devoted to the arch. From there, stairs (but no elevator) lead to a grand view at the top, even after dark. For more information about the arch, including a self-guided tour, see page 268.

Access: Museum only—**AE+A, AI, AL,** Level 2—Moderately accessible. To get to the arch from surrounding streets, you have to cross the huge traffic circle that surrounds it. Wheelchair users and other travelers with limited mobility should have a taxi drop them off right at the base of the arch itself (the only other option is an underground passage with stairs: twenty-five 6" steps down and thirty 6" steps back up). Once at the arch, a lift will take you to the museum on the third level, where you can enjoy some good views of Paris. The viewing terrace at the very top of the arch can only be reached by climbing 46 stairs (Level 4—Not accessible).

Cost, Hours, and Location: €7, covered by museum pass, April–Sept daily 10:00–23:00, Oct–March daily 10:00–22:30, Mo: Charles de Gaulle-Etoile, tel. 01 55 37 73 77.

▲**Old Opera (Opéra Garnier)**—This grand palace of the belle époque was built for Napoleon III and finished in 1875. (After completing this project, the architect—Charles Garnier—went south to do the casino in Monte Carlo.) From the grand avenue de l'Opéra, once lined with Paris' most fashionable haunts, the newly restored facade seems to say "all power to the wealthy." While huge, the actual theater fits only 2,000 spectators. The real show was before and after, when the elite of Paris—out to see and be seen—strutted their elegant stuff in the extravagant lobbies. Think of the grand marble stairway as a theater itself.

While the theater interior is wheelchair-accessible for theatergoers, the in-depth walking tours of the Opéra are not. However you get inside, imagine the place filled with the beautiful people of the day. The massive foundations straddle an underground lake (creating the mysterious world of *The Phantom of the Opera*). The actual red-velvet theater boasts a colorful ceiling by Marc Chagall (1964), playfully dancing around the eight-ton chandelier. Note the box seats next to the stage—the most expensive in the house, with an obstructed view of the stage but just right if you're there only to be seen. The elitism of this place prompted President François Mitterand to have a people's opera house built in the 1980s (symbolically on place de la Bastille, where the French Revolution started in 1789). This left the Opéra Garnier home only to a ballet and occasional concerts (usually no performances mid-July–mid-Sept). While the library/museum is of interest to opera buffs, non-disabled visitors will enjoy the second-floor grand foyer and Salon du Glacier, iced with decor typical of 1900.

American Express and the *Paris Story* film (listed below) are on the left side of the Opéra, and the venerable Galeries Lafayette department store (**AE, AI, AL, AT,** Level 1—Fully accessible) is just behind.

Access: AE, AL, AI, Level 1—Fully accessible. There is a ramp entry on rue Scribe and special seats accessible by lift for wheelchair users. Friendly customer service agent Sandrine (tel. 01 40 01 18 50) can help you with accessibility arrangements and ticketing. Non-disabled travelers enter through the front off place de l'Opéra.

Cost, Hours, and Location: €6, not covered by museum pass, daily 10:00–17:00 except when in use for performance, €10 English tours summers only, normally at 12:00 and 14:00, 90 min, includes entry, call to confirm; enter through the front off place de l'Opéra, Mo: Opéra, tel. 01 40 01 22 53.

Paris Story **Film**—This entertaining film offers a good and painless overview of the city's turbulent and brilliant past, covering 2,000 years in 45 fast-moving minutes. The theater's wide-screen projection and cushy chairs provide an ideal break from bad weather and weary bones and make this a fun activity to do with kids.

Access: Level 4—Not accessible. Slow walkers must climb stairs to get to the theater (no elevator).

Cost, Hours, and Location: €8, ages 6–18-€5, family of 4-€21, not covered by museum pass, get a 20 percent discount with this book, shows on the hour daily 9:00–19:00, next to Opéra at 11 rue Scribe, Mo: Opéra, tel. 01 42 66 62 06.

▲**La Défense and La Grande Arche**—Beam yourself out to this *Star Wars*-like complex of glass towers and men in suits to contemplate the future of Paris and to experience the ultimate contrast of old and new. The La Défense business and shopping center was first conceived nearly 60 years ago to create a U.S.-styled forest of skyscrapers to accommodate the business needs of the modern world. Today La Défense is home to 150,000 employees and 55,000 residents.

La Grande Arche is the centerpiece of this ambitious complex.

Inaugurated in 1989 on the 200th anniversary of the French Revolution, it was dedicated to human rights and brotherhood. The place is big—38 floors holding offices for 30,000 people on more than 200 acres. They say that Notre-Dame Cathedral could fit under its arch.

The complex at La Défense is an interesting study in 1960s land-use planning, directing lots of business and development away from downtown and allowing central Paris to retain its more elegant feel. This makes sense to most Parisians, regardless of whatever else they feel about this controversial complex.

For a good visit, explore the Grande Arche (Mo: La Défense), then roll or stroll among the glass buildings to the Esplanade de La Défense Métro station, and return home from there (by taxi or Métro). After enjoying the elegance of downtown Paris' historic, glorious monuments, you may agree that La Défense proves that man can build bigger, but not more beautiful.

Access: AE, AI, AL, AT, Level 1—Fully accessible. A combination of elevators, ramps, and stairlifts makes the Grande Arche accessible to wheelchair users. Don't be shy to ask staff for assistance (operating stair-lifts, finding the accessible route, etc.).

Cost, Hours, and Location: €8, under 18-€6, family deals, not covered by museum pass, daily 10:00–19:00, includes a film on its construction and art exhibits, RER or Mo: La Défense, follow signs to Grande Arche, tel. 01 49 07 27 57.

North Paris: Montmartre

▲▲**Sacré-Cœur and Montmartre**—This Byzantine-looking basilica, while only 130 years old, is impressive. One block from the basilica, the place du Tertre was the haunt of Toulouse-Lautrec and the original bohemians. Today it's mobbed with tourists and unoriginal bohemians, but it's still fun (go early in the morning to beat the crowds).

Access: AI, Level 4—Not accessible. Wheelchair users and others with limited mobility will probably want to skip the church interior. If you do go, take a taxi to the foot of the church steps. From there, you'll have to climb 26 steps with no railing to reach the entry. Once you're inside, it's all on one level.

Cost, Hours, and Location: Free, daily 7:00–23:00. Non-disabled travelers can pay €5 to climb the dome (Level 4—Not accessible; daily June–Sept 9:00–19:00, Oct–May 10:00–18:00). Disabled travelers should arrive by taxi (tell the driver to take you to the foot of the basilica steps). Non-disabled travelers and slow walkers can take the Métro to the Anvers stop (1 Métro ticket buys your way up the funicular and avoids all but the last 26 stairs) or the closer but less scenic Abbesses stop. A taxi to the top of the hill saves time and avoids sweat.

Pigalle—Paris' red-light district, the infamous "Pig Alley," is at the foot of butte Montmartre. *Oo la la.* It's more shocking than dangerous. Roll or stroll from place Pigalle to place Blanche, teasing desperate barkers and fast-talking temptresses. In bars, a €150 bottle of cheap champagne comes with a friend. Stick to the bigger streets, hang on to your wallet, and exercise good judgment. Cancan can cost a fortune, as can con artists in topless bars. After dark, countless tour buses line the streets, reminding us that tour guides make big bucks by bringing their groups to touristy nightclubs like the famous Moulin Rouge (Mo: Pigalle or Abbesses).

Northeast Paris: Marais Neighborhood and More

The Marais neighborhood extends along the Right Bank of the Seine from the Pompidou Center to the Bastille. It contains more pre-revolutionary lanes and buildings than anywhere else in town and is more atmospheric than touristy. It's medieval Paris. This is how much of the city looked until, in the mid-1800s, Napoleon III had Baron Haussmann blast out the narrow streets to construct broad boulevards (wide enough for the guns and ranks of the army, too wide for revolutionary barricades), thus creating modern Paris. Originally a swamp *(marais)* during the reign of Henry IV, this area became the hometown of the French aristocracy. In the 17th century, big shots built their private mansions *(hôtels)*, close to Henry IV's place des Vosges. When exploring the Marais, stick to the west-east axis formed by rue Sainte-Croix de la Bretonnerie, rue des Rosiers (heart of Paris' Jewish community), and rue St. Antoine. On Sunday afternoons, this trendy area pulses with shoppers and café crowds.

Northeast Paris

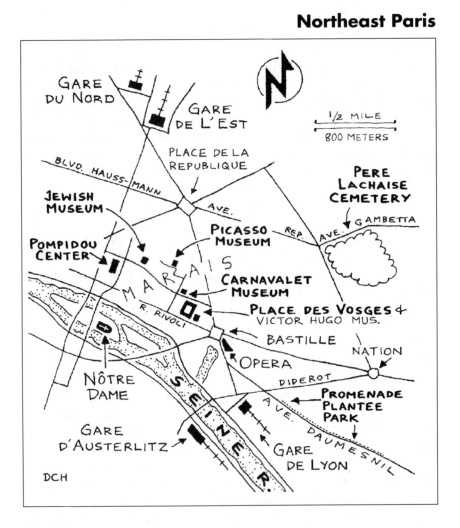

▲**Place des Vosges**—Study the architecture in this grand square: nine pavilions per side. Some of the brickwork is real, some is fake. If you are able, go to the center, where Louis XIII sits on a horse surrounded by locals enjoying their community park. Children frolic in the sandbox, lovers warm benches, and pigeons guard their fountains while trees shade this retreat from the glare of the big city. Henry IV built this centerpiece of the Marais in 1605. As hoped, this turned the Marais into Paris' most exclusive neighborhood. As the nobility flocked to Versailles in a later age, this too was a magnet for the rich and powerful of France. With the

Revolution, the aristocratic elegance of this quarter became working-class, filled with gritty shops, artisans, immigrants, and Jews. **Victor Hugo** lived at #6, and you can visit his house (**AE, AI, AT,** Level 1—Fully accessible; free, Tue–Sun 10:00–17:40, closed Mon, 6 place des Vosges, tel. 01 42 72 10 16).

Access: The park is Level 2—Moderately Accessible. The sidewalks around place des Voges are at street level, but to get into the courtyard at the square's center, you'll have to negotiate three stairs down, then another three back up (no railing).

▲▲**Pompidou Center**—Europe's greatest collection of far-out modern art, the Musée National d'Art Moderne, is housed on the fourth and fifth

floors of this newly renovated and colorful exoskeletal building. Once ahead of its time, this 20th-century (remember that century?) art has been waiting for the world to catch up with it. After so many Madonnas-and-Children, a piano smashed to bits and glued to the wall is refreshing. The Pompidou Center and its square are lively, with lots of people, street theater, and activity inside and out—a perpetual street fair. Kids of any age enjoy the fun, colorful fountains (called *Homage to Stravinsky*) on the square.

Access: AE, AI, AL, AT, Level 1—Fully accessible. The vast entry ramp has bumpy cobblestones, but if you like modern art, it's worth the trip to reach the fully accessible interior.

Cost, Hours, and Location: €5.50, free on first Sun of the month, covered by museum pass, audioguide–€4, Wed–Mon 11:00–21:00, closed Tue and May 1; to use escalator you need museum ticket or museum pass, good Café La Mezzanine on Level 1 is cheaper than cafés outside, Mo: Rambuteau, tel. 01 44 78 12 33.

▲▲**Jewish Art and History Museum (Musée d'Art et Histoire du Judaïsme)**—This fascinating museum is located in a beautifully restored Marais mansion and tells the story of Judaism throughout Europe, from the Roman destruction of Jerusalem to the theft of famous artworks during World War II. Helpful, free audioguides and many English explanations make this an enjoyable history lesson (red numbers on small signs indicate the number you should press on your audioguide). Move along at your own speed. The museum illustrates the cultural unity maintained by this continually dispersed population. You'll learn about the history of Jewish traditions from bar mitzvahs to menorahs, and see exquisite traditional costumes and objects around which daily life revolved. Don't miss the explanation of "the Dreyfus affair," a major event in French politics in the early 1900s. You'll also see photographs of and paintings by famous Jewish artists, including Chagall, Modigliani, and Soutine. A small, moving section is devoted to the deportation of Jews from Paris.

Access: AE, AI, AL, AT, ♥, Level 1—Fully accessible.

Cost, Hours, and Location: €6.50, ages 18–26-€4, under 18 free, not covered by museum pass, Mon–Fri 11:00–18:00, Sun 10:00–18:00, closed Sat, 71 rue du Temple, Mo: Rambuteau or Hôtel de Ville a few blocks away, tel. 01 53 01 86 60.

▲**Picasso Museum (Musée Picasso)**—Tucked into a corner of the Marais and worth ▲▲▲ if you're a Picasso fan, this museum contains the world's largest collection of Picasso's paintings, sculptures, sketches, and ceramics, and includes his small collection of Impressionist art. The art is well-displayed in a fine old mansion with a peaceful garden café. The room-by-room English introductions help make sense of Picasso's work—from the Toulouse-Lautrec-like portraits at the beginning of his career, to his gray-brown Cubist period, to his Salvador Dalí–like finish. The well-done €3 English guidebook helps Picassophiles appreciate the context of his art and learn more about his interesting life. Most will be happy reading the posted English explanations while moving at a steady pace through the museum—the ground and first floors satisfied our curiosity.

Access: AE, AI, AL, Level 1—Fully accessible. Leaving rue Thorigny, wheelchair users will need to cover 100 feet of bumpy cobblestones to reach the museum.

Cost, Hours, and Location: €5.50, free first Sun of month, covered by museum pass, Wed–Mon 9:30–18:00, closes at 17:30 Oct–March, closed Tue, 5 rue Thorigny, Mo: St. Paul or Chemin Vert, tel. 01 42 71 25 21.

▲▲**Carnavalet Museum**—The tumultuous history of Paris is well-displayed in this converted Marais mansion. Unfortunately, accessibility is difficult, and explanations are in French only, but many displays are fairly self-explanatory. You'll see paintings of Parisian scenes, French

Revolution paraphernalia, old Parisian store signs, a small guillotine, a model of 16th-century Ile de la Cité (notice the bridge houses), and rooms full of 15th-century Parisian furniture.

Access: Level 4—Not accessible (packed with stairs, no elevator).

Cost, Hours, and Location: Free, Tue–Sun 10:00–18:00, closed Mon, 23 rue de Sévigné, Mo: St. Paul, tel. 01 44 59 58 58.

▲**Promenade Plantée Park**—This two-mile-long, narrow garden walk on a viaduct was once a railroad and is now a joy. At times, stairs lead back down to the street between elevated segments. The shops below the viaduct's arches make for entertaining window-shopping.

Access: Level 4—Not accessible. With many stairs up and down, this is inaccessible to all but the most energetic slow walkers.

Cost, Hours, and Location: Free, opens Mon–Fri at 8:00, Sat–Sun at 9:00, closes at sunset. It runs from place de la Bastille (Mo: Bastille) along avenue Daumesnil to St. Mandé (Mo: Michel Bizot). To reach the park from place de la Bastille, take avenue Daumesnil (past opera building) to the intersection with avenue Ledru Rollin; walk up the stairs and through the gate.

▲**Père Lachaise Cemetery (Cimetière Père Lachaise)**—Littered with the tombstones of many of the city's most illustrious dead, this is your best one-stop look at the fascinating, romantic world of "permanent Parisians." More like a small city, the place is confusing, but maps will direct you to the graves of Frédéric Chopin, Molière, Edith Piaf, Oscar Wilde, Gertrude Stein, Jim Morrison, and Héloïse and Abélard. In section 97, a series of statues memorializing World War II makes the French war experience a bit more real (helpful €1.50 maps at flower store near entry, closes at dusk, across street from Métro stop, Mo: Père Lachaise or bus #69).

Access: Level 3—Minimally accessible. With lots of steps and cobbled, uneven terrain, the cemetery is best left to energetic slow walkers.

PALACE OF VERSAILLES

Every king's dream, Versailles was the residence of the French king and the cultural heartbeat of Europe for about 100 years—until the Revolution of 1789 ended the notion that God deputized some people to rule for Him on Earth. Louis XIV spent half a year's income of Europe's

richest country turning his dad's hunting lodge into a palace fit for a divine monarch. Louis XV and Louis XVI spent much of the 18th century gilding Louis XIV's lily. In 1837, about 50 years after the royal family was evicted, King Louis Philippe opened the palace as a museum. Europe's next-best palaces are Versailles wannabes.

Access: AE, AI, AL, AT, Level 1—Fully accessible. Loaner wheelchairs are available. Wheelchair accessibility is through entrance H. The elevator to the upper floor and loaner wheelchairs are also located here. The wheelchair-accessible toilet is located at the end of the tour (you can also use it before beginning the tour; ask the staff for help finding it). Once inside Versailles, the entire palace interior is fully accessible. The gardens around Versailles are also wheelchair-accessible (see "Getting around the Gardens," page 211). The Grand Trianon is accessible, but the Petit Trianon is only minimally so. Parts of the grounds, such as the Hamlet, are accessed via a rough path that may be challenging for wheelchair users.

Information: A helpful TI (**AE, AI,** Level 1—Fully accessible) is near Sofitel Hôtel between the Versailles R.G. station and the palace (May–Sept daily 9:00–19:00, Oct–April daily 9:00–18:00, tel. 01 39 24 88 88, www.chateauversailles.fr). You'll also find information booths inside the château (doors A, B-2, and C) and, in peak season, kiosks scattered around the courtyard. The useful brochure "Versailles Orientation Guide" explains your sightseeing options. A baggage check is available at door A.

Cost: Free for wheelchair user and companion; otherwise €7.50 (main palace and both Trianons are covered by museum pass); €5.50 after 15:30, under 18 free (the palace is also theoretically free for all teachers, professors, and architecture students). Admission is payable at entrances A, C, and D (wheelchair users report to entrance H). Tours cost extra (see "Touring Versailles," page 210). The Grand and Petit Trianons cost €5 together, €3 after 15:30 (both covered by museum pass). The gardens, which usually cost €3, are €5.50 on fountain "spray days" on summer weekends (gardens not covered by museum pass, see "Fountain Spectacles," page 211).

Hours: The **palace** is open May–Sept Tue–Sun 9:00–18:30, Oct–April Tue–Sun 9:00–17:30, closed Mon (last entry 30 min before

Versailles Town

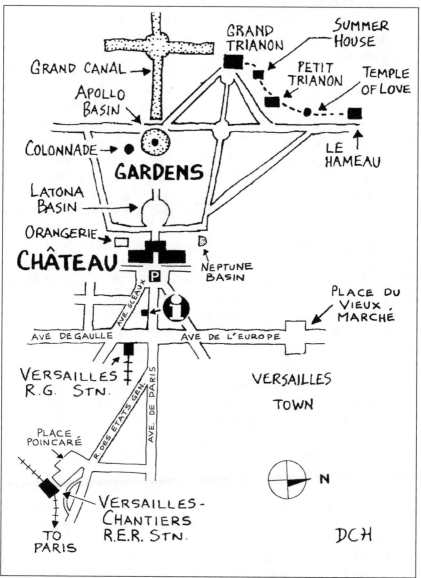

closing). The **Grand and Petit Trianon Palaces** are open daily April–Oct 12:00–18:00, Nov–March 12:00–17:00, closed Mon. The **garden** is open daily from 7:00 (8:00 in winter) to sunset (as late as 21:30 or as early as 17:30).

In summer, Versailles is especially crowded around 10:00 and 13:00, and all day Tue and Sun. Remember, the crowds gave Marie-Antoinette a pain in the neck, too, so relax and let them eat cake. For fewer crowds, go early or late: Either arrive by 9:00 (when the palace opens, touring the palace first, then the gardens) or after 15:30 (you'll get a reduced entry ticket, but you'll miss the last guided tours of the day, which generally depart at 15:00). If you arrive midday, see the gardens first and the palace later, at 15:00. The gardens and palace are great late. On our last visit, we were the only tourists in the Hall of Mirrors at 18:00...even on a Tuesday.

Touring Versailles: Versailles' highlights are the State Apartments, the magnificent Hall of Mirrors (both fully accessible), the lavish King's Private Apartments (not wheelchair-accessible), and the Opera House (not accessible). Most visitors are satisfied with a spin through the State Apartments, the gardens, and the Trianons. Versailles aficionados who are able find it worth their time (and money) to see the King's Private Apartments, which can be visited only with an audioguide or live guide (neither tour covered by museum pass).

Guided tours: The in-depth guided tours of Versailles are not wheelchair-accessible (there are stairs and other barriers along the route). Slow walkers can select a one-hour guided tour from a variety of themes, such as the daily life of a king or the lives of such lesser-known nobles as the well-coiffed Madame de Pompadour (€4, join first English tour available). Or consider the 90-minute tour (€6) of the King's Private Apartments (Louis XV, Louis XVI, and Marie-Antoinette) and the chapel. This tour, which is the only way visitors can see the sumptuous Opera House, can be long depending on the quality of your guide. Wheelchair users are welcome on these tours.

For a live tour, make reservations immediately upon arrival, as tours can sell out by 13:00 (first tours generally begin at 10:00, last tours depart usually at 15:00 but as late as 16:00).

The price of any tour is added to the €7.50 entry fee that non-disabled travelers pay to enter Versailles (entry covered by Paris museum pass, but tours are not). If you don't have a pass, keep your ticket as proof you've paid for admission in case you decide to take a guided tour after you've wandered through the palace by yourself.

Audioguide tours: The informative but dry audioguide costs €4.

Self-guided tour: To tour the palace on your own, join the line at entrance A if you need to pay admission. Those with a museum pass are allowed in through entrance B-2 without a wait (wheelchair riders use entrance H). Enter the palace and take a one-way roll or stroll through the State Apartments from the King's Wing, through the Hall of Mirrors, and out via the Queen's and Nobles' Wing.

The Hall of Mirrors was the ultimate hall of the day—250 feet long, with 17 arched mirrors matching 17 windows with royal garden views, 24 gilded candelabra, eight busts of Roman emperors, and eight classical-style statues (7 are ancient originals). The ceiling is decorated with stories of  Louis' triumphs. Imagine this place filled with silk gowns and powdered wigs, lit by thousands of candles. The mirrors—a luxurious rarity at the time—were a reflection of an age when aristocrats felt good about their looks and their fortunes. In another time altogether, this was the room in which the Treaty of Versailles was signed, ending World War I.

Before going downstairs at the end (elevator available), take a roll or stroll clockwise around the long room filled with the great battles of France murals. If you don't have *Rick Steves' Paris* or *Rick Steves' Mona Winks*, the guidebook called *The Châteaux, The Gardens, and Trianon* gives a room-by-room rundown.

Fountain Spectacles: Classical music fills the king's backyard, and the garden's fountains are in full squirt, on Sat July–Sept and on Sun early April-early Oct (schedule for both days: 11:00–12:00 & 15:30–17:00 & 17:20–17:30). On these "spray days," the gardens cost €5.50 (not covered by museum pass, ask for a map of fountains). Louis had his engineers literally reroute a river to fuel these fountains. Even by today's standards, they are impressive. Pick up the helpful brochure of the fountain show ("Les Grandes Eaux Musicales") at any information booth for a guide to the fountains. Also ask about the impressive *Les Fêtes de Nuit* nighttime spectacle (some Sat, July–mid-Sept).

Getting around the Gardens: It's a half-mile roll or stroll from the palace, down the canal, past the two mini-palaces to the Hamlet. The

Versailles Entrances

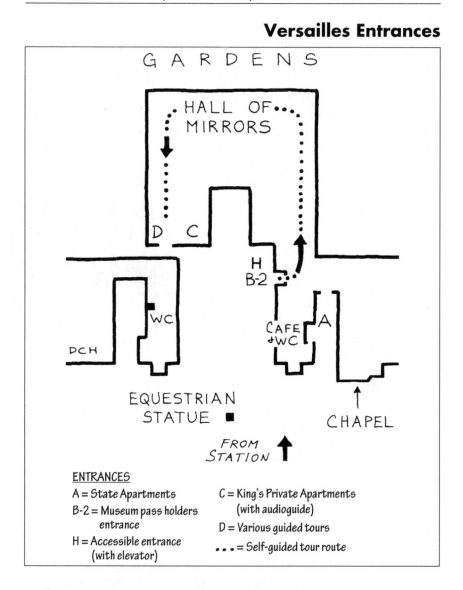

ENTRANCES

A = State Apartments

B-2 = Museum pass holders
   entrance

H = Accessible entrance
   (with elevator)

C = King's Private Apartments
   (with audioguide)

D = Various guided tours

••• = Self-guided tour route

gardens are wheelchair-accessible (**AE, AI,** Level 1—Fully accessible)—wheelchair riders can use the ramps (also used by tourist train and horse-drawn buggies) to access the dirt and small-stone pathways. There are several restaurants (accessible) and toilets (not accessible) sprinkled throughout the garden. The wheelchair-accessible toilet is located near the entrance of the Grand Trianon (see next page).

The fast-looking, slow-moving tourist train leaves from behind the chateau and serves the Grand Canal and the Trianons (Level 3—Minimally accessible; €5, 4/hr, 4 stops, you can hop on and off as you like; nearly worthless commentary).

Palace Gardens: The gardens offer a world of royal amusements.

Outside the palace is *l'orangerie.* Louis, the only person who could grow oranges in Paris, had a mobile orange grove that could be wheeled in and out of his greenhouses according to the weather. An accessible promenade leads from the palace to the Grand Canal, an artificial lake that, in Louis' day, was a mini-sea with nine ships, including a 32-cannon warship. France's royalty used to float up and down the canal in Venetian gondolas.

While Louis cleverly used palace life at Versailles to "domesticate" his nobility, turning otherwise meddlesome nobles into groveling socialites, all this pomp and ceremony hampered the royal family as well. For an escape from the public life at Versailles, they built more intimate palaces as retreats in their garden. Before the Revolution there was plenty of space to retreat—the grounds were enclosed by a 25-mile-long fence.

The beautifully restored **Grand Trianon Palace (AE, AI,** Level 1—Fully accessible) is as sumptuous as the main palace, but much smaller. With its pastel-pink colonnade and more human scale, this is a place you'd like to call home. The nearby **Petit Trianon (AE, AI+A,** Level 3—Minimally accessible), which has a fine neoclassical exterior and a skippable interior, was Marie-Antoinette's favorite residence (see "Cost" and "Hours," page 208).

You can almost see princesses bobbing gaily in the branches as you go through the enchanting forest, past the white marble temple of love (1778) to the queen's fake-peasant **Hamlet** (*le Hameau;* interior not tourable, exterior can be visited only via a gravelly, sandy path that may be difficult for wheelchair users). Palace life really got to Marie-Antoinette. Sort of a back-to-basics queen, she retreated further and further from her blue-blooded reality. Her happiest days were spent at the

Hamlet, under a bonnet, tending her perfumed sheep and her manicured gardens in a thatch-happy wonderland.

Cafés: The cafeteria and toilets are next to entrance A (stairs make them Level 4—Not accessible). You'll find a sandwich kiosk and a decent restaurant (**AE+A, AI,** Level 2—Moderately accessible) at the canal in the garden. A handy McDonald's is immediately across from the Versailles R.G. train station (fully accessible toilet without crowds).

Getting There: Slow walkers will take a RER-C train to Versailles R.G. or "Rive Gauche" (not wheelchair-accessible), near the palace. Wheelchair users: see "For Wheelchair Users," below.

Trains leave about five times an hour for the palace from these Paris RER stops: Gare d'Austerlitz, St. Michel, Musée d'Orsay, Invalides, Pont de l'Alma, and Champ de Mars-Tour Eiffel (€5 round-trip, 30 min one-way, line C5, direction: Versailles R.G.). Any train whose name starts with a *V* (e.g., "Vick") goes to Versailles; don't board other trains. Get off at the last stop (Versailles Rive Gauche), turn right out of the station, and turn left at the first boulevard. It's about a third of a mile to the palace.

When returning from Versailles, look through the windows past the turnstiles for the departure board. Any train leaving Versailles serves all downtown Paris RER line C stops (they're marked on the schedule as stopping at *"toutes les gares jusqu'à Austerlitz,"* meaning "all stations until Austerlitz").

Taxis for the 30-minute ride between Versailles and Paris cost about €25 one-way.

To reach Versailles from Paris by **car,** get on the *périphérique* freeway that circles Paris and take the toll-free autoroute A-13 toward Rouen. Follow signs into Versailles, then look for "château" signs and park in the huge lot in front of the palace (pay lot). An accompanying driver can drop the wheelchair user off in the palace courtyard (right at entrance H) before parking the car. The drive takes about 30 minutes one-way.

For Wheelchair Users: To reach Versailles from downtown Paris, wheelchair users have two options: RER or taxi. The RER train is much cheaper (€5 round-trip), but the only fully accessible RER station in Versailles is a good three-quarters of a mile from the palace—so you're in for a long roll. A taxi is more expensive, but it drops you off at the palace doorstep (about €50 round-trip, **AE+A,** Level 2—Moderately accessible; wheelchair users need to enter cab on their own, and driver will put folded wheelchair in trunk).

Realistically, the cheapest option might be to combine these methods: Take the RER to the Versailles-Chantiers station, then catch a taxi for the cheap and quick ride to the palace.

If you decide to take the RER train, start at the accessible Invalides Métro station in downtown Paris (has elevator). Arrive at the station early and ask for assistance at the ticket counter (they will prepare a lift for your use). Take the **RER-C train** (€5 round-trip, 30 min one-way, accessible toilet in first class) on line C7 (direction: Saint-Quentin-en-Yvelines) or C8 (direction: Versailles-Chantiers). Either train takes you to the Versailles-Chantiers station (has elevator). Upon arrival, pick up an information sheet at the *accueil* information kiosk in the station to help guide you the rest of the way. From here, you're three-quarters of a mile from the palace. Catch a taxi, or roll almost a half-mile on rue des Etats-Généraux (has curb cuts) to avenue de Paris. Then it's another quarter-mile on avenue de Paris (use bike path) to the palace. The entryway from the street to the palace is over large, rough, uneven cobblestones that can be challenging to traverse on wheels.

Town of Versailles: After the palace closes and the tourists go, the prosperous, wholesome town of Versailles feels a long way from Paris. In the pleasant town center, around place du Marché Notre-Dame, you'll find a variety of reasonable hotels, restaurants, cafés, and a few cobbled lanes. The square is a quarter-mile from the château (veer left when you leave château). The central market thrives on place du Marché on Sunday, Tuesday, and Friday until 13:00 (leaving the Versailles R.G. RER station, turn right and roll or stroll 10 min). Consider the wisdom of picking up or dropping your rental car in Versailles rather than in Paris. In Versailles, the Hertz and Avis offices are at Gare des Chantiers (served by Paris' Montparnasse station).

Sleeping in Versailles: If you want to sleep in Versailles to avoid the big-city crowds (and prices), consider **Hôtel d'Angleterre** (AE+A, AI, AR, AB+A, ♥,** Level 2—Moderately accessible). Away from the frenzy, this is a tranquil old place with smiling Polish Madame Kutyla in control. Rooms are comfortable and spacious. The hotel has three suitable rooms on the main floor with roomy (but not adapted) bathrooms. Park nearby in the château lot (Db-€58–88, extra bed-€15, just below palace to the right as you exit, 2 rue de Fontenay, tel. 01 39 51 43 50, fax 01 39 51 45 63, hotel.angleterre@voila.fr).

SHOPPING PARISIAN-STYLE

Even staunch anti-shoppers may be tempted to partake of chic Paris. Wandering among the elegant and outrageous boutiques provides a break from the heavy halls of the Louvre, and, if you approach it right, a little cultural enlightenment.

Here are some tips for avoiding *faux pas* and making the most of the experience.

French Etiquette: Before you enter a Parisian store, remember the following points.

- In small stores, always greet the clerk by saying *Bonjour,* plus the appropriate title *(Madame, Mademoiselle,* or *Monsieur).* When leaving, say, *Au revoir, Madame/Mademoiselle/Monsieur.*
- The customer is not always right. In fact, figure the clerk is doing you a favor by waiting on you.
- Except for in department stores, it's not normal for the customer to handle clothing. Ask first.
- Observe French shoppers. Then imitate.

Department Stores: Like cafés, department stores were invented here (surprisingly, not in America). Parisian department stores, monuments to a more relaxed and elegant era, begin with their spectacular perfume sections. Helpful information desks are usually nearby (pick up the handy store floor plan in English). Most stores have a good selection of souvenirs and toys at fair prices and reasonable restaurants; some have great view terraces. Choose from these great Parisian department stores: Galeries Lafayette (**AE, AI, AL, AT,** Level 1—Fully accessible; behind old Opéra Garnier, Mo: Opéra), Printemps (**AE, AI, AL, AT,** Level 1—Fully accessible; next door to Galeries Lafayette), and Samaritaine (**AE, AI, AL, AT,** Level 1—Fully accessible; near pont Neuf, Mo: Pont Neuf).

Boutiques: While boutiques are more intimate, sales clerks are more formal—mind your manners.

Here are four very different areas to explore. Streets and sidewalks are accessible, but some of the specific shops are not. If a place isn't accessible, just savor the window-shopping.

A roll or stroll from Sèvres-Babylone to St. Sulpice allows you to sample smart, classic clothing boutiques while enjoying one of Paris' prettier neighborhoods—for sustenance along the way, there's La Maison du Chocolat at 19 rue de Sèvres, selling handmade chocolates in exquisitely wrapped boxes.

The ritzy streets connecting place de la Madeleine and place Vendôme form a miracle mile of gourmet food shops, jewelry stores, four-star hotels, perfumeries, and exclusive clothing boutiques. Fauchon, on place de la Madeleine, is a bastion of over-the-top food products, hawking €7,000 bottles of Cognac (who buys this stuff?). Hédiard, across the square from Fauchon, is an older, more appealing, and accessible gourmet food shop. Next door, La Maison des Truffes sells black mushrooms for about €180 a pound, and white truffles from Italy for €2,500 a pound.

For more eclectic, avant-garde stores, peruse the artsy shops between the Pompidou Center and place des Vosges in the Marais.

For a contemporary, more casual, and less frenetic shopping experience, and to see Paris' latest urban renewal project, take the Métro to Bercy Village, a once-thriving wine-warehouse district that has been transformed into an outdoor shopping mall (Mo: Cour St. Emilion).

Flea Markets: Paris hosts several sprawling weekend flea markets (*marché aux puces,* mar-shay oh poos; literally translated, since *puce* is French for flea). While these markets are often moderately accessible, the crowds and tight aisles can make them unappealing to wheelchair users. These oversized garage sales date back to the Middle Ages, when middlemen would sell old, flea-infested clothes and discarded possessions of the wealthy at bargain prices to eager peasants. Today, some travelers find them claustrophobic, crowded, monster versions of those back home, though others enjoy them as French diamonds-in-the-rough and return happy.

The Puces St. Ouen (poos sahn-wahn) is the biggest and oldest of them all, with more than 2,000 vendors selling everything from flamingos to faucets (Sat 9:00–18:30, Sun–Mon 10:00–18:30, Mo: Porte de Clingancourt).

Street Markets: Several traffic-free street markets overflow with flowers, produce, fish vendors, and butchers, examples of the way most Parisians shopped before there were supermarkets and department stores. While some areas of these markets might be inaccessible, wheelchair users can generally find their way around them well enough. Good market streets include the rue Cler (Mo: Ecole Militaire), rue Montorgueil (Mo: Etienne Marcel), rue Mouffetard (Mo: Cardinal Lemoine or

Censier-Daubenton), and rue Daguerre (Mo: Denfert-Rochereau).
Browse these markets to collect a classy picnic (open daily except Sun
afternoons and Mon, also closed for lunch 13:00–15:00).

Souvenir Shops: Avoid souvenir carts in front of famous monuments. Prices and selection are better in shops and department stores.
The riverfront stalls near Notre-Dame sell a variety of used books, magazines, and tourist paraphernalia in the most romantic setting.

Whether you indulge in a new wardrobe, an artsy poster, or just one
luscious pastry, you'll find that a shopping excursion provides a priceless
slice of Parisian life.

NIGHTLIFE

Paris is brilliant after dark. Save energy from your day's sightseeing and
get out at night. Whether it's a concert at a church, an elevator up the
Arc de Triomphe, or a late-night café, experience the City of Light lit up.
If a **Seine River cruise** appeals, see "Tours," page 177.

Pariscope magazine (see "Tourist Information," page 168), offers a
complete weekly listing of music, cinema, theater, opera, and other special
events. *Paris Voice* newspaper, in English, has a monthly review of Paris
entertainment (available at any English-language bookstore, French-
American establishments, or the American Church, www.parisvoice.com).

Classical Concerts: For classical music on any night, consult
Pariscope magazine; the "Musique" section under "Concerts Classiques"
lists concerts (free and fee). You'll see posters at various churches, yet
accessibility varies; call ahead. Also consider daytime concerts in parks,
such as the Luxembourg Garden (**AE, AI,** Level 1—Fully accessible).
Even the Galeries Lafayette department store (**AE, AI, AL, AT,** Level
1—Fully accessible) offers concerts. Many concerts are free *(entrée libre),*
such as the Sunday atelier concert sponsored by the American Church
(Level 4—Not accessible; 17:00, Jan–June and Sept–Nov, 65 quai
d'Orsay, Mo: Invalides, RER: Pont de l'Alma, tel. 01 40 62 05 00,
www.acparis.org).

Opera: Paris is home to two well-respected opera venues. The Opéra
Bastille (**AE, AI, AL,** Level 1—Fully accessible) is the massive modern
opera house that dominates place de la Bastille. Come here for state-of-
the-art special effects and modern interpretations of classic ballets and

operas. In the spirit of this everyman's opera, unsold seats are available at a big discount to seniors and students 15 minutes before the show (Mo: Bastille). The Opéra Garnier (**AE, AI, AL,** Level 1—Fully accessible), Paris' first opera house, hosts opera and ballet performances. Come here for less expensive tickets and grand belle époque decor (ramp entry on rue Scribe and special seats accessible by lift for wheelchair users; Mo: Opéra, tel. 01 44 73 13 99). To get tickets for either opera house, call 01 44 73 13 00 (wheelchair users call 01 40 01 18 50), go to the opera ticket offices (open 11:00–18:00), or easiest, reserve on the Web at www.opera-de-paris.fr.

Bus Tours: Several companies offer after-dark tours of Paris. These trips are sold through your hotel (brochures in lobby) or directly at the offices listed below. You save no money by buying direct.

Paris Illumination Tours (**AE+A,** Level 2—Moderately accessible), run by Paris Vision, connect all the great illuminated sights of Paris with a 100-minute bus tour in 12 languages. Double-decker buses have huge windows, but customers continuing to the overrated Moulin Rouge get the most desirable front seats.

You'll board with a United Nations of tourists, get an audioguide, and listen to a tape-recorded spiel (interesting but occasionally hard to hear). Uninspired as it is, this provides an entertaining first-night overview of the city at its floodlit and scenic best (bring your city map to stay oriented as you go). Left-side seats are marginally better. Visibility is fine in the rain. You're always on the bus except for one five-minute cigarette break at the Eiffel Tower viewpoint (adults-€26, kids under 11 ride free, departures at 20:30 nightly all year, earlier off-season—call to confirm; also at 21:30 April–Oct only, departs from Paris Vision office at 214 rue de Rivoli, across the street from Mo: Tuileries, tel. 01 42 60 30 01, fax 01 42 86 95 36, www.parisvision.com).

SLEEPING

We've focused on a safe, handy, and colorful neighborhood: rue Cler. We list good hotels, helpful hints, and restaurants (see "Eating," page 231). If you'd prefer not to stay in the rue Cler neighborhood, we've also listed some

SLEEP CODE

(€1 = about $1.15, country code: 33)

Sleep Code: **S** = Single, **D** = Double/Twin, **T** = Triple, **Q** = Quad, **b** = bathroom, **s** = shower only, **no CC** = Credit Cards not accepted, * = French hotel rating system (0–4 stars). Nearly all hotels listed here will have someone who speaks English. You can assume a hotel takes credit cards unless you see "no CC" in the listing.

Please see "Accessibility Codes" sidebar on page 165 of this chapter for a quick guide to codes. For a more detailed explanation of Accessibility Levels and Codes, please see page 2 of the Introduction.

other options in the lively, trendy Marais district. Before reserving, read the descriptions of these two neighborhoods closely. Each offers different pros and cons, and your neighborhood is as important as your hotel for the success of your trip.

Reserve ahead for Paris, the sooner the better. Conventions clog Paris in September (worst), October, May, and June (very tough). In August, when Paris is quiet, some hotels offer lower rates to fill their rooms (if you're planning to visit Paris in the summer, the extra expense of an air-conditioned room can be money well spent). Most hotels accept telephone reservations, require prepayment with a credit-card number, and prefer a faxed follow-up to be sure everything is in order. For more information, see "Making Reservations" in this book's Introduction.

French hotels are rated by stars (indicated in this book by an *). One star is simple, two has most of the comforts, three is generally a two-star with a mini-bar and fancier lobby, and four is luxurious. Hotels with two or more stars are required to have an English-speaking staff. Nearly all hotels listed will have someone who speaks English.

Old, characteristic, budget Parisian hotels have always been cramped. Retrofitted with elevators, toilets, and private showers (as most are today), they are even more cramped. Even three-star hotel rooms are small and often not worth the extra expense in Paris. Some hotels include the hotel tax (*taxe du séjour,* about €1 per person per day), though most will add this to your bill.

Recommended hotels have an elevator unless otherwise noted. Quad rooms usually have two double beds. Because rooms with double beds and showers are cheaper than rooms with twin beds and baths, room prices vary within each hotel.

You can save as much as €20–25 by finding the increasingly rare room without a private shower, though some hotels charge for down-the-hall showers. Singles (except for the rare closet-type rooms that fit only one twin bed) are simply doubles used by one person. They rent for only a little less than a double.

You'll almost always have the option of breakfast at your hotel, which is pleasant and convenient—but, at €5–10, it's more than the price of breakfast at the corner café with less ambience (though you get more coffee at your hotel). Some hotels offer only the classic continental breakfast for about €5–8, but others offer buffet breakfasts for about €8–12 (cereal, yogurt, fruit, cheese, croissants, juice, and hard-boiled eggs)—which we usually spring for. While hotels hope you'll buy their breakfast, it's optional unless otherwise noted.

Get advice from your hotel for safe parking (consider long-term parking at Orly Airport and taxi in). Meters are free in August. Garages are plentiful (€14–23/day, with special rates through some hotels). Your hotelier can direct you to the nearest Internet café (*café internet,* kah-fay an-ter-net) and self-service launderette (*laverie automatique,* lah-vay-ree oh-to-mah-teek).

Rue Cler Orientation

Rue Cler, a village-like pedestrian street, is safe, tidy, colorful, and engaging. How such coziness lodged itself between the high-powered government district and the wealthy Eiffel Tower and Invalides areas, we'll never know. This is a neighborhood of wide, tree-lined boulevards, stately apartment buildings, and lots of Americans. The American Church, American Library, and American University call this area home. People with disabilities will find a warm welcome and more ♥'s per square block than anywhere else in Paris. The neighborhood streets are accessible for people using wheelchairs. Many of the stores are fully accessible, while others may have an entry step.

Become a local at a rue Cler café for breakfast or join the afternoon crowd for *une bière pression* (a draft beer). On rue Cler, you can eat and browse your way through a street full of tart shops, delis, cheese shops, and colorful outdoor produce stalls. Afternoon *boules* (lawn bowling) on the Esplanade des Invalides is a relaxing spectator sport (look for the dirt area to the upper right as you face Les Invalides). For an after-dinner cruise on the Seine, it's just a short roll or stroll to the river and the Bateaux-Mouches (see "Tours," page 177).

Your neighborhood **TI** is at the Eiffel Tower (**AE, AI,** Level 1— Fully accessible; May–Sept daily 11:00–18:40, closed Oct–April, tel. 01 45 51 22 15). There's a **post office** (**AE, AI,** Level 1—Fully accessible) at the end of rue Cler on avenue de la Motte Picquet, and a handy **SNCF train office** at 78 rue St. Dominique (**AE, AI,** Level 1—Fully accessible; Mon–Fri 9:00–19:00, Sat 10:00–12:30 & 14:00–18:00, closed Sun). Rue St. Dominique is the area's boutique-browsing street. **Cyber World Café** is at 20 rue de l'Exposition (**AE+A,** Level 2—Moderately accessible, one 8" doorstep; open daily, tel. 01 53 59 96 54).

The **American Church and Franco-American Center** is the community center for Americans living in Paris and should be one of your first contacts if you're planning to stay awhile (Level 4—Not accessible, fifteen 6" steps to enter; reception open Mon–Sat 9:00–22:00, Sun 9:00–19:30, 65 quai d'Orsay, tel. 01 40 62 05 00). Pick up copies of the *Paris Voice* for a monthly review of Paris entertainment, and *France-U.S.A. Contacts* for information on housing and employment through the community of 30,000 Americans living in Paris. The interdenominational services at 11:00 on Sunday, the coffee hour after church, and the free Sunday concerts (18:00, not every week, Sept–May only) are a great way to make some friends and get a taste of émigré life in Paris.

Key **Métro** stops are Invalides (Level 1—Fully accessible, has elevator), Ecole Militaire, and La Tour Maubourg. The mostly wheelchair-accessible **RER-C** line runs along the river, serving Versailles to the west and the Orsay Museum, Latin Quarter (St. Michel stop), and Austerlitz train station to the east (in rue Cler area, use Pont de l'Alma or Invalides RER stops).

Sleeping In the Rue Cler Neighborhood
(7th *arrondissement*, Mo: Ecole Militaire)
Rue Cler is the glue that holds this pleasant neighborhood together. From here you can roll or stroll to the Eiffel Tower, Napoleon's Tomb,

Rue Cler Hotels

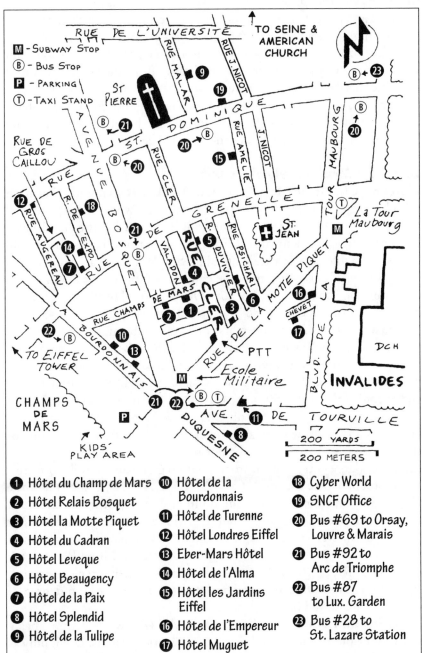

1. Hôtel du Champ de Mars
2. Hôtel Relais Bosquet
3. Hôtel la Motte Piquet
4. Hôtel du Cadran
5. Hôtel Leveque
6. Hôtel Beaugency
7. Hôtel de la Paix
8. Hôtel Splendid
9. Hôtel de la Tulipe
10. Hôtel de la Bourdonnais
11. Hôtel de Turenne
12. Hôtel Londres Eiffel
13. Eber-Mars Hôtel
14. Hôtel de l'Alma
15. Hôtel les Jardins Eiffel
16. Hôtel de l'Empereur
17. Hôtel Muguet
18. Cyber World
19. SNCF Office
20. Bus #69 to Orsay, Louvre & Marais
21. Bus #92 to Arc de Triomphe
22. Bus #87 to Lux. Garden
23. Bus #28 to St. Lazare Station

the Seine, and the Orsay and Rodin Museums. Hotels here are relatively spacious and a great value considering the elegance of the neighborhood and the high prices of the more cramped hotels of the trendy Marais.

Most of Rick Steves' readers stay in this neighborhood. If you want to disappear into Paris, choose a hotel away from the rue Cler. And if nightlife matters, sleep elsewhere.

There is only one Level 1 hotel in this neighborhood, near Métro stop La Tour Maubourg (listed below). The hotels listed below are within Camembert-smelling distance of rue Cler.

Level 2—Moderately Accessible

Hôtel du Champ de Mars (AE+A, AI+A, AR+A), with charming pastel rooms and helpful English-speaking owners Françoise and Stephane, is a homey rue Cler option. This plush little hotel has a Provence-style, small-town feel from top to bottom. Rooms are small, but comfortable and an excellent value. Single rooms can work as tiny doubles (one 4" entry step, no wheelchair-accessible rooms but one suitable room on ground floor; Sb-€66, Db-€72–76, Tb-€92, 30 yards off rue Cler at 7 rue du Champ de Mars, tel. 01 45 51 52 30, fax 01 45 51 64 36, www.hotel-du-champ-de-mars.com, stg@club-internet.fr).

Hôtel Relais Bosquet* (AE+A, AI, AR, AB+A) is modern, spacious, and a bit upscale, with snazzy, air-conditioned rooms, electric darkness blinds, and big beds. Gerard and his staff are politely formal and friendly (Sb-€125–150, standard Db-€145, spacious Db-€165, extra bed-€30, parking-€14, 19 rue du Champ de Mars, tel. 01 47 05 25 45, fax 01 45 55 08 24, www.relaisbosquet.com). The entryway has one 6" step. There is one large ground-floor room that is suitable for a wheelchair user (large entry and bathroom, but no grab bars for toilet or bath).

Hôtel la Motte Picquet (AE+A, AI+A, AR+A), at the end of rue Cler, is like staying in an antique dollhouse. Most of its 18 adorable, spendy rooms face a busy street, but the twins are on the quieter rue Cler (one 7" entry step, no accessible rooms but suitable room on ground floor; Sb-€105–121, Db-€129–165, 30 avenue de la Motte Picquet, tel. 01 47 05 09 57, fax 01 47 05 74 36, www.paris-hotel-mottepicquet.com). In the past, slow walkers and wheelchair users with a high degree of mobility have stayed here with satisfaction.

Hôtel du Cadran* (AE+A, AI+A, AR+A), while central, has a shiny lobby but no charm and tight, narrow, pricey rooms. Use it only as a last resort (Db-€152–170, 10 rue du Champ de Mars, air-con, tel. 01 40 62 67 00, fax 01 40 62 67 13, www.hotelducadran.com). There is one 6" entry step and a ground-floor room designated for wheelchair users (but it has a narrow entryway and lacks a wheelchair-accessible bathroom).

Level 3—Minimally Accessible

Grand Hôtel Lévêque** (AE+A, AI+A, ♥)** is ideally located, with a helpful staff (Christophe and female Pascale SE), a singing maid, and a Starship *Enterprise* elevator. It's a classic old hotel with well-designed rooms that have all the comforts, including air-conditioning and ceiling fans. It feels a bit frayed at the edges but remains a solid value (Sb–€56, Db-€86–106, Tb-€122 for 2 adults and 1 child only, breakfast-€7, 29 rue Cler, tel. 01 47 05 49 15, fax 01 45 50 49 36, www.hotel-leveque .com, info@hotelleveque.com). The entryway has one 4" step. There are no adapted rooms for wheelchair users; there are also no suitable ground-floor rooms, and the elevator is too small for a wheelchair.

Hôtel Beaugency** (AE+A, AI+A),** on a quieter street a short block off rue Cler, has 30 small, cookie-cutter rooms, and a lobby you can stretch out in. Rooms have automated air-conditioning that shuts off once you go to bed (Sb-€105, Db-€115–125, Tb-€145, first breakfast free with this book, 21 rue Duvivier, tel. 01 47 05 01 63, fax 01 45 51 04 96, www.hotel-beaugency.com). The doorway has one 3" step, another three 7" steps to the lobby, and then more 5" steps to the small elevator (23" wide and 34" deep). There are no suitable rooms for wheelchair users.

Near Rue Cler

The following listings are within a few blocks of rue Cler.

Level 2—Moderately Accessible

Hôtel de la Paix** (AE+A, AI, AR, AB, ♥),** a smart hotel located away from the fray on a quiet little street, offers 23 plush, well-designed rooms and is a good value (Sb-€61, Db-€91–100, Tb-€110–120, fine buffet breakfast, 19 rue du Gros-Caillou, tel. 01 45 51 86 17, fax 01 45 55 93 28, hotel.de.la.paix@wanadoo.fr). Wheelchair users are welcome here. One 3" entry step leads to a fully accessible room (including wheelchair-accessible toilet and roll-in shower).

Hôtel Splendid** (AE+A, AI, AR, AB+A, ♥)** is Art Deco modern, professional, and worth your while if you land one of its three suites with great Eiffel Tower views. Fifth-floor rooms have small terraces (one 4" entry step, 2 large rooms for wheelchair users but with no adapted toilets; Db-€126–150, Db suite-€200–225, 29 avenue de Tourville, tel. 01 45 51 24 77, fax 01 44 18 94 60, www.hotels-exclusive.com/hotels/splendid). This hotel has hosted wheelchair users in the past and welcomes persons with disabilities.

Hôtel de la Tulipe*** (AE+A, AI+A, AR, AB+A) is a unique place three blocks from rue Cler toward the river, with friendly Bernhard behind the desk. The smallish but artistically decorated rooms—each one different—come with little, stylish bathrooms and surround a seductive wood-beamed lounge and a peaceful, leafy courtyard (Db-€110–140, Tb-€170, 2-room suite-€220–250, no elevator, 33 rue Malar, tel. 01 45 51 67 21, fax 01 47 53 96 37, www.hoteldelatulipe.com). There is one 2" doorstep entry. One more interior 4" step leads to a large, open courtyard-access room that has worked for wheelchair users with assistance in the past (large bathroom is suitable but not adapted).

Hôtel de la Bourdonnais*** (AE, AI, AL, AR+A, AB+A, ♥) is a *très* Parisian place, mixing slightly faded Old World elegance with professional service, comfortable public spaces, and mostly spacious, traditionally decorated rooms (welcoming staff, accessible entry and elevator, but no specially adapted wheelchair-accessible rooms or bathrooms; avoid the few *petite* rooms, Sb-€120, Db-€150, Tb-€160, Qb-€180, 5-person suite-€210, air-con, 111 avenue de la Bourdonnais, tel. 01 47 05 45 42, fax 01 45 55 75 54, www.hotellabourdonnais.fr).

Hôtel de Turenne** (AE, AI, AL), with sufficiently comfortable, air-conditioned rooms and so-so bed quality, is a good value, particularly when it's hot. It also has five truly single rooms and several connecting rooms (one 2" entry step, accessible elevator but no accessible rooms; Sb-€61, Db-€71–83, Tb-€98, extra bed-€10, 20 avenue de Tourville, tel. 01 47 05 99 92, fax 01 45 56 06 04, hotel.turenne.paris7@wanadoo.fr).

Level 3—Minimally Accessible
Hôtel Londres Eiffel*** (AE, AI) is our closest listing to the Eiffel Tower and Champ de Mars park. It offers immaculate, warmly decorated rooms, cozy public spaces, Internet access, and air-conditioning. The helpful staff takes good care of their guests. It's less convenient to the Métro; handy bus #69 and the RER Pont de l'Alma stop are better options (Sb-€95–99, Db-€110–140, Tb-€150–165, extra bed-€17, 1 rue

Augerau, tel. 01 45 51 63 02, fax 01 47 05 28 96, www.londres-eiffel
.com, info@londres-eiffel.com). Although the entryway is wheelchair-
accessible, the elevator is quite small. Wheelchair users will have a difficult time here, but it works for slow walkers.

Eber-Mars Hôtel** (AE+A, AI+A, ♥), with helpful owner Jean-
Marc, is a good midrange value with larger-than-average rooms and a
beam-me-up-Jacques, coffin-sized elevator (one 4" step to enter, no specially adapted rooms, tiny elevator makes it difficult to reach rooms; small
Db-€75, large Db-€90–110, Tb-€135, extra bed-€25, pricey breakfast-
€10, 117 avenue de la Bourdonnais, tel. 01 47 05 42 30, fax 01 47 05 45
91, www.hotelseber.com).

Hôtel de l'Alma*** (AE+A, AI+A) is well-located on "restaurant
row," with cheery rooms, small bathrooms, a nice little courtyard, and
very reasonable rates (one 8" step to enter, no accessible elevator, no
accessible rooms; Sb-€80, Db-€90, includes breakfast, 32 rue de
l'Exposition, tel. 01 47 05 45 70, fax 01 45 51 84 47, www.alma-paris
-hotel.com, Carine SE).

Near Métro stop La Tour Maubourg

The next three listings are within two blocks of the intersection of avenue
de la Motte Picquet and boulevard de la Tour Marbourg.

Level 1—Fully Accessible

Hôtel les Jardins Eiffel*** (AE+A, AI, AR, AB, ♥), on a quiet street,
feels like a modern motel, but earns its three stars with professional service, its own parking garage, a spacious lobby, and 80 comfortable, air-
conditioned rooms (Db-€130–€160, extra bed-€21 or free for a child,
parking-€20/day, 8 rue Amélie, tel. 01 47 05 46 21, fax 01 45 55 28 08,
www.hoteljardinseiffel.com, Marie SE). Wheelchair users can avoid the
single 2" entry step and access the hotel's elevator in the garage. The
hotel has two wheelchair-accessible rooms (including adapted toilets and
bathtubs with grab bars; they will place bench in tub). They host many
wheelchair-using guests and are very welcoming.

Level 2—Moderately Accessible

Hôtel de l'Empereur** (AE, AI, AL) lacks intimacy but is roomy and
another good value. Its 38 pleasant, woody rooms come with sturdy furniture and all the comforts except air-conditioning. Streetside rooms

have views but some noise; fifth-floor rooms have small balconies and Napoleonic views (accessible entry and elevator, but no adapted rooms—though the hotel has accommodated wheelchair users in the past; Sb-€70–80, Db-€80–100, Tb-€120, Qb-€140, 2 rue Chevert, tel. 01 45 55 88 02, fax 01 45 51 88 54, www.hotelempereur.com, Alba SE).

Hôtel Muguet** (AE+A, AI, AR, ♥),** a peaceful, stylish, and immaculate hotel, gives you three-star comfort for a two-star price. This delightful hotel offers 48 tasteful, air-conditioned rooms, a greenhouse lounge, and a small garden courtyard. The hands-on owner, Catherine, gives her guests a restful and secure home in Paris (Sb-€87, Db-€97–105, Tb-€135, 11 rue Chevert, tel. 01 47 05 05 93, fax 01 45 50 25 37, www.hotelmuguet.com). There are two 8" steps at the entry and no specially adapted rooms. Three large rooms are designated for wheelchair users (but lack fully accessible bathrooms).

In the Marais Neighborhood
(4th *arrondissement,* Mo: St. Paul or Bastille)

Those interested in a more Soho/Greenwich Village locale should make the Marais their Parisian home. Only 15 years ago, it was a forgotten Parisian backwater, but now the Marais is one of Paris' most popular residential, tourist, and shopping areas. This is jumbled, medieval Paris at its finest, where classy stone mansions sit alongside trendy bars, antique shops, and fashion-conscious boutiques. The streets are a fascinating parade of artists, students, tourists, immigrants, and babies in strollers munching baguettes. The Marais is also known as a hub of the Parisian gay and lesbian scene. This area is *sans* doubt livelier (and louder) than the rue Cler area.

In the Marais, you have these sights close at hand: Picasso Museum, Carnavalet Museum, Victor Hugo's House, Jewish Art and History Museum, and the Pompidou Center. You're also a manageable roll or stroll from Paris' two islands (Ile St. Louis and Ile de la Cité), home to Notre-Dame and the Sainte-Chapelle. The Opéra Bastille, Promenade Plantée park, place des Vosges (Paris' oldest square), Jewish Quarter (rue des Rosiers), and nightlife-packed rue de Lappe are also nearby. (For sight descriptions, see "Northeast Paris," page 203; for the Opéra, see page 200.)

The Marais has two good open-air markets: the sprawling Marché de la Bastille on place de la Bastille (Thu and Sun until 12:30) and the

Marais Neighborhood

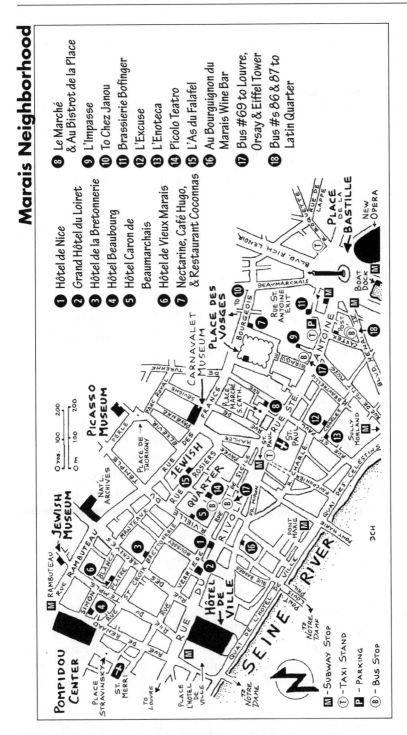

1. Hôtel de Nice
2. Grand Hôtel du Loiret
3. Hôtel de la Bretonnerie
4. Hôtel Beaubourg
5. Hôtel Caron de Beaumarchais
6. Hôtel de Vieux Marais
7. Nectarine, Café Hugo, & Restaurant Coconnas
8. Le Marché & Au Bistrot de la Place
9. L'Impasse
10. To Chez Janou
11. Brasserie Bofinger
12. L'Excuse
13. L'Enoteca
14. Picolo Teatro
15. L'As du Falafel
16. Au Bourguignon du Marais Wine Bar
17. Bus #69 to Louvre, Orsay & Eiffel Tower
18. Bus #s 86 & 87 to Latin Quarter

M - SUBWAY STOP
T - TAXI STAND
P - PARKING
B - BUS STOP

more intimate Marché de la place d'Aligre (daily 9:00–12:00, a few blocks behind Opéra on place d'Aligre).

Level 2—Moderately Accessible
Hôtel de Nice** (AE+A, AI+A, AL, AR+A, ♥), on the Marais' busy main drag, is a turquoise-and-rose "Marie-Antoinette does tie-dye" place. Its narrow halls are littered with paintings, and its 23 rooms are filled with thoughtful touches and include tight bathrooms. Twin rooms, which cost the same as doubles, are larger and on the street side—but have effective double-paned windows (narrow halls, tight spaces, stairs lead to lovely breakfast room; Sb-€68, Db-€105, Tb-€125, Qb-€135, extra bed-€20, 42 bis rue de Rivoli, Mo: Hôtel de Ville, tel. 01 42 78 55 29, fax 01 42 78 36 07).

Level 3—Minimally Accessible
Grand Hôtel du Loiret** (AE, AI) is a bare-bones and basic place where you get what you pay for (S-€37, Sb-€47–62, D-€42, Db-€56–72, Tb-€72–84, 8 rue des Mauvais Garçons, Mo: Hôtel de Ville, tel. 01 48 87 77 00, fax 01 48 04 96 56, hotelduloiret@hotmail.com).

Near the Pompidou Center
Level 2—Moderately Accessible
Hôtel de la Bretonnerie*** (AE, AI, AL, AR, AB+A, ♥), three blocks from the Hôtel de Ville, is a fine Marais splurge. It has an on-the-ball staff, a big, inviting lobby, elegant decor, and tastefully-appointed rooms with an antique, open-beam warmth (one large suitable room has large marble-floored bathroom, one small step up to toilet with enough space for a wheelchair to go up step, but no grab bars; perfectly good standard "classic" Db-€114, bigger "charming" Db-€148, Db suite-€190, Tb suite-€215, Qb suite-€245, between rue Vielle du Temple and rue des Archives at 22 rue Ste. Croix de la Bretonnerie, Mo: Hôtel de Ville, tel. 01 48 87 77 63, fax 01 42 77 26 78, www.bretonnerie.com, Francoise SE).

    Hôtel Beaubourg*** (AE+A, AI, AL, AR, ♥) is a good three-star value on a quiet street in the shadow of the Pompidou Center. Its 28 rooms are wood-beam comfy, and the inviting lounge is warm and pleasant (two entry steps, breakfast room in inaccessible basement but free room service; Db-€115, some with balconies-€135, twins are considerably larger than doubles, includes breakfast, 11 rue Simon Le Franc, Mo: Rambuteau, tel. 01 42 74 34 24, fax 01 42 78 68 11, htlbeaubourg @hotellerie.net).

Level 3—Minimally Accessible

Hôtel Caron de Beaumarchais*** (AE+A, AI+A, AL, AR+A) feels like a folk-museum, with its 20 sweet little rooms and a lobby cluttered with bits from an elegant 18th-century Marais house. Short antique collectors love this place (small back-side Db-€145, larger Db on the front-€160, air-con, 12 rue Vieille du Temple, Mo: Hôtel de Ville, tel. 01 42 72 34 12, fax 01 42 72 34 63, www.carondebeaumarchais.com).

Hôtel de Vieux Marais** (AE) is tucked away on a quiet street two blocks east of the Pompidou Center with bright, spacious, and well-designed rooms. The we-try-harder owner, Marie-Hélène, loves her work and gives this place its charm. Greet Leeloo, the hotel hound (Db-€110–140, extra bed-€23, air-con, just off rue des Archives at 8 rue du Plâtre, Mo: Rambuteau or Hôtel de Ville, tel. 01 42 78 47 22, fax 01 42 78 34 32, www.vieuxmarais.com).

EATING

The Parisian eating scene is kept at a rolling boil. Entire books (and lives) are dedicated to the subject. Paris is France's wine and cuisine melting pot. While it lacks a style of its own (only French onion soup is truly Parisian), it draws from the best of France. Paris could hold a gourmet's Olympics and import nothing.

Parisians eat long and well. Relaxed lunches, three-hour dinners, and endless hours sitting in outdoor cafés are the norm. They have a legislated 35-hour workweek and a self-imposed 36-hour eat-week. Local cafés, cuisine, and wines become a highlight of any Parisian adventure—sightseeing for your palate. Even if the rest of you is sleeping in a cheap hotel, let your taste buds travel first-class in Paris. (They can go coach in London.)

You can eat well without going broke, but choose carefully—you're just as likely to blow a small fortune on a mediocre meal as you are to dine wonderfully for €20. To save piles of euros, review the budget eating tips above and restaurant recommendations below, and consider dinner picnics (great take-out dishes available at *charcuteries*).

Restaurants open for dinner around 19:00, and small local favorites get crowded after 21:00. When lunch is served, it generally begins at 11:30 and goes until 14:00, with last orders taken at about 13:30. Beware: Many restaurants close Sunday and Monday. Most of the restaurants listed below accept credit cards.

Our recommendations are centered predominantly near the recommended hotels in the rue Cler and Marais neighborhoods; you can come home exhausted after a busy day of sightseeing and have a good selection of restaurants right around the corner. And evening is a fine time to explore these delightful neighborhoods. We've provided accessibility information for each place. Unless otherwise noted (by **AT** or **AT+A**), these restaurants do *not* have accessible toilets.

Tipping

Virtually all cafés and restaurants include a service charge in the bill (usually 15 percent), but it's polite to round up for a drink or meal well-served. This bonus tip is usually about 5 percent of the bill (e.g., if your bill is €19, leave €20). In the rare instance that service is not included (the menu states *service non compris*), tip 15 percent. When you hand your payment plus a tip to your waiter, you can say, *"C'est bon"* (say bohn), meaning, "It's good." If you order your food at a counter, don't tip.

Breakfast

Petit déjeuner (puh-tee day-zhu-nay) is typically *café au lait*, hot chocolate, or tea; a roll with butter and marmalade; and a croissant, though more hotels are starting to provide breakfast buffets with fruit, cereal, yogurt, and cheese (usually for a few extra euros and well worth it). While breakfasts are available at your hotel (about €5–10), they're cheaper at corner cafés (but no coffee refills; see also "Café Culture," page 234). It's fine to buy a croissant or roll at a bakery and eat it with your cup of coffee at a café. Better still, some bakeries offer worthwhile breakfast deals with juice, croissant, and coffee or tea for about €3 (the chain of bakeries called La Brioche Dorée is one example).

If the urge for an egg in the morning gets the best of you, drop into a café and order *une omelette or œufs sur le plat* (fried eggs). You could also buy or bring plastic bowls and spoons from home, buy a box of cereal and a small box of milk, and eat in your room before heading out for coffee.

Picnics

Great for lunch or dinner, Parisian picnics can be first-class affairs and adventures in high cuisine. Be daring. Try the smelly cheeses, ugly pâtés, sissy quiches, and minuscule (usually drinkable) yogurts. Local shopkeepers are accustomed to selling small quantities of produce. Try the tasty salads to go and ask for *une fourchette en plastique* (a plastic fork).

Gather supplies early for a picnic lunch; you'll probably visit several small stores to assemble a complete meal, and many close at noon. Look for a *boulangerie* (bakery), a *crémerie* or *fromagerie* (cheeses), a *charcuterie* (deli items, meats, and pâtés), an *épicerie* or *magasin d'alimentation* (small grocery store with veggies, drinks, and so on), and a *pâtisserie* (delicious pastries). While wine is taboo in public places in the United States, it's *pas de problème* in France.

Supermarchés offer less color and cost, more efficiency, and adequate quality. Department stores often have supermarkets in the basement along with top-floor cafeterias offering not really cheap but low-risk, low-stress, what-you-see-is-what-you-get meals. For a quick meal to go, look for food stands and bakeries selling take-out sandwiches and drinks. For an affordable restaurant meal, try a *créperie* or café.

In stores, unrefrigerated soft drinks and beer are one-half the price of cold drinks. Milk and boxed fruit juice are the most inexpensive drinks. Avoid buying drinks to go at streetside stands; you'll find them far cheaper in a shop. Try to keep a water bottle with you. Water quenches your thirst better and cheaper than anything you'll find in a store or café. We drink tap water in Paris and use that to refill our bottles.

For good lunch picnic sites, consider these suggestions. The Palais Royal (across the place du Palais Royal from the Louvre) is a good spot for a peaceful, royal picnic, as is the little triangular Henry IV Park on the west tip of Ile de la Cité. The pedestrian pont des Arts bridge, across from the Louvre, has unmatched views and plentiful benches. For great people-watching, try the Pompidou Center (by the *Homage to Stravinsky* fountains), the elegant place des Vosges (closes at dusk), the gardens at the Rodin Museum, and Luxembourg Garden.

Café Culture

French cafés (or *brasseries*) provide reasonable light meals and a refuge from museum and church overload. Feel free to order only a bowl of soup or a salad for lunch or dinner at a café.

Cafés generally open by 7:00, but closing hours vary. Unlike restaurants, which open only for lunch and dinner, meals are served throughout the day at cafés, so if you want a late lunch or an early dinner—find a café.

It's easier for the novice to sit and feel comfortable when you know the system. Check the price list first. Prices, which must be posted prominently, vary wildly between cafés. And cafés charge different prices for the same drink depending upon where you want drink it. Prices are posted: *comptoir* (counter/bar) or the more expensive *salle* (at a table). At large cafés, outside tables are most expensive and prices rise after 20:00.

Your waiter probably won't overwhelm you with friendliness. Notice how hard they work. They almost never stop. Cozying up to clients (French or foreign) is probably the last thing on their minds.

The **standard menu items** (generally served day and night) are the *croque monsieur* (grilled ham-and-cheese sandwich) and *croque madame* (*croque monsieur* with a fried egg on top). The *salade composée* (com-po-zay) is a hearty chef's salad. Sandwiches are least expensive but plain unless you buy them at the *boulangerie* (bakery). To get more than a piece of ham (*jambon*, zhahm-bohn) or chicken (*poulet*, poo-lay) on a baguette, order *jambon-* or *poulet-crudité* (crew-dee-tay), which means garnished with lettuce, tomatoes, cucumbers, and so on. Omelets come lonely on a plate with a basket of bread. The **daily special**—*plat du jour* (plah dew zhoor)—is your fast, hearty hot plate for €10–14. At most cafés (though never at a restaurant), feel free to order only appetizers—which many find lighter, more fun, and more interesting than entrées. Regardless of what you order, bread is free; to get more, just hold up your breadbasket and ask, *"Encore, s'il vous plaît."*

House **wine** at the bar is cheap (about €3 per glass, cheapest by the *pichet*, or pitcher), and the local beer is cheaper on tap (*une pression*, preh-syon) than in the bottle (*bouteille*, boo-tay). France's best **beer** is Alsatian; try Kronenbourg or the heavier Pelfort. *Une panaché* (pan-a-shay) is a refreshing French shandy (7-Up and beer). For a fun, bright, nonalcoholic drink of 7-Up with mint syrup, order *un diablo menthe* (dee-ah-bloh mahnt). Kids love the local lemonade (*citron pressé*, see-trohn preh-say) and the flavored syrups mixed with bottled water (*sirops à l'eau*, see-roh ah loh). The ice cubes melted after the last Yankee tour group left.

If you order **coffee or tea,** here's the lingo:

Coffee

* *un express* (uh nex-press) = shot of espresso
* *une noisette* (oon nwah-zette) = espresso with a shot of milk
* *café au lait* (kah-fay oh lay) = coffee with lots of milk. Also called *un grand crème* (large size; uh grahn krehm) or *un petit crème* (average size; uh puh-tee krehm)
* *un grand café noir* (uh grahn kah-fay nwahr) = cup of black coffee, closest to American style
* *un décaffiné* (uh day-kah-fee-nay) = decaf; can modify any of the above drinks

Tea

* *un thé nature* (tay nah-tour) = plain tea
* *un thé au lait* (uh tay oh lay) = tea with milk
* *un thé citron* (uh tay see-trohn) = tea with lemon
* *un infusion* (uhn an-few-see-yohn) = herbal tea

By law, the waiter must give you a glass of tap water with your coffee if you request it; ask for *un verre d'eau, s'il vous plaît* (uh vayr doh, see voo play).

Restaurants

Choose restaurants filled with locals, not places with big neon signs boasting, We Speak English. Consider your hotelier's opinion. If a restaurant doesn't post its menu *(la carte)* outside, move along.

If you want the menu, ask for *la carte* (and order à la carte like the locals do); if you ask for the *menu* (muh-noo), you'll get a fixed-price meal. *Menus,* which offer three or four courses, are generally a good value: You get your choice of soup, appetizer, or salad; your choice of three or four main courses with vegetables; plus a cheese course and/or a choice of desserts. Service is included, but wine and other drinks are generally extra. Restaurants that offer a *menu* for lunch often charge about €6 more for the same *menu* at dinner.

If you'd rather dine à la carte, ask the waiter for help deciphering the French. Go with his or her recommendations and anything *de la maison* (of the house), as long as it's not an organ meat (*tripes, rognons, andouillette*—yuck). Galloping gourmets should bring a menu translator; the *Marling Menu Master* is excellent. The *Rick Steves' French Phrase Book,* with a Menu Decoder, works well for most travelers. The wines are often listed in a separate *carte des vins.*

In France, an *entrée* is the first course and *le plat* is the main course. *Le plat* or *le plat du jour* (plate of the day) is the main course with vegetables (usually €10–14). If all you want is a salad, find a café instead. By American standards, the French undercook meats: rare or *saignant* (seh-nyahn) is close to raw; medium or *à point* (ah pwahn) is rare; and well-done or *bien cuit* (bee-yehn kwee), is medium.

Parisians are willing to pay for bottled water with their meal (*eau minérale,* oh mee-nay-rahl) because they prefer the taste over tap water. If you prefer a free pitcher of tap water, ask for *une carafe d'eau* (oon kah-rahf doh). Otherwise, you may unwittingly buy bottled water. To get inexpensive wine at a restaurant, order table wine in a pitcher (*un pichet,* pee-shay), rather than a bottle (though finer restaurants usually offer only bottles of wine). If all you want is a glass of wine, ask for *un verre de vin* (uh vehr duh van). A half carafe of wine is *un demi-pichet* (uh duh-mee pee-shay), a quarter carafe (ideal for one) is *un quart* (uh car).

To get a waiter's attention, simply say, *"S'il vous plaît"* (see voo play)—please.

Eating in the Rue Cler Neighborhood

The rue Cler neighborhood caters to its residents. Its eateries, while not destination places, have an intimate charm. Our favorites are small mom-and-pop places that love to serve traditional French food at good prices to a local clientele. You'll generally find great dinner *menus* for €20–30 and *plats du jour* for around €12–15. Eat early with tourists or late with locals.

Café du Marché (AE+A, AI, ❤, Level 2—Moderately accessible, one 3" entry step), with the best seats, coffee, and prices on rue Cler, serves hearty €9 salads and good €10 *plats du jour* for lunch or dinner to a trendy, smoky, mainly French crowd. This easygoing café is ideal if you want a light dinner (good dinner salads) or a more substantial but simple meal (Mon–Sat 11:00–23:00, close at 17:00 on Sun, at the corner of rue Cler and rue du Champ de Mars, tel. 01 47 05 51 27, well-run by Frank, Jack, and Bruno). Arrive before 19:30. It's packed at 21:00. A chalkboard lists the plates of the day—each a meal. You'll find similar dishes and prices with better (but smoky) indoor seating at nearby **Le Comptoir du Septième** (AE+A, AI, Level 2—Moderately accessible, two 8" entry steps), two blocks away on a busy street at the Ecole Militaire Métro stop (daily, 39 avenue de la Motte Picquet, tel. 01 45 55 90 20).

Café le Bosquet (AE, AI, ♥, Level 2—Moderately accessible, entry and main floor are fully accessible) is a vintage Parisian brasserie with dressy waiters and classic indoor or sidewalk tables on a busy street. Come here for a bowl of French onion soup, a salad, or a three-course set *menu* for €16 (closed Sun, many choices from a fun menu, the house red wine is plenty good, 46 avenue Bosquet, at the corner of rue du Champs de Mars and avenue Bosquet, tel. 01 45 51 38 13). This place has regular wheelchair-using customers.

Léo le Lion (AE+A, AI, ♥, Level 2—Moderately accessible, one 3" entry step), a warm, charming souvenir of old Paris, is popular with locals. Expect to spend €25 per person for fine à la carte choices (closed Sun, 23 rue Duvivier, tel. 01 45 51 41 77).

At **L'Affriolé** (AE+A, AI, ♥, Level 2—Moderately accessible, one 4" entry step), you'll compete with young professionals for a table. This small and trendy place is well-deserving of its rave reviews. Item selections change daily and the wine list is extensive, with some good bargains (€32 *menu*, closed Sun, 17 rue Malar, tel. 01 44 18 31 33). The staff has welcomed wheelchair users through the years.

Au Petit Tonneau (AE+A, AI, ♥, Level 2—Moderately accessible, one 4" entry step) is a purely Parisian experience. Fun-loving owner-chef Madame Boyer prepares everything herself, wearing her tall chef's hat like a crown as she rules from her family-style kitchen. The small dining room is plain and a bit smoky (allow €35/person with wine, open daily, 20 rue Surcouf, tel. 01 47 05 09 01).

Thoumieux (AE, AI, ♥, Level 2—Moderately accessible), the neighborhood's classy, traditional Parisian brasserie, is a local institution and deservedly popular. It's big and dressy, with formal but good-natured waiters. They serve a €14 lunch *menu*, a €31 dinner *menu* (3 courses with wine), and really good *crème brulée* (daily, 79 rue St. Dominique, tel. 01 47 05 49 75).

Le P'tit Troquet (AE+A, AI, ♥, Level 2—Moderately accessible, one 3" entry step) is a petite place taking you back to Paris in the 1920s, gracefully and earnestly run by Dominique. The delicious three-course

Rue Cler Restaurants

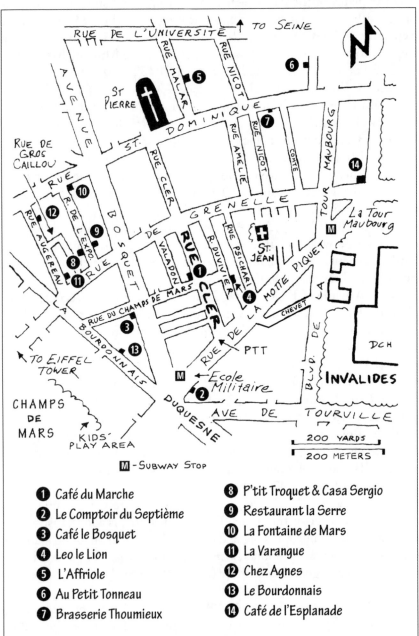

1. Café du Marche
2. Le Comptoir du Septième
3. Café le Bosquet
4. Leo le Lion
5. L'Affriole
6. Au Petit Tonneau
7. Brasserie Thoumieux
8. P'tit Troquet & Casa Sergio
9. Restaurant la Serre
10. La Fontaine de Mars
11. La Varangue
12. Chez Agnes
13. Le Bourdonnais
14. Café de l'Esplanade

€27 *menu* comes with fun, traditional choices (closed Sun, 28 rue de l'Exposition, tel. 01 47 05 80 39).

Restaurant la Serre (AE+A, AI, ♥, Level 2—Moderately accessible, one 7" entry step) is crowded and small, but reasonably priced (*plats du jour* €11–15, closed Sun–Mon, good onion soup and duck specialties, 29 rue de l'Exposition, tel. 01 45 55 20 96, Margot).

La Casa di Sergio (AE+A, AI, ♥, Level 2—Moderately accessible) is *the* place for gourmet Italian cuisine served family-style. Only Sergio could make us enthusiastic about Italian food in Paris. Sergio, a people-loving Sicilian, says he's waited his entire life to open a restaurant like this. Eating here involves a little trust...just let Sergio spoil you (€26–34 *menus,* closed Sun, 20 rue de l'Exposition, tel. 01 45 51 37 71). While there is one 6" doorstep and a small entryway, Sergio has been known to take the door off the hinges to allow a wheelchair user into his restaurant—you will feel welcome here.

La Fontaine de Mars (AE+A, AI, ♥, Level 2—Moderately accessible, one 3" entry step) is a longtime favorite for locals, charmingly situated on a classic tiny Parisian street and jumbled square. It's a happening scene, with tables jammed together for the serious business of good eating. Reserve in advance or risk eating upstairs without the fun street-level ambience (allow €40/person with wine, nightly, 129 rue St. Dominique, where rue de l'Exposition and rue St. Dominique meet, tel. 01 47 05 46 44).

La Varangue (AE+A, AI+A, ♥, Level 3—Minimally accessible, one large 10" entry step) is an entertaining one-man show featuring English-speaking Phillipe, who ran a French catering shop in Pennsylvania for three years, then returned to Paris to open his own place. He lives upstairs, and clearly has found his niche serving a Franco-American clientele who are all on a first-name basis. The food is cheap and good (try his snails and chocolate cake—but not together), the tables are few, and he opens early, at 18:00. Norman Rockwell would dig his tiny dining room (€10 *plats du jour* and a €14.50 *menu,* closed Sun, always a veggie option, 27 rue Augereau, tel. 01 47 05 51 22).

Chez Agnès (AE+A, AI+A, ♥, Level 2—Moderately accessible, one 6" entry step) is the smallest restaurant listed in this chapter. Eccentric and flowery, it's truly a family-style place where engaging Agnès (with dog Gypsy at her side) does it all—working wonders in her minuscule kitchen, and serving, too, without a word of English. Don't come for a quick dinner; she expects to get to know you (€23 *menu*, closed Mon, 1 rue Augereau, tel. 01 45 51 06 04).

Le Bourdonnais (AE+A, AI, ♥, Level 2—Moderately accessible, narrow entry, one 6" entry step), boasting one Michelin star, is the neighborhood's intimate gourmet splurge. You'll find friendly but formal service in a plush and very subdued 10-table room. Micheline Coat, your hostess, will treat you well (€43 lunch *menu*, €66 dinner *menu*, daily, 113 avenue de la Bourdonnais, tel. 01 47 05 47 96).

Café de l'Esplanade (AE+A, AI, Level 2—Moderately accessible, 2" entry step with wide door, wheelchair users are seated close to door), the latest buzz, is your opportunity to be surrounded by chic, yet older and sophisticated Parisians enjoying top-notch traditional cuisine as foreplay. There's not a tourist in sight. It's a sprawling place—half its tables with well-stuffed chairs fill a plush, living-room-like interior, and the other half are lined up outside under its elegant awning facing the street, valet boys, and car park. Dress competitively, as this is *the* place to be seen in the 7th *arrondissement* (€20 *plats du jour,* plan on €45 plus wine for dinner, open daily, reserve—especially if you want a curbside table, smoke-free room in the back, bordering Les Invalides at 52 rue Fabert, tel. 01 47 05 38 80).

Picnicking: The rue Cler is a moveable feast that gives "fast food" a good name. The entire street is clogged with connoisseurs of good eating. Only the health-food store goes unnoticed. A festival of food, the street is lined with people whose lives seem to be devoted to their specialty: polished produce, rotisserie chicken, crêpes, or cheese.

For a magical picnic dinner at the Eiffel Tower, assemble it in no fewer than five shops on rue Cler and lounge on the best grass in Paris (the police don't mind after dusk), with the dogs, Frisbees, a floodlit tower, and a cool breeze in the parc du Champ de Mars.

The accessible **crêpe stand** next to Café du Marché does a wonderful top-end dinner crêpe for €4. **Asian delis** (generically called *Traiteur Asie*) provide tasty, low-stress, low-price, take-out treats; most delis are accessible (€6 dinner plates, 2 delis have tables on the rue Cler—one across from Grand Hôtel Lévêque, and the other near rue du Champ de Mars). A good, small, **late-night grocery (AE, AI, ♥,** Level 1—Fully accessible) is at 197 rue de Grenelle, open daily until midnight.

In the Marais Neighborhood

The trendy Marais is filled with locals enjoying good food in colorful and atmospheric eateries. The scene is competitive and changes all the time. Here is an assortment of places—all handy to recommended hotels—that offer a memorable experience and good food at reasonable prices. For maximum ambience, go to the place des Vosges or place du Marché Ste. Catherine. For locations, see map on page 229.

Eating at place des Vosges: This elegant square, built by King Henry IV in 1605, put the Marais on the aristocratic map. And today the posh ambience survives with several good places offering romantic meals under its venerable arches, overlooking a peaceful park.

The mod and pastel **Nectarine (AE+A, AI,** Level 2—Moderately accessible, one 4" entry step, accessible street dining with heaters) at #16 is a teahouse serving healthy salads, quiches, and inexpensive *plats du jour* both day and night. Its fun menu lets you mix and match omelets and crêpes (daily, tel. 01 42 77 23 78). Next door, **Café Hugo (AE, AI, AT+A, ♥,** Level 2—Moderately accessible, wheelchair-friendly with accessible street dining) is a typical bistro serving good traditional favorites such as €6 onion soup and €5 crêpes (open daily, named for the square's most famous resident). **Restaurant Coconnas (AE, AI, AT+A, ♥,** Level 2—Moderately accessible) at #2 is a welcoming place that has a large, accessible interior, fine ambience, and attentive staff (open daily, tel. 01 42 78 58 16).

Restaurants on place du Marché Ste. Catherine: This tiny square just off rue St. Antoine is an international food festival cloaked in extremely Parisian, leafy-square ambience. On a balmy evening, this is clearly a neighborhood favorite, with five popular restaurants offering €20–30 meals. Most of the restaurants here are accessible, but lack accessible toilets (**AE, AI,** Level 2—Moderately accessible). Survey the square and you'll find two French-style bistros (**Le Marché** and **Au Bistrot de la Place,** both open daily), a fun Italian place, a popular Japanese/Korean restaurant, and a Russian eatery with an easy but adventurous menu. You'll eat under the trees surrounded by a futuristic-in-1800 planned residential quarter.

Eating elsewhere in the Marais: The streets beyond the Ste. Catherine and Vosges squares offer plenty of other appealing choices.

L'Impasse (AE+A, AI, Level 2—Moderately accessible, one 4" entry step), a cozy, neighborhood bistro on a quiet alley, serves an enthusiastically

French, €26 three-course *menu* (great escargots, scallops, and steak). Françoise, a former dancer and artist, runs the place *con brio* and, judging by the clientele, she's a fixture in the neighborhood. It's a spacious place where everything is made fresh (closed Sun, 4 impasse de Guéménée, tel. 01 42 72 08 45). Françoise promises anyone with this book a free glass of *byrrh*—it's pronounced "beer," but it's a French port-like drink. The restaurant is next to a self-serve launderette (open nightly until 21:30—clean your clothes while you dine).

Chez Janou (**AE+A, AI, AT+A,** Level 3—Minimally accessible, tough three 8" entry steps with no railing), a Provençal bistro, tumbles out of its corner building and fills its broad sidewalk with keen eaters. At first glance, you know this is a find. It's relaxed and charming, yet youthful and bustling with energy. The style is French Mediterranean, with an emphasis on vegetables (€14 *plats du jour,* €27 3-course *menu* that changes with the season, open daily, a block beyond place des Vosges at 2 rue Roger Verlomme, tel. 01 42 72 28 41).

Brasserie Bofinger (**AE, AI,** Level 2—Moderately accessible, accessible door to right of main entrance), an institution for over 100 years, is famous for fish and traditional cuisine with an Alsatian flair. Boys shuck and stack seafood platters out front. Inside, you're surrounded by brisk, black-and-white-attired waiters in plush rooms reminiscent of the Roaring Twenties. The non-smoking room is best—under the grand 1919 *coupole.* The €31 three-course (with wine) *menu* is a good value (open daily, reservations smart, 5 rue de la Bastille, don't be confused by the lesser "Petite" Bofinger across the street, tel. 01 42 72 87 82).

L'Excuse (**AE+A, AI,** Level 2—Moderately accessible, one 6" entry step), one of the neighborhood's top restaurants, is a good splurge for a romantic, dressy evening in a hushed atmosphere, with lounge-lizard music and elegant Mediterranean nouveau cuisine. The plates are petite but creative and presented with panache (€37 *menu,* closed Sun, reserve ahead, request downstairs—ideally by the window, 14 rue Charles V, tel. 01 42 77 98 97).

L'Enoteca (**AE+A, AI,** Level 2—Moderately accessible, one 2" entry step) is a high-energy, half-timbered wine bar/restaurant dishing up reasonable Italian cuisine (no pizza) with a tempting antipasti bar. It's a relaxed, open setting with busy, blue-aproned waiters serving two floors of local eaters (allow €30 for meals with wine, daily, 25 rue Charles V, across from L'Excuse at rue St. Paul and rue Charles V, tel. 01 42 78 91 44).

Picolo Teatro (AE, AI+A, Level 2—Moderately accessible), small and crowded, is the place vegetarians should go for a fine meal (closed Mon, near rue des Rosiers, 6 rue des Ecouffes, tel. 01 42 72 17 79).

L'As du Falafel (AE+A, AI, Level 2—Moderately accessible, one 4" entry step)—a small establishment in an Orthodox Jewish neighborhood—serves inexpensive Jewish cuisine with bustling ambience (closed Sat, tasty falafels for €5, 34 rue des Rosiers).

Au Bourguignon du Marais (AE+A, AI, Level 2—Moderately accessible, challenging entry), a small wine bar south of rue de Rivoli, is a place that wine-lovers shouldn't miss. Gentle English-speaking Jacques offers excellent Burgundy wines that blend well with his fine, though limited, selection of *plats du jour* (allow €45 with wine, closed Sat–Sun, call by 19:00 to reserve, 52 rue François Miron, tel. 01 48 87 15 40).

On Ile St. Louis

The Ile St. Louis is a romantic and peaceful place to window-shop for plenty of promising dinner possibilities. Cruise the island's main street for a variety of options, from cozy *crêperies* to Italian (intimate pizzeria and upscale) to typical brasseries (several with fine outdoor seating facing the bridge to Ile de la Cité). After dinner, sample Paris' best sorbet. Then stroll or roll across to the Ile de la Cité to see an illuminated Notre-Dame. All listings below line the island's main drag, the rue St. Louis-en-l'Ile (see map on page 261). Consider skipping dessert to enjoy the best ice cream in Paris.

Le Tastevin and **Auberge de la Reine Blanche** (both AE, AI, Level 2—Moderately accessible) are two little family-run places that serve top-notch traditional French cuisine with white-tablecloth, candlelit elegance in small, 10-table rooms under heavy wooden beams. Their *menus* start with three courses at about €29 and offer plenty of classic choices that change with the season for freshness. Le Tastevin at #46, run by Madame Puisieux, is a little more intimate (daily, tel. 01 43 54 17 31). Auberge de la Reine Blanche is a bit more touristy—but in the best sense—with friendly Françoise and her crew working hard to please in a characteristic little place with dollhouse furniture on the walls and a two-dove welcoming committee at the door (closed Wed, #30, tel. 01 46 33 07 87). Reservations are smart for each.

Café Med (AE+A, AI, Level 2—Moderately accessible, two 6" entry steps), closest to Notre-Dame at #77, is best for inexpensive salads, crêpes, and lighter *menus* in a tight but cheery setting (daily, very limited wine list, tel. 01 43 29 73 17, charming Eva SE).

Nos Ancêtres les Gaulois and **La Taverne du Sergeant Recruteur** (both **AE+A, AI,** Level 2—Moderately accessible, one 8" entry step), next door to each other, are famous for their rowdy, medieval cellar atmosphere. They serve all-you-can-eat buffets with straw baskets of raw veggies (cut whatever you like with your dagger), massive plates of pâté, a meat course, and all the wine you can stomach for €36. The food is just food; burping is encouraged. If you want to eat a lot, drink a lot of wine, and holler at your friends while receiving smart-aleck buccaneer service, these food fests can be fun. Nos Ancêtres les Gaulois, or "Our Ancestors the Gauls," has bigger tables and seems made-to-order for local stag parties (daily from 19:00, # 39, tel. 01 46 33 66 07). If you'd rather be surrounded by drunk tourists than locals, pick La Taverne du Sergeant Recruteur. The "Sergeant Recruteur" used to get young Parisians drunk and stuffed here, then sign them into the army (daily from 19:00, #41, tel. 01 43 54 75 42).

Ice cream dessert: Half the people you'll see on Ile St. Louis are licking an ice cream cone, because this is the home of *les glaces Berthillon*. The original **Berthillon** shop, at 31 rue St. Louis-en-l'Ile, is marked by the line of salivating customers (**AE+A, AI,** Level 2—Moderately accessible; closed Mon–Tue). It's so popular that the wealthy people who can afford to live on this fancy island complain about the congestion it causes. For a less famous but at least as tasty treat, the homemade Italian gelato a block away at **Amorino Gelati** is giving Berthillon competition (**AE+A, AI+A,** Level 2—Moderately accessible); they offer little tastes and bigger portions—Berthillon doesn't need to (no line, easier to see what you want, 47 rue St. Louis-en-l'Ile, tel. 01 44 07 48 08). Having some of each is a fine option.

TRANSPORTATION CONNECTIONS

Paris is Europe's rail hub, with six major train stations, each serving different regions: Gare de l'Est (eastbound trains), Gare du Nord (northern France and Europe), Gare St. Lazare (northwestern France), Gare d'Austerlitz (southwestern France and Europe), Gare de Lyon (southeastern France and Italy), and Gare Montparnasse (northwestern France and TGV service to France's southwest). Any train station can give you schedule information, make reservations, and sell tickets for any destination. Buying tickets is handier from an SNCF neighborhood office (e.g., Louvre, Invalides, Orsay, Versailles, airports) or at your neighborhood travel agency—worth the small fee (SNCF signs in their window indicate they sell train tickets). For schedule information, call 08 36 35 35 35 (€0.50/min, English sometimes available).

All six train stations have Métro, bus, and taxi service. All have banks or change offices, ATMs, information desks, telephones, cafés, baggage storage (*consigne automatique*, none at Gare St. Lazare), newsstands, and clever pickpockets. Each station offers two types of rail service: long distance to other cities, called *Grandes Lignes* (major lines); and suburban service to outlying areas, called *banlieue* or RER. Both *banlieue* and RER trains serve outlying areas and the airports; the only difference is that *banlieue* lines are operated by SNCF (France's train system) and RER lines are operated by RATP (Paris' Métro and bus system). Paris train stations can be intimidating, but if you slow down, take a deep breath, and ask for help, you'll find them manageable and efficient. Bring a pad of paper for clear communication at ticket/info windows. All stations have helpful *accueil* (information) booths; the bigger stations have roving helpers, usually in red vests.

Access: Most of Paris' train stations are generally accessible, though each station has areas that a wheelchair user can't access. Most platforms can be reached by wheelchair, but sometimes the wheelchair user will be assisted by staff. Most stations have accessible toilets and elevators. When you arrive at any station, ask an attendant for assistance, or report to the *accueil* (information) booth.

SNCF, the French rail company, has a telephone number with detailed recorded information about accessibility for every station in France (tel. 08 00 15 47 53). The catch: It's all in French. In a pinch, recruit a hotelier or another friendly local to call for you.

Below, we've listed specific access information only for the Gare du Nord station, which you'll use to connect to most destinations in this book (e.g., London, Amsterdam, Bruges, and the Rhine via Köln).

Station Overview

Here's an overview of Paris' major train stations. Métro, RER, buses (BUS), and taxis are well-signposted at every station. When arriving,

Paris Train Stations

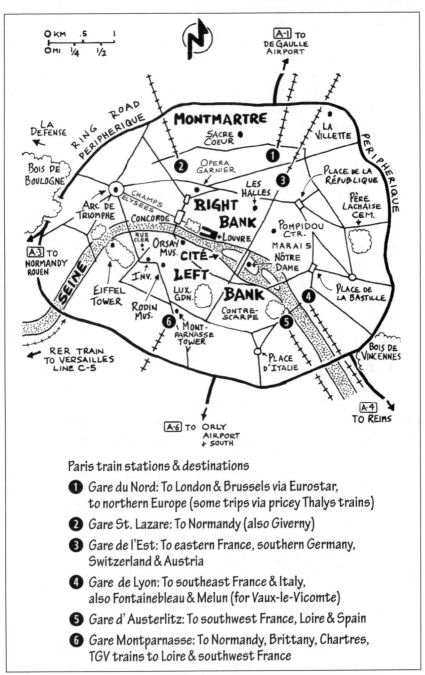

Paris train stations & destinations

❶ Gare du Nord: To London & Brussels via Eurostar,
to northern Europe (some trips via pricey Thalys trains)

❷ Gare St. Lazare: To Normandy (also Giverny)

❸ Gare de l'Est: To eastern France, southern Germany,
Switzerland & Austria

❹ Gare de Lyon: To southeast France & Italy,
also Fontainebleau & Melun (for Vaux-le-Vicomte)

❺ Gare d' Austerlitz: To southwest France, Loire & Spain

❻ Gare Montparnasse: To Normandy, Brittany, Chartres,
TGV trains to Loire & southwest France

follow signs for *Grandes Lignes–SNCF* to find the main tracks.

Gare du Nord

This vast station serves cities in northern France and international destinations north of Paris, including Copenhagen, the Thalys train to Brussels and Amsterdam (see "To Brussels and Amsterdam by Thalys Train," page 250), and the Eurostar train to London (see Eurostar information on page 141 of the London chapter). If arriving on the Eurostar from London and moving on to Bruges or Amsterdam, get your ticket here upon arrival to save hassle later on.

Allow plenty of time to navigate the huge Gare du Nord. If you arrive by Métro, follow *Grandes Lignes* signs (main lines) and keep going up until you reach the tracks at street level. *Grandes Lignes* depart from tracks 3–21, suburban *(banlieue)* lines from tracks 30–36, and RER trains depart from tracks 37–44 (tracks 41–44 are 1 floor below). Glass train information booths *(accueil)* are scattered throughout the station and information staff circulate to help (all rail staff are required to speak English).

The tourist information kiosk opposite track 16 is a hotel reservation service for Accor chain hotels (they also have free Paris maps). Information booths for the **Thalys** (high-speed trains to Brussels and Amsterdam) are opposite track 8. All non-Eurostar ticket sales are opposite tracks 3–8. Passengers departing on **Eurostar** (London via Chunnel) must buy tickets and check in on the second level, opposite track 6. (Note: Britain's time zone is 1 hour earlier; times listed on Eurostar tickets are local times.) Monet-esque views over the trains and peaceful, air-conditioned cafés hide on the upper level, past the Eurostar ticket windows. Storage lockers, baggage check, taxis, and rental cars are at the far end, just opposite track 3.

Access: AE, AI, AT, Level 2—Moderately accessible (some parts of the station are accessible only by escalator, not elevator). Wheelchair users can find an accessible toilet along the side of track 3 (€0.40, push a button near door to be let in). Another accessible toilet is located near track 36 (€0.40). The platforms are at street level, so elevators are not needed to leave the station. There are accessible elevators to the lower level, where car rentals and the Métro are located. As you go toward the exit with the taxi stand, you'll find the elevators located just inside the doorway on the right-hand side (go to the floor marked –1).

Key destinations served by Gare du Nord *Grandes Lignes:* **London** Eurostar via Chunnel (12–15/day, 3 hrs, tel. 08 36 35 35 39; see Eurostar Information, page 141), **Brussels** (12/day, 1.5 hrs, see "To Brussels and Amsterdam by Thalys Train," page 250), **Bruges** (18/day, 2 hrs, change in Brussels, 1 direct), **Amsterdam** (10/day, 4 hrs; see "To Brussels and Amsterdam by Thalys Train," page 250), **Köln** (7/day, 4 hrs), **Copenhagen** (1/day, 16 hrs, 2 night trains), **Koblenz** (6/day, 5 hrs, change in Köln).

By *banlieue*/**RER lines: Chantilly-Gouvieux** (hrly, fewer on weekends, 35 min), **Charles de Gaulle Airport** (2/hr, 30 min, runs 5:30–23:00, track 4), **Auvers-sur-Oise** (2/hr, 1 hr, transfer at Pontoise).

Gare Montparnasse

This big and modern station covers three floors, serves lower Normandy and Brittany, and offers TGV service to the Loire Valley and southwestern France, as well as suburban service to Chartres. At street level, you'll find a bank, *banlieue* trains (serving Chartres; you can also reach the *banlieue* trains from the second level), and ticket windows in the center, just past the escalators. Lockers *(consigne automatique)* are on the mezzanine level between levels 1 and 2. Most services are provided on the second level, where the *Grandes Lignes* arrive and depart (ticket windows to the far left with your back to glass exterior). *Banlieue* trains depart from tracks 10 through 19. The main rail information office is opposite track 15. Taxis are to the far left as you leave the tracks.

Key destinations served by Gare Montparnasse: Chartres (20/day, 1 hr, *banlieue* lines), **Pontorson-Mont St. Michel** (5/day, 4.5 hrs, via Rennes, then take bus; or take train to Pontorson via Caen, then bus from Pontorson), **Dinan** (7/day, 4 hrs, change in Rennes and Dol), **Bordeaux** (14/day, 3.5 hrs), **Sarlat** (5/day, 6 hrs, change in Bordeaux, Libourne, or Souillac), **Toulouse** (11/day, 5 hrs, most require change, usually in Bordeaux), **Albi** (7/day, 6–7.5 hrs, change in Toulouse, also night train), **Carcassonne** (8/day, 6.5 hrs, most require changes in Toulouse and Bordeaux, direct trains take 10 hrs), **Tours** (14/day, 1 hr).

Gare de Lyon

This huge and bewildering station offers TGV and regular service to southeastern France, Italy, and other international destinations (for more trains to Italy, see "Gare de Bercy," next page). Don't leave this station without checking out Le Train Bleu Restaurant, up the stairs opposite track G.

Grande Ligne trains arrive and depart from one level but are divided into two areas (tracks A–N and 5–23). They are connected by the long platform along tracks A and 5, and by the hallway adjacent to track A and opposite track 9. This hallway has all the services, ticket windows, ticket information, banks, shops, and access to car rental. *Banlieue* ticket windows are just inside the hall adjacent to track A *(billets Ile de France)*. *Grandes Lignes* and *banlieue* lines share the same tracks. A helpful tourist office (Mon–Sat 8:00–20:00, closed Sun) and a train information office are both opposite track L. From the RER or Métro, follow signs for *Grandes Lignes Arrivées* and take the escalator up to reach the platforms. Train information booths *(accueil)* are opposite tracks G and 11. Baggage check is down the stairs opposite track 13. Taxis stands are well-marked in front of the station and one floor below.

Key destinations served by Gare de Lyon: Vaux-le-Vicomte (train to Melun, hrly, 30 min), **Fontainebleau** (nearly hrly, 45 min), **Beaune** (12/day, 2.5 hrs, most require change in Dijon), **Dijon** (15/day, 1.5 hrs), **Chamonix** (9/day, 9 hrs, change in Lyon and St. Gervais, direct night train), **Annecy** (8/day, 4–7 hrs), Lyon (16/day, 2.5 hrs), **Avignon** (9/day in 2.5 hrs, 6/day in 4 hrs with change), **Arles** (14/day, 5 hrs, most with change in Marseille, Avignon, or Nîmes), **Nice** (14/day, 5.5–7 hrs, many with change in Marseille), **Venice** (3/day, 3/night, 11–15 hrs, most require changes), **Rome** (2/day, 5/night, 15–18 hrs, most require changes), **Bern** (9/day, 5–11 hrs, most require changes, night train).

Gare de Bercy

This smaller station handles some night train service to Italy during renovation work at the Gare de Lyon (Mo: Bercy, 1 stop east of Gare de Lyon on line 14).

Gare de l'Est

This single floor station (with underground Métro) serves eastern France and European points east of Paris. Train information booths are at tracks 1, 18, and 26; ticket windows are in the big hall opposite track 8; luggage storage is through the hall opposite track 12.

Key destinations served by Gare de l'Est: Colmar (12/day, 5.5 hrs, change in Strasbourg, Dijon, or Mulhouse), **Strasbourg** (14/day, 4.5 hrs, many require changes), **Reims** (12/day, 1.5 hrs), **Verdun** (5/day, 3 hrs, change in Metz or Chalon), **Munich** (5/day, 9 hrs, some require changes, night train), **Vienna** (7/day, 13–18 hrs, most require changes, night train), **Zürich** (10/day, 7 hrs, most require changes, night train), **Prague** (2/day, 14 hrs, night train).

Gare St. Lazare

This relatively small station serves upper Normandy, including Rouen and Giverny. All trains arrive and depart one floor above street level. Follow signs to *Grandes Lignes* from the Métro to reach the tracks. Ticket windows are in the first hall on the second floor. *Grandes Lignes* (main lines) depart from tracks 17–27; *banlieue* (suburban) trains depart from 1–16. The train information office *(accueil)* is opposite track 15. There's a post office along track 27, and WCs are opposite track 19. There is no baggage check.

Key destinations served by Gare St. Lazare: **Giverny** (train to Vernon, 5/day, 45 min; then bus or taxi 10 min to Giverny), **Rouen** (15/day, 75 min), **Honfleur** (6/day, 3 hrs, via Lisieux, then bus), **Bayeux** (9/day, 2.5 hrs, some with change in Caen), **Caen** (12/day, 2 hrs).

Gare d'Austerlitz

This small station provides non-TGV service to the Loire Valley, southwestern France, and Spain. All tracks are at street level. The information booth is opposite track 17, and all ticket sales are in the hall opposite track 10. Baggage consignment (if open) and car rental are near *porte* 27 (along the side, opposite track 21).

Key destinations served by Gare d'Austerlitz: **Amboise** (8/day in 2 hrs, 12/day in 1.5 hrs with change in St. Pierre-des-Corps), **Cahors** (7/day, 5–7 hrs, most with changes), **Barcelona** (1/day, 9 hrs, change in Montpellier, night trains), **Madrid** (2 night trains only, 13–16 hrs), **Lisbon** (1/day, 24 hrs).

To Brussels and Amsterdam by Thalys Train

The pricey Thalys train has the monopoly on routes to Brussels and Amsterdam. (And if you're headed to Bruges, you'll first have to change trains in Brussels.) Without a railpass, you'll pay about €80–100 second-class for the Paris–Amsterdam train or about €60–80 second-class for the Paris–Brussels train. Even with a railpass, you need to pay for reservations (€14/second class, €30/first class). Wheelchair users and one companion get discounted first-class fares with minimal restrictions. Anyone should book at least a day ahead as seats are limited (toll tel. 08 25 84 25 97).

Access: AE+A, AI, AT, Level 2—Moderately accessible. Wheelchair users can pay for second class on Thalys trains, but reserve first-class accessible seats at no additional charge. Wheelchair users should alert Thalys at the time of booking that they will need assistance, then arrive 30 minutes before departure so Thalys staff can prepare for boarding with ramps. On Thalys trains, only first class is accessible, with designated spaces for wheelchairs. Train cars 1, 11, and 21 have a seat with a mobile base to make transfers easier. These three cars also have accessible toilets.

To London by Eurostar Train

The fastest, most accessible, and most convenient way to get to London is by rail—through the "Chunnel." For information on this option, see page 141.

Airports
Charles de Gaulle Airport

Paris' primary airport has two main terminals: T-1 and T-2, and two lesser terminals, T-3 and T-9. SAS, United, US Airways, KLM, Northwest, and Lufthansa all normally use T-1. Air France dominates T-2, though you'll also find Delta, Continental, American, British Airways, and Air Canada. Smaller airlines use T-3 and charter flights leave from T-9. Airlines sometimes switch terminals, so verify your terminal before flying. Terminals are connected every few minutes by a free *navette* (shuttle bus; **AE, AI,** Level 2—Moderately accessible; line #1). The RER (Paris subway) stops at T-2 and T-3 terminals, and the TGV (stands for *train à grande vitesse,* tay-zhay-vay) station is at T-2. There is no bag storage at the airport. Beware of pickpockets on *navettes* between terminals and (worse) on RER trains. Do not take an unauthorized taxi from the men greeting you on arrival (official taxi stands are well signed).

Those flying to or from the United States will almost certainly use T-1 or T-2. Below is information for each terminal. For flight information, call 01 48 62 22 80.

General Airport Access: AE, AI, AL, AT+A, Level 2—Moderately accessible. Although Charles de Gaulle airport has basic accessibility features, wheelchair users have reported that this can be a challenging place to navigate. The TI's *"Passager a mobilite reduite"* guide lists the accessibility of the airport and its hotels and restaurants.

TERMINAL 1 (T-1): This circular terminal covers three floors—arrival (*arrivées,* top floor), departure (*départs,* one floor down) and shops/boutiques (basement level). For information on getting to Paris, see "Transportation between Charles de Gaulle Airport and Paris," next page. On the **arrival** level you'll find a variety of services at these gates:

- Gate 36 (called *Meeting Point*): ADP, a quasi–tourist office, sells museum passes, offers free maps, and provides tourist/hotel information (daily 7:00–22:00). A nearby *Relay* store sells phone cards. To find the shuttle buses (*navettes,* **AE, AI,** Level 2—Moderately accessible) for Terminal 2 and the RER trains to Paris, take the elevator down to level *(niveau)* 2, then go outside (line #1 serves T-2 including the TGV station; line #2 goes directly to the RER station).
- Gate 34: Outside are Air France buses to Paris and Orly Airport.
- Gate 32: ATMs. Outside are Roissy Buses to Paris (buy tickets inside at gate 30 or from driver).
- Gate 22: SNCF train ticket office.
- Gate 20: Taxis outside.
- Gate 16: A bank with lousy rates for currency exchange.
- Gates 10–24: Car-rental offices.

The **departure level** *(niveau 3)* is limited to flight check-in, though you will find ADP information desks here. Those departing from T-1 will find restaurants, a PTT (post office), a pharmacy, boutiques, and a handy grocery store one floor below the ticketing desks (level 2 on the elevator).

Access for Terminal 1: **AE, AI, AL, AT,** Level 1—Fully accessible, but the toilets and elevators can be hard to find. If you'll be taking the train to Paris, check in with the RER-SNCF information booth to prepare for your journey—they will show you to the elevator. For general assistance for persons with reduced mobility, call 01 48 62 28 24.

TERMINAL 2 (T-2): This long, horseshoe-shaped terminal is divided into several sub-terminals (or Halls), each identified by a letter. Halls are connected with each other, the RER, the TGV station, and T-1 every five minutes with free *navettes* or shuttle buses (**AE, AI,** Level 2—Moderately accessible; line #1 runs to T-1). Here is where you should find these key carriers: in Hall A—Air France, Air Canada, and American Airlines; in Hall C—Delta, Continental, and more Air France; and in Hall D—British Airways. The RER and TGV stations are below the Sheraton Hotel (access by *navettes* or on foot). Stops for *navettes,* Air France buses, and Roissy Buses are all clearly marked and near each Hall (see "Transportation between Charles de Gaulle Airport and Paris," below). ADP information desks are located near gate 5 in each Hall. Car-rental offices, post offices, pharmacies, and ATMs *(point d'argent)* are also well-signed.

Access for Terminal 2: **AE, AI, AL, AT+A,** Level 2—Moderately accessible. While the interior of the terminal is fully accessible, not all toilet areas are accessible. If using the train to get into Paris, check in with the RER-SNCF information booth to prepare for your journey. For general assistance for persons with reduced mobility, call 01 48 62 59 00.

Transportation between Charles de Gaulle Airport and Paris: The most accessible route downtown is via taxi or with an airport shuttle.

Taxis with luggage will run €40–55 with bags. If taking a cab to the airport, ask your hotel to call for you (the night before if you must leave early). You can request a minibus with a ramp for accessibility, which costs more than a normal taxi. (See "Getting around Paris," page 172.)

Airport shuttle minivans get you affordably from either of Paris' airports to or from your hotel. Reserve from home and they'll pick you up at the airport; plan on a 30-minute wait (prices for **AE+A,** Level 2—Moderately accessible van: €23 for 1 person, €27 for 2 people, €41 for 3 people, €55 for 4 people). Be clear on where and how you are to meet your driver. **Golden Air** is reliable and has standard vans as well as a fully-accessible minivan, available for an additional fee (**AE, AI,** Level 1, €130 for wheelchair user plus up to 5 other passengers, reserve a week in advance, tel. 01 47 37 06 56, fax 01 47 37 57 23, www.goldenair.net).

Sleeping at Charles de Gaulle Airport: Hôtel Ibis** (**AE, AI, AL, AR, AB,** Level 1—Fully accessible), outside the RER Roissy Rail station at T-3 (the first RER stop coming from Paris), offers standard and predictable accommodations (three rooms on each floor are fully accessible; Db-€90, near *navette* stop, free shuttle bus to all terminals, tel. 01 49 19 19 19, fax 01 49 19 19 21, h1404sb@accor-hotels.com). **Novotel***** (**AE, AI, AL, AR, AB,** Level 1—Fully accessible) is next door and the next step up (one room on each floor is fully accessible; Db-€155–170, tel. 01 49 19 27 27, fax 01 49 19 27 99, h1014@accor-hotels.com).

Orly Airport

This airport feels small. Orly has two terminals: Sud and Ouest. International flights arrive at Sud. After exiting Sud's baggage claim (near gate H), you'll see signs directing you to city transportation, car rental, and so on. Turn left to enter the main terminal area, and you'll find exchange offices with bad rates, an ATM, the ADP (a quasi–tourist office that offers free city maps and basic sightseeing information, open until 23:00), and an SNCF French rail desk (closes at 18:00, sells train tickets and even Eurailpasses, next to ADP). On the lower level, you'll find a sandwich bar, toilets, a bank (same bad rates), a newsstand (buy a phone card), and a post office (great rates for cash or American Express traveler's checks). Car-rental offices are located in the parking lot in front of the terminal. For flight info on any airline serving Orly, call 01 49 75 15 15.

Transportation between Orly Airport and Paris: Taxis, airport shuttles, and several efficient public-transportation routes link Orly with central Paris. Wheelchair users will find taxis and minibuses to be the most convenient option. The gate locations listed below apply to Orly Sud, but the same transportation services are available from both terminals.

Taxis are to the far right as you leave the terminal, at gate M. Allow €26–35 with bags for a taxi into central Paris. (For access, see "Getting around Paris," page 172.)

Airport shuttle minivans are ideal for single travelers or families of four or more (see "Charles de Gaulle Airport," page 251, for a good company to contact; from Orly, figure about €18 for 1 person, €12/person for 2 people, less for larger groups and kids).

Sleeping near Orly Airport: Hôtel Ibis** (AE, AI, AL, AR, AB, Level 1—Fully accessible) is reasonable, basic, and close by (9 fully accessible rooms; Db-€60, tel. 01 56 70 50 60, fax 01 56 70 50 70, h1413@accor-hotels.com). **Hôtel Mercure***** (AE, AI, AL, AR, AB, Level 1—Fully accessible) provides more comfort for a price (6 fully accessible rooms; Db-€120–135, tel. 01 49 75 15 50, fax 01 49 75 15 51, h1246@accor-hotels.com). Both have free shuttles to the terminal.

HISTORIC PARIS ROLL OR STROLL

From Notre-Dame to Sainte-Chapelle

Paris has been the capital of Europe for centuries. We'll start where it did, on the Ile de la Cité, with forays into both the Left and Right Banks, on a tour that laces together the story of Paris: Roman, medieval, the Revolution, café society, the literary scene of the 1920s, and the modern world.

Allow at least four hours to complete this self-guided three-mile tour, including sightseeing. If the distance seems too long, break it into pieces to make it more manageable. Stops along this walk have varying

ACCESSIBILITY CODE CHART

CODE	MEANING
AE	Accessible Entryway
AE+A	Accessible Entry with Assistance
AI	Accessible Interior
AI+A	Accessible Interior with Assistance
AT	Accessible Toilet
AT+A	Accessible Toilet with Assistance
AL	Accessible Lift (elevator)
AL+A	Accessible Lift with Assistance

For the full chart, or a more detailed explanation of codes, please see page 2 of the Introduction.

Historic Paris Roll or Stroll

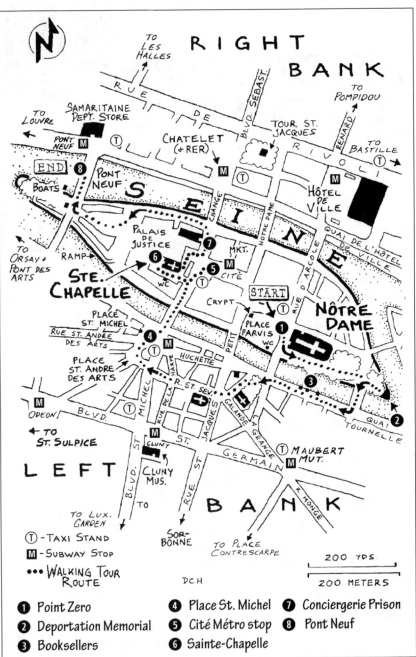

① Point Zero
② Deportation Memorial
③ Booksellers
④ Place St. Michel
⑤ Cité Métro stop
⑥ Sainte-Chapelle
⑦ Conciergerie Prison
⑧ Pont Neuf

degrees of accessibility (as noted). Skip those portions that do not suit your mobility level, and move on to the next stop.

Begin at Notre-Dame. To get there, take a taxi or ride the Métro to Cité, Hôtel de Ville, or St. Michel and roll or stroll to the big square facing the cathedral.

Notre-Dame Cathedral

Cathedral Access: AE, AI+A, Level 2— Moderately accessible. The entryway and three-fourths of the main floor are wheelchair-accessible. There are three 6" steps to enter the area of the Mass and the treasury.

Tower Access: Level 4—Not accessible (400 steps).

Cost, Hours, and Location: Cathedral entry is free; open daily 8:00–18:45. Ask about free English tours, normally held on Wed and Thu at 12:00 and Sat at 14:30. The **treasury** costs €2.50 (not covered by museum pass); daily 9:30–17:30. Mo: Cité, Hôtel de Ville, or St. Michel. Climbing the **tower** costs €5.50 (covered by museum pass); daily April–Sept 9:30–19:30, Oct–March 10:00–18:00, last entry 45 min before closing, arrive early to avoid long lines.

There are clean, but not accessible, toilets in front of the church near Charlemagne's statue (twenty-five 7" steps).

The Sight: The **cathedral facade** is worth a close look. The church is dedicated to "Our Lady" (Notre-Dame). Mary is center stage—cradling

Jesus, surrounded by the halo of the rose window. Adam is on the left and Eve is on the right.

Below Mary and above the arches is a row of 28 statues known as the Kings of Judah. During the French Revolution, these Biblical kings were mistaken for the hated French kings. The citizens stormed the church, crying, "Off with their heads!" All were decapitated but have since been recapitated.

Notre-Dame Facade

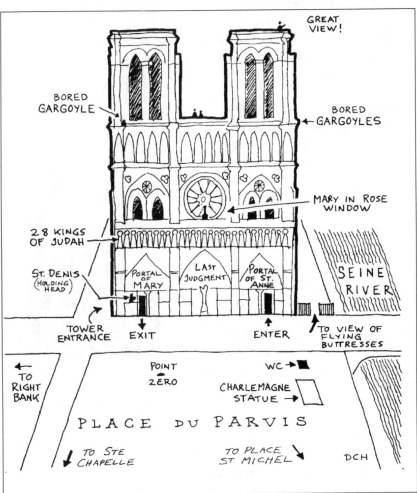

GREAT VIEW!

BORED GARGOYLE

BORED GARGOYLES

MARY IN ROSE WINDOW

28 KINGS OF JUDAH

ST. DENIS (HOLDING HEAD)

PORTAL OF MARY

LAST JUDGMENT

PORTAL OF ST. ANNE

SEINE RIVER

TOWER ENTRANCE

EXIT

ENTER

TO VIEW OF FLYING BUTTRESSES

POINT ZERO

WC

CHARLEMAGNE STATUE →

TO RIGHT BANK

PLACE DU PARVIS

TO STE CHAPELLE

TO PLACE ST. MICHEL

DCH

Speaking of decapitation, look at the carving above the doorway on the left. The man with his head in his hands is St. Denis. Back when there was a Roman temple on this spot, Christianity began making converts. The fourth-century bishop of Roman Paris, Denis, was beheaded. But these early Christians were hard to keep down. The man who would become St.

Denis got up, tucked his head under his arm, and headed north until he found just the right place to meet his maker: Montmartre. (Although the name "Montmartre" comes from the Roman "Mount of Mars," later generations—thinking of their beheaded patron St. Denis—preferred a less pagan version, "Mount of Martyrs.") The Parisians were convinced of this miracle, Christianity gained ground, and a church soon replaced the pagan temple.

Medieval art was OK if it embellished the house of God and told Bible stories. For a fine example, move to the base of the central column (at the foot of Mary, about where the head of St. Denis could spit if he were really good). Working around from the left, find God telling a barely created Eve, "Have fun but no apples." Next, a sexy serpent makes apples à la mode. Finally, Adam and Eve, now ashamed of their nakedness, are expelled by an angel. This is a tiny example in a church covered with meaning.

Now move to the right and study the carving above the **central portal.** It's the end of the world, and Christ sits on the throne of Judgment (just under the arches, holding his hands up). Below him an angel and a demon weigh souls in the balance. The "good" stand to the left, looking up to heaven. The "bad" ones to the right are chained up and led off to...Versailles on a Tuesday. The "ugly" ones must be the crazy sculpted demons to the right, at the base of the arch.

Wander through the interior. You'll be routed around the ambulatory, much as medieval pilgrims would have been. Don't miss the rose windows filling each of the transepts. Back outside, go around the church through the park on the riverside for a close look at the flying buttresses.

The neo-Gothic 300-foot **spire** is a product of the 1860 reconstruction. Around its base are apostles and evangelists (the green men) as well as Eugène-Emmanuel Viollet-le-Duc, the architect in charge of the work. Notice how the apostles look outward, blessing the city, while the architect (at top, seen from behind the church) looks up, admiring his spire.

The archaeological **crypt** is a worthwhile

15-minute stop with your museum pass (Level 3—Minimally accessible, fourteen 6" steps down to the entryway, inside is mostly wheelchair accessible; €3.50, Tue–Sun 10:00–17:30, closed Mon, enter 100 yards in front of church). You'll see Roman ruins, trace the street plan of the medieval village, and see diagrams of how the earliest Paris grew and grew, all thoughtfully explained in English.

If you're hungry near Notre-Dame, the nearby Ile St. Louis has inexpensive crêperies and grocery stores open daily on its main drag. Plan a picnic for the quiet, accessible, bench-filled park immediately behind the church (public toilet, but not easily accessible).

• *Behind Notre-Dame, cross the street and enter through the iron gate into the park at the tip of the island. Wheelchair users go left on the sidewalk to the corner and cross where there is a light and curb cuts. Go right down the sidewalk to the entrance near the river. From here, if you are able, take the twenty-six 7" stairs down to the...*

Deportation Memorial (Mémorial de la Déportation)

Access: Level 4—Not accessible. The memorial can be reached only by going down twenty-six 7" stairs.

Cost, Hours, and Location: Free, April–Sept daily 10:00–12:00 & 14:00–19:00; Oct–March daily 10:00–12:00 & 14:00–17:00; east tip of the Ile de la Cité, behind Notre-Dame and near Ile St. Louis, Mo: Cité.

The Sight: This memorial to the 200,000 French victims of the Nazi concentration camps draws you into their experience. As you descend, the city around you disappears. Surrounded by walls, you have become a prisoner. Your only freedom is your view of the sky and the tantalizing glimpse of the river below.

Enter the single-file chamber ahead (28" wide). Inside, the circular plaque in the floor reads, "They descended into the mouth of the earth and they did not return." A hallway stretches in front of you, lined with 200,000 lighted crystals, one for each French citizen that died. Flickering at the far end is the eternal flame of hope. The tomb of the unknown deportee lies at your feet. Above, the inscription reads, "Dedicated to the living memory of the 200,000 French deportees sleeping in the night and the fog, exterminated in the Nazi concentration camps."

Above the exit as you leave is the message you'll find at all Nazi sights: "Forgive, but never forget."

Ile St. Louis

Back on street level, look across the river to the Ile St. Louis. If the Ile de la Cité is a tug laden with the history of Paris, it's towing this classy little residential dinghy laden only with boutiques, famous sorbet shops, and restaurants (see page 243). This island wasn't developed until much later (18th century). What was a swampy mess is now harmonious Parisian architecture. The accessible pedestrian bridge, pont St. Louis, connects the two islands, leading right to rue St. Louis-en-l'Ile. This spine of the island is lined with interesting shops. A short roll or stroll takes you to the famous Berthillon ice-cream parlor (**AE+A, AI+A,** Level 2—Moderately accessible, one 4" entry doorstep and one interior 4" step; at #31).

Ile St. Louis

1. La Tastevin
2. Auberge de la Reine Blanche
3. Café Med
4. Rests. Nos Ancêtres les Gaulois & La Taverne du Sergeant Recruteur
5. Les Glaces Berthillon Ice Cream
6. Amorino Gelati

• *Loop back to the pedestrian bridge along the parklike quays (go north to the river and turn left). This accessible pathway is about as peaceful and romantic as Paris gets.*

Before heading to the opposite end of the Ile de la Cité, loop through the Latin Quarter (as indicated on the map). From the Deportation Memorial, cross the bridge onto the Left Bank and enjoy the riverside view of Notre-Dame. Window-shop among the green book stalls, browsing through used books, vintage posters, and souvenirs. At the little park and church (over the bridge from the front of Notre-Dame), venture inland a few blocks, basically arcing through the Latin Quarter and returning to the island two bridges down at place St. Michel.

Latin Quarter

This area, which gets its name from the language used here when it was an exclusive medieval university district, lies between Luxembourg Gardens and the Seine, centering around the Sorbonne University and boulevards St. Germain and St. Michel. This is the core of the Left Bank—it's crowded with international eateries, far-out bookshops, street singers, and jazz clubs. For colorful wandering and

café sitting, afternoons and evenings are best (Mo: St. Michel).

Along rue St. Séverin you can still see the shadow of the medieval sewer system (the street slopes into a central channel of bricks). In the days before plumbing and toilets, when people still went to the river or neighborhood wells for their water, "flushing" meant throwing it out the window. Certain times of day were flushing times. Maids on the fourth floor would holler *"Faites attention à l'eau!"* ("Look out for the water!") and heave it into the streets, where it would eventually be washed down into the Seine.

Consider a visit to the Cluny Museum for its medieval art and unicorn tapestries (Level 3—Minimally accessible; see page 197). The accessible park behind the museum makes a delightful picnic spot (access at corner of boulevards St. Michel and St. Germain).

Place St. Michel (facing the St. Michel bridge) is the traditional core of the Left Bank's artsy, liberal, hippie, Bohemian district of poets,

philosophers, winos, and tourists. In less-commercial times, place St. Michel was a gathering point for the city's malcontents and misfits. Here, in 1871, the citizens took the streets from the government troops, set up barricades *Les Mis*-style, and established the Paris Commune. In World War II the locals rose up against their Nazi oppressors (read the plaques by St. Michel fountain). And in the spring of 1968, a time of social upheaval all over the world, young students—battling riot batons and tear gas—took over the square and demanded change.

• *From place St. Michel, look across the river and find the spire of Sainte-Chapelle church and its weathervane angel (below). Cross the river on pont St. Michel and continue along boulevard du Palais. On your left you'll see the high-security doorway to Sainte-Chapelle. But first, carry on another 30 yards and turn right at a wide pedestrian street, the rue de Lutèce.*

Cité "Métropolitain" Stop

Of the 141 original turn-of-the-20th-century subway entrances, this is one of 17 survivors now preserved as a national art treasure. The curvy, plantlike iron work is a textbook example of Art Nouveau, the style that rebelled against the erector-set squareness of the Industrial Age (e.g., Mr. Eiffel's tower).

The flower market right here on place Louis Lépine is a pleasant detour. On Sundays this square chirps with a busy bird market. And across the way is the Prefecture de Police, where Inspector Clouseau of *Pink Panther* fame used to work and where the local resistance fighters took the first building from the Nazis in August 1944, leading to the Allied liberation of Paris a week later.

Pause here to admire the view. Sainte-Chapelle is a pearl in an ugly architectural oyster, part of a complex of buildings that includes the Palace of Justice (to the right of Sainte-Chapelle, behind the fancy gates).

• *Return to the entrance of Sainte-Chapelle. Everyone needs to pass through a metal detector to get in. Free, suitable toilets are ahead on the left. Wheelchair-accessible toilets are near the Palace of Justice entrance, with one 4" curb to negotiate and a long ramp with no railing.*

The line into the church may be long. (Museum-card holders can go directly in; pick up the excellent English info sheet.) After going through the security area and the cobblestone pathway, find the wheelchair-accessible entry-way ramp (listed as the exit). Enter the humble ground floor of...

Sainte-Chapelle

Access: Lower level only—**AE, AI, AT+A,** Level 2—Moderately accessible. Unfortunately, the upstairs chapel can be reached only by climbing a narrow spiral staircase (Level 4—Not accessible, though slow walkers can try it—it's worth the climb).

Cost, Hours, and Location: Free for wheelchair users, otherwise €5.50, €8 combo-ticket covers inaccessible Conciergerie, both covered by museum pass, daily 9:30–18:00, Mo: Cité, tel. 01 44 07 12 38 for concert information.

The Sight: Sainte-Chapelle is a triumph of Gothic church architecture and a cathedral of glass like no other. It was speedily built from 1242 to 1248 for St. Louis IX (France's only canonized king) to house the supposed Crown of Thorns. Its architectural harmony is due to the fact that it was completed under the direction of one architect in only six years—unheard of in Gothic times. (Notre-Dame took more than 200 years to build.)

The design clearly shows an *ancien regime* approach to worship. The basement was for staff and other common folk. Royal Christians worshiped upstairs. The ground-floor paint job, a 19th-century restoration, is a reasonably accurate copy of the original.

If you can manage stairs, climb the spiral staircase to the **Chapelle Haute.** Fill the place with choral music, crank up the sunshine, face the top of the altar, and really believe that the Crown of Thorns was there, and this becomes one awesome space.

"Let there be light." In the Bible, it's clear: Light is divine. Light shining through stained glass was a symbol of God's grace shining down to earth. Gothic architects used their new technology to turn dark stone buildings into lanterns of light. The glory of Gothic shines brighter here than in any other church.

Sainte-Chapelle Area

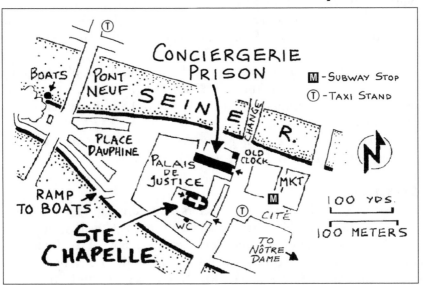

There are 15 separate panels of stained glass (6,500 square feet— two-thirds of it 13th-century original), with more than 1,100 different scenes, mostly from the Bible.

The altar was raised up high to better display the relic—the Crown of Thorns—around which this chapel was built. The supposed crown cost King Louis IX three times as much as this church. Today it is kept in the Notre-Dame Treasury and shown only on Fridays during Lent.

Louis' little private viewing window is in the wall to the right of the altar. Louis, both saintly and shy, liked to go to church without dealing with the rigors of public royal life. Here he could worship while still dressed in his jammies.

Lay your camera on the ground and shoot the ceiling. Those ribs growing out of the slender columns are the essence of Gothic.

Palais de Justice

Back outside, as you roll or stroll around the church exterior, look down and notice how much Paris has risen in the 800 years since Sainte-Chapelle was built. You're in a huge complex of buildings that has housed the local government since ancient Roman times. It was the site of the original Gothic palace of the early kings of France. The only surviving medieval parts are the Sainte-Chapelle church and the Conciergerie prison.

Most of the site is now covered by the giant Palais de Justice, home of France's supreme court (built in 1776). *"Liberté, Egalité, Fraternité"* over the doors is a reminder that this was also the headquarters of the revolutionary government.

• *Now pass through the big iron gate to the noisy boulevard du Palais. The building to the right of the Palais de Justice is the...*

Conciergerie

Access: Level 4—Not accessible. Visitors must negotiate a flight of stairs to get into the accessible courtyard and lobby of the Conciergerie.

Cost, Hours, and Location: Courtyard and lobby—Free. Interior—€5.50, €8 combo-ticket covers Sainte-Chapelle, both covered by museum pass, daily April–Sept 9:30–18:30, Oct–March 10:00–17:00, good English descriptions.

The Sight: This former prison is a gloomy place. Kings used it to torture and execute failed assassins. The leaders of the Revolution put it to similar good use. The tower next to the entrance, called "the babbler," was named for the painful sounds that leaked from it.

Look at the stark lettering above the doorways. This was a no-nonsense revolutionary time. Everything, even lettering, was subjected to the test of reason. No frills or we chop 'em off.

The lobby, with an English-language history display, is free. Marie-Antoinette was imprisoned here. During a busy eight-month period in the Revolution, she was one of 2,600 prisoners kept here on the way to the guillotine. The interior, with its huge vaulted and pillared rooms, echoes with history but is pretty barren. You can see Marie-Antoinette's cell, housing a collection of her mementos. In another room, a list of those made "a foot shorter at the top" by the "national razor" includes ex-King Louis XVI, Charlotte Corday (who murdered Jean-Paul Marat in his bathtub), and the chief revolutionary who got a taste of his own medicine, Maximilien de Robespierre.

• *Back outside, turn left on boulevard du Palais and head toward the river (north). On the corner is the city's oldest public clock. The mechanism of the present clock is from 1334, and even though the case is Baroque, it keeps on ticking.*

Turn left onto quai de l'Horloge and continue west along the river, past the round medieval tower called "the babbler." The bridge up ahead is the...

Pont Neuf

This "new bridge" is now Paris' oldest. Built during Henry IV's reign (c. 1600), its 12 arches span the widest part of the river. The fine view includes the park on the tip of the island (note Seine tour boats), the Orsay Museum, and the Louvre. These turrets were originally for vendors and street entertainers. In the days of Henry IV, who originated the promise of "a chicken in every pot," this would have been a lively scene.

• *For a scenic, relaxing finale to this tour, consider a boat ride on the Seine. The **Vedettes de Pont-Neuf** (AE, AI, Level 1—Fully accessible) leave from the tip of the island (€9.50; see page 178); to reach the boats via an accessible ramp, traverse some cobblestones one block upriver (east) of the bridge on the south side of the island. The ramp will lead you along the riverfront and under the pont Neuf to the boat dock.*

*At pont Neuf, you're also close to La Samaritaine department store (**AE, AI, AL, AT**, Level 1—Fully accessible), across the bridge on the Right Bank. Near La Samaritaine, you'll also find a Métro stop (pont Neuf) and taxi stands to connect you to the rest of Paris.*

CHAMPS-ELYSEES ROLL OR STROLL

Don't leave Paris without experiencing the Champs-Elysées (zhahn-zay-lee-zay). This is Paris at its most Parisian: monumental sidewalks, stylish shops, grand cafés, and glimmering showrooms. This tour covers about three miles. If this tour seems like too much for you, break it down into several different outings (taxis roll down the Champs-Elysées frequently and Métro stops are located every three blocks). Take your time and enjoy. It's a great roll or stroll day or night.

The tour begins at the Arc de Triomphe, located in the middle of a huge traffic circle. Arrive by taxi (ask to be let off right at the arch) or by Métro (get off at Charles de Gaulle-Etoile—not accessible—and follow signs to Arc de Triomphe). If you decide against visiting the arch, start this tour at the top of the Champs-Elysées, across from the arch (skip down to "The Champs-Elysées" on page 272).

Arc de Triomphe

Access: Museum only—**AE+A, AI, AL,** Level 2—Moderately accessible. The elevator goes only as far as the museum (offers some city views). From there, 46 stairs lead to the observation deck atop the arch.

The arch is connected to the top of the Champs-Elysées via an underground walkway (twenty-five 6" steps down and thirty 6" steps back up).

The Sight: Begun in 1809, the arch was intended to honor Napoleon's soldiers, who, in spite of being vastly outnumbered by the Austrians, scored a remarkable victory at the battle of Austerlitz. Napoleon died prior to its completion. But it was finished in time for his 1840 funeral procession to pass underneath, carrying his remains (19

ACCESSIBILITY CODE CHART

CODE	MEANING
AE	Accessible Entryway
AE+A	Accessible Entry with Assistance
AI	Accessible Interior
AI+A	Accessible Interior with Assistance
AT	Accessible Toilet
AT+A	Accessible Toilet with Assistance
AL	Accessible Lift (elevator)
AL+A	Accessible Lift with Assistance

For the full chart, or a more detailed explanation of codes, please see page 2 of the Introduction.

years dead) from exile in St. Helena to Paris. The arch is dedicated to the glory of all French armies.

On **top** of the Arc de Triomphe, survey the panorama of Paris that spreads out before you. Follow the huge axis that stretches all the way from the Louvre, up the Champs-Elysées, straight down the avenue de la Grande Armée to a forest of skyscrapers in La Défense. Notice the contrast between the skyscrapers and the uniform heights of the buildings closer to the arch. Former French President François Mitterand had the huge, white **Grande Arche de la Défense** built as a centerpiece of this mini-Manhattan. The wide boulevard lined with grass and trees a little to your left is avenue Foch (named after a WWI hero) and is the best address to have in Paris (the Shah of Iran and Aristotle Onassis had homes here). The huge park at the end of avenue Foch is the Bois de Boulogne.

From the Champs-Elysées side, scan the cityscape of downtown Paris. Notice the symmetry. The beauty of Paris—basically a flat basin with a river running through it—is man-made. The key to this beauty is the relationship between the width of its grand boulevards and the uniformity in the height and design of the buildings. To the right, the rude **Montparnasse Tower** looks lonely out there, standing like the box the Eiffel Tower came

Champs-Elysées Roll or Stroll

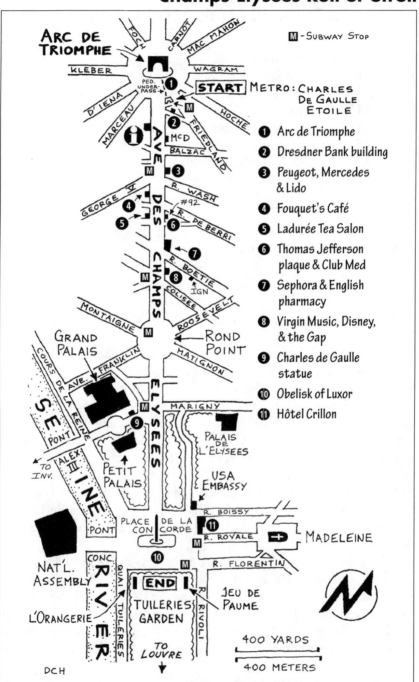

M – SUBWAY STOP

START METRO: CHARLES
DE GAULLE
ETOILE

❶ Arc de Triomphe

❷ Dresdner Bank building

❸ Peugeot, Mercedes
& Lido

❹ Fouquet's Café

❺ Ladurée Tea Salon

❻ Thomas Jefferson
plaque & Club Med

❼ Sephora & English
pharmacy

❽ Virgin Music, Disney,
& the Gap

❾ Charles de Gaulle
statue

❿ Obelisk of Luxor

⓫ Hôtel Crillon

400 YARDS

400 METERS

in. It served as a wake-up call in the early 1970s to preserve the building-height restriction and strengthen urban design standards.

The 12 boulevards that radiate from the Arc de Triomphe were part of Baron Haussmann's master plan for Paris: the creation of a series of major boulevards, intersecting at diagonals with monuments (such as the Arc de Triomphe) as centerpieces of those intersections. His plan did not anticipate the automobile—obvious when you watch the traffic scene below. Gaze down at what appears to be a chaotic traffic mess. But watch how smoothly it really functions. Cars entering the circle have the right of way (the only one in France this way); those in the circle must yield. Still, there are plenty of accidents, often caused by tourists oblivious to the rules. Tired of disputes, insurance companies split the fault and damages of any Arc de Triomphe accident 50–50. The trick is to make a parabola—get to the center ASAP and then begin working your way out two avenues before you want to exit.

Look straight down the **avenue des Champs-Elysées.** Louis XIV opened the lower end—a short extension of the Tuileries Garden leading to Versailles Palace—in 1667. This date is considered the birth of Paris as a grand city. The Champs-Elysées soon became the place to cruise in your carriage. (It still is today—traffic can be jammed up even at midnight.) One hundred years later, the café scene arrived.

Like its Roman ancestors, this arch has served as a parade gateway for triumphal armies (French or foe) and important ceremonies. From 1940 to 1944, a large swastika flew from here as Nazis goose-stepped down the Champs-Elysées. Allied troops marched triumphantly under this arch in August 1944.

Descend the arch and head to the worn eagle directly underneath. You're surrounded by names of French victories since the Revolution—19th century on the arch, 20th century in the pavement. On the columns you'll see lists of generals (with a line under the names of those who died in battle). Then find the bronze plaque at the foot of the **Tomb of the Unknown Soldier** (from World War I). Every

day at 18:30 since just after World War I, the flame is rekindled and new flowers set in place. National parades start and end here with one minute of silence.

Head out to the traffic circle on the Champs-Elysées side and study the arch. On your right, the arch's massive column is decorated by its most famous sculpture. *The Departure of the Volunteers,* or *La Marseillaise,* was a rousing effort to rally the troops with what looks like an ugly reincarnation of Joan of Arc. On the left, Napoleon poses confidently with an overcome-with-awe Paris—crowned by her city walls—kneeling at his imperial feet.

• *Cross the giant traffic circle (by underground walkway or wave down a taxi) to get to the top of...*

The Champs-Elysées

Look down the wide boulevard. The Louvre is the building at the very end of the avenue through the Tuileries Garden. This guided tour goes straight down the Champs-Elysées to the Tuileries. Notice how the left sidewalk is more sunny and popular with pedestrians. We'll start on the more interesting left side but cross over later for the exhilarating view from the center of the avenue's 10 lanes and a peek at two fancy cafés.

The *nouveau* Champs-Elysées, revitalized in 1994, has new street benches, lamps, broader sidewalks, and an army of green-suited workers armed with high-tech pooper-scoopers. The plane trees (a kind of sycamore that does well in big city pollution) are reminiscent of the big push Napoleon III made, planting 600,000 trees to green up the city.

Until the 1960s, this boulevard was pure elegance. Locals actually dressed up to come here. From the 1920s through the 1960s this was a street of top-end hotels, cafés, and residences; the McDonald's would have been unthinkable back then. Then in 1963 the government pumped up the neighborhood's commercial metabolism by bringing in the RER (commuter underground). Suburbanites had easy access and *bam*—there went the neighborhood.

In 1985, a law prohibited the demolition of the old elegant building fronts that once gave the boulevard a uniform grace. As a consequence, many of today's modern businesses hide behind preserved facades. Imagine the boulevard pre-'63, with only the finest structures lining both sides all the way to the palace gardens.

Start your descent. The first tiny street you cross, rue de Tilsitt, is part of a shadow ring road—an option for drivers who'd like to avoid the chaos of the arch, complete with stoplights. Pop around the corner (left) to one of a dozen uniformly U-shaped pavilions that were part of the original 1853 grand design. Peek into the foyer—of what is currently the **Dresdner Bank** office (**AE, AI,** Level 2—Moderately accessible, one 2" entry step)—for a glimpse of 19th-century Champs-Elysées elegance.

Back on the main drag, begin your downhill roll or stroll. The coming of **McDonald's** was a shock to the boulevard (**AE, AI, AT,** Level 1—Fully accessible). At first it was allowed only white arches painted on the window. Today it spills out onto the sidewalk—providing it has café-quality chairs and flower boxes. (There's a public toilet nearby, but for a wheelchair-accessible toilet, McDonald's is ideal).

At the fancy **car dealerships,** you can pick up your new sedan and a leather jacket and purse to match. Peugeot is at #136 (**AE+A, AI,** Level 2—Moderately accessible, three 6" entry steps) showing off their futuristic concept cars next to the classic models. The flashy Mercedes showroom at #118 is like an English-language car show (**AE+A, AI,** Level 2—Moderately accessible, one 8" entry step). In the 19th century, this was an area for horse stables; today, it's the district of garages, limo companies, and car dealerships.

Next to Mercedes is the famous **Lido** (**AE+A, AI,** Level 2—Moderately accessible, two 6" entry steps), Paris' largest cabaret—check out the photos, perky R-rated video, and prices. Moviegoing on the Champs-Elysées is also popular. Check to see if there are films you recognize, then look for the showings *(séances);* a "v.o." *(version originale)* next to the time indicates the film will be in its original language.

Now cross the boulevard. Spend one traffic-light cycle at the island midstream enjoying the view. Look up at the arch with its rooftop bristling with tourists. Notice the architecture—old and elegant, new, and new behind old facades.

Fouquet's café-restaurant (**AE+A, AI,** Level 2—Moderately accessible, one 3" entry step, #99), under the red awning, serves very expensive coffee. The setting is stuffy but tops. Since the early 1900s, Fouquet's has been a favorite of French actors and actresses. The golden plaques in the pavement honor winners of France's Oscar-like film awards, the Césars.

A block downhill is **Ladurée** (green and purple awning), a classic 19th-century tea salon/restaurant/*pâtisserie* (**AE, AI, AL,** Level 2—

Moderately accessible, accessible entry on left side, #75). Its interior is right out of the 1860s. Wander around...even peeking into the cozy rooms upstairs (accessible elevator). A coffee here is *très élégant*. The bakery makes traditional macaroons, cute little cakes, and gift-wrapped finger sandwiches.

Cross back to the lively side. At #92, a wall plaque marks the place Thomas Jefferson lived while minister to France (1785–1789). A plaque just below marks the spot where Robert Birlinger died fighting the Germans during the liberation of Paris in August 1944.

The nearby **Club Med** is a reminder of the French commitment to the vacation. Since 1936 the French, by law, have enjoyed one month of paid vacation. In the swinging '60s, Club Med made hedonism accessible to the middle-class French masses.

At #74, glide down **Sephora's** ramp into a vast hall of cosmetics and perfumes (**AE, AI, AL,** Level 2—Moderately accessible, elevator to left of entry; daily 10:00–24:00). It's thought-fully laid out: the entry hall is lined with the new products—all open and ready (with disposable white sniff strips) to sample. Women's perfumes line the left wall, and men's line the (shorter) right wall—organized alphabetically by company, from Armani to Versace. Stop first at the central "wheel of scents." The woman here helps shoppers explore their  needs. She dishes up samples until you find the scent of your dreams and then assembles a list of products to match. The wheel of scents is organized like a wheel of color (clockwise from fresh to strong). Follow the labeled progression: fresh, sea, flower, fruit, herb, wood, spicy, amber, and leather. Lemon is freshest. *Civette*—eau de cow pie—is strongest. (I'm not kidding...give it a whiff. Now you can mark your territory.) The best-seller: chocolate. Worst seller? Guess. Grab a basket and follow your nose. The mesmerizing music, chosen just for Sephora, actually made me crave cosmetics. Halfway down on your left in red flashing numbers are the current prices of perfumes *(cours des parfums)* in cities throughout the world—allowing jet-setters to comparison shop.

The English **pharmacy** (**AE+A, AI,** Level 2—Moderately accessible, one 3" entry step) is open until midnight at the corner on rue La

Boétie, and map-lovers can detour one block down this street to the Espace IGN (Institut Géographique National), France's version of the National Geographic Society (**AE, AI,** Level 2—Moderately accessible; Mon–Fri 9:30–19:00, Sat 11:00–12:30 & 14:00–18:30, closed Sun).

Virgin Megastore (AE+A, AI, Level 2—Moderately accessible, one 5" entry step) sells a world of music one block farther down the Champs-Elysées. The Disney, Gap, and Quicksilver stores are reminders of global economics—the French seem to love these stores as much as Americans do.

At the **Rond-Point,** the shopping ends and the park begins. (Unfortunately for wheelchair users, the curb cuts end here, too.) This leafy circle is always colorful, lined with flowers or seasonal decorations, whether thousands of pumpkins at Halloween or hundreds of decorated trees at Christmas).

A block past the Rond-Point at the next intersection you find a new statue of Charles de Gaulle—striding out as he did the day Paris was liberated in 1944. Cross the street halfway. On the pedestrian island look right to see the glass- and steel-domed **Grand and Petit Palais** exhibition halls, built for the 1900 World's Fair (**AE, AI,** Level 2—Moderately accessible; entrances accessible, ticket agent can assist); note that the Petit Palais is closed until 2005 for renovation. Impressive temporary exhibits fill the huge Grand Palais (on right, €8, not covered by museum pass), while the Petit Palais (left side), when it reopens in 2005, will display its permanent collection of 19th-century paintings by Delacroix, Cézanne, Monet, Picasso, and other masters (free).

Beyond the two palaces, the Alexander Bridge leads over the Seine to the golden dome of Les Invalides. This exquisite bridge, spiked with golden statues and ironwork lamps, was built to celebrate a turn-of-the-20th-century treaty between France and Russia. Like the Grand and Petit Palais, it's a fine example of belle époque exuberance.

Les Invalides was built by Louis XIV as a veteran's hospital for his battle-weary troops. The esplanade leading up Les Invalides—possibly the largest patch of accessible grass in Paris—gives soccer balls and Frisbees a rare-in-Paris welcome.

Return to the sunny side of the street, where curb cuts make a welcome reappearance. From here, it's a straight shot down the last stretch of the Champs-Elysées to **place de la Concorde,** the 21-acre square with the obelisk. (If you want to go the center of the square, use the crosswalk.) During the Revolution, this was the place de la Révolution. About

2,000 heads lost their bodies here during the Reign of Terror. The guillotine sat here. A bronze plaque in the ground in front of the obelisk memorializes the place where Louis XVI and Marie-Antoinette, among many others, were made "a foot shorter on top." Three worked the guillotine: One managed the blade, one held the blood bucket, and one caught the head, raising it high to the roaring crowd.

The 3,300-year-old **obelisk of Luxor** now forms the centerpiece of place de la Concorde. It was carted here from Egypt in 1829, a gift to the French king. The gold pictures on the obelisk tell the story of its incredible journey.

The obelisk also forms a center point along a line locals call the "royal perspective." From this straight line (Louvre—Obelisk—Arc de Triomphe—Grand Arche de la Défense) you can hang a lot of history. The Louvre symbolizes the old regime (divine-right rule by kings and queens). The obelisk and place de la Concorde symbolize the people's revolution (cutting off the king's head). The Arc de Triomphe calls to mind the triumph of nationalism (victorious armies carrying national flags under the arch). And the huge modern arch in the distance, surrounded by the headquarters of multinational corporations, heralds a future in which business entities are more powerful than nations.

On the north side of place de la Concorde is **Hôtel Crillon,** Paris' most exclusive hotel. It's just left of the twin buildings that guard the entrance to rue Royale (which leads to the Greek-style church of the Madeleine). This hotel is so fancy that one of its belle époque rooms is displayed in New York's Metropolitan Museum of Art. Eleven years before the king lost his head on this square, Louis XVI met with Benjamin Franklin in this hotel to sign a treaty recognizing the United States as an independent country. (The heavily fortified American embassy is located next door.) For a memorable splurge, consider high tea at Hôtel de Crillon.

And from the base of the Champs-Elysées, the beautiful **Tuileries Garden** leads through the iron gates to the Louvre. Relax next to the pond or find one of the cafés in the gardens.

BELGIUM

- 12,000 square miles, a little larger than Maryland
- 10 million people (830 per square mile)
- €1 = about $1.15

Belgium falls through the cracks. It's nestled between Germany, France, and Britain, and it's famous for waffles, sprouts, and endive—no wonder many travelers don't even consider a stop here. But many who do visit remark that Belgium is one of Europe's best-kept secrets. There are tourists—but not as many as the country's charms merit.

Ten million Belgians are packed into a country only a little bigger than Maryland. At 830 people per square mile, it's the second most densely populated country in Europe (after the Netherlands). This population concentration, coupled with a dense and well-lit rail and road system, causes Belgium to shine at night when viewed from space, a phenomenon NASA astronauts call the "Belgian Window."

It's here in Belgium that Europe comes together: Where Romance languages meet Germanic languages, where Catholics meet Protestants, and where the new Europe is growing, sprouting from the seed planted 40 years ago by the Benelux union. Because of Belgium's international importance as the capital of the European Union, more than 25 percent of its residents are foreigners. Belgium flies the flag of Europe more vigorously than any other place on the continent.

The country is split between the French-speaking Walloons in the south and the Dutch-speaking Flemish people (60 percent of the population) in the north. Talk to locals to learn how deep the cultural rift is. Belgium's capital, Brussels, while mostly French-speaking, is officially bilingual. The country also has a small minority of German-speaking people.

With all this diversity, English bridges the gap—it's almost universally spoken in Belgium, especially in the Flemish half (Dutch-speaking, including Bruges). But if you want to win points, learn a couple of key Dutch words: "hello" is *hallo* (hol-LOH), "please" is *alstublieft* (AHL-stoo-bleeft), and "thank you" is *dank u wel* (dahnk yoo vehl). For

Belgium

language help in French-speaking Belgium (including Brussels), see page 159 and the "French Survival Phrases" near the end of this book.

Belgians brag that they eat as much as the Germans and as well as the French. They are among the world's leading beer consumers and carnivores. And yes, they really do eat waffles here. While Americans think of "Belgian" waffles for breakfast, the Belgians (who don't eat waffles or pancakes for breakfast) think of *wafels* as Liège-style (dense, sweet, eaten plain, and heated up) and Brussels-style (lighter, often with powdered sugar or whipped cream and fruit, served in teahouses only in the afternoons from 14:00–18:00). You'll see waffles sold at restaurants and takeaway stands.

Bruges is the best first bite of Belgium. It's a wonderfully preserved medieval Flemish gem that expertly nurtures the tourist industry, bringing the town a prosperity it hasn't enjoyed since 500 years ago, when—as one of the largest cities in the world—it helped lead northern Europe out of the Middle Ages.

ACCESSIBILITY IN BELGIUM

Access for people with disabilities is generally good in Belgium, particularly in public spaces, though English-language publications and English-speaking organizations are in short supply.

The **Belgium Tourist Office** will provide information to help you plan your visit (780 3rd Avenue, Suite 1501, New York, NY 10017, tel. 212/758-8130, fax 212/355-7675, www.visitbelgium.com, info@visitbelgium.com).

BRUGES

(Brugge)

With Renoir canals, pointy gilded architecture, vivid time-tunnel art, and stay-awhile cafés, Bruges is a heavyweight sightseeing destination as well as a joy. Where else can you roll or stroll along a canal, munch mussels, wash them down with the world's best beer, savor heavenly chocolate, and see Flemish Primitives and a Michelangelo, all within 300 yards of a bell tower that jingles every 15 minutes? And there's no language barrier.

The town is Brugge (BROO-ghah) in Flemish, or Bruges (broozh) in French and English. Its name comes from the Viking word for "wharf." Right from the start, Bruges was a trading center. In the 11th century, the city grew wealthy on the cloth trade.

By the 14th century, Bruges' population was 40,000—as large as London's. As the middleman in the sea trade between northern and southern Europe, it was one of the biggest cities in the world and an economic powerhouse. In addition, Bruges was the most important cloth market in northern Europe.

In the 15th century, while England and France were slogging it out in the Hundred Years' War, Bruges was at peace, and the favored residence of the powerful Dukes of Burgundy. Commerce and the arts boomed. The artists Jan van Eyck and Hans Memling had studios here. But by the 16th century, the harbor had silted up and the economy had collapsed. The Burgundian court left, Spain conquered Belgium in 1548, and Bruges' Golden Age abruptly ended. For generations, Bruges was known as a mysterious and dead city. In the 19th century, a new port, Zeebrugge, brought renewed vitality to the area. And in the 20th century, tourists discovered the town.

Today Bruges prospers because of tourism: It's a uniquely well-pre-

ACCESSIBILITY CODES

These codes offer a quick overview of what to expect. If applicable, more specific details about the facility (e.g., exact number and height of steps, special instructions for gaining entry) are explained in each listing.

CODE	MEANING
AE	Accessible Entryway
AE+A	Accessible Entry with Assistance
AI	Accessible Interior
AI+A	Accessible Interior with Assistance
AT	Accessible Toilet
AT+A	Accessible Toilet with Assistance
AL	Accessible Lift (elevator)
AL+A	Accessible Lift with Assistance
AR	Accessible Hotel Room
AR+A	Accessible Hotel Room with Assistance
AB	Accessible Hotel Bathroom
AB+A	Accessible Hotel Bathroom with Assistance
♥	Caring, welcoming attitude regarding accessibility

For more detailed information, please refer to the full Accessibility Codes chart on page 4 of the Introduction. For more information on Accessibility Levels, see page 2.

served Gothic city and a handy gateway to Europe. It's no secret, but even with the crowds, it's the kind of city where you don't mind being a tourist.

ACCESSIBILITY IN BRUGES

Bruges is an Easy Access city, far better than Paris. We found more wheelchair users in Bruges than any other city on our trip. Although there are cobblestones everywhere, there's usually a smooth sidewalk in

IF YOU NEED MEDICAL HELP

Start with your hotel staff. They are accustomed to handling medical problems. Here are some other resources to try:

To contact a doctor, call 050-391-528 (during the day) or 050-364-030 (at night, from 20:00–8:00). To summon an ambulance, call 100. For medical supplies, try Thuiszorg Winkel in the city center (closed Sun, Oude Burg 23, tel. 050-440-352, thuiszorgwinkel.brugge@cm.be).

the midst so you can easily wheel your way through the cobbles. While keeping its beauty and history intact, Bruges manages to open its arms to people at all levels of mobility.

The city's pamphlet *Accessibility Guide Bruges,* which covers services, sights, churches, hotels, restaurants, cafés, parking places, and public toilets, makes an excellent companion to this book (find it online or buy at the TIs for €1, English version available, Municipal Council for Persons with a Disability, Tourist Office, Burg 11, tel. 050-448-686, www.accessiblebruges.be, info@accessiblebruges.be).

Belgian trains and Bruges' city buses are generally accessible. Tours in Bruges are less accessible: Bus tours are Level 2, boat tours are Level 3.

Many of Bruges' top sights are at least partly accessible to travelers with limited mobility. Fully accessible (Level 1) sights include Market and Burg squares; most of the Church of Our Lady and the Memling Museum; the lower chapel of the Basilica of the Holy Blood; and the Bell Tower's Exhibition Hall (but not the top of the tower). The Groeninge Museum, Town Hall Gothic Room, and Begijnhof are moderately accessible (Level 2). The Straffe Hendrik Brewery tour and Renaissance Hall are minimally accessible (Level 3). Only a handful of sights—such as the top of the Bell Tower and the Gruuthuse Museum—are not accessible (Level 4).

Bruges' ultimate sight—the town itself—is open to all. And the best way to enjoy it is to get lost on the back streets, away from the lace shops and ice-cream stands.

ORIENTATION

The tourists' Bruges (you'll be sharing it) is a piece of land roughly half a square mile in size, contained within a canal, or moat. Nearly everything of interest and importance is within a cobbled swath between the train station and Market Square. Many of our quiet and charming recommended accommodations lie just beyond Market Square.

Tourist Information

The main office (**AE, AI, AL,** Level 2—Moderately accessible) is on Burg Square (use the elevator in the courtyard to the right of the steps to the Expositie; April–Sept Mon–Fri 9:30–18:30, Sat–Sun 10:00–12:30 & 14:00–18:30; Oct–March Mon–Fri 9:30–17:00, Sat–Sun 9:30–13:00 & 14:00–17:30, lockers, money-exchange desk, non-accessible €0.25 toilet in courtyard, tel. 050-448-686, www.brugge.be). The other TI is at the train station (**AE, AI,** Level 2—Moderately accessible; generally open Tue–Sat 10:00–13:00 & 14:00–18:00, closed Sun–Mon).

The TIs sell a great €1 Bruges visitor's guide with a map and listings of all of the sights and services. Wheelchair users will appreciate the thorough *Accessibility Guide Bruges* (€1, see "Accessibility in Bruges," page 281). And you can pick up a bimonthly English-language program called *events@brugge*. The TIs have information on train schedules and on the

---

MUSEUM TIPS

Admission prices are steep but include great audioguides—so plan on spending some time and getting into it. The information number for all museums is 050-448-711.

Combo-Ticket: The TIs and participating museums sell a museum combo-ticket (any 5 museums for €15). Since the Groeninge and Memling museums cost €8 each, anyone interested in art will save money with this pass.

Dark Monday: In Bruges, nearly all sights are open Tuesday through Sunday year-round from 9:30 to 17:00 and closed on Monday. If you're in Bruges on a Monday, consider a boat, bus, or walking tour (see "Tours of Bruges," page 286).

Bruges

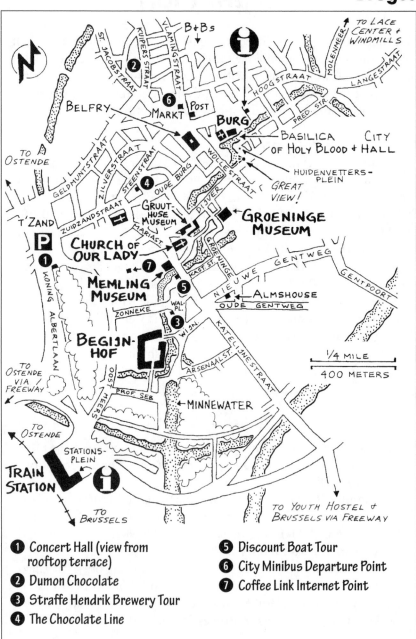

1. Concert Hall (view from rooftop terrace)
2. Dumon Chocolate
3. Straffe Hendrik Brewery Tour
4. The Chocolate Line
5. Discount Boat Tour
6. City Minibus Departure Point
7. Coffee Link Internet Point

many tours available (see "Tours of Bruges," next page). Many hotels give free maps with more detail than the map the TIs sell.

Arrival in Bruges

By Train: Coming in by train you'll see the square bell tower marking the main square. Upon arrival, stop by the station TI (described above). The station lacks ATMs but has lockers (from €2, daily 6:00–24:00).

Access: The station (**AE, AI, AL, AT,** Level 2) is moderately accessible to all mobility levels, but only platforms 5–10 are accessible by elevator. There is a wheelchair-accessible toilet near the train information booth (attendant with key on duty at baggage room daily 7:00–19:00).

Getting to the Center: The cheapest way to get to the town center is by **bus** (**AE, AI, AL,** Level 1—Fully accessible). All buses have transfer lifts for wheelchairs and go directly to the Market Square. Simply get on any bus, pay €1, and in four minutes you're there. The €1 tickets are good for an hour. A day pass costs €3. Buses #4 and #8 go farther, to the northeast part of town (the windmills).

Note that nearly all city buses go directly from the train station to the Market Square and fan out from there. They then return to Market Square (bus #2 stops at post office on square; other buses stop at library on nearby Kuiperstraat) and go directly back to the station.

The **taxi** fare from the train station to most hotels is around €6 (**AE+A,** Level 2—Moderately accessible; tel. 050-334-444). Wheelchair users must be able to transfer to the taxi—the driver is willing to assist and to place the chair in the trunk.

If you want to get into town on your own power, note that the train station is about a mile from the center. The sidewalks and streets are cobblestone, often with rough seams. Some curb cuts have 2" steps, and it can be a challenge to switch from one side of the street to the other. This might be a good time to consider a bus or taxi. But if you'd rather walk or roll, cross the busy street and canal in front of the station, head up Oostmeers, and turn right on Steenstraat to reach Market Square.

By Car: Park at the train station for just €2.50 per day; show your parking receipt for a free bus ride into town. There are pricier (€9/day) underground parking garages at 't Zand and around town, and these garages are well-marked. Driving in Bruges is very complicated because of the one-way system.

Helpful Hints

Internet Access: The relaxing **Coffee Link** (**AE+A, AI+A, AT,** Level 2—Moderately accessible, one 2" entry step, one 4" step up to computers), with mellow music, pleasant art, and 16 terminals, is centrally located across from the Church of Our Lady (€2.20/30 min, daily 10:00–20:00, Mariastraat 38, tel. 050-349-973).

Laundry: Bruges' most convenient place to do laundry is **Belfort Auto Wash** (**AE, AI+A,** Level 2—Moderately accessible, non-accessible toilet; open daily 8:30–22:00, just off Market Square in an arcade at Sint Jakobsstraat 51, tel. 050-335-902). A less central launderette is at Gentpoortstraat 28 (**AE, AI+A,** Level 2—Moderately accessible, steep ramp leads to second level; daily 7:00–22:00).

Shopping: Shops are open from 9:00 to 18:00, a little later on Friday. Grocery stores are usually closed on Sunday. The main shopping street, Steenstraat, stretches from Market Square to the square called 't Zand.

Market Days: Wednesday morning (Market Square) and Saturday morning ('t Zand) are bustling market days. On Saturday and Sunday afternoons, a flea market hops along Dijver in front of the Groeninge Museum.

Post Office: It's on Market Square near the bell tower (Level 3—Minimally accessible; Mon–Fri 9:00–19:00, Sat 9:30–12:30, closed Sun, tel. 050-331-411). There are no ramps, since the P.O. is part of a monument (four 8" entry steps).

Best Town View: The best view without a climb is from the rooftop terrace of Bruges' concert hall, the Concertgebouw (**AE, AI, AL,** Level 2—Moderately accessible). This seven-story building, built in 2002, is the city's only modern highrise (daily 11:00–23:00, free elevator, on edge of old town on 't Zand). Non-disabled travelers can climb the bell tower (Level 4—Not accessible) overlooking the Market Square for a fine vista.

Tours of Bruges

Walking Tour—Local guides lead small groups through the core of town (€5, daily July–Aug, Sat–Sun only in June and Sept, depart from TI at 15:00, 2 hrs, no tours off-season). Wheelchair users have been part of these tours for years. Though earnest, the tours are heavy on history and in two languages, so they may be less than peppy. Still, to propel you beyond the pretty gables and canal swans of Bruges, they're good medicine.

A private two-hour guided tour costs €40 (reserve at least 3 days in advance through TI, tel. 050-448-685); consider Christian Scharle (mobile 0476-493-203, tmb@skynet.be).

Bruges by Boat—The most relaxing and scenic (though not informative) way to see this city of canals is by boat, with the captain narrating. Boats leave from all over town (€5.50, 4/hr, 10:00–17:00, 30-min rides, little difference between tours).

Access: AE+A, Level 3—Minimally accessible. Boats leave from platforms that are reached by climbing down stairs. Wheelchair users must be able to step down into these small boats; you leave your wheelchair at the platform.

City Minibus Tour—City Tour Bruges gives a rolling overview of virtually every sight in Bruges in an 18-seat, two-skylight minibus with dial-a-language headsets and video support (€9.50, 50 min). The tour leaves hourly from Market Square (10:00–19:00 in summer, until 18:00 in spring and fall, less in winter, tel. 050-355-024). The narration, while clear, is slow-moving and boring.

Access: AE+A, Level 2—Moderately accessible. Wheelchair users must be able to climb the three steps into and out of the bus. The tour operator will fold and store the wheelchair on the bus.

Horse-and-Buggy Tour—You'll see buggies around town ready to take you for a clip-clop tour (€28/30 min, price is per carriage, not per person).

Access: AE+A, Level 2—Moderately accessible. Wheelchair users must be able to climb into the carriage. The driver will fold and store the chair.

Tours from Bruges

Daytours in Flanders Fields Minibus Tours—This company offers those with extra time excellent and entertaining all-day tours through the rarely-visited Flemish countryside. Tours include World War I battlefields, trenches, memorials, poppy-splattered fields, and a visit to the Flanders Fields Museum in Ieper, called Ypres in French. Frank, the guide, loves leading his small groups on this fascinating day trip (€59, €5 discount when booked direct with this book, Wed–Sun 9:00–17:00, no

BRUGES AT A GLANCE

▲▲▲**Groeninge Museum** World-class collection of mainly Flemish art. **Hours:** Tue–Sun 9:30–17:00, closed Mon. **Access:** Level 2—Moderately accessible.

▲▲**Bell Tower** 366 steps to a worthwhile view and a carillon close-up. **Hours:** Daily 9:30–17:00. **Access:** Bell Tower is Level 4—Not accessible; Exhibition Hall is Level 1—Fully accessible.

▲▲**Burg Square** Historic square with TI, sights, and impressive architecture. **Hours:** Always open. **Access:** Level 1—Fully accessible.

▲▲**St. Jans Hospital/Memling Museum** Art by the greatest of the Flemish Primitives. **Hours:** Tue–Sun 9:30–17:00, closed Mon. **Access:** Level 1—Fully accessible.

▲▲**Church of Our Lady** Tombs and church art, including Michelangelo's Madonna and Child. **Hours:** Tue–Sun 9:00–12:30 & 13:30–17:00, closed Mon. **Access:** Level 2—Moderately accessible.

▲▲**Begijnhof** Benedictine nuns' peaceful courtyard and Begijn's House museum. **Hours:** Courtyard always open, museum open daily 10:00–12:00 & 13:45–17:30, off-season closes at 17:00. **Access:** Level 2—Moderately accessible.

▲▲**Straffe Hendrik Brewery Tour** Fun and handy tour, includes beer. **Hours:** Daily on the hour 11:00–16:00, Oct–March

tours Mon and Tue, hotel pick-ups, call 050-346-060 or toll-free 0800-99133 to book, www.visitbruges.com).

Access: AE+A, Level 2—Moderately accessible. Wheelchair users need to be able to get on and off the bus. Frank will be happy to assist. Some of the sights (cemeteries and trenches) may be a challenge, and the wheelchair user will have to decide whether to engage in that part of the tour.

11:00 and 15:00 only. **Access:** Level 4—Not accessible.

▲**Market Square** Main square that is the modern heart of the city, with carillon bell tower. **Hours:** Always open. **Access:** Most of the square is Level 1—Fully accessible.

▲**Basilica of the Holy Blood** Romanesque and Gothic church housing relic of the blood of Christ. **Hours:** April–Sept daily 9:30–12:00 & 14:00–18:00, Oct–March Thu–Tue 10:00–12:00 & 14:00–16:00, Wed 10:00–12:00. **Access:** Lower Chapel is Level 1—Fully accessible; Upper Chapel and Treasury are Level 4—Not accessible.

▲**Town Hall's Gothic Room** Beautifully restored hall from 1400. **Hours:** Daily 9:30–17:00. **Access:** Level 2—Moderately accessible.

▲**Gruuthuse Museum** 15th-century mansion with furniture, tapestries, even a guillotine. **Hours:** Tue–Sun 9:30–17:00, closed Mon. **Access:** Level 4—Not accessible.

▲**Chocolate** Sample Bruges' specialty: Try Dumon, The Chocolate Line, Sweertvaegher, and on and on. **Hours:** Shops generally open 10:00–18:00. **Access:** These three shops are all Level 2—Moderately accessible.

If the tour above is full, adventurous slow walkers could consider a similar but more physically demanding package offered by **Quasimodo Countryside Tours** (Level 4—Not accessible; €45, €38 if under 26, 30-seat non-smoking bus, includes a picnic lunch, lots of walking, reserve by calling 050-370-470 or free call 0800-97525, www.quasimodo.be). The bus leaves from the Park Hotel on 't Zand.

SIGHTS

These sights are listed in order from Market Square to Burg Square to the cluster of museums around the Church of our Lady to the Begijnhof (less than a quarter-mile from beginning to end). For a self-guided tour and more information on each sight, see the Bruges Roll or Stroll, page 310.

▲**Market Square (Markt)**—Ringed by banks, the post office, lots of restaurant terraces, great old gabled buildings, and the bell tower, this is the modern heart of the city (most city buses run from here to the train station). Under the bell tower are two great Belgian french-fry stands, a quadrilingual Braille description of the old town, and a metal model of the tower. In Bruges' heyday as a trading center a canal came right up to this square.

Geldmuntstraat, just off the square, is a delightful street with many fun and practical shops and eateries.

Access: Most of the square is fully accessible (Level 1), but the cobblestone streets (with 2" curbs) vary in degree of roughness. Geldmuntstraat (**AE+A,** Level 2—Moderately accessible) has 4" curbs, with curb cuts down to one or two inches. Some stores have wheelchair-accessible entryways, others have entry steps.

▲▲**Bell Tower (Belfort)**—Most of this bell tower has presided over Market Square since 1300. The octagonal lantern was added in 1486, making it 290 feet high—that's 366 steps. (See Bruges Roll or Stroll, page 310.)

Access: Bell Tower is Level 4—Not accessible; Exhibition Hall **AE, AI, AL, AT,** is Level 1—Fully accessible. While the Bell Tower requires a long, steep climb, you can reach the Exhibition Hall on the second floor by elevator (in the courtyard, down the hallway toward the toilet). The toilet off courtyard is wheelchair-accessible (€0.30, ask attendant for key).

Cost and Hours: €5, daily 9:30–17:00, ticket window closes 45 min early.

▲▲**Burg Square**—The opulent square called Burg is Bruges' civic center, historically the birthplace of the city and the site of the ninth-century castle of the first Count of Flanders. Today the easily-accessed square is the scene of outdoor concerts and home of the TI (**AE, AI, AL,** Level 2—Moderately accessible; €0.25 non-accessible toilet). For more information, see Bruges Roll or Stroll, page 310.

▲**Basilica of the Holy Blood**—Originally the Chapel of Saint Basil, the church is famous for its relic of the blood of Christ which, according to tradition, was brought to Bruges in 1150 after the Second Crusade. The relic is in the Upper Chapel; the dark, solid, and accessible Lower Chapel is a fine example of Romanesque style. See Bruges Roll or Stroll, page 310.

Access: Lower Chapel **AE, AI,** is Level 1—Fully accessible; Upper Chapel and adjacent Treasury are Level 4—Not accessible (up thirty-seven 7" steps).

Cost and Hours: Treasury—€1.25, April–Sept daily 9:30–12:00 & 14:00–18:00, Oct–March Thu–Tue 10:00–12:00 & 14:00–16:00, Wed 10:00–12:00 only, tel. 050-336-792.

▲**Town Hall's Gothic Room**—Your ticket gives you a room full of Bruges history, in the form of old town maps and paintings and a grand, beautifully restored "Gothic Hall" from 1400. Its painted and carved wooden ceiling features hanging arches. Trace the story of Bruges via the series of late-19th-century wall murals. See Bruges Roll or Stroll, page 310.

Access: AE, AI, AL, Level 2—Moderately accessible. The Gothic Room is upstairs and accessible by elevator.

Cost, Hours, and Location: €2.50, includes audioguide and admission to Renaissance Hall, daily 9:30–17:00, Burg 12.

Renaissance Hall (Brugse Vrije)—This is just one ornate room with an impressive Renaissance chimney. Underwhelming to most, the hall is a hit with heraldry fans. See Bruges Roll or Stroll, page 310.

Access: AE+A, AI+A, Level 3—Minimally accessible. The entry-way is at the end of three 8" steps, a long landing, and two 7" steps.

Cost, Hours, and Location: €2.50, includes audioguide and admission to City Hall's Gothic Room, Tue–Sun 9:30–12:00 & 13:30–17:00, closed Mon, entry in corner of square at Burg 11a.

▲▲▲**Groeninge Museum**—This museum houses a world-class collection of mostly Flemish art, from van Eyck to Memling to René Magritte. The highlight is the Flemish Primitives—under-appreciated, pre-Renaissance artwork created in and around Bruges, characterized by remarkable detail work, strict warts-and-all realism, and a strange sense of perspective. See Bruges Roll or Stroll, page 310.

Access: AE+A, AI, AT, Level 2—Moderately accessible. The two 3" steps at the museum's entrance are wheelchair-accessible after a museum staff member puts a ramp in place—ask for assistance. The rest of the museum is accessible, including a unisex adapted toilet in the men's restroom.

Cost, Hours, and Location: €8, Tue–Sun 9:30–17:00, closed Mon, Dijver 12, tel. 050-448-751.

▲**Gruuthuse Museum**—Once a wealthy brewer's home, this is a sprawling smattering of everything from medieval bedpans to a guillotine. The collection mostly celebrates Bruges' golden age (15th century), with a fine display of beautiful and enlightening tapestries. See Bruges Roll or Stroll, page 310.

Access: Level 4—Not accessible. There are six 6" steps at the entry, and the building includes many levels accessible only by steps, sometimes winding and narrow.

Cost, Hours, and Location: €6, Tue–Sun 9:30–17:00, closed Mon, Dijver 17.

▲▲**Church of Our Lady**—The church stands as a memorial to the power and wealth of Bruges in its heyday. A delicate *Madonna and Child* by Michelangelo is near the apse (to the right if you're facing the altar). It's said to be the only Michelangelo statue to leave Italy in his lifetime (thanks to the wealth generated by Bruges' cloth trade). If you like tombs and church art, pay to wander through the Michelangelo-free, art-filled apse. See Bruges Roll or Stroll, page 310.

Access: AE, AI, Level 2—Moderately accessible. The church is wheelchair-accessible, with the exception of a small room (up two 8" steps) at the end of the apse. The nearest accessible toilet is across the street at the Visitors Center of the Memling Museum (see below).

Cost, Hours, and Location: Apse-€2.50, Tue–Sun 9:00–12:00 & 13:30–17:00, closed Mon, Mariastraat.

▲▲**St. Jans Hospital/Memling Museum**—The former monastery/hospital complex has two entrances—one is to a welcoming Visitors Center and the other to the Memling Museum. The museum, in the monastery's former church, was once a medieval hospital and now contains six much-loved paintings by the greatest of the Flemish Primitives, Hans Memling. See Bruges Roll or Stroll, page 310.

Access: AE, AI, AL, AT, Level 1—Fully accessible with the exception of a corner room (two 8" steps). You'll find an elevator (on the right side of the inside entry) and an accessible unisex toilet (€.30, located in men's room at Visitors Center). Loaner wheelchairs are available.

Cost, Hours, and Location: Visitor Center is free. Museum costs €8, includes fine audioguide, Tue–Sun 9:30–17:00, closed Mon, across the street from the Church of Our Lady, Mariastraat 38.

▲▲**Begijnhof**—Inhabited by Benedictine nuns, Begijnhof almost makes you want to don a habit and fold your hands as you pass under its wispy trees and whisper past its frugal little homes. For a good slice of Begijnhof life, visit the simple Begijn's House museum to the left of the entry gate. See Bruges Roll or Stroll, page 310.

Access: AE+A, AI+A, Level 2—Moderately accessible. The cobblestones in the Begijnhof are heavy and rough, making for a bone-jarring wheelchair ride. The museum has one 4" entry step, one 4" step to visit the kitchen, one 8" step to the courtyard, and two 7" steps to see the sleeping quarters.

Museum Cost and Hours: €2 with English explanations, daily 10:00–12:00 & 13:45–17:30, off-season closes at 17:00.

Minnewater—Just south of the Begijnhof is Minnewater, an idyllic world of flower boxes, canals, swans, and tour boats packed like happy egg cartons. See Bruges Roll or Stroll, page 310.

Almshouses—Making your way back from the Begijnhof to the town center, you might detour along Nieuwe Gentweg to visit one of about 20 almshouses in the city. At #8, go through the door marked *Godshuis de Meulenaere 1613* (free) into the peaceful courtyard. This was a medieval form of housing for the poor. The rich would pay for someone's tiny room here in return for lots of prayers.

Access: AE+A, AI, Level 2—Moderately accessible. There are two 6" steps at the almshouse entry.

Bruges Experiences: Chocolate, Beer, and Lace

▲**Chocolate**—Bruggians are connoisseurs of fine chocolate. You'll be tempted by chocolate-filled display windows all over town. While Godiva is the best big-factory/high-price/high-quality brand, there are plenty of smaller, family-run places in Bruges that offer exquisite handmade chocolates.

Perhaps Bruges' smoothest and creamiest chocolates are at **Dumon** (**AE+A,** Level 2—Moderately accessible). Madam Dumon and her children (Stefaan and Christophe) make their top-notch chocolate daily and sell it fresh just off Market Square (€1.70/100 grams, Thu–Tue 10:00–18:00, closed Wed, old chocolate molds on display in basement, Eiermarkt 6, tel. 050-346-282, www.chocolatierdumon.com). Their ganache, a dark creamy combo, wows chocoholics. The Dumons don't provide English labels because they believe it's best to describe their chocolates in person. If you're using a wheelchair, roll up to the window to the left of the entrance and they'll serve you samples there.

Locals and tourists alike flock to **The Chocolate Line** (**AE+A, AI,** Level 2—Moderately accessible, wooden ramp available to cover the 8" step—ask) for their *"gastronomique"* varieties—unique concoctions such as Havana cigar (marinated in rum, cognac, and Cuban tobacco leaves—so therefore technically illegal in the United States), lemon grass, ginger (shaped like a Buddha), saffron curry (a white elephant), and a spicy chili. Try the sheets of chocolate with crunchy roasted cocoa beans. The kitchen—busy whipping up their 80 varieties—is on display in the back (€3.20/100 grams, Mon–Sat 9:30–18:00, Sun from 10:30, Simon Stevinplein 19, between Church of Our Lady and Market Square, tel. 050-341-090).

The smaller **Sweertvaegher** (**AE+A, AI,** Level 2—Moderately accessible, one 4" entry step), near Burg Square, features top-quality chocolate (€2.60/100 grams) that's darker rather than sweeter, made with fresh ingredients and no preservatives (Tue–Sun 9:30–18:15, closed Mon, Philipstockstraat 29, tel. 050-338-367).

▲▲**Straffe Hendrik Brewery Tour**—Belgians are Europe's beer connoisseurs. This fun and handy tour is a great way to pay your respects. While the tour won't work for wheelchair users (Level 4—Not accessible, lots of very steep steps), energetic beer-loving slow walkers could manage. The happy gang at this working family brewery gives entertaining and informative 45-minute, three-language tours (often by friendly Inge, €4 including a beer, great rooftop panorama, daily on the hour 11:00–16:00, 11:00 and 15:00 are your best times to avoid groups, Oct–March 11:00 and 15:00 only, 1 block past church and canal, take a right down skinny Stoofstraat to #26 on Walplein, tel. 050-332-697). For more on beer, see "Belgian Beers," page 306.

Lace and Windmills by the Moat—About a half-mile from the center in the northeast end of town are four windmills strung out along a pleasant grassy setting on the "big moat" canal (between Kruispoort and Dampoort, on Bruges side of the moat). One windmill (St. Janshuismolen; Level 4—Not accessible) is open to visitors (€2, daily 9:30–12:30 & 13:30–17:00, closed Oct–April, at the end of Carmersstraat). The ramps to the base of the windmills are steep and rugged, and the windmills themselves are not accessible.

To actually see lace being made, drop by the nearby **Lace Centre (AE, AI,** Level 2—Moderately accessible, one 2" entry step), where ladies toss bobbins madly while their eyes go bad (Mon–Fri 10:00–12:00 & 14:00–18:00, until 17:00 on Sat, closed Sun, Peperstraat 3, tel. 050-330-072). One €2 ticket includes

Lace Centre entry and afternoon demonstrations, plus entry to a small lace museum called **Kantcentrum (AE+A, AI,** Level 2—Moderately accessible, one 6" entry step) and the adjacent **Jeruzalem Church (AE+A, AI,** Level 2—Moderately accessible, one 6" entry step and tight 22" doorway).

SLEEPING

Hotels

Level 1—Fully Accessible
The adjacent **Novotel** and **Ibis** hotels **(AE, AI, AL, AR, AB)** have three accessible rooms apiece. The Ibis, in a former 15th-century convent, has been updated completely inside and out for accessibility, including an entrance ramp (Db-€59–89, elevator, parking, Katelijnestraat 65A, tel. 050-337-575, fax 050-336-419, www.hotels-belgium.com/brugge/ibis.htm).

SLEEP CODE

(€1 = about $1.15, country code: 32)

Sleep Code: **S** = Single, **D** = Double/Twin, **T** = Triple, **Q** = Quad, **b** = bathroom, **s** = shower only, **no CC** = Credit Cards not accepted. Unless otherwise noted, credit cards are accepted. Everyone speaks English.

Most places are located between the train station and the old center, with the most distant (and best) being a few blocks beyond Market Square to the north and east. Bruges is most crowded Friday and Saturday evenings Easter through October—with July and August weekends being worst.

Bruges is a great place to sleep, with Gothic spires out your window, no traffic noise, and the cheerily out-of-tune carillon heralding each new day at 8:00 sharp. (Thankfully, the bell tower is silent from 22:00 to 8:00.)

Please see "Accessibility Codes" sidebar on page 281 of this chapter for a quick guide to codes. For a more detailed explanation of Accessibility Levels and Codes, please see page 2 of the Introduction.

The Novotel, in a new, Scandinavian-style building, is also completely accessible (Db-€114–121, elevator, pool, restaurant, parking-€9, Katelijnestraat 65B, tel. 050-337-533, fax 050-336-556, www.hotels -belgium.com/brugge/novotel.htm).

Level 2—Moderately Accessible

Hotel Patritius (AE, AI, AR, AB+A), family-run and centrally located, is a grand circa-1830 neoclassical mansion with 16 stately rooms, a plush lounge and breakfast room, and a courtyard garden (small Db-€85, Db-€90–99, Tb-€130, free parking, Ridderstraat 11, tel. 050-338-454, fax 050-339-634, www.hotelpatritius.be, hotel.patritius@proximedia.be, Garrett and Elvi Spaey). There is an elevator accessed outside the hotel and one suitable room with an accessible toilet (but bathtub is not accessible). This unit sleeps four and includes a second room that allows privacy for a companion.

Bruges Hotels

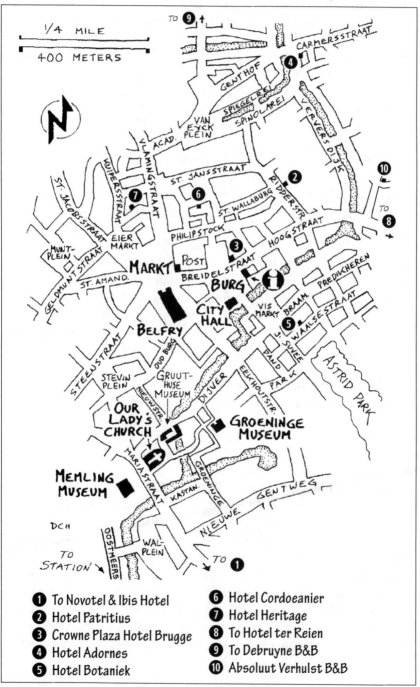

1/4 MILE

400 METERS

1. To Novotel & Ibis Hotel
2. Hotel Patritius
3. Crowne Plaza Hotel Brugge
4. Hotel Adornes
5. Hotel Botaniek
6. Hotel Cordoeanier
7. Hotel Heritage
8. To Hotel ter Reien
9. To Debruyne B&B
10. Absoluut Verhulst B&B

Crowne Plaza Hotel Brugge (AE+A, AI, AL, AR, AB) is the most modern, comfortable, and central hotel option. It's just like a fancy American hotel, each of its 96 air-conditioned rooms equipped with a magnifying mirror and trouser press (Db-€225–240, prices drop as low as €180 on weekdays and off-season, elevator, pool, Burg 10, tel. 050-446-844, fax 050-446-868, www.crowneplaza.com). The wheelchair access is through the attached De Linde restaurant—you have to negotiate one 8" step to reach the accessible revolving door. They have one room with accessible toilet and shower.

Hotel Adornes (AE, AI, AR, AB+A) is small and classy—a great value. It has 20 comfy rooms with full, modern bathrooms in a 17th-century canalside house, and offers free parking, free loaner bikes, and a cellar lounge with games and videos (Db-€90–110 depending upon size, singles take a double for nearly the same cost, Tb-€125, Qb-€135, elevator, near Van Nevel B&B, mentioned below, and Carmersstraat at St. Annarei 26, tel. 050-341-336, fax 050-342-085, www.adornes.be, hotel.adornes@proximedia.be, Nathalie runs the family business, Britt provides a warm welcome). The hotel is accessible by wheelchair through the courtyard in back. One large ground-floor room works for guests using wheelchairs. While the toilet and bathtub are not specially adapted, the bathroom is large enough to maneuver a wheelchair.

Level 3—Minimally Accessible

Hotel Botaniek (AE+A, AI, AL, AR+A, AB+A, three 8" entry steps) has three stars, nine rooms, and a quiet location a block from Astrid Park (Db-€92, big Db-€96, Tb-€105, Qb-€115, 8 percent discount for 3 nights, elevator, Waalsestraat 23, tel. 050-341-424, fax 050-345-939, www.botaniek.be, hotel.botaniek@pi.be).

Hotel Cordoeanier (AE+A, AI, AR, AB+A, three 7" entry steps), a family-run place, rents 22 bright, simple, modern rooms on a quiet street two blocks off Market Square (Sb-€52–65, Db-€65–70, Tb-€72–80, Qb-€85, Quint/b-€97, higher prices are for bigger rooms, Internet access, Cordoeanierstraat 16, tel. 050-339-051, fax 050-346-111, www.cordoeanier.be, Kris, Veerle, Guy, and family). The hotel has two ground-floor rooms with wheelchair-accessible toilets, but not baths.

Hotel Heritage (AE+A, AI, AL, AB+A, four 7" entry steps) offers 24 rooms in a completely modernized old building. It's tastefully decorated and has all the amenities. It's a great splurge (standard Db-€135, superior Db-€177, deluxe Db-€218, singles take a double for nearly the same cost, extra bed-€40, suites available, air-con, non-smoking, elevator, free Internet access, sauna, tanning bed, Niklaas Desparsstraat 11, a block north of Market Square, tel. 050-444-444, fax 050-444-440, www.hotel-heritage.com, info@hotel-heritage.com, run by cheery and hardworking Johan and Isabelle). When making reservations, alert the staff to your needs; they are willing to assist during your stay.

In a jam, you might try this large, well-located hotel of lesser value: **Hotel ter Reien (AE+A, AI, AL, AR+A, AB+A,** one 4" step at the more accessible rear entrance, reserve rooms nearest the elevator, no bathrooms adapted for wheelchair users; 26 rooms, Db-€90, Langestraat 1, tel. 050-349-100, hotel.ter.reien@online.be).

Bed-and-Breakfasts

B&Bs, run by people who enjoy their work, offer fine value but limited accessibility. They typically have rooms on upper floors reachable only by steep staircases. While none would be suitable for wheelchair users, the two listings below have relatively few stairs and are satisfactory for slow walkers. Parking is generally easy on the street.

Level 3—Minimally Accessible

Debruyne B&B (AE+A, AI, AR+A, AB+A, ♥), run by Marie-Rose and her architect husband, Ronny, offers artsy, original decor (check out the elephant-sized doors—Ronny's design) and genuine warmth. If the Gothic is getting medieval, this is refreshingly modern (Sb-€50, Db-€55, Tb-€75, 1-night stay-€10 extra per room, no CC, non-smoking, free Internet, half-mile north of Market Square, Lange Raamstraat 18, tel. 050-347-606, fax 050-340-285, www.bedandbreakfastbruges.com). Two of the rooms are on the ground floor, but can be reached only by climbing steps. Marie-Rose has hosted wheelchair users before and is willing to help guests tackle the nine 5" steps to the breakfast room and also to serve meals in the guest's room. The bathrooms are suitable but not adapted.

Absoluut Verhulst is a great, modern-feeling B&B in a 400-year-old house, run by friendly Frieda and Benno. It presents a challenge for even slow walkers, but if you have your heart set on staying at a B&B, this one has fewer stairs than most (Sb-€50, Db-€75, huge and lofty suite-€95 for 2, €115 for 3, and €125 for 4, 1-night stays pay €10 extra per room, no

CC, 5-min walk east of Market Square at Verbrand Nieuwland 1, tel. & fax 050-334-515, www.b-bverhulst.com, b-b.verhulst@pandora.be).

EATING

Belgium is where France meets the North, and you'll find a good mix of both Flemish and French influences in Bruges. We've included accessibility information for each place. Unless otherwise noted (by **AT** or **AT+A**), these restaurants do *not* have accessible toilets.

Tipping

It generally isn't necessary to tip in restaurants (15 percent service is usually already included in the menu price). Still, feel free to tip about 5 percent if the service is good. In bars, you can round up to the next euro ("keep the change") if you get table service rather than order at the bar.

Belgian Specialties

These are popular throughout Belgium.

Moules: Mussels are served everywhere, either cooked plain *(nature)*, with white wine *(vin blanc)*, with shallots or onions *(marinière)*, or in a tomato sauce *(provençale)*. You get a big-enough-for-two bucket and a pile of fries. Go local by using one empty shell to tweeze out the rest of the *moules.* When the mollusks are in season, from about mid-July through April, you'll get the big Dutch mussels. Locals take a break in May and June, when only the puny Danish kind is available.

Frites: Belgian fries (*Vlaamse frites*, or Flemish fries) taste so good because they're deep-fried twice—once to cook, and once to brown. The natives eat them with mayonnaise, not ketchup.

Flemish Specialties

These specialties are traditional to Bruges.

Carbonnade: Rich beef stew flavored with onions and beer.

Chou rouge à la flamande: Red cabbage with onions and prunes.

Flamiche: Cheese pie with onions.

Flemish asparagus: White asparagus (fresh in springtime) in cream sauce.

Lapin à la flamande: Marinated rabbit braised in onions and prunes.

Soupe à la bière: Beer soup.

Stoemp: Mashed potatoes and vegetables.

Waterzooi: Creamy meat stew (chicken, eel, or fish).

...à la flamande: Anything cooked in the local Flemish style.

Brussels Specialties

You can find these specialties in Bruges, though they're technically "native" to Brussels (which tends toward French cuisine).

Anguilles au vert: Eel in green herb sauce.

Caricoles: Sea snails, very local and seasonal, usually sold hot by street vendors.

Cheeses: Remoudou and Djotte de Nivelles are made locally.

Choux de Bruxelles: Brussels sprouts (in cream sauce).

Crevettes: Shrimp, often served as croquettes (minced and stuffed in breaded, deep-fried rolls).

Croque monsieur: Grilled ham-and-cheese sandwich.

Endive: Typical Belgian vegetable (also called chicorée or chicon) served as a side dish.

Filet américain: Beware, for some reason steak tartare (raw) is called American.

Tartine de fromage blanc: Open-face cream-cheese sandwich, often enjoyed with a kriek (cherry-flavored) beer.

...à la brabançonne: Anything cooked in the local Brabant (Brussels) style, such as *faisan* (pheasant) *à la brabançonne.*

Desserts and Snacks

Gaufres: Waffles, sold hot in small shops.

Dame blanche: Hot fudge sundae.

Spekuloos: Spicy gingerbread biscuits, served with coffee.

Pralines: Belgian filled chocolates.

Pistolets: Round croissants.

Cramique: Currant roll.

Craquelin: Currant roll with sugar sprinkles.

Restaurants

Bruges' specialties include mussels cooked a variety of ways (one order can feed two), fish dishes, grilled meats, and french fries. Don't eat before 19:30 unless you like eating alone. Tax and service are always included. You'll find plenty of affordable, touristy restaurants on floodlit squares and along dreamy canals. Bruges feeds 3.5 million tourists a year, and most are seduced by a high-profile location. These can be fine experiences for the magical setting and views, but the quality of food and service is low. We wouldn't blame you for eating at one of these places, but we won't recommend any. We prefer the candle-cool bistros that flicker on back streets.

The Flemish Pot (AE, AI, AT, ❤, Level 1—Fully accessible)— a.k.a. The Little Pancake House—is a cute restaurant serving delicious, inexpensive pancake meals (savory and sweet) and homemade *wafels* for lunch. Then at 18:00, enthusiastic chefs Mario and Rik stow their waffle irons and pull out a traditional menu of vintage Flemish plates (good €15 dinner *menu*, daily 10:00–22:00, just off Geldmuntstraat at Helmstraat 3, tel. 050-340-086).

Restaurant Chez Olivier (AE, AI, ❤, Level 2—Moderately accessible, barrier-free entry, wheelchair-using regulars)—a classy, white-tablecloth, 10-table place—is considered the best fancy French cuisine splurge in town. While delicate Anne serves, her French husband, Olivier, is busy cooking up whatever he found freshest that day. While you can order à la carte, it's wise to go with the recommended daily *menu* (3-course lunch €35, 4-course dinner-€55, wine adds €20, 12:00–13:30 & 19:00–21:30, closed Sun and Thu, reserve for dinner, Meestraat 9, tel. 050-333-659).

Rock Fort (AE+A, AI, Level 2—Moderately accessible, staff can help with the two 2" entry steps) is a chic new eight-table place with a modern, fresh coziness and a high-powered respect for good food. Two young chefs (Peter and Hermes) give their French cuisine a creative twist, and have become the talk of the town after just a few months in business, (€10 Mon–Fri lunch special with coffee, €15–20 beautifully presented dinner plates, Thu–Tue 12:00–14:30 & 18:00–23:00, closed Wed and at lunch on Sun, great pastas and salads, reservations smart for dinner, Langestraat 15, tel. 050-334-113).

Restaurant de Koetse (AE+A, AI, AT+A, ❤, Level 2—Moderately accessible, popular with wheelchair users, one 2" entry step) is a good bet

Bruges Restaurants

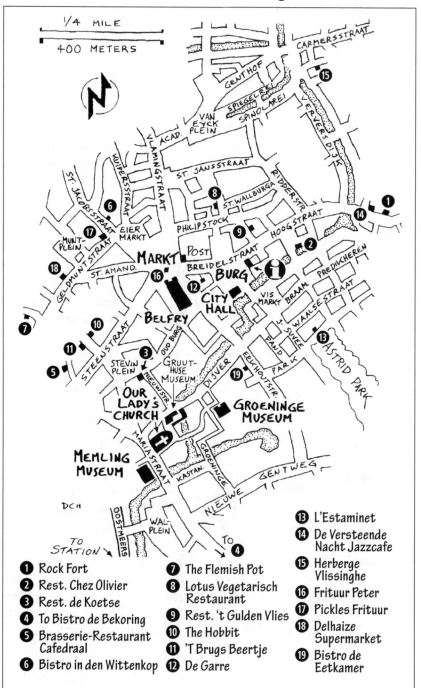

¼ MILE

400 METERS

13 L'Estaminet
14 De Versteende Nacht Jazzcafe
15 Herberge Vlissinghe
16 Frituur Peter
17 Pickles Frituur
18 Delhaize Supermarket
19 Bistro de Eetkamer

1 Rock Fort
2 Rest. Chez Olivier
3 Rest. de Koetse
4 To Bistro de Bekoring
5 Brasserie-Restaurant Cafedraal
6 Bistro in den Wittenkop

7 The Flemish Pot
8 Lotus Vegetarisch Restaurant
9 Rest. 't Gulden Vlies
10 The Hobbit
11 'T Brugs Beertje
12 De Garre

for central, affordable, quality local-style food. The ambience is traditional, yet fun and kid-friendly. The cuisine is Belgian and French with a stress on grilled meat, seafood, and mussels (3-course meals for €25, €20 plates include vegetables and a salad, Fri–Wed 12:00–15:00 & 18:00–22:00, closed Thu, smoke-free section, wheelchair accessible, Oude Burg 31, tel. 050-337-680). The suitable toilet has enough room to maneuver a wheelchair, but there are no grab bars.

Bistro de Eetkamer (AE+A, AI, Level 2—Moderately accessible, one 7" entry step) is an intimate eight-table place offering stay-awhile elegance, uppity service, and fine French/Italian cuisine—but only to those with a reservation (fine 4-course €42 menu, Thu–Mon 12:00–14:00 & 18:30–22:00, closed Tue–Wed, just south of Market Square, Eekhoutstraat 6, tel. 050-337-886).

Bistro de Bekoring (AE+A, AI, ♥, Level 2—Moderately accessible, one 8" step down at entry)—a cute, candlelit Gothic place—is tucked within two almshouses that were joined together. Rotund and friendly Chef Roland and his wife Gerda love serving traditional Flemish food from a small menu (€30 dinners, Wed–Sat open from 12:00 and from 18:30, closed Sun–Tue, out past Begijnhof at Arsenaalstraat 53, tel. 050-344-157).

Brasserie-Restaurant Cafedraal (AE, AI, Level 2—Moderately accessible) is boisterous and fun-loving, serving a local crowd good-quality modern European cuisine with the accent on French and fish. The high-ceilinged room is rustic but elegantly candlelit and the back bar sparkles in a brown way (€10 2-course lunches, €24 dinner plates, Tue–Sat 12:00–15:00 & 18:00–23:00, closed Sun–Mon, Zilverstraat 38, tel. 050-340-845).

Bistro in den Wittenkop (AE, AI, Level 2—Moderately accessible), very Flemish, is a cluttered, laid-back, old-time place specializing in the beer-soaked equivalent of beef bourguignon (€15–19 main courses, Tue–Sat 12:00–14:00 & 18:00–24:00, closed Sun–Mon, terrace in back, Sint Jakobsstraat 14, tel. 050-332-059).

Lotus Vegetarische Restaurant (AE+A, AI, Level 2—Moderately accessible, one 4" entry step) serves good vegetarian lunch plates (€9 *plat du jour* offered daily), salads, and homemade chocolate cake in a smoke-free, pastel-elegant setting without a trace of tie-dye (Mon–Sat 11:45–14:00, closed Sun, just off Burg at Wapenmakersstraat 5, tel. 050-331-078).

Restaurant 't Gulden Vlies (AE, AI, Level 2—Moderately accessible)—romantic and candlelit, quiet and less "ye olde" than the other places—serves when the others are closed. The *menu* is Belgian and French with a creative twist (€16 plates, €25 monthly menu, Wed–Sun 19:00–03:00, closed Mon–Tue, Mallebergplaats 17, tel. 050-334-709).

The Hobbit (AE+A, AI, ♥, Level 2—Moderately accessible, staff can help with the one 4" entry step) is a popular grill house across the street from the recommended bar 't Brugs Beertje (listed below). It features an entertaining menu, including all-you-can-eat spareribs with salad for €13—nothing fancy, just good basic food in a fun traditional setting (daily 18:00–24:00, Kemelstraat 8–10, tel. 050-335-520).

Bars Offering Light Meals, Beer, and Ambience

Stop into one of the city's atmospheric bars for a light meal or a drink with great Bruges ambience. Straffe Hendrik (Strong Henry), a potent and refreshing local brew, is—even to a Bud Light kind of guy—obviously great beer. If you're not big on beer, you might enjoy *kriek* (cherry-flavored) or *frambozen* (raspberry-flavored) *Bier*. For more on beer, see next page.

Any pub or restaurant carries the basic beers, but for a selection of more than several hundred types, including brews to suit any season, drink at **'t Brugs Beertje (AE+A, AI+A, ♥,** Level 2—Moderately accessible, welcoming but crowded, with tight spaces and a 2" entry step). For a light meal, consider their traditional cheese plate (Thu–Tue 16:00–24:00, closed Wed, Kemelstraat 5, tel. 050-339-616).

De Garre (AE+A, AI, Level 3—Minimally accessible, six 8" entry steps), with a huge selection of brews, is another good place to gain an appreciation of the Belgian beer culture. Rather than a noisy pub scene, it has a dressier sit-down-and-focus-on-your-friend-and-the-fine-beer ambience (daily 12:00–24:00, off Breidelstraat, between Burg and Markt, on tiny Garre alley, tel. 050-341-029). Access here is a challenge, but worth the effort. Since the restaurant is part of a monument, no architectural changes are permitted.

L'Estaminet (AE+A, AI, AT+A, Level 2—Moderately accessible, staff can help with the one 4" entry step, suitable toilet accessed by another 4" step) is a youthful, trendy, jazz-filled eatery. Away from the tourists, it's popular with local students who come for hearty €7 spaghetti (11:30–24:00, closed Mon afternoon and all day Thu, facing peaceful Astrid Park at Park 5, tel. 050-330-916).

BELGIAN BEERS

Belgium has about 350 different varieties of beer, more than any other country, and the locals take their beers as seriously as the French regard their wines. Even small café menus include six to eight varieties. Connoisseurs can be confused by the many choices, and casual drinkers probably won't like every kind offered, since some varieties don't even taste like beer. Belgian beer is generally yeastier and higher in alcohol than beers in other countries.

In Belgium, certain beers are paired with certain dishes. To bring out their flavor, different beers are served at cold, cool, or room temperature, and each has its own distinctive glass. Whether wide-mouthed, tall, and fluted, or with or without a stem, the glass is meant to highlight the beer's qualities. One of my favorite Belgian beer experiences is drinking a Kwak beer in its traditional tall glass. The glass, which widens at the base, stands in a wooden holder, and you pick the whole apparatus up—frame and glass— and drink. As you near the end, the beer in the wide bottom comes out at you quickly, with a "Kwak! Kwak! Kwak!"

To get a draft beer, ask for *een pintje* (a pint, pronounced ayn pinch-ya). Cheers is *proost*. The colorful cardboard coasters make nice, free souvenirs.

Here's a breakdown of types of beer, with some common brand names you'll find either on tap or in bottles. (Some beers require a second fermentation in the bottle, so they're only available in bottles.) This list is just a start, and you'll find many beers that don't fall into these neat categories. For encyclopedic information on Belgian beers, visit www.belgianstyle.com or www.beerhunter.com.

Ales (Blonde/Red/Amber/Brown): Ales are easily recognized by their color. Try a blonde or golden ale (Leffe Blonde, Duvel, Straffe Hendrik, Kwak), a rare and bitter sour red (Rodenbach), an amber (Palm, De Koninck), or a brown (Leffe Bruin).

Lagers: These are the light, sparkling, Budweiser-type beers. Popular brands include Jupiler, Stella Artois, and Maes.

Lambics: Perhaps the most unusual and least beer-like, lambics are stored for years in wooden casks, fermenting from wild yeasts that occur naturally in the air. Tasting more like a dry and bitter cider or champagne, pure lambic is often blended with fruits or herbs to improve the taste. Homebrewed lambics—such as *gueuze, faro, lambic doux,* and *lambic blanche*—are on tap in old cafés. Only *gueuze,* a blend of aged and young ale, is sold commercially in bottles. Some brand names include Cantillon, Lindemans, and Mort Subite ("sudden death").

Fruit lambics include those made with cherries *(kriek),* raspberries *(frambozen* or *framboise),* peaches *(peche),* or black currants *(casis).* The result for each is a tart beer, similar to a dry pink champagne.

White *(Witte)*: Based on wheat instead of hops, these milky-yellow summertime beers are often served with a lemon slice. White beer, similar to a Hefeweizen in the United States, is often flavored with spices like orange peel or coriander. Hoegaarden is the name to look for.

Trappist beers: For centuries, between their vespers and matins, Trappist monks have been brewing heavily fermented beers. Three typical Trappist beers (from the Westmalle monastery) are *Tripel,* with a blonde color, served cold with a frothy head; *Dobbel,* which is dark, sweet and served cool; and *Singel,* made especially by the monks for the monks, and considered a fair trade for a life of celibacy. Other Trappist monasteries include Rochefort, Chimay, Westvleteren, and Orval.

Strong beers: The potent brands include Duvel (meaning "devil" because of its high octane, camouflaged by a pale color), Verboden Vrucht (literally "forbidden fruit," with Adam and Eve on the label), and the not-for-the-fainthearted brands of Judas, Satan, and Lucifer. Gouden Carolus is considered the strongest beer in Belgium, and Delerium Tremens speaks for itself.

De Versteende Nacht Jazzcafé (AE+A, AI, Level 2—Moderately accessible, one 2" entry step) is another popular young hangout serving vegetarian dishes, salads, and pastas on Langestraat (€12.50 meals, Tue–Thu 19:00–24:00, Fri–Sat 18:00–24:00, closed Sun–Mon, live jazz on Wed from 21:00, at #11, tel. 050-343-293).

Herberghe Vlissinghe (AE+A, AI, Level 2—Moderately accessible), the oldest pub in town (1515), serves hot snacks in a great atmosphere (Wed–Sun open from 11:00 on, closed Mon–Tue, Blekersstraat 2, tel. 050-343-737).

Fries, Fast Food, and Picnics

Local french fries *(frites)* are a treat. Proud and traditional *frituurs* serve tubs of fries and various local-style shish kebabs. Belgians dip their *frites* in mayonnaise, but ketchup is there for the Yankees (along with spicier sauces). For a quick, cheap, and scenic meal, hit a *frituur* and savor them by the steps and benches overlooking Market Square, about 50 yards past the post office. The best fries in town are from **Frituur Peter** (Level 1—Fully accessible)—twin take-away carts on the Market Square at the base of the bell tower (daily 10:00–24:00).

Pickles Frituur (AE+A, AI, Level 2—Moderately accessible, one 8" entry step), a block off Market Square, is handy for sit-down fries. Run by Marleen, its forte is greasy, fast, deep-fried Flemish corn dogs. The "menu 2" comes with three traditional gut bombs (Mon–Sat 11:00–24:00, at the corner of Geldmuntstraat and Sint Jakobstraat, tel. 050-337-957).

Delhaize Supermarket (AE, AI, Level 2—Moderately accessible) is great for picnics (push-button produce-pricer lets you buy as little as one mushroom, Mon–Sat 9:00–18:00, Fri until 18:30, closed Sun, 3 blocks off the Market Square on Geldmuntstraat). The small **Delhaize grocery** (Level 3—Minimally accessible, narrow aisles prevent wheelchair access, but slow walkers will be fine) is on Market Square opposite the bell tower (Mon–Sat 9:00–12:00 & 14:00–18:00, Sun 14:00–18:00). For midnight munchies, you'll find Indian-run corner grocery stores.

TRANSPORTATION CONNECTIONS

At the Bruges train station, check in at the ticket counter at least 15 minutes before departure to arrange for assistance along the way and at your destination. To use the accessible toilet, ask for the key at the baggage claim. They can also set up a ramp for you, or provide other help boarding.

From Brussels, an hour away by train, all of Europe is at your fingertips. Train info: tel. 050-302-424. The Brussels Zuid/Midi train station is accessible to people using wheelchairs and the Brussels Centraal and Noord stations have recently been retrofitted to improve accessibility. The bathrooms are independently operated and are accessible.

By train to: Brussels (2/hr, usually at :33 and :59, 1 hr, €10), **Ghent** (4/hr, 40 min), **Ostende** (3/hr, 15 min), **Köln** (6/day, 4 hrs), **Paris** (hrly via Brussels, 2.5 hrs, must pay supplement of €10.50 second class, €21 first class, even with a railpass), **Amsterdam** (hrly, 3.5 hrs, transfer in Antwerp or Brussels), **Amsterdam's Schiphol Airport** (hrly, 3.5 hrs, transfer in Antwerp or Brussels, €35).

Trains from England: Bruges is an ideal "welcome to Europe" stop after London. Take the Eurostar train from London to Brussels under the English Channel (8/day, 2.5 hrs), then transfer, continuing to Bruges (2/hr, 1 hr). For more on the Eurostar train, see page 141.

BRUGES ROLL OR STROLL

This tour, which takes you from Market Square to the Burg to the cluster of museums around the Church of Our Lady (the Groeninge, Gruuthuse, and Memling), shows you the best of Bruges. Note that museums are open Tue–Sun 9:30–17:00, closed Mon.

If the route (2/3-mile) seems too long to cover in a day, break it up into manageable pieces. Skip the portions or museums that don't suit your mobility level, and simply move on to the next stop. Wheelchair users can use the bike lanes—just be alert to the many bicycle riders sharing the paths.

Market Square (Markt)

Access: Most of the square is fully accessible (Level 1), but the cobblestone streets (with 2" curbs) vary in degree of roughness.

The pleasant, shop-lined street just off the square, Geldmuntstraat (**AE+A,** Level 2—Moderately accessible), has 4" curbs, with curb cuts down to one or two inches. Some stores have entries that are wheelchair-accessible; others have steps.

The Sight: Ringed by banks, the post office, lots of restaurant terraces, great old gabled buildings, and the bell tower, this is the modern heart of the city. And, in Bruges' heyday as a trading center, this was also the center.

The "typical" old buildings here were rebuilt in the 19th century in an exaggerated neo-Gothic style (Bruges is often called "more Gothic than Gothic"). This pre-Martin Luther style was a political statement by this Catholic town.

A canal came right up to this square. Imagine boats moored where

ACCESSIBILITY CODE CHART

CODE	MEANING
AE	Accessible Entryway
AE+A	Accessible Entry with Assistance
AI	Accessible Interior
AI+A	Accessible Interior with Assistance
AT	Accessible Toilet
AT+A	Accessible Toilet with Assistance
AL	Accessible Lift (elevator)
AL+A	Accessible Lift with Assistance

For the full chart, or a more detailed explanation of codes, please see page 2 of the Introduction.

the post office stands today. In the 1300s, farmers shipped their cotton, wool, flax, and hemp to the port at Bruges. Before loading it onto outgoing boats, the industrious locals would spin, weave, and dye it into a finished product.

By 1400, the economy was shifting away from textiles and toward more refined goods such as high-fashion items, tapestries, chairs, jewelry, and paper—a new invention replacing parchment that was made in Flanders with cotton that was shredded, soaked, and pressed.

The square is adorned with **flags,** including the red-white-and-blue lion flag of Bruges, the black-yellow-red flag of Belgium, and the blue-with-circle-of-stars flag of the European Union.

The **statue** depicts two friends, Jan Breidel and Pieter de Coninc, clutching sword and shield and looking toward France during their 1302 people's uprising against the French king. The rebels identified potential French spies by demanding they repeat two words—shield and friend *(schild en vriend)*—that only Flemish locals (or foreigners with phlegm) could pronounce. They won Flanders its freedom. Cleverly using hooks to pull knights from their horses, it was the medieval world's first victory of foot-soldiers over horse-knights and of common people over nobility. The French knights, thinking that fighting these Flemish peasants

Bruges Roll or Stroll

1 Market Square
2 Bell Tower
3 Breidelstraat
4 Burg Square
5 Basilica of the Holy Blood
6 Town Hall
7 Renaissance Hall
8 Crowne Plaza Hotel (atop old ruins)
9 Blinde Ezelstraat
10 Fish Market
11 Huidevettersplein
12 Postcard view
13 Groeninge Museum
14 Gruuthuse Museum
15 Church of Our Lady
16 Memling Museum
17 Begijnhof
18 Minnewater

would be a cakewalk, had worn their dress uniforms. The peasants had a field day afterwards scavenging all the golden spurs from the fallen soldiers after the Battle of the Golden Spurs (1302).

Geldmuntstraat, a block west of the square, has fun shops and eateries. Nearby Steenstraat is the main shopping street and is packed with people.

Bell Tower (Belfort)

Access: The Bell Tower is Level 4—Not accessible; Exhibition Hall is **AE, AI, AL, AT,** Level 1—Fully accessible. While the Bell Tower requires a long, steep climb, you can reach the Exhibition Hall on the second floor by elevator (in the courtyard, down the hallway toward the toilet). The toilet off courtyard is wheelchair-accessible (€0.30, ask attendant for key).

Cost and Hours: €5, daily 9:30–17:00, ticket window closes 45 min early.

The Sight: Most of this Bell Tower has stood over Market Square since 1300. The octagonal lantern was added in 1486, making it 290 feet high. The tower combines medieval crenellations, pointed Gothic arches, round Roman arches, flamboyant spires, and even a few small flying buttresses (two-thirds of the way up).

Try some French fries from either stand at the bottom of the tower. Look for the small metal model of the tower, the Braille description of the old town, and the carillon concert schedule (listed with photos of player at keyboard, just inside courtyard at base of Bell Tower).

If you can handle the 366 steps, climb the tower (€5, no wheelchair access). Just before you reach the top, peek into the carillon room. The 47 bells can be played mechanically with the giant barrel and movable tabs (as they are on each quarter hour) or with a manual keyboard (as they are during concerts). The carillon player uses his fists and feet rather than fingers. Be there on the quarter hour, when things ring. It's *bellissimo* at the top of the hour.

Atop the tower, survey the town. On the horizon you can see the towns along the North Sea coast.

• *Facing the Bell Tower, turn left (east) onto traffic-free...*

Breidelstraat

Lace, waffles, chocolates, tapestry—Bruges' many treats are sold here.
And beer? Turn right down the narrow alleyway midway along the block
to find the tiny De Garre bar, which serves more than a hundred Belgian
beers in a smoky, local atmosphere (**AE+A, AI,** Level 3—Minimally
accessible, six 8" entry steps, daily 12:00–24:00, tel. 050-341-029).

• *Thread yourself through the lace and waffles to Burg Square.*

Burg Square

The opulent square called Burg is
Bruges' historical birthplace, political
center, and religious heart. Today it's the
scene of outdoor concerts and home of
the TI.

Pan the square to see six centuries of
architecture. Starting with the view of
the bell tower above the rooftops, sweep
counterclockwise 360 degrees. You'll go
from Romanesque (the interior of the fancy gray-brick **Basilica of the
Holy Blood** in the corner) to the pointed Gothic arches and prickly
steeples of the white sandstone **Town Hall** to the well-proportioned
Renaissance windows of the **Old Recorder's House** (next door, under
the gilded statues), to the elaborate 17th-century Baroque of the
Provost's House (past the TI and the park behind you). The **park** at the
back of the square is the site of a cathedral that was demolished during
the French Revolutionary period. Today the foundation is open to the
public in the Crowne Plaza Hotel basement (described below).

• *Complete your spin and make your way to the small, fancy, gray-and-gold
building in the corner of the Burg Square.*

Basilica of the Holy Blood

Access: Lower Chapel is **AE, AI,** Level 1—Fully accessible; Upper
Chapel and adjacent Treasury are Level 4—Not accessible (up thirty-
seven 7" steps).

Cost, Hours: Treasury—€1.25, April–Sept daily 9:30–12:00 &
14:00–18:00, Oct–March Thu–Tue 10:00–12:00 & 14:00–16:00, Wed
10:00–12:00 only, tel. 050-336-792.

The Sight: The gleaming gold knights and ladies on the church's gray facade remind us that the double-decker church was built (c. 1150) by a brave Crusader to house the drops of Christ's blood he brought back from Jerusalem.

Lower Chapel: Enter the accessible Lower Chapel through the door labeled *Basiliek*. Inside, the stark and dim decor reeks of the medieval piety that drove crusading Europeans on Christian jihads against Muslims. With heavy columns and round arches, the style is pure Romanesque. The annex along the right

aisle displays somber statues of Christ being tortured and entombed, plus a 12th-century relief panel over a doorway of St. Basil, a fourth-century scholarly monk, being baptized by a double-jointed priest and a man-sized Dove of the Holy Spirit.

• *Leave the Lower Chapel and go outside. If you need to avoid stairs, head directly to the Town Hall (see listing below). Otherwise, take the staircase to reach the...*

Upper Chapel: After being gutted by Napoleon's secular-humanist crusaders in 1797, the Upper Chapel's original Romanesque decor was redone in a neo-Gothic style. The nave is colorful, with a curved wooden ceiling, painted walls, and stained-glass windows of the dukes who ruled Flanders and their duchesses.

The painting at the main altar tells how the Holy Blood got here. Derrick of Alsace, having wrested Jerusalem *(Hierosolyma)* and Bethlehem *(Bethlema)* from Muslim control in the Second Crusade, kneels (left) before the grateful Christian patriarch of Jerusalem, who rewards him with the relic. Derrick returns home (right) and kneels before

THE LEGEND OF THE HOLY BLOOD

Several drops of Christ's blood, washed from his lifeless body by Joseph of Arimathea, were preserved in a crystal phial in Jerusalem. After Derrick of Alsace, who received the relic for his success in the Second Crusade, donated it to the city of Bruges, the old, dried blood suddenly turned to liquid. This miracle was repeated every Friday for the next two centuries, and verified by thousands of pilgrims from around Europe who flocked here to adore it. The blood dried up for good in 1325.

Every year on Ascension Day (the 40th day after Easter), Bruges' bankers, housewives, and waffle-vendors put on old-time costumes for the parading of the phial through the city. Crusader knights re-enact the bringing of the relic, Joseph of Arimathea re-washes Christ's body, and ladies in medieval costume with hair tied up in horn-like hairnets come out to wave flags, while many of Bruges' citizens just take the day off.

Bruges' bishop to give him the phial of blood.

The relic itself—some red stuff preserved inside a clear, six-inch tube of rock-crystal—is kept in the adjoining room (through the three arches). It's in the tall silver tabernacle on the altar. (Unless it's Friday, the tabernacle's doors will be closed, so you can't actually see the phial of blood.) On holy days, the relic is shifted across the room, and displayed on the throne under the canopy.

The Treasury (Next to Upper Chapel): For €1.25 you can see the impressive gold-and-silver, gem-studded, hexagonal reliquary that the phial of blood is paraded around in on feast days (c. 1600, left wall). The phial is placed in the "casket" at the bottom of the four-foot structure. On the wall, flanking the shrine, are paintings of kneeling residents who, for centuries, have tended the shrine and organized the pageantry as part of the 31-member Brotherhood of the Holy Blood. Elsewhere in the room are the Brothers' ceremonial necklaces, clothes, chalices, and so on.

In the display case by the entrance, find the lead box that protected the phial of blood from Protestant extremists (1578) and French revolutionaries (1797) bent on destroying this glaring symbol of Catholic mumbo-jumbo. The broken rock-crystal tube with gold caps on either end is a replica of the phial, giving an idea of what the actual relic looks like. Opposite the reliquary are the original cartoons (from 1541) that provided the designs for the basilica's stained glass.

Town Hall (Stadhuis)

Access: AE, AI, AL, Level 2—Moderately accessible. The Gothic Room is upstairs and accessible by elevator. There are no accessible toilets available.

Cost, Hours, and Location: Entrance Hall-free, Gothic Room-€2.50, includes audioguide and admission to Renaissance Hall, daily 9:30–17:00, Burg 12.

The Sight: Built around 1400, when Bruges was a thriving bastion of capitalism with a population of 35,000, this building served as a model for town halls elsewhere, including Brussels. The white sandstone facade is studded with statues of knights, nobles, and saints with prickly Gothic steeples over their heads. A colorful double band of cities' coats of arms includes those of Bruges *(Brugghe)* and Dunquerke. (Back then, Bruges' jurisdiction included many towns in present-day France.) The building is still the Town Hall, and it's not unusual to see couples arriving here to get married.

Entrance Hall: The free ground-level lobby (closed on weekends) is draped with colorful banners representing the different professions in town. Pick them out: candlestick makers, painters, pig ranchers, weavers, blacksmiths, and cloth makers.

The adjacent hallway is a picture gallery with scenes from Belgium's history, from the Spanish Bourbon king to the arrival of Napoleon, shown meeting the town mayor here at the Town Hall in 1803.

The painting at the far left end of the lobby (behind ticket desk) shows the event that symbolically ended Bruges' glory days. Mary of Burgundy lies absolutely flat on her back, having tumbled from a horse, as peasants rush to help. When she died at age 25 (in 1482), her husband Maximilian inherited Bruges. The town was soon swallowed up in Maximilian's huge Holy Roman Empire, ruled from afar by kings in Austria and Spain, who did nothing as the town's harbor and economy silted up.

Gothic Room: Some of modern democracy's roots lie in this ornate room where, for centuries, the city council met to discuss the town's affairs. In 1464, one of Europe's first parliaments, the Estates-General of the Low Countries, convened here. The fireplace at the far end bears a proclamation from 1305, which says, "All the artisans, laborers...and citizens of Bruges are free—all of them" (...providing they pay their taxes).

The elaborately carved and painted wooden ceiling (a reconstruction from 1800) features Gothic-style tracery in gold, red, and black. Five dangling arches hang down the center ("pendentives"), now adorned with modern floodlights. Notice the New Testament themes carved into the circular medallions that decorate the points where the arches meet.

The **wall murals** are late-19th-century Romantic paintings depicting episodes in the city's history. Start with the biggest painting along the left wall, and work clockwise, following the numbers found on the walls:

1. Hip, hip...hooray! Everyone cheers, flags wave, trumpets blare, and dogs bark, as Bruges' knights, dressed in gold with black Flemish lions, return triumphant after driving out French oppressors and winning Flanders' independence. The Battle of the Golden Spurs (1302) is remembered every July 11, now the Flemish national holiday.

2. Perhaps Bruges' high-water mark came at this elaborate ceremony, when Philip the Good of Burgundy (seated, in black) assembled his court here in Bruges and solemnly founded the knightly Order of the Golden Fleece (1430).

3. The Crusader knight, Derrick of Alsace, returns from Jerusalem and kneels at the entrance of St. Basil's Chapel to present the relic of Christ's Holy Blood (1150).

4. A nun carries a basket of bread in this scene from St. Jans Hospital.

5. A town leader stands at the podium and hands a sealed document to a German businessman, renewing the Hanseatic League's business

license. Membership in this club of trading cities was a key to Bruges' prosperity.

6. As peasants cheer, a messenger of the local duke proclaims the town's right to self-government (1190).

7. The mayor visits a Bruges painting studio to shake the hand of Jan van Eyck, the greatest Flemish Primitive painter (1433). Jan's wife, Margareta is there, too. In the 1400s, Bruges rivaled Florence and Venice as Europe's cultural capital. See the town in the distance, out van Eyck's window.

8. Skip it.

9. City fathers grab a ceremonial trowel from a pillow to lay the fancy cornerstone of the Town Hall (1376). Bruges' familiar towers stand in the background.

10. Skip it.

11. It's a typical market day at the Halls (the courtyard behind the bell tower). Arabs mingle with Germans in fur-lined coats and beards in a market where they sell everything from armor to lemons.

12. A bishop blesses a new canal (1404) as ships sail right by the city. This was Bruges in its heyday before the silting of the harbor. At the far right, the two bearded men with moustaches are the brothers who painted these murals.

In the adjoining room, old paintings and maps show how little the city has changed over the centuries. **Map #8** (on the right wall) shows in exquisite detail the city as it looked in 1562. (The map is oriented with south on top.) Find the bell tower, the Church of Our Lady, and Burg Square, which back then was bounded on the north by a cathedral. Notice the canal (on the west) leading from the North Sea right to Market Square. A moat circled the city with its gates, unfinished wall, and 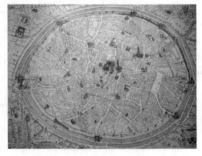 28 windmills (4 of which survive today). The mills pumped water to the town's fountains, made paper, ground grain, and functioned as the motor of the Middle Ages. Most locals own a copy of this map that shows how their neighborhood looked 400 years ago.

• *In the southeast corner of Burg Square is the...*

Renaissance Hall (Brugse Vrije)

Access: AE+A, AI+A, Level 3—Minimally accessible. The entry is at the end of three 8" steps, a long landing, and two 7" steps.

Cost, Hours, and Location: €2.50, includes audioguide and admission to City Hall's Gothic Room, Tue–Sun 9:30–12:00 & 13:30–17:00, closed Mon, entry in corner of square at Burg 11a.

The Sight: This elaborately decorated room with a grand Renaissance chimney was designed by Bruges' Renaissance man, Lancelot Blondeel (in 1531), and carved out of oak. If you're into heraldry, the symbolism (explained in the free English flier) makes this room worth a five-minute stop. If you're not, you'll wonder where the rest of the museum is.

The centerpiece of the incredible carving is the Holy Roman Emperor, Charles V. This celebrates 200 years of Spanish rule. The hometown duke, on the far left, is related to Charles V. By making the connection to the Holy Roman Emperor clear, this carved family tree of Bruges' nobility helped substantiate their power. Notice the closely guarded family jewels. And check out the expressive little cherubs.

Crowne Plaza Hotel

Access: AE+A, AI, AL, AT, Level 2—Moderately accessible. The wheelchair access is through the De Linde restaurant, which is connected to the hotel—you have to negotiate one 8" step to reach the accessible revolving door. Once inside, you can reach the ruins by elevator.

Location: Burg 10, tel. 050-446-844, fax 050-446-868, www .crowneplaza.com.

The Sight: One of the city's newest buildings (1992) sits atop the ruins of the town's oldest structures. In around 900, when Viking ships regularly docked here to rape and pillage, Baldwin Iron Arm built a fort *(castrum)* to protect his Flemish people. In 950, the fort was converted into St. Donatian's church, which became one of the city's largest.

Ask politely at the hotel's reception desk to see the archeological site—ruins of both the fort and the church—in their basement. Providing there's no conference going on, they'll let you go downstairs (via the accessible elevator; downstairs you'll also find an adapted toilet).

In the basement of the modern hotel are conference rooms lined with old stone walls and display cases of objects found in the ruins of earlier structures. On the immediate left hangs a document announcing the "Vente de Materiaux" (sale of material). When Napoleon destroyed the church in the early 1800s, its bricks were auctioned off. A local builder bought them at auction, and now the pieces of the old cathedral are embedded in other buildings throughout Bruges.

See the oak pilings once driven into this former peat bog to support the fort and shore up its moat. Paintings show the immensity of the church that replaced it. The curved stone walls you'll notice are from the foundations of the ambulatory around the church altar.

Excavators found a town water hole—a bonanza for archaeologists—turning up the refuse of a thousand years of habitation—pottery, animal skulls, rosary beads, dice, coins, keys, thimbles, pipes, spoons, and Delftware.

Don't miss the 14th-century painted sarcophagus—painted quickly for burial with the crucifixion on the west end and the Virgin and Child on the east.

• *Back on the Burg Square, roll or stroll south under the Goldfinger family down the alleyway called...*

Blinde Ezelstraat

Midway down on the left side (knee level), see an original iron hinge from the city's south gate, back when the city was ringed by a moat and closed up at 22:00. On the right wall a few feet higher, a black patch shows just how grimy the city had become before a 1960s cleaning. Despite the cleaning and a few fanciful reconstructions, the city looks today much as it did in centuries past.

• *Cross the bridge over what was the 13th-century city moat. On your left are the arcades of the...*

Fish Market (Vismarkt)

The North Sea is just 12 miles away, and the fresh catch is sold here (Tue–Sat 6:00–13:00). Once a thriving market, today it is being replaced by souvenir stalls.

• *Take an immediate right (west), entering a courtyard called...*

Huidevettersplein

This tiny, picturesque, restaurant-filled square was originally the head-quarters of the town's skinners and tanners. On the facade of the Hotel Duc de Bourgogne, four old relief panels show scenes from the leather tanners—once a leading Bruges industry. First they tan the hides in a bath of acid; then, with tongs, they pull it out to dry; then they beat it to make soft; and finally, they scrape and clean it to make it ready to sell.

• *Continue a few feet to Rozenhoedkaai street, where you can look back and get a great...*

Postcard View

The bell tower reflected in a quiet canal lined with old houses—the essence of Bruges. Seeing buildings rising straight from the water makes you understand why this was the Venice of the North. Can you see the Bell Tower's tilt? It leans about four feet. The tilt has been carefully monitored since 1740, but no change has been detected.

Looking left (west) down the Dijver canal (past a flea market on weekends) looms the huge spire of the Church of Our Lady, the tallest brick spire in the Low Countries. Between you and the church is the Europa College (a post-graduate institution where the laws, economics, and politics of a united Europe are taught) and two fine museums.

• *Two blocks away on Dijver street is the...*

Groeninge Museum

Access: AE+A, AI, AT, Level 2—Moderately accessible. The two 3" steps at the museum's entrance are wheelchair-accessible after a museum staff member puts a ramp in place—ask for assistance. The rest of the museum is accessible, including a unisex adapted toilet in the men's restroom.

Cost and Hours: €8, Tue–Sun 9:30–17:00, closed Mon, Dijver 12, tel. 050-448-751.

The Sight: This sumptuous collection of paintings

takes you from 1400 to 1945. While the museum has plenty of worthwhile modern art, the highlights are its vivid and pristine Flemish Primitives. ("Primitive" here means before the Renaissance.) Flemish art is shaped by its love of detail, its merchant patrons' egos, and the power of the Church. Lose yourself in the halls of Groeninge: Gaze across 15th-century canals, into the eyes of reassuring Marys, and through town squares littered with leotards, lace, and lopped-off heads.

• *Next door is the...*

Gruuthuse Museum

Access: Level 4—Not accessible. There are six 6" steps at the entry, and the building includes many levels accessible only by stairs, sometimes winding and narrow.

Cost, Hours, and Location: €6, Tue–Sun 9:30–17:00, closed Mon, Dijver 17.

The Sight: The 15th-century mansion of a wealthy Bruges merchant displays period furniture, tapestries, coins, and musical instruments. Nowhere in the city do you get such an intimate look at the materialistic revolution of Bruges' glory days.

With the help of the excellent and included audioguide, just browse through rooms of secular objects that are both functional and beautiful. Here are some highlights:

In the first room (or Great Hall) the big fireplace, oak table, and tapestries attest to the wealth of Louis Gruuthuse, who got rich providing a special herb used to spice up beer.

Tapestries like the ones you see here were a famous Flemish export product, made in local factories out of raw wool imported from England and silk from the Orient (via Italy). Both beautiful and useful (as insulation), they adorned many homes and palaces throughout Europe.

These **four tapestries** (of nine originals) tell a worldly story of youthful lustiness that upsets our stereotypes about supposed medieval piousness. The first tapestry, the *Soup-eating Lady* (on the left) shows a shepherd girl with a bowl of soup in her lap. The horny shepherd lad cuts a slice of bread (foreplay in medieval symbolism) and saucily asks (read the archaic French cartoon bubbles) if he can "dip into the goodies in her lap," if you catch my drift. On the right, a woman brazenly strips off her socks to dangle her feet in water while another woman lifts her dress to pee.

The next tapestry, called *The Dance,* shows couples freely dancing together under the apple tree of temptation. *The Wedding Parade* (opposite wall) shows where all this wantonness leads—marriage. Music plays, the table is set and the meat's on the BBQ, as the bride and groom enter...reluctantly. The bride smiles, but she's closely escorted by two men, while the scared groom (center) gulps nervously. From here, next stop is *Old Age* (smaller tapestry), and the aged shepherd is tangled in a wolf trap. "Alas," reads the French caption, "he was once so lively, but marriage caught him, and now he's trapped in its net."

In Room 2 see the *Bust of Charles V* (on top of an oak chest) and ponder the series of marriages that made Charles (1500–1558), the grandson of a Flemish girl, the powerful ruler of most of Europe, including Bruges. Mary of Burgundy (and Flanders) married powerful Maximilian I of Austria. Their son married Ferdinand and Isabella of Spain's daughter, and when little Charles was born to them, he inherited all his parents' lands and more. Charles' son, Philip II (see his bust opposite), a devout Catholic, brought persecution and war to the Protestant Low Countries.

The Gruuthuse mansion abuts the Church of Our Lady. Upstairs you'll find a chapel with a window overlooking the huge church. The family could attend services without leaving home, with their private box seats looking down into the choir. From the balcony, you can look down on two reclining gold statues in the church that mark the tombs of Charles the Bold and his daughter, Mary of Burgundy (the grandmother of powerful Charles V).

The last room (ground floor, near the entrance) deals with old-time justice. In 1796, the enlightened city of Bruges chose the newfangled guillotine as its humane form of execution. This 346-pound model was tested on sheep before being bloodied twice for executions on the Market Square. Also see branding irons, a small workbench for slicing off evil-doers' members, and posts to chain up criminals for public humiliation.

Leaving the museum, contemplate the mountain of bricks towering 400 feet above as they have for 600 years. You're heading for that church.
• *Return to the main street, then go left to Mariastraat and the church. If you're on foot, take the interesting back way to the church (includes six 6" steps over rough cobblestone). At the Arentshuis Museum entrance, duck under the arch at #16 and into a quiet courtyard. Veer right and cross a tiny 19th-*

century bridge. From the bridge, look up at the corner of the Gruuthuse mansion, where there's a teeny-tiny window, a toll-keeper's lookout. The bridge gives you a close-up look at Our Lady's big buttresses and round apse. The church entrance is around the front.

Church of Our Lady

Access: AE, AI, Level 2—Moderately accessible. The church is wheelchair-accessible, with the exception of a small room (up two 8" steps) at the end of the apse. The nearest accessible toilet is across the street at the Memling Museum (see below).

Cost, Hours, and Location: Apse €2.50, Tue–Sun 9:00–12:00 & 13:30–17:00, closed Mon, Mariastraat.

The Sight: The church stands as a memorial to the power and wealth of Bruges in its heyday. A delicate *Madonna and Child* by **Michelangelo (1504)** is near the apse (free, to the right as you enter), somewhat overwhelmed by the ornate Baroque niche it sits in. It's said to be the only Michelangelo statue to leave Italy in his lifetime, bought in Tuscany by a wealthy Bruges business-man, who's buried beneath it.

As Michelangelo chipped away at the master-piece of his youth, *David*, he took breaks by carving this (1504). Mary, slightly smaller than life-size, sits while young Jesus stands in front of her. Their expressions are mirror images of each other—serene but a bit melancholy, with downcast eyes, as though pondering the young child's dangerous future. Though they're lost in thought, their hands instinc-

tively link, tenderly. The white Carrara marble is highly polished, something Michelangelo only did when he was certain he'd got it right.

If you like tombs and church art, pay to wander through the apse (accessible except for the small room at the end). The highlight is the reclining statues marking the tombs of the last local rulers of Bruges, Mary of Burgundy and her father Charles the Bold. The dog and lion at their feet are sym-bols of fidelity and courage.

In 1482, when 25-year-old Mary of Burgundy tumbled from a horse and died, she left behind a toddler son and a husband about to become Holy Roman Emperor. Beside her lies her father, Charles the Bold, who also died prematurely, in war. Their twin deaths meant Bruges belonged to Austria, and would soon be swallowed up by Emperor Maximilian's empire. Trade routes shifted, and goods now flowed through Antwerp, then Amsterdam, as Bruges' North Sea port filled with silt. After these three blows, Bruges began four centuries of economic decline.

To the left of the main altar is a balcony overlooking the altar. It's actually part of the Gruuthuse mansion next door, giving that wealthy noble family a private box seat for Mass.

• *Just across Mariastraat from the church entrance is the entrance to the St. Jans Hospital's Visitors Center (**AE, AI, AT**, Level 1—Fully accessible). The Memling Museum, which fills that hospital's church, is 20 yards south on Mariastraat.*

Memling Museum

Access: AE, AI, AL, AT, Level 1—Fully accessible except for corner room with two 8" steps. An elevator is on the right side of the inside entry. The accessible unisex toilet is in the men's room in the Visitors Center. Loaner wheelchairs are available.

Cost, Hours, Location: €8 includes fine audioguide, Tue–Sun 9:30–17:00, closed Mon, across the street from the Church of Our Lady, Mariastraat 38.

The Sight: This medieval hospital (newly opened after 2 years of renovation) contains six much-loved paintings by the greatest of the Flemish Primitives, Hans Memling. His *Mystical Wedding of St. Catherine* triptych deserves a close look. Catherine and her "mystical groom," the baby Jesus, are flanked by a headless John the Baptist and a pensive John the Evangelist. The chairs are there so you can study it. If you understand the Book of Revelation, you'll understand St. John's wild and intricate vision. The St. Ursula Shrine, an ornate little mini-church in the same room, is filled with impressive detail.

• *Continue south on Mariastraat. From here the lacy cuteness of Bruges crescendos as you approach the...*

Begijnhof

Access: AE+A, AI+A, Level 2—Moderately accessible. The cobble-stones in the Begijnhof are rough, making for a teeth-rattling wheelchair ride. The museum has one 4" entry step, one 4" step to visit the kitchen, one 8" step to the courtyard, and two 7" steps to see the sleeping quarters. The toilet is not wheelchair-accessible.

Museum Cost and Hours: €2 with English explanations, daily 10:00–12:00 & 13:45–17:30, off-season closes at 17:00.

The Sight: The peaceful courtyard (free) is lined with small buildings. The simple museum to the left of the entry gate gives you a sense of beguine life (Level 2, see Access above).

Begijnhofs (gutturally: buh-HHHINE-hof) were built to house women of the lay order called *beguines,* who spent their lives in piety and service (without having to take the same vows a nun would). For military and other reasons, there were more women than men in the medieval Low Countries. The order of *beguines* offered women (often single or widowed) a dignified place to live and work. When the order died out, many *begijnhofs* were taken over by towns for subsidized housing, but some, like this one, became homes for nuns.

In the church, the rope that dangles from the ceiling is yanked by a nun around 17:15 to announce a sung vespers service.

• *Exiting opposite the way you entered you'll hook left (over some big, rough cobbles) and see a lake with silver swans...*

Minnewater

Just south of the Begijnhof is Minnewater, a tranquil lake-filled park with canals and swans. This was once far from quaint—a busy harbor where the small boats shuttled cargo from the big ocean-going ships into town. From this point the cargo was transferred again to flat-bottomed boats that went through the town's canals to their respective warehouses and Market Square.

When locals see these swans they remember the 15th-century mayor—famous for his long neck—who collaborated with the Austrians.

The townsfolk beheaded him as a traitor. The Austrians warned them that similarly long-necked swans would inhabit the place to forever remind them of this murder. And they do.

• *You're a 1/3-mile roll or stroll from the train station (where you can catch a bus or taxi to Market Square) or a 2/3-mile roll or stroll from Market Square—take your pick.*

THE NETHERLANDS

- 14,000 square miles, a little larger than Maryland
- 16 million people (1,150 people per square mile; 15 times the population density of the United States)
- €1 = about $1.15

Holland: Windmills, wooden shoes, tulips, cheese, and great artists. In its 17th-century glory days, tiny Holland was a world power—politically, economically, and culturally—with more great artists per square mile than any other country.

Today, the Netherlands is Europe's most densely populated country and also one of its wealthiest and best organized. A generation ago, Belgium, the Netherlands, and Luxembourg created the nucleus of a united Europe when they joined to form the Benelux Economic Union.

Efficiency is a Dutch custom. The average income is higher than in the United States. Though only 8 percent of the labor force is made up of farmers, 70 percent of the land is cultivated, and you'll travel through vast fields of barley, wheat, sugar beets, potatoes, and flowers.

"Holland" is just a nickname for the Netherlands. North Holland and South Holland are the largest of the 12 provinces that make up the Netherlands. The word Netherlands means "lowlands," and the country is so named because half of it is below sea level, reclaimed from the sea (or rivers). That's why the locals say, "God made the Earth, but the Dutch made Holland." Modern technology and plenty of Dutch elbow grease have turned much of the sea into fertile farmland. Though a new, 12th province—Flevoland, near Amsterdam—has been drained, dried, and populated in the last 100 years, Dutch reclamation projects are essentially finished.

The Dutch pride themselves on their frankness, and they like to split the bill. Traditionally, Dutch cities have been open-minded, loose, and liberal (to attract sailors in the days of Henry Hudson). And today,

The Netherlands

Amsterdam is a capital of alternative lifestyles—a city where nothing's illegal as long as nobody gets hurt. From marijuana to prostitution, you can get it all—legally—in the Netherlands.

But contrary to nervous Americans' expectations, Holland is safe. The buzzword here is "social control," meaning that neighborhood security comes not from iron shutters, heavily armed cops, and gated communities, but from neighbors looking out for each other. Everyone knows everyone in this tight-knit neighborhood. If Magrit doesn't buy bread for two days, the baker asks around. Unlike in many big cities, there's no chance that anyone here could lie dead in his house unnoticed for weeks. Video surveillance cameras watch prostitutes, while prostitutes survey the streets, buzzing for help if they spot trouble. Watch the men who watch the women who watch out for their neighbors across the street who watch the flower shop on the corner—"social control."

You'll find almost no language barrier anywhere in the Netherlands, as all well-educated folks, nearly all young people, and the majority of people in the tourist trade speak English. Still, take a few minutes to learn some polite Dutch pleasantries. Just like in Flemish-speaking Belgium, "Hello" is *hallo* (hol-LOH), "please" is *alstublieft* (AHL-stoo-bleeft), and "thank you" is *dank u wel* (dahnk yoo vehl).

In the Netherlands, you'll find basic Dutch fare, with plenty of cheese and bread. For some variety, try ethnic specialties from the country's former colonies such as Indonesia and Surinam. For dessert, sample a gooey, super-sweet *stroopwafel* (syrup waffle) or a dessert pancake *(pannenkoeken)*.

Amsterdam is Holland's highlight. While the freewheeling capital does have a quiet side, travelers who prefer small towns can sleep in nearby Haarlem (see page 398) and side-trip into the big city.

ACCESSIBILITY IN THE NETHERLANDS

Due to a strong commitment to equal rights, access for people with disabilities is generally good in the Netherlands.

The **Netherlands Board of Tourism** offers helpful resources. The Web site offers some accessibility information for people with disabilities, including a searchable database of hotels and other attractions (355 Lexington Avenue, 19th Floor, New York, NY 10017, tel. 888/GOHOLLAND, fax 212/370-9507, www.holland.com, info@goholland.com).

The **National Association for the Handicapped** is available to answer questions about accessibility in Holland (Mon–Fri 9:30–13:00, closed Sat–Sun, tel. 020/291-6600).

Mobility International Netherlands provides information on international tours and exchanges for people with disabilities (Heidestein 7, Driebergen, tel. 034/382-1795, fax 034/381-6776, jaberend@worldonline.nl).

AMSTERDAM

Amsterdam is a progressive way of life housed in Europe's most 17th-century city. Physically, it's built upon millions of pilings. But, more than that, it's built on good living, cozy cafés, great art, street-corner jazz, stately history, and a spirit of live and let live. It has more than 700,000 people and about as many bikes. It also has more canals than Venice and about as many tourists.

During its Golden Age in the 1600s, Amsterdam was the world's richest city, an international sea-trading port and the cradle of capitalism. Wealthy, democratic burghers built a planned city of canals lined with trees and townhouses topped with fancy gables. Immigrants, Jews, outcasts, and political rebels were drawn here by its tolerant atmosphere. Painters like young Rembrandt captured it on canvas. But all this history is only the beginning.

Approach the city not as a historian, but as an ethnologist observing a strange culture. Roll or stroll through any neighborhood and see things that are commonplace here but rarely found elsewhere. Carillon bells chime quaintly in neighborhoods selling sex as young professionals smoke pot with impunity next to old ladies in bonnets selling flowers. Observe the neighborhood's "social control," where a man feels safe in his home knowing he's being watched by the hookers next door.

The Dutch people are open, honest, and refreshingly blunt. As connoisseurs of world culture, they appreciate Rembrandt paintings, Indonesian food, and the latest French film—but with an unsnooty, blue-jeans attitude.

Be warned: Amsterdam, a bold experiment in freedom, may box your Puritan ears. Take it all in, then pause to watch the sun set—at 10:00 p.m.—and see the Golden Age reflected in a quiet canal.

ACCESSIBILITY IN AMSTERDAM

For travelers with limited mobility, Amsterdam is both challenging and rewarding. While locals have a friendly attitude toward people with disabilities, they also have great respect for the historical nature of their beautiful (and largely non-accessible) canalside buildings. The city has strict rules about making adaptations to monumental structures—useful for historical preservation, not so helpful for accessibility. The good news is that attitudes regarding accessibility are slowly improving.

ACCESSIBILITY CODES

These codes offer a quick overview of what to expect. If applicable, more specific details about the facility (e.g., exact number and height of steps, special instructions for gaining entry) are explained in each listing.

CODE	MEANING
AE	Accessible Entryway
AE+A	Accessible Entry with Assistance
AI	Accessible Interior
AI+A	Accessible Interior with Assistance
AT	Accessible Toilet
AT+A	Accessible Toilet with Assistance
AL	Accessible Lift (elevator)
AL+A	Accessible Lift with Assistance
AR	Accessible Hotel Room
AR+A	Accessible Hotel Room with Assistance
AB	Accessible Hotel Bathroom
AB+A	Accessible Hotel Bathroom with Assistance
♥	Caring, welcoming attitude regarding accessibility

For more detailed information, please refer to the full Accessibility Codes chart on page 4 of the Introduction. For more information on Accessibility Levels, see page 2.

The streets and sidewalks of Amsterdam have a certain freedom of movement: thousands of bikes mingling and merging with cars and pedestrians. Wheelchair users here are smart to adapt to the chaos—maneuvering their way through the streets, across trolley tracks, along the pink bike-only paths, and on the sidewalks. Stay alert and keep a steady line as you make your way through this bustling city.

Many Amsterdam sights are fully accessible to travelers with limited mobility (Level 1): Rijksmuseum, Van Gogh Museum, Heineken Brewery, Anne Frank House Museum (but not the house interior), Begijnhof, Amsterdam History Museum (except the carillon loft), Gassan Diamonds tour, Dutch Theater, Dutch Resistance Museum, and Tropical Museum.

Other sights are only moderately accessible (Level 2): Amsterdam Film Museum, Westerkerk (except for the tower), Holland Experience 3-D Movie, Jewish History Museum, De Hortus Botanical Garden, and Marijuana and Hemp Museum.

Unfortunately, these Amsterdam sights are not accessible to travelers with limited mobility (Level 3 or 4): the interior of the Anne Frank House, the loft at the Amsterdam History Museum, Rembrandt's House, and Amstelkring Museum.

ORIENTATION

(area code: 020)

Amsterdam's central train station, on the north edge of the city, is your starting point (TI and trams fanning out to all points). Damrak is the main street axis, connecting the station with Dam Square (people-watching and hangout center) and its Royal Palace. From this spine, the city spreads out like a fan, with 90 islands, hundreds of bridges, and a series of concentric canals (named "Prince's," "Gentleman's," and "King's") laid out in the 17th century, Holland's Golden Age. Amsterdam's major sights are within walking distance of Dam Square.

To the east of Damrak is the old part of the city (today's Red Light District); the west is the new part, with the Anne Frank House and the Jordaan neighborhood. Museums and Leidseplein nightlife cluster at the south edge of the city center.

Amsterdam

Arrival in Amsterdam

By Train: Amsterdam swings, and the hinge that connects it to the world is its perfectly central Centraal Station. Go out the door, and you're in the heart of the city (and its tram hub). Straight ahead is Damrak street, leading to Dam Square. With your back to the entrance of the station, the TI and GVB public-transit offices are just ahead and to your left. And on your right is a vast, multistoried bike garage.

Access: AE, AI, AL, AT, Level 1—Fully accessible. All train platforms have wheelchair-accessible elevators (except platform 15). There is a wheelchair-accessible toilet (€0.35) in the Balcon Restaurant, located on platform 2.

Contact the Disability Service Line in advance if you'll be arriving by train and want help making arrangements for assistance, including getting to a taxi to your destination (tel. 030/235-7822, daily 7:00–23:00, call at least 3 hrs ahead). This service is available at larger stations throughout the Netherlands.

By Plane: See "Transportation Connections," at the end of this chapter.

Tourist Information

There are four VVV offices ("VVV" is Dutch for TI—tourist information office; all are **AE, AI,** Level 2—Moderately accessible): inside the train station at track 2 (wheelchair-accessible elevator, press outside button to get staff's attention; Mon–Sat 8:00–20:00, Sun 9:00–17:00); in front of the train station (daily 9:00–17:00); on Leidsestraat (less crowded, daily 9:00–19:00); and at the airport (daily 7:00–22:00).

Avoid the crowded, inefficient offices if you can. For €0.60 a minute, you can save yourself a trip by calling the TI toll line at 0900-400-4040 (Mon–Fri 9:00–17:00). Also see www.amsterdam.nl (City of Amsterdam) and www.holland.com (Netherlands Board of Tourism). If you're staying in nearby Haarlem, use the helpful, friendly, and rarely crowded Haarlem TI (see page 398) to answer most of your Amsterdam questions and provide you with the brochures. Consider buying a city map (€2), *Day by Day* entertainment calendar (€1.50), and any of the (€1.50) walking-tour brochures ("Discovery Tour through the Center," "The Former Jewish Quarter," and "Walks through Jordaan"; these aren't designed for wheelchair users, but they contain interesting information).

At Amsterdam's Centraal Station, GWK Change has hotel reserva-

IF YOU NEED MEDICAL HELP

Your hotel is the best first point of contact. But if you need to get help on your own, Amsterdam's main hospital is the Academic Medical Center (Meibergdreef 9, tel. 020/566-9111). For emergencies, dial 112. The emergency pharmacy number is 020/212-1568. And you can reach the Netherlands Disabled Assistance at 030/291-7822 (daily 7:00–23:00).

tion windows whose clerks sell phone cards (local and international) and cheaper city maps (€1.60) and can answer basic tourist questions with shorter lines. They're located in the west tunnel at the right end of the station as you leave the platform (tel. 020/627-2731).

Don't use the TI (or GWK) to book a room; you'll pay €5 per person and your host loses 13 percent—meaning you'll likely pay a higher rate. The phone system is easy, everyone speaks English, and the listings in this book are a better value than the potluck booking you'd get from the TI.

Helpful Hints

Theft Alert: Tourists are considered green and rich, and the city has more than its share of hungry thieves—especially on trams and at the many hostels. Keep your valuables hidden by wearing a money belt or neck pouch.

Street Smarts: A *plein* is a square, *kerk* means church, *gracht* means canal, and most canals are lined by streets with the same name. When finding your way around town, beware of silent transportation (trams and bicycles). Slow walkers shouldn't walk on tram tracks or pink bicycle paths, but wheelchair users will find that bike paths are sometimes the only way to go.

Shop Hours: Many shops close all day Sunday and Monday morning.

Happy Birthday: On the Queen's Birthday on April 30, Amsterdam turns into a gigantic garage sale/street market.

Maps: The free and cheap tourist maps can be confusing. Consider paying a bit more for a top-notch map (about €2, sold at newsstands), such as the Carto Studio Centrumkaart Amsterdam or, better yet, the "Amsterdam: Go Where the Locals Go" map by Amsterdam Anything.

Telephones: Calling the United States from a phone booth is very cheap—you'll get about three minutes for a euro. Handy telephone cards (€5 or €10) are sold at TIs, the GVB public-transit office (in front of train station), tobacco shops, post offices, and train stations. Amsterdam's emergency telephone number is 112.

Accessible Toilets: Your best bets for wheelchair-accessible toilets are modern **restaurants** (for example, McDonald's south of Dam Square on the pedestrian Kalvestraat, or near the restaurant inside the Krasnapolsky Grand Hotel on Dam Square 9) or major **museums** (including the Anne Frank House, van Gogh Museum, Rijksmuseum, Stedelijk Modern Art Museum, and many more—as listed below).

Getting around Amsterdam

The helpful GVB transit-information office (**AE, AI,** Level 2— Moderately accessible) is in front of the train station and next to the TI. Its free multilingual *Public Transport Amsterdam Tourist Guide* includes a transit map and explains ticket options and tram connections to all the sights.

By Taxi

Amsterdam's taxis (**AE+A,** Level 2—Moderately accessible) are expensive (€2.50 drop and €1.50 for each kilometer). You can wave them down, find a rare taxi stand, or call one for a pick-up (tel. 020/677-7777). The driver will assist the wheelchair user and place the folded wheelchair in the trunk. While taxis are often not a good value, they can save time, energy, and frustration if you're unsure of your route.

By Bus, Tram, and Métro

Trams #2 and #5 travel the north-south axis from Centraal Station to Dam Square to Leidseplein to Museumplein. Tram #14 goes east-west (Westerkerk-Dam Square-Muntplein-Waterlooplein-Plantage). If you get lost in Amsterdam, 10 of the city's 17 trams take you back to the central train station.

The Métro (underground train) is used mostly for commuting to the suburbs, but it does connect Centraal Station with some

PRONUNCIATION OF PLACE NAMES

Dam (dahm) Amsterdam's main square
Damrak (DAHM-rock) Main street between train station and
  Dam Square
Spui (shpow, Both a street and square
  rhymes with cow)
Rokin (roh-KEEN) Street connecting Dam Square
  and Spui
Kalverstraat Pedestrian street off Dam Square
  (KAL-ver-strot)
Leidseplein Lively square
  (LIDE-zuh-pline)
Jordaan (zhor-DAHN) Neighborhood in southwest
  Amsterdam
Museumplein (myoo- Square with Rijks and Van Gogh
  ZAY-um-pline) museums
gracht (hhkkrockt, canal
  gutturally)
straat (strot) street
plein (pline) public square
huis (house) house
kerk (kerk) church

sights east of Damrak (Nieuwmarkt-Waterlooplein-Weesplein).

Access: The newest trams are wheelchair-accessible. The handy tram #5 has all accessible cars, and trams #7, #10, and #13 are phasing in the new cars. Older trams are not accessible—with entry steps and very narrow aisles, and also often a post at the entry. If your destination is not on an accessible tram route, and you use a wheelchair, take a taxi instead. Some, but not all, stops on the handy Nieuwmarkt-Waterlooplein-Weesplein line on the Métro are wheelchair-accessible; check with the GVB transit-information office (in front of train station) or ticket-seller before purchasing your ticket.

Tickets and passes: Individual **tickets** cost €1.70 and give you an hour on the buses, trams, and Métro system (pay as you board on trams

AMSTERDAM AT A GLANCE

▲▲▲**Rijksmuseum** Best collection anywhere of the Dutch masters: Rembrandt, Frans Hals, Jan Vermeer, and Jan Steen. **Hours:** Daily 10:00–17:00, sometimes 9:00–21:00. **Access:** Level 1—Fully accessible.

▲▲▲**Van Gogh Museum** 200 paintings by this angst-ridden artist. **Hours:** Daily 10:00–18:00, until 22:00 on Friday. **Access:** Level 1—Fully accessible.

▲▲▲**Anne Frank House** Young Anne's hideaway during the Nazi occupation. **Hours:** Daily April–Aug 9:00–21:00, Sept–March 9:00–19:00. **Access:** House is Level 4—Not accessible; adjacent museum is Level 1—Fully accessible.

▲▲**Dutch Resistance Museum** History of the Dutch struggle against the Nazis. **Hours:** Tue–Fri 10:00–17:00, Sat–Mon 12:00–17:00. **Access:** Level 1—Fully accessible.

▲▲**Amstelkring Museum** Catholic church hidden in the attic of a 17th-century merchant's house. **Hours:** Mon–Sat 10:00–17:00, Sun 13:00–17:00. **Access:** Level 4—Not accessible.

▲▲**Red-Light District** Women of the world's oldest profession on the job. **Hours:** Best between noon and evening—avoid late night. **Access:** Level 1—Fully accessible.

▲▲**Vondelpark** City park and concert venue. **Hours:** Always open. **Access:** Level 1—Fully accessible.

▲**History Museum** Shows city's growth from fishing village to trading capital to today. Includes some Rembrandts and a playable carillon. **Hours:** Mon–Fri 10:00–17:00, Sat–Sun 11:00–17:00.

Access: Museum is Level 1—Fully accessible; carillon loft is Level 4—Not accessible.

▲**Rembrandt's House** The master's reconstructed house, displaying his etchings. **Hours:** Mon–Sat 10:00–17:00, Sun 13:00–17:00. **Access:** Level 3—Minimally accessible.

▲**Dutch Theater** Moving memorial in former Jewish detention center. **Hours:** Daily 11:00–16:00. **Access:** Level 1—Fully accessible.

▲**Tropical Museum** Re-creations of tropical-life scenes. **Hours:** Daily 10:00–17:00. **Access:** Level 1—Fully accessible.

▲**Begijnhof** Quiet courtyard lined with picturesque houses. **Hours:** Daily 10:00–17:00. **Access:** Level 1—Fully accessible.

▲**Leidseplein** Lively square with cafés and street musicians. **Hours:** Always open, best on sunny afternoons. **Access:** Level 1—Fully accessible.

▲**Museumplein** Square with art museums, street musicians, crafts, and nearby diamond demos. **Hours:** Always open. **Access:** Level 1—Fully accessible.

▲**Diamonds** Tours at shops throughout the city. **Hours:** Generally daily 9:00–17:00. **Access:** Generally Level 1—Fully accessible.

▲**Heineken Brewery** Best beer tour in Europe. **Hours:** Tue–Sun 10:00–18:00, closed Mon. **Access:** Level 1—Fully accessible.

▲**Marijuana and Hemp Museum** All the dope, from history and science to memorabilia. **Hours:** Daily 11:00–22:00. **Access:** Level 2—Moderately accessible.

and buses; for the Métro, buy tickets from machines or ticket-sellers).

Strip tickets are cheaper than individual tickets. Any downtown bus or tram ride costs two strips (good for 1 hour of transfers). A card with 15 strips costs €6.50 and can be purchased at the GVB transit-information office, machines at the train station, post offices, airport, or tobacco shops throughout the country. Shorter strip tickets (2, 3, and 8 strips) are also sold on some buses and trams but are more expensive. Strip tickets are good on buses all over the Netherlands (the further you go, the more strips you'll use, such as 6 strips for Haarlem to the airport), and you can share them with your partner.

A €5.80 **Day Card** gives you unlimited transportation on the buses and Métro for a day in Amsterdam; you'll almost break even if you take three trips (valid until 6:00 the following morning; buy as you board or at the GVB transit-information office, which also sells a better-value 2-day version for €9; sometimes costs €0.50 more if you buy it on board).

The **Amsterdam Pass** offers unlimited use of the tram, bus, and Métro as well as free or discounted admissions to many city sights and boat rides (€26/24 hrs, €36/48 hrs, €46/72 hrs, sold at GVB transit-information office and TIs). If you'll be using the tram a lot and visiting lots of museums, this pass can save you about a third on your transportation and sightseeing. (Note that it doesn't include the Anne Frank House).

By Foot or Wheels
The longest roll or stroll a tourist would take is from the station to the Rijksmuseum (about 1.5 miles). Watch out for silent but potentially dangerous bikes and trams.

By Boat
Several companies do "hop-on, hop-off" tours with several stops to shuttle tourists between sights, but none is fully wheelchair-accessible. "Canal Bus" (€15 for all-day ticket), with only three steps to the boat, offers better access than "Museum Boat" (€13.50), with several steps to the dock and then more to the boat (both boats: every 30 min in summer, every 45 min off-season, departures 9:30–17:00, 7 stops, live quadrilingual guide). The sales booths in front of the Centraal Station (and the boats)

Amsterdam Sights

offer free brochures listing museum times and admission prices.

These boats are designed as transportation, but for wheelchair users and slow walkers, taxis and trams are more accessible and convenient. If you want a boat experience, the easier option is a nonstop tour, which gives more information, covers more distance, and costs less (see "Tours of Amsterdam," below).

By Car
Forget it—frustrating one-ways, terrible parking, and meter maids with a passion for "booting" cars wrongly parked.

Tours of Amsterdam
Canal-Boat Tours—These long, low, tourist-laden boats leave continually from several docks around the town for a relaxing, if uninspiring, one-hour quadrilingual introduction to the city. The **Rederij Noord-Zuid** (**AE, AI,** Level 1—Fully accessible) across from the Casino at Liedseplein has four fully wheelchair-accessible boats (call 2 days ahead to get schedule for accessible boats; €8.50, daily 10:00–21:00, Stadhouderskade 25, tel. 020/679-1370). Canal cruises also depart from the Rondvaart Kooij dock, near Spui, but those boats are only moderately accessible (**AE+A,** Level 2, must walk down 3 steps; €6.50). No fishing allowed—but bring your camera. Some prefer to cruise at night, when the bridges are illuminated.

Private Guide—Ab Walet is a likeable, hard-working, and knowledgeable local guide who enjoys personalizing tours for Americans interested in knowing his city better. He specializes in history and architecture and exudes a passion for Amsterdam (wheelchair riders and slow walkers welcome, €70/half day, €120/day, tel. 020/671-2588, mobile 06/2069-7882, abwalet@yahoo.com). Ab says that his favorite clients are elderly folks who just enjoy taking their time seeing the sights.

SIGHTS

Southwest Amsterdam
▲▲▲**Rijksmuseum**—Built to house the nation's great art, the Rijksmuseum owns several thousand paintings, including an incomparable collection of Dutch masters: Rembrandt, Vermeer, Hals, and Steen. The

Rijksmuseum

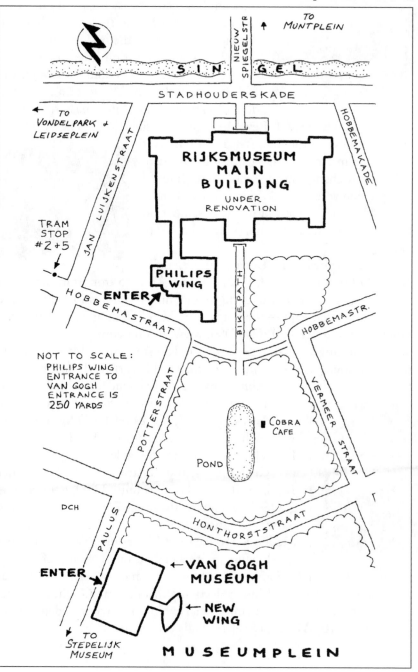

museum has made it easy for you to focus on the highlights, because they're all that's on display while most of the building undergoes several years of renovation (due to reopen in the summer of 2008). Wander through the Rijksmuseum's Philips Wing for a delightful dose of 17th-century Dutch masterpieces.

Access: AE, AI, AT, Level 1—Fully accessible. Wheelchair users can cut to the head of the line. Ask at the entry for assistance in finding the accessible entrance (which may change during renovation). Interior lifts provide access to all floors. A wheelchair-accessible toilet is located in the basement on the "A" entry side. Loaner wheelchairs are available.

Cost, Hours, and Location: €9, daily 10:00–17:00, sometimes 9:00–21:00, tram #2 or #5 from train station to Hobbemastraat, where the entrance of Philips Wing is located, on the south side of the Rijks—the part of the huge building nearest the Van Gogh Museum, tel. 020/674-7000, www.rijksmuseum.nl.

▲▲▲**Van Gogh Museum**—Near the Rijksmuseum, this remarkable museum showcases 200 paintings by the troubled artist whose art seemed to mirror his life. The exhibition hall (usually included with admission) features temporary exhibits of 1840–1920 art.

Access: AE, AI, AT, Level 1—Fully accessible. Wheelchair users can cut to the head of the line. Loaner wheelchairs are available.

Cost, Hours, and Location: €9, €2.50 if under 18, daily 10:00–18:00, Fri until 22:00, good audio-guide–€4, Paulus Potterstraat 7, tel. 020/570-5200, www.vangoghmuseum.nl.

Stedelijk Modern Art Museum—Next to the Van Gogh Museum, this place is fun, far-out, refreshing, and will reopen in 2005 after renovation. It has mostly post-1945 art but also a sometimes-outstanding collection of Monet, van Gogh, Cézanne, Picasso, and Chagall, and many special exhibitions (www.stedelijk.nl).

Access: AE, AI, AT, Level 1—Fully accessible.

Van Gogh Museum

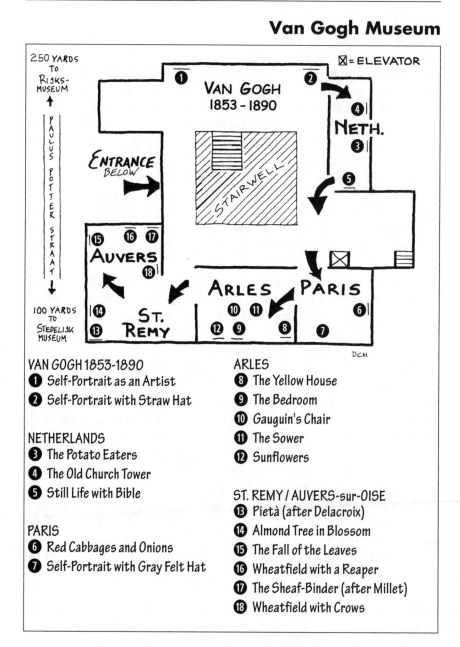

VAN GOGH 1853-1890
① Self-Portrait as an Artist
② Self-Portrait with Straw Hat

NETHERLANDS
③ The Potato Eaters
④ The Old Church Tower
⑤ Still Life with Bible

PARIS
⑥ Red Cabbages and Onions
⑦ Self-Portrait with Gray Felt Hat

ARLES
⑧ The Yellow House
⑨ The Bedroom
⑩ Gauguin's Chair
⑪ The Sower
⑫ Sunflowers

ST. REMY / AUVERS-sur-OISE
⑬ Pietà (after Delacroix)
⑭ Almond Tree in Blossom
⑮ The Fall of the Leaves
⑯ Wheatfield with a Reaper
⑰ The Sheaf-Binder (after Millet)
⑱ Wheatfield with Crows

▲**Museumplein**—Bordered by the Rijks, Van Gogh, and Stedelijk museums and the Concertgebouw (classical music hall), this fully accessible square is interesting even to art haters. Amsterdam's best acoustics are found underneath the Rijksmuseum, where street musicians perform everything from chamber music to Mongolian throat singing. Mimes, human statues, and crafts booths dot the square. Coster Diamonds offers tours on stone-cutting and polishing. Skateboarders careen across a concrete tube, while locals enjoy a park bench or a coffee at the Cobra café.

Access: Level 1—The square is fully accessible and has adapted toilets.

▲**Heineken Brewery**—The leading Dutch beer is no longer brewed here, but this old brewery now welcomes visitors to a slick and entertaining beer-appreciation experience. It's really the most enjoyable beer tour we've encountered in Europe. You'll learn as much as you want, marvel at the huge vats and towering ceilings, see videos, and go on rides. "What's it like to be a Heineken bottle and be filled with one of the best beers in the world? Try it for yourself." An important section recognizes a budding problem of our age—vital to people as well as beer—this planet's scarcity of clean water. With globalization, corporations are well on the way to owning the world's water supplies.

Access: AE, AI, AL, AT, Level 1—Fully accessible.

Cost, Hours, and Location: €7.50 for self-guided hour-long tour and 3 beers or soft drinks, must be over age 18, Tue–Sun 10:00–18:00, last entry 17:00, closed Mon, tram #16, #24, or #25 to Stadhouderskade 78, an easy roll or stroll from Rijksmuseum, tel. 020/523-9666.

▲**Leidseplein**—Brimming with cafés, this people-watching mecca is an impromptu stage for street artists, accordionists, jugglers, and unicyclists. Sunny afternoons are liveliest. The Boom Chicago theater fronts this square (see page 375). Roll or stroll down nearby Lange Leidsedwarsstraat (1 block north) for a taste-bud tour of ethnic eateries, from Greek to Indonesian.

Access: Level 1—Fully accessible. The sidewalks in this area are all wheelchair-accessible, and you'll also find accessible canal-boat tours (see "Tours of Amsterdam," page 344).

▲▲**Vondelpark**—This huge and lively city park is popular with the Dutch—families with little kids, romantic couples, strolling seniors, and hippies sharing blankets and beers. It's a popular venue for free summer concerts. On a sunny afternoon, it's a hedonistic scene that seems to say "parents...relax."

Access: Level 1—Fully accessible. Wheelchair users can travel on the bikeway or on the two dirt paths on either side of the bikeway.

Amsterdam Film Museum—It's actually not a museum but a movie theater. In its three 80-seat theaters, it shows several films a day, from small foreign productions to 70mm classics drawn from its massive archives.

Access: AE+A, AI+A, Level 2—Moderately accessible. Wheelchair users will find barriers both at the entry and inside the building.

Cost, Hours, and Location: €6.25, films always shown in the original language, often English subtitles, Vondelpark 3, tel. 020/589-1400, www.filmmuseum.nl.

Central Amsterdam, near Dam Square

▲▲▲**Anne Frank House**—A pilgrimage for many, this house offers a fascinating look at the hideaway of young Anne during the Nazi occupation of the Netherlands. Pick up the English pamphlet at the door. The exhibit offers thorough coverage of the Frank family, the diary, the stories of others who hid, and the Holocaust. In summer, skip the hour-long daytime lines by arriving after 18:00 (last entry is 20:30) and visit after dinner. For an interesting glimpse of Holland under the Nazis, rent the powerful movie *Soldier of Orange* before you leave home.

ANNE FRANK TAGEBUCH

Access: House is Level 4—Not accessible, with many stairs and tight hallways; adjacent museum is **AE, AI, AT,** Level 1—Fully accessible. In the museum, wheelchair users and other travelers with limited mobility can watch a "virtual" tour of the house. Ask for entry at the ticket booth.

Cost, Hours, and Location: €7.50, April–Aug daily 9:00–21:00, Sept–March daily 9:00–19:00, Prinsengracht 267, near Westerkerk, tel. 020/556-7100, www.annefrank.nl.

Central Amsterdam

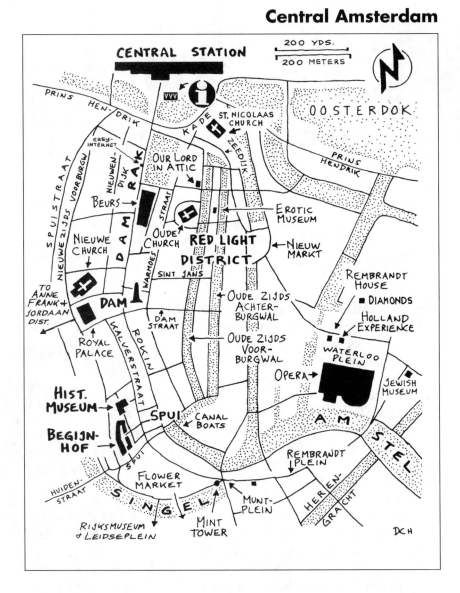

Westerkerk—Near the Anne Frank House, this landmark church (generally open April–Sept 11:00–15:00) has a barren interior, Rembrandt's body buried somewhere under the pews, and Amsterdam's tallest steeple. The non-accessible tower is open by tour only. The mandatory €3 guided tour (in English and Dutch) tells of the church and its carillon and takes you up to see the view (45 min, departures on the hour, April–Sept Mon–Sat 10:00–17:00, last trip at 17:00, closed Sun and in Oct–March).

Access: AE, AI, Level 2—The church is accessible except for the tower.

▲**Begijnhof**—Entering this tiny, idyllic courtyard in the city center, you escape into the charm of old Amsterdam. Notice house #34, a 500-year-old wooden structure (rare since repeated fires taught city fathers a trick called brick). Peek into the hidden Catholic church, dating from the time when post-Reformation Dutch Catholics couldn't worship in public. It's opposite the English Reformed church, where the Pilgrims worshiped while waiting for their voyage to the New World (marked by a plaque near the door; often closed). Be considerate of the people who live around the courtyard.

Access: AE, AI, Level 1—Fully accessible. The entrance on the east side of the courtyard has no steps. The courtyard has fully accessible pathways. The hidden Catholic church (**AE+A, AI,** Level 2—Moderately accessible) has large doors and two 2" steps, one on either side of the landing.

Cost, Hours, and Location: Free, daily 10:00–17:00, on Begijnensteeg lane, just off Kalverstraat between #130 and #132, pick up flier at office near entrance, open weekdays 10:00–16:00.

▲**Amsterdam History Museum**—Follow the city's growth from fishing village to world trader to hippie haven. This creative and hardworking museum features Rembrandt's paintings, fine English descriptions, and a (non-accessible) carillon loft. The loft comes with push-button recordings of the town bell tower's greatest hits and a self-serve carillon "keyboard" that lets visitors ring a few bells. The museum's free pedestrian corridor—lined with old-time group portraits—is a powerful teaser.

Access: Museum is **AE, AI, AT,** Level 1—Fully accessible. The loft is Level 4—Not accessible. The museum has wheelchair-accessible elevators (that do not go to the loft) and an adapted toilet (near David and Goliath café). Loaner wheelchairs are available.

Cost, Hours, and Location: €6.50, Mon–Fri 10:00–17:00, Sat–Sun 11:00–17:00, good-value restaurant, next to Begijnhof, Kalverstraat 92, tel. 020/523-1822.

Southeast Amsterdam

To reach these sights from the train station, take tram #9, #14, or #20 (all **AE+A,** Level 2—Moderately accessible).

Waterlooplein Flea Market—For more than a hundred years, the Jewish Quarter flea market has raged daily except Sunday on Waterlooplein (behind the Rembrandt House). The long, narrow park-like square is filled with stalls selling cheap clothes, hippie stuff, old records, tourist knickknacks, and garage-sale junk.

▲**Rembrandt's House**—This place offers a 10-minute introductory video (Dutch and English showings alternate); Rembrandt's reconstructed house (filled with exactly what his bankruptcy inventory of 1656 said he owned); a reconstructed studio; a printer explaining the etching process; then, for the finale, several rooms of original Rembrandt etchings. You'll find no paintings, but the etchings are marvelous and well described.

Access: AE, AT, Level 3—Minimally accessible. The house itself is not accessible, but the video and gallery of etchings are. There is an adapted toilet.

Cost, Hours, and Location: €7, half-price for wheelchair users, see combo-ticket deal in Holland Experience listing below, Mon–Sat 10:00–17:00, Sun 13:00–17:00, Jodenbreestraat 4, tel. 020/520-0400.

Holland Experience—Bragging "Experience Holland in 30 minutes," this 3-D movie takes you traveling with three clowns through an idealized montage of Dutch clichés. There are no words but lots of images and special effects as you rock with the boat and get spritzed with perfume while viewing the tulips.

Access: AE, AI, Level 2—Moderately accessible. There is no accessible toilet.

Cost, Hours, and Location: €8.50, €2 discount with this book, or show this book and get €1.25 off the €13.50 combo-ticket with Rembrandt's House, daily 10:00–18:00 on the hour, adjacent to Rembrandt's house at Jodenbreestraat 8, tel. 020/422-2233.

▲**Diamonds**—Many shops in the "city of diamonds" offer tours. These tours come with two parts: a chance to see experts behind magnifying glasses polishing the facets of precious diamonds, followed by a visit to an intimate sales room to see (and perhaps buy) a tiny, shiny souvenir. The handy, professional Gassan Diamonds facility fills a huge warehouse a block from Rembrandt's House. You'll get a security sticker and join a

Southeast Amsterdam

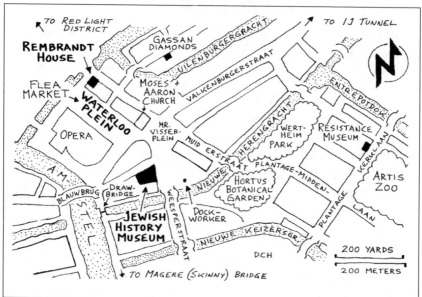

tour to see a polisher at work and hear a general explanation of the process (free, 15 min). Then you'll have an opportunity to have color and clarity described and illustrated with diamonds ranging in value from $100 to $30,000. Get a free cup of coffee from the café.

Access: AE, AI, AL, AT, Level 1—Fully accessible.

Cost, Hours, and Location: Free tours daily 9:00–17:00, Nieuwe Uilenburgerstraat 173, tel. 020/622-5333, www.gassandiamonds.com.

Jewish History Museum—Four historic synagogues have been joined by steel and glass to make one modern complex telling the story of the Jews in Amsterdam through the centuries.

Access: AE+A, AI, AT, Level 2—Moderately Accessible. Wheelchair users enter through a side door; ring the bell to gain entrance.

Cost, Hours, and Location: €6.50, daily 11:00–17:00, good and accessible kosher café, Jonas Daniel Meijerplein 2, tel. 020/626-9945.

De Hortus Botanical Garden—This is a unique oasis of tranquility within the city (no mobile phones allowed because "our collection of plants is a precious community, treat it with respect"). One of the oldest botanical gardens in the world, it dates from 1638, when medicinal herbs

JEWS IN AMSTERDAM

In 1940, one in ten Amsterdammers was Jewish, and most lived in the neighborhood behind Waterlooplein. Jewish traders had long been welcome in a city that cared more about business than religion. In the late 1500s, many Sephardic Jews from Spain and Portugal immigrated, fleeing persecution. (The philosopher Baruch Spinoza's ancestors were among them.) In the 1630s, Yiddish-speaking Eastern European Jews (Ashkenazi) poured in. By 1700, the Jewish Quarter was a bustling, exotic, multicultural world, with more people speaking Portuguese, German, and Yiddish than Dutch.

Jews were not first-class citizens. They needed the city's permission to settle there, and they couldn't hold public office (but then neither could Catholics under Calvinist rule). Still, the Jewish Quarter was not a ghetto (enforced segregation), there were no special taxes, and cosmopolitan Amsterdam was well acquainted with all types of beliefs and customs.

In 1796, Jews were given full citizenship. In exchange, they were required to learn the Dutch language and submit to the city's legal system...and the Jewish culture began assimilating into the Dutch.

In 1940, Nazi Germany occupied the Netherlands. On February 22, 1941, the Nazis began rounding up Jews—herding hundreds of them to Jonas Daniel Meijerplein to be shipped to extermination camps in Eastern Europe. The citizens responded with a general strike that shut down the entire city, a heroic gesture honored today with a statue of a striking dockworker on Jonas Daniel Meijerplein. Despite the strike, the roundups continued. By war's end, more than 100,000 of the city's 130,000 Jews had died.

Today, about 25,000 Jews live in Amsterdam, and the Jewish Quarter has blended in with the modern city.

were grown here. Today, among its 6,000 different kinds of plants—most of which were collected by the Dutch East India Company in the 17th and 18th centuries—you'll find medicinal herbs, cacti, several greenhouses (one with a fluttery butterfly house—a hit with kids), and a tropical palm house. Much of it is thoughtfully described in English: "A Dutch merchant snuck a coffee plant out of Ethiopia, which ended up in this garden in 1706. This first coffee plant in Europe was the literal granddaddy of the coffee cultures of Brazil—long the world's biggest coffee producer."

Access: AE, AI+A, AT, Level 2—Moderately accessible. Loaner wheelchairs are available. While the "Museum Maps" rate the garden as wheelchair-accessible, the stone path makes it a challenge, especially in the spots where the stones are at their deepest. They do have a wheelchair-accessible toilet.

Cost, Hours, and Location: €6, Mon–Fri 9:00–17:00, Sat–Sun 11:00–17:00, until 16:00 in winter, Plantage Middenlaan 2A, tel. 020/625-9021.

▲Dutch Theater (Hollandsche Schouwburg)—This is a moving memorial. Once a lively theater in the Jewish neighborhood, this was used as an assembly hall for local Jews destined for Nazi concentration camps. On the wall, 6,700 family names pay tribute to the 104,000 Jews deported and killed by the Nazis. Upstairs is a small history exhibit on local Jews during World War II. The ruined theater actually offers little to see but plenty to think about—notice the hopeful messages that visiting school groups attach to the wooden tulips.

Access: AE, AI, AT, Level 1—Fully accessible. Enter to the left of the main door (ring bell to gain entry). Loaner wheelchairs are available.

Cost, Hours, and Location: Free, daily 11:00–16:00, Plantage Middenlaan 24, tel. 020/626-9945.

▲▲Dutch Resistance Museum (Verzetsmuseum)—This is an impressive look at how the Dutch resisted their Nazi occupiers from 1940 to 1945. You'll see propaganda movie clips, study forged ID cards under a magnifying glass, and read of ingenious, clever, and courageous efforts to hide local Jews from the Germans. And at the end of the war, Nazi helmets were turned into bedpans.

Access: AE, AI, AT, Level 1—Fully accessible, including an adapted toilet. If you need a loaner wheelchair, reserve it in advance.

Cost, Hours, and Location: €5, free for a wheelchair user's companion, but a solo wheelchair user pays; Tue–Fri 10:00–17:00, Sat–Mon 12:00–17:00, closed April 30, well described in English, recommended accessible café adjacent, tram #9 (**AE+A,** Level 2—Moderately accessible) from station, Plantage Kerklaan 61, tel. 020/620-2535. Amsterdam's famous zoo is just across the street.

▲**Tropical Museum (Tropenmuseum)**—As close to the Third World as you'll get without lots of vaccinations, this imaginative museum offers wonderful re-creations of tropical-life scenes and explanations of Third World problems. Ride the elevator to the top floor, and work your way down through this immense collection opened in 1926 to give the Dutch a peek at their vast colonial holdings. Don't miss the display case allowing you to see and hear the world's most exotic musical instruments. The accessible Ekeko cafeteria serves tropical food.

Access: AE, AI, AT, Level 1—Fully accessible, including an adapted toilet. Loaner wheelchairs are available.

Cost, Hours, and Location: €7, daily 10:00–17:00, tram #9 (**AE+A,** Level 2—Moderately accessible) to Linnaeusstraat 2, tel. 020/568-8215.

Red Light District

▲▲**Amstelkring Museum (Our Lord in the Attic)**—Near the train station in the Red Light District, you'll find a hidden Catholic church filling the attic of a 17th-century merchant's townhouse.

Access: Level 4—Not accessible. The many stairs leading to this attic make it accessible only to energetic slow walkers.

Cost, Hours, and Location: €4.50, Mon–Sat 10:00–17:00, Sun 13:00–17:00, Oudezijds Voorburgwal 40, tel. 020/624-6604.

Red Light District—Europe's most touristed ladies of the night shiver and shimmy as they have since 1700 in 450 display-case windows between the Oudezijds Achterburgwal and Oudezijds Voorburgwal, surrounding the Oude Kerk (Old Church). Drunks and druggies make the streets uncomfortable for tourists late at night, but it's a fascinating place to roll or stroll at any other time after noon.

The neighborhood, one of Amsterdam's oldest, has had prostitutes since 1200. Prostitution is entirely legal here and women are generally entrepreneurs, renting a space and running their own businesses. Popular prostitutes net around €300 a day (S&F, €25–50) and fill out tax returns.

Access: The Red Light District neighborhood is fully accessible.

Sex Museums—Amsterdam has two sex museums: one in the Red Light District and one a block in front of the train station on Damrak. While visiting one can be called sightseeing, visiting both is hard to explain. Here's a comparison:

The **Erotic Museum in the Red Light District** is less offensive, with five floors relying heavily on badly-dressed dummies acting out the roles that women of the neighborhood play. It also has a lot of uninspired paintings, videos, old photos, and sculpture (**AE, AI,** Level 2—Moderately accessible; €5, daily 11:00–24:00, along the canal at Oudezijds Achterburgwal 54, tel. 020/624-7303).

The **Damrak sex museum** goes deeper, telling the story of pornography from Roman times through 1960. Every sexual deviation is uncovered in its various displays, and the nude and pornographic art is a cut above that of the other sex museum. Also interesting are the early French pornographic photos and memorabilia from Europe, India, and Asia. You'll find a Marilyn Monroe tribute and some S&M displays, too. The museum's first floor is moderately accessible (**AE, AI**), but the upper level is not (€2.50, daily 10:00–23:30, Damrak 18, a block in front of train station).

▲**Hash, Marijuana, and Hemp Museum**—This is a collection of dope facts, history, science, and memorabilia. While small, it has a shocker finale: the high-tech grow room in which dozens of varieties of marijuana are cultivated in optimal hydroponic (among other) environments. Some plants stand five feet tall and shine under the intense grow lamps. The view is actually through glass walls into the neighboring "Sensi Seed Bank" Grow Shop,  which sells carefully cultivated seeds and all the gear needed to grow them. It's an interesting neighborhood.

Access: AE, AI, Level 2—Moderately accessible. There is no accessible toilet.

Cost, Hours, and Location: €6, daily 11:00–22:00, Oudezijds Achterburgwal 148, tel. 020/623-5961.

The **Cannabis College Foundation,** "dedicated to ending the global war against the cannabis plant through public education," is next door at #124.

Access: Level 3—Minimally accessible. There are seven 8" entry steps and no accessible toilets.

Cost and Hours: Free, daily 11:00–19:00, tel. 020/423-4420, www.cannabiscollege.com.

SLEEPING

Greeting a new day overlooking a leafy canalside scene—graceful bridges, historic gables, and bikes clattering on cobbles—is a fun part of experiencing Amsterdam. But Amsterdam is a tough city for budget accommodations, and any room under €140 will have its rough edges. Amsterdam has few hotels that combine accessibility and affordability; we've listed the best values here. We've also listed some fully accessible splurges. Accessible hotels that are central and near the canals have their challenges, but they also contribute to the city's Old World character.

Amsterdam is jammed during convention periods, the Queen's Birthday (April 30), and on summer weekends. Many hotels will not take weekend bookings for people staying less than three nights.

Parking in Amsterdam is even worse than driving. You'll pay €32 a day to park safely in a garage—which can be blocks from your hotel.

If you'd rather trade big-city action for small-town coziness, consider sleeping in Haarlem, half an hour away by train (see page 398).

Near the Train Station, Rembrandt Square, and the Jordaan
Level 1—Fully Accessible
Albus Grand Hotel (AE, AI, AL, AR, AB, ♥) is a modern yet warm and elegant three-star hotel (with four-star amenities) that offers a friendly welcome and excellent value. It's centrally located just off Rembrandt Square near the Flower Market (Db-€135–180 depending

Amsterdam Hotels

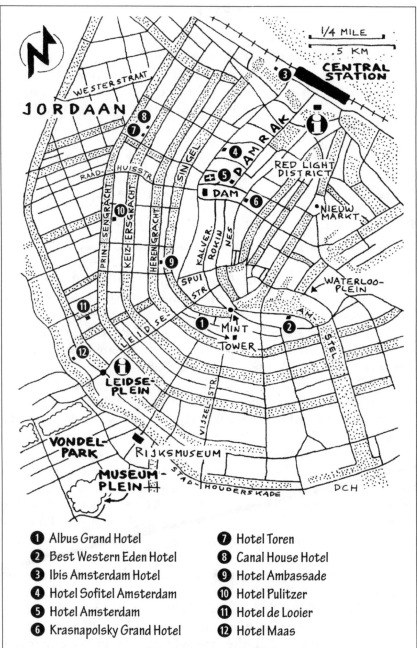

1. Albus Grand Hotel
2. Best Western Eden Hotel
3. Ibis Amsterdam Hotel
4. Hotel Sofitel Amsterdam
5. Hotel Amsterdam
6. Krasnapolsky Grand Hotel
7. Hotel Toren
8. Canal House Hotel
9. Hotel Ambassade
10. Hotel Pulitzer
11. Hotel de Looier
12. Hotel Maas

SLEEP CODE

(€1 = about $1.15, country code: 31, area code: 020)
Sleep Code: **S** = Single, **D** = Double/Twin, **T** = Triple, **Q** = Quad,
b = bathroom, **s** = shower only, **no CC** = Credit Cards not accepted. Nearly everyone speaks English in the Netherlands, and prices include breakfast unless noted. Credit cards are accepted unless otherwise noted.

Please see "Accessibility Codes" sidebar on page 333 of this chapter for a quick guide to codes. For a more detailed explanation of Accessibility Levels and Codes, please see page 2 of the Introduction.

on season, Vijzelstraat 49, tel. 020/530-6215, fax 020/530-6299, www .albusgrandhotel.com, info@albusgrandhotel.com). There are several adapted rooms for full accessibility.

Best Western Eden Hotel (AE, AI, AL, AR, AB) is close to the Flower Market on a canal near Rembrandt Square (Db-€135–180 depending on season, Amstel 144, tel. 020/530-7888, fax 020/624-2946, res.eden@hotelgroup.com). There is one fully adapted room and five other ground-floor rooms that are suitable for wheelchair users.

Ibis Amsterdam Hotel (AE, AI, AL, AR, AB) is a modern and efficient 187-room place, towering over the train station and a multistory bicycle garage. It offers a central location, comfort, and good value without a hint of charm (Db-€163, family-€189, €5 extra on weekends, skip breakfast and save €13 per person, book long in advance, air-con, smoke-free rooms on request, Stationsplein 49, tel. 020/638-9999, fax 020/620-0156, www.ibishotel.com, h1556-fo@accor-hotels.com). The hotel has one fully adapted room (#701), including an adapted bathroom and shower.

Hotel Sofitel Amsterdam (AE, AI, AL, AR, AB) is an upscale modern chain hotel tastefully set in a restored 17th-century building just off Dam Square. Everything is first class—including the prices. They have an excellent central location, a restaurant and bar, an adapted room for full accessibility, and all the top-end amenities to make your stay

comfortable (Db-€255–305 depending on season, Nieuwezijds Voorburgwal 67, tel. 020/627-5900, fax 020/623-8932, h1159@accor
-hotels.com).

Level 2—Moderately Accessible
Hotel Amsterdam (AE, AI, AL, AR+A, ♥), on Dam Square, is large and
well-maintained, combining modern comforts with a historic location
(Db-€185–210 depending on season, Damrak 93-94, tel. 020/555-0666,
fax 020/620-4716, www.hotelamsterdam.nl, info@hotelamsterdam.nl).
Even though the rooms have not been adapted, they are suitable for wheelchair users. The hotel has hosted wheelchair users in the past, and the staff
is eager to offer assistance. The hotel also has a fully accessible restaurant.

Between Dam Square and
the Anne Frank House
Level 1—Fully Accessible
Krasnapolsky Grand Hotel (AE, AI, AL, AR, AB)—not to be confused
with the Grand Hotel next door—is more than 130 years old but has
been modernized to include one wheelchair-accessible room (flexible
rates, usually Db-€175, Dam 9, tel. 020/554-9111, fax 020/622-8607,
www.nh-hotels.com, nhkrasnapolsky@nh-hotels.nl). They welcome
wheelchair users, and the staff is ready to assist as needed. The adapted
room includes a fully wheelchair-accessible toilet and shower. The hotel
also has two wheelchair-accessible restaurants, with an accessible toilet
nearby.

Level 3—Minimally Accessible
Hotel Toren (AE+A, AI+A—even the elevator leads to stairs on each
floor) is a chandeliered historic mansion in a pleasant, quiet canalside
setting in downtown Amsterdam. This splurge hotel, run by Eric and
Petra Toren, is classy yet friendly and two blocks northeast of the Anne
Frank House. The least expensive four-star hotel in town, it's a great
value (Sb-€100–120, Db-€125–160, deluxe canalside Db-€215, Tb-
€160–185, "bridal suites" for €205–230, prices vary with season, 10 percent discount for cash with this book, breakfast buffet-€12, air-con,
Keizersgracht 164, tel. 020/622-6352, fax 020/626-9705, www.toren.nl).
Bernarda, who runs the bar, is an excellent source of local advice.

Canal House Hotel (AE+A, AI+A), a few doors down, offers a rich 17th-century atmosphere. Above generous and elegant public spaces, tangled antique-filled halls lead to 26 spacious, tastefully appointed rooms. Evenings come with candlelight and soft music (Sb-€140, Db-€150, big Db-€190, elevator, Keizersgracht 148, tel. 020/622-5182, fax 020/624-1317, www.canalhouse.nl, info@canalhouse.nl).

Hotel Ambassade (AE+A, AI+A)—lacing together 60 rooms in 10 houses—is an amazingly elegant and fresh place, sitting aristocratically but daintily on the Herengracht. Its public rooms are palatial, with a library and plush antique furnishings. A family-run hotel this size is unusual (Sb-€158, Db-€188, Db suite-€260, Tb-€220, extra bed-€30, 5 percent tax, breakfast-€15—and actually worth it—elevator, free Internet access, Herengracht 341, tel. 020/555-0222, www.ambassade-hotel.nl, info@ambassade-hotel.nl).

In the Jordaan
Level 2—Moderately Accessible
Hotel Pulitzer (AE, AI, AL, AR+A, ♥) is a five-star splurge, a refined and traditional blend of old and new. The hotel has connected and restored several 17th- and 18th-century canal houses into a hotel, restaurant, bar, business center, and art gallery—pure luxury set on the Prinsengracht canal in Jordaan (Db-€275–450 depending on season, Prinsengracht 315-331, tel. 020/523-5235, fax 020/627-6753, www .sheraton.com/pulitzer, res100_amsterdam@starwoodhotels.com). The elevators will take an average-sized wheelchair, the lobby has an adapted toilet, and the rooms are suitable (but not adapted) for wheelchair users.

Level 3—Minimally Accessible
Hotel de Looier (AE, AI, AL) is a place with three fading stars in the Jordaan a five-minute roll or stroll from the Leidseplein (Db-€110–130 depending on season, Derde Looiersdwarsstraat 75, tel. 020/625-1855, fax 020/627-5320). The bedrooms and bathrooms are not adapted, but are suitable for some. There is an accessible restaurant and bar in the lobby.

In the Spui and Leidseplein Neighborhoods

The area around Amsterdam's rip-roaring nightlife center (Leidseplein) is colorful, comfortable, and convenient. These places are within a block or two of Leidseplein but in generally quiet and characteristic settings.

Level 1—Fully Accessible

Hotel Maas (AE, AI, AL, AR, AB) is a big, quiet, and stiffly hotelesque place. Though it's on a busy street rather than a canal, it's a handy option (S-€80, Sb-€105, one D-€95, Db-€145, suite-€205, prices vary with view and room size, extra person-€20, hearty breakfast, elevator, tram #1, #2, or accessible #5 from station; Leidsekade 91, tel. 020/623-3868, fax 020/622-2613, www.hotelmaas.nl, info@hotelmaas.nl). They have a few adapted rooms and are welcoming to wheelchair users.

EATING

Traditional Dutch food is basic and hearty, with lots of bread, cheese, soups, and fish. Lunch and dinner are served at American times (roughly 12:00–14:00 and 18:00–21:00). Expect tobacco smoke—in bars, cafés, restaurants, everywhere. You don't have to like it, but expect it.

Waiters constantly say *"Alstublieft"* (AHL-stoo-bleeft). It's a catch-all polite word meaning "please," "here's your order," "enjoy," and "you're welcome." You can respond with a thank you by saying *"Dank u wel"* (dahnk yoo vehl).

Dutch treats include cheese, pancakes *(pannenkoeken),* gin *(jenever),* light pilsner-type beer, and "syrup waffles" *(stroopwafel).*

Experiences you owe your tongue in Holland: trying a raw herring (outdoor herring stands are all over), lingering over coffee in a "brown café," sipping an old *jenever* with a new friend, and consuming an Indonesian feast—a *rijsttafel.*

We've included accessibility information for each place. Unless otherwise noted (by **AT** or **AT+A**), these restaurants do *not* have accessible toilets.

Amsterdam Restaurants and Coffeeshops

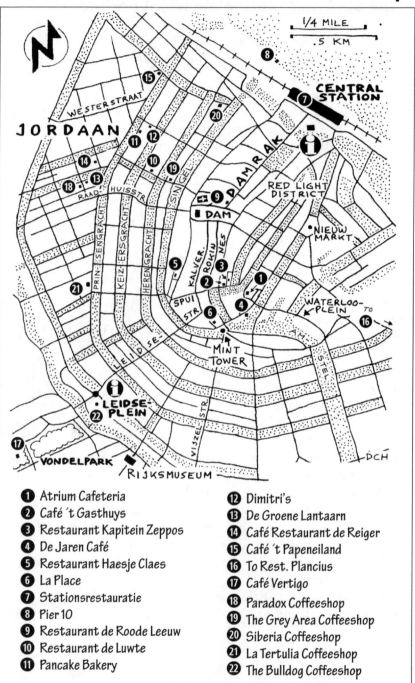

1. Atrium Cafeteria
2. Café 't Gasthuys
3. Restaurant Kapitein Zeppos
4. De Jaren Café
5. Restaurant Haesje Claes
6. La Place
7. Stationsrestauratie
8. Pier 10
9. Restaurant de Roode Leeuw
10. Restaurant de Luwte
11. Pancake Bakery
12. Dimitri's
13. De Groene Lantaarn
14. Café Restaurant de Reiger
15. Café 't Papeneiland
16. To Rest. Plancius
17. Café Vertigo
18. Paradox Coffeeshop
19. The Grey Area Coffeeshop
20. Siberia Coffeeshop
21. La Tertulia Coffeeshop
22. The Bulldog Coffeeshop

Budget Tips: Get a sandwich to go, and have a canalside picnic. Sandwiches *(broodjes)* of delicious cheese on fresh bread are cheap at snack bars, delis, and *broodje* restaurants. Ethnic fast-food stands abound, offering a variety of meats wrapped in pita bread. Easy to buy at grocery stores, yogurt in the Netherlands (and throughout Northern Europe) is delicious and drinkable right out of its plastic container.

Types of Eateries

Any place labeled *restaurant* will serve full meals for lunch or dinner. But there are other places to fill the tank.

An *eetcafé* is a simple restaurant serving basic soups, salads, sandwiches, and traditional meat-and-potatoes meals in a generally comfortable but no-nonsense setting.

A *salon de thé* serves tea and coffee, yes, but also croissants, pastries, and sandwiches for a light brunch, lunch, or afternoon snack.

Cafés are all-purpose establishments, serving light meals at meal times and coffee, drinks, and light snacks the rest of the day and night. *Bruin* cafés ("brown cafés," named for their nicotine-stained walls) are usually a little more bar-like, with dimmer lighting, wood paneling, and more tobacco smoke.

A *proeflokal* is a bar (with light snacks) for tasting wine, spirits, or beer.

Coffeeshop is the code word for an establishment where cannabis is sold and consumed, though most also offer drinks and munchies, too.

There's no shortage of stand-up, take-out places serving fast-food, sandwiches, and all kinds of quick ethnic fare.

No matter what the type of establishment, it will probably be *gezellig*—a much-prized Dutch virtue, meaning an atmosphere of relaxed coziness.

Tipping

The Dutch are easygoing. Pay as you go or pay after? Usually it's your choice. Tip or don't tip? Your call. Wait for table service or order at the bar? Whatever you do, you won't be scolded for your *faux pas,* as you might be in France. Dutch establishments are *gezellig.* Still, here are some guidelines:

Tipping is not necessary in restaurants (15 percent service is usually already included in the menu price), but a tip of about 5 percent is a nice reward for good service. In bars, rounding up to the next euro ("keep the change") is appropriate if you get table service rather than order at the bar.

When ordering drinks in a café or bar, you can just pay as you go (especially if the bar is crowded), or wait until the end to settle up, as many locals do. If you get table service, take the cue from your waiter.

Cafés with outdoor tables generally do not charge more if you eat outside (unlike in France or Italy).

Typical Meals

Breakfast: Breakfasts are big by Continental standards—bread, meat, cheese, and maybe an egg or omelet. Hotels generally put out a buffet spread including juice and cereal.

Lunch: Simple sandwiches are called *broodjes* (most commonly made with cheese and/or ham). An open-face sandwich of ham and cheese topped with two fried eggs is an *uitsmijter* (OUTS-mi-ter). Soup is popular for lunch.

Dinner: It's the biggest meal of the day, consisting of meat or seafood with boiled potatoes, cooked vegetables, and a salad. Hearty stews are served in winter. These days, many people eat more vegetarian fare.

Sweets: Try *poffertjes* (small sugared doughnuts without holes), *pannenkoeken* (pancakes with fruit and cream), *stroopwafels* (syrup waffles), and *appelgebak* (apple pie).

Local Specialties

Cheeses: Edam (covered with red wax) or Gouda (HOW-dah). Gouda can be young or old: *jong* is mellow, and *oude* is salty, crumbly, and strong, sometimes seasoned with cumin or cloves.

French Fries: Sold at stands and commonly served with mayonnaise (ketchup and curry sauce are often available) on a paper tray or in a newspaper cone. *Vlaamse frites* are made from whole potatoes, not pulp.

Haring **(herring):** Fresh raw herring, marinated or salted, sold at stands and often served with onions or pickles, sometimes with sour cream on a thick, soft, white bun.

Hutspot: Hearty meat stew with mashed potatoes, onions, and carrots, especially popular on winter days.

Kroketten **(croquettes):** Log-shaped rolls of meats and vegetables (kind of like corn dogs) breaded and deep-fried, sold at delis. Look for *bitterballen* (meatballs), *frikandelen* (sausage), or *vlammetjes* (spring rolls).

Pannenkoeken: Either sweet dessert pancakes or crêpe-like dinner pancakes.

Ethnic Foods

If you're not in the mood for meat and potatoes, sample some of Amsterdam's abundant ethnic offerings.

Indonesian (Indisch): The tastiest "Dutch" food is Indonesian, from the Netherlands' former colony. Find any Indisch restaurant and experience a *rijsttafel* (rice table). With as many as 30 spicy dishes and a big bowl of rice (or noodles), a *rijsttafel* can be split and still fill two hungry tourists. *Nasi rames* is a cheaper, smaller version of a *rijsttafel*. Another popular dish is *bami goreng*—stir-fried noodles served with meat, vegetables, and *rijsttafel* items. *Nasi goreng* is like *bami* but comes with fried rice. *Sate* is skewered meat and *gado-gado* consists of steamed vegetables and hard-boiled eggs with peanut sauce. Among the most common sauces are peanut, red chili *(sambal)*, and dark soy.

Middle Eastern: Try a *shoarma* (roasted lamb with garlic in pita bread, served with bowls of different sauces), falafel (fried chickpea balls in pita bread), gyros, or *doner kebab* (Turkish gyro).

Surinamese (Surinaamse): Surinamese cuisine is a mix of Caribbean and Indonesian influences, featuring *roti* (spiced chicken wrapped in a tortilla) and rice (white or fried) served with meats in sauces (curry and spices). Why Surinamese food in Amsterdam? In 1667, Holland traded New York City ("New Amsterdam") to Britain in exchange for the small country of Surinam (which borders Guyana on the northeast coast of South America). For the next three centuries, Surinam (renamed Dutch Guyana) was a Dutch colony, which is why it has indigenous Indians, Creoles, and Indonesian immigrants who all speak Dutch. When Surinam gained independence in 1975, 100,000 Surinamese emigrated to Amsterdam, sparking a rash of Surinamese fast-food outlets.

Drinks

Beer: Order "a beer" and you'll get a *pils*, a light lager/pilsner-type beer in a 10-ounce glass with a thick head leveled off with a stick. (Typical brands are Heineken, Grolsch, Oranjeboom, and Amstel.) A common tap beer is Palm Speciale, an amber ale served in a stemmed, wide-mouth glass. Belgian beers are popular, always available in bottles and sometimes on tap. *Witte* (white) beer is light-colored and summery, sometimes served with a lemon slice (it's like American Hefeweizen but yeastier).

Jenever: This is Dutch gin made from juniper berries. *Jong* (young) is sharper; *oude* (old) is mellow. Served chilled, *jenever* (yah-NAY-ver) is meant to be chugged with a *pils* chaser (this combination is called a *kopstoot*—head-butt). While cheese gets harder and sharper with age, *jenever* grows smooth and soft. Old *jenever* is best.

Liqueur: You'll find a variety of local fruit brandies and cognacs.

Wine: Dutch people drink a lot of fine wine, but it's almost all imported.

Coffee: The Dutch love their coffee, enjoying many of the same drinks (espresso, cappuccino) served in American or Italian coffee shops. Coffee usually comes with a small spice cookie. A *koffie verkeerd* (fer-KEERT, "coffee wrong") is an espresso with a lot of steamed milk.

Orange Juice: Many café/bars have a juicer for making fresh-squeezed orange juice.

Water: The Dutch (unlike many Europeans) drink tap water with meals, but many prefer mineral water, still or sparkling (Spa brand is popular).

Restaurants

Of Amsterdam's thousand-plus restaurants, no one knows which are best. We suggest that you pick an area and wander. The rowdy food ghetto thrives around Leidseplein. Roll or stroll along Leidsedwarsstraat, the restaurant row. The area around Spui Canal and that end of Spuistraat is also trendy and a bit less rowdy. For fewer crowds and more charm, find something in the Jordaan district. The best advice: your hotelier's. Most keep a reliable eating list for their neighborhood and know which places keep their travelers happy.

Here are some handy places to consider.

Near Spui in the Center

The first four places all cluster along the colorful, student-filled Grimburgwal lane near the intersection of Spui and Rokin (midway between Dam Square and the Mint Tower).

The city university's **Atrium (AE, AI, AT** Level 1—Fully accessible), housed in an old hospital, is a great budget cafeteria (€5.50 meals, Mon–Fri 11:00–15:00 & 17:00–19:00, closed Sat–Sun, from Spui, roll or stroll west down Landebrug Steeg past the canalside Café 't Gasthuys 3 blocks to Oudezijds Achterburgwal 237, go through arched doorway on the right, tel. 020/525-3999). Once inside, find the Manager's Office and ask to have the gate to the food lines unlocked, and if needed, the key to the adapted toilet.

Café 't Gasthuys (AE+A, Level 2—Moderately accessible, two 3" entry steps and narrow aisles leading to one wheelchair-accessible table), one of Amsterdam's many brown cafés, serves light meals and good sandwiches and offers indoor or peaceful canalside tables (daily 12:00–24:00, Grimburgwal 7, tel. 020/624-8230).

Restaurant Kapitein Zeppos (AE, AI, Level 2—Moderately accessible, one 2" entry step, double doors open for easier access)—named for a Belgian TV star from the 1960s—serves French-Dutch food in a relatively big and festive setting. The light lunch specials—soups and sandwiches—cost €5–10. Dinners go for about €20 (daily 11:00–15:30 & 17:30–23:00, just off Grimburgwal at Gebed Zonder End 5, tel. 020/624-2057).

De Jaren Café (AE+A, AI, Level 2—Moderately accessible, four 6" entry steps, another 2" step at end of landing) is a stark and trendy place for soup, salads, sandwiches, or just coffee over a newspaper. On a sunny day, its canalside patio is popular with yuppies (daily 10:00–24:00, Nieuwe Doelenstraat 20-22, just up from Muntplein, tel. 020/625-5771).

Restaurant Haesje Claes (AE, AI, Level 2—Moderately accessible), famous as *the* place for traditional Dutch cooking in the center, is big and fast enough to be a standard for tour groups (daily 12:00–22:00, Spuistraat 275, tel. 020/624-9998). Wheelchair access is through the entrance at Nieuwezijds Voorburgwal 320 or through the door on the side between the buildings. The area around the restaurant is a huge and festive bar scene.

La Place (Level 3—Minimally accessible, lots of stairs), a cafeteria on the ground floor of a department store, is a festival of fresh, appealing food served cafeteria-style. It has a no-smoking section and a small outdoor terrace upstairs (Mon–Sat 10:00–20:00, Thu until 21:00, Sun 12:00–20:00, it's in La Marché at the end of Kalverstraat, near Mint Tower, corner of Rokin and Muntplein, tel. 020/622-0171).

In and near the Train Station

Stationsrestauratie (AE, AI, AT, Level 1—Fully accessible) is a surprisingly classy, budget, self-service option inside the station on platform 2 (Mon–Sat 7:00–21:30, Sun from 8:00). The entire platform 2 is lined with eateries, including the tall, venerable, 1920s-style First Class Grand Café. Many of the restaurants are wheelchair-accessible. There is one adapted toilet (in the "Balcon" restaurant).

Pier 10 (AE+A, AI, Level 2—Moderately accessible, two 2" entry steps, narrow door navigable with assistance), once an old fishing shack, is now a charmingly simple little restaurant offering cozy harborfront dining (may be closed during renovation of train station). It's at the end of a dock in the shadow of (but ignoring) the huge train station. Reserve a place in the tiny five-table front room (two seatings: 18:30 and 21:30) where it's just you and the harbor traffic by candlelight (€30 meals, fun but small menu, seafood and modern European, daily from 17:30, De Ruyterkade Steiger 10, tel. 020/624-8276).

Near Dam Square

Restaurant de Roode Leeuw (AE, AI, AT, Level 1—Fully accessible, hotel receptionist has key for accessible toilet) is a grand place offering a respite from the crush of Damrak. You'll get a menu filled with Dutch traditions, dressy service, and plenty of tourists (€18–22 main dish, 3-course menu with lots of intriguing choices for €30, daily 12:00–22:00, Damrak 93-94, tel. 020/555-0666).

Near the Anne Frank House and in the Jordaan District

These are all within a few scenic blocks of Anne Frank's house, providing handy lunches and atmospheric dinners in Amsterdam's most characteristic neighborhood. Fully accessible places are generally hard to find in the Jordaan—if you need a Level 1 restaurant, look elsewhere.

Restaurant de Luwte (AE+A, AI, Level 2—Moderately accessible, one 2" entry step) is painfully romantic on a picturesque street overlooking a canal, with lots of candles, a muted but fresh modern interior, and French Mediterranean cuisine (€18 main courses, €35 for a full meal, big dinner salads for €15, daily 18:00–22:00, Leliegracht 26, tel. 020/625-8548).

The **Pancake Bakery** (AE+A, AI, Level 2—Moderately accessible, staff will assist with three 7" entry steps) serves good pancakes in a nothing-special family atmosphere. The menu features a fun selection of ethnic-themed pancakes—including Indonesian, for those who want two experiences in one (€8.50 pancakes, splitting OK, daily 12:00–21:30, Prinsengracht 191, tel. 020/625-1333).

Dimitri's (AE+A, Level 2—Moderately accessible, outdoor tables accessible, indoor seating up three 10" steps and through narrow door) is a nondescript little place serving creative salads, with a few outdoor tables on a street filled with bikes and cobbles (€9 main-course salads, breakfasts too, daily 8:00–22:00, Prinsenstraat 3, tel. 020/627-9393).

De Groene Lantaarn (AE, AI+A, Level 2—Moderately accessible, six 6" steps with railing after entry) is fun for fondue. The menu offers fish, meat, and Dutch cheese with salad and fruit for €17–22 (Thu-Sun from 18:00, closed Mon–Wed, a few blocks into the Jordaan at Bloemgracht 47, tel. 020/620-2088).

Café Restaurant de Reiger (AE+A, Level 2—Moderately accessible, three 8" entry steps and small doorway) must offer the best cooking of any *eetcafé* in the Jordaan. It's famous for its fresh ingredients and delightful bistro ambience. In addition to an English menu, ask for a translation of the €15 daily specials on the chalkboard. The café, which is crowded late and on weekends, takes no reservations but you're welcome to have a drink at the bar while you wait (daily 11:00–15:30 & 18:00–22:30, glass of house wine for €2.50, veggie options, non-smoking section, Nieuwe Leliestraat 34, tel. 020/624-7426).

Café 't Papeneiland (AE+A, AI, Level 2—Moderately accessible, staff can assist with the one 7" entry step) is a classic brown café. With Delft tiles, an evocative old stove, and a stay-awhile perch overlooking a canal with welcoming benches, it's been the neighborhood hangout since the 17th century. Though the café serves light meals, most come here to nurse a drink and chat (overlooking northwest end of Prinsengracht at #2, tel. 020/624-1989).

Near the Botanical Garden and Dutch Resistance Museum

Restaurant Plancius (AE, AI, Level 1—Fully accessible, use door facing museum and sidewalk, accessible toilet in nearby museum), adjacent to the Dutch Resistance Museum, is a mod, handy spot for lunch. With good indoor and outdoor tables, it's popular with the broadcasters from the nearby local TV studios (creative breakfasts and light lunches €5–8, daily 10:00–22:00, Plantage Kerklaan 61a, tel. 020/330-9469).

Near Vondelpark

Café Vertigo (AE+A, AI, Level 2—Moderately accessible, accessible outdoor tables, interior access through Film Museum with staff assistance) offers a fun selection of excellent soups and sandwiches. The service can be slow, but if you grab an outdoor table, you can watch the world spin by (daily 11:00–24:00, beneath Film Museum, Vondelpark 3, tel. 020/612-3021).

SMOKING

Tobacco

A third of the Dutch people smoke tobacco. Holland has a long tradition as a smoking culture, being among the first to import the tobacco plant from the New World. Tobacco shops such as the House of Hajenius glorify the habit (see page 391). Still, the Dutch version of the Surgeon General is finally waking up to the drug's many potential health problems. Since 2002, warning stickers bigger than America's are required on cigarette packs, and some of them are almost comically blunt, such as: "Smoking will make you impotent...and then you die." (The warnings prompted gag stickers like, "If you can read this, you're healthy enough," and "Life can kill you.") Smoking was recently prohibited on trains. It's unclear how much this will be obeyed or enforced.

Marijuana

Amsterdam, Europe's counterculture mecca, thinks the concept of a "victimless crime" is a contradiction in terms. Heroin and cocaine are strictly illegal in the Netherlands, and the police stringently enforce laws prohibiting their sale and use. But, while hard drugs are definitely out, marijuana causes about as much excitement as a bottle of beer.

Throughout the Netherlands you'll see "coffeeshops"—pubs selling marijuana. The minimum age for purchase is 18. Coffeeshops can sell up to five grams of marijuana per person per day. Locals buy marijuana by asking, "Can I see the cannabis menu?" The menu looks like the inventory of a drug bust. Display cases show various joints or baggies for sale. The Dutch include a little tobacco in their prerolled joints. To avoid the tobacco, you either need to roll your own (get cigarette papers free with your baggie, dispensed like toothpicks) or borrow a bong. Baggies of marijuana usually cost €5—smaller contents mean better quality.

Pot should never be bought on the street in Amsterdam. Well-established coffeeshops are considered much safer. Coffeeshop owners have an interest in keeping their trade safe and healthy. They warn Americans, unused to the strength of the local stuff, to try a lighter leaf.

To learn more about marijuana, drop by Amsterdam's Cannabis College or the Hash, Marijuana, and Hemp Museum. To see where cannabis growers buy their seeds, stop by the Sensi Seed Bank Store. The college, museum, and store are all located on Oudezijds Achterburgwal street.

Coffeeshops: Most of downtown Amsterdam's coffeeshops feel grungy and foreboding to anyone over 30. The neighborhood places (and those in small towns around the countryside) are much more inviting to people without piercings, tattoos, and favorite techno artists. We've listed a few places with a more pub-like ambience for Americans wanting to go local, but within reason.

Paradox (AE, AI, Level 2—Moderately accessible, one accessible table on same level as entry) is the most *gezellig* (cozy) coffeeshop we found—a mellow, graceful place. The manager, Ludo, is patient with descriptions and is happy to explain all your options. This is a rare coffeeshop that serves light meals. The juice is fresh, the music is easy, and the neighborhood is charming. Colorful murals with bright blue skies are all over the walls, creating a fresh and open feeling (loaner bongs, games, daily 10:00–20:00, 2 blocks from Anne Frank House at 1e Bloemdwarsstraat 2, tel. 020/623-5639).

The Grey Area coffeeshop **(AE+A,** Level 2—Moderately accessible, two 10" entry steps, narrow door) is a cool, welcoming, and smoky hole-in-the-wall appreciated among local aficionados as a seven-time winner of Amsterdam's Cannabis Cup award. Judging by the proud autographed photos on the wall, many famous Americans have dropped in. You're welcome to just nurse a bottomless cup of coffee (open Tue–Sun high noon to 20:00, closed Mon, between Dam Square and Anne Frank House at Oude Leliestraat 2, tel. 020/420-4301, www.greyarea.nl, run by two friendly Americans, Steven and John).

Siberia Coffeeshop (AE, AI, ♥, Level 2—Moderately accessible, lots of room) is central but feels cozy, with a friendly canalside ambience (daily 11:00–23:00, Internet access, helpful staff, fun English menu that explains the personalities of each item, a variety of €4 bags, Brouwersgracht 11).

La Tertulia (AE, AI, ♥, Level 2—Moderately accessible, one wheelchair-accessible table near entry door) is a sweet little mother-daughter-run place with pastel décor and a cheery terrarium ambience (Tue–Sat 11:00–19:00, closed Sun–Mon, games, sandwiches, brownies, Prinsengracht 312, www.coffeeshopamsterdam.com).

The Bulldog (mostly Level 3—Minimally accessible) is the high-profile, leading touristy chain of coffeeshops. They are young but welcoming, with reliable selections. They're pretty comfortable for green tourists wanting to just hang out for a while. The flagship branch, in a former police station right on Leidseplein, is handy, offering fun outdoor tables where you can watch the world skateboard by (daily 9:00–01:00, Leidseplein 17, tel. 020/625-6278, www.bulldog.nl).

NIGHTLIFE

Amsterdam hotels serve breakfast until 11:00 because so many people—visitors and locals—live for nighttime in Amsterdam. On summer evenings, people flock to the main squares for drinks at outdoor tables. Leidseplein is the glitziest, surrounded by theaters, restaurants, and nightclubs.

Boom Chicago is a free, irreverent magazine that lists festivals, plays, films, dance, and live music, from rock to classical. It gives you the best rundown on the youth and nightlife scene, and offers a €3 discount on the Boom Chicago R-rated comedy theater act listed below (magazine free at TIs and many bars). *Uitkrant,* also free at TIs, is in Dutch, but it's just a calendar of events, and anyone can figure out the name of the event and its date, time, and location. There's also *What's On in Amsterdam, Time Out Amsterdam,* the Thursday edition of many Dutch papers, and the *International Herald Tribune*'s special Netherlands inserts (all sold at newsstands).

The **AUB ticket office** (**AE, AI,** Level 2—Moderately accessible) at Stadsschouwburg Theater (Leidseplein 26, tel. 0900-0191) is the best one-stop-shopping box office for theater, classical music, and major rock shows.

Music: You'll find classical music at the Concertgebouw (**AE, AI, AT,** Level 1—Fully accessible; at the far south end of Museumplein, tel. 020/675-4411) and at the former Beurs (**AE, AI,** Level 2—Moderately accessible; on Damrak, tel. 020/627-0466), and opera and dance at the opera house on Waterlooplein (**AE, AI,** Level 2—Moderately accessible; tel. 020/551-8100). In summer, Vondelpark hosts open-air concerts.

Comedy: Boom Chicago (**AE, AI, AT, ♥,** Level 1—Fully accessible), an R-rated comedy theater act, was started 10 years ago by a group of Americans on a graduation tour. They have been entertaining tourists and locals alike ever since. The show is a series of rude, clever, and high-powered skits offering a raucous look at Dutch culture and local tourism (€18, Sun–Thu at 20:15, Fri–Sat 19:30 and 22:45, dinner seating early in the 270-seat Leidseplein Theater, Leidseplein 12, tel. 020/423-0101, www.boomchicago.nl). They do four shows: *Best of Boom* (a collection of their greatest hits over the years), a new show for locals and return customers, and two improv shows. Meals are optional and a good value.

Movies: Catch modern movies in the 1920s setting of the classic Tuschinski Theater (**AE+A, AI,** Level 2—Moderately accessible, four 7" entry steps; between Muntplein and Rembrandtplein on Reguliers-breestraat 26-28). It's not unusual for movies at many cinemas to be sold out—consider buying tickets during the day.

TRANSPORTATION CONNECTIONS

Amsterdam's train-information center requires a long wait. Save lots of time by getting train tickets and information in a small-town station, at the airport upon arrival, or from a travel agency. For phone information, dial 0900-9292 for local trains or 0900-9296 for international trains (€0.50/min, daily 7:00–24:00, wait through recording and hold... hold...hold...). The numbers listed are frustrating phone trees in Dutch and—if you wait—maybe in English.

By train to: Schiphol Airport (6/hr, 20 min, €3), **Haarlem** (6/hr, 15 min, €5.50 same-day return; see "Amsterdam to Haarlem Train Tour," page 405), **The Hague** (2/hr, 50 min), **Rotterdam** (4/hr, 1 hr), **Bruges** (hrly, 3.5–4.25 hrs, 1-3 transfers; transfers are timed closely—be alert and check with conductor), **Brussels** (2/hr, 3 hrs, €30), **Ostende** (hrly, 4 hrs, change in Antwerp), **London** (8/day, 6.5 hrs, with transfer to Eurostar Chunnel train in Brussels, Eurostar discounted with railpass, www.eurostar.com), **Copenhagen** (5/day, 10 hrs, transfer in Osnabrück and Hamburg; or 3-hr train to Duisberg and transfer to 11-hr night train), **Frankfurt** (8/day, 5–6 hrs, transfer in Köln or Duisburg), **Munich** (7/day, 9 hrs, transfer in Mannheim, Hanover, or Köln, one 11-hr direct night train), **Bonn** (10/day, 3 hrs, some direct but most transfer in Köln), **Bern** (5/day, 9 hrs, one direct but most transfer in Basel, Köln, or Brussels), **Paris** (5/day, 5 hrs, required fast train from Brussels with €11 supplement).

Amsterdam's Schiphol Airport

Schiphol (SKIP-pol) Airport, like most of Holland, is English-speaking, accessible, user-friendly, and below sea level. Its banks offer fair rates (24 hrs daily, in arrival area).

The most accessible way into either Amsterdam or Haarlem from the airport is by **taxi** (**AE+A,** Level 2—Moderately accessible); figure €35 to Amsterdam, €45 to Haarlem. The airport also has easy **train** connections with **Amsterdam** (**AE, AI,** Level 2—Moderately accessible; 6/hr, 20 min, €3) and **Haarlem** (**AE, AI,** Level 2—Moderately accessible; 4/hr, 40 min, transfer at Amsterdam-Sloterdijk, €4.55).

The airport has a train station of its own. You can validate your Eurailpass and hit the rails immediately or, to stretch your train pass, buy an inexpensive ticket into Amsterdam today and start the pass later.

Schiphol flight information (tel. 0900-7244-7465, €0.10/min) can give you flight times and your airline's Amsterdam number for reconfirmation before going home (€0.45/min to climb through its phone tree). To reach the airlines, dial: KLM at 020/649-9123 or 020/474-7747, Northwest is same as KLM, Martinair at 020/601-1222, SAS at 0900-746-63727, American Airlines at 06/022-7844, British Airways at 023/554-7555, and easyJet at 023/568-4880.

If you have time to kill at Schiphol, check out the Dutch Masters. The Rijksmuseum loans a dozen or so of its masterpieces from the

Golden Age to the Rijksmuseum Schiphol, a free little art gallery behind the passport check between piers E and F.

Access: AE, AI, AL, AT, Level 1—The airport is fully accessible.

Sleeping at Schiphol: Ibis Amsterdam Airport Hotel (AE, AI, AL, AT, AR, AB, Level 1—Fully accessible) is a modern and efficient 644-room place. It offers close proximity to the airport, comfort, and good value (Db-€100, book long in advance, air-con, non-smoking rooms, Schipholweg 181, reservation tel. 020/502-5111, reception tel. 020/502-5100, fax 020/657-0199, www.ibishotel.com). This hotel has one wheelchair-accessible room, including an adapted bathroom and shower.

Central Station

AMSTERDAM ROLL OR STROLL

From the Train Station to the Rijksmuseum

Amsterdam today looks much as it did in its Golden Age, the 1600s. It's a retired sea captain of a city, still in love with life, with a broad outlook and a salty story to tell.

Take a Dutch-sampler tour from one end of the old center to the other, tasting all Amsterdam has to offer along the way. It's your best single roll or stroll through Dutch clichés, democratic people-squares, businesses, afternoon happy-hour hangouts, and, yes, Amsterdam's 800-year history.

ACCESSIBILITY CODE CHART

CODE	MEANING
AE	Accessible Entryway
AE+A	Accessible Entry with Assistance
AI	Accessible Interior
AI+A	Accessible Interior with Assistance
AT	Accessible Toilet
AT+A	Accessible Toilet with Assistance
AL	Accessible Lift (elevator)
AL+A	Accessible Lift with Assistance

For the full chart, or a more detailed explanation of codes, please see page 2 of the Introduction.

Amsterdam Roll or Stroll Overview

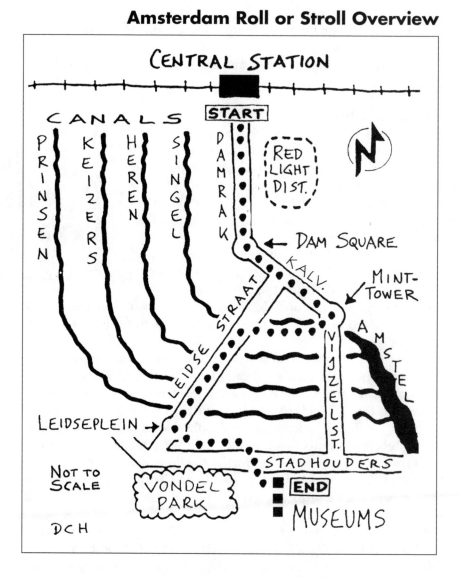

CENTRAL STATION

START

CANALS

PRINSEN KEIZERS HEREN SINGEL DAMRAK

RED LIGHT DIST.

N

← DAM SQUARE

KALV.

MINT-TOWER →

LEIDSE STRAAT

VIJZELST.

AMSTEL

LEIDSEPLEIN →

NOT TO SCALE

STADHOUDERS

VONDEL PARK

END

MUSEUMS

DCH

Start at the central-as-can-be train station. You'll roll or stroll about three miles, heading down Damrak to Dam Square, continuing south down the pedestrian street, Kalverstraat, to the Mint Tower, then wafting through the Bloemenmarkt (flower market), before continuing south to Leidseplein and bearing left to the Rijksmuseum. Trams #5 (accessible) or #2 (not accessible) head back to Centraal Station from the southwest corner of the Rijksmuseum. If this tour seems too long, you can break it up into several outings.

Beware of silent transport—trams and bikes. Stay off the tram tracks and yield to bell-ringing bikers.

Centraal Station

Here, where today's train travelers enter the city, sailors of yore disembarked from seagoing ships to be met by street musicians, pickpockets, hotel-runners, and ladies carrying red lanterns. When the station was built at the former harbor mouth, Amsterdam lost some of its harbor feel, but it's still a bustling port of entry.

The Centraal Station, of warm red brick and prickly spires, is the first of several neo-Gothic buildings we'll see from the late 1800s, built during Amsterdam's economic revival. One of the towers has a clock dial; the other tower's dial is a weathervane—watch the hand twitch as the wind gusts.

Emerging from the train station, the city spreads out before you in a series of concentric canals. Ahead of you stretches the street called Damrak, leading south to Dam Square, a half-mile away. To the left of Damrak is the city's old *(oude)* side, to the right is the new *(nieuwe)*.

The big church towering above the old side (at about 10 o'clock) is the St. Nicholas church, built in the 1880s when Catholics—after two centuries of oppression—were finally free to worship in public. The church marks the beginning of the Red Light District. The city's biggest bike garage, a multi-storied wonder, is on your right (in front of the Ibis Hotel).

• *We'll basically head south from here to the Rijksmuseum. The art museum and the station—designed by the same architect—stand like bookends holding the old town together. Follow the crowds south on Damrak, going along the right side of the street.*

Damrak

Roll or stroll past every Dutch cliché at the tourist shops: wooden shoes, plastic tulips, Heineken fridge magnets, and windmill saltshakers. Listen to a hand-cranked barrel organ. Order french fries (called *Vlaamse frites,*

Amsterdam Roll or Stroll, Part 1

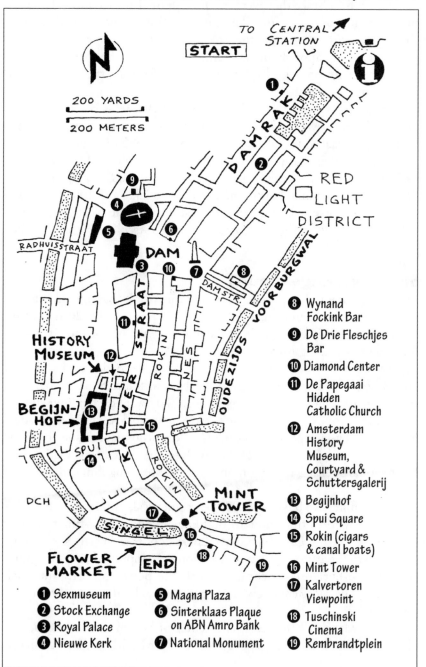

TO CENTRAL STATION

START

RED LIGHT DISTRICT

200 YARDS
200 METERS

RADHUISSTRAAT

DAM

HISTORY MUSEUM

BEGIJN-HOF →

SPUI

DCH

FLOWER MARKET

END

MINT TOWER

8 Wynand Fockink Bar
9 De Drie Fleschjes Bar
10 Diamond Center
11 De Papegaai Hidden Catholic Church
12 Amsterdam History Museum, Courtyard & Schuttersgalerij
13 Begijnhof
14 Spui Square
15 Rokin (cigars & canal boats)
16 Mint Tower
17 Kalvertoren Viewpoint
18 Tuschinski Cinema
19 Rembrandtplein

1 Sexmuseum
2 Stock Exchange
3 Royal Palace
4 Nieuwe Kerk
5 Magna Plaza
6 Sinterklaas Plaque on ABN Amro Bank
7 National Monument

or Flemish fries, since they were invented in the Low Countries) and dip them in mayonnaise, not ketchup. Eating international cuisine (Indonesian *rijsttaffel,* Argentine steaks, Middle Eastern *shoarma*) is like going local in cosmopolitan Amsterdam. And you'll find the city's most notorious commodity displayed disease-free at the Amsterdam Sexmuseum.

The street was once a riverbed, where the Amstel River flowed north into the IJ (eye) river behind today's train station. Both rivers then emptied into a vast inlet of the North Sea (the Zuiderzee), making Amsterdam a major seaport. Today, the Amstel is channeled into canals, its former mouth has been covered by the Centraal Station, the North Sea inlet has been diked off to make an inland lake, and 100,000 ships a year reach the open waters by sailing west through the North Sea Canal.
• *The long brick building with the square clock tower, along the left side of Damrak, is the...*

Stock Exchange (Beurs)

Built from nine million bricks on 4,880 tree trunks hammered into the marshy soil, the Beurs van Berlage (named for an early 20th-century Amsterdam architect with vision) stands as a symbol of the city's long tradition as a trading town.

Back when "stock" meant whatever could be loaded and unloaded onto a boat, Amsterdammers gathered here to trade. Soon, rather than trading goats, chickens, and kegs of beer, they were exchanging slips of paper and "futures" at one of the world's first stock exchanges. Traders needed money-changers who needed bankers who made money by lending money...and Amsterdam of the 1600s became one of the world's first great capitalist cities, loaning money to free-spending kings, dukes, and bishops.

This impressive building (1903)—geometrical, minimal, no frills—is one of the world's first modern buildings, emphasizing function over looks. In 1984, the Exchange moved next door (see the stock-exchange read-out) to the Euronext complex—a joint attempt by France, Belgium, and the Netherlands to compete with the power of Britain's stock exchange. The old Beurs now hosts concerts and a museum for temporary exhibits.

Amsterdam still thrives as the center of Dutch businesses such as Heineken, Shell Oil, Philips Electronics, KLM Airlines, and Unilever.

Amsterdammers have always had a reputation of putting business above ideological differences, staying neutral while trading with both sides.

• *Damrak opens into...*

Dam Square

The city got its start right here, around 1250, when fishermen in this marshy delta settled along the built-up banks of the Amstel River. They crossed the river with a *damme,* creating a small village called "Amstel-damme." Soon the fishermen were trading with German riverboats traveling downstream and with seafaring boats docking from Stockholm, Hamburg, and

London. Dam Square was the center of it all.

The dam over the Amstel divided the *damrak* (meaning outer harbor—for sea traffic) from the *rokin* (inner harbor—for river traffic). Land trade routes converged here as well, and a customs house stood here. Today the Damrak and Rokin (roh-KEEN) are major roads and the city's palace and major department stores face the square, where mimes, jugglers, and human statues mingle with locals and tourists. This is the historic heart of the city. As the symbolic center of the Netherlands, it's where political demonstrations begin and end.

Pan the square clockwise to find: the Royal Palace (the large domed building on the west side), Nieuwe Kerk (New Church), an ABN AMRO bank, Damrak, the proud old De Bijenkorf department store ("the beehive"), Krasnapolsky Grand Hotel, the white phallic obelisk of the National Monument, Rokin street, touristy Madame Tussaud's, and the entrance to pedestrian-only Kalverstraat.

Royal Palace

The name is misleading, since Amsterdam is one of the cradles of modern democracy. For centuries, this was the Town Hall of a self-governing community that prided itself on its independence and thumbed its nose at royalty. The current building, from 1652, is appropriately classical (like the democratic Greeks), with a triangular pediment featuring—fittingly for Amsterdam—denizens of the sea cavorting with Neptune (with his green copper trident.)

After the city was conquered by the French under Napoleon, he imposed a monarchy on Holland, making his brother Louis the King of the Netherlands (1808). Louis used the city hall as his "Royal Palace," giving it the current name. When Napoleon was overthrown, the victorious powers dictated that the Netherlands remain a monarchy, under a noble Dutch family called the House of Orange. If the current Queen Beatrix is in town, this is, technically, her residence (her permanent home is in the Royal Palace at The Hague). Amsterdam is the nominal capital of the Netherlands, but all governing activity is at The Hague (a city 30 miles southwest).

Nieuwe Kerk

In 1980, Queen Beatrix said, "I do" in the Nieuwe Kerk, where the Netherlands' monarchs are crowned, wed, and buried. The "New" church is 600 years old (younger than the 700-year-old "Old" church in the Red Light District). The sundial above the entrance once served as the city's official timepiece.

The church's bare, spacious, well-lit interior (**AE, AI, AT,** Level 1—Fully accessible; often occupied by temporary art exhibits) looks quite different from the ornate Baroque-crusted churches found in the rest of Europe. In 1566, clear-eyed Protestant extremists throughout Holland marched into Catholic churches (like this once was), lopped off the heads of holy statues, stripped gold-leaf angels from the walls, urinated on Virgin Marys, and shattered stained-glass windows in a wave of anti-Catholic vandalism.

This Iconoclasm (icon-breaking) of 1566 started an 80-year war against Spain and the Hapsburgs, leading finally to Dutch independence in 1648. Catholic churches like this one were converted to the new dominant religion, Calvinist Protestantism (today's Dutch Reformed Church). From then on, Dutch churches downplayed the "graven images" and "idols" of ornate religious art.

The Nieuwe Kerk is now a symbolic religious center of the Netherlands. When Beatrix dies or retires, her son (Crown Prince Willem Alexander) will parade to the center of the church, sit in front of

> # CITY ON A SANDBAR
>
> Amsterdam is built upon millions of wooden pilings. The city was founded on unstable mud, which sits on stable sand. In the Middle Ages, buildings were made of wood, which rests lightly and easily on mud. But with devastating fires repeatedly wiping out entire neighborhoods, stone became the building material of choice. It was fire-resistant but too heavy for a mud foundation. For more support, pilings were driven 30 feet through the mud and into the sand. The Royal Palace sits upon 13,000 such pilings—still solid after 300 years. (The wood survives fine if kept wet and out of the air.) Since World War II, concrete rather than wood has been used, with foundations driven 60 feet deep through the first layer of sand, through more mud, and into a second layer of sand. And today's biggest buildings have foundations sinking as much as 120 feet deep.

the golden choir screen, and—with TV lights glaring and flashbulbs popping—be crowned the next sovereign.

Access: The church entry and interior are wheelchair-accessible. The associated restaurant (to the right) is also fully accessible and has adapted toilets.

• *Looking between the Royal Palace and the Nieuwe Kerk, you'll see the fanciful brick facade of the Magna Plaza shopping center, marking the way to the Anne Frank House and the Jordaan neighborhood. Back in Dam Square, on the wall of the ABN AMRO bank, find the colorful little stone plaque of...*

Sinterklaas—St. Nicholas

Jolly old St. Nicholas (Nicolaas in Dutch) is the patron saint of seafarers (see the three men in a tub) and of Amsterdam, and is also the model for Sinterklaas—the guy we call Santa Claus. Every year in late November, Holland's Santa Claus arrives by boat near the Centraal Station (from his legendary home in Spain), rides a white horse up Damrak with his black servant, Peter, and arrives triumphant in this square while thousands of kids cheer.

December 5th is the Dutch Christmas (though many celebrate the 25th as well), when they exchange presents, and Sinterklaas leaves goodies in good kids' wooden shoes. (Smart kids maximize capacity by putting out big boots.)

Around the corner in Damrak, the bank has an ATM machine and Chip-loader *(Oplaadpunt)*. The ATM is familiar, but what's that small keypad next to it? It's for loading up the Dutch cash card—an attempt to eliminate the need for small change. With the keypad, the Dutch transfer money from their account onto a card with a computer chip. Then they can make purchases at stores by inserting the card into a pay point, like Americans buy gas from the pump.

National Monument

The obelisk, which depicts a crucified Christ, men in chains, and howling dogs, was built in 1956 as a WWII memorial. Now it's considered a monument for peace.

Nazis occupied Holland from 1940–1945. They deported 100,000 Amsterdam Jews, driving young Anne Frank and her family into hiding. Near the end of the war, the "Hunger Winter" of 1944–1945 killed thousands and forced many to survive on tulip bulbs. Today, Dutch people in their 70s—whose growth-spurt years coincided with the Hunger Winter—are easy to identify because they are uniformly short.

Circling the Square

You're at the center of Amsterdam. To the east a few blocks is the top of the Red Light District. Amsterdam is the world capital of experimental theater, and several edgy theaters line the street called the Nes (stretching south from the Krasnapolsky Grand Hotel).

Office workers do afternoon happy hours at crowded **bars** that stock *jenevers* and liqueurs in wooden kegs. De Drie Fleschjes, a particularly casual pub, is tucked right behind the Nieuwe Kerk. More upscale Wynand Fockink (100 yards down the alley along the right side of

Krasnapolsky Grand Hotel) serves fruit brandies produced in their adjoining distillery, which you can visit (Level 3—Minimally accessible; doorway is accessible, but interior is jammed with bottles and barrels). Though the brew is bottled and distributed all over Holland, what you get here in the home-office bar is some of the best Fockink liqueur in the world.

At the **Amsterdam Diamond Center** (where Rokin street meets Dam Square), see cutters and jewelry-setters handling diamonds, plus some small educational displays and fake versions of big, famous stones. Since the 1500s, the city has been one of the world's diamond capitals. Eighty percent of industrial diamonds (for making drills and such) pass through here, as well as cut and polished jewels like the Koh-i-Nohr diamond.

• *From Dam Square, head south on...*

Kalverstraat

This pedestrian-only street is lined with many familiar franchise stores and record shops. This has been a shopping street for centuries and today is notorious among locals as the place for cheesy, crass materialism. For smaller and more elegant stores, try the adjacent district called De Negen Straatjes (the nine little streets) with 190 shops mingling with the canals (about 4 blocks west of Kalverstraat).

• *About 120 yards along (across from the McDonald's), go into...*

"De Papegaai" Hidden Catholic Church (Petrus en Paulus Kerk)

This Catholic church (**AE+A, AI**, Level 2—Moderately accessible, daily 10:00–17:00), while not exactly "hidden" (you found it), keeps a low profile even now that Catholicism has been legalized in Amsterdam. In the late 1500s, with Protestants fighting Catholics and the Dutch fighting Spanish invaders, Amsterdam tried to stay neutral, doing business with all parties. Finally in 1578, Protestant extremists (following the teachings of Reformer John Calvin) took political control of the city. They expelled Catholic leaders and bishops, outlawed the religion, and allied

Amsterdam with anti-Spanish forces in an action known to historians as The Alteration.

For the next two centuries, Amsterdam's Catholics were driven underground. Catholicism was illegal but tolerated, as long as it was not done in public, but in humble, unadvertised places like this, and for personal use only.

Today the church, which asks for a mere "15 minutes for God" *(een kwartier voor God)*, stands as a metaphor for how marginal religion has always been in highly commercial and secular Amsterdam.

Access: The wheelchair user can ring a bell to gain entry through the regular door instead of trying to get through the revolving door. The interior of the church is accessible, with flat aisles.

• *Seventy yards farther along, at #92, where Kalverstraat crosses Wijde Kapel Steeg, look to the right at an archway leading to the...*

Courtyard of the Amsterdam History Museum

On the arch is Amsterdam's coat of arms—a red shield with three Xs and a crown. Not a reference to the city's sex trade, the X-shaped crosses (which appear everywhere in the city) represent the crucifixion of St. Andrew, the patron saint of fishermen, and symbolize heroism, determination, and mercy. The crown dates to 1489, when Holy Roman Emperor Maximilian of Austria paid off a big loan from city bankers and, as thanks for the cash, gave the city permission to use his prestigious trademark, the Hapsburg crown, atop their shield.

In the middle of the alleyway stands an alms box (with a sealed-over coin slot). The relief above the door (dated 1581) shows boys around a dove, reminding all who pass that this was an orphan home and asking for charity. Go inside the courtyard (fully accessible).

You'll see the pleasant David and Goliath café (**AE, AI, AT,** Level 1—Fully accessible), watched over by a giant statue of Goliath and a knee-high David (from 1650). In the courtyard are the lockers for the orphan's uniforms and an accessible pay toilet.

• *The courtyard leads to another accessible courtyard with the best city-history museum in town, the Amsterdam History Museum (**AE, AI, AT**, Level 1—*

Fully accessible except for carillon loft, loaner wheelchairs available, see page 351). In between the two courtyards (on the left) is an accessible glassed-in passageway (free, daily 10:00–17:00) lined with paintings, called the...

Schuttersgalerij (Civic Guards Gallery)

In these group portraits from Amsterdam's Golden Age (early 1600s), look into the eyes of the frank, dignified men (and occasionally women) with ruffs and lace collars who made Amsterdam the most prosperous city in Europe, sending trading ships to distant colonies, and pocketing interest from loans. The weapons they carry are mostly symbolic, since these "Civic Guards" who once protected the town had become more like fraternal organizations of business bigwigs.

The **Civic Guard of Captain Arent ten Grootenhuys from 1608** (fourth painting on the left wall, bottom level) is typical of this highly-stylized genre. The company sits in two rows. In the center is the young flag-bearer (with rolled-up flag). Just to the left is Captain G., recognizable because he holds the traditional captain's pike (a long axe-like weapon topped with a spearhead-shaped tip). This "captain" was really a successful businessman, one of the founders of the Dutch East India Company. His lieutenant (right of center, with elaborate armor) cocks a partisan (pike with a sword-like tip). Others wield hatchet-headed halberds.

Everyone looks straight out, with every face lit perfectly. They each paid for their own portrait and wanted it right. It took masters like Rembrandt and Frans Hals to take the starch out of the collars and compose more natural scenes.

• *The Gallery offers a shortcut to the Begijnhof, 70 yards farther south. But if the Gallery is closed, backtrack to Kalverstraat, continue south, then turn right on Begijnensteeg. This leads to the entrance into the walled courtyard (**AE, AI,** Level 1—Fully accessible; free, daily 10:00–17:00) called the...*

Begijnhof

This quiet courtyard (gutturally: buh-HHHINE-hof) lined with houses around a church has sheltered women since 1346. In early times, rich women gave up their wealth to live in Christian poverty here as part of the lay order called *Beguines*. Poor

women and widows lived here as well, spinning wool and making lace to earn their keep.

In 1578, when Catholicism was outlawed, the Dutch Reformed Church (and the city) took over many Catholic charities—such as this place. Many Dutch women, widowed by the hazards of overseas trade, find a retirement home here. The last Beguine died in 1971, but the Begijnhof still provides subsidized housing to single women in need (mostly Catholic seniors and students). The Begijnhof is just one of about 75 *hofjes* (housing projects surrounding courtyards) that dot Amsterdam.

Begin the Beguine visit at the statue of one of these charitable sisters. She faces the Wooden House *(Houten Huys)* at #34. The city's oldest, it dates from 1477. Originally the whole city was built of wood. To the left of the house is a display of carved gable stones that once adorned house fronts and served as street numbers (and still do at #19 and at #26, the former Mother Superior's house).

The brick-faced **English Church** (Engelse Kerk, from 1420) was the Beguine church until 1607, when it became Anglican. Fleeing persecution in England, the Pilgrims (strict Protestants) stopped here in tolerant Amsterdam and prayed in this church before the Mayflower carried them to religious freedom at Plymouth Rock in America. (It has English services on Sundays at 10:30; otherwise it's often closed.)

The "hidden" **Catholic Church** faces the English Church (enter through a low-profile doorway). Amsterdam's oppressed 17th-century Catholics, who refused to worship as Protestants, must have eagerly awaited the day when, in the 19th century, they were legally allowed to say Mass. You can go inside (**AE+A, AI,** Level 2—Moderately accessible; one 2" entry step, then large heavy door, then another 2" step and another door).

Today, Holland is still divided religiously, but without the bitterness. Roughly a third are Catholic, a third Protestant...and a third list themselves as "unchurched."

• *From the Begijnhof, backtrack to busy Kalverstraat, then turn right, continuing south. Pause at the busy intersection with Spuistraat and get oriented.*

Spui and the Rokin

To the right down Spuistraat is the square called **Spui** (rhymes with cow). Lined with cafés and bars, it's one of the city's more popular spots

for nightlife and sunny afternoon people-watching.

A half-block to the left is the busy street called **Rokin** (ro-KEEN). A statue of Wilhelmina (1860–1962) on the Rokin shows the Queen riding daintily sidesaddle. In real life, she was the iron-willed inspiration for Dutch Resistance against the Nazis. The present Queen Beatrix is Wilhelmina's granddaughter.

Nearby, canal cruises depart from the Rondvaart Kooij dock (**AE+A,** Level 2—Moderately accessible, must walk down 3 steps; €6.50).

On Rokin, the **House of Hajenius (AE+A, AI,** Level 2—

Moderately accessible), is a temple of cigars, a "paradise for the connoisseur" showing "175 years of tradition and good taste." Entering this sumptuous Art Deco building with painted leather ceilings is stepping back to 1910. The brown-capped canisters are for smelling fine pipe tobacco. Take a whiff. The personal humidifiers (read the explanation) allow locals to call in an order and have their cigar waiting for them in just the right humidity. Upstairs in back is a small free museum (Rokin 92, www.hajenius.com).

Access: One 6" entry step leads to the accessible ground floor. The upper-level museum is up eleven narrow 5" steps.

• *Continue up Kalverstraat toward the...*

Mint Tower

The tower, which marks the limit of the medieval walled city, served as one of the original gates (the steeple was added later, in 1620). The city walls were girdled by a moat—the Singelgracht canal. Until about 1500, the area beyond here was nothing but marshy fields and a few farms on reclaimed land.

On the way to the Mint Tower, you'll pass department stores with cafeterias. At the end of Kalverstraat, the Vroom & Dreesman

Amsterdam Roll or Stroll, Part 2

⓴ Flower Market	㉔ Stadsschouwburg	㉘ Bulldog Café
㉑ Koningsplein	㉕ AUB box office	㉙ Rijksmuseum
㉒ Metz & Co.	㉖ Melkweg	㉚ Trams #2 & #5
㉓ Smartshop	㉗ Restaurant Row	(2 locations)

department store is one of Holland's oldest chains. Inside, La Place is a sprawling self-service cafeteria, handy for a quick and healthy lunch (Level 3—Minimally accessible, has stairs). Across the street, the Kalvertoren shopping complex offers a top-floor viewpoint and café (**AE, AI, AL,** Level 2—Moderately accessible; venture into the glass atrium and slide up the wild elevator).

From the busy intersection at Muntplein, look left (at about 10 o'clock) down Reguliersbreestraat. A long block east of here (where you see trees) is Rembrandtplein, another major center for nightlife. Halfway down the block is the massive easyInternetcafé (**AE, AI,** Level 2— Moderately accessible; open 24/7, €1/40 min, Reguliersbreestraat 33). Near it, the twin green domes mark the exotic Tuschinski Theater (**AE+A, AI,** Level 2—Moderately accessible; four 7" entry steps, accessible lobby), where you can see modern movies in a sumptuous Art Deco setting. Sit inside and stare at the ever-changing ceiling, imagining this place during the roaring '20s (Reguliersbreestraat 26–28).

• *Just past the Mint Tower, turn right and head west along the south bank of the Singel canal, which is lined with the greenhouse shops of the...*

Flower Market (Bloemenmarkt)

Cut flowers, plants, bulbs, seeds, and garden supplies attest to Holland's reputation for growing flowers. Tulips, imported from Turkey in the 1600s, grew well in the sandy soil of the dunes and reclaimed land. By the 1630s, the country was in the grip of a full-blown tulip mania, where a single bulb sold for as much as a house, and fortunes were won and lost. Finally, in 1637, the market plummeted, and the tulip became just one of many beauties in  the country's flower arsenal. Today Holland is a major exporter of flowers. Certain seeds are certified and OK to bring back into the United States (merchants have the details).

• *The long Flower Market ends at the next bridge, where you'll see a square named...*

Koningsplein

Choke down a raw herring—the commodity that first put Amsterdam on the trading map—with locals who flock to this popular outdoor herring stand (one 12" step to reach ordering platform). Hollandse nieuwe means the herring are in season.

• *From Koningsplein, we'll turn left, heading straight to Leidseplein. At first the street southward is just labeled Koningsplein (Scheltema, Amsterdam's leading bookstore, is at Koningsplein 20; AE, AI, AL, Level 2—Moderately accessible), but it soon becomes...*

Leidsestraat

Between here and Leidseplein you'll cross several grand canals, following a street lined with fashion and tourist shops, and crowded with shoppers, tourists, bicycles, and trams. Trams must wait their turn to share a single track as the street narrows.

The once-grand, now-frumpy Metz & Co. department store (**AE, AI, AL, Level 2**—Moderately accessible; where Leidsestraat crosses Herengracht) offers a rare above-the-rooftops panorama of the city from its fully accessible sixth-floor café.

Looking left down Herengracht, you'll see the "Golden Curve" of the canal, lined with grand classical-style gables.

• *Past the posh stores of Laura Ashley, DKNY, and Lush, find a humble establishment where Leidsestraat crosses the Keizersgracht canal.*

"When Nature Calls" Smartshop

"Smart shops" like this one (**AE+A, AI**, Level 2—Moderately accessi-

ble) are clean, well-lighted, fully professional retail outlets that sell powerful drugs, many of which are illegal in the U.S. Their "natural" drugs include harmless nutrition boosters (royal jelly), harmful but familiar tobacco, herbal versions of popular dance-club drugs (herbal Ecstasy), powerful psychoactive plants (psilocybin mushrooms), and joints that are an unpredictable mix of

CANALS

Amsterdam's canals tamed the flow of the Amstel River, creating pockets of dry land to build on. The city's 100 canals are about 10 feet deep, crossed by some 1,200 bridges, fringed with 100,000 Dutch elm and lime trees, and filled with 2,000 houseboats. A system of locks (back near the Centraal Station) controls the flow outward to (eventually) the North Sea and the flow inward of the incoming tide. The locks are opened periodically to flush out the system.

It's amazing how quiet and peaceful this big city of more than 700,000 can be. Some of the boats in the canals look pretty funky by day, but Amsterdam is an unpretentious, anti-status city. When the sun goes down and the lights come on, people cruise the sparkling canals with an on-board hibachi and a bottle of wine, and even scows can become chick magnets.

marijuana and other substances, sold under exotic names like "Herbal Love." The big item: marijuana seeds.

Prices are clearly marked, with brief descriptions of the drugs, their ingredients, and effects. The knowledgeable salespeople can give more information on their "100 percent natural products that play with the human senses."

Still, my fellow Americans, *caveat emptor!* We've grown used to thinking: "If it's legal, it must be safe (if it's not, I'll sue)."

While perfectly legal and above-board, some of these substances can cause powerful, often unpleasant reactions. Even if you've smoked marijuana (itself a potent mind alterant), use caution with less familiar drugs. (Keizersgracht 508, daily 10:00–22:00, www.whennaturecalls.nl).

Access: Two exterior 3" entry steps, then two more 8" steps after the landing. The rest of the store is very small, packed with display cases.

• *Leidsestraat empties into the square called...*

Leidseplein

Filled with outdoor tables under trees, ringed with cafés, theaters, and night-clubs, bustling with tourists, diners, trams, mimes, and fire-eaters, and lit by sun- or lantern-light, Leidseplein is the city's liveliest square.

Do a 360-degree spin: Leidseplein's south side is bordered by the city's main serious theater, the **Stadsschouwburg,** which dates back to the 17th-century Golden Age (present building from 1890). To the right, down a lane behind the big theater, stands the **Melkweg** (Milky Way, **AE, AI,** Level 2—Moderately accessible), the once-revolutionary, now-institutional entertainment complex housing all things youth-oriented under one roof (Lijnbaansgracht 234a); go into

the lobby or check out posters plastered on walls to find out who's playing tonight. On the east end of Leidseplein is the **Bulldog Café and Coffeeshop** (Level 3—Minimally accessible), the flagship of several café/bar/coffeeshops in town. (Notice the sign above the door—it once housed the police bureau.) A small green-and-white decal in the window indicates that it's a city-licensed "coffeeshop," where marijuana is sold and smoked legally. On Leidseplein's west side is the Boom Chicago nightclub theater (at #12), presenting English-language spoofs of politics, Amsterdam, and tourists (**AE, AI, AT, ♥,** Level 1—Fully accessible). The neighborhood beyond Haagen Dazs and Burger King is the **restaurant ghetto,** featuring countless Thai, Brazilian, Indian, Italian, Indonesian, and even a few Dutch eateries.

• *From Leidseplein, tram #5 (with accessible cars) or #2 (not always accessible) zip you back to the station where you began this tour. The Rijksmuseum— with the greatest collection of Dutch masterpieces in the country—is a short*

roll or stroll away (see page 344). Behind the Rijksmuseum is the always enter-
taining Museumplein and the Van Gogh Museum (page 346). The accessible
Heineken Brewery museum is a half-mile east of the Rijks on Stadhouders-
kade. You can also catch trams #5 and #2 back to the station from the
Rijksmuseum.

HAARLEM

Cute, cozy, yet real, Haarlem makes a fine home base or a good day-trip destination, giving you small-town warmth with easy connections to wild and crazy Amsterdam (15 min by train).

Bustling Haarlem gave America's Harlem its name back when New York was "New Amsterdam," a Dutch colony. For centuries Haarlem has been a market town, buzzing with shoppers heading home with fresh bouquets, nowadays by bike.

Enjoy the market on Monday (clothing) or Saturday (general), when the square bustles like a Brueghel painting with cheese, fish, flowers, and families. Make yourself at home, and buy some flowers to brighten your hotel room.

ACCESSIBILITY IN HAARLEM

Haarlem is not ideal in terms of accessibility. We've listed only the most accessible hotels and restaurants. The best local resource is the *Holiday Magazine* (see below).

ORIENTATION

(area code: 023)
Tourist Information
Haarlem's TI (a.k.a. VVV; **AE, AI,** Level 2—Moderately accessible), at the train station, is friendlier, more helpful, and less crowded than

ACCESSIBILITY CODES

These codes offer a quick overview of what to expect. If applicable, more specific details about the facility (e.g., exact number and height of steps, special instructions for gaining entry) are explained in each listing.

CODE	MEANING
AE	Accessible Entryway
AE+A	Accessible Entry with Assistance
AI	Accessible Interior
AI+A	Accessible Interior with Assistance
AT	Accessible Toilet
AT+A	Accessible Toilet with Assistance
AL	Accessible Lift (elevator)
AL+A	Accessible Lift with Assistance
AR	Accessible Hotel Room
AR+A	Accessible Hotel Room with Assistance
AB	Accessible Hotel Bathroom
AB+A	Accessible Hotel Bathroom with Assistance
♥	Caring, welcoming attitude regarding accessibility

For more detailed information, please refer to the full Accessibility Codes chart on page 4 of the Introduction. For more information on Accessibility Levels, see page 2.

Amsterdam's. Ask your Amsterdam questions here (Mon–Fri 9:30–17:30, Sat 10:00–14:00, closed Sun, tel. 0900/616-1600, €0.50/min, helpful parking brochure). The €1 *Holiday Magazine* has a good accessibility section (free if you buy the fine €2 town map). The TI also sells a €2 self-guided walking-tour map for over-achievers. The little computer terminal prints out free maps anytime on the curb outside the TI.

Arrival in Haarlem: Haarlem's train station has elevators that allow wheelchair users access from the platform to the street level. As you leave the station (which has lockers), the TI is on your right and the bus station is across the street. Two parallel streets flank the train station

Haarlem

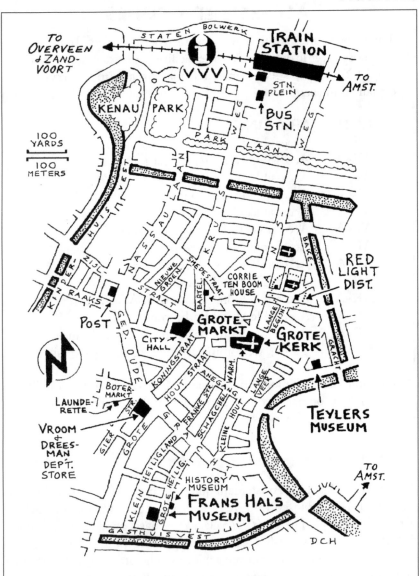

(Kruisweg and Jansweg). Head up either street, and you'll reach the town square and church in six wheelchair-accessible blocks (narrow sidewalks and lots of pedestrians). If you need help, ask a local person to point you toward the *Grote Markt* (Main Square).

Parking is expensive on the streets and €1 an hour in several central garages. Two main garages let you park overnight for €1 (at the train station and near Die Raeckse Hotel).

Helpful Hints

Laundry: My Beautiful Launderette is handy and cheap (€5 wash and dry, self-service, bring change, daily 8:30–20:30, €8 full service available Mon–Fri 9:00–17:00, near Vroom & Dreesman department store at Boter Markt 20).

Parade: On April 24, 2004, an all-day **Flower Parade** of floats wafts through eight towns, including Haarlem.

Local Guide: For a local guide, consider Walter Schelfhout (€75/2 hrs, tel. 023/535-5715).

SIGHTS

▲▲**Market Square (Grote Markt)**—Haarlem's market square, where 10 streets converge, is the town's delightful centerpiece...as it has been for 700 years. To enjoy a coffee or beer here, simmering in Dutch good living, is a quintessential European experience. In a recent study, the Dutch were found to be the most content people in Europe. And later, the people of Haarlem were found to be the most content in the Netherlands. Observe. Sit and gaze at the church, appreciating the same

scene Dutch artists captured in oil paintings that now hang in museums.

Just a few years ago, trolleys ran through the square and cars were parked everywhere. But today it's a wheelchair-accessible people zone, with market stalls filling the square on Mondays and Saturdays and café tables on other days.

This is a great place to build a picnic with Haarlem finger foods—raw herring, local cheese (Gouda and Edam), a *frikandel* (little corn-dog sausage), french fries with mayonnaise, *stroopwafels* (waffles with syrup), *poffertjes* (little sugar doughnuts), or one of many different ethnic foods (falafel, *shoarma*, Indonesian). Overseeing the square is the...

L. J. Coster statue: Forty years before Gutenberg "invented" the first printing press, this man carved the letter "A" out of wood, dropped it into some wet sand and saw the imprint it left. He got the idea of making movable type out of wood (and later he may have tried using lead). For Haarlemmers, that was good enough and they credit their man, L. J. Coster, with inventing modern printing. In the statue, Coster (c. 1370–1440) holds up a block of movable type and points to himself, saying: "I made this." How much Coster did is uncertain, but Gutenberg trumped him by building a printing press, casting type in metal, and pounding out the Bible.

Town Hall: This has been the site of Haarlem's town hall since about 1100 (when William the Conqueror ruled England). Remember that while most of medieval Europe was ruled by kings, dukes, and barons, Haarlem has been largely self-governing since 1425. The town hall was rebuilt after a 1351 fire, and the facade is from 1630. (The entry is wheelchair-accessible, with a fully adapted toilet—one of the few in town.)

The town drunk used to hang out on the bench in front of the town hall, where he'd expose himself to newlyweds coming down the stairs. The Dutch, rather than arrest the man, moved the bench.

Meat Market (Vleeshall), 1603: The fine Flemish Renaissance building nearest the cathedral is the old meat hall. Built by the rich butchers and leatherworkers guilds, the meat market was on the ground floor, the leather upstairs, and the cellar was filled with ice to keep the meat preserved. It's decorated with carved bits of early advertising—sheep and cows for sale.

▲**Church (Grote Kerk)**—This 15th-century Gothic church (now Protestant) is worth a look, if only for its Oz-like organ (from 1738, 100 feet high, its 5,000 pipes impressed both Handel and Mozart). Note how the organ, which fills the west end, seems to steal the show from the altar.

Access: AE+A, AI, Level 2—Moderately accessible. There is a tall step and a ledge to get in the door, but the interior is accessible. There is no accessible toilet.

Cost, Hours, and Location: €1.50, Mon–Sat 10:00–16:00, closed Sun to tourists, tel. 023/532-4399. The church is on the Market Square; to enter, find the small Entrée sign behind the church at Oude Groenmarkt 23.

Organ Concert: Consider attending (even part of) a concert to hear Holland's greatest pipe organ (regular free concerts Tue at 20:15 mid-May–mid-Oct, additional concerts Thu at 15:00 July–Aug, confirm schedule at TI or at www.bavo.nl).

▲▲**Frans Hals Museum**—Haarlem is the hometown of Frans Hals, and this refreshing museum—an almshouse for old men back in 1610—displays many of his greatest paintings. Enjoy lots of Frans Hals group portraits and the take-me-back paintings of old-time Haarlem. A 17th-century artist's painting *Proverbs* illustrates 72 old Dutch proverbs. To peek into old Dutch ways, identify some with the help of the English-language key.

Access: AE, AI+A, AT, Level 2—Moderately accessible. Most of the interior is accessible, except for a couple of steps into two rooms and four steps into another room. They have one loaner wheelchair (first come, first served).

Cost, Hours, and Location: €5.40, wheelchair user pays but companion goes free (only if companion pushes wheelchair), Tue–Sat 11:00–17:00, Sun 12:00–17:00, closed Mon, Groot Heiligland 62, tel. 023/511-5775, www.franshalsmuseum.nl.

History Museum—This small museum, across the street from the Frans Hals Museum, offers a glimpse of old Haarlem. Request the English version of the 10-minute video. Study the large-scale model of Haarlem in 1822 while its fortifications were still intact, and enjoy the new "time machine" computer and video display that shows you various aspects of life in Haarlem at different points in history. The adjacent architecture center (free) may be of interest to architects.

Access: AE, AI, AT, Level 1—Fully accessible.

Cost, Hours, and Location: €1, Tue–Sat 12:00–17:00, Sun 13:00–17:00, closed Mon, Groot Heiligland 47, tel. 023/542-2427.

Corrie ten Boom House—Haarlem is home to Corrie ten Boom, popularized by *The Hiding Place,* an inspirational book and movie about the Ten Boom family's experience protecting Jews from the Nazis. Corrie ten Boom gives the other half of the Anne Frank story—the point of view of those who risked their lives to hide Dutch Jews during the Nazi occupation (1940–1945).

The clock shop was the Ten Boom family business. The elderly father and his two daughters—Corrie and Betsy, both in their 50s—lived above the store and in the brick building attached in back (along Schoutensteeg alley). Corrie's bedroom was on the top floor at the back. This room was tiny to start with, but the family built a second, secret room at the very back—the hiding place, where they could hide six or seven Jews at a time.

Devoutly religious, the family had a long tradition of tolerance, having for generations hosted prayer meetings here in their home for both Jews and Christians.

The Gestapo, tipped off that the family was harboring Jews, burst into the Ten Boom house. Finding a suspicious number of ration coupons, the Nazis arrested the family but failed to find the six Jews in the hiding place (who later escaped). Corrie's father and sister died while in prison, but Corrie survived the Ravensbrück concentration camp to tell her story in her memoir.

Access: Level 4—Not accessible. Unfortunately, since it has many levels and tight hallways, this museum is best left to energetic slow walkers.

Cost, Hours, and Location: The Ten Boom House is open for 60-minute English tours; the tours are sometimes mixed with preaching. Donation accepted, April–Oct Tue–Sat 10:00–16:00, Nov–March Tue–Sat 11:00–15:00, closed Mon, 50 yards north of Market Square at Barteljorisstraat 19, tel. 023/531-0823. The clock-shop people get all wound up if you go inside; wait in the little side street at the door, where tour times are posted.

▲**Teylers Museum**—Famous as the oldest museum in Holland, Teylers is interesting mainly as a look at a 200-year-old museum—fossils, minerals, and primitive electronic gadgetry. New exhibition halls (with rotating exhibits) have freshened up the place. Stop by if you enjoy mixing, say, Renaissance sketches with pickled extinct fish.

Access: AE+A, AI, AT, Level 2—Moderately accessible. Wheelchair users gain entrance by alerting the staff inside the entry (three 6" steps). Loaner wheelchairs are available.

Cost, Hours, and Location: €5.50, Tue–Sat 10:00–17:00, Sun 12:00–17:00, Spaarne 16, tel. 023/531-9010.

Red Lights—Roll or stroll through a little red light district as precious as a Barbie doll—and legal since the 1980s (2 blocks northeast of Market Square, off Lange Begijnestraat, no senior or student discounts). Don't miss the mall marked by the red neon sign reading *t'Steegje*. The nearby *t'Poortje* (office park) costs €6.

AMSTERDAM TO HAARLEM TRAIN TOUR

Since you may be commuting from Amsterdam to Haarlem, here's a tour to keep you entertained. Departing from Amsterdam, grab a seat on the right (with your back to Amsterdam, top deck if possible). Everything is on the right unless we say on the left.

You're riding the oldest train line in Holland. Across the harbor behind the Amsterdam station, the tall brown skyscraper is the corporate office of **Shell Oil.** The Dutch had the first multinational corporation (the United East India Company, back in the 17th century). And today this international big-business spirit survives with companies like Shell and Philips.

Leaving Amsterdam, you'll see the cranes and ships of its harbor—sizable but nothing like the world's biggest in nearby Rotterdam.

On your left, find the old **windmill.** In front of it, the little garden plots and cottages are escapes for big-city people who probably don't even have a balcony.

Coming into the Sloterdijk Station (where trains connect for Amsterdam airport), you'll see huge office buildings, such as Dutch Telecom KPN. These grew up after the station made commuting easy.

Look for the **drive-in brothel** less than a mile past Sloterdijk Station, 50 yards to the right of the tracks (just before a long line of modern windmills—see the pink urinals and the purple door). A yellow sign says, *Tippel Zone—open 21:00. (Tippel* is the sound a mouse makes when it runs through the house at night.) There's an oval driveway with pink "bus stops" for browsing, a lounge building, and blue privacy stalls behind (including 2 for bikers). The lounge has a clinic with a nurse and counselors to keep the women healthy. If a prostitute is diagnosed with AIDS, she gets a subsidized apartment to encourage her to quit the business. Shocking as this may seem to some, it's a good example of a pragmatic solution to a problem—getting the most dangerous prostitutes off the streets to combat the spread of AIDS.

Passing through a forest and by some houseboats, you enter a *polder*—reclaimed land. This is an ecologically sound farm zone, run without chemicals. Cows, pigs, and chickens run free—they're not raised in cages. The train tracks are on a dike, which provides a solid foundation not susceptible to floods. This way the transportation system functions right through any calamity. Looking out at the distant dike, remember you're in the most densely populated country in Europe. On the horizon, sleek, modern windmills whirl.

On the right, just after the tall green-and-white telecom tower, find a big, beige-and-white building. This is the **mint,** where currency is printed (top security, no advertising). This has long been a family business—see the name: Johan Enschede.

As the train slows down, you're passing through the Netherlands' biggest train-car maintenance facility and entering Haarlem. Look left. The domed building is a prison, built in 1901 and still in use. The windmill burned down in 1932 and was just rebuilt in 2002.

When you cross the Spaarne River, you'll see the great church spire towering over Haarlem as it has since medieval times—back when a fortified wall circled the town. Notice the white copy of the same spire capping the smaller church between the prison and the big church. This was the original sandstone steeple that stood atop the big church, until structural problems forced them to move it to another church and build a new spire for the big church. Hop out into one of Holland's oldest stations. Art Nouveau decor from 1908 survives all around.

SLEEPING

Level 1—Fully Accessible
Hotel Joops (yopes, rhymes with ropes; **AE, AI, AL, AR, AB, ❤**), with 20 comfortable rooms, is located just behind the church (Db-€90, Tb-€100, Qb-€120, breakfast buffet-€9.50, Internet access, Oude

---

SLEEP CODE

(€1 = about $1.15, country code: 31, area code: 023)
The helpful Haarlem TI, just outside the train station, can nearly always find you a €20 bed in a private home (usually not accessible)—for a €4.50-per-person fee plus a cut of your host's money. Avoid this if you can; it's cheaper to reserve calling direct. Nearly every Dutch person you'll encounter speaks English.

Haarlem is most crowded in April and May (especially Easter weekend) and in July and August.

The listed prices include breakfast unless otherwise noted and usually include the €1.70-per-person-per-day tourist tax. To avoid this town's louder-than-normal street noises, forgo views for a room in the back. Hotels and the TI have a useful parking brochure.

Please see "Accessibility Codes" sidebar on page 399 of this chapter for a quick guide to codes. For a more detailed explanation of Accessibility Levels and Codes, please see page 2 of the Introduction.

Groenmarkt 20, tel. 023/532-2008, fax 023/532-9549, Joops@easynet.nl). They have many wheelchair-accessible bedrooms that share one wheelchair-accessible bathroom and shower in the hall on the first floor. To reach the front desk, you'll have to manage one 2" entry step.

Level 3—Minimally Accessible
Both of these hotels, with stairs and tight hallways, are best for slow walkers.

Hotel Amadeus, on Market Square, has 15 small, bright, and basic rooms. Some have views of the square. This characteristic hotel, ideally located above an early 20th-century dinner café, is relatively quiet. Its lush old lounge/breakfast room on the second floor (no elevator) overlooks the square, and Mike and Inez take good care of their guests (Sb-€57.50, Db-€80, Tb-€105, Qb-€110, includes tax, 2-night stay and cash get you a 5 percent discount, steep climb to lounge, then an elevator, Grote Markt

Haarlem Hotels and Restaurants

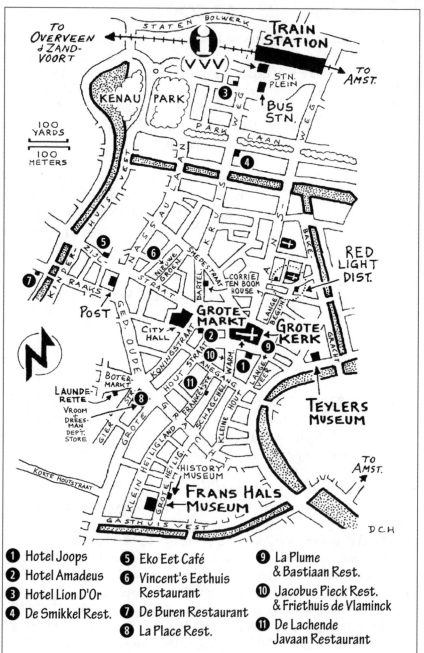

① Hotel Joops
② Hotel Amadeus
③ Hotel Lion D'Or
④ De Smikkel Rest.

⑤ Eko Eet Café
⑥ Vincent's Eethuis
   Restaurant
⑦ De Buren Restaurant
⑧ La Place Rest.

⑨ La Plume
   & Bastiaan Rest.
⑩ Jacobus Pieck Rest.
   & Friethuis de Vlaminck
⑪ De Lachende
   Javaan Restaurant

10, tel. 023/532-4530, fax 023/532-2328, www.amadeus-hotel.com, info@amadeus-hotel.com). The hotel also runs a six-terminal Internet café (€1.20/15 min, 25 percent discount with this book; second floor, no elevator).

Hotel Lion D'Or is a classy, 34-room business hotel with all the professional comforts and a handy location. Don't expect a warm welcome (Sb-€135–155, Db-€165–185, extra bed-€30, elevator, some nonsmoking rooms, across the street from train station at Kruisweg 34, tel. 023/532-1750, fax 023/532-9543, www.goldentulip.nl/hotels/gtliondor, reservations@hotelliondor.nl).

EATING

For details on eating Dutch, see "Eating," page 363 of the Amsterdam chapter. Unless otherwise noted (by **AT** or **AT+A**), these restaurants do not have accessible toilets.

Between Market Square (Grote Markt) and the Train Station

Pancakes for dinner? **Pannekoekhuis De Smikkel** (**AE+A, AI,** Level 2—Moderately accessible, one 4" entry step) serves a selection of more than 50 dinner (meat, cheese, etc.) and dessert pancakes. The €8 pancakes are filling; smaller sizes are available (daily 12:00–21:00, Sun from 16:00, closed Mon in winter, 2 blocks in front of station, Kruisweg 57, tel. 023/532-0631).

Enjoy a sandwich or coffee surrounded by trains and 1908 architecture in the classy **Foodcourt Haarlem Station** (**AE, AI,** Level 2—Moderately accessible; daily 7:30–20:00, between tracks #3 and #6 at the station).

On or near Zijlstraat

Eko Eet Café (**AE, AI,** Level 2—Moderately accessible) is great for a cheery, tasty vegetarian meal (€11 *menu*, daily 17:30–21:30, Zijlstraat 39, tel. 023/532-6568).

Vincent's Eethuis (**AE+A, AI,** Level 2—Moderately accessible, one 5" entry step, then another 2" step, wide-open interior) serves the best cheap, basic Dutch food in town. This former St. Vincent's soup kitchen now feeds more gainfully employed locals than poor (€6, friendly staff, Mon–Fri 16:30–19:30, closed Sat–Sun, Nieuwe Groenmarkt 22).

The cheery **De Buren** (**AI,** Level 3—Minimally accessible, narrow entry) offers handlebar-mustache fun, serving happy locals traditional Dutch food such as *draadjesvlees* (beef stew with applesauce). Gerard and Marjo love their work. Enjoy their entertaining and creative menu, made especially for you (€11–16 dinners, "you choose the sauce," Wed–Sun 17:00–22:00, closed Mon–Tue, back garden terrace, outside the tourist area at Brouwersvaart 146, follow Raaks Straat west across the canal from Die Raeckse Hotel, tel. 023/534-3364).

Between the Market Square and Frans Hals Museum

La Place (**AE, AI, AL, AT,** Level 1—Fully accessible) serves a healthy budget lunch with Haarlem's best view. Sit on the top floor or roof garden of the Vroom & Dreesman department store (Mon 11:00–17:30, Tue–Sat 9:30–17:30, Thu until 20:30, closed Sun, on the corner of Grote Houtstraat and Gedempte Oude Gracht). Find the accessible lift at the back corner of the store and take it to the sixth floor.

Bastiaan (**AE, AI,** Level 2—Moderately accessible) serves good Mediterranean cuisine in a classy atmosphere (€16 dinners, Tue–Sat from 18:00, closed Sun–Mon, Lange Veerstraat 8, tel. 023/532-6006).

La Plume steak house (**AE+A, AI,** Level 2—Moderately accessible, staff can assist with the one 4" entry step) is noisy with a happy, local, and carnivorous crowd (€12–18 meals, daily from 17:30, Lange Veerstraat 1, tel. 023/531-3202).

Jacobus Pieck Eetlokaal (Level 3—Minimally accessible, three 6" entry steps, narrow landing, and tight aisles) is popular with locals for its fine-value "global cuisine" (€9.50 plate of the day, great €5 sandwiches, Mon 10:00–17:00, Tue–Sat 10:00–22:00, closed Sun, Warmoesstraat 18, behind church, tel. 023/532-6144).

Friethuis de Vlaminck (Level 3—Minimally accessible) is the place for a cone of old-fashioned french fries (€1.55, Warmoesstraat 3, Tue–Sat until 18:00, closed Sun–Mon, behind church).

De Lachende Javaan (**AE, AI,** Level 2—Moderately accessible) serves the best Indonesian food in town. The €18 *rijsttafel* is excellent (Tue–Sun from 17:00, closed Mon, Frankestraat 27, tel. 023/532-8792).

TRANSPORTATION CONNECTIONS

By train to: Amsterdam (6/hr, 15 min, €3.20 one-way, €5.50 same-day return, ticket not valid on "Lovers Train," a misnamed private train that runs hrly), **Delft** (2/hr, 40 min), **Hoorn** (4/hr, 1 hr), **The Hague** (4/hr, 35 min), and **Alkmaar** (2/hr, 30 min).

To **Schiphol Airport:** by **taxi** (about €45) or by **train** (4/hr, 40 min, transfer at Amsterdam-Sloterdijk, €4.55).

GERMANY

(Deutschland)

- Germany is 136,000 square miles (like Montana)
- Population is 77 million (about 570 per square mile, declining slowly)
- 1 euro (€) = about $1.15

Deutschland is energetic, efficient, and organized. It is Europe's muscle man—both economically and wherever people line up (Germans have a reputation for pushing ahead). Its bustling cities hold 85 percent of its people, and average earnings are among the highest on earth. Ninety-seven percent of the workers get one-month paid vacations, and, during the other 11 months, they create a gross national product that's about one-third of the United States' and growing. Germany has risen from the ashes of World War II to become the world's fifth-largest industrial power, ranking fourth in steel output and nuclear power and third in automobile production. Germany shines culturally, beating out all but two countries in production of books, Nobel laureates, and professors.

Germany is young by European standards. In 1850, there were 35 independent countries in what is now Germany. In medieval times there were 350, each with its own weights, measures, coinage, king, and lotto. "Germany" was finally united in 1871 by Otto von Bismarck. Over the next century, it lost two World Wars and was split down the middle during the Cold War.

While its East-West division lasted about 40 years, historically Germany has been divided between north and south. While northern Germany was barbarian, is Protestant, and assaults life aggressively, southern Germany was Roman, is Catholic, and enjoys a more relaxed tempo of life. The American image of Germany is beer-and-pretzel Bavaria (probably because that was "our" sector after the war). This historic north-south division is less pronounced these days, as Germany becomes a more mobile society. The big chore facing Germany today is integrating the wilted economy of what was East Germany into the powerhouse economy of the West. This monumental task has given the West higher taxes (and second thoughts).

Germany

Most Germans in larger towns and the tourist trade speak at least some English. Still, you'll get more smiles by using the German pleasantries. In smaller, nontouristy towns, German is the norm. German—like English, Dutch, Swedish, and Norwegian—is a Germanic language, making it easier on most American ears than Romance languages (such as French and Italian). The most important phrases: "Hello" is *guten Tag* (GOO-tehn tahg), "please" is *bitte* (BIT-teh), and "thank you" is *danke* (DAHNG-keh). For more, see the "Survival Phrases" near the end of this book (excerpted from *Rick Steves' German Phrase Book*).

For most visitors, the rich pastries, wine, and beer provide the fondest memories of Germanic cuisine. The wine (85 percent whites) is particularly good from the Mosel and Rhine areas. Germany is also a big beer country. The average German, who drinks 40 gallons of beer a year, knows that *dunkles* is dark, *helles* is light, *Flaschenbier* is bottled, and *vom Fass* is on tap. *Pils* is barley-based, *Weize* is wheat-based, and *Malzbier* is the malt beer that children learn with. *Radler* is half beer and half lemon-lime soda. As for treats, gummi bears are local gumdrops with a cult following (beware of imitations—you must see the word *Gummi*), and Nutella is a chocolate-hazelnut spread that may change your life.

Germany's tourist route today—Rhine, Romantic Road, Bavaria—was yesterday's trade route, connecting its most prosperous medieval cities. Your best first glance at Germany is the Rhine River Valley. We've featured this romantic region in this book, along with two convenient, interesting big cities nearby: Köln, which is directly on the Rhine train line, and Frankfurt, connected by its airport to most anywhere in the world.

ACCESSIBILITY IN GERMANY

Even though the Rhine Valley is hilly and often inaccessible, Germany generally has good access. The western half of the country, bombed during World War II, has been rebuilt into more modern styles that often meet good accessibility standards. Bigger cities such as Frankfurt and Köln are relatively flat and offer decent access.

Under the slogan "Tourism without Barriers," Germany is offering a wide range of travel packages that include barrier-free accommodation, activities, and services. Germany even celebrated the "Year of the Disabled" in 2003.

The **German National Tourist Office** can help you plan your visit (122 East 42nd Street, 52nd Floor, New York, NY 10168, tel. 212/661 7200, fax 212/6617174, www.visits-to-germany.com, gntony@aol.com).

For information specific to people with disabilities, see www.germany -tourism.de/e/1583.html. This useful Web site lists the accessibility of many public buildings and offers advice on accessible travel in Frankfurt, Mainz, Wiesbaden, and Munich.

Transportation

Facilities at German airports and train stations are usually good. Throughout the German transportation system, symbols provide guidance for those who do not speak the language. In most big cities, subways have at least some accessible stations and trains—ask for a map with access marked.

Organizations

Bifos helps people with disabilities find resources to assist them during a stay in Germany. They also rent accessible vans (Jordanstrasse 5, Kassel, tel. 0561/728-8540, fax 0561/728-8529, bifos@t-online.de).

NatKo runs tours for the disabled (tel. 06131/250-410, fax 06131/214-848, German-only Web site: www.natko.de).

The **Federal Association for the Disabled** (Bundesverband Selbsthilfe Körperbehinderter) can answer basic questions on access (Altkrautheimer Strasse 20, Krautheim, tel. 06294/42810, fax 06294/428-179).

Two independent living centers that can provide information concerning disability-related resources and travel destinations in Germany are **CIL Mainz** (Rheinstrasse 45, Mainz, tel. 06131/146-743, fax 06131/146-74440, zsl@mainz-online.de) and **Zentrum Selbstbestimmtes Leban Behinderter** (Luitpoldstrasse 42, Erlangen, tel. 09131/810-4690, fax 09131/204-572, info@zsl-erlangen.de).

RHINE VALLEY

The Rhine Valley is storybook Germany, a fairy-tale world of legends and robber-baron castles. Cruise the most castle-studded stretch of the romantic Rhine as you listen for the song of the treacherous Loreley. Explore the castle-crowned villages of Bacharach and St. Goar. And for real hands-on castle thrills, roll or stroll through the Rhineland's greatest castle, Rheinfels.

Nearby destinations—Köln and Frankfurt—offer a modern, big-city German experience, and much better accessibility than those quaint Rhine villages. Köln is an urban Jacuzzi that keeps the Rhine churning. It's home to Germany's greatest Gothic cathedral and its best collection of Roman artifacts, a world-class art museum, and a healthy dose of German urban playfulness. And Frankfurt, while not on the Rhine, is the closest major transportation hub. Many Americans stream in to and out of Europe through Frankfurt's huge airport—but consider staying for a while to check out the city's lively square and gaze at its towering skyscrapers.

ACCESSIBILITY IN THE RHINE VALLEY

The Rhine Valley is the least accessible destination covered in this book, but we've included it because the Rhine is Germany's most worthwhile sight. Though beautiful and enticing, the Rhine Valley presents wheelchair riders with many barriers: steep hillside villages, lots of stairs and narrow passageways, small train stations with stairs instead of elevators, and unevenly cobbled public spaces. Slow walkers have a few more options.

ACCESSIBILITY CODES

These codes offer a quick overview of what to expect. If applicable, more specific details about the facility (e.g., exact number and height of steps, special instructions for gaining entry) are explained in each listing.

CODE	MEANING
AE	Accessible Entryway
AE+A	Accessible Entry with Assistance
AI	Accessible Interior
AI+A	Accessible Interior with Assistance
AT	Accessible Toilet
AT+A	Accessible Toilet with Assistance
AL	Accessible Lift (elevator)
AL+A	Accessible Lift with Assistance
AR	Accessible Hotel Room
AR+A	Accessible Hotel Room with Assistance
AB	Accessible Hotel Bathroom
AB+A	Accessible Hotel Bathroom with Assistance
♥	Caring, welcoming attitude regarding accessibility

For more detailed information, please refer to the full Accessibility Codes chart on page 4 of the Introduction. For more information on Accessibility Levels, see page 2.

The big cities of Köln and Frankfurt offer the best accessibility, from their train stations and hotels to their best sights. From there, accessibility goes down as quaintness goes up: Mid-size Rhine towns like Koblenz have more barriers, and Bacharach and St. Goar, the Rhine's most charming villages, have very poor accessibility (especially train stations and hotels). The good news is that travelers of all mobility levels can take advantage of the valley's best experience: a lazy boat cruise down the Rhine (or, even more accessible, a quick zip along the river by train).

Rhine Valley

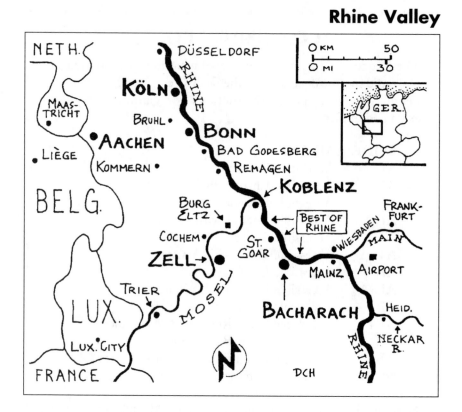

For a wheelchair user, the best Rhine experience begins in Köln (a convenient first stop in Germany if you're coming from London, Paris, Bruges, or Amsterdam). From there, take a train along the Rhine to Frankfurt (following the self-guided Rhine Blitz Tour, page 425). Frankfurt's international airport is a convenient departure point for returning home. To add more adventure to your trip, break up the Köln-to-Frankfurt journey with a boat cruise along the best part of the Rhine. Slow walkers and more adventurous and mobile wheelchair users may want to spend more time in the Rhine's quaintest villages—Bacharach and St. Goar—and venture by taxi up to St. Goar's Burg Rheinfels. But hotels in Bacharach and St. Goar are not at all accessible; wheelchair users may prefer to stay in Köln or Frankfurt instead, or at the fully accessible INNdependence Hotel in Mainz (managed by the village's disabled community and convenient to Frankfurt's airport).

As you decide which Rhineland activities best suit your abilities, keep in mind that with uneven terrain and lots of stairs, the castles are tough—even for non-disabled travelers. Sometimes it's better to "visit with your eyes" rather than go there in person. To castle or not to castle, the choice is yours.

The Rhine

Ever since Roman times, when this was the Empire's northern boundary, the Rhine has been one of the world's busiest shipping rivers. You'll see a steady flow of barges with 1,000- to 2,000-ton loads. Tourist-packed buses, hot train tracks, and highways line both banks.

Many of the castles were "robber-baron" castles, put there by petty rulers (there were 350 independent little countries in medieval Germany) to levy tolls on passing river traffic. A robber baron would put his castle on, or even in, the river. Then, often with the help of chains and a tower on the opposite bank, he'd stop each ship and get his toll. There were 10 customs stops in the 60-mile stretch between Mainz and Koblenz alone (no wonder merchants were early proponents of the creation of larger nation-states).

Some castles were built to control and protect settlements, and others were the residences of kings. As times changed, so did the lifestyles of the rich and feudal. Many castles were abandoned for more comfortable mansions in the towns.

Most Rhine castles date from the 11th, 12th, and 13th centuries. When the pope successfully asserted his power over the German emperor in 1076, local princes ran wild over the rule of their emperor. The castles saw military action in the 1300s and 1400s, as emperors began reasserting their control over Germany's many, many kingdoms.

The castles were also involved in the Reformation wars, in which Europe's Catholic and "protesting" dynasties fought it out using a fragmented Germany as their battleground. The Thirty Years' War (1618–1648) devastated Germany. The outcome: Each ruler got the freedom to decide if his people would be Catholic or Protestant, and one-third of Germany was dead. Production of Gummi Bears ceased entirely.

The French—who feared a strong Germany and felt the Rhine was the logical border between them and Germany—destroyed most of the

RHINE TRANSPORT ACCESSIBILITY

Note that boat access is better (and ramps less steep) when the river level is higher. Some boats are more accessible than others (the boats named *Stolzenfels*, *Rüdesheim*, and *Drachenfels* are the least accessible). Call ahead to find out when the most accessible boat will arrive at the town you're interested in.

Town	Train Station	K-D Boat Dock
Köln	Level 1—Fully accessible.	Level 2—Moderately accessible, with shore ramps.
Koblenz	Level 1—Fully accessible.	Level 2—Moderately accessible, with shore ramps.
St. Goar	Level 4—Not accessible; 23-6" steps lead down to long landing, then another nine 6" steps down to street.	Level 2—Moderately accessible, with shore ramps.
Bacharach	Level 4—Not accessible; 23-6" steps lead down to long landing, then another 24-6" steps up to town.	Level 2—Moderately accessible, with shore ramps.
Mainz	Level 1—Fully accessible.	Level 2—Moderately with shore ramps.
Frankfurt (not on Rhine)	Level 1—Fully accessible.	N/A

castles prophylactically (Louis XIV in the 1680s, the revolutionary army in the 1790s, and Napoleon in 1806). They were often rebuilt in neo-Gothic style in the Romantic Age—the late 1800s—and today are enjoyed as restaurants, hotels, hostels, and museums.

For information on Rhine castles, visit www.burgen-am-rhein.de. For more on the Rhine, visit www.loreleytal.com (heavy on hotels but has maps, photos, and a little history).

Getting around the Rhine

While the Rhine flows north from Switzerland to Holland, the scenic stretch from Mainz to Koblenz hoards all the touristic charm. Studded with the crenellated cream of Germany's castles, it bustles with boats, trains, and highway traffic. Travelers have fun exploring with a mix of big steamers, tiny ferries *(Fähre)*, trains, and bikes.

By Boat

While many travelers do the entire trip by boat, the most scenic hour is from St. Goar to Bacharach. Sit on the top deck with your handy Rhine map-guide (or the kilometer-keyed tour in this chapter) and enjoy the parade of castles, towns, boats, and vineyards.

There are several boat companies, but most travelers sail on the bigger, more expensive, and romantic **Köln-Düsseldorfer (K-D)** line. Your journey is free if you have a consec-utive-day Eurailpass or a dated Eurail Flexipass, Eurail Selectpass, or German railpass (but it uses up a day of any flex-ipass). Otherwise you'll pay about €8.40 for the first hour, then progressively cheaper per hour. The recommended Bacharach–St. Goar trip costs €8.40 one-way, €10.20 round-trip; it's half-price on Monday and Friday for seniors over 60 (tel. 06741/1634 in St. Goar, tel.  06743/1322 in Bacharach, www.k-d.com). Boats run daily in both directions from April through October, with no boats off-season. Complete, up-to-date schedules are posted in any station, Rhineland hotel, TI, bank, current Thomas Cook Timetable, or at www.euraide.de/ricksteves (confirm times before your departure). You can purchase tickets at the dock up to five minutes before the boat leaves. The boat is rarely full. Romantics will plan to catch the old-time *Goethe* (**AE+A, AI, AT,** Level 2—Moderately accessible), which sails each direction once a day (see "Rhine Cruise Schedule" in this chapter; confirm time locally).

RHINE CRUISE SCHEDULE

Boats run May through September and on a reduced schedule for parts of April and October; no boats run November through March. These times are based on the 2003 schedule. Check www.euraide.de/ricksteves for any changes.

Koblenz	Boppard	St. Goar	Bacharach
—	9:00	10:15	11:25
*9:00	*11:00	*12:20	*13:35
11:00	13:00	14:15	15:25
14:00	16:00	17:15	18:25
13:10	11:50	10:55	10:15
14:10	12:50	11:55	11:15
—	13:50	12:55	12:15
18:10	16:50	15:55	15:15
*20:10	*18:50	*17:55	*17:15

Riding the "Nostalgic Route," you'll take the 1913 steamer Goethe *(AE+A, AI, AT, Level 2—Moderately accessible), with working paddle wheel and viewable engine room (departing Koblenz at 9:00 and Bacharach at 17:15).*

K-D Line Access: AE+A, AI, AL, AT, Level 2—Moderately accessible. Aside from requiring some assistance boarding (which can be more or less difficult, depending on the river level), K-D boats offer very good accessibility. You'll enter by ramp, sometimes with a small gap (staff will assist). Most of the boats have fully accessible interiors, including adapted toilets and elevators. The least-accessible boats are named *Stolzenfels, Rüdesheim,* and *Drachenfels*—call ahead to be sure you don't wind up on one of these (classified by K-D as non-accessible for boarding, with little accessibility once on board).

The smaller **Bingen-Rüdesheimer** line is slightly cheaper than K-D. Railpasses aren't valid on this cruise. Buy tickets on the boat. They offer three two-hour round-trip St. Goar-to-Bacharach trips daily in summer (about €7.50 one-way, €9.50 round-trip; departing St. Goar at 11:00, 14:10, and 16:10, departing Bacharach at 10:10, 12:00, and 15:00; tel. 06721/14140, www.bingen-ruedesheimer.com),

Bingen-Rüdesheimer Access: AE+A, AI, AL, AT, Level 2— Moderately accessible. Bingen-Rüdesheimer boats are wheelchair-accessible, with better access at St. Goar (ramps only, no steps) than at Bacharach (one 7" entry step). The ramp into the boat is steep, but boat staff is willing to help. Some boats have wheelchair-accessible bathrooms, plus ramps or elevators to the top deck. Call ahead for a schedule of the most-accessible boats.

By Train

Hourly milk-run trains down the Rhine hit every town: St. Goar to Bacharach—12 min; Bacharach to Mainz—60 min; Mainz to Frankfurt, 45 min. Some train schedules list St. Goar but not Bacharach as a stop, but any schedule listing St. Goar also stops at Bacharach. Tiny stations are unmanned; buy tickets at the platform machines or on the train. Prices are cheap (e.g., €2.60 between St. Goar and Bacharach).

Train Access: Trains range from Level 2—Moderately accessible to Level 3—Minimally accessible. Some trains have wheelchair-accessible cars (including accessible toilets). Ask at the station which trains are accessible. Sometimes the train floor does not meet the level of the platform, so there can be a gap to get on or off of a train. Catch the conductor's attention to assist with boarding and let him know of your destination to get assistance disembarking.

Station Access: Stations in bigger towns and cities (Köln, Koblenz, Mainz, Frankfurt) are fully accessible. Wheelchair users who'd like extra help can call the Mobility Service Center (MobilitätsServiceZentrale, tel. 0180-551-2512, Mon–Fri 8:00–20:00, Sat 8:00–14:00, closed Sun); they arrange assistance for train travelers, except at small stations such as St. Goar and Bacharach. The small, quaint Rhine villages suffer from very poor accessibility at their train stations. In St. Goar (Level 4—Not accessible), twenty-three 6" steps lead down to a long landing, then it's another nine 6" steps down to the street. From the platform in Bacharach (Level 4—Not accessible), twenty-three 6" steps lead down to a long landing, then it's another twenty-four 6" steps back up to the town. If possible, arrive in these two towns by car or by boat to avoid the accessibility difficulties at their train stations.

Best of the Rhine

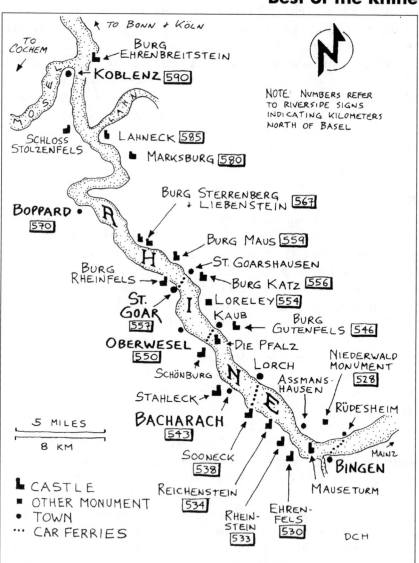

By Ferry

While there are no bridges between Koblenz and Mainz, you'll see car ferries (usually family-run for generations) about every three miles. Ferries near St. Goar and Bacharach cross the river every 10 minutes daily in the summer from about 6:00 to 20:00, connecting Bingen–Rüdesheim, Lorch–Niederheimbach, Engelsburg–Kaub, and St. Goar–St.Goarshausen (adult-€1, car and driver-€2.80, pay on the boat).

DER ROMANTISCHE RHEIN BLITZ ZUG FAHRT

One of Europe's great train thrills is zipping along the Rhine in this fast train tour (worth ▲▲▲). Here's a quick and easy, from-the-train-window tour (also works for car, or best by boat; you can cut in anywhere) that skips the syrupy myths filling normal Rhine guides. For more information than necessary, buy the handy *Rhine Guide from Mainz to Cologne* (€4.50 book with foldout map, at most shops or TIs). Or for skimpy information and a longer, prettier map, try the *Long Rhine Tour* map (€5.20).

Sit on the left (river) side of the train or boat going south from Koblenz. While nearly all of the castles listed are viewed from this side, we'll note the times when you should cross to (or look out of) the other side.

You'll notice large black-and-white kilometer markers along the riverbank. Rick erected these years ago to make this tour easier to follow. They tell the distance from the Rhinefalls, where the Rhine leaves Switzerland and becomes navigable. Now the river-barge pilots have accepted these as navigational aids as well. We're tackling just 60 kilometers (36 miles) of the 1,320-kilometer-long (820-mile) Rhine. Your Blitz Rhine Tour starts at Koblenz and heads upstream to Bingen. If you're going the other direction, it still works. Just hold the book upside down.

If you have limited time, try the recommended, shorter St. Goar-to-Bacharach cruise, included as part of the trip below.

Km 590: Koblenz—This Rhine blitz starts with Romantic Rhine thrills—at Koblenz. Koblenz is not a nice city (it was really hit hard in

World War II), but its place as the historic *Deutsche Ecke* (German corner)—the tip of land where the Mosel joins the Rhine—gives it a certain historic charm. Koblenz, derived from the Latin for "confluence," has Roman origins. Explore the park, noticing the reconstructed memorial to the Kaiser. Across the river, the yellow Ehrenbreitstein Castle now houses a hostel. It's a six-block roll or stroll from the station to the Koblenz boat dock (or catch a taxi). Accommodations for Koblenz are listed on page 450.

Km 585: Burg Lahneck—Above the modern autobahn bridge over the Lahn River, this castle *(Burg)* was built in 1240 to defend local silver mines; the castle was ruined by the French in 1688 and rebuilt in the 1850s in neo-Gothic style. Burg Lahneck faces another Romantic rebuild, the yellow Schloss Stolzenfels.

Km 580: Marksburg—This castle (black and white with the 3 modern chimneys behind it, just after town of Spay) is the best-looking of all the Rhine castles and the only surviving medieval castle on the Rhine. Because of its commanding position, it was never attacked. It has a great medieval interior and is now a museum (unfortunately not accessible; €4.50, daily April–Oct 10:00–18:00, Nov–March 11:00–17:00, call ahead to see if a rare English tour is scheduled, tel. 02627/206, www.marksburg.de). The three modern smokestacks vent Europe's biggest car-battery recycling plant just up the valley.

Km 570: Boppard—Once a Roman town, Boppard has some impressive remains of fourth-century walls. Notice the Roman towers and the substantial chunk of Roman wall near the train station, just above the main square.

Km 567: Burg Sterrenberg and Burg Liebenstein—These are the "Hostile Brothers" castles across from Bad Salzig. Take the wall between the castles (actually designed to improve the defenses of both castles), add two greedy and jealous brothers and a fair maiden, and create your own legend. Burg Liebenstein is now a fun, friendly, and affordable family-run hotel.

Km 560: While you can see nothing from here, a 19th-century lead mine functioned on both sides of the river with a shaft actually tunneling completely under it.

Km 559: Burg Maus—The Maus ("Mouse") got its name because the next castle was owned by the Katzenelnbogen family. ("Katze" means "cat.") In the 1300s, it was considered a state-of-the-art fortification...until

Napoleon had it blown up in 1806 with state-of-the-art explosives. It was rebuilt true to its original plans around 1900.

Km 557: St. Goar and Rheinfels Castle—Cross to (or look out) the other side of the train. The pleasant town of St. Goar was named for a sixth-century hometown monk. It originated in Celtic times (really old) as a place where sailors would stop, catch their breath, send home a postcard, and give thanks after surviving the seductive and treacherous Loreley crossing. St. Goar is worth a stop to explore its mighty Rheinfels Castle. For accessibility and accommodations, see page 438.

Now back to the river side of the train...

Km 556: Burg Katz—Burg Katz (Katzenelnbogen) faces St. Goar from across the river. Together, Burg Katz (built in 1371) and Rheinfels Castle had a clear view up and down the river and effectively controlled traffic. There was absolutely no duty-free shopping on the medieval Rhine. Katz got Napoleoned in 1806 and rebuilt around 1900. Today, it's under a rich and mysterious Japanese ownership. It's technically a hotel—Germany wouldn't allow its foreign purchase for private use—but it's so expensive, nobody's ever stayed there. Below the castle, notice the derelict grape terraces—worked since the eighth century, but abandoned only in the last generation. The Rhine wine is particularly good because the slate absorbs the heat of the sun and stays warm all night, resulting in sweeter grapes. Wine from the flat fields above the Rhine gorge is cheaper and good only as "table wine." The wine from the steep side of the Rhine gorge—harder to grow and harvest—is tastier and more expensive.

About Km 555: A statue of the Loreley, the beautiful but deadly nymph (see next listing for legend), combs her hair at the end of a long spit—built to give barges protection from vicious icebergs that occasionally rage down the river in the winter. The actual Loreley, a cliff, is just ahead.

Km 554: The Loreley—Steep a big slate rock in centuries of legend and it becomes a tourist attraction, the ultimate Rhinestone. The Loreley (flags on top, name painted near shoreline), rising 450 feet over the narrowest and deepest point of the Rhine, has long been important. It was a holy site in pre-Roman days. The legend says that the fine echoes here—thought to be ghostly voices—fertilized the legendary soil.

Because of the reefs just upstream (at kilometer 552), many ships never made it to St. Goar. Sailors (after days on the river) blamed their misfortune on a *wunderbares Fräulein* whose long blonde hair almost covered her

428 Rick Steves' Easy Access Europe

RHINE RIVER TRADE AND BARGE WATCHING

The Rhine is great for barge-watching. There's a constant parade of action, and each boat is different. Since ancient times, this has been a highway for trade. Today, the world's biggest port (Rotterdam) waits at the mouth of the river.

Barge workers are almost a subculture. Many own their own ships. The captain (and family) live in the stern. Workers live in the bow. The family car often decorates the bow like a shiny hood ornament. In the Rhine town of Kaub, there was a boarding school for the children of the Rhine merchant marine—but today it's closed, since most captains are Dutch, Belgian, or Swiss. The flag of the boat's home country flies in the stern (German; Swiss; Dutch—horizontal red, white, and blue; or French—vertical red, white, and blue). Logically, imports go upstream (Japanese cars, coal, and oil) and exports go downstream (German cars, chemicals, and pharmaceuticals). A clever captain manages to ship goods in each direction.

Tugs can push a floating train of up to five barges at once. Upstream it gets steeper and they can push only one at a time. Before modern shipping, horses dragged boats upstream (the faint remains of towpaths survive at points along the river). From 1873

body. Heinrich Heine's *Song of Loreley* (the CliffsNotes version is on local postcards) tells the story of a count who sent his men to kill or capture this siren after she distracted his horny son, causing him to drown. When the soldiers cornered the nymph in her cave, she called her father (Father Rhine) for help. Huge waves, the likes of which you'll never see today, rose from the river and carried Loreley to safety. And she has never been seen since.

But alas, when the moon shines brightly and the tour buses are parked, a soft, playful Rhine whine can still be heard from the Loreley. As you pass, listen carefully ("Sailors...sailors...over my bounding mane").

Km 552: Killer reefs, marked by red-and-green buoys, are called the "Seven Maidens." Okay, one goofy legend: The prince of Schönburg to 1900, they laid a chain from Bonn to Bingen, and boats with cogwheels and steam engines hoisted themselves upstream. Today, 265 million tons travel each year along the 530 miles from Basel on the Swiss border to Rotterdam on the Atlantic.

Riverside navigational aids are of vital interest to captains who don't wish to meet the Loreley. Boats pass on the right unless they clearly signal otherwise with a large blue sign. Since downstream ships can't stop or maneuver as freely, upstream boats are expected to do the tricky do-si-do work. Cameras monitor traffic all along and relay warnings of oncoming ships via large triangular signals posted before narrow and troublesome bends in the river. There may be two or three triangles per signpost, depending upon how many "sectors," or segments, of the river are covered. The lowest triangle indicates the nearest stretch of river. Each triangle tells if there's a ship in that sector. When the bottom side of a triangle is lit, that sector is empty. When the left side is lit, an oncoming ship is in that sector.

Castle (*ober* Oberwesel) had seven spoiled daughters who always dumped men because of their shortcomings. Fed up, he invited seven of his knights up to the castle and demanded that his daughters each choose one to marry. But they complained that each man had too big a nose, was too fat, too stupid, and so on. The rude and teasing girls escaped into a riverboat. Just downstream, God turned them into the seven rocks that form this reef. While this story probably isn't entirely true, there's a lesson in it for medieval children: Don't be hard-hearted.

Km 550: Oberwesel—Cross to (or look out) the other side of the train. Oberwesel was a Celtic town in 400 B.C., then a Roman military station. It now boasts some of the best Roman wall and medieval tower remains on the Rhine and the commanding Schönburg Castle. Notice how many of the train tunnels have entrances designed like medieval turrets—they were actually built in the Romantic 19th century. OK, back to the river side.

Km 546: Burg Gutenfels and Pfalz Castle: The Classic Rhine View—Burg Gutenfels (see white painted "Hotel" sign) and the ship-shape Pfalz Castle (built in the river in the 1300s) worked very effectively to tax medieval river traffic. The town of Kaub grew rich as Pfalz raised its chains when boats came and lowered them only when the merchants had paid their duty. Those who didn't pay spent time touring its prison, on a raft at the bottom of its well. In 1504, a pope called for the destruction of Pfalz, but a six-week siege failed. Notice the overhanging outhouse (tiny white room—with faded medieval stains—between two wooden ones).

In Kaub, a green statue honors the German field marshal Gebhard Leberecht von Blücher. He was Napoleon's nemesis. In 1813, as Napoleon fought his way back to Paris after his disastrous Russian campaign, he stopped at Mainz—hoping to fend off the Germans and Russians pursuing him by controlling that strategic bridge. Blücher tricked Napoleon. By building the first major pontoon bridge of its kind here at the Pfalz Castle, he crossed the Rhine and outflanked the French. Two years later, Blücher and Wellington teamed up to defeat Napoleon once and for all at Waterloo.

Km 544: The "Raft Busters"—Immediately before Bacharach, at the top of the island, buoys mark a gang of rocks notorious for busting up rafts. The Black Forest is upstream. It was poor, and wood was its best export. Black Foresters would ride log booms down the Rhine to the Ruhr (where there were timber-fortified coal-mine shafts) or to Holland (where logs were sold to shipbuilders). If they could navigate the sweeping bend just before Bacharach and then survive these "raft busters," they'd come home reckless and romantic, the German folkloric equivalent of American cowboys after payday.

Km 543: Bacharach and Burg Stahleck—Cross to (or look out) the other side of the train. Bacharach is an adorable village, but has poor accessibility (see details next page; accommodations are listed on page 447). Some of the Rhine's best wine is from this town, whose name means "altar to Bacchus." Local vintners brag that the medieval Pope Pius II ordered it by the cartload. The 13th-century Burg Stahleck, perched above the town, is now a hostel.

Look across the river to see...

Km 540: Lorch—This pathetic stub of a castle is barely visible from the road. Notice the small car ferry (3/hr, 10 min), one of several along the bridgeless stretch between Mainz and Koblenz. Now look inland to see the next four castles.

Km 538: Castle Sooneck—Built in the 11th century, this castle was twice destroyed by people sick and tired of robber barons.

Km 534: Burg Reichenstein, and **Km 533: Burg Rheinstein**— These are two of the first castles to be rebuilt in the Romantic era. Both are privately owned, tourable, and connected by a pleasant trail.

Km 530: Ehrenfels Castle—Opposite Bingerbrück and the Bingen station, you'll see the ghostly Ehrenfels Castle (clobbered by the Swedes in 1636 and by the French in 1689). Since it had no view of the river traffic to the north, the owner built the cute little *Mäuseturm* (Mouse Tower) on an island (the yellow tower you'll see near the train station today). Rebuilt in the 1800s in neo-Gothic style, it's now used as a Rhine navigation signal station. Look over the river.

Km 528: Niederwald Monument—Across from the Bingen train station on a hilltop is the 120-foot-high Niederwald monument, a memorial built with 32 tons of bronze in 1877 to commemorate "the reestablishment of the German Empire." A lift takes tourists to this statue from the famous and extremely touristy wine town of Rüdesheim.

From here, the Romantic Rhine becomes the industrial Rhine, and our tour is over.

Bacharach

Once prosperous from the wine and wood trade, Bacharach (BAHKH-ah-rahkh, with a guttural kh sound) is now just a pleasant half-timbered village of a thousand people working hard to keep its tourists happy. Accommodations are listed on page 447.

Accessibility in Bacharach: Bacharach is a quaint, old, cobbled town—less than ideal for wheelchair users. Note that the train station has very poor access, with no elevator and lots of steps. Arrival in Bacharach is much easier by car or, better yet, by K-D boat (the dock is fully accessible). For train station and boat accessibility, see "Getting around the Rhine," page 421. There are two wheelchair-accessible toilets

Bacharach

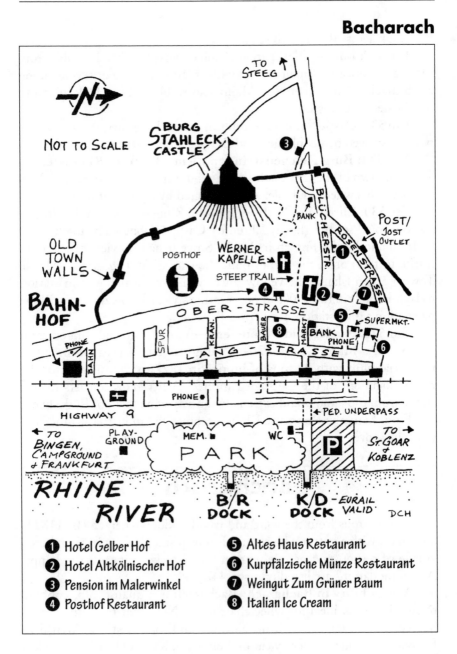

TO STEEG ↑

BURG STAHLECK CASTLE

NOT TO SCALE

BANK

BLÜCHERSTR.

ROSEN-STRASSE

POST/ JOST OUTLET

OLD TOWN WALLS

POSTHOF

WERNER KAPELLE

STEEP TRAIL

BAHN-HOF

OBER - STRASSE

SPUR

KRAN.

BAUER

MARKT

BANK

SUPER MKT.

PHONE

BAHN

LANG - STRASSE

PHONE

PHONE •

HIGHWAY 9

PED. UNDERPASS

TO BINGEN, CAMPGROUND & FRANKFURT

PLAY-GROUND

MEM. ■

PARK

WC

P

TO St GOAR & KOBLENZ

RHINE RIVER

B/R DOCK

K/D DOCK

EURAIL VALID

DCH

1 Hotel Gelber Hof
2 Hotel Altkölnischer Hof
3 Pension im Malerwinkel
4 Posthof Restaurant

5 Altes Haus Restaurant
6 Kurpfälzische Münze Restaurant
7 Weingut Zum Grüner Baum
8 Italian Ice Cream

in town: one is near the K-D boat dock (€0.50), and the other is in the courtyard near the Posthof TI office (free).

Tourist Information: The TI (**AE+A, AI, AT,** Level 2—Moderately accessible) is on the main street in the Posthof courtyard next to the church. The staff is willing to assist wheelchair users (April–Oct Mon–Fri 9:00–17:00, Sat 10:00–16:00, closed Sun; Nov–March Mon–Fri 9:00–12:00, closed Sat–Sun, Internet access-€6/hr, Oberstrasse 45, tel. 06743/919-303, www.bacharach.de or www.rhein-nahe-touristik.de, Herr Kuhn and his team SE). The TI stores bags for day-trippers, provides ferry schedules, and sells the handy *Rhine Guide from Mainz to Cologne* (€4.50).

Shopping: The Phil Jost beer-stein stores carry most everything a shopper could want. The more accessible shop (**AE, AI,** Level 2—Moderately accessible) is next to the post office at Rosenstrasse 16 (barrier-free entryway and wide aisles; Mon–Fri 8:30–18:00, Sat 8:30–17:00, closed Sun, ships overseas, 10 percent discount with this book, tel. 06743/1224, www.phil-jost-germany.com). The other branch (Level 3—Minimally accessible, three 8" steps and an obstructed, narrow entry) is across from the church in the main square (same hours as above and also open Sun 10:00–17:00). The Josts offer sightseeing advice, send faxes, and reserve German hotels for travelers (reasonable charge for phone and fax fees).

Local Guides: Get acquainted with Bacharach by taking a tour. Charming Herr Rolf Jung, retired headmaster of the Bacharach school, is a superb English-speaking guide. Herr Jung is accustomed to including wheelchair users and slow walkers in his tours (€30, 90 min, call to reserve, tel. 06743/1519). If Herr Jung is not available, the TI has a list of other English-speaking guides, or take the self-guided tour, described below.

Introductory Bacharach Roll or Stroll

Start at the Köln–Düsseldorfer ferry dock (next to a fine picnic park). View the town from the parking lot. The Rhine used to lap against Bacharach's town wall, just over the present-day highway. Every few years the river floods, covering the highway with about 10 feet of water. The **castle** on the hill is a youth hostel. Two of its original 16 towers are visible from here (up to five if you look real hard). The huge

roadside wine keg declares this town was built on the wine trade.

Reefs up the river forced boats to unload upriver and reload here. Consequently, Bacharach became the biggest wine trader on the Rhine. A riverfront crane hoisted huge kegs of prestigious "Bacharach" wine (which in practice was from anywhere in the region). The tour buses next to the dock and the flags of the biggest spenders along the highway remind you today's economy is basically tourism.

At the big town map and accessible public toilet (€0.50), take the underpass, ascend on the steep ramp to the left, continue the short distance further to the left, then pass under the train tracks through the medieval gate (one out of an original fifteen 14th-century gates). Travel across rough cobblestones for 100 feet and continue to the end of the street (Bauerstrasse) over medium-rough cobblestones and an asphalt-paved street to Bacharach's main street, Oberstrasse. (Left will take you to the train station.)

Travel right to the golden horn that hangs over the old **Posthof** (**AE, AI, AT,** Level 1—Fully accessible; TI, free accessible toilet at back of courtyard and non-accessible toilet upstairs in smaller courtyard). The post horn symbolizes the postal service throughout Europe. In olden days, when the postman blew this, traffic stopped and the mail sped through. This post station dates from 1724, when stagecoaches ran from Köln to Frankfurt.

Enter the courtyard—once a carriage house and inn that accommodated Bacharach's first VIP visitors. Notice the fascist eagle (from 1936, on the left as you enter) and the fine view of the two-tone Protestant **church** on the right and a ruined chapel above. The Posthof is the home of the **Rhineland Museum,** which hopes to open in 2004 with a cultural landscape exhibit on the Rhine Valley, well described in English. Manager Bitz's vision even includes wine-tasting (www.mittelrheintal.de).

Two hundred years ago, Bacharach's main drag was the only road along the Rhine. Napoleon widened it to fit his cannon wagons. Proceed to the church, passing the **Italian Ice Cream** café (**AE+A, AI,** Level 2—Moderately accessible), where friendly Mimo serves his special invention: tasty Riesling wine-flavored gelato (one entry step; €0.60 per scoop, opposite Posthof at Oberstrasse 48). Continue past the steps between the Posthof and the church (they lead to the castle).

The church marks the town center. If you enter the church (Level 3—Minimally accessible, eleven 7" entry steps; English info on table near door), you'll find grotesque capitals, brightly painted in medieval style, and a mix of round Romanesque and pointed Gothic arches. Left of the altar, some medieval frescoes survive where an older Romanesque arch was cut by a pointed Gothic one.

Across from the church is the half-timbered, red-and-white Altes Haus (from 1368), the oldest house in town. Continue down Oberstrasse past the Altes Haus to the **old mint** *(Münze)*, marked by a crude coin in its sign. Across from the mint, the wine garden of Fritz Bastian is the liveliest place in town after dark (see "Eating," page 448). Above you in the vineyards stands a ghostly black-and-gray tower.

Take the next left (Rosenstrasse) and wander 100 yards up to the **well.** Notice the sundial and the wall painting of 1632 Bacharach with its walls intact.

If you have limited mobility, end the tour here, skip the next paragraph, and read the rest of the tour for its historical detail. Adventurous slow walkers can continue, climbing the tiny-stepped lane behind the well up into the vineyard and to the tower. The slate steps (four 7" steps to a rough, narrow, uphill path, then eighteen 6"-to-11" steps to another narrow, rough path) lead to a small, extremely steep path through the vineyard that deposits you at a viewpoint atop the stubby remains of the old town wall (if signs indicate that the path is closed, get as close to the tower base as possible).

A grand medieval town spreads before you. When Frankfurt had 15,000 residents, medieval Bacharach had 4,000. For 300 years (1300–1600), Bacharach was big, rich, and politically powerful.

From this perch, you can see the chapel ruins and six surviving **city towers.** Visually trace the wall to the castle. The castle was actually the capital of Germany for a couple of years in the 1200s. When Barbarossa, the Holy Roman Emperor, went away to fight the Crusades, he left his brother (who lived here) in charge of his vast realm. Bacharach was home of one of seven electors who voted for the Holy Roman Emperor in 1275. To protect their own power, these elector-princes did their best to choose the weakest guy on the ballot. The elector from Bacharach helped select a two-bit prince named Rudolf von Hapsburg (from a two-bit castle in Switzerland). The underestimated Rudolf brutally silenced the robber barons along the Rhine and established the mightiest dynasty in European history. His family line, the Hapsburgs, ruled the Austro-Hungarian Empire until 1918.

Plagues, fires, and the Thirty Years' War (1618–1648) finally did Bacharach in. The town has slumbered for several centuries, with a population of about a thousand. And today the royal castle houses commoners—40,000 overnights annually by youth hostelers.

In the mid-19th century, painters such as Turner and writers such as Victor Hugo were charmed by the Rhineland's romantic mix of past glory, present poverty, and rich legend. They put this part of the Rhine on the old "grand tour" map as the "Romantic Rhine." Victor Hugo pondered the ruined 15th-century chapel, which you can see under the castle. In his 1842 travel book, *Rhein Reise (Rhine Travels)*, he wrote, "No doors, no roof or windows, a magnificent skeleton puts its silhouette against the sky. Above it, the ivy-covered castle ruins provide a fitting crown. This is Bacharach, land of fairy tales, covered with legends and sagas." If you're enjoying the Romantic Rhine, thank Victor Hugo and company.

To get back into town, return to the sundial and explore other surrounding streets.

St. Goar

St. Goar is a classic Rhine town—its hulk of a castle overlooking a half-timbered shopping street and leafy riverside park busy with sightseeing ships and contented strollers. From the boat dock, the main drag—a pedestrian mall without history—cuts through town before winding up to the castle. Rheinfels Castle, once the mightiest on the Rhine, is the single best Rhineland ruin to explore. Accommodations are listed on page 449.

Accessibility in St. Goar: Like other small Rhine villages, St. Goar suffers from poor accessibility. The main drag is accessible, as is the riverfront pathway. But most shops in town have a few entry steps, and none of the town's three public toilets (one at each end of town, a third up at the castle) is wheelchair-accessible.

Tourist Information: The helpful St. Goar TI (**AE+A, AI,** Level 2—Moderately accessible; three 7" entry steps) books rooms, offers a free left-luggage service, and sells the *Rhine Guide from Mainz to Cologne* (€4.50). It's on the pedestrian street, three blocks from the K-D boat dock and train station (May–Oct Mon–Fri 8:00–12:30 & 14:00–17:00,

St. Goar

BURG RHEINFELS CASTLE

DCH

TRAIL TO BACHARACH

TRAIN STATION

TO BACHARACH + FRANKFURT

ULMENHOF TOWER

SCHLOSSBERG

BISMARCK-

YOUTH HOSTEL

PHONE

OBER-STRASSE

HEER-STRASSE

HIGHWAY 9

PHONE

HEER-STRASSE

WC

HARBOR

P A R K

BUS PARKING

TO BOPPARD, KOBLENZ

P

KD DOCK (EURAIL VALID)

R H I N E RIVER

BR DOCK

FERRY

TO LORELEY

ST. GOARSHAUSEN

NOT TO SCALE

❶ Rheinfels Castle Hotel & Rest.
❷ To Landsknecht Hotel
❸ Hotel am Markt & Rest.
❹ Tourist Office
❺ Post Office
❻ Montag Shops

Sat 10:00–12:00, closed Sun; Nov–April until 16:30 and closed Sat–Sun, tel. 06741/383).

Picnic: St. Goar's waterfront park is hungry for a picnic. The small Edeka **supermarket** (**AE, AI,** Level 2—Moderately accessible) on the main street is great for foraging (Mon–Fri 8:00–18:30, Sat 8:00–13:00, closed Sun).

Shopping: The friendly and helpful Montag family runs the Hotel Montag (Michael) and three shops (steins—Misha; Steiffs—Maria; and cuckoo clocks—Marion), all at the base of the castle hill road. The stein shop (**AE, AI,** Level 2—Moderately accessible; one of the few stores in town without steps) under the hotel has Rhine guides, fine steins, and copies of Rick's Germany guidebook. All three shops offer 10 percent off any of their souvenirs (including Hummels) for travelers with this book (€5 minimum purchase). On-the-spot VAT refunds cover about half your shipping costs (if you're not shipping, they'll give you VAT form to claim refund at airport). The Montags' teddy bear store has four 7" entry steps, while the clock shop has five 6" entry steps, with staff willing to assist.

St. Goar's Rheinfels Castle

Sitting like a dead pit bull above St. Goar, this mightiest of Rhine castles (worthy of ▲▲▲) rumbles with ghosts from its hard-fought past. Burg Rheinfels (built in 1245) withstood a siege of 28,000 French troops in 1692. But in 1797, the French Revolutionary army destroyed it.

Rheinfels *was* huge. Once the biggest castle on the Rhine, it was used for ages as a quarry, and today—while still mighty—it's only a small

fraction of its original size. This hollow but interesting shell offers your single best hands-on ruined-castle experience on the river. Rather than wander aimlessly, visit the castle by following what you can of our self-guided tour (see below). The castle map is mediocre; the English booklet is better, with history and illustrations (€1.80). If planning to explore the mine tunnels, bring a flashlight, buy a tiny one (€2.60 at entry), or do it by candlelight (museum sells candles with matches, €0.50). If it's damp, be careful of slippery stones. An inaccessible WC is in the castle courtyard under the stairs to the restaurant entry.

Access: Range from Level 2—Moderately accessible to Level 4—Not accessible. With lots of uneven terrain, steps, and levels, this castle presents a challenge for wheelchair users. But more adventurous wheelchair users and slow walkers will want to visit the castle—for the Rhine view, if nothing else—and, if able to go up hills and over uneven terrain, can explore quite a bit of the grounds. Even the most adventurous, though, will likely encounter difficulty with some of the castle's steep, narrow stairs and tight passageways.

Cost, Hours, and Location: €4, family card-€10, mid-March–Oct daily 9:00–18:00, last entry at 17:00, Nov–mid-March only Sat–Sun 11:00–17:00. The guided tours of the castle are excellent but not accessible

St. Goar's Rheinfels Castle

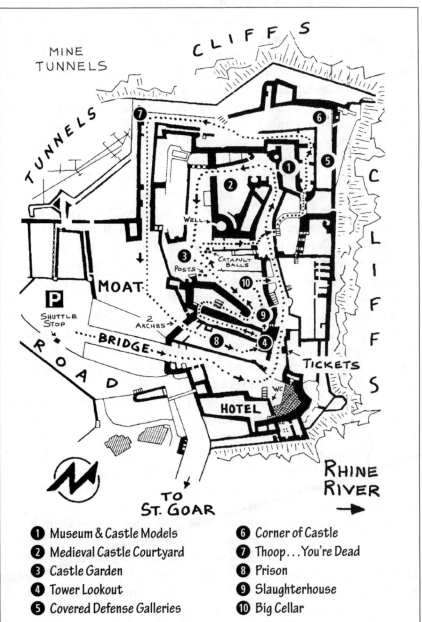

1. Museum & Castle Models
2. Medieval Castle Courtyard
3. Castle Garden
4. Tower Lookout
5. Covered Defense Galleries
6. Corner of Castle
7. Thoop . . . You're Dead
8. Prison
9. Slaughterhouse
10. Big Cellar

(instead, do what you are able of the self-guided tour, below). There's free luggage-check service at the ticket office (tel. 06741/7753). To get to the castle from St. Goar's boat dock or train station, take a €5 taxi ride (**AE+A,** **Level 2**—Moderately accessible; €6 for a minibus, tel. 06741/7011), or the kitschy "tschu-tschu" tourist train, complete with lusty music (**AE+A,** **Level 2**—Moderately accessible, driver will assist wheelchair user in stepping up to seat, then will load folded wheelchair into front of train; €2 one-way, €3 round-trip, 7-min trip, 3/hr, daily 10:00–17:00, runs from square between station and dock, also stops at Hotel Montag, tel. 06741/2030). Slow walkers with stamina could hike up the steep hill up to the castle (potentially dangerous by wheelchair: 18" wide sidewalk, 17 percent grade, short curved section through railroad underpass).

Self-Guided Tour: This tour was designed for people without mobility problems, though we've provided details so that those with limited mobility who want to give it a try will know what to expect.

From the ticket gate, enter the complex (the 8-foot-wide, 14-foot-tall gate will be opened for wheelchair users). Go straight uphill, over the rough cobblestones and a rutted path. Pass *Grosser Keller* on the left (where we'll end this tour), head through an internal gate past the *zu den gedeckten Wehrgängen* sign on the right (where we'll pass later) uphill to the museum, which is in the only finished room of the castle (**AE+A,** **AI, Level 2**—Moderately accessible, one 6" entry step through 5-foot-wide wooden door; daily 9:30–12:00 & 13:00–17:30).

1. Museum and Castle Model: The seven-foot-tall carved stone *(Keltische Säule von Pfalzfeld)* immediately inside the door—a tombstone from a nearby Celtic grave—is from 400 years before Christ. There were people here long before the Romans...and this castle. The chair next to the door is an old library chair. If you smile sweetly, the man behind the desk may demonstrate—pull the back forward and it becomes stairs for getting to the highest shelves.

The sweeping castle-history exhibit in the center of the room is well-described in English. The massive fortification was the only Rhineland castle to withstand Louis XIV's assault during the 17th century. At the far end of the room is a model reconstruction of the castle showing how much bigger it was before French revolutionary troops destroyed it in the 18th century. Study this. Find where you are (hint: look for the tall tower). This was the living quarters of the original castle, which was only the smallest ring of buildings around the tiny central courtyard (13th century). The ramparts were added in the 14th century. By 1650, the fortress was largely complete. Ever since its destruction by the French in 1769, it's had no military value. While no WWII bombs were wasted on this ruin, it served St. Goar as a quarry for generations. The basement of the museum (accessible only via a winding staircase) shows the castle pharmacy and an exhibit on Rhine region odds and ends, including tools and an 1830 loom. Look for the photos of ice breaking on the Rhine— which, with global warming, hasn't been necessary since 1963.

Exit the museum and go 30 yards directly out, slightly uphill on the dirt path into the castle courtyard.

2. Medieval Castle Courtyard: Five hundred years ago, the entire castle circled this courtyard. The place was self-sufficient and ready for a siege with a bakery, pharmacy, herb garden, animals, brewery, well (top of yard), and livestock. During peacetime, 300 to 600 people lived here; during a siege there would be as many as 4,500. The walls were plastered and painted white. Bits of the original 13th-century plaster survive.

Continue on the dirt path through the courtyard, out *Erste Schildmauer,* turn left into the next courtyard, and head to the two old, black, upright posts. Find the pyramid of stone catapult balls on your left.

3. Castle Garden: Catapult balls like these were too expensive not to recycle. If ever used, they'd be retrieved after the battle. Across from the balls is a well—essential for any castle during the age of siegeing. Look in (one 18" step). The old posts are for the ceremonial baptizing of new members of the local trading league. While this guild goes back centuries, today it's a social club that fills this court with a huge wine party the third weekend of each September.

All but the hardiest of slow walkers will want to call it quits here and head back to the entry gate; otherwise, climb the cobbled path up to the castle's best viewpoint—up where the German flag waves (4 flights of stairs: eleven 8" steps, seventeen 6" steps, sixteen 8" steps, nineteen curving 10" steps).

4. Highest Castle Tower Lookout: Enjoy a great view of the river, castle, and the forest that was once all part of this castle. Remember, the fortress once covered five times the land it does today. Notice how the other castles (across the river) don't poke above the top of the Rhine canyon. That would make them easy for invading armies to see.

Return to the catapult balls, head down the dirt road and through the tunnel, veer left through the arch marked *zu den gedeckten*

Wehrgängen, go down two flights of stairs (twenty-five 7" steps, then thirteen 6" steps) and stop at the top of the next staircase before turning left into the dark covered passageway. From here, you'll begin a rectangular tour taking you completely around the perimeter of the castle. But first, take a look at the...

5. *Covered Defense Galleries:* Soldiers—the castle's "minutemen"—had a short commute: defensive positions on the outside, home in the holes below on the left. Even though these living quarters were padded with straw, life was unpleasant. A peasant was lucky to live beyond age 45.

Now go left through the dark gallery and to the corner of the castle, (where you'll see a white painted arrow at eye level) and down two more flights of steps (ten 8" steps, then seven 10" steps). Position yourself with your back to the arrow on the wall.

6. *Corner of Castle:* Look up. A three-story, half-timbered building originally rose beyond the highest stone fortification. The two stone tongues near the top just around the corner supported the toilet. (Insert your own joke here.) Turn around. The crossbow slits below the white arrow were once steeper. The bigger hole on the riverside was for hot pitch.

Follow that white arrow along the outside to the next corner. Midway you'll pass stairs on the right leading down *zu den Minengängen*—the mine tunnels (sign on upper left; the adventurous with flashlights could poke around in the tunnels). Continue on, going level to the corner. At the corner, turn left.

7. *Thoop...You're Dead.* Look ahead at the smartly placed crossbow-arrow slit. While you're lying there, notice the stonework. The little round holes were for scaffolds used as they built up. They indicate this stonework is original. Notice also the fine stonework on the chutes. More boiling pitch...now you're toast, too.

Continue along the castle wall around the corner. At the railing, look up the valley and uphill where the sprawling fort stretched. Below, just outside the wall, is land where attackers would gather. The mine tunnels are under there, waiting to blow up any attackers.

Continue along the perimeter, jog left, go down five 10" steps and into an open field, and go toward the wooden bridge. You may detour here into the passageway (on right) marked *13 Hals Graben.* The "old" wooden bridge is actually modern. Angle left through two arches (before the bridge) and through the rough entry to *Verliess* (prison) on the left.

8. *Prison:* This is one of six dungeons. You entered through a door prisoners only dreamed of 400 years ago. They came and went through the little square hole in the ceiling. The holes in the walls supported timbers that thoughtfully gave as many as 15 residents something to sit on to keep them out of the filthy slop that gathered on the floor. Twice a day they were given bread and water. Some prisoners actually survived more than two years in here. The town could torture and execute; the castle had permission only to imprison criminals in these dungeons. Consider this: According to town records, the two men who spent the most time down here—2.5 years each—died within three weeks of regaining their freedom. Perhaps after a diet of bread and water, feasting on meat and wine was simply too much.

Continue through the next arch, under the white arrow, and turn left and go 30 yards to the *Schlachthaus.*

9. Slaughterhouse: Any proper castle was prepared to survive a six-month siege. With 4,000 people, that's a lot of provisions. The cattle that lived within the walls were slaughtered in this room. The castle's mortar was congealed here (by packing all the organic waste from the kitchen into kegs and sealing it). Notice the drainage gutters. "Running water" came through from drains built into the walls (to keep the mortar dry and therefore strong...and less smelly).

Back outside, climb the modern stairs (nine 8" steps) to the left. A skinny passage leads you into the...

10. Big Cellar: This *Grosser Keller* was a big pantry. When the castle was smaller, this was the original moat—you can see the rough lower parts of the wall. The original floor was 13 feet deeper. The drawbridge rested upon the stone nubs on the left. When the castle expanded, the moat became this cellar. Above the entry, holes mark spots where timbers made a storage loft, perhaps filled with grain. In the back, an arch leads to the wine cellar where finer wine was kept. Part of a soldier's pay was wine...table wine. This wine was kept in a single 180,000-liter stone barrel, which generally lasted about 18 months.

The count owned the surrounding farmland. Farmers got to keep 20 percent of their production. Later, in more liberal feudal times, the nobility let them keep 40 percent. Today the German government leaves the workers with 60 percent...and provides a few more services.

You're free. Climb out (seventeen 8" steps), turn right, and leave. For coffee on a great view terrace, visit the Rheinfels Castle Hotel (see "Eating," page 449), opposite the entrance.

Koblenz

The Rhine and Mosel rivers flow together at a confluence known as "German Corner" (Deutsche Ecke)—home to Koblenz, one of the oldest towns in Germany (recently celebrating its 2,000th birthday). While not quite matching up to Bacharach and St. Goar for quaintness, Koblenz has its own advantages: It's far more accessible than those smaller Rhine towns, and it's a good place to catch a boat going south to see the best parts of the Rhine.

Accessibility in Koblenz: The townsfolk are trying to modernize their little city without losing its historic vibe. Most museums, sights, and churches are accessible to wheelchair users. The free TI map (see "Tourist Information," below) gives accessibility information for Koblenz's sights. For any additional help you need that the TI can't provide, contact **Der Kreis Club Behinderter** (tel. 0261/14447, a short taxi ride from the station at Am Alten Hospital 3a, www.der-kreis-cbf.de).

For a quick guide to Accessibility Codes, please see page 417 of this chapter. For a detailed explanation of Accessibility Codes, please see page 2 of the Introduction.

Arrival in Koblenz: The **train station** is fully accessible (if you need assistance, ask at the Service Point). There are ramps to the street on both the north and south exits of the train station. The south ramp takes you to the taxis and the TI.

The **boat dock** (with both Rhine and Mosel boats) is five blocks on Markenbildchenweg Strasse from the station. At the river, you can access a ramp a half-block upstream from the boat dock (to avoid eight 7" steps).

Tourist Information: Koblenz's TI (**AE, AI, ♥,** Level 2— Moderately accessible) is friendly and helpful (Mon–Fri 9:00–19:00, Sat–Sun 10:00–19:00, until 18:00 Oct–April, closed Sun Nov–March, just south of the station at Bahnhofplatz 7, tel. 0261/303-880; fully accessible toilet at nearby McDonald's). The free TI map shows all the streets in Koblenz that are accessible for wheelchair users, lists Koblenz's 18 most historically significant sights (including accessibility notes), and tells the story of this historic confluence.

Koblenz

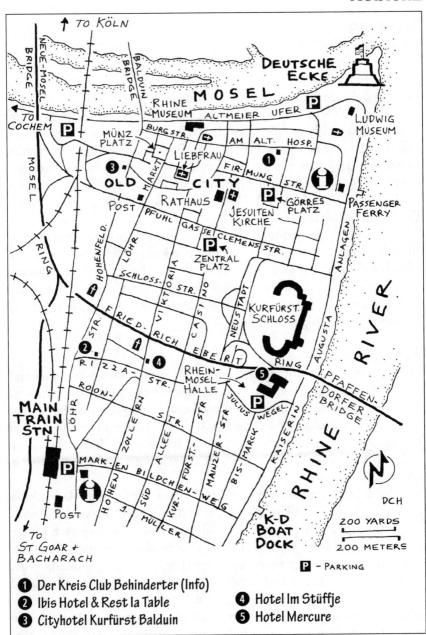

1. Der Kreis Club Behinderter (Info)
2. Ibis Hotel & Rest la Table
3. Cityhotel Kurfürst Balduin
4. Hotel Im Stüffje
5. Hotel Mercure

SLEEPING AND EATING ON THE RHINE

Sleeping
(country code: 49)

The Rhine is an easy place for cheap sleeps, but accessible rooms can be hard to come by. In terms of sheer quaintness, Bacharach and St. Goar are the best towns for an overnight stop (10 miles, apart, connected by milk-run trains, riverboats, and a riverside bike path). Slow walkers, and highly mobile wheelchair users traveling with a companion, will want to consider these listings first. Bacharach is a more interesting town, but St. Goar has the famous castle. Parking in Bacharach is simple along the highway next to the tracks (3-hr daytime limit is generally not enforced) or in the boat parking lot. Parking in St. Goar is tighter; ask at your hotel.

Those with limited mobility will find far better options in some of the valley's larger towns (or in big cities like Köln or Frankfurt; see accessible hotel listings later in this chapter). For wheelchair users traveling alone, we've listed some good, accessible options in the towns of Koblenz and Mainz—both of which also have access to the region's best activity, the Rhine boat cruise.

Eating

Germans eat lunch and dinner about when we do. Order house specials whenever possible. Pork, fish, and venison are good, and don't miss the bratwurst and sauerkraut. Potatoes are the standard vegetable, but *Spargel* (giant white asparagus) is a must in season. The bread and pretzels in the basket on your table often cost extra. If you need a break from pork, order the *Salatteller*. Great beers and white wines abound. Go with whatever beer is on tap.

We've included the most accessible restaurants for each place. Unless otherwise noted (by **AT** or **AT+A**), they do *not* have accessible toilets.

Tipping: Tipping is an issue only at restaurants that have waiters and waitresses. Don't tip if you order your food at a counter. At restaurants with wait staff, the service charge (10–15 percent) is usually listed on the menu and included in your bill. When the service is included, there's no need to tip beyond that, but if you like to tip and you're pleased with the service, you can round up the bill (but not more than five percent). If the service is not included, tip up to 10 percent. Rather than

SLEEP CODE

(€1 = about $1.15)

Sleep Code: **S** = Single, **D** = Double/Twin, **T** = Triple, **Q** = Quad, **b** = bathroom, **s** = shower only, **no CC** = Credit Cards not accepted, **SE** = Speaks English, **NSE** = No English. All hotels speak some English. Breakfast is included and credit cards are accepted unless otherwise noted.

Please see "Accessibility Codes" sidebar on page 417 of this chapter for a quick guide to codes. For a more detailed explanation of Accessibility Levels and Codes, please see page 2 of the Introduction.

leaving coins on the table, Germans usually pay with paper, saying how much they'd like the bill to be (e.g., for an €8.10 meal, give a €20 bill and say *"Neun Euro"*—9 euros—to get €11 change).

Sleeping in Bacharach
(area code: 06743)
See map on page 432 for locations.

Level 3—Minimally Accessible
Hotel Gelber Hof (AE+A, AI+A, AL, AR, AB+A) has been operated by the Mades family since 1728—a whopping 275 years (Renate and Heiner have been in charge for the last 35). Inside you'll find modern, well-cared-for rooms (accessible toilets in hallway—ramp to sink available upon request; Sb-€65, Db-€70, closed Nov–Easter, one block from church at 26 Blücherstrasse, tel. 06743/910-100, fax 06743/910-1050, www.hotel-gelber-hof.com, mades@hotel-gelber-hof.com).

Hotel Altkölnischer Hof (AE+A, AI+A), a grand old building near the church, rents 20 rooms with modern furnishings (and some balconies) over an Old World restaurant. Public rooms are old-time elegant (call to reserve larger room for wheelchair access, bathrooms not accessible, staff will place wooden ramp over two steps on side entry, small elevator fits wheelchair only if it's folded; Sb-€48–70, small or dark Db-€62–65, bright new Db-€72–82, new Db with balcony-€80–105, elevator, closed Nov–March, Blucherstrasse 2, tel. 06743/1339 or 06743/2186, fax 06743/2793, www.hotel-bacharach-rhein.de, altkoelnischer-hof @t-online.de).

Level 4—Not Accessible

This place could work for an energetic slow walker or driver.

Pension im Malerwinkel sits like a grand gingerbread house just outside the wall at the top end of town in a little neighborhood so charming it's called "Painters' Corner" *(Malerwinkel)*. The Vollmer family's 20-room place is super-quiet and comes with a sunny garden on a brook and easy parking (twenty-one 7" steps with no elevator, call ahead for larger room; Sb-€35, Db-€55–58 for 1 night, €50 for 2 nights, €47 for 3 nights, no CC, some rooms have balconies but most face parking lot; from town center walk uphill and up the valley 10 min—allowing a slow pace—until you pass the old town gate and look left to Blücherstrasse 41, tel. 06743/1239, fax 06743/93407, www.im-malerwinkel .de, pension@im-malerwinkel.de).

Eating in Bacharach

You can easily find inexpensive (€10–15), atmospheric restaurants offering indoor and outdoor dining.

Posthof Restaurant (AE, AI, AT, Level 1—Fully accessible) is a historic carriage house—a stopping place for centuries of guests—newly opened as a restaurant. The menu is trendier, with free German tapas (ask), seasonal specials, and local "as organic as possible" produce. You'll sit in a half-timbered cobbled courtyard (€5–15, good salads and veggie dishes, fun kids' play area, daily 11:00 until late, Oberstrasse 45, tel. 06743/599-663).

These next three places are neighbors.

Altes Haus (AE+A, AI, Level 2—Moderately accessible), the oldest building in town, serves reliably good food with Bacharach's most romantic atmosphere (€9–15, Thu–Tue 12:00–15:30 & 18:00–21:30, closed Wed and Dec–Easter, dead center by the church, tel. 06743/1209). Find the cozy little dining room with photos of the opera singer who sang about Bacharach, adding to its fame. You can enter the restaurant through the large door in front (three 7" steps), or if your wheelchair is less than 22" wide, use the back door (two 7" steps).

Kurpfälzische Münze (AE, AI, Level 2—Moderately accessible, one 2" entry step, 2 accessible tables) is more expensive but a popular standby for its sunny terrace and classy candlelit interior (€7–21, daily 10:00–22:00, in the old mint, a half-block down from Altes Haus, tel. 06743/1375).

Wine-Tasting: Drop in on entertaining Fritz Bastian's **Weingut zum Grüner Baum** wine bar (**AE+A, AI,** Level 2—Moderately accessible; also offers soup and cold cuts, good ambience indoors and out, just past Altes Haus; Mon–Wed and Fri from 13:00, Sat–Sun from 12:00, closed Thu and Feb–mid-March, tel. 06743/1208). As the president of the local vintner's club, Fritz is on a mission to give travelers an understanding of the subtle differences among the Rhine wines. Groups of two to six people pay €13.50 for a "carousel" of 15 glasses of 14 different white wines, one lonely red, and a basket of bread. Your mission: Team up with others using Rick's books to rendezvous here after dinner. Spin the lazy Susan, share a common cup, and discuss the taste. Fritz insists, "After each wine, you must talk to each other."

Sleeping in St. Goar
(area code: 06741)

Level 2—Moderately Accessible
Rheinfels Castle Hotel (AE+A, AI, AL, AR) is the town splurge. Actually part of the castle but an entirely new building, this luxury 57-room place is good for those with money and a car (Db-€130–154 depending on river views and balconies, extra bed-€34, elevator, free parking, indoor pool and sauna, dress-up restaurant, Schlossberg 47, tel. 06741/8020, fax 06741/802-802, www.schlosshotel-rheinfels.de, info @burgrheinfels.de). Access to the exterior ramp is available upon request. The rooms are large enough for wheelchair users, but the bathrooms are not. They have hosted wheelchair users in the past, and are willing to assist.

Level 3—Minimally Accessible
Landsknecht Hotel (AE+A, AI+A, AR), with 30 modern rooms, is located a mile north of the town square on the Rhine (Db-€65–130 depending on size of room, closed Jan–Feb, free parking, Rheinuferstrasse, St.Goar, tel. 06741/2011, fax 06741/7499, www.hotel-landsknecht.de, info@hotel-landsknecht.de). An accessible walkway leads from town to the

hotel along the river. At the parking lot, use the moderately steep driveway to the rear of the hotel to reach the rooms. For the registration desk and restaurant, go through the front door (two 6" steps). The rooms are wheelchair-accessible, but the bathrooms are not.

Level 4—Not Accessible
Hotel am Markt, well-run by Herr and Frau Velich, is rustic with all the modern comforts. It features a hint of antler with a pastel flair, 18 bright rooms (enter through side door, then five 5" steps into hallway and twenty 7.5" steps to hotel rooms, bathroom not wheelchair-accessible), and a good restaurant (see listing below). It's a good value and a stone's throw from the boat dock and train station (S-€35, Sb-€43, standard Db-€59, bigger riverview Db-€69, Tb-€82, Qb-€88, 20 percent cheaper off-season, closed Nov–Feb, Am Markt 1, tel. 06741/1689, fax 06741/1721, www.hotelammarkt1.de, hotel.am.markt@gmx.de).

Eating in St. Goar
Head up to **Rheinfels Castle Hotel** for your Rhine splurge (**AE+A, AI, AL,** Level 2—Moderately accessible) for its incredible view terrace in an elegant setting (€8–15 dinners, daily 18:30–21:15, reserve a table by the window). To enter, go through the parking lot and locked gate—which must be opened by staff—then down the ramp, through hallways, and to the elevator.

Hotel Am Markt (**AE+A, AI,** Level 3—Minimally accessible) serves good traditional meals—plenty of game and fish—at fair prices (€5–16) with good atmosphere and service. To enter, use the three 5" steps on the side, travel across the patio, and go up two 7" front entry steps; the staff can assist you during non-peak times.

Sleeping in Koblenz
(area code: 0261)
Each of these four hotels is fully accessible with adapted rooms, and all are located conveniently close to the station (or within a short taxi trip).

Level 1—Fully Accessible
Ibis Hotel (**AE, AI, AL, AR, AB**) is an inexpensive, modern chain hotel a short roll or stroll from the train station (4 adapted rooms; Db-€49–64, Rizzastrasse 42, tel. 0261/30240, fax 0261/302-4240, www.ibishotel.com).

Cityhotel Kurfürst Balduin (AE, AI, AL, AR, AB) is a centrally located, modern business-class hotel (Sb-€58, Db-€96, Hohenfelder Strasse 12, tel. 0261/13320, fax 0261/332-100, www.cityhotel-koblenz .de, info@cityhotel-koblenz.de).

Hotel Im Stüffje (AE, AI, AL, AR, AB) is a quaint old-style hotel that has been retrofitted for accessibility (Sb-€60, Db-€80, Tb-€105, Hohenzollernstrasse 5–7, tel. 0261/915-220, fax 0261/915-2244, www .handicap-hotel.de, hotel-im-stueffje@t-online.de).

Hotel Mercure (AE, AI, AL, AR, AB) is a modern 168-room chain hotel near the station (Db-€120, Julius-Wegeler-Strasse 6, tel. 0261/1360, fax 0261/136-1199, www.mercure.de, h2004@accor-hotels.com).

Eating in Koblenz

Restaurant la Table (AE, AI, AT, Level 1—Fully accessible) in Ibis Hotel and the restaurant in **Hotel Im Stüffje (AE, AI, AT,** Level 1) are fully accessible (see above).

Sleeping in Mainz
(area code: 06131)

Consider spending the night in the town of Mainz—if for no other reason than to take advantage of the wonderful INNdependence Hotel. The town is also close to Frankfurt and the Frankfurt Airport.

Arrival in Mainz: The Mainz **train station** is fully accessible **(AE, AI, AL, AT).** To reach the TI, leave the station, go across the courtyard and bus stops, and into the left end of the building (Im Brückenturm am Rathaus, tel. 06131/286-210). To get from the **boat dock** to the TI, you can catch the accessible bus, take a taxi, or roll or stroll up Kaiserstrasse from the riverfront Adenauer-Ufer (a 45-minute trek).

INNdependence Hotel is fully accessible **(AE, AI, AL, AR, AB, ♥),** run by the Mainz disabled community. These hospitable folks are justifiably proud of their establishment (Sb-€70, Db-€85, Gleiwitzer Strasse 4, tel. 06131/250-5380, fax 06131/211-451, www.inndependence .de, info@inndependence.de).

Ibis Mainz (AE, AI, AL, AR, AB) belongs to the inexpensive, no-frills Ibis hotel chain (some adapted rooms; Db-€89, less off-season, Holzhofstrasse 2, tel. 06131/934-240, fax 06131/234-126, www.ibis hotel.com).

TRANSPORTATION CONNECTIONS

Milk-run trains stop at all Rhine towns each hour, starting as early as 6:00. Koblenz, Boppard, St. Goar, Bacharach, Bingen, and Mainz are each about 15 minutes apart. From Koblenz to Mainz takes 75 minutes. To get a faster big train, go to Mainz (for points east and south) or Koblenz (for points north, west, and along Mosel). Train info: tel. 01805-996-633. (For station access information, see "Getting around the Rhine—By Train," page 423.)

From Mainz to: Bacharach/St. Goar (hrly, 1 hr), **Cochem** (hrly, 2.5 hrs, change in Koblenz), **Köln** (3/hr, 90 min, change in Koblenz), **Baden-Baden** (hrly, 1.5 hrs), **Munich** (hrly, 4 hrs), **Frankfurt** (3/hr, 45 min), **Frankfurt Airport** (4/hr, 25 min).

From Koblenz to: Köln (4/hr, 1 hr), **Berlin** (2/hr, 5.5 hrs, up to 2 changes), **Frankfurt** (3/hr, 1.5 hrs, 1 change), **Cochem** (2/hr, 50 min), **Trier** (2/hr, 2 hrs), **Brussels** (12/day, 4 hrs, change in Köln), **Amsterdam** (12/day, 4.5 hrs, up to 5 changes).

From Frankfurt to: Bacharach (hrly, 1.5 hrs, change in Mainz; first train to Bacharach departs at 6:00, last train at 20:45), **Koblenz** (hrly, 90 min, changes in Mannheim or Wiesbaden), **Rothenburg** (hrly, 3 hrs, transfers in Würzburg and Steinach), **Würzburg** (hrly, 2 hrs), **Nürnberg** (hrly, 2 hrs), **Munich** (hrly, 4 hrs, 1 change), **Amsterdam** (8/day, 5 hrs, up to 3 changes), **Paris** (9/day, 6.5 hrs, up to 3 changes).

From Bacharach to: Frankfurt Airport (hrly, 1.5 hrs, change in Mainz, first train to airport departs about 5:40, last train 21:30).

Köln (Cologne)

Germany's fourth-largest city, big, no-nonsense Köln has a compact and lively center. The Rhine was the northern boundary of the Roman Empire and, 1,700 years ago, Constantine—the first Christian emperor—made "Colonia" the seat of a bishopric. Five hundred years later, under Charlemagne, Köln became the seat of an archbishopric. With 40,000 people living within its walls, it was the largest German city and an important cultural and religious center throughout the Middle Ages. To many, the city is most famous for its toilet water. "Eau de Cologne" was first made here by an Italian chemist in 1709.

Köln

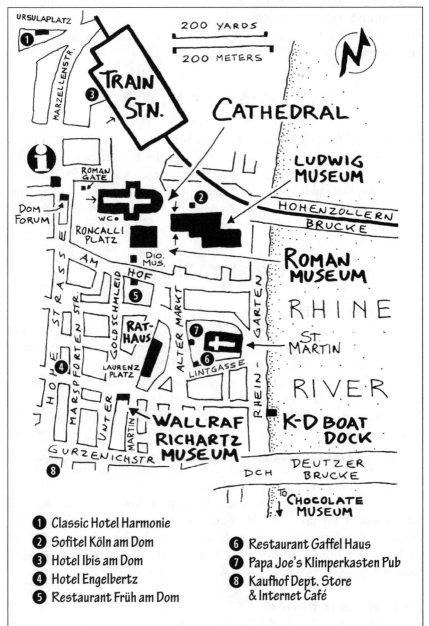

1. Classic Hotel Harmonie
2. Sofitel Köln am Dom
3. Hotel Ibis am Dom
4. Hotel Engelbertz
5. Restaurant Früh am Dom
6. Restaurant Gaffel Haus
7. Papa Joe's Klimperkasten Pub
8. Kaufhof Dept. Store & Internet Café

Even after WWII bombs destroyed 95 percent of Köln (population down from 800,000 to 40,000), it has remained, after a remarkable recovery, a bustling commercial and cultural center as well as a fun, colorful, and pleasant-smelling city.

ACCESSIBILITY IN KÖLN

As a big, modern city, Köln offers much better accessibility than other Rhine destinations in this chapter. The wheelchair user can move freely between the boat dock, train station, hotels, restaurants, and museums.

For a quick guide to Access Codes, please see page 417 of this chapter. For a detailed explanation of Accessibility Codes, please see page 2 of the Introduction.

ORIENTATION

(area code: 0221)

Köln's old-town core, bombed out then rebuilt quaint, is traffic-free and includes a park and bike path along the river. From the cathedral/TI/train station, Hohe Strasse leads into the shopping action.

The Roman arch in front of the cathedral reminds us that even in Roman times this was an important trading street and a main road through Köln. In medieval times, when Köln was a major player in the trade heavyweight Hanseatic League, two major trading routes crossed here. This "high street" thrived. Following its complete destruction in World War II, it emerged once again as an active trading street—the first pedestrian shopping mall in Germany.

For a quick old-town ramble, roll or stroll down Hohe Strasse and take a left at the city hall (Rathaus) to the river (where K-D Rhine cruises start). Enjoy the quaint old town and the waterfront park. The Hohenzollernbrücke, crossing the Rhine at the cathedral, is the busiest railway bridge in the world (30 trains/hr all day long).

Tourist Information

Köln's energetic TI (**AE, AI,** Level 2—Moderately accessible), opposite the church entry, has free city maps, a program of private guided tours (e.g., architecture, medieval Köln, Romanesque churches; call TI to reserve) and several brochures (Mon–Sat 9:00–21:00, Sun 10:00–18:00, July–Aug Mon–Sat until 22:00, Unter Fettenhennen 19, tel. 0221/2213-0400, www.koelntourismus.de). Köln's **WelcomeCard** (€9/24 hrs, €14/48 hrs) provides use of the city's transit system, a 50 percent discount on major museums (Römisch-Germanisches, Ludwig, and Wallraf-Richartz), and smaller discounts on other museums (like the Chocolate Museum). For information on the museums, visit www.museenkoeln.de. Note that many of Köln's museums are closed on Monday.

Arrival in Köln

Köln couldn't be easier to visit—its three important sights cluster within two blocks of its TI and train station. This super pedestrian zone is a constant carnival of people.

Köln's bustling **train station** (AE, AI, AL, AT, Level 1—Fully accessible) has everything you need: a food court, juice bar, drugstore, shopping mall with grocery store, pricey WC (€1), travel center (*Reisezentrum*, Mon–Fri 5:30–23:00, Sat–Sun until 22:30), and lockers (€2/24 hrs, put money in and wait 30 seconds for door to open; next to Reisezentrum).

If you **drive** to Köln, follow signs to *Zentrum*, then continue to the huge Parkhaus Am Dom pay lot under the cathedral (€1.50/hr, €13/day).

SIGHTS

Köln's Cathedral (Dom)

The Gothic Dom, Germany's most exciting church (worth ▲▲▲), looms immediately up from the train station.

Cathedral Access: AE, AI, AL, Level 1—Fully accessible. From the train station, roll or stroll to the front of the cathedral to access the entry. There is also an accessible glass lift that takes you up the side of this colossal structure. The toilets are difficult to reach, but there is a free, accessible toilet next door in the Ludwig Museum. The tower, with 509 steps, is not accessible.

Köln's Cathedral

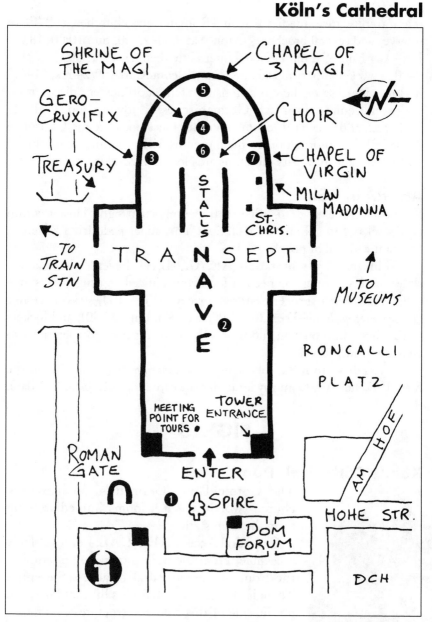

Cost and Hours: Church free (tower €2), daily 10:00–19:30, but no tourist visits during church services daily at 18:30, Sun also at 12:00 & 17:00; get schedule at Dom Forum office or www.koelner-dom.de.

Tours: The one-hour English-only **tours** are reliably excellent; wheelchair users are welcome (€4, Mon–Sat at 10:30 and 14:30, Sun at 14:30, meet inside front door of Dom, tel. 0221/9258-4730). Your tour ticket also gives you free entry to the English-language 20-minute video in the Dom Forum directly after the tour (see "Dom Forum," page 460).

Self-guided Tour: If you don't take the official tour, follow this seven-stop tour (note that stops 3–7 are closed during confession on Sat 14:00–18:00).

1. Roman Gate and Cathedral Exterior: The square in front of the cathedral has been a busy civic meeting place since ancient times. A Roman temple stood where the cathedral stands today. The north gate of the Roman city, from A.D. 50, marks the start of Köln's 2,000-year-old main street.

Look for the life-size replica tip of a spire. The real thing is 515 feet above you. The cathedral facade, while finished according to the original 13th-century plan, is "neo-Gothic" from the 19th century.

Postcards show the church after the 1945 bombing. The red brick building—to your right as you face the church—is the Diocesan Museum. The Roman museum is beside the church on the right, and the Ludwig modern-art museum is behind that.

Go inside the church, to the pews in the center of the nave.

2. Nave: If you feel small, you're supposed to. The 140-foot-tall ceiling reminds us of our place in the vast scheme of things. Lots of stained glass—enough to cover three football fields—fills the church with light, representing God.

The church was begun in 1248. The choir—the lofty area from the center altar to the far end ahead of you—was finished in 1322. Later, with the discovery of America and routes to the Indies by sea, trade shifted away from inland ports like Köln. Funds dried up and eventually the building stopped. For 300 years the finished end of the church was walled off and functioned as a church while the unfinished torso (where you are now) waited. For centuries the symbol of Köln's skyline was a huge crane that sat atop the unfinished west spire.

With the rise of German patriotism in the early 1800s, Köln became a symbol of German unity. And the Prussians—the movers and shakers behind German unity—mistakenly considered Gothic a German style. They initiated a national tax that funded the speedy completion of this gloriously Gothic German church. Seven hundred workers (compared to 100 in the 14th century) finished the church in just 38 years (1842–1880). The great train station was built in the shadow of the cathedral's towering spire.

The glass windows in the front of the church are medieval. The glass surrounding you in the nave is not as old, but it's precious nevertheless. The glass on the left is Renaissance. That on the right—a gift from Ludwig I, father of "Mad" King Ludwig of touristic fame—is 19th-century Bavarian.

While 95 percent of Köln was destroyed by WWII bombs, the structure of the cathedral survived fairly well. In anticipation of the bombing, the glass and art treasures were taken to shelters and saved. The new "swallow's nest" organ above you was installed to celebrate the cathedral's 750th birthday in 1998. Relics (mostly skulls) fill cupboards on each side of the nave. The guys in the red robes are cathedral cops, called *Schweizers* (after the Swiss guard at the Vatican); if a service is getting ready to start, they might hustle you out.

3. Gero-Crucifix: As you go through the gate into the oldest part of the church, look for the mosaic of the ninth-century church on the floor. It shows a saint holding the Carolingian Cathedral, which stood on this spot for several centuries before this one was built.

Ahead of you on the left, the Chapel of the Cross features the oldest surviving monumental crucifix from north of the Alps. Carved in 976 with a sensitivity 300 years ahead of its time, it shows Jesus not suffering and not triumphant—but with eyes closed...dead. He paid the price for our sins. It's quite a twofer: great art and powerful theology in one. The cathedral has three big pilgrim stops: this crucifix, the Shrine of the Magi, and the *Madonna of Milan* (both coming up).

Continue to the front end of the church, stopping to look at the big golden reliquary in the glass case behind the high altar.

4. Shrine of the Magi: Relics were a big deal in the Middle Ages. Köln's acquisition of the bones of the Three Kings in the 12th century put it on the pilgrimage map and brought in enough money to justify the construction of this magnificent place. By some stretch of medieval Christian logic, these relics also justified the secular power of the local king. This reliquary, made in about 1200, is the biggest and most splendid we've seen. It's seven feet of gilded silver, jewels, and enamel. Old Testament prophets line the bottom, and 12 New Testament apostles—with a wingless angel in the center—line the top.

Inside sit the bones of the Magi...three skulls with golden crowns. So what's the big deal about these three kings of Christmas-carol fame? They were the first to recognize Jesus as the savior and the first to come as pilgrims to worship him. They inspired medieval pilgrims and countless pilgrims since. For a thousand years, a theme of this cathedral has been that life is a pilgrimage...a search for God.

5. *Chapel of the Three Magi:* The center chapel, at the far end, is the oldest. It also has the church's oldest window (center, from 1265). It has the typical design: a strip of Old Testament scenes on the left with a theologically and visually parallel strip of New Testament scenes on the right (e.g., on bottom panels: to the left, the birth of Eve; to the right, the birth of Mary with her mother Anne on the bed).

Later, glass (which you saw lining the nave) was painted and glazed. This medieval window is actually colored glass, which is assembled like a mosaic. It was very expensive. The size was limited to what pilgrim donations could support. Notice the plain, budget design higher up.

6. *Choir:* Peek into the center zone between the high altar and the carved wooden central stalls. (You can usually only get inside if you take the tour.) This is surrounded by 13th- and 14th-century art: carved oak stalls, frescoed walls, statues painted as they would have been, and original stained glass high above. Study the fanciful oak carvings. The woman cutting the man's hair is a Samson-and-Delilah warning to the sexist men of the early Church.

7. *Chapel of the Virgin:* The nearby chapel faces one of the most precious paintings of the important Gothic "School of Köln."

The Patron Saints of Köln was painted in 1442 by Stefan Lochner. Notice the photographic realism and believable depth. There are literally dozens of identifiable herbs in the grassy foreground. During the 19th century, the city fought to have it in the museum. The Church went to court to keep it. The judge ruled that it could stay in the cathedral only as long as a Mass was said before it every day. For more than a

hundred years, that happened at 18:30. Now, 21st-century comfort has trumped 19th-century law—in winter, services take place in the warmer Sacraments Chapel instead. (For more on the "School of Köln" art style, see Wallraf-Richartz Museum, below).

Overlooking the same chapel, the *Madonna of Milan* sculpture (1290), associated with miracles, was a focus of pilgrims for centuries.

As you head for the exit, find the statue of St. Christopher (with Jesus on his shoulder and the pilgrim's staff). Since 1470, pilgrims and travelers have looked up at him and taken solace in the hope that their patron saint is looking out for them. Go in peace.

Treasury—The newly built treasury sits outside the cathedral's left transept (when you exit through the front door, turn right and continue right around the building to the gold pillar that reads *Schatzkammer*). The six dim, hushed rooms are housed in the cathedral's 13th-century stone cellar vaults. Spotlights shine on black cases filled with gilded chalices and crosses, medieval reliquaries (bits of chain, bone, cross, and cloth in gold-crusted glass capsules), and plenty of fancy bishop garb: intricately embroidered miters and vestments, rings with fat gemstones, and six-foot gold crosiers.

Access: AE, AI, AL, Level 1—Fully accessible.

Cost and Hours: €4, daily 10:00–18:00, lockers at entry with €1 coin deposit, tel. 0221/1794-0300. Displays come with brief English descriptions, but the fine little €4 book sold inside the cathedral shop provides extra information.

Dom Forum—This helpful visitor center, across from the entry of the cathedral, is a good place to take a break (**AE, AI,** Level 1—Fully accessible; Mon–Fri 10:00–18:30, Sat 10:00–17:00, Sun 13:00–17:00, plenty of info, welcoming lounge with €0.50 coffee, free but non-accessible WC downstairs, tel. 0221/9258-4720). They offer an English-language "multivision" video on the history of the church daily at 11:30 and 15:30 (starts slow but gets a little better, 20 min, €1.50 or included with church tour, www.domforum.de).

Diocesan Museum—This museum contains some of the cathedral's finest art (**AE+A, AI,** Level 2—Moderately accessible, one 4" entry step with no railing; free, Fri–Wed 10:00–18:00, closed Thu, brick building to right of Roman Museum, Roncalliplatz 2, tel. 0221/257-7672, www.kolumba.de).

More Sights

▲▲Römisch-Germanisches Museum—Germany's best Roman museum offers minimal English among its elegant and fascinating display of Roman artifacts: fine glassware, jewelry, and mosaics. The permanent collection is downstairs and upstairs; temporary exhibits are on the ground floor.

Budget travelers can view the museum's prize piece, a fine mosaic floor, free from the front window. Once the dining-room floor of a rich merchant, this is actually its original position (the museum was built around it). It shows scenes from the life of Dionysus...wine and good times, Roman style. The tall monument over the Dionysus mosaic is the mausoleum of a first-century Roman army officer. Upstairs you'll see a reassembled, arched original gate to the Roman city with the Roman initials for the town, "CCAA," still legible, and incredible glassware that Roman Köln was famous for producing. The gift shop's €0.50 brochure provides too little, and the €12 book too much (detailed descriptions for this museum and about Roman artifacts displayed in other German cities).

Access: AE, AI, AL, Level 1—Fully accessible. A free, accessible toilet is at the nearby Ludwig Museum.

Cost, Hours, and Location: €3.60, 50 percent discount with WelcomeCard, Tue–Sun 10:00–17:00, closed Mon, Roncalliplatz 4, tel. 0221/2212-4590.

▲▲Ludwig Museum—Next door and more enjoyable, this museum—in a slick and modern building—offers a stimulating trip through the art of the last century and American Pop and post-WWII art. Artists include German and Russian Expressionists, the Blue Rider School, and Pablo Picasso. The floor plan is a mess. Just enjoy the art. The Agfa History of Photography exhibit is three rooms with no English; look for the pigeon with the tiny vintage camera strapped to its chest. Exhibits are fairly well-described in English.

Access: AE, AI, AL, AT, Level 1—Fully accessible.

Cost, Hours, and Location: €5.10, often more due to special exhibitions, 50 percent discount with WelcomeCard, Tue 10:00–20:00, Wed–Fri 10:00–18:00, Sat–Sun 11:00–18:00, closed Mon, last entry 30 min before closing, Bischofsgartenstrasse 1, tel. 0221/2212-6165. There's a classy but pricey cafeteria with a reasonable salad bar at the entry level.

▲▲**Wallraf-Richartz Museum**—Housed in a building-sized cinderblock near City Hall, this minimalist museum features a world-class collection of old masters, from medieval to northern Baroque and Impressionist. You'll see the best collection anywhere of Gothic School of Köln paintings (1300–1550), offering an intimate peek into those times. Included is German, Dutch, Flemish, and French art with masters such as Albrecht Dürer, Peter Paul Rubens, Rembrandt, Frans Hals, Jan Steen, Vincent van Gogh, Pierre-Auguste Renoir, Claude Monet, Edvard Munch, and Paul Cézanne.

Access: AE, AI, AL, AT, Level 1—Fully accessible.

Cost, Hours, and Location: €5.10, 50 percent discount with WelcomeCard, Tue 10:00–20:00, Wed–Fri 10:00–18:00, Sat–Sun 11:00–18:00, closed Mon, English descriptions, Martinstrasse 39, tel. 0221/2212-1119.

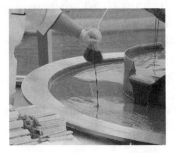

Imhoff-Stollwerck Chocolate Museum—Chocoholics love this place (cleverly billed as the "Mmmuseum"). The museum takes you on a well-described-in-English tour from the origin of the cocoa bean to the finished product. You can see displays on the culture of chocolate and watch treats trundle down the conveyor belt in the functioning chocolate factory, the museum's highlight. The top floor's exhibit of chocolate advertising is fun. Sample sweets from the chocolate fountain, or take some home from the fragrant choc-full gift shop.

Access: AE, AI, AL, AT, ♥, Level 1—Fully accessible.

Cost, Hours, and Location: €5.50, €5 with WelcomeCard, Tue–Fri 10:00–18:00, Sat–Sun 11:00–19:00, closed Mon, last entry 1 hr before closing, Rheinauhafen 1a, a 3/4-mile roll or stroll south of station on riverfront between Deutzer and Severins bridges, tel. 0221/931-8880, www.schokoladenmuseum.de.

Käthe Kollwitz Museum—This museum offers the largest collection of this woman's powerful Expressionist art, welling from her experiences living in Berlin during the tumultuous first half of the last century.

Access: AE, AI, AL, Level 1—Fully accessible. The entry and store interior are accessible for a person using a wheelchair. The glass elevator is accessible, as is the lift in the museum. You will need to ask the ticket agent for access to the elevator in order to visit the fourth-floor exhibits.

Cost, Hours, and Location: €3, Tue–Fri 10:00–18:00, Sat–Sun 11:00–18:00, closed Mon, Neumarkt 18–24, tel. 0221/227-2363, www.kollwitz.de. To find the museum, enter Neumarkt Passage, go to the glass-domed center courtyard, and take the elevator to the fifth floor.

SLEEPING AND EATING IN KÖLN

(area code: 0221)

Köln is *the* convention town in Germany. Consequently, the town is either jam-packed with hotel prices in the €180 range, or empty and hungry. Unless otherwise noted, prices listed are the non-convention weekday rates and breakfast is included. Prices are much higher during conventions, but soft on weekends (always ask) and for slow-time drop-ins. To find out which conventions are in town when you are, visit www.koelnmesse.de. Unlisted smaller conventions can lead to small price increases. Big conventions in nearby Düsseldorf can also fill up rooms and raise rates in Köln. Outside of convention times the TI can always get you a discounted room in a business-class hotel (for a €3 fee).

For a quick guide to Access Codes, please see page 417 of this chapter. For a detailed explanation of Accessibility Codes, please see page 2 of the Introduction.

Level 1—Fully Accessible

Classic Hotel Harmonie (AE, AI, AL, AR, AB) is all class, striking a perfect balance between modern and classic. Its 72 rooms include some luxurious "superior" rooms (with hardwoods and swanky bathrooms, including a foot-warming floor) that become affordable on weekends. So *this* is how the other half lives (Sb-€75–95, Db-€115, €20 less on non-convention weekends if you ask, superior room-€20 extra, some rooms have train noise so request quiet room, non-smoking rooms, air-con, elevator, Ursulaplatz 13-19, tel. 0221/16570, fax 0221/165-7200, www.classic-hotel-harmonie.de, harmonie@classic-hotels.com).

Sofitel Köln am Dom (AE, AI, AL, AR, AB) is a modern, upscale chain hotel offering full accessibility, professionalism, and all the amenities (Db-€170–320 depending on season, tel. 0221/20630, fax 0221/206-3527, just below the Dom on Kurt-Hackenberg-Platz, h1306@accor-hotels.com).

Level 2—Moderately Accessible

Hotel Ibis am Dom (AE, AI, AL, AR), a huge budget chain with a 71-room modern hotel right at the train station, offers comfort in a tidy, affordable package (no accessible toilets in rooms; Sb-€77, Db-€89; convention rate: Sb-€109, Db-€121; breakfast-€9, air-con, non-smoking rooms, elevator, Hauptbahnhof, entry across from station's Reisezentrum, tel. 0221/912-8580, fax 0221/9128-58199, www.ibishotel.com, h0739 @accor-hotels.com). The hotel's fine restaurant is accessible (with nearby accessible toilet).

Level 3—Minimally Accessible

Hotel Engelbertz (AE, AL) is a fine, family-run, 40-room place a few blocks from the station and cathedral at the end of the pedestrian mall (Sb-€68 and Db-€96, convention rate Db-€186, readers with this book can request a discount during non-convention times, elevator, just off Hohe Strasse at Obenmarspforten 1–3, tel. 0221/257-8994, fax 0221/257-8924, www.hotel-engelbertz.de, info@hotel-engelbertz.de). Although the entry and lobby are wheelchair-accessible, the rooms and bathrooms are too small and cramped for wheelchair users.

Eating in Köln

Kölsch is both the dialect spoken here and the city's distinct type of beer (pale, hoppy, and highly fermented). You'll find plenty of places to enjoy both in the streets around Alter Markt (2 blocks off river).

Hotel Ibis am Dom Restaurant (AE, AI, AT, Level 1—Fully accessible) has an upscale dining room with a welcoming staff (see hotel listing above).

Touristy **Früh am Dom (AE, AI, AT,** Level 1—Fully accessible), close to the cathedral and train station, offers three floors of drinking and dining options; the main floor is best for wheelchair users (Am Hof 12–14, tel. 0221/261-3211)).

Gaffel Haus (AE+A, AI+A, Level 3—Minimally accessible) serves good local food (near Lintgasse at Alter Markt 20–22, tel. 0221/257-7692). The staff can assist with the one 6" entry step and three more 6" steps up to tables.

Papa Joe's Klimperkasten (AE, AI, Level 2—Moderately accessible, barrier-free entry and accessible tables) wins the atmosphere award in a dark pub packed with memorabilia and nightly live jazz (Alter Markt 50–52, tel. 0221/258-2132).

TRANSPORTATION CONNECTIONS

Köln

By train to: Cochem (2/hr, 1.75 hrs), **Bacharach** or **St. Goar** (hrly, 1.5 hrs, 1 change), **Frankfurt Airport** (every 2 hrs direct, or 3/hr, 2 hrs, change in Mainz), **Koblenz** (4/hr, 1 hr), **Bonn** (6/hr, 20 min), **Trier** (3/hr, 3 hrs, change in Koblenz), **Aachen** (3/hr, 1 hr), **Paris** (7/day, 4 hrs), **Amsterdam** (every 2 hrs, 3.5 hrs, up to 4 changes). Train info: tel. 01805-996-633.

Frankfurt

Frankfurt offers a good look at today's no-nonsense modern Germany. There's so much more to this country than castles and old cobbled squares. While the city leads Germany in skyscrapers—mostly bank headquarters—one-third of Frankfurt is green space. Especially in the area around the train station, you'll notice the fascinating multi-ethnic flavor of the city. A third of its 650,000 residents carry foreign passports.

Frankfurt is a major transportation hub for trains and flights. Many tourists treat the city as a place to transfer, but if your travels bring you here, consider staying awhile. Even two or three hours in the city leaves you with some powerful impressions. The great sights are 15 minutes from the train station, which is 15 minutes from the airport. For years, Frankfurt was a place to avoid—a sterile, business-minded city known to Germans as "Bankfurt" or "Krankfurt" (*krank* means "sick"). But the city has recently rejuvenated its cultural landscape, and today's Frankfurt has a special energy that makes it worth a look.

ACCESSIBILITY IN FRANKFURT

As a modern city (largely destroyed and rebuilt after World War II), Frankfurt offers good accessibility. For a quick guide to Accessibility

Codes, please see page 417 of this chapter. For a detailed explanation of Accessibility Codes, please see page 2 of the Introduction.

ORIENTATION

(area code: 069)

Tourist Information: Frankfurt has several TIs. The most central is inside the train station's main entry, offering an abundance of brochures and a free hotel-booking service (**AE, AI, AT,** Level 1—Fully accessible; Mon–Fri 8:00–21:00, Sat–Sun 9:00–18:00, tel. 069/2123-8800, www .frankfurt-tourismus.de). Buy the city/subway map (the basic €0.50 version is fine—skip the detailed €1 map) and consider the Frankfurt Welcome brochure (€0.50). The TI sells the all-day city transit pass (*Tageskarte,* €4.60), Museum Ticket (€8, valid 2 days, covers 24 museums), and Frankfurt Card (see below), and offers bus tours of the city (see below). You'll find other TIs in Römerberg (Mon–Fri 9:30–17:30, Sat–Sun 10:00–16:00), on the pedestrian shopping street Zeil, and at the airport.

The **Frankfurt Card** (€7.50/1 day, €11/2 days, sold at TI) gives you a transit pass (including connections to and from the airport), 50 percent off all major museums, and 25 percent off the city bus tour (which virtually pays for the pass). It's hard to do enough in a day to make the card pay for itself. Note that most museums are closed Monday and, depending on what the city decides, may be free and open until 20:00 on Wednesday (confirm at any TI).

The basic **city bus tour** (**AE+A,** Level 2—Moderately accessible) gives a 2.5-hour orientation to Frankfurt, including Römerberg, Goethe's House, and (in summer only) the Main Tower. Wheelchair users need to be able to transfer into the bus; wheelchairs are folded and stored under the bus (€25, 25 percent discount with Frankfurt Card, recorded narration, April–Oct daily at 10:00 and 14:00, Nov–March daily at 14:00). The bus picks up at the Römerberg TI first, then 15 minutes later at the Hauptbahnhof TI.

Local Guide: Elisabeth Lücke loves her city and shares it very well (€45/hr, reserve in advance, tel. 06196/45787, www.elisabeth-luecke.de).

Frankfurt

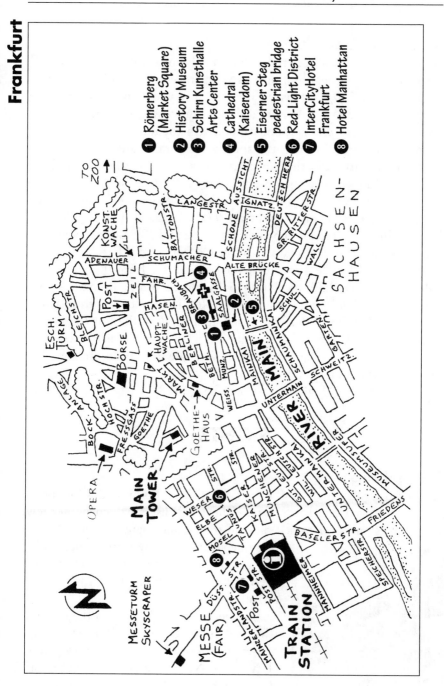

1 Römerberg (Market Square)
2 History Museum
3 Schirn Kunsthalle Arts Center
4 Cathedral (Kaiserdom)
5 Eiserner Steg pedestrian bridge
6 Red-Light District
7 InterCityHotel Frankfurt
8 Hotel Manhattan

Arrival in Frankfurt

By Train: The Frankfurt train station (Hauptbahnhof; **AE, AI, AT,** Level 1—Fully accessible) bustles with travelers. This is Germany's busiest station: 350,000 travelers make their way to 25 platforms to catch 1,800 trains every day. While it was big news when it opened in the 1890s, it's a dead-end station, which, with today's high-speed trains, makes it outdated. In fact, the speedy ICE trains are threatening to bypass Frankfurt altogether unless it digs a tunnel to allow for a faster pass-through stop (a costly project is now in the discussion stage).

The TI is in the main hall just inside the front door. There is one wheelchair-accessible toilet, near track 9 (key available upon request from Railway Information booth behind tracks 12 and 13). Lockers and baggage check are in the main hall across from the TI (€2/day, daily 6:00–20:00). More lockers are at track 24, across from the post office (Mon–Fri 7:00–19:30, Sat 8:00–16:00, closed Sun, automatic stamp machine outside). Inquire about train tickets in the Reisezentrum across from track 9 (daily 6:00–23:00). Pick up a snack at the fine food court across from tracks 4 and 5. The station is a few blocks from the convention center (Messe), a three-minute subway ride from the center, or a 12-minute shuttle train from the airport.

By Plane: See "Frankfurt Airport," page 473.

SIGHTS

Römerberg

This brief sightseeing tour connects the main sights around Römerberg, Frankfurt's lively Market Square. Wheelchair users will encounter few curb cuts, some semi-buried railroad tracks, and many sections of cob-

blestone sidewalks. There are no accessible toilets along the route of this tour (ideally, use the one at the train station when you arrive).

To get to Römerberg from the station, it's a 3/4-mile taxi ride, roll, or stroll (up Kaiserstrasse) or three-minute subway ride (Level 4—Not accessible; elevator at Römerberg stop but not at train station; cars aren't accessible, with post in middle of entry). All but the most energetic slow walkers should take a taxi to Römerberg. If you decide to tackle the U-Bahn, follow blue U signs and find a ticket box. Push the green *Kurzstrecke* button (short ride, €1.15), then follow signs to U-4 (direction Seckbacher Landstrasse) or U-5 (direction Preungesheim). Choose the track with the best *Nächste Abfahrt* (next departure) time and go two stops to Römerberg.

Exiting, go downhill to...

Römerberg—Frankfurt's Market Square (Level 1—Fully accessible) was the birthplace of the city. The town hall *(Römer)* houses the *Kaisersaal,* or Imperial Hall, where Holy Roman Emperors celebrated their coronations. Today the *Römer* houses the city council and mayor's office. The cute row of half-timbered houses (rebuilt in 1983) opposite the *Römer* is typical of Frankfurt's quaint old center before WWII. Go past the red-and-white church downhill toward the river to Frankfurt's...

History Museum—While most won't want to spend time in the actual museum upstairs (not accessible; €4, 2 floors of artifacts, paintings, and displays without a word of English), the models in the ground-floor annex are fascinating and wheelchair-accessible (€1, follow signs to *Altstadtmodelle,* English film and explanations). Study the maps of medieval Frankfurt. The wall surrounding the city was torn down in the early 1800s to make the ring of parks and lakes you see on your modern map. The long, densely packed row of houses on the eastern end of town was Frankfurt's Jewish ghetto from 1462 to 1796. The five original houses that survive make up today's Jewish Museum. (Frankfurt is the birthplace of Anne Frank and the banking Rothschild family.) The big model in the middle of the room shows the town in the 1930s. Across from it, you can see the horror that befell the town in 1940, 1943, and on the "fatal night" of March 23, 1944. This last Allied bombing accomplished its goal of demoralizing the city. Find the facade of the destroyed city hall—where you just were. The film behind this model is a good 15-minute virtual tour of Frankfurt through the ages (ask them to change the language to English for you—*"Auf Englisch, bitte?"*). At the model of today's Frankfurt, orient yourself, then locate the riverfront (to detour to the riverfront, go left when you exit the museum; you'll find the grassy park and fun Eiserner Steg pedestrian bridge—**AE, AL,** Level 1—Fully accessible) and the long, skinny "pistol" (the Schirn arts exhibition center) pointing at the cathedral—where you're heading on this self-guided tour.

Access: To gain entry to the museum, wheelchair users need to press the outside button to notify the staff. The ground floor is **AE+A, AI,** Level 2—Moderately accessible; the upper floor is not accessible.

Hours and Location: Tue, Thu, and Sun 10:00–17:00, Wed 16:00–20:00, Fri 10:00–14:00, Sat 13:00–17:00, closed Mon, Saalgasse 19, tel. 069/2123-0702, www.historisches-museum.frankfurt.de.

Leaving the museum, turn right to...

Saalgasse—Literally "long hall street," this lane of postmodern build-ings echoes the higgledy-piggledy build-ings that stood here until World War II (right side of street is wheelchair-accessi-ble over medium-rough cobblestones). In the 1990s, famous architects from around the world were each given a ruined house of the same width and told to design a new building to reflect the building that stood there before the war. Which one is an upside-down half-timbered house with  the sun and sky? (Hint: Animals are on the ground floor.)

Saalgasse leads to some ancient **Roman ruins (AE+A,** Level 2— Moderately accessible, ramp near church entrance leads to four 6" steps for access to full exhibit) next to the cathedral. The grid of stubs was the  underfloor of a Roman bath (allowing the floor to be heated). The small mon-ument in the middle of the ruins com-memorates the A.D. 794 meeting of Charlemagne (king of the Franks and first Holy Roman Emperor) with the local bishop—the first official mention of a town called Frankfurt. When Charlemagne and the Franks were flee-ing the Saxons, a white deer led them to the easiest place to cross the Main—where the *Franks* could *ford* the river—hence, Frankfurt. The skyscraper with the yellow emblem in the distance is Norman Foster's Commerce Bank building, the tallest office block in Europe (985 feet tall). Next to it, with the red and white antenna, is the Main Tower, which you can visit (see below).

St. Bartholomew's Cathedral (Kaiserdom)—Ten Holy Roman Emperors were elected and crowned in this cathedral from 1562 to 1792. The church was destroyed in World War II, rebuilt, and reopened in 1955. Twenty-seven scenes from the life of St. Bartholomew (Bartholomäus in German) flank the high altar and ring the choir. Everything of value was moved to safety before the bombs came. But the delightful red sandstone chapel of Sleeping Mary (to the left of the high altar), carved and painted in the 15th century, was too big to move—so it was fortified with sandbags. The altarpiece and the fine stained glass next to it survived the bombing (**AE, AI,** Level 2—Moderately accessible; free, Sat–Thu 9:00–12:00 & 14:30–17:00, closed Fri, enter on side opposite river).

From the cathedral, it's a short roll or stroll back to Römerberg or to the Zeil, Frankfurt's lively department store pedestrian boulevard. Or visit the...

Main Tower—Finished in 2000 and housing the Helaba Bank, this tower offers the best public viewpoint from a Frankfurt skyscraper. A 45-second ear-popping elevator ride takes you to the 55th floor, 650 feet above the city. Here you can survey the city, from Frankfurt's ultimate viewpoint.

Access: The observation deck is Level 4—Not accessible (must climb 50 steps from elevator to deck). But wheelchair users and other visitors with limited mobility (and companions) will be accompanied to the part of the roof next to the restaurant, just below the observation deck, where you'll enjoy similar views.

Cost, Hours, and Location: Free passage to restaurant deck for limited-mobility visitors and their companions, otherwise €4.50 to observation deck, daily 10:00–22:00, Fri–Sat until 23:00, enter at Neue Mainzer Strasse 52, near corner of Neue Schlesingerstrasse, tel. 069/913-201.

SLEEPING

(area code: 069)

Avoid driving or sleeping in Frankfurt, especially during the city's numerous trade fairs (about 7 days a month—normally not in summer), which send hotel prices skyrocketing (visit www.messefrankfurt.com for a complete schedule of fairs). Pleasant Rhine towns are just a quick train ride or drive away. But if you must spend the night in Frankfurt, here are two places within a block of the train station (and its fast and handy train to the airport). This isn't the safest neighborhood; be careful after dark and don't wander into seedy-feeling streets.

For a rough idea of directions to hotels, position yourself with your back to the main entrance of the train station and use an imaginary clock as a compass: InterCityHotel is across the street at 9:00 (exit near gate 24, follow the signs to the Hotel), and Hotel Manhattan is across the street at 10:00. To sleep at the airport, see "Frankfurt Airport," next page.

For a quick guide to Access Codes, please see page 417 of this chapter. For a detailed explanation of Accessibility Codes, please see page 2 of the Introduction.

Level 1—Fully Accessible
InterCityHotel Frankfurt (AE, AI, AL, AR, AB) has 384 modern rooms (including one wheelchair-accessible room with fully adapted bathroom) and offers four-star amenities (Sb-€68, Db-€136, elevator, Poststrasse 8, tel. 069/273-910, fax 069/2739-1999, www.intercityhotel .de, frankfurt@intercityhotel.de).

Level 2—Moderately Accessible
Hotel Manhattan (AE, AI, AL, AR, AB+A), with 60 sleek, arty rooms, is beautifully located across from the station. An unusual mix of warm and accommodating staff with all the business-class comforts, it's a good splurge on a first or last night in Europe (Sb-€87, Db-€102, show this book to get a 10 percent break during non-convention times, further discount when really slow—including weekends, kids under 12 free, elevator, free Internet access, Düsseldorfer Strasse 10, tel. 069/269-5970, fax 069/ 2695-97777, www.manhattan-hotel.com, manhattan-hotel@t-online.de, manager Michael Rosen SE). They have one room set aside for wheelchair users (toilet is accessible, bath/shower is not).

TRANSPORTATION CONNECTIONS

Frankfurt am Main
By train to: Mainz (3/hr, 40 min), **Bacharach** (hrly, 1.5 hrs, change in Mainz), **Koblenz** (hrly, 1.5 hrs, 1 change), **Köln** (2/hr, 1.25 hrs),

Rothenburg (hrly, 3 hrs, changes in Würzburg and Steinach; the tiny Steinach–Rothenburg train often leaves from track 5, shortly after the Würzburg train arrives), **Würzburg** (hrly, 2 hrs), **Nürnberg** (hrly, 2 hrs), **Munich** (hrly, 4 hrs, 1 change), **Baden-Baden** (2/hr, 1.5 hrs, up to 3 changes), **Freiburg** (hrly, 2 hrs, change in Mannheim), **Bonn** (hrly, 2 hrs, 1 change), **Berlin** (hrly, 6 hrs), **Amsterdam** (8/day, 5 hrs, up to 3 changes), **Bern** (hrly, 4.5 hrs, changes in Mannheim and Basel), **Brussels** (hrly, 5 hrs, change in Köln), **Copenhagen** (6/day, 9 hrs, change in Hamburg), **London** (6/day, 8 hrs, 3 changes), **Milan** (hrly, 9 hrs, 2 changes), **Paris** (9/day, 6.5 hrs, up to 3 changes), **Vienna** (8/day, 8 hrs, 2 changes). Train info: tel. 01805-996-633.

Frankfurt Airport (Flughafen)

The airport is user-friendly. There are two separate terminals (if you don't know which terminal you're flying out of, call the airline—see "Airport Info," below). An accessible skyline train connects the two terminals. All trains and subways operate out of Terminal 1. Taxis serve both terminals. The airport offers accessible toilets, showers, a baggage check desk (daily 6:00–22:00, €3.50 per bag/day), lockers (€3–5/24 hrs, depending on size), ATMs, fair banks with long hours, a grocery store (daily 6:30–21:45, Terminal 1, on level 0 between sectors A and B), a post office, a train station, a business lounge (Europe City Club—€15 for anyone with a plane ticket, on departure level), easy car-rental pickup, plenty of parking, an information booth, a pharmacy (7:00–21:30, Terminal 1), a casino, and even McBeer. McWelcome to Germany. If you're meeting someone, each terminal has a hard-to-miss "meeting point" near where those arriving pop out.

Access: Travelers with limited mobility will be transported by electric cart to the baggage claim or the gate. If using a gate-checked wheelchair, ask for assistance in order to gain access to the elevator that will take you to the lower level. The toilets located in the arrival halls are accessible; toilets at the baggage-claim area are not. Taxis will take wheelchair users if the baggage and wheelchair will fit in the trunk (**AE+A,** Level 2—Moderately accessible). For train station access, see "Trains," next page.

Airport Info (in English): For flight information, call 01805-372-4636 (www.frankfurt-airport.de). The airport operator (tel. 069/6900) can transfer you to any of the airlines for booking or confirmation. Or contact the airlines directly (wait for an announcement in English): Lufthansa—tel. 01803-803-803; American Airlines—tel. 01803-242-324; Delta—tel. 01803-337-880; Northwest/KLM—toll tel. 0190-510-045 (€0.62/min). Pick up the free brochure "Your Airport-Assistant" for a map and detailed information on airport services (available at the airport and at most Frankfurt hotels).

Trains: The airport has its own train station, where train travelers can validate railpasses or buy tickets. To connect by train to Frankfurt or beyond, check in with the airport's Deutsche Bahn (DB) Information Booth (located in airport's regional train station, Terminal 1, Level O, Booth 316). The DB staff can assist the wheelchair user to the appropriate train platform, and then onto the train. The DB staff will also contact train personnel at train stations for either interim or final destination assistance disembarking. (Smaller, unmanned stations—such as in Bacharach and St. Goar—do not offer this service.)

By train to: Mainz (3/hr, 30 min), **Bacharach** (hrly, 1 hr, change in Mainz), **Koblenz** (2/hr, 1.5 hrs), **Köln** (2/hr, 1 hr), **Rothenburg** (hrly, 3 hrs, with transfers in Würzburg and Steinach), **Würzburg** (2/hr, 2 hrs), **Nürnberg** (hrly, 2 hrs), **Munich** (2/hr, 4 hrs, 1 change), **Baden-Baden** (hrly, 1.5 hrs, 1 change), and **international destinations** (such as Paris, London, Milan, Amsterdam, Vienna, and many more).

Sleeping at Frankfurt Airport

You can sleep at the airport, but you'll pay a premium and miss out on seeing Frankfurt. But if you must, the airport **Sheraton** (**AE, AI, AL, AT, AR, AB,** Level 1—Fully accessible) has one fully adapted room for wheelchair users (#3081) and a thousand standard, international business-class rooms (rates vary wildly depending on season and conventions, but Db usually around €200–250, about 25 percent discount with major corporate ID—try anything, AAA and senior discounts, kids up to 18 free in the room, includes big breakfast, non-smoking rooms, fitness club, Terminal 1, tel. 069/69770, fax 069/6977-2351, www.sheraton.com/frankfurt, salesfrankfurt@sheraton.com). Most other bedrooms are accessible for wheelchair users, but without adapted bathrooms. The staff can assist wheelchair users in getting between the airport and the hotel.

APPENDIX

European National Tourist Offices in the United States

Belgian National Tourist Office: 780 Third Avenue #1501, New York, NY 10017, tel. 212/758-8130, fax 212/355-7675, www.visitbelgium.com, info@visitbelgium.com. Hotel and city guides; brochures for ABC lovers—antiques, beer, and chocolates; map of Brussels; and a list of Jewish sights.

Visit Britain: 551 Fifth Avenue #701, New York, NY 10176, tel. 800/462-2748, fax 212/986-1188, www.visitbritain.com, travelinfo @visitbritain.org. Request the Britain Vacation Planner. Free maps of London and Britain. Regional information, garden tour map, and urban cultural activities brochure.

French Government Tourist Office: For questions and brochures (on regions, barging, and the wine country), call 410/286-8310. Ask for the France Guide, with good accessibility information. Materials delivered in 4 to 6 weeks are free; there's a $4 shipping fee for information delivered in 5 to 10 days.

Their Web site is www.franceguide.com, their e-mail address is info@franceguide.com, and their offices are...

In New York: 444 Madison Avenue, 16th floor, New York, NY 10022, fax 212/838-7855.

In California: 9454 Wilshire Boulevard #310, Beverly Hills, CA 90212, fax 310/276-2835.

German National Tourist Office: 122 East 42nd Street, 52nd Floor, New York, NY 10168, tel. 212/661-7200, fax 212/661-7174, www.visits-to-germany.com, gntony@aol.com. Maps, Rhine schedules, castles, and city and regional information.

Netherlands Board of Tourism: 355 Lexington Avenue, 19th Floor, New York, NY 10017, tel. 888/GO-HOLLAND, fax 212/370-9507, www.holland.com, info@goholland.com. Great country map, events calendar, and seasonal brochures; $5 donation requested for mailing (pay on receipt).

U.S. Embassies and Consulates

Belgium: U.S. Embassy, Regentlaan 27 Boulevard du Régent, Brussels, tel. 02/508-2111, www.usembassy.be

Britain: U.S. Embassy, 24 Grosvenor Square, Tube: Bond Street, London, tel. 020/7499-9000, www.usembassy.org.uk

France: U.S. Embassy, 2 avenue Gabriel, Mo: Concorde, Paris, tel. 01 43 12 22 22, www.amb-usa.fr

Germany: U.S. Embassy, Neustadtische Kirchstrasse 4-5, Berlin, tel. 030/832-9233, www.usembassy.de

The Netherlands: U.S. Consulate General at Museumplein 19, Amsterdam (for passport concerns), tel. 020/575-5309, www.usemb.nl /consul.htm; U.S. Embassy at Lange Voorhout 102, The Hague, tel. 070/310-9209, www.usemb.nl

Let's Talk Telephones

To make international calls, you need to break the codes: the international access codes and country codes (see below). For information on making local, long-distance, and international calls, see "Telephones" in this book's introduction.

International Access Codes

When dialing direct, first dial the international access code (011 if you're calling from the U.S.A. or Canada; 00 if you're calling from Europe). All European countries use "00" as their international access code.

Country Codes

After you've dialed the international access code, dial the code of the country you're calling.

Austria—43	Greece—30
Belgium—32	Ireland—353
Britain—44	Italy—39
Canada—1	Morocco—212
Czech Rep.—420	Netherlands—31
Denmark—45	Norway—47
Estonia—372	Portugal—351
Finland—358	Spain—34
France—33	Sweden—46
Germany—49	Switzerland—41
Gibraltar—350	U.S.A.—1

Numbers and Stumblers

• Europeans write a few of their numbers differently than we do: 1 = 1, 4 = 4 , 7= 7. Learn the difference or miss your train.

• Europeans write dates as day/month/year (Christmas is 25/12/05).

• Commas are decimal points, and decimals are commas. A dollar and a half is 1,50. There are 5.280 feet in a mile.

• When counting with fingers, start with your thumb. If you hold up your first finger to request one item, you'll probably get two.

• What we Americans call the second floor of a building is the first floor in Europe.

• Europeans keep the left "lane" open for passing on escalators and moving sidewalks. Keep to the right.

EUROPEAN CALLING CHART

Just smile and dial, using this key: AC = Area Code, LN = Local Number.

European Country	Calling long distance within...	Calling from the U.S.A./Canada to...	Calling from another European country to...
Austria	AC (Area Code) + LN (Local Number)	011 + 43 + AC (without the initial zero) + LN	00 + 43 + AC (without the initial zero) + LN
Belgium	LN	011 + 32 + LN (without initial zero)	00 + 32 + LN (without initial zero)
Britain	AC + LN	011 + 44 + AC (without initial zero) + LN	00 + 44 + AC (without initial zero) + LN
Croatia	AC + LN	011 + 385 + AC (without initial zero) + LN 00 + 385 + AC	(without initial zero) + LN
Czech Republic	LN	011 + 420 + LN	00 + 420 + LN
Denmark	LN	011 + 45 + LN	00 + 45 + LN
Finland	AC + LN	011 + 358 + AC (without initial zero) + LN	00 + 358 + AC (without initial zero) + LN
France	LN	011 + 33 + LN (without initial zero)	00 + 33 + LN (without initial zero)
Germany	AC + LN	011 + 49 + AC (without initial zero) + LN	00 + 49 + AC (without initial zero) + LN
Greece	LN	011 + 30 + LN	00 + 30 + LN
Hungary	06 + AC + LN	011 + 36 + AC + LN	00 + 36 + AC + LN

Ireland	AC + LN	011 + 353 + AC (without initial zero) + LN	00 + 353 + AC (without initial zero) + LN
Italy	LN	011 + 39 + LN	00 + 39 + LN
Netherlands	AC + LN	011 + 31 + AC (without initial zero) + LN	00 + 31 + AC (without initial zero) + LN
Norway	LN	011 + 47 + LN	00 + 47 + LN
Poland	AC + LN	011 + 48 + AC (without initial zero) + LN	00 + 48 + AC (without initial zero) + LN
Portugal	LN	011 + 351 + LN	00 + 351 + LN
Slovenia	AC + LN	011 + 386 + AC (without initial zero) + LN	00 + 386 + AC (without initial zero) + LN
Spain	LN	011 + 34 + LN	00 + 34 + LN
Sweden	AC + LN	011 + 46 + AC (without initial zero) + LN	00 + 46 + AC (without initial zero) + LN
Switzerland	LN	011 + 41 + LN (without initial zero)	00 + 41 + LN (without initial zero)
Turkey	AC (if no initial zero is included, add one) + LN	011 + 90 + AC (without initial zero) + LN	00 + 90 + AC (without initial zero) + LN

- The instructions above apply whether you're calling a fixed phone or mobile phone.
- The international access codes (the first numbers you dial when making an international call) are 011 if you're calling from the U.S.A./Canada, or 00 if you're calling from anywhere in Europe.
- To call the U.S.A. or Canada from Europe, dial 00, then 1 (the country code for the U.S.A and Canada), then the area code and number. In short, 00 + 1 + AC + LN = Hi, Mom!

Metric Conversion (approximate)

1 inch = 25 millimeters   32 degrees F = 0 degrees C
1 foot = 0.3 meter   82 degrees F = about 28 degrees C
1 yard = 0.9 meter   1 ounce = 28 grams
1 mile = 1.6 kilometers   1 kilogram = 2.2 pounds
1 centimeter = 0.4 inch   1 quart = 0.95 liter
1 meter = 39.4 inches   1 square yard = 0.8 square meter
1 kilometer = 0.62 mile   1 acre = 0.4 hectare

Temperature Conversion

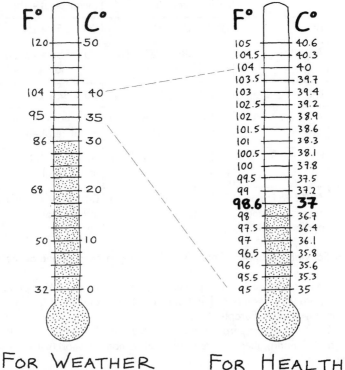

FOR WEATHER   FOR HEALTH

Climate

Here is a list of average temperatures (first line—average daily low; second line—average daily high; third line—days of no rain).

J	F	M	A	M	J	J	A	S	O	N	D

BELGIUM • Brussels

J	F	M	A	M	J	J	A	S	O	N	D
30°	32°	36°	41°	46°	52°	54°	54°	51°	45°	38°	32°
40°	44°	51°	58°	65°	72°	73°	72°	69°	60°	48°	42°
10	11	14	12	15	15	14	13	17	14	10	12

BRITAIN • London

J	F	M	A	M	J	J	A	S	O	N	D
36°	36°	38°	42°	47°	53°	56°	56°	52°	46°	42°	38°
43°	44°	50°	56°	62°	69°	71°	71°	65°	58°	50°	45°
16	15	20	18	19	19	19	20	17	18	15	16

FRANCE • Paris

J	F	M	A	M	J	J	A	S	O	N	D
34°	34°	39°	43°	49°	55°	58°	58°	53°	46°	40°	36°
43°	45°	54°	60°	68°	73°	76°	75°	70°	60°	50°	44°
14	14	19	17	19	18	19	18	17	18	15	15

GERMANY • Berlin

J	F	M	A	M	J	J	A	S	O	N	D
23°	23°	30°	38°	45°	51°	55°	54°	48°	40°	33°	26°
35°	38°	48°	56°	64°	70°	74°	73°	67°	56°	44°	36°
15	12	18	15	16	13	15	15	17	18	15	16

NETHERLANDS • Amsterdam

J	F	M	A	M	J	J	A	S	O	N	D
31°	31°	34°	40°	46°	51°	55°	55°	50°	44°	38°	33°
40°	42°	49°	56°	64°	70°	72°	71°	67°	57°	48°	42°
9	9	15	14	17	16	14	13	11	11	9	10

Basic French Survival Phrases

Good day.	**Bonjour**.	bohn-zhoor
Mrs./Mr.	**Madame/Monsieur**	mah-dahm/muhs-yur
Do you speak English?	**Parlez-vous anglais?**	par-lay-voo ahn-glay
Yes./No.	**Oui./Non.**	wee/nohn
I understand.	**Je comprends.**	zhuh kohn-prahn
I don't understand.	**Je ne comprends pas.**	zhuh nun kohn-prahn pah
Please.	**S'il vous plaît.**	see voo play
Thank you.	**Merci.**	mehr-see
I'm sorry.	**Désolé.**	day-zoh-lay
Excuse me.	**Pardon.**	par-dohn
(No) problem.	**(Pas de) problème.**	(pah duh) proh-blehm
It's good.	**C'est bon.**	say bohn
Goodbye.	**Au revoir.**	oh vwahr
one/two	**un/deux**	uhn/duh
three/four	**trois/quatre**	twah/kah-truh
five/six	**cinq/six**	sank/sees
seven/eight	**sept/huit**	seht/weet
nine/ten	**neuf/dix**	nuhf/dees
How much is it?	**Combien?**	kohn-bee-an
Write it?	**Ecrivez?**	ay-kree-vay
Is it free?	**C'est gratuit?**	say grah-twee
Included?	**Inclus?**	an-klew
Where can I find...?	**Où puis-je trouver...?**	oo pwee-zhuh troo-vay
Do you have an elevator?	**Vous avez un ascenseur?**	vooz ah-vay uhn ah-sahn-sur
I'd like/We'd like...	**Je voudrais/ Nous voudrions...**	zhuh voo-dray/ noo voo-dree-ohn
...a room.	**...une chambre.**	ewn shahn-bruh
...the bill.	**...l'addition.**	lah-dee-see-ohn
...a ticket to ___.	**...un billet pour ___.**	uhn bee-yay poor
Is it possible?	**C'est possible?**	say poh-see-bluh
Where is...?	**Où est...?**	oo ay
...the train station	**...la gare**	lah gar
...the bus station	**...la gare routière**	lah gar root-yehr
...tourist information	**...l'office du tourisme**	loh-fees dew too-reez-muh
Where are the toilets?	**Où sont les toilettes?**	oo sohn lay twah-leht
men	**hommes**	ohm
women	**dames**	dahm
left/right	**à gauche/à droite**	ah gohsh/ah dwaht
straight	**tout droit**	too dwah
When does this open/ close?	**Ça ouvre/ferme**	sah oo-vruh/fehrm
At what time?	**À quelle heure?**	ah kehl ur
Just a moment.	**Un moment**.	uhn moh-mahn
now/soon/later	**maintenant/bientôt/ plus tard**	man-tuh-nahn/bee-an-toh/ plew tar
today/tomorrow	**aujourd'hui/demain**	oh-zhoor-dwee/duh-man

When using the phonetics, try to nasalize the n sound.

For more user-friendly French phrases, check out *Rick Steves' French Phrase Book and Dictionary* or *Rick Steves' French, Italian & German Phrase Book and Dictionary.*

Basic German Survival Phrases

Good day.	Guten Tag.	**goo**-ten tahg
Do you speak English?	Sprechen Sie Englisch?	**shprekh**-en zee **eng**-lish
Yes./No.	Ja./Nein.	yah/**nīn**
I (don't) understand.	Ich verstehe (nicht).	ikh fehr-**shtay**-heh (nikht)
Please.	Bitte.	**bit**-teh
Thank you.	Danke.	**dahng**-keh
I'm sorry.	Es tut mir leid.	es toot meer līt
Excuse me.	Entschuldigung.	ent-**shool**-dee-goong
(No) problem.	(Kein) Problem.	(kīn) proh-**blaym**
(Very) good.	(Sehr) gut.	(zehr) goot
Goodbye.	Auf Wiedersehen.	owf **vee**-der-zayn
one/two	eins/zwei	īns/tsvī
three/four	drei/vier	drī/feer
five/six	fünf/sechs	fewnf/zex
seven/eight	sieben/acht	zee-ben/ahkht
nine/ten	neun/zehn	noyn/tsayn
How much is it?	Wieviel kostet das?	**vee**-feel **kos**-tet dahs
Write it?	Schreiben?	**shrī**-ben
Is it free?	Ist es umsonst?	ist es oom-**zohnst**
Included?	Inklusive?	in-kloo-**see**-veh
Where can I find...?	Wo kann ich finden...?	voh kahn ikh **fin**-den
Do you have an elevator?	Haben Sie einen Lift?	**hah**-ben zee **i**-nen lift
I'd like/	Ich hätte gern/	ikh **het**-teh gehrn
We'd like...	Wir hätten gern...	veer **het**-ten gehrn
...a room.	...ein Zimmer.	īn **tsim**-mer
...the bill.	...die Rechnung.	dee **rekh**-noong
...a ticket to ___.	...eine Fahrkarte nach___.	ī-neh **far**-kar-teh nahkh
Is it possible?	Ist es möglich?	ist es **mur**-glikh
Where is...?	Wo ist..?	voh ist
...the train station	...der Bahnhof	dehr **bahn**-hohf
...the bus station	...der Busbahnhof	dehr **boos**-bahn-hof
...tourist information	...das Touristen-informationsbüro	dahs too-ris-ten-in-for-maht-see-**ohns**-bew-roh
...toilet	...die Toilette	dee toh-**leh**-teh
men	herren	**hehr**-ren
women	damen	**dah**-men
left/right	links/rechts	links/rekhts
straight	geradeaus	geh-rah-deh-**ows**
When is this open/closed?	Um wieviel Uhr ist hier geöffnet/ geschlossen?	oom **vee**-feel oor ist heer geh-**urf**-net/ geh-**shlos**-sen
At what time?	Um wieviel Uhr?	oom **vee**-feel oor
Just a moment.	Moment.	moh-**ment**
now/soon/later	jetzt/bald/später	yetzt/bahld/**shpay**-ter
today/tomorrow	heute/morgen	**hoy**-teh/**mor**-gen

When using the phonetics, pronounce ī as the long i sound in "light."

For more user-friendly German phrases, check out *Rick Steves' German Phrase Book and Dictionary* or *Rick Steves' French, Italian & German Phrase Book and Dictionary*.

Slow Walkers: Faxing Your Hotel Reservation

You can photocopy this form and fax it to the hotel (it's also online at
www.ricksteves.com/slowwalker).

To: _____ @ _____
         hotel   *fax*

From: _____ @ _____
          name   *fax*

Today's date: ____ /_____ /____
                  day   *month* *year*

Dear Hotel _____,

My name: _____

Total number of people: _____ Number of rooms: _____

Single____ Double____ Twin____ Triple____

With private bathroom____ Bathroom down the hall____

Number of nights: _____

Arriving: ____ /_____ /____
           day   *month* *year*

Departing: ____ /_____ /____
            day   *month* *year*

I have difficulty walking. I have the following needs:

No stairs___ Very few stairs___ Ground floor room___ Elevator___

Room near elevator or hotel entrance___

If you have a suitable room available, please reserve it for me. Please fax or email confirmation of
my reservation, along with the type of room reserved and the price. Please also inform me of
your cancellation policy. After I hear from you, I will send my credit card information as a
deposit to hold the room. Thank you.

_____
Name

_____
Address

_____
City   *State*   *Zip Code*   *Country*

_____
Fax

_____
E-mail Address

Wheelchair Users: Faxing Your Hotel Reservation

You can photocopy this form and fax it to the hotel (it's also online at www.ricksteves.com/wheelchair).

To: _____ @ _____
                    hotel   fax

From: _____ @ _____
                    name   fax

Today's date: ___ /_____ /___
                    day   month   year

Dear Hotel _____,

I use a wheelchair and would like to stay at your hotel if you have a room that meets my needs.

Total number of people: _____   Number of rooms: _____

Single____ Double____ Twin____ Triple____

With private bathroom____ Bathroom down the hall____

Number of nights: _____

Arriving: ___ /_____ /___ Departing: ___ /_____ /___
                day   month   year   day   month   year

My wheelchair measurements are ____cm (width) and ____cm (height).

I have the following needs:

_____ No steps at the hotel entrance or to my hotel room

_____ Doorways at hotel entrance and in the hotel room wide enough for my wheelchair

_____ A ground-floor room or an elevator large enough for my wheelchair

_____ An adapted bathroom with these features: _____ low sink, _____ roll-in shower,

_____ grab bars for tub, _____ handheld shower nozzle, _____ grab bars for toilet

If you have a suitable room available, please reserve it for me. Please fax or email confirmation of my reservation, along with the type of room reserved and the price. Please also inform me of your cancellation policy. After I hear from you, I will send my credit card information as a deposit to hold the room. Thank you.

_____
Name

_____
Address

_____
City   State   Zip Code   Country

_____
Fax

_____
E-mail Address

Road Scholar Feedback for *Easy Access Europe*

Your feedback helps us improve this guidebook for future travelers. Please fill this out, attach any additional tips/favorite discoveries if you like, and send it to us. You can also post your feedback on our Graffiti Wall at www.ricksteves .com. Thanks! **Rick**

Do you or your traveling companion(s) use a wheelchair?

Yes____ No____Sometimes____

Are you or your traveling companion a slow walker (who managed without a wheelchair)?

Yes____ No____

Please list cities visited in terms of ease of accessibility (from the easiest to the most difficult):

_____

_____

What was most helpful about this book?

_____

_____

Did this book steer you wrong in any way? If so, how?

_____

_____

What would you like to see improved in this book?

_____

_____

Any Easy Access tips or discoveries you'd like to share?

_____

_____

Please send to: ETBD, Box 2009, Edmonds, WA 98020

INDEX

ABOUT THE AUTHORS

RICK STEVES

RICK STEVES is on a mission: to help make European travel acces-

sible and meaningful for Americans. Rick has spent 100 days every year since 1973 exploring Europe. He's researched and written 24 travel guidebooks. He writes and hosts the public television series Rick Steves Europe, now in its seventh season. With the help of his hardworking staff of 60 at Europe through the Back Door, Rick organizes and leads tours of Europe and offers an information-packed Web site (www.rick-steves.com). Rick, his wife (and favorite travel partner) Anne, and their two teenage children, Andy and Jackie, call Edmonds, just north of Seattle, home.

DR. KEN PLATTNER

DR. KEN PLATTNER has spent 26 years as a family therapist,

professor of comparative religion, and hospital chaplain. When he's not travel-ing, Ken leads men's groups, presides at weddings, and provides therapy for people with disabilities. He's on the Board of Directors of Hope Counseling Centers and the ManKind Project International, and is the spokesman and moderator of the Denver Mayor's Commission for People with Disabilities. Ken and his wife Carol live in the mountains just outside Denver, happily sharing an empty nest with enough dreams and hobbies to last forever. Ken's Web site is www.kenplattner.com.

FREE-SPIRITED TOURS FROM

Rick Steves

Small Groups
Great Guides
Guaranteed Prices
No Grumps

Best of Europe ■ Eastern Europe ■ Turkey
Italy ■ Village Italy ■ South Italy ■ Britain
Ireland ■ France ■ Heart of France
South of France ■ Spain/Portugal
Germany/Austria/Switzerland
Scandinavia ■ London ■ Paris ■ Rome
Venice ■ Florence ■ Prague ■ Barcelona

Looking for a one, two, or three-week tour that's run in the Rick Steves style? Check out Rick Steves' educational, experiential tours of Europe.

Rick's tours are an excellent value compared to "mainstream" tours. Here's a taste of what you'll get...

- **Small groups:** With just 24-28 travelers, you'll go where typical groups of 40-50 can only dream.

- **Big buses:** You'll travel in a full-size 40-50 seat bus, with plenty of empty seats for you to spread out and be comfortable.

- **Great guides:** Our guides are hand-picked by Rick Steves for their wealth of knowledge and giddy enthusiasm for Europe.

- **No tips or kickbacks:** To keep your guide and driver 100% focused on giving you the best travel experience, we pay them good salaries—and prohibit them from taking tips and merchant kickbacks.

- **All sightseeing:** Your price includes all group sightseeing, with no hidden charges.

- **Central hotels:** You'll stay in Rick's favorite small, characteristic, locally-run hotels in the center of each city, within walking distance of the sights you came to see.

- **Peace of mind:** Your tour price is guaranteed for 2004; deposits are 100% refundable for two weeks; we include prorated trip interruption/cancellation coverage; single travelers don't need to pay an extra supplement; you can easily save a seat online at www.ricksteves.com.

Interested? Visit **www.ricksteves.com** or call (425) 771-8303 for a free copy of Rick Steves' 2004 Tour Catalog!

Rick Steves' Europe Through the Back Door
130 Fourth Avenue North, PO Box 2009, Edmonds, WA 98020 USA
Phone: (425) 771-8303 ■ Fax: (425) 771-0833 ■ www.ricksteves.com

Free, fresh travel tips, all year long.

Visit **www.ricksteves.com**
to get Rick's free
64-page newsletter… and more!

Rick Steves

COUNTRY GUIDES 2004

Best of Europe
Best of Eastern Europe
France
Germany, Austria & Switzerland
Great Britain
Ireland
Italy
Scandinavia
Spain & Portugal

CITY GUIDES 2004

Amsterdam, Bruges & Brussels
Florence & Tuscany
London
Paris
Provence & The French Riviera
Rome
Venice

MORE EUROPE FROM RICK STEVES

Europe 101
Europe Through the Back Door 2004
Mona Winks
Postcards from Europe

More Savvy. More Surprising. More Fun.

PHRASE BOOKS & DICTIONARIES

French, Italian & German

French

German

Italian

Portuguese

Spanish

VHS RICK STEVES' EUROPE

The Best of Ireland

Bulgaria, Eastern Turkey, Slovenia
    & Croatia

The Heart of Italy

London & Paris

Prague, Amsterdam & the Swiss Alps

Romantic Germany & Berlin

Rome, Caesar's Rome, Sicily

South England, Heart of England & Scotland

Southwest Germany & Portugal

Travel Skills Special

Venice & Veneto 2003

DVD RICK STEVES' EUROPE

Rick Steves' Europe
    All Thirty Shows 2000-2003

Britain & Ireland

Exotic Europe

Germany, the Swiss Alps
    & Travel Skills

Italy